The Pragmatics Reader

D1556003

The Pragmatics Reader is an indispensable set of readings for all students studying pragmatics at advanced undergraduate and postgraduate levels. Combining key classic texts with newer extracts covering current developments in contemporary pragmatics, each reading has been carefully selected both to showcase the best thinking and latest research and also to reflect the international nature of the field.

The 30 varied readings, including four specially commissioned papers, have been organized into eight themed sections:

- Linguistic pragmatics
- Post-Gricean pragmatics
- Indexicality
- Historical pragmatics
- Politeness, face and impoliteness
- Cross-cultural and intercultural pragmatics
- Pragmatics and conversation – development and impairment
- Pragmaticians on pragmatics.

Each of these sections is supported and enhanced by substantial editorial commentaries, pre-reading, in-reading and post-reading activities and suggestions for further reading, both in print and online. The book also features a general introduction, a glossary of key terms, and a conclusion that explores the relationship between pragmatic theory and practice before anticipating the future directions of the subject.

Dawn Archer is a Reader in Corpus Linguistics and Research Lead for Linguistics at the University of Central Lancashire. She is the author of *Historical Sociopragmatics: Questions and Answers in the English Courtroom (1640–1760)* and editor of *What's in a Word-List? Investigating Word Frequency and Keyword Extraction.*

Peter Grundy is an Honorary Fellow in the English Language Centre at Durham University, having been a Senior Lecturer in Linguistics and Deputy Dean of Arts prior to his retirement. He is author of *Doing Pragmatics*, now in its third edition, and is on the editorial boards of *Intercultural Pragmatics* and *Asian Journal of ELT*, and is a past President of IATEFL.

The Pragmatics Reader

Edited by

Dawn Archer and Peter Grundy

Routledge
Taylor & Francis Group

LONDON AND NEW YORK

First published 2011
by Routledge
2 Park Square, Milton Park, Abingdon, Oxon OX14 4RN

Simultaneously published in the USA and Canada
by Routledge
270 Madison Ave, New York, NY 10016

Routledge is an imprint of the Taylor & Francis Group, an informa business

Typeset in Perpetua and Bell Gothic by
Florence Production Ltd, Stoodleigh, Devon
Printed and bound in Great Britain by
The MPG Books Group

British Library Cataloguing in Publication Data
A catalogue record for this book is available from the British Library

Library of Congress Cataloging in Publication Data
The pragmatics reader/edited by Dawn Archer and Peter Grundy.
    p.cm.
  Includes bibliographical references and index.
 1. Pragmatics. 2. Linguistics. I. Archer, Dawn. II. Grundy, Peter.
P99.4.P72P7462011
 401'.45–dc22   2010032702

ISBN: 978–0–415–54659–1 (hbk)
ISBN: 978–0–415–54660–7 (pbk)

Contents

Acknowledgements and permissions

The editors are extremely grateful to many inspiring colleagues and to the generations of students who we have kept in mind throughout as we put together this Reader. We hope that they – and you – agree with us that the texts that follow provide a representative overview of Pragmatics and, importantly, are also fun to work with.

Several people deserve a special mention. Louisa Semlyen at Routledge teamed us up in the first place, and we thank her for this, for her vision in conceiving this Reader and for her persistence in seeing that it happened! We also owe a very great deal to David Cox at Routledge, who guided us gently as well as assiduously through the editing process from the commission stage to the beautiful book you hold in your hands. In addition, we'd like to thank Andrew Craddock, for his copy-editing assistance, Andrew Watts and Julia Mitchell, for their production assistance, and Matthew Davies, whose help with the References has been invaluable.

Last, but far from least, the editors and publisher would like to thank the following copyright holders for permission to reprint material:

Section 2: Post-Gricean Pragmatics

Austin, J.L. (1962) *How to Do Things With Words.* 7,000 words by permission of Oxford University Press.

Searle, J.R., 'Indirect speech acts'. This article was published in Cole, P. and Morgan, J.L. (eds), *Syntax and Semantics: speech acts.* Vol. 3, pp. 59–82. © Elsevier 1975. Reproduced with permission.

Grice, Paul H., 'Logic and conversation'. This article was published in Cole, Peter and Morgan, J.L. (eds), *Syntax and Semantics: speech acts.* Vol. 3. (1975). New York: Academic Press, pp. 41–58. © Academic Press 1975. Reproduced with permission.

Seuren, P.A.M. (1998) *Western Linguistics,* 25: 426–8, 430–41. Oxford: Blackwell Publishers. © P.A.M. Seuren 1998. Reproduced with permission of Blackwell Publishing.

Stalnaker, R.C. (1974) 'Pragmatic presuppositions' In: Munitz, M.K. and Unger, P.K. (eds) *Semantics and Philosophy.* New York: New York University Press, pp. 197–214. © New York University 1974.

Section 3: Post-Gricean Pragmatics

3.1 Neo-Griceans

Levinson, Stephen C. (2000) *Presumptive Meanings: the theory of generalized conversational implicature*, pp. 112–18, 166–7, 170–3, 177–80. © 2000 Massachusetts Institute of Technology, by permission of The MIT Press.

3.2 Relevance theoretic pragmatics

From 'Relevance theory', by Blakemore, D. In: Verschueren, J., Östman, J.-O. and Blommaert, J. (eds) *Handbook of Pragmatics* (1995), pp. 443–52. With the kind permission of John Benjamins Publishing Company, Amsterdam/Philadelphia, www.benjamins.com.
Carston, R. (2002) 'Explicature'. In: Carston, R. (ed.) *Thoughts and Utterances: the Pragmatics of Explicit Communication*. Oxford: Blackwell Publishing, pp. 116–25. © 2002 R. Carston. Reproduced with permission of Blackwell Publishing.
Sperber, D. and Wilson, D. (1998) 'The mapping between the mental and public lexicon'. In Carruthers, P. and Boucher, J. (eds) *Thought and Language*. © 1998 Peter Carruthers and Jill Boucher, published by Cambridge University Press, reprinted with permission.

Section 4: Indexicality

Levinson, S.C. (2004) 'Deixis'. In: Horn, L.R. and Ward, G. (eds) *The Handbook of Pragmatics*. Oxford: Blackwell Publishing, 100–21. © 2004 S.C. Levinson. Reproduced with permission of Blackwell Publishing.
Rubba, J. (1996) 'Alternate grounds in the interpretation of deictic expressions'. In: Fauconnier, G. and Sweetser, E. (eds) *Spaces, Worlds and Grammar*. Chicago, Illinois: University of Chicago Press, pp. 227-61. © 1996 University of Chicago. Reproduced with permission.
Verschueren, J. (2000) 'Notes on the role of metapragmatic awareness', *Pragmatics*, 10(4): 439–56. Reproduced with permission.
The editors would also like to thank Sladjana Hrkalovic for permission to use her photograph of the Quayside at Newcastle upon Tyne.

Section 5: Historical pragmatics

Traugott, E.C. (1999) 'The role of pragmatics in semantic change'. In: Verschueren, J. (ed.) *Pragmatics in 1998*. Vol. 2. Antwerp: IPra, pp. 93–102. Reproduced with permission.
Brinton, Laurel J. (1996) *Pragmatic Markers in English: grammaticalization and discourse functions*. Berlin: Mouton de Gruyter. Reproduced with permission.
Jucker, A. and Taavitsainen, I. (2000) From 'Diachronic speech act analysis: insults from flyting to flaming'. In: Jucker, A. and Taavitsainen, I. (2000) *Journal of Historical Pragmatics* 1(1): 67–95 (abridged). With the kind permission of John Benjamins Publishing Company, Amsterdam/Philadelphia, www.benjamins.com

Section 6: Politeness, face and impoliteness

Goffman, E. (1967) 'On facework: an analysis of ritual elements in social interaction'. Approximately 4,251 words (pp. 5–46) from *Interaction Ritual* by Erving Goffman (Penguin Books 1971, 1972). © 1967 Erving Goffman. Reproduced with permission from Penguin Books and Random House.

Brown, P. and Levinson, S.C. (1987) *Politeness*. © 1978, 1987 Cambridge University Press. Reproduced with permission.

Locher, M. and Watts, R.J. (2008) 'Relational work and impoliteness: negotiating norms of linguistic behaviour'. In: Bousfield, D. and Locher, M. (eds) *Impoliteness in Language: studies on its interplay with power in theory and practice*. Berlin: Mouton de Gruyter, pp. 77–97. Reproduced with permission.

Culpeper, J. (2005) 'Impoliteness and entertainment in the television quiz show *The Weakest Link*', *Journal of Politeness Research* 1(1): 35–72.

Section 7: Cross-cultural and intercultural pragmatics

Blum-Kulka, S. and House, J. (1989) 'Investigating cross-cultural pragmatics'. In: Blum-Kulka, S., House, J. and Kasper, G. (eds) *Cross-cultural Pragmatics: requests and apologies*. Norwood, New Jersey: Ablex, pp. 11–25.

Cook, H.M. (2001) 'Why can't learners of JFL distinguish polite from impolite speech styles?', in Rose, K.R. and Kasper, G. (eds) *Pragmatics in Language Teaching*, pp. 80–102, Cambridge: Cambridge University Press.

Section 8: Pragmatics and conversation – development and impairment

Ninio, A. and Snow, C. (1996) *Pragmatic Development: essays in developmental science*. Boulder, Colorado: Westview Press. Chapter 7: 'Children as conversationalists'. © 1996 Anat Ninio, Catherine Snow. Reprinted by permission of Westview Press, a member of the Perseus Books Group.

Schegloff, E.A. (1999) 'Discourse, pragmatics, conversation, analysis'. *Discourse Studies* (1)4: 418–26. © 1999 A.E. Schegloff. Reprinted by Permission of SAGE.

Hamilton, H.E. (1994) *Conversations with an Alzheimer's Patient: an interactional sociolinguistic study*. © 1994 Cambridge University Press, reproduced with permission.

Section 9: Pragmaticians on pragmatics

Kopytko, R. (1995) 'Against rationalistic pragmatics', *Journal of Pragmatics* 23: 475–91. © 1995, with permission from Elsevier.

Pressman, J. (1994) 'Pragmatics in the late twentieth century: countering recent historiographic neglect', *Pragmatics* (4)4: 461–89. Reproduced with permission.

Briggs, C.L. (1997) 'From the ideal, the ordinary, and the orderly to conflict and violence in pragmatic research', *Pragmatics* (7)4: 451–9. Reproduced with permission.

The editors would also like to thank Hodder Education for permission to include in the glossary a considerable number of glossary entries from Grundy, P. (1994) *Doing Pragmatics*. 3rd edition. © 2008 Hodder Education.

Using this book

The Pragmatics Reader contains an editors' introduction, eight themed sections, a concluding section and a glossary. You will find at least three, and sometimes as many as six, related readings in each of the themed sections. The conclusion brings together some of the ideas in the preceding sections as part of its discussion regarding the theory and practice of Pragmatics, and tries to anticipate areas in which we expect Pragmatics to develop.

Each themed section opens with its own introduction. This is followed by a pre-reading activity, an in-reading activity, the text, and a post-reading activity – a format we repeat for each reading in the section. The section then concludes with suggestions for further reading. Depending on their number, these are sometimes fully referenced and sometimes in list form (in which case, the full reference can be found at the end of the Reader).

The pre-reading activities are designed to set you thinking in the right direction before you read the text. We hope the few minutes each takes will turn out to be time well spent. You should also read through the in-reading activity before you start to read the text, so that you know what to do as you read in order to get the most from the text. The texts themselves vary greatly in the challenge they present – do not expect to understand each of them at first reading, and remember that reading slowly and with care, often guided by the in-reading activity, may lead to a deeper understanding than reading rapidly. At the end of each text, you will find two or three post-reading activities. Often these can be done in class with fellow students. Whether you do them by yourself or with colleagues, they are meant to help you to make sense of what you have read and to think through its wider implications.

We have made a special effort to make *The Pragmatics Reader* pedagogically engaging and we very much hope that you'll enjoy the reading activities described above. We also hope the glossary will help to make the readings as accessible as possible. To this end, we would advise you to read through the glossary items before beginning your reading proper.

We are always interested in any feedback you may have, which you can send to us care of Routledge. We hope that any subsequent editions of this Reader will be improved further as a result of your experience, so please do let us know how you get on. We hope you enjoy reading *The Pragmatics Reader* as much as we have enjoyed putting it together, and we wish you a very successful encounter with Pragmatics.

Dawn Archer
Peter Grundy

SECTION 1

Introduction

1 The proper study of pragmatics

IF, AS ALEXANDER POPE CLAIMED, 'the proper study of mankind is man', what should we say is the proper study of pragmatics?

Certainly, a Pragmatics Reader ought to begin with a definition. Let's imagine, then, that we're at the start of the Hundred Metre final at the Pragmatics Olympics, the athletes coiled on their starting blocks. Suddenly, one of them is up and away, with a definition of pragmatics emblazoned on his vest:

> Linguistic pragmatics can, very roughly and rather broadly, be described as *the science of language use*

(which you just may recognize as the first sentence of the first edition of the *Journal of Pragmatics*). But the runners are barely into their stride when 'bang-bang', a double discharge. Yes, it's a false start. Several more such false starts follow:

> For the purpose of this publication, pragmatics can be briefly defined as the cognitive, social, and cultural study of language and communication.

(Another opening sentence, this one from Verschueren *et al.* 1995: ix).

> Pragmatics as we now know it has radiated outward from that aspect of human inferential behavior Grice calls implicature, the aspect of speaker meaning that differentiates what is (strictly) said from what is (more broadly) meant.
>
> (Horn and Ward 2004: xii)

> Pragmatics studies the use of language in human communication as determined by the conditions of society.
>
> (Mey 2001: 6)

> Pragmatics is the study of those relations between language and context that are grammaticalized, or encoded in the structure of a language.
>
> (Levinson 1983: 9)

Finally, a single discharge. This time, no one has anticipated the start. And the first to show? A veteran with many races under his belt. The legend on his vest says simply:

> The study of meaning in context.

In presenting a series of definitions, we are doing what most pragmaticians who try to delimit our discipline do; we've worked through a series of false starts, as we first consider and then reject several candidate definitions. We allowed 'The study of meaning in context' to get off to a clean start on this occasion, not because it's an exhaustive or particularly insightful definition in itself, but because it would be hard to find any pragmatician who would reject it out of hand. It is at least a partial definition, and one which captures the essential nature of our interest.

2 The centrality of context

The centrality of context is recognized not only in many of the definitions of our discipline that pragmaticians offer (e.g. Levinson above), but also in the theoretical and applied work of many scholars whose insights have shaped our subject. This applies equally to those who approach pragmatics from philosophical, cognitive, or sociocultural perspectives. You won't be surprised to discover, therefore, that many of the contributors to this Reader discuss context in considerable detail and that only one of the thirty-one authors whose work you are about to read fails to use the term *context* overtly. But then this work is precisely about the conditions (i.e. contexts) under which utterances may be said to be felicitous.

As a definition, however, 'the study of meaning in context' isn't entirely unproblematic either, and for at least two reasons. The first is to do with the phrase 'meaning in context' itself, and the implicature it seems to favour, that meaning is determined *by* context. Indeed, we don't have to read far in the literature to find pragmatic meanings labelled 'context-dependent', a designation which again seems to invite the taken-for-granted assumption that context determines meaning. But what about the other possibility – that, far from being presumptive, context is actually created by use? This concept is explored in Duranti and Goodwin's landmark collection of papers, *Rethinking Context*. The editors begin predictably enough: 'Context has long been a key concept both in the field of pragmatics and in ethnographically oriented studies of language use as well as quantitative ones' (1992: 1). But it's not long before they encourage us to rethink the presumptive view of context:

> Instead of viewing context as a set of variables that statically surround strips of talk, context and talk are now argued to stand in a mutually reflexive relationship to each other, with talk, and the interpretive work it generates, shaping context as much as context shapes talk.
>
> (Duranti and Goodwin 1992: 31)

This perspective is especially clear in Schegloff's paper in *Rethinking Context*, which argues that rather than being given, context may in fact be what's new. The suggestion that the context may be what's new and the utterance what's given seems like a useful perspective, especially as we consider the 'presumption of relevance', a given that a hearer accords to an utterance as he seeks to maximize its 'contextual effects' in the relevance theoretic account of pragmatics.

A second reason why the definition of pragmatics as 'the study of meaning in context' is problematic is to do with the scope of 'context'. Once again, we don't have to read far in the literature to find contexts, which we know in reality to be virtually infinite, presented as simple scenarios evident to both speaker and hearer. A typical example is A and B's conversation about their mutual friend, C, who works in a bank in Grice's 'Logic and conversation'. In the same paper, Grice illustrates how the maxims guide (non-verbal) behaviour in two very simple (and unlikely) scenarios involving himself and the reader, first mending a car and then making a cake. But, of course, real interactions involve, not model persons such as A and B, but muddle persons such as ourselves, operating in complex social contexts in which we may have different roles and statuses, and to which we bring different personal experiences, encyclopaedic knowledge and types of personality. In other words, in the pragmatics literature, 'context' is what an author decides it should be for the purposes of their theory. On the one hand, it may be reduced to mending a car and the number of screws that a rational person would hand to a person self-evidently needing that number. On the other, it can take account of a virtually unlimited social reality. And to complicate things further, context isn't necessarily limited only to a quantitative continuum of this kind. As well as being treated as an external phenomenon, something out there in the world if you like, context can also be thought of as an internal phenomenon or mental construct, as in 'contextual effect' and its later substitute, 'cognitive effect', in Sperber and Wilson's account of relevance.

If we bring together our two reservations about the definition of pragmatics as 'the study of meaning in context', an interesting, and perhaps predictable, pattern emerges:

- If we view context as presumptive, we're likely also to view it reductively and take a rationalistic view of pragmatic actions. This is a hallmark of the 'Anglo-American' approach evident in the work of linguistic philosophers such as Austin and Grice, in which pragmatics may be seen alongside syntax and semantics, and phonetics and phonology as a component, or even a level, in a linguistic theory. As theory-builders, pragmaticians of this kind will be concerned about abstractions such as 'the semantics-pragmatics interface' and the role of pragmatics in the lexicon. What such pragmaticians study in the final analysis is the nature of human language and the mechanisms that appear to underlie the production and, especially, interpretation of utterances. Their approach is normative as they attempt to make generalizations that hold across all such instances of use.
- If we view context as emergent, we're likely to view it as complex and take a data-driven or empirical view of pragmatic actions. This is a hallmark of the 'continental' European approach in which pragmaticians work alongside conversation analysts, discourse analysts, sociolinguists, (linguistic) anthropologists and other researchers studying actually occurring language. As field workers, such pragmaticians will be concerned about what constitutes an appropriate data set and which analytic method is most appropriate to it – perhaps becoming for the moment ethnomethodologists or participant observers as they try to identify defining regularities in the speech patterns of groups of language users. What such

pragmaticians study is the use of language in human interaction and the social structures that are reflected in and created by this use. Their approach is appropriate to the particularity of the instances of language use that they hope to understand.

Given the broadness of these generalizations, a caveat is of course in order here. We don't want to suggest that those who work in the rationalistic tradition are entirely unconcerned with what constitutes an appropriate data set, even if their data will typically be invented rather than naturally occurring. One could hardly study presupposition without choosing one's data very carefully, for example. However, there's a distinction to be drawn between choosing data to illustrate a theory and being concerned to ensure that the chosen data represent a social reality on the basis of which a theory may be proposed.

Despite this caveat, we think it's fair to say that the kind of pragmatics each of us does will be determined by the extent to which we limit the scope of 'context' in our study of 'meaning in context'.

In this Reader, we have tried to choose must-read texts whose authors take differing views with regard to the degree to which context is (a) presumptive or emergent, and (b) can be legitimately limited, both in domain and extent. In this way, we hope to strike a fair balance between differing and sometimes competing accounts of the proper study of pragmatics. In particular, we hope to avoid the censure Jacob Mey delivered to the editors of an important collection of papers, who, he said, reminded him of 'the famous Lord Nelson, who only reluctantly would put his spy-glass to his good eye, preferring not to see what he didn't like' (Mey 2005: 349).

3 Meaning and the semantics/pragmatics interface

But what of 'meaning', alongside which 'context' seems to be a very simple notion indeed?

Some definitions of pragmatics appeal to the distinction between those meanings that are taken to be pragmatic and those that are not. A good example can be found in Levinson's list of candidate definitions of pragmatics: 'Pragmatics is the study of all those aspects of meaning not captured in a semantic theory' (1983: 12). A semantic theory is generally held to account for (1) our knowledge of the meanings of words and the context-independent rules that allow us to combine them into meaningful sentences, and (2) our understanding of sentences as true or false (with appropriate satisfaction conditions for non-declarative structures), an ability which necessarily entails the correlative ability to identify referents. We might, following Trask (1999: 243), think of these meanings as *intrinsic* to the linguistic expression containing them. Levinson's pragmatics, 'all those aspects of meaning not captured in a semantic theory', are then *extrinsic* to the linguistic expression that prompts their recovery in a given context. In differentiating 'natural' and 'non-natural' meaning, Grice makes a similar distinction, as do those who distinguish sentence meaning and speaker meaning, and as we all do in recognizing that there's a difference between what is said and what is meant.

However, as pragmatic theories have developed over time, it's become clear that not everyone recognizes the difference between sentence meaning and speaker meaning in quite the same way. Take the case of someone asking a question of the kind that invites the specification of a time or a location as an answer. We may say in response, 'Six o'clock' or 'London', meaning 'Roberta's coming at six o'clock' or 'I met him in London'. Are these more elaborated meanings, sentence meanings or speaker meanings? Elliptical utterances of this kind suggest that 'what is said' isn't fully accounted for by the meaning of the linguistic expressions they contain. This alerts us to a further difficulty posed by defining pragmatics as 'the study of meaning in context'. Not surprisingly, this difficulty is taken up in some of the readings in this volume, and in particular in Section 3.2.

4 Approaches to pragmatics

At this point, we want to return to the definition of pragmatics proposed by the second athlete to anticipate the starting pistol: 'For the purpose of this publication, *pragmatics* can be briefly defined as *the cognitive, social, and cultural study of language and communication.*' This definition is given in the opening sentence of the preface to the Benjamins *Handbook of Pragmatics*, edited by Verschueren *et al.* The editors then expand upon the definition on the first page of their introduction:

> Pragmatics does not deal with language *as such* but with *language use* and the relationships between language form and language use. Obviously, using language involves *cognitive* processes, taking place in a *social* world with a variety of *cultural* constraints.
>
> (Verschueren *et al.* 1995: 1)

In editing this Reader, we've come to a similar but slightly different view of the way the pragmatic territory has been divided up. This isn't surprising since Verschueren *et al.* take a language-use and exclude a language-component view of the proper study of pragmatics. Our task as editors of this Reader has been to bring together a representative collection of the most influential writings in the field over fifty years or so. Whatever one's view of the proper study of pragmatics, these clearly include language-component views of pragmatics. It seems to us that the readings in this collection represent three perspectives on pragmatics, which we will label philosophical, cognitive and sociocultural. Of course, these are not exclusive categories. A cognitive perspective, for example, might well, in fact probably would, have implications for the component perspective. Similarly, an intention of the kind made manifest in a speech act can be considered from a philosophical perspective (e.g. how do desires and beliefs relate to intentions?), from a cognitive perspective (e.g. how are intentions represented in the mind? What is the corresponding thought for any particular speech act?), and from a socio-cultural perspective (e.g. how are intentions most appropriately presented in a range of different social settings?).

In listing these perspectives in the order 'philosophical, cognitive, sociocultural', we are to some extent representing a historical evolution in the focus of pragmatics and to some extent privileging the philosophical (although not without reservation). Largely for historical reasons, this ordering principle is also reflected in the structure of the Reader, whose first seven readings (Section 2, **Linguistic pragmatics**, and Section 3.1, **Neo-Gricean pragmatics**) are predominantly philosophical or rationalistic in the approach they take. Several of the readings in this section, coming as they do relatively early in the history of pragmatics, are concerned precisely with whether the phenomena they analyse are semantic or pragmatic. Thus Austin establishes that intentionality is a non-truth conditional property of utterances and both Seuren and Stalnaker argue the at one time minority view that presuppositions are meanings-in-context. Like Austin, Grice was an 'ordinary language' philosopher interested in the ways in which natural languages differ from formal languages, and in particular in their ability to convey meanings that are not formally stated. His influential paper outlining implicature is included here alongside other readings, which (1) subscribe to the position that ultimately there is a reason or a set of reasons that motivates each action or utterance and that if we can work those reasons out, we can identify what someone means by what they say, and (2) explicitly draw upon Grice's theoretical explanation for the process by which hearers might distinguish 'what is said' from *what is meant beyond what is said*. For example, Searle draws from Grice's idea of communication being a cooperative activity when explaining the (albeit largely unconscious) steps by means of which speakers use implicit means to signal their intent.

The next four readings (Section 3.2, **Relevance theory**) approach pragmatics from a cognitive perspective. That's to say, these readings take the view that the ultimate aim of the pragmatician is to work out how inferred meanings are processed and represented in the mind. The pragmatic use of language, including overt procedural indications of required constraints on interpretation, provides data from which we hope to establish a cognitively plausible account of communication. In this respect, there's a parallel with the objectives of Chomsky's generative linguistics in which realised syntactic structures are seen as evidence of a set of underlying mental abilities.

The three readings that follow in Section 4, **Indexicality**, explore what might be described as the keyhole area in pragmatics – keyhole in the sense that deixis grammaticalizes aspects of temporal, spatial and speaker context and is thus the keyhole through which we glimpse the room beyond, the room in which all uses of language, and not just deictics, are necessarily contextualized and contextualizing. While they each explore indexicality, the readings in this section are ordered so as to reflect increasing degrees of commitment to a sociocultural approach to pragmatics.

Similar things might be said about the three readings in the following section (Section 5, **Historical pragmatics**), with the first two readings adopting more of a 'pragmalinguistic' approach (Leech 1983) representative of the Anglo-American perspective we briefly describe above, and the third reading adopting more of a 'sociopragmatic' approach representative of the 'continental' European approach. Thus, Traugott draws on the rationalistic ideas of Grice and Levinson to demonstrate 'the central role' that pragmatic inferencing and implied meaning play in semantic change. Brinton moves on from semantic change to provide insights into the grammaticalization of pragmatic markers and, in the reading we include here, the various uses of *I guess* in Chaucer (e.g. as an intimacy signal, for ironic modesty and to suggest to the audience that they were free to respond when, in fact, their responses were being carefully manipulated). The most overtly sociocultural of the three readings, Jucker and Taavitsainen, also addresses issues of face in their discussion of the diachronic development of *insults/insulting*. Their main focus, however, centres upon their argument that speech acts are best considered as 'fuzzy concepts' sharing a multidimensional pragmatic space across time as well as place.

The four readings in Section 6, **Politeness, face and impoliteness**, pick up on and extend the theme of im/politeness and facework. The first reading, by Goffman, constitutes a sociological approach, but is included here to reflect Goffman's widely recognized influence on the field of im/politeness. The most cited – and, arguably, still the most influential – linguistic politeness work, Brown and Levinson's *Some Universals in Language Usage* is also included. Brown and Levinson's approach is rationalistic: they start from the assumption that Model Persons (MPs) have both a positive face (a want to be liked/valued) and a negative face (a want to be unimpeded in their actions) and that, in order to protect face (their own and others'), MPs will seek to avoid face-threatening acts or use strategies designed to minimize the threat to face. The two remaining readings focus on (linguistic) *im*politeness. Culpeper offers a means of capturing impoliteness in a way that 'mirrors' Brown and Levinson, in that it includes categories such as 'bald on record *im*politeness', 'positive *im*politeness' and 'negative *im*politeness'. He also draws on Goffman's notions of *incidental* and *accidental* face threat to explain face aggravation which does not constitute impoliteness. The Locher and Watts reading rejects the use of 'models' to predict or explain post-factum why impoliteness has been produced, in favour of an approach which prioritizes the participants' perspective(s) and, in particular, their use of 'expectation frames'.

The three readings in Section 7, **Cross-cultural and intercultural pragmatics**, focus on the use of language outside the culture of which speakers might be said to be native members, and on the communication and skill acquisition problems posed by such unfamiliar contexts.

The second reading in this section, Cook's paper on the extent to which L2 propositional meanings on the one hand and pragmatic meanings on the other are more or less opaque to learners, begins with the following observation: 'Although language is a symbolic system used to describe objects in the world, it is also a major tool by which we communicate who we are, what we are doing, and how we feel towards addressees and the events around us.' How then do we communicate who we are and how we feel in an appropriate way when in an unfamiliar culture or when using a lingua franca? The first two readings in this section are also notably applied in the sense that they measure the extent to which users in cross-cultural situations recognize pragmatic phenomena, in one case speech acts, in another the politeness effects of (Japanese) sentence-final particles. The first reading also illustrates the use of an instrument of measurement designed specifically for pragmatic research.

Section 8, **Pragmatics and conversation – development and impairment**, takes a different approach from the other sections in this Reader. What we are seeking to do here is to demonstrate the overlap between the pragmatic approach to language and other disciplines such as Conversation Analysis and Interactional Sociolinguistics. We do this via our focus on 'conversation'. We also use this section to introduce work which investigates the pragmatic competence of individuals and which, in consequence, continues the applied theme introduced in Section 7. The focus, here, is more clinical, however. For example, Ninio and Snow outline the development of conversational skills in children whose pragmatic development is considered to be in the normal range, using the Ninio and Wheeler Taxonomy and Coding System, and Schegloff and Hamilton use, respectively, a conversation analytic approach and an interactional sociolinguistic approach to gauge the pragmatic skills of Alvin (a commisurotomy patient) and Elsie (an Alzheimer's patient). Significantly, Schegloff and Hamilton both come to the same conclusion in regard to the dangers of relying solely on laboratory-based testing when seeking to gauge pragmatic abilities in pragmatically impaired adults and, perhaps somewhat more predictably, spell out how their own approaches, in conjunction with laboratory-based testing, might offer clinicians a more thorough understanding of a pragmatically-impaired individual's *actual* pragmatic competence.

All discussion and writing in our field makes an implicit contribution to the proper-study-of-pragmatics debate, and many pragmaticians, as we've seen, also make explicit contributions. What's special about the three readings in Section 9, **Pragmaticians on pragmatics**, is that they each question some of these implicit and explicit contributions and draw attention to the way in which the scales have been tipped in favour of particular 'traditions' or 'schools'. In this respect, these three readings echo, albeit in different ways, the disquiet already evident in the opening of Kecskes's paper in Section 7, which highlights the 'overwhelming emphasis on the decisive role of context, socio-cultural factors and cooperation' in recent research in pragmatics 'while ignoring the role of the individual's prior experience, existing knowledge and egocentrism'.

The readings in Section 9 also remind us that the terms we have used to describe approaches to the study of pragmatics also have long histories of their own. So if we describe an approach as 'philosophical' or 'cognitive' or 'sociocultural', we link it to a very considerable body of existing work, a great deal of which may not be principally linguistic. Thus in his paper 'Against rationalistic pragmatics', Roman Kopytko argues that in their construction of a universal theory of politeness, Brown and Levinson are motivated by the utilitarianism of Bentham and Mill, which in turn draws on the rationalism of Hobbes, Locke and Descartes. In order to construct a supposedly universal theory, Brown and Levinson, according to Kopytko, adopt a grossly reductive view of data and an analytical method which privileges reason as the only explanatory motive. In a sense, therefore, their rationalistic approach shows little advance over methods available in the past. You can perhaps decide for yourself whether a seventeenth century 'treatise on politeness' might also have invoked the sort of P(ower), D(istance) and (Imposition) R(anking) equation that Brown and Levinson propose.

Another theme that Section 9 confronts is the factionalization of our discipline inherent in the philosophical, cognitive and sociocultural approaches that we identify. In choosing to write about 'historiographic neglect', Pressman's 'Pragmatics in the late twentieth century: countering recent historiographic neglect' draws attention to the tendency to chronicle pragmatics in a way which is biased in favour of a linguistic orientation and which ignores the work of scholars who follow a sociocultural orientation. This conspiracy view of the way those in positions of influence have written the chronicle of pragmatics is echoed by Jacob Mey in the review of the important collection (Horn and Ward 2004) mentioned on page 3. According to Mey, Horn and Ward 'have completely silenced any voices that did not sound proper in the symphonic version they have put together on the basis of their chosen themes' (Mey 2005: 350).

Section 9 therefore reads a little like the *Star Wars* of pragmatics. We leave you to judge who represents the good and who the bad in these epic struggles, hoping perhaps that the various schools and traditions will in the fullness of time turn out, like the protagonists in that galaxy far, far away, to be closely related members of an estranged family with a lot more in common than they had supposed. With this in mind, Dawn Archer's concluding section, Section 10, Theory and practice in pragmatics, encourages you to reflect upon two related issues: the extent to which 'theory' and 'application' are bedfellows within pragmatics at the turn of the twenty-first century, and the field's ongoing relevance/usefulness to knowledge, culture and society in its various guises.

5 Down the passage which we did not take / Towards the door we never opened / Into the rose-garden (T.S. Eliot, 'Burnt Norton', *The Four Quartets*)

The absence at the beginning of this introduction of the customary reference to Morris's definition of pragmatics ('the relation of signs to interpreters' (1938: 6)) or Bar-Hillel's suggestion that the 'pragmatic wastebasket' might after all contain sufficient material on which the build a theory in its own right (1971: 405) is deliberate: we take the view that our subject has passed the time when we need to retrace the first steps of its early history. Who after all would begin an account of the current state of generative syntax with a reference to its historical beginnings in Chomsky's *Syntactic Structures*? Who still needs to counter the 'conception of pragmatics as a fairly thin icing on a substantial semantic cake', a position Carson attributes to Burton-Roberts, when, as she puts it:

> It follows from the view of pragmatics emerging from the cognitively based, relevance theoretic framework, that exactly the reverse is the case: pragmatic inference is natural and substantial, and encoded meaning may be not only minimal, but also unnatural from the point of view of what utterances communicate.
>
> (Carson 2002: 311)

At the time of writing, pragmatics is a field supported by two of the most important journals in linguistics, *Journal of Pragmatics*, now well into its fourth decade of publication, and *Pragmatics*, the journal of the International Pragmatics Association, now into its third decade of publication. These journals, and others that have frequently carried pragmatics articles, have been joined over the years by several other new journals, notably *Journal of Linguistic Anthropology*, *Discourse Studies*, *Intercultural Pragmatics*, *Journal of Historical Pragmatics* and *Journal of Politeness Research*. Even the most cursory glance at these journals reveals a vast range of areas and methods, only a small proportion of which we have been able to represent in this blue riband collection of readings.

6 Some concluding comments

In this introduction, we have argued that:

1   The proper study of pragmatics is meaning in context. But at the same time, we need to take into account that pragmaticians vary greatly in the extent to which they view context as either presumptive or emergent and in the contextual scope they consider it appropriate to take into account.
2   Pragmaticians take up different positions on the issue of the semantics/pragmatics interface.
3   Pragmaticians typically bring one of three perspectives to the study of meaning in context: a philosophical / philosophy of mind perspective, a cognitive / theory of mind perspective and a sociocultural / language in society perspective.
4   The ultimate aim of the philosophical and cognitive approaches to pragmatics is to understand the role of pragmatics in a wider theory of language. The ultimate aim of sociocultural approaches is to understand the contribution of the pragmatic features of language use to our understanding of social organization.

And one further thought: the study of human behaviour, and especially the study of language, aims ultimately to understand the tacit knowledge underlying overt behaviour. Tacit knowledge is by definition inaccessible to our conscious awareness. And yet it's perhaps in our pragmatic uses of language, and the metapragmatic awareness that we experience, that we seem sometimes to come closest to making a connection between what we do and what we know.

This introduction began with an analogy drawn from athletics. A different, and arguably better analogy might be drawn from football, where a team such as Manchester United or Real Madrid is made up of players from many different countries. The players in the squad, thirty-one of them in total, possess a range of dazzling but sometimes difficult-to-reconcile skills. You are the manager. How are you going to bring them together as a united team?

SECTION 1 FURTHER READING

The two historic texts mentioned above are often seen as motivating the view of pragmatics as a field of study in its own right:

Bar-Hillel, Y. (1971) 'Out of the pragmatic wastebasket', *Linguistic Inquiry* 2: 401–7.
Morris, C. (1938) *Foundations of the Theory of Signs* (*International Encyclopedia of Unified Science*, Vol. 1, No. 2), Chicago, Illinois: University of Chicago Press.

You might also want to read two textbook chapters widely considered to contain stimulating discussions of approaches to pragmatics:

Levinson, S.C. (1983) *Pragmatics*, Cambridge: University of Cambridge Press, Chapter 1.
Mey, J.L. (2001) *Introduction to Pragmatics* (2nd edition), Oxford: Blackwell Publishers, Chapter 1.

The first and the Jubilee editorials of the *Journal of Pragmatics* present a 'continental' view of the domain of pragmatic studies:

Haberland, H. and Mey, J.L. (1977) 'Editorial: linguistics and pragmatics', *Journal of Pragmatics* 1 (1): 1–12.
Haberland, H. and Mey, J.L. (2002) 'Editorial: linguistics and pragmatics: 25 years after', *Journal of Pragmatics* 34 (1): 1671–82.

For the opportunity to rethink context, a good place to start is:

Duranti, A. and Goodwin, C. (eds) (1992) *Rethinking Context*, Cambridge: Cambridge University Press, especially the introduction and chapters by Goodwin and Goodwin, Gumperz, Hanks, and Schegloff.

Horn and Ward's *The Handbook of Pragmatics* contains two outstanding chapters on the semantics/pragmatics interface:

Bach, E. (2004) 'Pragmatics and the philosophy of language', in L.R. Horn and G. Ward (eds) *The Handbook of Pragmatics*, pp. 463–87, Oxford: Blackwell.
Recanati, F. (2004b) 'Pragmatics and semantics', in L.R. Horn and G. Ward (eds) *The Handbook of Pragmatics*, pp. 442–62, Oxford: Blackwell.

SECTION 2

Linguistic pragmatics

Introduction

T HE FIVE READINGS IN THIS SECTION cover the three central areas of linguistic pragmatics: speech acts, conversational implicature, and presupposition. Speech act theory was developed by two language philosophers, J.L. Austin and John Searle. Their seminal work is represented in the first two readings in this section. These readings are followed by H.P. Grice's paper 'Logic and conversation', which proposes the theory of conversational implicature and is widely regarded as the most important text in linguistic pragmatics. The two final readings in the section trace out the history of presupposition, and weigh the arguments for treating it as a semantic or a pragmatic phenomenon.

Speech acts

The work of the speech act theorists, J.L. Austin and John Searle, has been hugely influential in shaping modern pragmatics up to the present day (for more details, see Section 10). Yet, both Austin and Searle were language philosophers by training: they were members of the Oxford-based group, the Ordinary Language Philosophers, who believed that the established view of language philosophy (e.g. truth-conditional semantics) was incorrectly trying to reduce meaning to truth, even though 'many sentences both in the language of philosophy and in everyday language aren't *intended* to be true or false' (Wharton 2010b: 453). In response, Austin (and later, Searle) began to advocate studies based on *ordinary* as opposed to *ideal* language, as was common among language philosophers in the mid-twentieth century, so that researchers might capture how interlocutors will use language *to do things* (i.e. to perform actions).

Austin's *How To Do Things With Words* is recognized as the canonical work on the performative: the class of verbs which, when stated, also perform an action (cf. 'I promise', 'I bet', etc.). Edited initially by J.O. Urmson after Austin's premature death from cancer, and later by Urmson and Marina Sbisà, the book is faithful to the exploratory lecture series Austin delivered in 1955, at Harvard University. Our reading is taken from the second edition of *How To Do Things With Words*, published by Oxford University Press, and includes sections of Lectures I, II, VIII, and IX. The first part of our reading relates to Austin's notion of the performative utterance, which, initially, is described as being distinct from the constative (i.e. statements which can be judged to be true or false (see Austin 1962: 3)). But you should be aware that Austin ultimately abandons this dichotomy – so that he might argue for a new framework for the study of language, based on the notion of a speech act. As such, the bulk of our reading focuses on Austin's argument that a speech act has three distinct levels: the 'locutionary' level (the words as they are uttered or written), the 'illocutionary' level (the speaker's/writer's intention behind the words, that is, their associated force) and the 'perlocutionary' level (the intended effect of the illocution on the hearer). Take, for example, the different ways by which we might get someone to leave the room. A typical request might be *Can you leave the room* or even *Please leave the room* while a typical prediction/order might be *You will leave the room*. Of course, for any of these speech acts to be felicitous, the target would need to comply – by leaving the room.

For reasons of space, we are unable to include Austin's final lecture elaborating his five 'very general' classes of illocutionary acts, as part of our reading. However, as Austin refers to these classes at the end of the reading as it is included here, we explain them below for you:

- 'verdictives' capture judgements as to fact or value (typical examples given by Austin include the acts of *estimating, reckoning* or *appraising*);
- 'exercitives' capture the exercising of authority, rights or influence (e.g. *appointing, voting, ordering, urging, advising, warning*);
- 'commissives' capture the undertaking of commitments or espousals (e.g. via the act of *promising*);
- 'behabitives' capture reactions to events or lines of conduct in the social context (e.g. *apologizing, congratulating, commending, condoling, cursing, challenging*); and
- 'expositives' capture 'how . . . utterances fit [discoursally] into the course of an argument or conversation' (typical examples given by Austin are 'I reply', 'I argue', 'I concede', etc.).

It's worth noting, here, that Austin allowed for the existence of both marginal cases of these classes and also overlaps between them. As such, this particular reading offers an interesting contrast to that of Jucker and Taavitsainen (2000) in Section 5 (**Historical pragmatics**), which promotes a prototype approach to speech acts. Indeed, Jucker and Taavitsainen prefer to see speech acts as 'fuzzy concepts which show both diachronic and synchronic variation' in a multidimensional 'pragmatic space'.

Searle's main contributions to speech act theory, and pragmatics more generally, develop against the background of Austin's work – and also Grice's work on conversational implicature, which we discuss below. Indeed, according to Tim Wharton (2010b: 455), his 1969 book *Speech Acts* 'is an attempt to integrate the speech act framework within a modern linguistic theory' and that, without Searle, 'speech act theory would arguably still be a subject . . . taught on philosophy courses, as opposed to courses on linguistics and pragmatics'. Rather than take our reading from *Speech Acts*, however, we have opted to include Searle's (1975a) paper on 'Indirect speech acts', which was published in Peter Cole and Jerry L. Morgan's (1975) edited collection, *Syntax and Semantics: Speech Acts*. Vol. 3.

Before we provide a synopsis of 'Indirect speech acts', we briefly want to alert you to one of Searle's contributions to speech act theory, which, although not explicitly covered in our reading, is drawn upon implicitly – Searle's use of 'directives' and 'commissives' to explain how we make sense of indirect speech acts. 'Directives' and 'commissives' represent two of the five speech act types within Searle's taxonomy of illocutionary acts (Searle 1969), which also includes 'assertives', 'expressives' and 'declaratives'. Like Austin's 'very general classes' (see above), these speech act types prioritize illocutionary force. But Searle distinguishes between his types using three specific criteria: illocutionary point, direction of fit and expressed psychological state. For example, assertives capture those speech acts that aim to represent something as being the case and, as such, offer the speaker a means of making their words fit the world of belief (e.g. *reporting*). Expressives, on the other hand, capture those speech acts that aim to express a psychological state and, as such, make the words fit the world of feeling (e.g. *apologizing* or *reprimanding*). Commissives and directives share a common feature – the undertaking of an action. However, whereas commissives commit the speaker to doing something and, as such, capture speech acts that attempt to make the world fit the words *via the speaker* (e.g. *promising*), directives aim to get a target (or targets) to do something and, as such, attempt to make the world fit the words *via the target* (e.g. *ordering*). Last but not least, declaratives constitute a special group of speech acts, which are institutional in nature, and thus can only be used felicitously by people with special roles in society. Their purpose is to make something the case. In a very real sense, then, they literally change the world of the target (as when a judge passes sentence on a defendant).

An aspect of Searle's approach, which is covered explicitly by our 'Indirect Speech Acts' reading, is his suggestion that, to be successful, a speech act would need to fulfil certain 'rules' or conditions; namely, a propositional content rule, preparatory rules, a sincerity rule and an essential rule. Thus, in the case of a promise, the propositional rule would be 'S pledges to do A'; the preparatory rules, that 'S believes that A is in H's best interest and that S can do A'; the sincerity rule, that 'S intends to do A'; and the essential rule, that 'S undertakes an obligation to do A for H'. According to Searle, this is the case regardless of whether the speech act is direct – such that there is a mapping of form and function (e.g. a question, which utilises an interrogative structure) – or indirect – such that it is performed in a way that reveals a mismatch between form and function (e.g. a directive, which utilises the form of an interrogative). Our reading largely represents Searle's original chapter in *Syntax and Semantics: Speech Acts*. Vol. 3, except for a few omitted paragraphs in the introduction and also the 'Sample case', 'Some putative facts' and 'Extending the analysis' sections. As such, it captures Searle's hypothesis that we can get from the literal illocution to the primary illocutionary act of an indirect speech act by means of ten (and perhaps more) inferential steps, and that these steps rely on our implicit understanding of the felicity conditions of direct speech acts plus the context of utterance plus 'certain general principles of conversation' (cf. Grice). In the case of requests, for example, Searle identified:

- Directives that primarily focus on preparatory condition(s), e.g. by addressing H's ability to perform A ('Can you be a little more quiet?') or by querying H's desire or willingness to do A ('Would you mind not making so much noise?').
- Directives that primarily focus on the sincerity condition, e.g. by addressing S's wish or want that H will do/cease to do A ('I'd rather you didn't do that anymore').
- Directives that primarily focus on the essential condition, e.g. by specifically addressing that H do/not do A ('Quit making that awful racket') or by providing reasons for H to do/not do A ('It might help if you shut up').

Any of the above elements can also be embedded inside another, according to Searle. Thus, we can make requests such as the following: *Would it be too much if I suggested that you could possibly make a little less noise?*, which attend to both H's ability (i.e. the preparatory condition of a request) and S's wish or want that H will cease to do A (i.e. the sincerity condition), as well as the propositional content condition: that H make less noise.

Like Brown and Levinson (see Section 6, **Politeness, face and impoliteness**), Searle suggests that 'politeness is the chief motivation for the indirect forms' of directives, to the extent that 'certain forms are conventionally used as polite requests'. One reason why such 'polite requests' become 'conventional devices' is their idiomaticity, according to Searle – although, as Searle acknowledges, the ultimate selection 'of forms . . . will, in all likelihood, vary from one language to another' (cf. Section 7, **Cross-cultural and intercultural pragmatics**).

Implicature

H.P. Grice was an Oxford-educated English philosopher of language, whose working life (like Searle's) was spent largely in the US. Grice's contribution to pragmatics is probably even more influential than Austin's and Searle's, not least because, in a very real way, his work – and, in particular, the distinction he proposed between semantics (as a theory of linguistic meaning) and pragmatics (as the study of language use) – allowed for the co-existence of truth-conditional semantics and speech act theory. The reading we reproduce here, 'Logic and Conversation', represents Lecture II of Grice's 1967 William James Lecture series, also delivered at Harvard, and omits only the introductory 'philosophical logic' section prior to the Implicature section (i.e. 22–4). We have chosen this particular reading, taken from *Studies in the Way of Words*, because it describes Grice's (now extremely) well-known Cooperative Principle (henceforth CP), and its attendant conversational maxims (Quantity, Quality, Relation and Manner), as well as Grice's notion of implicature. As the reading will make clear, Grice introduced his CP to account for the notion of implicature, that is, cases in which (in intuitive terms) a speaker *says* one thing, but *means* something over and above the words they have said. Consider, for example, the following exchange:

> Peter: Do you want some coffee?
> Mary: Coffee would keep me awake.

Notice that Mary's response to Peter's question is indirect: rather than answering a yes-no question using *yes* or *no*, she responds with information about what coffee does to her metabolism. Now, depending on the context, we might interpret this response as a *no* (because Mary will be going to bed soon, for example) or as a *yes* (because Mary has some work to finish, and needs to remain alert). Such implicatures are 'conversational' in nature, according to Grice: that is, they are 'a component of speaker meaning that constitutes an aspect of what is meant in a speaker's utterance without being part of what is said' (Horn 2004: 3) and, hence, must be derived via the CP and its maxims. As such, they are different from 'conventional' implicatures, which arise from the *conventionally inferred meanings* associated with particular lexical items and/or linguistic constructions (see, for example, the meanings which are triggered by the words *therefore, but, even, so*, etc.). In essence, the CP ('Make your contribution such as is required, at the stage at which it occurs, by the accepted purpose or direction of the talk exchange in which you are engaged') allows participants to assume that, when they converse, they are involved in a mutually-beneficial and cooperative endeavour – unless they are given evidence to the contrary. As such, when interactants ask questions such as 'Do you want some coffee?' and receive answers such as 'Coffee would keep me awake', they will try to find an explanation by which the latter might be understood as an answer to the former. It is at this point that Grice's maxims come into play: for example, if we were to adopt a Gricean perspective, we might explain the above example as a flout of the Maxim of Relation ('Be relevant').

As Wharton (2010c: 257) states, 'It is important not to confuse Grice's claims about the rational, cooperative nature of conversations with the much stronger claim (which Grice certainly did *not* endorse) that *all* conversations are cooperative, and that the maxims are *always* obeyed'. In fact, Grice listed three ways in which the maxims may fail to be fulfilled in addition to *flouting* (i.e. breaking the maxims as a means of triggering the hearer's search for an implicit meaning), namely:

- a speaker might *violate* a maxim covertly, in an attempt to deceive their interlocutor(s);
- a speaker might *opt out* of the CP and maxims by, for example, making it clear that they are unwilling to participate in the conversation with or unwilling to provide the requested information to their interlocutor(s), etc.; or
- a speaker might be faced with a 'clash' of maxims, with the result that they cannot fulfill one of the maxims without violating one of the others.

In addition, researchers such as Jenny Thomas (1995) have pointed out that speakers can also *infringe* or *suspend* the maxims. *Infringements* occur when the speaker fails to observe a maxim or maxims, but the non-observance stems from imperfect linguistic performance rather than any intention to deceive. Reasons for this type of non-observance include the speaker having an imperfect command of the language and the speaker's linguistic performance being (temporarily) impaired in some way (because of alcohol, drugs, etc.). In contrast, we talk about the *suspension* of a maxim or maxims in cases where there is no (or there is perceived to be no) expectation on the part of the interlocutor(s) that they must be fulfilled.

There are problems with the notion of the CP and its maxims, which Grice himself recognized. For example, he was concerned that the notion of 'being relevant' conceals 'different kinds and focuses of relevance there may be, how these shift in the course of a talk exchange, how to allow for the fact that subjects of conversation are legitimately changed, and so on'. In spite – and, we might argue, because – of such issues, classical Gricean theory has given rise to new theoretical approaches, some of which are discussed in detail in this Reader.

Presupposition

A presupposition is an uncontroversial background assumption that a hearer accommodates in order to focus on the non-presupposed content of an utterance. Imagine, for example, that it's midnight at Elsinore in the opening scene of *Hamlet*, and Barnado reports for guard duty. Although he sees the shadowy figure of the sentinel he has come to replace, he can't identify him, and calls out, 'Who's there?'. Barnado's question presupposes the existence of the person addressed (there is someone there) and asks that person to identify themselves. Does the presupposition arise because the context provides sufficient evidence for this assumption to be accepted? (It certainly seems that the utterance would make little sense without making such an assumption.) Or does the presupposition arise because the interrogative structure has an underlying propositional form which presupposes the existence of the person addressed and requests this person to identify themselves (i.e. the presupposition is an entailment of the sentence)? Put simply, is presupposition a pragmatic or a semantic phenomenon?

Although distinguishing a presupposition from an assertion (or, in the case of 'Who's there?', from a question or open proposition) is straightforward enough, many of the questions surrounding presupposition are anything but straightforward. This is not only because trying to determine whether presupposition is a semantic or a pragmatic phenomenon is no easy matter, but also because there are a range of other issues that call for difficult judgements. These include the 'projection problem' (the circumstances under which presuppositions survive when the utterances with which they are associated are embedded in higher clauses), the issue of whether definite descriptions are existential (i.e. presuppose the existence of a referent), and whether presupposition can be accounted for in the two-value, true/false logic that Aristotle proposed and that, for obvious reasons, we are reluctant to abandon.

Not surprisingly, the resulting literature is extensive, not only in terms of range but also in terms of historical ancestry, since the phenomenon of presupposition has been recognized from the earliest days of Western philosophy. For this reason, the first reading in this sub-section is taken from Pieter Seuren's remarkable work *Western Linguistics: An Historical Introduction*. The text reproduced here is a compilation which includes two paragraphs taken from the introductory chapter 'Linguistics from Antiquity till the seventeenth century' and a large part of the Chapter 6 section, 'Cognitive semantics: discourse-dependency', which deals with presupposition. We have edited this section so as to try and present the complex history of the study of presupposition from the earliest European philosophers to contemporary linguists and logicians in as accessible a way as possible.

In the opening paragraphs, Seuren distinguishes two approaches to the study of language, which he terms 'formalist' and 'ecolinguistic'. Broadly, formalists try to fit natural language into abstract or logical systems, and ecolinguists expect their study of natural language to identify phenomena that don't slot neatly into pre-existing frameworks. Seuren shows how this distinction is especially relevant in the study of presupposition, where the formalist position is that all sentences are either true (T) or false (F). Ecolinguists, on the other hand, are willing to entertain the notion that some phenomena may not conform to a two-value logic of this kind. The clash between formalist and empirical approaches to pragmatics is implicit in many of the later readings in this volume and resurfaces explicitly in Section 9 where Roman Kopytko argues that rationalistic approaches can result in the contradictory notion of a 'decontextualized pragmatics'.

Leaning towards an ecolinguistic position, Seuren examines a number of issues, including existential presupposition and negation. If you accept the theory of *existential presupposition*, you believe that a definite description presupposes the existence of a referent. Thus, 'presupposition failure' occurs when a definite description cannot be matched with a referent, as in a proposition such as *the present King of France*. Seuren shows how Strawson's view of a sentence such as *The present King of France is bald* as neither T nor F requires a *gapped bivalent logic*, which acknowledges not only the two values T and F, but also this third additional possibility. But as we can also use definite descriptions to refer to entities that do not exist, such as *The Loch Ness Monster*, we should perhaps abandon the formalist notion of existential presupposition altogether in favour of an ecolinguistic account of definite descriptions that takes into account the extensional nature of the terms used.

Seuren goes on to show that the 'neither T nor F' possibility cannot capture the facts of negation, which may sometimes preserve a presupposition and sometimes cancel it. Thus, *Mary hasn't recovered from flu* may sometimes assert the continuation of an illness whose earlier existence is presupposed and sometimes assert that Mary hasn't recovered from an illness because she never had that illness in the first place. So we seem to have three values for the sentence: T_1 when Mary hasn't recovered from flu and F when she has, and T_2 when she didn't have flu in the first place and so couldn't recover from it for that reason. So a *bivalent logic*, whether *gapped* or not, is impossible. The ecolinguistic solution is to treat Mary's having been ill with flu as a default assumption which will be confirmed (probably) or disconfirmed (possibly) in the discourse domain in which it occurs. So if the speaker and the addressee both know that Mary has been lucky enough not to have had flu when everyone else has had it, then the default assumption that Mary had flu does not go through. Equally, where the speaker but not the addressee knows that Mary hasn't had flu, the speaker can say *Mary hasn't recovered from flu – she didn't have it in the first place*. In some accounts, this kind of negation is termed *metalinguistic*, because it corrects a 'default assumption' triggered by the preceding linguistic structure.

One final nail in the formalist coffin is provided by *only* sentences, where the T_2 possibility isn't available. *Only Mary has recovered from flu* and its negation *Not only Mary has recovered from flu* both presuppose that Mary has recovered (i.e. we cannot get a Mary-hasn't-recovered-from-flu-because-she-never-had-it reading). So, however we look at it, it's impossible to get a tidy formalist solution for *negation*.

Interestingly, a default assumption theory of presupposition of the kind Seuren espouses enables us to preserve the view of presupposition as an entailment surviving sentence negation, since if a sentence containing a presupposition is admissible in a discourse domain, the presupposed element of such a sentence must also be admissible when that sentence is negated. Thus, we have a pragmatic, context-sensitive solution to a semantic claim that cannot be upheld on formalist grounds.

Seuren therefore concludes that presupposition is a pragmatic phenomenon. First, the formalist position which would apply a *bivalent logic* to all sentences doesn't hold water. Second, presuppositions appear to be default assumptions which may be blocked either for 'logical' reasons (information already present in the discourse domain rules out the presupposition) or for 'cognitive' reasons (the default assumption fails to represent a recognizable state of affairs in a given context). Thus, in the discourse domain in which Mary never caught flu, the default assumption that she had flu, which would usually arise from *Mary hasn't recovered from flu*, is blocked for logical reasons.

Discourse domains are contextual constructions entertained by speakers and hearers. Although Stalnaker does not use the term discourse domain in his paper 'Pragmatic presuppositions', he does argue that presuppositions are related to the particular contexts or situations in which statements are made, and reflect, not properties of language, but the common background beliefs and assumptions of speakers and addressees. In Stalnaker's view, a presupposition is a speaker- and not a sentence-meaning. It's simply inappropriate to talk about *the present King of France* given our background knowledge. Equally, we don't need to worry about whether *the present King of France is bald* lacks a truth value since it isn't (to use Strawson's term) an 'occasion sentence'.

One thing that can be said for the formalist, semantic view of presupposition is that it provides an (albeit problematic) explanation of presupposition as an entailment that survives negation. Stalnaker sets out to provide what he calls 'intuitively natural explanations' of a series of presuppositional phenomena. These explanations reflect 'the ordinary notion of presupposition' and appeal to the notion of 'common ground we can take for granted'. Thus, presuppositions are assumptions that are logical or natural or uncontroversial in given contexts involving particular speakers and addressees.

As we might expect, Stalnaker's paper isn't without its critics. However, his view of presuppositions as 'constraints on the contexts in which statements can be made' makes it much more difficult to sustain the formalist view of presuppositions as 'constraints on the truth-conditions of propositions expressed in making statements', which has dominated Western linguistics since the time of Aristotle.

Apart from four paragraphs, which we judge less central to Stalnaker's argument, his paper is reproduced in full below.

J.L. AUSTIN

HOW TO DO THINGS WITH WORDS

PRE-READING

As we make clear above, speech acts are utterances that *do things*. In the reading that follows, Austin highlights 'I do (take this woman to be my lawful wedded wife)' as uttered in the course of a marriage ceremony, 'I name this ship the *Queen Elizabeth*' as uttered when smashing a bottle against the hull, and 'I bet you sixpence it will rain tomorrow' as three typical examples of utterances that *do things*. We also drew your attention to the 'very general classes' of speech acts above, which Austin developed as a means of grouping together similar speech acts, and we summarized these classes for you. Before you read the following extract from *How To Do Things With Words* re-read our summaries of the Verdictive class, the Exercitive class, the Commissive class, the Behabitive class and the Expositive class until you are very familiar with them. Then try to determine which of these classifications best captures Austin's 'I do', 'I name this ship . . .', and 'I bet . . .' examples.

IN-READING

Austin states that:

1   While the 'uttering of the words is [. . .] usually a, or even *the,* leading incident in the performance of' acts such as 'marrying, betting, bequeathing, christening or what not', it is possible to perform such acts 'in some other way' (by which he means non-verbally). Austin provides, as examples, 'effect[ing] marriage by cohabiting', and betting 'with a totalisator machine by putting a coin in a slot'. When you get to this point in the reading, stop and consider to what extent betting on slot machines is a different activity from making a bet with someone face-to-face? What, if any, are the similarities and the differences (beyond the former being a silent activity)? Are there any acts that you can think of, which must be affected via speech to be considered felicitous? For example, are marriage and co-habitation the same thing, within your culture? Why/why not?

2   There are three ways in which illocutionary acts are bound up with effects – 'securing uptake', 'taking effect' and 'inviting a response'. Austin further states that 'these are all distinct from the producing of effects . . . characteristic of the perlocutionary act'. As you

read Austin's sub-section on the **Distinctions between illocutionary and perlocutionary acts**, summarize in your own words what each of these ways – 'securing uptake', 'taking effect' and 'inviting a response' – involve, linguistically.

■ ■ ■

HOW TO DO THINGS WITH WORDS
J.L. AUSTIN

[. . .] Utterances can be found [. . .] such that

A. they do not 'describe' or 'report' or constate anything at all, are not 'true or false'; and
B. the uttering of the sentence is, or is a part of, the doing of an action, which again would not *normally* be described as, or as 'just', saying something.

This is far from being as paradoxical as it may sound [. . .]: indeed, the examples now to be given will be disappointing.
[. . .]

'I do (sc. take this woman to be my lawful wedded wife)'—as uttered in the course of the marriage ceremony.

'I name this ship the *Queen Elizabeth*'—as uttered when smashing the bottle against the stem.

'I give and bequeath my watch to my brother'—as occurring in a will.

'I bet you sixpence it will rain tomorrow.'

In these examples it seems clear that to utter the sentence (in, of course, the appropriate circumstances) is not to *describe* my doing of what I should be said in so uttering to be doing or to state that I am doing it: it is to do it. None of the utterances cited is either true or false: I assert this as obvious and do not argue it. It needs argument no more than that 'damn' is not true or false: it may be that the utterance 'serves to inform you'—but that is quite different. To name the ship *is* to say (in the appropriate circumstances) the words 'I name, &c.'. When I say, before the registrar or altar, &c., 'I do', I am not reporting on a marriage: I am indulging in it.
[. . .]

Can saying make it so?

Are we then to say things like this:
    'To marry is to say a few words', or
    'Betting is simply saying something'?

Such a doctrine sounds odd or even flippant at first, but with sufficient safeguards it may become not odd at all.

A sound initial objection to them may be this; and it is not without some importance. In very many cases it is possible to perform an act of exactly the same kind *not* by uttering words, whether written or spoken, but in some other way. For example, I may in some places effect marriage by cohabiting, or I may bet with a totalisator machine by putting a coin in a slot. We should then, perhaps, convert the propositions above, and put it that 'to say a few certain words is to marry' or 'to marry is, in some cases, simply to say a few words' or 'simply to say a certain something is to bet'.

[. . .] The uttering of the words is [. . .] usually a, or even *the*, leading incident in the performance of the act (of betting or what not), the performance of which is also the object of the utterance, but it is far from being usually, even if it is ever, the *sole* thing necessary if the act is to be deemed to have been performed. Speaking generally, it is always necessary that the *circumstances* in which the words are uttered should be in some way, or ways, *appropriate*, and it is very commonly necessary that either the speaker himself or other persons should *also* perform certain *other* actions, whether 'physical' or 'mental' actions or even acts of uttering further words. Thus, [. . .] for (Christian) marrying, it is essential that I should not be already married with a wife living, sane and undivorced, and so on: for a bet to have been made, it is generally necessary for the offer of the bet to have been accepted by a taker (who must have done something, such as to say 'Done') [. . .]

[. . .]

Let us [. . .] concentrate [. . .] on [. . .] this matter of 'the appropriate circumstances'. To bet is not [. . .] merely to utter the words 'I bet, &c.': someone might do that all right, and yet we might still not agree that he had in fact, or at least entirely, succeeded in betting. To satisfy ourselves of this, we have only to announce our bet after the race is over. Besides the uttering of the words [. . .], a good many other things have as a general rule to be right and to go right if we are to be said to have happily brought off our action. What these are we may hope to discover by looking at and classifying types of case in which something *goes wrong* and the act—marrying, betting, bequeathing, christening, or what not—is therefore at least to some extent a failure: the utterance is then, we may say, not indeed false but in general *unhappy*. And for this reason we call the doctrine of *the things that can be and go wrong* on the occasion of such utterances, the doctrine of the *Infelicities*.

[. . .]

Locutionary, illocutionary, and perlocutionary acts

[. . .] To perform a locutionary act is in general, we may say, also and *eo ipso* to perform an *illocutionary* act, as I propose to call it. Thus in performing a locutionary act we shall also be performing such an act as:

asking or answering a question,
giving some information or an assurance or a warning,
announcing a verdict or an intention,
pronouncing sentence,
making an appointment or an appeal or a criticism,
making an identification or giving a description,

and the numerous like.

[. . .]
[. . .] [T]o perform a locutionary act, and therein an illocutionary act, may also be to perform an act of another kind. Saying something will often, or even normally, produce certain consequential effects upon the feelings, thoughts, or actions of the audience, or of the speaker, or of other persons: and it may be done with the design, intention, or purpose of producing them; and we may then say, thinking of this, that the speaker has performed an act in the nomenclature of which reference is made either (C. *a*), only obliquely, or even (C. *b*), not at all, to the performance of the locutionary or illocutionary act. We shall call the performance of an act of this kind the performance of a 'perlocutionary' act, and the act performed, where suitable—essentially in cases falling under (C. *a*)—a 'perlocution'. Let us not yet define this idea any more carefully [. . .] but simply give examples:

(E. 1)

Act (A) or Locution
He said to me 'Shoot her!' [. . .]

Act (B) or Illocution
He urged (or advised, ordered, &c.) me to shoot her.

Act (C. *a*) or Perlocution
He persuaded me to shoot her.

Act (C. *b*)
He got me to (or made me, &c.) shoot her.

(E. 2)

Act (A) or Locution
He said to me, 'You can't do that'.

Act (B) or Illocution
He protested against my doing it.

Act (C. *a*) or Perlocution
He pulled me up, checked me.

Act (C. *b*)
He stopped me, he brought me to my senses, &c.
He annoyed me.
[. . .]

We have here then [. . .] three kinds of acts—the locutionary, the illocutionary, and the perlocutionary [. . .]
[. . .]
[. . .] Our interest is essentially to fasten on the second [. . .] and contrast it with the other two. There is a constant tendency in philosophy to elide this in favour of one or other of the other two. Yet it is distinct from both. [. . .] Speaking of the 'use of "language" for arguing or warning' looks just like speaking of 'the use of "language" for persuading, rousing, alarming'; yet the former may, for rough contrast, be said to be *conventional*, in the sense that at least it could be made explicit by the performative formula; but the latter could not. Thus

we can say 'I argue that' or 'I warn you that' but we cannot say 'I convince you that' or 'I alarm you that'. Further, we may entirely clear up whether someone was arguing or not without touching on the question of whether he was convincing anyone or not.

[. . .] To take this farther, let us be quite clear that the expression 'use of language' can cover other matters even more diverse than the illocutionary and perlocutionary acts and obviously quite diverse from any with which we are here concerned. For example, we may speak of the 'use of language' *for* something, e.g. for joking; and we may use 'in' in a way different from the illocutionary 'in', as when we say 'in saying "*p*" I was joking' or 'acting a part' or 'writing poetry'; or again we may speak of 'a poetical use of language' as distinct from 'the use of language in poetry'. These references to 'use of language' have nothing to do with the illocutionary act. For example, if I say 'Go and catch a falling star', it may be quite clear what both the meaning and the force of my utterance is, but still wholly unresolved which of these other kinds of things I may be doing. There are etiolations, parasitic uses, etc., various 'not serious' and 'not full normal' uses. The normal conditions of reference may be suspended, or no attempt made at a standard perlocutionary act, no attempt to make you do anything, as Walt Whitman does not seriously incite the eagle of liberty to soar.

[. . .] Furthermore, there may be some things we 'do' in some connexion with saying something which do not seem to fall, intuitively at least, exactly into any of these roughly defined classes, or else seem to fall vaguely into more than one; [. . .] for example, *insinuating*, as when we insinuate something in or by issuing some utterance, seems to involve some convention, as in the illocutionary act; but we cannot *say* 'I insinuate . . . ', and it seems like implying to be a clever effect rather than a mere act. A further example is evincing emotion. We may evince emotion in or by issuing an utterance, as when we swear; but once again we have no use here for performative formulas and the other devices of illocutionary acts. We might say that we use swearing *for* relieving our feelings. We must notice that the illocutionary act is a conventional act: an act done as conforming to a convention.

The next three points that arise do so importantly because our acts are *acts*.

[. . .] Acts of all our three kinds necessitate, since they are the performing of actions, allowance being made for the ills that all action is heir to. We must systematically be prepared to distinguish between 'the act of doing *x*', i.e. achieving *x*, and 'the act of attempting to do *x*'.

In the case of illocutions we must be ready to draw the necessary distinction, not noticed by ordinary language except in exceptional cases, between

(*a*) the act of attempting or purporting (or affecting or professing or claiming or setting up or setting out) to perform a certain illocutionary act, and
(*b*) the act of successfully achieving or consummating or bringing off such an act.

[. . .]

[. . .] Since our acts are actions, we must always remember the distinction between producing effects or consequences which are intended or unintended; and (i) when the speaker intends to produce an effect it may nevertheless not occur, and (ii) when he does not intend to produce it or intends not to produce it it may nevertheless occur. To cope with complication (i) we invoke the distinction between attempt and achievement; to cope with complication (ii) we invoke the normal linguistic devices of disclaiming (adverbs like 'unintentionally' and so on) which we hold ready for general use in all cases of doing actions.

[. . .] Furthermore, we must, of course, allow that as actions they may be things that we do not exactly *do*, in the sense that we did them, say, under duress or in any other such way. [. . .]

[. . .] Finally we [. . .] have the idea of an 'act' as a fixed physical thing that we do, as distinguished from conventions and as distinguished from consequences. But

(a) the illocutionary act and the locutionary act involve conventions: compare with them the act of doing obeisance. It is obeisance only because it is conventional and it is done only because it is conventional. [. . .]

(b) the perlocutionary act always includes some consequences, as when we say 'By doing x I/he was doing y' [. . .] That we can import an arbitrarily long stretch of what might also be called the 'consequences' of our act into the nomenclature of the act itself is, or should be, a fundamental commonplace of the theory of our language about all 'action' in general. Thus if asked 'What did he do?', we may reply either 'He shot the donkey' or 'He fired a gun' or 'He pulled the trigger' or 'He moved his trigger finger', and all may be correct. [. . .] If in such cases we *mention* both a B act (illocution) and a C act (perlocution) we shall say '*by* B-ing he C-ed' rather than '*in*-B-ing . . . ' This is the reason for calling C a *per*locutionary act as distinct from an illocutionary act.

[. . .]

Distinctions between illocutionary and perlocutionary acts [. . .]

[. . .] [T]he illocutionary act as distinct from the perlocutionary [act] is connected with the production of effects in certain senses:

(1) Unless a certain effect is achieved, the illocutionary act will not have been happily, successfully performed. This is not to say that the illocutionary act is the achieving of a certain effect. I cannot be said to have warned an audience unless it hears what I say and takes what I say in a certain sense. An effect must be achieved on the audience if the illocutionary act is to be carried out.

  How should we best put it here? And how can we limit it? Generally the effect amounts to bringing about the understanding of the meaning and of the force of the locution. So the performance of an illocutionary act involves the securing of *uptake*.

(2) The illocutionary act 'takes effect' in certain ways, as distinguished from producing consequences in the sense of bringing about states of affairs in the 'normal' way, i.e. changes in the natural course of events. Thus 'I name this ship the *Queen Elizabeth*' has the effect of naming or christening the ship; then certain subsequent acts such as referring to it as the *Generalissimo Stalin* will be out of order.

(3) We have said that many illocutionary acts invite by convention a response or sequel. Thus an order invites the response of obedience and a promise that of fulfilment. The response or sequel may be 'one-way' or 'two-way': thus we may distinguish arguing, ordering, promising, suggesting, and asking to, from offering, asking whether you will and asking 'Yes or no?' If this response is accorded, or the sequel implemented, that requires a second act by the speaker or another person; and it is a commonplace of the consequence-language that this cannot be included under the initial stretch of action.

Generally we can, however, always say 'I got him to' with such a word. This does make the act one ascribed to me and it is, when words are or may be employed, a perlocutionary act. Thus we must distinguish 'I ordered him and he obeyed' from 'I *got him* to obey'. The general implication of the latter is that other additional means were employed to produce this consequence as ascribable to me, inducements, personal presence, and influence which may amount to duress; there is even very often an illocutionary act distinct from merely ordering, as when I say 'I got him to do it by stating x'.

So here are three ways, securing uptake, taking effect, and inviting a response, in which illocutionary acts are bound up with effects; and these are all distinct from the producing of effects which is characteristic of the perlocutionary act.

The perlocutionary act may be either the achievement of a perlocutionary object (convince, persuade) or the production of a perlocutionary sequel. Thus the act of warning may achieve its perlocutionary object of alerting and also have the perlocutionary sequel of alarming, and an argument against a view may fail to achieve its object but have the perlocutionary sequel of convincing our opponent of its truth ('I only succeeded in convincing him'). What is the perlocutionary object of one illocution may be the sequel of another. For example, warning may produce the sequel of deterring and saying 'Don't', whose object is to deter, may produce the sequel of alerting or even alarming. Some perlocutionary acts are always the producing of a sequel, namely those where there is no illocutionary formula: thus I may surprise you or upset you or humiliate you by a locution, though there is no illocutionary formula 'I surprise you by . . . ', 'I upset you by . . . ', 'I humiliate you by . . . '

It is characteristic of perlocutionary acts that the response achieved, or the sequel, can be achieved additionally or entirely by non-locutionary means: thus intimidation may be achieved by waving a stick or pointing a gun. Even in the cases of convincing, persuading, getting to obey and getting to believe, we may achieve the response non-verbally; but if there is no illocutionary act, it is doubtful whether this language characteristic of perlocutionary objects should be used. Compare the use of 'got him to' with that of 'got him to obey'. However, this alone is not enough to distinguish illocutionary acts, since we can for example warn or order or appoint or give or protest or apologize by non-verbal means and these are illocutionary acts. Thus we may cock a snook or hurl a tomato by way of protest.

More important is the question whether these responses and sequels can be achieved by non-conventional means. Certainly we can achieve the same perlocutionary sequels by non-conventional means (or as we say 'unconventional' means), means that are not conventional at all or not for that purpose; thus I may persuade someone by gently swinging a big stick or gently mentioning that his aged parents are still in the Third Reich. Strictly speaking, there cannot be an illocutionary act unless the means employed are conventional, and so the means for achieving it non-verbally must be conventional. But it is difficult to say where conventions begin and end; thus I may warn him by swinging a stick or I may give him something by merely handing it to him. But if I warn him by swinging a stick, then swinging my stick is a warning: he would know very well what I meant: it may seem an unmistakable threatening gesture. Similar difficulties arise over giving tacit consent to some arrangement, or promising tacitly, or voting by a show of hands. But the fact remains that many illocutionary acts cannot be performed except by saying something. This is true of stating, informing (as distinct from showing), arguing, giving estimates, reckoning, and finding (in the legal sense); it is true of the great majority of verdictives and expositives as opposed to many exercitives and commissives.

[. . .]

POST-READING

Now that you have completed your reading, we would like you to grade the usefulness of Austin's distinctions between the 'locutionary', 'illocutionary' and 'perlocutionary' characteristics of speech acts (where 5 is *very useful* and 1 is *not essential*). Which – if any – does Austin seem to prioritise? If there is evidence to suggest that one is prioritised over the others, do you find this problematic at all? Why/why not?

JOHN R. SEARLE

INDIRECT SPEECH ACTS*

PRE-READING

When uttered at UK dinner tables, *Can you pass the salt?* has the form of an interrogative, but functions as a request that H give the salt-shaker to S. A closely related phrase – roughly translated as *Can you give me the salt?* – seems to work in the same way in many other languages. Before reading 'Indirect Speech Acts', write down as many examples as you can of utterances that, like *Can you pass/give me the salt?*, display a similar mismatch between form and function (or 'literal' meaning and illocutionary force) in either English or another language with which you are familiar.

IN-READING

1   Searle provides a detailed description of why, as hearers, we take *Can you pass the salt?* to be a request that we give the salt-shaker to S and not a literal question about our ability to pass it to them. When you get to this point in the reading (indicated by the first | in the margin), decide which of these ten steps are absolutely essential in your view and which are not as essential – and why. To what extent do you think Searle is actually suggesting that we systematically go through such an inferential process when we are the target of requests?

2   Searle suggests that 'in order to be a plausible candidate at all for use as an indirect speech act, a sentence has to be idiomatic. But within the class of idiomatic sentences, some forms tend to become entrenched as conventional devices for indirect speech acts'. As you come to Searle's discussion of 'Problem 1' (indicated by the second | in the margin), summarize the various points that Searle makes in regard to the relationship between speech acts, indirectness and idiomaticity.

■ ■ ■

INDIRECT SPEECH ACTS
JOHN R. SEARLE

[. . .]

The problem posed by indirect speech acts is the problem of how it is possible for the speaker to say one thing and mean that but also to mean something else. And since meaning consists in part in the intention to produce understanding in the hearer, a large part of that problem is that of how it is possible for the hearer to understand the indirect speech act when the sentence he hears and understands means something else. The problem is made more complicated by the fact that some sentences seem almost to be conventionally used as indirect requests. [. . .]

In Searle (1969: Chapter 3) I suggested that many such utterances could be explained by the fact that the sentences in question concern conditions of the felicitous performance of the speech acts they are used to perform indirectly – preparatory conditions, propositional content conditions, and sincerity conditions – and that their use to perform indirect speech acts consists in indicating the satisfaction of an essential condition by means of asserting or questioning one of the other conditions. [. . .] The answer originally suggested in Searle (1969) seems to me incomplete, and I want to develop it further here. The hypothesis I wish to defend is simply this: In indirect speech acts the speaker communicates to the hearer more than he actually says by way of relying on their mutually shared background information, both linguistic and nonlinguistic, together with the general powers of rationality and inference on the part of the hearer. To be more specific, the apparatus necessary to explain the indirect part of indirect speech acts includes a theory of speech acts, certain general principles of cooperative conversation [. . .] and mutually shared factual background information of the speaker and the hearer, together with an ability on the part of the hearer to make inferences. It is not necessary to assume the existence of any conversational postulates (either as an addition to the theory of speech acts or as part of the theory of speech acts) nor any concealed imperative forces or other ambiguities. We will see, however, that in some cases, convention plays a most peculiar role.

[. . .]

A sample case

Let us begin by considering a typical case of the general phenomenon of indirection:

(1) *Student X: Let's go to the movies tonight.*

(2) *Student Y: I have to study for an exam.*

The utterance of (1) constitutes a proposal in virtue of its meaning, in particular because of the meaning of *Let's*. [. . .]

[. . .]

The utterance of (2) [. . .] would normally constitute a rejection of the proposal, but not in virtue of its meaning. In virtue of its meaning it is simply a statement about Y. Statements of this form do not, in general, constitute rejections of proposals, even in cases in which they are made in response to a proposal. Thus, if Y had said:

I have to eat popcorn tonight.

or:

I have to tie my shoes.

in a normal context, neither of these utterances would have been a rejection of the proposal. [. . .] How does X know that the utterance is a rejection of the proposal? and [. . .] How is it possible for Y to intend or mean the utterance of (2) as a rejection of the proposal? In order to describe this case, let us introduce some terminology. Let us say that the PRIMARY illocutionary act performed in Y's utterance is the rejection of the proposal made by X, and that Y does that by way of performing a SECONDARY illocutionary act of making a statement to the effect that he has to prepare for an exam. [. . .]

A brief reconstruction of the steps necessary to derive the primary illocution from the literal illocution would go as follows. (In normal conversation, of course, no one would consciously go through the steps involved in this reasoning.)

STEP 1:   *I have made a proposal to Y, and in response he has made a statement to the effect that he has to study for an exam (facts about the conversation).*

STEP 2:   *I assume that Y is cooperating in the conversation and that therefore his remark is intended to be relevant (principles of conversational cooperation).*

STEP 3:   *A relevant response must be one of acceptance, rejection, counterproposal, further discussion, etc. (theory of speech acts).*

STEP 4:   *But his literal utterance was not one of these, and so was not a relevant response inference from Steps 1 and 3).*

STEP 5:   *Therefore, he probably means more than he says. Assuming that his remark is relevant, his primary illocutionary point must differ from his literal one (inference from Steps 2 and 4).*

This step is crucial. Unless a hearer has some inferential strategy for finding out when primary illocutionary points differ from literal illocutionary points, he has no way of understanding indirect illocutionary acts.

STEP 6:   *I know that studying for an exam normally takes a large amount of time relative to a single evening, and I know that going to the movies normally takes a large amount of time relative to a single evening (factual background information).*

STEP 7:   *Therefore, he probably cannot both go to the movies and study for an exam in one evening (inference from Step 6).*

STEP 8:   *A preparatory condition on the acceptance of a proposal, or on any other commissive, is the ability to perform the act predicated in the propositional content condition (theory of speech acts).*

STEP 9:   *Therefore, I know that he has said something that has the consequence that he probably cannot consistently accept the proposal (inference from Steps 1, 7, and 8).*

STEP 10: *Therefore, his primary illocutionary point is probably to reject the proposal (inference from Steps 5 and 9).*

It may seem somewhat pedantic to set all of this out in 10 steps; but if anything, the example is still underdescribed – I have not, for example, discussed the role of the assumption of sincerity, or the ceteris paribus conditions that attach to various of the steps. Notice, also, that the conclusion is probabilistic. It is and ought to be. This is because the reply does not necessarily constitute a rejection of the proposal. Y might have gone on to say:

I have to study for an exam, but let's go to the movies anyhow.

I have to study for an exam, but I'll do it when we get home from the movies.

The inferential strategy is to establish, first, that the primary illocutionary point departs from the literal, and second, what the primary illocutionary point is.

The argument of this chapter will be that the theoretical apparatus used to explain this case will suffice to explain the general phenomenon of indirect illocutionary acts. That apparatus includes mutual background information, a theory of speech acts, and certain general principles of conversation. In particular, we explained this case without having to assume that sentence (2) is ambiguous or that it is 'ambiguous in context' or that it is necessary to assume the existence of any 'conversational postulates' in order to explain X's understanding the primary illocution of the utterance. The main difference between this case and the cases we will be discussing is that the latter all have a generality of FORM that is lacking in this example. I shall mark this generality by using **bold** type for the formal features in the surface structure of the sentences in question. In the field of indirect illocutionary acts, the area of directives is the most useful to study because ordinary conversational requirements of politeness normally make it awkward to issue flat imperative sentences (e.g., *Leave the room*) or explicit performatives (e.g., *I order you to leave the room*), and we therefore seek to find indirect means to our illocutionary ends (e.g., *I wonder if you would mind leaving the room*). In directives, politeness is the chief motivation for indirectness.

Some sentences 'conventionally' used in the performance of indirect directives

Let us begin, then, with a short list of some of the sentences that could quite standardly be used to make indirect requests and other directives such as orders. At a pretheoretical level these sentences naturally tend to group themselves into certain categories.[1]

GROUP 1: *Sentences concerning H's ability to perform A:*

[. . .]
Can you *pass the salt?*
Could you *be a little more quiet?*
You could *be a little more quiet.*
You can *go now* (this may also be a permission = *you may go now*).
Are you able *to reach the book on the top shelf?*
Have you *got change for a dollar?*

GROUP 2: *Sentences concerning S's wish or want that H will do A:*

I would like you to *go now.*
I want you to *do this for me, Henry.*
I would/should appreciate it if you would/could *do it for me.*
I would/should be most grateful if you would/could *help us out.*
I'd rather you didn't *do that any more.*
I'd be very much obliged if you would *pay me the money back soon.*
I hope you'll *do it.*
I wish you wouldn't *do that.*

GROUP 3: *Sentences concerning H's doing A:*

> *Officers **will** henceforth wear ties at dinner.*
> ***Will you** quit making that awful racket?*
> ***Would you** kindly get off my foot?*
> ***Won't you** stop making that noise soon?*
> ***Aren't you** going to eat your cereal?*

GROUP 4: *Sentences concerning H's desire or willingness to do A:*

> ***Would you be willing** to write a letter of recommendation for me?*
> ***Do you want** to hand me that hammer over there on the table?*
> ***Would you mind** not making so much noise?*
> ***Would it be convenient for you** to come on Wednesday?*
> ***Would it be too much (trouble) for you** to pay me the money next Wednesday?*

GROUP 5: *Sentences concerning reasons for doing A:*

> ***You ought** to be more polite to your mother.*
> ***You should** leave immediately.*
> ***Must you** continue hammering that way?*
> ***Ought you** to eat quite so much spaghetti?*
> ***Should you** be wearing John's tie?*
> ***You had better** go now.*
> ***Hadn't you better** go now?*
> ***Why not** stop here?*
> ***Why don't you** try it just once?*
> ***Why don't you be** quiet?*
> ***It would be better for you (for us all) if you would** leave the room.*
> ***It wouldn't hurt if you** left now.*
> ***It might help if you** shut up.*
> ***It would be better if you** gave me the money now.*
> ***It would be a good idea if you** left town.*
> ***We'd all be better off if you'd** just pipe down a bit.*

This class also contains many examples that have no generality of form but obviously, in an appropriate context, would be uttered as indirect requests, e.g.:

> *You're standing on my foot.*
> *I can't see the movie screen while you have that hat on.*

Also in this class belong, possibly:

> ***How many times have I told you (must I tell you)** not to eat with your fingers?*
> ***I must have told you a dozen times not to** eat with your mouth open.*
> ***If I have told you once I have told you a thousand times not to** wear your hat
>   in the house.*

GROUP 6: *Sentences embedding one of these elements inside another; also, sentences embedding an explicit directive illocutionary verb inside one of these contexts:*

> **Would you mind awfully if I asked you if you could** write me a letter of recommendation?
> **Would it be too much if I suggested that you could possibly** make a little less noise?
> **Might I ask you** to take off your hat?
> **I hope you won't mind if I ask you if you could** leave us alone.
> **I would appreciate it if you could** make less noise.[2]

This is a very large class, since most of its members are constructed by permitting certain of the elements of the other classes.

Some putative facts

[. . .]

FACT 1: *The sentences in question do not have an imperative force as part of their meaning.* This point is sometimes denied by philosophers and linguists, but very powerful evidence for it is provided by the fact that it is possible without inconsistency to connect the literal utterance of one of these forms with the denial of any imperative intent, e.g.:

> I'd like you to do this for me, Bill, but I am not asking you to do it or requesting that you do it or ordering you to do it or telling you to do it.

> I'm just asking you, Bill: Why not eat beans? But in asking you that I want you to understand that I am not telling you to eat beans; I just want to know your reasons for thinking you ought not to.

FACT 2: *The sentences in question are not ambiguous as between an imperative illocutionary force and a nonimperative illocutionary force.* I think this is intuitively apparent, but in any case, an ordinary application of Occam's razor places the onus of proof on those who wish to claim that these sentences are ambiguous. One does not multiply meanings beyond necessity. Notice, also, that it is no help to say they are 'ambiguous in context,' for all that means is that one cannot always tell from what the sentence means what the speaker means by its utterance, and that is not sufficient to establish sentential ambiguity.

FACT 3: *Notwithstanding Facts 1 and 2, these are standardly, ordinarily, normally – indeed, I shall argue, conventionally – used to issue directives.* There is a systematic relation between these and directive illocutions in a way that there is no systematic relation between *I have to study for an exam* and rejecting proposals. Additional evidence that they are standardly used to issue imperatives is that most of them take *please*, either at the end of the sentence or preceding the verb, e.g.:

> I want you to stop making that noise, please.
> Could you please lend me a dollar?

When *please* is added to one of these sentences, it explicitly and literally marks the primary illocutionary point of the utterance as directive, even though the literal meaning of the rest of the sentence is not directive.

It is because of the combination of Facts 1, 2, and 3 that there is a problem about these cases at all.

FACT 4: *The sentences in question are not, in the ordinary sense, idioms.* An ordinary example of an idiom is *kicked the bucket* in *Jones kicked the bucket.* The most powerful evidence I know that these sentences are not idioms is that in their use as indirect directives they admit of literal responses that presuppose that they are uttered literally. Thus, an utterance of *Why don't you be quiet, Henry?* admits as a response an utterance of *Well, Sally, there are several reasons for not being quiet. First, . . .* Possible exceptions to this are occurrences of *would* and *could* in indirect speech acts, and I will discuss them later.

Further evidence that they are not idioms is that, whereas a word-for-word translation of *Jones kicked the bucket* into other languages will not produce a sentence meaning 'Jones died,' translations of the sentences in question will often, though by no means always, produce sentences with the same indirect illocutionary act potential of the English examples. Thus, e.g., *Pourriez-vous m'aider?* and *Können Sie mir helfen?* can be uttered as indirect requests in French or German. I will later discuss the problem of why some translate with equivalent indirect illocutionary force potential and some do not.

FACT 5: *To say they are not idioms is not to say they are not idiomatic.* All the examples given are idiomatic in current English, and – what is more puzzling – they are idiomatically used as requests. In general, nonidiomatic equivalents or synonyms would not have the same indirect illocutionary act potential. Thus, *Do you want to hand me the hammer over there on the table?* can be uttered as a request, but *Is it the case that you at present desire to hand me that hammer over there on the table?* has a formal and stilted character that in almost all contexts would eliminate it as a candidate for an indirect request. Furthermore, *Are you able to hand me that hammer?*, though idiomatic, does not have the same indirect request potential as *Can you hand me that hammer?* That these sentences are IDIOMATIC and are IDIOMATICALLY USED AS DIRECTIVES is crucial to their role in indirect speech acts. I will say more about the relations of these facts later.

FACT 6: *The sentences in question have literal utterances in which they are not also indirect requests.* Thus, *Can you reach the salt?* can be uttered as a simple question about your abilities (say, by an orthopedist wishing to know the medical progress of your arm injury). *I want you to leave* can be uttered simply as a statement about one's wants, without any directive intent. At first sight, some of our examples might not appear to satisfy this condition, e.g.:

Why not stop here?
Why don't you be quiet?

But with a little imagination it is easy to construct situations in which utterances [such as] these would be not directives but straight-forward questions. Suppose someone had said *We ought not to stop here.* Then *Why not stop here?* would be an appropriate question, without necessarily being also a suggestion. Similarly, if someone had just said *I certainly hate making all this racket*, an utterance of (*Well, then*) *Why don't you be quiet?* would be an appropriate response, without also necessarily being a request to be quiet.

It is important to note that the intonation of these sentences when they are uttered as indirect requests often differs from their intonation when uttered with only their literal illocutionary force, and often the intonation pattern will be that characteristic of literal directives.

FACT 7: *In cases where these sentences are uttered as requests, they still have their literal meaning and are uttered with and as having that literal meaning.* I have seen it claimed that they have different meanings 'in context' when they are uttered as requests, but I believe that is obviously false. The man who says I want you to do it means literally that he wants you to do it. The point is that, as is always the case with indirection, he means not only what he says but something more as well. What is added in the indirect cases is not any additional or different SENTENCE meaning, but additional SPEAKER meaning. Evidence that these sentences keep their literal meanings when uttered as indirect requests is that responses that are appropriate to their literal utterances are appropriate to their indirect speech act utterances (as we noted in our discussion of Fact 4), e.g.:

> *Can you pass the salt?*
> *No, sorry, I can't, it's down there at the end of the table.*
> *Yes, I can. (Here it is.)*

FACT 8: *It is a consequence of Fact 7 that when one of these sentences is uttered with the primary illocutionary point of a directive, the literal illocutionary act is also performed.* In every one of these cases, the speaker issues a directive BY WAY OF asking a question or making a statement. But the fact that his primary illocutionary intent is directive does not alter the fact that he is asking a question or making a statement. Additional evidence for Fact 8 is that a subsequent report of the utterance can truly report the literal illocutionary act.

Thus, e.g., the utterance of *I want you to leave now, Bill* can be reported by an utterance of *He told me he wanted me to leave, so I left*. Or, the utterance of *Can you reach the salt?* can be reported by an utterance of *He asked me whether I could reach the salt*. Similarly, an utterance of *Could you do it for me, Henry; could you do it for me and Cynthia and the children?* can be reported by an utterance of *He asked me whether I could do it for him and Cynthia and the children*.

This point is sometimes denied. I have seen it claimed that the literal illocutionary acts are always defective or are not 'conveyed' when the sentence is used to perform a nonliteral primary illocutionary act. As far as our examples are concerned, the literal illocutions are always conveyed and are sometimes, but not in general, defective. For example, an indirect speech act utterance of *Can you reach the salt?* may be defective in the sense that S may already know the answer. But even this form NEED not be defective. (Consider, e.g., *Can you give me change for a dollar?*.) Even when the literal utterance is defective, the indirect speech act does not depend on its being defective.

An explanation in terms of the theory of speech acts

The difference between the example concerning the proposal to go to the movies and all of the other cases is that the other cases are systematic. What we need to do, then, is to describe an example in such a way as to show how the apparatus used on the first example will suffice for these other cases and also will explain the systematic character of the other cases.

I think the theory of speech acts will enable us to provide a simple explanation of how these sentences, which have one illocutionary force as part of their meaning, can be used to perform an act with a different illocutionary force. Each type of illocutionary act has a set of conditions that are necessary for the successful and felicitous performance of the act. To illustrate this, I will present the conditions on two types of acts within the two genuses, directive and commissive (Searle 1969: Chapter 3).

A comparison of the list of felicity conditions on the directive class of illocutionary acts and our list of types of sentences used to perform indirect directives show that Groups 1–6 of types can be reduced to three types: those having to do with felicity conditions on the performance of a directive illocutionary act, those having to do with reasons for doing the act, and those embedding one element inside another one. Thus, since the ability of H to perform A (Group 1) is a preparatory condition, the desire of S that H perform A (Group 2) is the sincerity condition, and the predication of A of H (Group 3) is the propositional content condition, all of Groups 1–3 concern felicity conditions on directive illocutionary acts. Since wanting to do something is a reason par excellence for doing it, Group 4 assimilates to Group 5, as both concern reasons for doing A. Group 6 is a special class only by courtesy, since its elements either are performative verbs or are already contained in the other two categories of felicity conditions and reasons.

	Directive (Request)	*Commissive (Promise)*
Preparatory condition	H is able to perform A.	S is able to perform A. H wants S to perform A.
Sincerity condition	S wants H to do A.	S intends to do A.
Propositional content condition	S predicates a future act A of H.	S predicates a future act A of S.
Essential condition	Counts as an attempt by S to get H to do A.	Counts as the undertaking by S of an obligation to do A.

Ignoring the embedding cases for the moment, if we look at our lists and our sets of conditions, the following generalizations naturally emerge:

GENERALIZATION 1: *S can make an indirect request (or other directive) by either asking whether or stating that a preparatory condition concerning H's ability to do A obtains.*

GENERALIZATION 2: *S can make an indirect directive by either asking whether or stating that the propositional content condition obtains.*

GENERALIZATION 3: *S can make an indirect directive by stating that the sincerity condition obtains, but not by asking whether it obtains.*

GENERALIZATION 4: *S can make an indirect directive by either stating that or asking whether there are good or overriding reasons for doing A, except where the reason is that H wants or wishes, etc., to do A, in which case he can only ask whether H wants, wishes, etc., to do A.*

It is the existence of these generalizations that accounts for the systematic character of the relation between the sentences in Groups 1–6 and the directive class of illocutionary acts. Notice that these are generalizations and not rules. The rules of speech acts (or some of them) are stated in the list of conditions presented earlier. That is, for example, it is a rule of the directive class of speech acts that the directive is defective if the hearer is unable to perform the act, but it is precisely not a rule of speech acts or of conversation that one can perform a directive by asking whether the preparatory condition obtains. The theoretical task is to show how that generalization will be a consequence of the rule, together with certain other information, namely, the factual background information and the general principles of conversation.

Our next task is to try to describe an example of an indirect request with at least the same degree of pedantry we used in our description of the rejection of a proposal. Let us take the simplest sort of case: At the dinner table, X says to Y, *Can you pass the salt?* by way of asking Y to pass the salt. Now, how does Y know that X is requesting him to pass the salt instead of just asking a question about his abilities to pass the salt? Notice that not everything will do as a request to pass the salt. Thus, if X had said *Salt is made of sodium chloride* or *Salt is mined in the Tatra mountains*, without some special stage setting, it is very unlikely that Y would take either of these utterances as a request to pass the salt. Notice further that, in a normal conversational situation, Y does not have to go through any conscious process of inference to derive the conclusion that the utterance of *Can you pass the salt?* is a request to pass the salt. He simply hears it as a request. This fact is perhaps one of the main reasons why it is tempting to adopt the false conclusion that somehow these examples must have an imperative force as part of their meaning or that they are 'ambiguous in context,' or some such. What we need to do is offer an explanation that is consistent with all of Facts 1–8 yet does not make the mistake of hypostatizing concealed imperative forces or conversational postulates. A bare-bones reconstruction of the steps necessary for Y to derive the conclusion from the utterance might go roughly as follows:

STEP 1:   Y has asked me a question as to whether I have the ability to pass the salt (fact about the conversation).

STEP 2:   I assume that he is cooperating in the conversation and that therefore his utterance has some aim or point (principles of conversational cooperation).

STEP 3:   The conversational setting is not such as to indicate a theoretical interest in my salt-passing ability (factual background information).

STEP 4:   Furthermore, he probably already knows that the answer to the question is yes (factual background information). (This step facilitates the move to Step 5, but is not essential.)

STEP 5:   Therefore, his utterance is probably not just a question. It probably has some ulterior illocutionary point (inference from Steps 1, 2, 3, and 4). What can it be?

STEP 6:   A preparatory condition for any directive illocutionary act is the ability of H to perform the act predicated in the propositional content condition (theory of speech acts).

STEP 7:   Therefore, X has asked me a question the affirmative answer to which would entail that the preparatory condition for requesting me to pass the salt is satisfied (inference from Steps 1 and 6).

STEP 8:   We are now at dinner and people normally use salt at dinner; they pass it back and forth, try to get others to pass it back and forth, etc. (background information).

STEP 9:   He has therefore alluded to the satisfaction of a preparatory condition for a request whose obedience conditions it is quite likely he wants me to bring about (inference from Steps 7 and 8).

STEP 10: Therefore, in the absence of any other plausible illocutionary point, he is probably requesting me to pass him the salt (inference from Steps 5 and 9).

The hypothesis being put forth in this chapter is that all the cases can be similarly analyzed. According to this analysis, the reason I can ask you to pass the salt by saying *Can you pass the salt?* but not by saying *Salt is made of sodium chloride* or *Salt is mined in the Tatra mountains* is that your ability to pass the salt is a preparatory condition for requesting you to pass the salt in a way that the other sentences are not related to requesting you to pass the salt. But obviously, that answer is not by itself sufficient, because not all questions about your abilities are requests. The hearer therefore needs some way of finding out when the utterance is just a question about his abilities and when it is a request made by way of asking a question about his abilities. It is at this point that the general principles of conversation (together with factual background information) come into play.

The two features that are crucial, or so I am suggesting, are, first, a strategy for establishing the existence of an ulterior illocutionary point beyond the illocutionary point contained in the meaning of the sentence, and second, a device for finding out what the ulterior illocutionary point is. The first is established by the principles of conversation operating on the information of the hearer and the speaker, and the second is derived from the theory of speech acts together with background information. The generalizations are to be explained by the fact that each of them records a strategy by means of which the hearer can find out how a primary illocutionary point differs from a secondary illocutionary point.

The chief motivation – though not the only motivation – for using these indirect forms is politeness. Notice that, in the example just given, the *Can you* form is polite in at least two respects. Firstly, X does not presume to know about Y's abilities, as he would if he issued an imperative sentence; and, secondly, the form gives – or at least appears to give – Y the option of refusing, since a yes-no question allows *no* as a possible answer. Hence, compliance can be made to appear a free act rather than obeying a command.

Some problems

[. . .] Even supposing that this pattern of analysis could be shown to be successful in many more cases, there are still several problems that remain:

PROBLEM 1: The biggest single problem with the foregoing analysis is this: If, as I have been arguing, the mechanisms by which indirect speech acts are meant and understood are perfectly general – having to do with the theory of speech acts, the principles of cooperative conversation, and shared background information – and not tied to any particular syntactical form, then why is it that some syntactical forms work better than others. Why can I ask you to do something by saying *Can you hand me that book on the top shelf?* but not, or not very easily, by saying *Is it the case that you at present have the ability to hand me that book on the top shelf?*

Even within such pairs as:

Do you want to do A?
Do you desire to do A?

and:

Can you do A?
Are you able to do A?

there is clearly a difference in indirect illocutionary act potential. Note, for example, that the first member of each pair takes *please* more readily than the second. Granting that none of these pairs are exact synonyms, and granting that all the sentences have some use as indirect requests, it is still essential to explain the differences in their indirect illocutionary act potential. How, in short, can it be the case that some sentences are not imperative idioms and yet function as forms for idiomatic requests?

The first part of the answer is this: The theory of speech acts and the principles of conversational cooperation do, indeed, provide a framework within which indirect illocutionary acts can be meant and understood. However, within this framework certain forms will tend to become conventionally established as the standard idiomatic forms for indirect speech acts. While keeping their literal meanings, they will acquire conventional uses as, e.g., polite forms for requests.

It is by now, I hope, uncontroversial that there is a distinction to be made between meaning and use, but what is less generally recognized is that there can be conventions of usage that are not meaning conventions. I am suggesting that *can you, could you, I want you to*, and numerous other forms are conventional ways of making requests (and in that sense it is not incorrect to say they are idioms), but at the same time they do not have an imperative meaning (and in that sense it would be incorrect to say they are idioms). Politeness is the most prominent motivation for indirectness in requests, and certain forms naturally tend to become the conventionally polite ways of making indirect requests.

If this explanation is correct, it would go some way toward explaining why there are differences in the indirect speech forms from one language to another. The mechanisms are not peculiar to this language or that, but at the same time the standard forms from one language will not always maintain their indirect speech act potential when translated from one language to another. Thus, *Can you hand me that book?* will function as an indirect request in English, but its Czech translation, *Mužete mi podat tu Knížku?* will sound very odd if uttered as a request in Czech.

A second part of the answer is this: In order to be a plausible candidate for an utterance as an indirect speech act, a sentence has to be idiomatic to start with. It is very easy to imagine circumstances in which: *Are you able to reach that book on the top shelf?* could be uttered as a request. But it is much harder to imagine cases in which *Is it the case that you at present have the ability to reach that book on the top shelf?* could be similarly used. Why?

I think the explanation for this fact may derive from another maxim of conversation having to do with speaking idiomatically. In general, if one speaks unidiomatically, hearers assume that there must be a special reason for it, and in consequence, various assumptions of normal speech are suspended. Thus, if *I* say, archaically, *Knowest thou him who calleth himself Richard Nixon?*, you are not likely to respond as you would to an utterance of *Do you know Richard Nixon?*

Besides the maxims proposed by Grice, there seems to be an additional maxim of conversation that could be expressed as follows: *Speak idiomatically unless there is some special reason not to.* For this reason, the normal conversational assumptions on which the possibility of indirect speech acts rests are in large part suspended in the nonidiomatic cases.

The answer, then, to Problem 1 is in two parts. In order to be a plausible candidate at all for use as an indirect speech act, a sentence has to be idiomatic. But within the class of idiomatic sentences, some forms tend to become entrenched as conventional devices for indirect speech acts. In the case of directives, in which politeness is the chief motivation for the indirect forms, certain forms are conventionally used as polite requests. Which kinds of forms are selected will, in all likelihood, vary from one language to another.

PROBLEM 2: Why is there an asymmetry between the sincerity condition and the others such that one can perform an indirect request only by asserting the satisfaction of a sincerity condition, not by querying it, whereas one can perform indirect directives by either asserting or querying the satisfaction of the propositional content and preparatory conditions?

Thus, an utterance of *I want you to do it* can be a request, but not an utterance of *Do I want you to do it?* The former can take *please*, the latter cannot. A similar asymmetry occurs in the case of reasons: *Do you want to leave us alone?* can be a request, but not *You want to leave us alone.*[3] Again, the former can take *please*, the latter cannot. How is one to explain these facts?

I believe the answer is that it is odd, in normal circumstances, to ask other people about the existence of one's own elementary psychological states, and odd to assert the existence of other people's elementary psychological states when addressing them. Since normally you are never in as good a position as I am to assert what I want, believe, intend, and so on, and since I am normally not in as good a position as you to assert what you want, believe, intend, and so on, it is, in general, odd for me to ask you about my states or tell you about yours. We shall see shortly that this asymmetry extends to the indirect performance of other kinds of speech acts.

PROBLEM 3: Though this chapter is not intended as being about English syntactical forms, some of the sentences on our lists are of enough interest to deserve special comment. Even if it should turn out that these peculiar cases are really imperative idioms, like *how about ...?*, it would not alter the general lines of my argument; it would simply shift some examples out of the class of indirect speech acts into the class of imperative idioms.

One interesting form is *why not plus verb*, as in *Why not stop here?* This form, unlike *Why don't you?*, has many of the same syntactical constraints as imperative sentences. For example, it requires a voluntary verb. Thus, one cannot say *Why not resemble your grandmother?* unless one believes that one can resemble someone as a voluntary action, whereas one can say *Why not imitate your grandmother?* Furthermore, like imperative sentences, this form requires a reflexive when it takes a second-person direct object, e.g., *Why not wash yourself?* Do these facts prove that the *Why not . . . ?* (and the *why . . . ?*) forms are imperative in meaning? I think they are not. On my account, the way an utterance of *why not?* works is this: In asking *Why not stop here?* as a suggestion to stop here, S challenges H to provide reasons for not doing something on the tacit assumption that the absence of reasons for not doing something is itself a reason for doing it, and the suggestion to do it is therefore made indirectly in accordance with the generalization that alluding to a reason for doing something is a way of making an indirect directive to do it. This analysis is supported by several facts. First, as we have already seen, this form can have a literal utterance in which it is not uttered as a suggestion; second, one can respond to the suggestion with a response appropriate to the literal utterance, e.g., *Well, there are several reasons for not stopping here. First, . . .* And third, one can report an utterance of one of these, without reporting any directive illocutionary forces, in the form *He asked me why we shouldn't stop there.* And here the occurrence of the practical *should* or *ought* (not the theoretical *should* or *ought*) is sufficient to account for the requirement of a voluntary verb.

Other troublesome examples are provided by occurrences of *would* and *could* in indirect speech acts. Consider, for example, utterances of *Would you pass me the salt?* and *Could you hand me that book?* It is not easy to analyze these forms and to describe exactly how they differ in meaning from *Will you pass me the salt?* and *Can you hand me that book?* Where, for example, are we to find the *if* clause, which, we are sometimes told, is required by the so-called subjunctive use of these expressions? Suppose we treat the *if* clause as *if I asked you to.* Thus, *Would you pass me the salt?* is short for *Would you pass me the salt if I asked you to?*

There are at least two difficulties with this approach. First, it does not seem at all plausible for *could*, since your abilities and possibilities are not contingent on what I ask you to do. But second, even for *would* it is unsatisfactory, since *Would you pass me the salt if I asked you to?* does not have the same indirect illocutionary act potential as the simple *Would you pass me the salt?* Clearly, both forms have uses as indirect directives, but, equally clearly, they are not equivalent. Furthermore, the cases in which *would* and *could* interrogative forms DO have a nonindirect use seem to be quite different from the cases we have been considering, e.g., *Would you vote for a Democrat?* or *Could you marry a radical?* Notice, for example, that an appropriate response to an utterance of these might be, e.g., *Under what conditions?* or *It depends on the situation.* But these would hardly be appropriate responses to an utterance of *Would you pass me the salt?* in the usual dinner table scene we have been envisaging.

Could seems to be analyzable in terms of *would* and possibility or ability. Thus, *Could you marry a radical* means something like *Would it be possible for you to marry a radical? Would*, like *will*, is traditionally analyzed either as expressing want or desire or as a future auxiliary.

The difficulty with these forms seems to be an instance of the general difficulty about the nature of the subjunctive and does not necessarily indicate that there is any imperative meaning. If we are to assume that *would* and *could* have an imperative meaning, then it seems we will be forced to assume, also, that they have a commissive meaning as well, since utterances of *Could I be of assistance?* and *Would you like some more wine?* are both normally offers. I find this conclusion implausible because it involves an unnecessary proliferation of meanings. It violates Occam's razor regarding concepts. It is more economical to assume that *could* and *would* are univocal in *Could you pass the salt?, Could I be of assistance?, Would you stop making that noise?,* and *Would you like some more wine?.* However, a really satisfactory analysis of these forms awaits a satisfactory analysis of the subjunctive. The most plausible analysis of the indirect request forms is that the suppressed *if* clause is the polite *if you please* or *if you will.*

Extending the analysis

I want to conclude this chapter by showing that the general approach suggested in it will work for other types of indirection besides just directives. [. . .]

[. . .] [T]he richest mine for examples is provided by commissives, and a study of the examples of sentences used to perform indirect commissives (especially offers and promises) shows very much the same patterns that we found in the study of directives. Consider the following sentences, any of which can be uttered to perform an indirect offer (or, in some cases, a promise).

Sentences concerning the preparatory conditions:

A.   that S is able to perform the act:

   Can I help you?
   I can do that for you.
   I could get it for you.
   Could I be of assistance?

B.   that H wants S to perform the act:

   Would you like some help?
   Do you want me to go now, Sally?
   [. . .]

Sentences concerning the sincerity condition:

   I intend to do it for you.
   I plan on repairing it for you next week

Sentences concerning the propositional content condition:

[. . .]
I am going to give it to you next time you stop by.
Shall I give you the money now?

Sentences concerning S's wish or willingness to do A:

I want to be of any help I can.
I'd be willing to do it (if you want me to).

Sentences concerning (other) reasons for S's doing A:

I think I had better leave you alone.
[. . .]
You need my help, Cynthia.

Notice that the point made earlier about the elementary psychological states holds for these cases as well: One can perform an indirect illocutionary act by asserting, but not by querying, one's own psychological states; and one can perform an indirect illocutionary act by querying, but not by asserting, the presence of psychological states in one's hearer.

Thus, an utterance of *Do you want me to leave?* can be an offer to leave, but not *You want me to leave.* (Though it can be, with the tag question *You want me to leave, don't you?*) Similarly, *I want to help you out* can be uttered as an offer, but not *Do I want to help you out?*

The class of indirect commissives also includes a large number of hypothetical sentences:

If you wish any further information, just let me know.
If I can be of assistance, I would be most glad to help.
If you need any help, call me at the office.

In the hypothetical cases, the antecedent concerns either one of the preparatory conditions, or the presence of a reason for doing A, as in *If it would be better for me to come on Wednesday, just let me know.* Note also that, as well as hypothetical sentences, there are iterated cases of indirection. Thus, e.g., *I think I ought to help you out* can be uttered as an indirect offer made by way of making an indirect assertion. These examples suggest the following further generalizations:

GENERALIZATION 5: *S can make an indirect commissive by either asking whether or stating that the preparatory condition concerning his ability to do A obtains.*

GENERALIZATION 6: *S can make an indirect commissive by asking whether, though not by stating that, the preparatory condition concerning H's wish or want that S do A obtains.*

GENERALIZATION 7: *S can make an indirect commissive by stating that, and in some forms by asking whether, the propositional content condition obtains.*

GENERALIZATION 8: *S can make an indirect commissive by stating that, but not by asking whether, the sincerity condition obtains.*

GENERALIZATION 9: *S can make an indirect commissive by stating that or by asking whether there are good or overriding reasons for doing A, except where the reason is that S wants or desires to do A, in which case he can only state but not ask whether he wants to do A.*

[. . .]

Notes

*   © John R. Searle.

1   In what follows, I use the letters *H*, *S*, and *A* as abbreviations for 'hearer,' 'speaker,' and 'act' or 'action.'

2   This form is also included in Group 2.

3   This point does not hold for the etymologically prior sense of *want* in which it means 'need.'

■ ■ ■

POST-READING

1   Thus far, we have focused primarily on *Can you pass the salt,* an utterance that utilizes a typical English pattern – *can you x* – and, as such, is conventionally heard as a request for H to do something (for more details, see, e.g., Yule 1996: 56). However, as not all indirect speech acts are as conventional as the *can you* pattern, we want to give you an opportunity to think about indeterminacy and the problems it might pose to speech act theorists. Take, for example, the utterance, *If I were you, I'd leave town straight away.* According to Leech (1983), this particular locution can function as advice, a warning or a threat, depending on the contextual circumstances. Can you explain the circumstances, in Searlean terms? You may find it helpful to compare the preparatory conditions, essential conditions and sincerity conditions for these particular speech acts as a means of determining similarities and/or differences.

2   Leech (1983) also points out that utterances such as *If I were you, I'd leave town straight away* can be indeterminate within a situational context shared by S and H: for example, S can claim that they had offered H 'a piece of advice, given from the friendliest of motives' (Leech 1983: 23–4) even when H insists they 'heard' a threat: and we will have no way of knowing whether S actually *intended* to offer H some advice, and H has misunderstood their intent, or S was strategically utilizing the utterance's ambiguity to their advantage so that, to paraphrase Leech, they can have their cake and eat it. To what extent does this suggest that the **meaning** of speech acts needs to be a negotiation between S and H (i.e. needs to account for both S's illocutionary intent and H's inferential processes)? To what extent does it also problematize Searle's hypothesis (in, e.g., Step 2) that – to make sense of indirectness – we have to assume S and H are 'cooperating in the conversation and that therefore [their] utterance[s have] some aim or point' beyond that of deceiving one another?

H.P. GRICE

LOGIC AND CONVERSATION

PRE-READING

In our introduction, we explained how Grice developed his CP and its maxims so that we could capture cases in which a speaker says one thing, but means something over and above the meaning of the words themselves. Before reading 'Logic and conversation', come up with five examples where you have said something fully expecting your interlocutors to look for a meaning beyond the words you actually uttered.

IN-READING

We have marked the first occurrence of each of the following words (using | in the margin): *implicate, implicature, implicated, say, maxims, Quality, Quantity, Relation, Manner, violate, opt out, clash, flout, infringement*. When you come to each item, write down an initial definition for them. When these words re-occur, as you read, return to your initial definitions, so that you can determine whether/the extent to which they are still applicable or need revising in light of your expanding knowledge base.

■ ■ ■

LOGIC AND CONVERSATION
H.P. GRICE

[. . .]

Implicature

Suppose that A and B are talking about a mutual friend, C, who is now working in a bank. A asks B how C is getting on in his job, and B replies, *Oh quite well, I think; he likes his colleagues, and he hasn't been to prison yet*. At this point, A might well inquire what B was implying, what he was suggesting, or even what he meant by saying that C had not yet been to prison. The answer might be any one of such things as that C is the sort of person likely to yield to the temptation provided by his occupation, that C's colleagues are really very unpleasant and treacherous people, and so forth. It might, of course, be quite unnecessary for A to make such an inquiry of B, the answer to it being, in the context, clear in advance. It is clear that whatever B implied, suggested, meant in this example, is distinct from what B said, which was simply that C had not been to prison yet. I wish to introduce, as terms of art, the verb *implicate* and the related nouns *implicature* (cf. *implying*) and *implicatum* (cf. *what is implied*). The point of this maneuver is to avoid having, on each occasion, to choose between this or that member of the family of verbs for which *implicate* is to do general duty. I shall, for the time being at least, have to assume to a considerable extent an intuitive understanding of the meaning of *say* in such contexts, and an ability to recognize particular verbs as members of the family with which *implicate* is associated. I can, however, make one or two remarks that may help to clarify the more problematic of these assumptions, namely, that connected with the meaning of the word *say*.

In the sense in which I am using the word *say*, I intend what someone has said to be closely related to the conventional meaning of the words (the sentence) he has uttered. Suppose someone to have uttered the sentence *He is in the grip of a vice*. Given a knowledge of the English language, but no knowledge of the circumstances of the utterance, one would know something about what the speaker had said, on the assumption that he was speaking standard English, and speaking literally. One would know that he had said, about some particular male person or animal *x*, that at the time of the utterance (whatever that was), either (1) *x* was unable to rid himself of a certain kind of bad character trait or (2) some part of *x*'s person was caught in a certain kind of tool or instrument (approximate account, of course). But for a full identification of what the speaker had said, one would need to know (a) the identity of *x*, (b) the time of utterance, and (c) the meaning, on the particular occasion of utterance, of the phrase *in the grip of a vice* [a decision between (1) and (2)]. This brief indication of my use of *say* leaves it open whether a man who says (today) *Harold Wilson is a great man* and another who says (also today) *The British Prime Minister is a great man* would, if each knew that the two singular terms had the same reference, have said the same thing. But whatever decision is made about this question, the apparatus that I am about to provide will be capable of accounting for any implicatures that might depend on the presence of one rather than another of these singular terms in the sentence uttered. Such implicatures would merely be related to different maxims.

In some cases the conventional meaning of the words used will determine what is *implicated*, besides helping to determine what is said. If I say (smugly), *He is an Englishman; he is, therefore, brave*, I have certainly committed myself, by virtue of the meaning of my words, to its being the case that his being brave is a consequence of (follows from) his being an Englishman. But while I have said that he is an Englishman, and said that he is brave, I do not want to say that I have *said* (in the favored sense) that it follows from his being an Englishman that he is brave, though I have certainly indicated, and so implicated, that this is so. I do not want to say that my utterance of this sentence would be, *strictly speaking*, false should the consequence in question fail to hold. So *some* implicatures are conventional, unlike the one with which I introduced this discussion of implicature.

I wish to represent a certain subclass of nonconventional implicatures, which I shall call *conversational* implicatures, as being essentially connected with certain general features of discourse; so my next step is to try to say what these features are. The following may provide a first approximation to a general principle. Our talk exchanges do not normally consist of a succession of disconnected remarks, and would not be rational if they did. They are characteristically, to some degree at least, cooperative efforts; and each participant recognizes in them, to some extent, a common purpose or set of purposes, or at least a mutually accepted direction. This purpose or direction may be fixed from the start (e.g., by an initial proposal of a question for discussion), or it may evolve during the exchange; it may be fairly definite, or it may be so indefinite as to leave very considerable latitude to the participants (as in a casual conversation). But at each stage, *some* possible conversational moves would be excluded as conversationally unsuitable. We might then formulate a rough general principle which participants will be expected (ceteris paribus) to observe, namely: Make your conversational contribution such as is required, at the stage at which it occurs, by the accepted purpose or direction of the talk exchange in which you are engaged. One might label this the Cooperative Principle.

On the assumption that some such general principle as this is acceptable, one may perhaps distinguish four categories under one or another of which will fall certain more specific *maxims* and submaxims, the following of which will, in general, yield results in accordance with the Cooperative Principle. Echoing Kant, I call these categories *Quantity*, *Quality*, *Relation*, and *Manner*. The category of Quantity relates to the quantity of information to be provided, and under it fall the following maxims:

1. Make your contribution as informative as is required (for the current purposes of the exchange).
2. Do not make your contribution more informative than is required.

(The second maxim is disputable; it might be said that to be over-informative is not a transgression of the Cooperative Principle but merely a waste of time. However, it might be answered that such overinformativeness may be confusing in that it is liable to raise side issues; and there may also be an indirect effect, in that the hearers may be misled as a result of thinking that there is some particular *point* in the provision of the excess of information. However this may be, there is perhaps a different reason for doubt about the admission of this second maxim, namely, that its effect will be secured by a later maxim, which concerns relevance.)

Under the category of Quality falls a supermaxim—"Try to make your contribution one that is true"—and two more specific maxims:

1. Do not say what you believe to be false.
2. Do not say that for which you lack adequate evidence.

Under the category of Relation I place a single maxim, namely, "Be relevant." Though the maxim itself is terse, its formulation conceals a number of problems that exercise me a good deal: questions about what different kinds and focuses of relevance there may be, how these shift in the course of a talk exchange, how to allow for the fact that subjects of conversation are legitimately changed, and so on. I find the treatment of such questions exceedingly difficult, and I hope to revert to them in later work.

Finally, under the category of Manner, which I understand as relating not (like the previous categories) to what is said but, rather, to *how* what is said is to be said, I include the supermaxim—"Be perspicuous"—and various maxims such as:

1. Avoid obscurity of expression.
2. Avoid ambiguity.
3. Be brief (avoid unnecessary prolixity).
4. Be orderly.

And one might need others.

It is obvious that the observance of some of these maxims is a matter of less urgency than is the observance of others; a man who has expressed himself with undue prolixity would, in general, be open to milder comment than would a man who has said something he believes to be false. Indeed, it might be felt that the importance of at least the first maxim of Quality is such that it should not be included in a scheme of the kind I am constructing; other maxims come into operation only on the assumption that this maxim of Quality is satisfied. While this may be correct, so far as the generation of implicatures is concerned it seems to play a role not totally different from the other maxims, and it will be convenient, for the present at least, to treat it as a member of the list of maxims.

There are, of course, all sorts of other maxims (aesthetic, social, or moral in character), such as "Be polite," that are also normally observed by participants in talk exchanges, and these may also generate nonconventional implicatures. The conversational maxims, however, and the conversational implicatures connected with them, are specially connected (I hope) with the particular purposes that talk (and so, talk exchange) is adapted to serve and is primarily employed to serve. I have stated my maxims as if this purpose were a maximally effective exchange of information; this specification is, of course, too narrow, and the scheme needs to be generalized to allow for such general purposes as influencing or directing the actions of others.

As one of my avowed aims is to see talking as a special case or variety of purposive, indeed rational, behavior, it may be worth noting that the specific expectations or presumptions connected with at least some of the foregoing maxims have their analogues in the sphere of transactions that are not talk exchanges. I list briefly one such analogue for each conversational category:

1. *Quantity*. If you are assisting me to mend a car, I expect your contribution to be neither more nor less than is required. If, for example, at a particular stage I need four screws, I expect you to hand me four, rather than two or six.
2. *Quality*. I expect your contributions to be genuine and not spurious. If I need sugar as an ingredient in the cake you are assisting me to make, I do not expect you to hand me salt; if I need a spoon, I do not expect a trick spoon made of rubber.
3. *Relation*. I expect a partner's contribution to be appropriate to the immediate needs at each stage of the transaction. If I am mixing ingredients for a cake, I do not expect to be handed a good book, or even an oven cloth (though this might be an appropriate contribution at a later stage).
4. *Manner*. I expect a partner to make it clear what contribution he is making and to execute his performance with reasonable dispatch.

These analogies are relevant to what I regard as a fundamental question about the Cooperative Principle and its attendant maxims, namely, what the basis is for the assumption which we seem to make, and on which (I hope) it will appear that a great range of implicatures depends, that talkers will in general (ceteris paribus and in the absence of indications to the contrary) proceed in the manner that these principles prescribe. A dull but, no doubt at a certain level, adequate answer is that it is just a well-recognized empirical fact that people do behave in these ways; they learned to do so in childhood and have not lost the habit of doing so; and, indeed, it would involve a good deal of effort to make a radical departure from the habit. It is much easier, for example, to tell the truth than to invent lies.

I am, however, enough of a rationalist to want to find a basis that underlies these facts, undeniable though they may be; I would like to be able to think of the standard type of conversational practice not merely as something that all or most do *in fact* follow but as something that it is *reasonable* for us to follow, that we *should not* abandon. For a time, I was attracted by the idea that observance of the Cooperative Principle and the maxims, in a talk exchange, could be thought of as a quasi-contractual matter, with parallels outside the realm of discourse. If you pass by when I am struggling with my stranded car, I no doubt have some degree of expectation that you will offer help, but once you join me in tinkering under the hood, my expectations become stronger and take more specific forms (in the absence of indications that you are merely an incompetent meddler); and talk exchanges seemed to me to exhibit, characteristically, certain features that jointly distinguish cooperative transactions:

1. The participants have some common immediate aim, like getting a car mended; their ultimate aims may, of course, be independent and even in conflict—each may want to get the car mended in order to drive off, leaving the other stranded. In characteristic talk exchanges, there is a common aim even if, as in an over-the-wall chat, it is a second-order one, namely, that each party should, for the time being, identify himself with the transitory conversational interests of the other.
2. The contributions of the participants should be dovetailed, mutually dependent.
3. There is some sort of understanding (which may be explicit but which is often tacit) that, other things being equal, the transaction should continue in appropriate style unless both parties are agreeable that it should terminate. You do not just shove off or start doing something else.

But while some such quasi-contractual basis as this may apply to some cases, there are too many types of exchange, like quarreling and letter writing, that it fails to fit comfortably. In any case, one feels that the talker who is irrelevant or obscure has primarily let down not his audience but himself. So I would like to be able to show that observance of the Cooperative Principle and maxims is reasonable (rational) along the following lines: that anyone who cares about the goals that are central to conversation/communication (such as giving and receiving information, influencing and being influenced by others) must be expected to have an interest, given suitable circumstances, in participation in talk exchanges that will be profitable only on the assumption that they are conducted in general accordance with the Cooperative Principle and the maxims. Whether any such conclusion can be reached, I am uncertain; in any case, I am fairly sure that I cannot reach it until I am a good deal clearer about the nature of relevance and of the circumstances in which it is required.

It is now time to show the connection between the Cooperative Principle and maxims, on the one hand, and conversational implicature on the other.

A participant in a talk exchange may fail to fulfill a maxim in various ways, which include the following:

1. He may quietly and unostentatiously *violate* a maxim; if so, in some cases he will be liable to mislead.
2. He may *opt out* from the operation both of the maxim and of the Cooperative Principle; he may say, indicate, or allow it to become plain that he is unwilling to cooperate in the way the maxim requires. He may say, for example, *I cannot say more; my lips are sealed.*
3. He may be faced by a *clash:* He may be unable, for example, to fulfill the first maxim of Quantity (Be as informative as is required) without violating the second maxim of Quality (Have adequate evidence for what you say).
4. He may *flout* a maxim; that is, he may blatantly fail to fulfill it. On the assumption that the speaker is able to fulfill the maxim and to do so without violating another maxim

(because of a clash), is not opting out, and is not, in view of the blatancy of his performance, trying to mislead, the hearer is faced with a minor problem: How can his saying what he did say be reconciled with the supposition that he is observing the overall Cooperative Principle? This situation is one that characteristically gives rise to a conversational implicature; and when a conversational implicature is generated in this way, I shall say that a maxim is being *exploited*.

I am now in a position to characterize the notion of conversational implicature. A man who, by (in, when) saying (or making as if to say) that *p* has implicated that *q*, may be said to have conversationally implicated that *q*, provided that (1) he is to be presumed to be observing the conversational maxims, or at least the Cooperative Principle; (2) the supposition that he is aware that, or thinks that, *q* is required in order to make his saying or making as if to say *p* (or doing so in *those* terms) consistent with this presumption; and (3) the speaker thinks (and would expect the hearer to think that the speaker thinks) that it is within the competence of the hearer to work out, or grasp intuitively, that the supposition mentioned in (2) is required. Apply this to my initial example, to B's remark that C has not yet been to prison. In a suitable setting A might reason as follows: "(1) B has apparently violated the maxim 'Be relevant' and so may be regarded as having flouted one of the maxims conjoining perspicuity, yet I have no reason to suppose that he is opting out from the operation of the Cooperative Principle; (2) given the circumstances, I can regard his irrelevance as only apparent if, and only if, I suppose him to think that C is potentially dishonest; (3) B knows that I am capable of working out step (2). So B implicates that C is potentially dishonest."

The presence of a conversational implicature must be capable of being worked out; for even if it can in fact be intuitively grasped, unless the intuition is replaceable by an argument, the implicature (if present at all) will not count as a conversational implicature; it will be a conventional implicature. To work out that a particular conversational implicature is present, the hearer will rely on the following data: (1) the conversational meaning of the words used, together with the identity of any references that may be involved; (2) the Cooperative Principle and its maxims; (3) the context, linguistic or otherwise, of the utterance; (4) other items of background knowledge; and (5) the fact (or supposed fact) that all relevant items falling under the previous headings are available to both participants and both participants know or assume this to be the case. A general pattern for the working out of a conversational implicature might be given as follows: "He has said that *p*; there is no reason to suppose that he is not observing the maxims, or at least the Cooperative Principle; he could not be doing this unless he thought that *q*; he knows (and knows that I know that he knows) that I can see that the supposition that he thinks that *q* is required; he has done nothing to stop me thinking that *q*; he intends me to think, or is at least willing to allow me to think, that *q*; and so he has implicated that *q*."

Examples of conversational implicature

I shall now offer a number of examples, which I shall divide into three groups.

GROUP A: *Examples in which no maxim is violated, or at least in which it is not clear that any maxim is violated.*

A is standing by an obviously immobilized car and is approached by B; the following exchange takes place:

(1) A: *I am out of petrol.*
   B: *There is a garage round the corner.*

(Gloss: B would be infringing the maxim "Be relevant" unless he thinks, or thinks it possible, that the garage is open, and has petrol to sell; so he implicates that the garage is, or at least may be open, etc.)

In this example, unlike the case of the remark *He hasn't been to prison yet*, the unstated connection between B's remark and A's remark is so obvious that, even if one interprets the supermaxim of Manner, "Be perspicuous," as applying not only to the expression of what is said but also to the connection of what is said with adjacent remarks, there seems to be no case for regarding that supermaxim as infringed in this example. The next example is perhaps a little less clear in this respect:

(2) A: *Smith doesn't seem to have a girlfriend these days.*
    B: *He has been paying a lot of visits to New York lately.*

B implicates that Smith has, or may have, a girlfriend in New York. (A gloss is unnecessary in view of that given for the previous example.)

In both examples, the speaker implicates that which he must be assumed to believe in order to preserve the assumption that he is observing the maxim of Relation.

GROUP B: *Examples in which a maxim is violated, but its violation is to be explained by the supposition of a clash with another maxim.*

A is planning with B an itinerary for a holiday in France. Both know that A wants to see his friend C, if to do so would not involve too great a prolongation of his journey:

(3) A: *Where does C live?*
    B: *Somewhere in the South of France.*

(Gloss: There is no reason to suppose that B is opting out; his answer is, as he well knows, less informative than is required to meet A's needs. This *infringement* of the first maxim of Quantity can be explained only by the supposition that B is aware that to be more informative would be to say something that infringed the second maxim of Quality. "Don't say what you lack adequate evidence for," so B implicates that he does not know in which town C lives.)

GROUP C: *Examples that involve exploitation, that is, a procedure by which a maxim is flouted for the purpose of getting in a conversational implicature by means of something of the nature of a figure of speech.*

In these examples, though some maxim is violated at the level of what is said, the hearer is entitled to assume that that maxim, or at least the overall Cooperative Principle, is observed at the level of what is implicated.

(1a) *A flouting of the first maxim of Quantity.*

A is writing a testimonial about a pupil who is a candidate for a philosophy job, and his letter reads as follows: "Dear Sir, Mr. X's command of English is excellent, and his attendance at tutorials has been regular. Yours, etc." (Gloss: A cannot be opting out, since if he wished to be uncooperative, why write at all? He cannot be unable, through ignorance, to say more, since the man is his pupil; moreover, he knows that more information than this is wanted. He must, therefore, be wishing to impart information that he is reluctant to write down. This supposition is tenable only if he thinks Mr. X is no good at philosophy. This, then, is what he is implicating.)

Extreme examples of a flouting of the first maxim of Quantity are provided by utterances of patent tautologies like *Women are women* and *War is war*. I would wish to maintain that at the level of what is said, in my favored sense, such remarks are totally noninformative and so, at that level, cannot but infringe the first maxim of Quantity in any conversational context. They are, of course, informative at the level of what is implicated, and the hearer's identification of their informative content at this level is dependent on his ability to explain the speaker's selection of this particular patent tautology.

(1b) *An infringement of the second maxim of Quantity, "Do not give more information than is required," on the assumption that the existence of such a maxim should be admitted.*

A wants to know whether *p*, and B volunteers not only the information that *p*, but information to the effect that it is certain that *p*, and that the evidence for its being the case that *p* is so-and-so and such-and-such.

B's volubility may be undesigned, and if it is so regarded by A it may raise in A's mind a doubt as to whether B is as certain as he says he is ("Methinks the lady doth protest too much"). But if it is thought of as designed, it would be an oblique way of conveying that it is to some degree controversial whether or not *p*. It is, however, arguable that such an implicature could be explained by reference to the maxim of Relation without invoking an alleged second maxim of Quantity.

(2a) *Examples in which the first maxim of Quality is flouted.*

Irony. X, with whom A has been on close terms until now, has betrayed a secret of A's to a business rival. A and his audience both know this. A says *X is a fine friend.* (Gloss: It is perfectly obvious to A and his audience that what A has said or has made as if to say is something he does not believe, and the audience knows that A knows that this is obvious to the audience. So, unless A's utterance is entirely pointless, A must be trying to get across some other proposition than the one he purports to be putting forward. This must be some obviously related proposition; the most obviously related proposition is the contradictory of the one he purports to be putting forward.)

Metaphor. Examples like *You are the cream in my coffee* characteristically involve categorial falsity, so the contradictory of what the speaker has made as if to say will, strictly speaking, be a truism; so it cannot be *that* that such a speaker is trying to get across. The most likely supposition is that the speaker is attributing to his audience some feature or features in respect of which the audience resembles (more or less fancifully) the mentioned substance.

It is possible to combine metaphor and irony by imposing on the hearer two stages of interpretation. I say *You are the cream in my coffee*, intending the hearer to reach first the metaphor interpretant "You are my pride and joy" and then the irony interpretant "You are my bane."

Meiosis. Of a man known to have broken up all the furniture, one says *He was a little intoxicated.*

Hyperbole. Every nice girl loves a sailor.

(2b) Examples in which the second maxim of Quality, "Do not say that for which you lack adequate evidence," is flouted are perhaps not easy to find, but the following seems to be a specimen. I say of X's wife, *She is probably deceiving him this evening.* In a suitable context, or with a suitable gesture or tone of voice, it may be clear that I have no adequate reason for supposing this to be the case. My partner, to preserve the assumption that the conversational game is still being played, assumes that I am getting at some related proposition for the acceptance of which I do have a reasonable basis. The related proposition might well be that she is given to deceiving her husband, or possibly that she is the sort of person who would not stop short of such conduct.

(3) *Examples in which an implicature is achieved by real, as distinct from apparent, violation of the maxim of Relation* are perhaps rare, but the following seems to be a good candidate. At a genteel tea party, A says *Mrs. X is an old bag.* There is a moment of appalled silence, and then B says *The weather has been quite delightful this summer, hasn't it?* B has blatantly refused to make what he says relevant to A's preceding remark. He thereby implicates that A's remark should not be discussed and, perhaps more specifically, that A has committed a social gaffe.

(4) *Examples in which various maxims falling under the super-maxim "Be perspicuous" are flouted. Ambiguity.* We must remember that we are concerned only with ambiguity that is deliberate, and that the speaker intends or expects to be recognized by his hearer. The problem the hearer has to solve is why a speaker should, when still playing the conversational game, go out of his way to choose an ambiguous utterance. There are two types of cases:

(a) Examples in which there is no difference, or no striking difference, between two interpretations of an utterance with respect to straightforwardness; neither interpretation is notably more sophisticated, less standard, more recondite or more far-fetched than the other. We might consider Blake's lines: "Never seek to tell thy love, Love that never told can be." To avoid the complications introduced by the presence of the imperative mood, I shall consider the related sentence, *I sought to tell my love, love that never told can be.* There may be a double ambiguity here. *My love* may refer to either a state of emotion or an object of emotion, and *love that never told can be* may mean either "Love that cannot be told" or "love that if told cannot continue to exist." Partly because of the sophistication of the poet and partly because of internal evidence (that the ambiguity is kept up), there seems to be no alternative to supposing that the ambiguities are deliberate and that the poet is conveying both what he would be saying if one interpretation were intended rather than the other, and vice versa; though no doubt the poet is not explicitly saying any one of these things but only conveying or suggesting them (cf. "Since she [nature] pricked thee out for women's pleasure, mine be thy love, and thy love's use their treasure").

(b) Examples in which one interpretation is notably less straightforward than another. Take the complex example of the British General who captured the province of Sind and sent back the message *Peccavi*. The ambiguity involved ("I have Sind"/"I have sinned") is phonemic, not morphemic; and the expression actually used is unambiguous, but since it is in a language foreign to speaker and hearer, translation is called for, and the ambiguity resides in the standard translation into native English.

Whether or not the straightforward interpretant ("I have sinned") is being conveyed, it seems that the nonstraightforward interpretant must be. There might be stylistic reasons for conveying by a sentence merely its nonstraightforward interpretant, but it would be pointless, and perhaps also stylistically objectionable, to go to the trouble of finding an expression that nonstraightforwardly conveys that p, thus imposing on an audience the effort involved in finding this interpretant, if this interpretant were otiose so far as communication was concerned. Whether the straightforward interpretant is also being conveyed seems to depend on whether such a supposition would conflict with other conversational requirements, for example, would it be relevant, would it be something the speaker could be supposed to accept, and so on. If such requirements are not satisfied, then the straightforward interpretant is not being conveyed. If they are, it is. If the author of *Peccavi* could naturally be supposed to think that he had committed some kind of transgression, for example, had disobeyed his orders in capturing Sind, and if reference to such a transgression would be relevant to the presumed interests of the audience, then he would have been conveying both interpretants: otherwise he would be conveying only the nonstraightforward one.

Obscurity. How do I exploit, for the purposes of communication, a deliberate and overt violation of the requirement that I should avoid obscurity? Obviously, if the Cooperative Principle is to operate, I must intend my partner to understand what I am saying despite the obscurity I import into my utterance. Suppose that A and B are having a conversation in the presence of a third party, for example, a child, then A might be deliberately obscure, though not too obscure, in the hope that B would understand and the third party not. Furthermore, if A expects B to see that A is being deliberately obscure, it seems reasonable to suppose that, in making his conversational contribution in this way, A is implicating that the contents of his communication should not be imparted to the third party.

Failure to be brief or succinct. Compare the remarks:

(a) *Miss X sang "Home Sweet Home."*
(b) *Miss X produced a series of sounds that corresponded closely with the score of "Home Sweet Home."*

Suppose that a reviewer has chosen to utter (b) rather than (a). (Gloss: Why has he selected that rigmarole in place of the concise and nearly synonymous *sang*? Presumably, to indicate some striking difference between Miss X's performance and those to which the word *singing* is usually applied. The most obvious supposition is that Miss X's performance suffered from some hideous defect. The reviewer knows that this supposition is what is likely to spring to mind, so that is what he is implicating.)

Generalized conversational implicature

I have so far considered only cases of what I might call "particularized conversational implicature"—that is to say, cases in which an implicature is carried by saying that *p* on a particular occasion in virtue of special features of the context, cases in which there is no room for the idea that an implicature of this sort is normally carried by saying that *p*. But there are cases of generalized conversational implicature. Sometimes one can say that the use of a certain form of words in an utterance would normally (in the absence of special circumstances) carry such-and-such an implicature or type of implicature. Noncontroversial examples are perhaps hard to find, since it is all too easy to treat a generalized conversational implicature as if it were a conventional implicature. I offer an example that I hope may be fairly noncontroversial.

Anyone who uses a sentence of the form *X is meeting a woman this evening* would normally implicate that the person to be met was someone other than X's wife, mother, sister, or perhaps even close platonic friend. Similarly, if I were to say *X went into a house yesterday and found a tortoise inside the front door*, my hearer would normally be surprised if some time later I revealed that the house was X's own. I could produce similar linguistic phenomena involving the expressions *a garden, a car, a college*, and so on. Sometimes, however, there would normally be no such implicature ("I have been sitting in a car all morning"), and sometimes a reverse implicature ("I broke a finger yesterday"). I am inclined to think that one would not lend a sympathetic ear to a philosopher who suggested that there are three senses of the form of expression *an X:* one in which it means roughly "something that satisfies the conditions defining the word *X,*" another in which it means approximately "an X (in the first sense) that is only remotely related in a certain way to some person indicated by the context," and yet another in which it means "an X (in the first sense) that is closely related in a certain way to some person indicated by the context." Would we not much prefer an account on the following lines (which, of course, may be incorrect in detail): When someone, by using the form of expression *an X,* implicates that the X does not belong to or is not otherwise closely connected with some identifiable person, the implicature is present because the speaker has failed to be specific in a way in which he might have been expected to be specific, with the consequence that it is likely to be assumed that he is not in a position to be specific. This is a familiar implicature situation and is classifiable as a failure, for one reason or another, to fulfill the first maxim of Quantity. The only difficult question is why it should, in certain cases, be presumed, independently of information about particular contexts of utterance, that specification of the closeness or remoteness of the connection between a particular person or object and a further person who is mentioned or indicated by the utterance should be likely to be of interest. The answer must lie in the following region: Transactions between a person and other persons or things closely connected with him are liable to be very different as regards their concomitants and results from the same sort of transactions involving only remotely connected persons or things; the concomitants and results, for instance, of my finding a hole in my roof are likely to be very different from the concomitants and results of my finding a hole in someone else's roof. Information, like money, is often given without the giver's knowing to just what use the recipient will want to put it. If someone to whom a transaction is mentioned gives it further consideration, he is likely to find himself wanting the answers to further questions that the speaker may not be able to identify in advance; if the appropriate specification will be likely to enable the hearer to answer a considerable variety of such questions for himself, then there is a presumption that the speaker should include it in his remark; if not, then there is no such presumption.

Finally, we can now show that, conversational implicature being what it is, it must possess certain features:

1. Since, to assume the presence of a conversational implicature, we have to assume that at least the Cooperative Principle is being observed, and since it is possible to opt out of the observation of this principle, it follows that a generalized conversational implicature can be canceled in a particular case. It may be explicitly canceled, by the addition of a clause that states or implies that the speaker has opted out, or it may be contextually canceled, if the form of utterance that usually carries it is used in a context that makes it clear that the speaker is opting out.

2. Insofar as the calculation that a particular conversational implicature is present requires, besides contextual and background information, only a knowledge of what has been said (or of the conventional commitment of the utterance), and insofar as the manner of expression plays no role in the calculation, it will not be possible to find another way of saying the same thing, which simply lacks the implicature in question, except where some special feature of the substituted version is itself relevant to the determination of an implicature (in virtue of one of the maxims of Manner). If we call this feature nondetachability, one may expect a generalized conversational implicature that is carried by a familiar, nonspecial locution to have a high degree of nondetachability.

3. To speak approximately, since the calculation of the presence of a conversational implicature presupposes an initial knowledge of the conventional force of the expression the utterance of which carries the implicature, a conversational implicatum will be a condition that is not included in the original specification of the expression's conventional force. Though it may not be impossible for what starts life, so to speak, as a conversational implicature to become conventionalized, to suppose that this is so in a given case would require special justification. So, initially at least, conversational implicata are not part of the meaning of the expressions to the employment of which they attach.

4. Since the truth of a conversational implicatum is not required by the truth of what is said (what is said may be true—what is implicated may be false), the implicature is not carried by what is said, but only by the saying of what is said, or by "putting it that way."

5. Since, to calculate a conversational implicature is to calculate what has to be supposed in order to preserve the supposition that the Cooperative Principle is being observed, and since there may be various possible specific explanations, a list of which may be open, the conversational implicatum in such cases will be disjunction of such specific explanations; and if the list of these is open, the implicatum will have just the kind of indeterminacy that many actual implicata do in fact seem to possess.

■ ■ ■

POST-READING

1   Grice suggests that irony and metaphors constitute a *flout* of the first maxim of Quality: 'Do not say what you believe to be false', but suggests that *flouts* of the second Quality maxim ('Do not say that for which you lack adequate evidence') are rare. Why might this be the case? Can you think of an example (real or made up) which would constitute a flout of the second Quality maxim?

2   When you read Austin's text, you will have noticed that he seems to use 'sentence/s' and 'utterance/s' interchangeably. Thanks to Grice, this has now changed: put simply, researchers will systematically distinguish between sentences (and sentence meaning) and utterances (and utterance interpretation). Can you tease out these differences, in your own words? If it helps, you might start by distinguishing between semantics and pragmatics. In respect to utterances and utterance interpretation, you might also think about Grice's *what is said* and whether this is the same as – or different from – what S *intends by what is said* and what H *infers from what is said*.

PIETER A.M. SEUREN

WESTERN LINGUISTICS
An historical introduction

PRE-READING

1   If you have already studied presupposition, make a list of all the structures you can think of which are sometimes said to trigger or induce presuppositions.
2   If you are new to presupposition, try to identify the background assumptions implicit in the following:
   •   She has lost her driving licence.
   •   The largest real fraction.
   •   Only pragmatics is interesting.
   •   The King of France is bald.
   •   Have you been happier since your wife died?
   •   Joe regrets that his son lives in Kentucky.
   •   Only Trevor was caught.
   •   That Trevor died did not surprise her.

IN-READING

This reading contains a number of ideas and concepts familiar in the study of philosophy that may be new to you. These include the *Paradox of the Horns, Frege's compositional calculus, bivalence, the Principle of the Excluded Middle (PEM), the Principle of the Excluded Third (PET)* and *occasion sentences*. When you come across each of these in the reading, return to this point and make sure that you understand the explanation given below. To save you trying to keep the book open at two pages at the same time, you might consider photocopying the explanations below and keeping them to hand as you read.

•   *The Paradox of the Horns.* A modern version might be called *The Paradox of the Driving Licence.* The sentence *She has lost her driving licence* presupposes that she once had a driving licence and asserts that she has now lost it. If we negate this sentence (*She has not lost her driving licence*), there are two interpretations:
   (1) She had a driving licence before (presupposition) and has not lost it now (assertion).
   (2) She has not lost her driving licence because she never had a driving licence to lose.

In (1), the presupposition in the affirmative sentence 'survives' negation (i.e. negation is restricted to the assertion), but in (2) the presupposition in the affirmative sentence does not survive the unrestricted negation. Grundy (2008: 66) has a similar example where a Catholic priest says 'At least we won't have to give up sex'.

- *Frege's compositional calculus.* We call a means of calculating the truth value of a formal or natural language structure a *calculus*. Aristotle was the first logician who proposed a calculus, distinguishing *predicates*, which assign properties, and *subjects* or *terms* of reference, to which properties may be assigned by predicates. A resulting sentence may be T, or true (it matches a state of affairs in the world), or F, or false (there is no case in the world in which we see the stated property assigned to the term of reference).
- *Bivalence.* The view of sentences as either T or F.
- *The Principle of the Excluded Middle (PEM).* There is no category between T and F (such as neither T nor F).
- *The Principle of the Excluded Third (PET).* All propositions are unequivocally T or F (i.e. there's no *if* about it). We cannot say of a proposition that it's T or F conditionally. Seuren argues that Geach should not treat a sentence such as *The present King of France is bald* as conditionally T or F depending on there being a single King of France. Placing conditions on the ability to determine truth value in this way violates PET and is thus tantamount to postulating that a sentence may be neither T nor F, which violates PEM.
- *Occasion sentences.* Occasion sentences are 'anchored' in the real world, so that their truth value is a consequence of their matching or not matching any corresponding state of affairs. For Strawson, it makes no sense to determine truth value except by this criterion, so that in cases where a term such as *the present King of France* cannot be anchored, the containing sentence lacks a truth value.

■ ■ ■

WESTERN LINGUISTICS: AN HISTORICAL INTRODUCTION
PIETER A.M. SEUREN

[. . .]

For the formalists, language is a formal system describable in terms of rules for the acoustic or visual expression of meanings, and whatever appears to go against the system tends to be regarded as a nuisance, attributable to deplorable interference from outside sources. Formalists tend to play down the fact that language occurs as a natural faculty of the human race and is therefore an empirical object to be approached by hypotheses that aim at empirical adequacy. They prefer to approach the task of analysing language with a formal system that has been developed elsewhere, usually in logic or mathematics, and tend to impose their a priori, preconceived system on what they perceive as the facts of language. Keen observation of facts is not their strongest point. Instead, they usually underestimate the difficulties posed by natural languages. And when these are pointed out to them they are prepared to take them into account only to the extent that their system is not messed up too badly. Facts that might show the unviability of their approach are usually ruled out of order and attributed to the weakness (or dumbness) of the humans who use language. For them, language is a product of ingenuity, 'something which we could have cooked up ourselves . . . had this not, in effect, already been done (perhaps none too well)' (Travis 1981:1).

In the ecologistic approach, on the other hand, language is primarily seen as a product of nature, and hence as an object for empirical research. The expectation is that language, like nature, will manifest itself in all kinds of unexpected variations on and deviations from an as yet largely unknown rule or norm system. Regularities are wonderful, but, as in the rest of nature, they are not always readily detectable and they tend to leave room for idiosyncrasies or, as they are commonly called, exceptions. For an ecologist, language is an object of wonder, a 'storehouse of unimaginable complexities and surprises, to be discerned by looking very closely' (Travis 1981:1), and, we may add, by exerting patience and mulling over the facts in our minds until a bright idea springs up and shows them in their true light.

[. . .]

6.2.3 Presuppositions

We shall now pass on to a discussion of presuppositions, a phenomenon in the semantics of language that does not fit at all into the established logical mould and is a prime example of how an ecologistic method of analysis can supplement, and to some extent supplant, the purely logical analysis.

6.2.3.1 History of the presupposition problem

6.2.3.1.1 EUBULIDES OF MEGARA

The Megarian school of philosophy
Presuppositions already caused Aristotle trouble. The trouble came from Megara, a town about thirty miles west of Athens. Megara had a small philosophy school that had been founded by a follower of Socrates called Euclides (±450–380 BC). His successor at the school was Eubulides, who originated from Miletus in Asia Minor. Little is known about Eubulides' life. He is said to have offered hospitality to Plato and some of his fellow Socratics immediately after Socrates' death in 399, when, for political reasons, they thought it safer to leave Athens (Plato, in fact, exiled himself from Athens till 387). It is also said that he took over the Megarian school in 380. Tradition has it, moreover, that he taught rhetoric to Demosthenes (384–322), the great Athenian public orator and politician who was the main obstacle to Macedonian power over Athens. If these reports are reliable he must have been Aristotle's senior by at least thirty-five years.

The links with Socrates, Plato and Demosthenes are relevant in that they show a political affiliation. Eubulides apparently sided with the Athenian nationalist party, who opposed Macedonian domination and were thus set against Alexander's reign, and also against Aristotle's presence in Athens.*

Eubulides' paradoxes
Eubulides is known in the history of philosophy for his so-called paradoxes, four in number. The most famous one is the *Liar Paradox*, which comes about, in its simplest form, when a sentence says of itself that it is false, or when two sentences say of each other that they are false. The paradox is that when such sentences are true they are at the same time false, and when they are false they are at the same time true. This paradox was a well-known riddle in Antiquity, and a frequent source of worry to Medieval as well as modern logicians. Tarski

considered it important enough to set up his famous distinction between object language and metalanguage to get rid of it, adding the injunction that the two should never be mixed.

The paradox is also found in St. Paul's Epistle to Titus (I. 12–13). In a diatribe against the evil Cretans, he writes, apparently unaware of the paradox:

> One of their own prophets said: 'Cretans always lie, the wicked beasts and lazy bellies', and he spoke the truth.

The 'prophet' in question is usually identified as the half-mythical Cretan poet Epimenides (6th century BC), which is why the paradox is also often called the *Epimenidan Paradox*.

Another paradox is the *Electra Paradox*,** also called the *Paradox of the Hooded Man*. [. . .]

Then there is the *Paradox of the Heap*, or the *Sorites* (from the Greek word *sōrós* 'heap'). It runs as follows. One grain of sand in an hourglass does not make a heap. Two grains do not make a heap. Ten grains do not make a heap. Five hundred grains, however, do make a heap. At what stage does it become true to say that there is a heap of sand? The implication is that there is an intermediate 'grey' area where it is neither entirely true nor entirely false to say that there is a heap. This paradox would seem to call into doubt the Aristotelian Principle of Bivalence, in particular the Principle of the Excluded Middle. It is a plea for recognition of the inherent vagueness of many common predicates.

Finally, we have the *Paradox of the Horns*, expressed as a somewhat salacious joke about cuckolds (unappreciated by Aristotle, one presumes):

> What you have not lost you still have. But you have not lost your horns. So you still have horns.

If this reasoning were correct one could argue that every person who has never worn horns wears them. It is this paradox that will occupy us in the present section. Kneale and Kneale's comment is as follows:

> [Paradoxes] of the fourth type show that if a statement (e.g. 'You have lost horns') involves a presupposition (e.g. that you once had horns) it may be negated either in a restricted way with acceptance of the same assumption or in an unrestricted way without acceptance of that presupposition.
>
> Kneale and Kneale (1962:114)

We shall see below that this comment is precisely right.
[. . .]

6.2.3.1.3 FREGE'S APPROACH TO PRESUPPOSITIONS

The modern history of presupposition theory probably starts with a footnote in Frege (1884),[1] [. . .] For Frege, the use of a definite term normally presupposes ('setzt voraus') the real existence of its reference object. When we say *The moon is smaller than the earth* we presuppose that there is a real moon and a real earth, and we say of the former that it is smaller than the latter (Frege 1892: 31). Only if this presupposition is fulfilled can the sentence have a truth value. If it is not fulfilled the sentence may still have a sense or meaning, as happens in fictional, often literary, contexts but it lacks a truth value. Most sentences in Homer's *Odyssey*, for example, are without a truth value:

Why is the thought not sufficient for us? Because and to the extent that we care about its truth value. This is not always the case. When we listen to an epic poem, for example, it is, besides the euphony of the language, only the sense of the sentences and the images and feelings evoked by them that will captivate us. But as soon as we ask if it is all true we take leave of the artistic pleasure and embark on a scientific investigation. For that reason it is a matter of total indifference to us whether the name *Ulysses*, for example, has a reference as long as we take the poem to be no more than a work of art. It is, therefore, the effort to achieve truth that pushes us forward everywhere from the sense to the reference.

Frege (1892: 33)

This argument is part of Frege's vision of a compositional calculus. [. . .] [T]he truth value of a simple sentence is computed by feeding the term extensions into the function denoted by the predicate. Since predicates denote characteristic functions, the resulting value is a truth value. Now, clearly, if one of the terms lacks an extension there is no, or a deficient, input to the predicate function and no truth value can result.

The notion of presupposition is not at all prominent in Frege (1892). The term *presuppose* ('voraussetzen') is not a technical term in that article. It is used in its ordinary, natural meaning, only to support the thesis that truth values can be computed compositionally by means of a categorial calculus. It is not until Strawson takes up the issue again, more than half a century later, that presupposition theory takes off as a serious part of semantics.

Meanwhile we note that Frege and Strawson discussed only *existential presupposition*. The presupposition that Eubulides presented in his Paradox of the Horns was of a different kind, to do with the lexical predicate *have lost*. And the presuppositions associated with terms like *only*, as studied by Peter of Spain and Walter Burley, are different again.† [. . .]

6.2.3.1.4 GEACH ON PRESUPPOSITIONS

There is a curious little article of 1950, written by Peter Geach, then at Cambridge, where the concept of presupposition is used in, let us say, the old-fashioned way, not restricted to existential presupposition. The article is a critique of Russell's Theory of Descriptions (see 6.1.2.3), first on account of its failure to recognize presuppositions in ordinary language, then on account of Russell and Whitehead's defective definition of the iota operator in *Principia Mathematica*. About the former, Geach writes:

On Russell's view 'the King of France is bald' is a false assertion. This view seems to me to commit the fallacy of 'many questions'. To see how this is so, let us take a typical example of the fallacy: the demand for 'a plain answer — yes or no!' to the question 'have you been happier since your wife died?' Three questions are here involved:

1. Have you ever had a wife?
2. Is she dead?
3. Have you been happier since then?

The act of asking question 2 presupposes an affirmative answer to question 1; if the true answer to 1 is negative, question 2 *does not arise*. The act of asking question 3 presupposes an affirmative answer to question 2; if question 2 does not arise, or if the answer to it is negative, question 3 *does not arise*. When a question does not arise, the only proper way of answering it is to say so and explain the reason; the 'plain' affirmative or negative answer, though grammatically possible, is *out of place*. (I do not call it 'meaningless' because the word is a mere catchword nowadays.) This does not go against the laws of contradiction and excluded middle; what these laws tell us is that *if* the question arose 'yes' and 'no' would be exclusive alternatives.

Similarly, the question 'Is the present King of France bald?' involves two other questions:

4. Is anybody at the moment a King of France?
5. Are there at the moment different people each of whom is a King of France? And it does not arise unless the answer to 4 is affirmative and the answer to 5 is negative.

Geach (1950: 84–5)

We shall see below that Geach is wrong in saying that this does not violate the law of excluded middle. What Geach has in mind is a gapped bivalent logic, which does violate PET, and hence the law of excluded middle. But the interesting thing about this article is that it takes us back to Peter of Spain and Walter Burley, with the additional benefit that the existential presupposition is brought in line with other kinds of presupposition. [. . .]

6.2.3.1.5 STRAWSON'S ANALYSIS OF PRESUPPOSITIONS

[. . .]

Occasion sentences restored

Strawson begins with restoring occasion sentences to their rightful position. Russell had undertaken to make them disappear by analysing definite descriptions in terms of quantifiers. His basically Aristotelian programme, which was later continued by Quine, consisted in reducing all occasion sentences to eternal sentences. Strawson pointed out that it is much more sensible to say that sentences as such, that is as types, do not have a truth value and should not be expected to have one. Only assertive sentences that are actually uttered, or conceived, in an appropriate context, statements in his terminology, can be expected to have a truth value.

The normal or prototypical sentence has to be anchored in discourse to acquire a truth value. Suppose I produce the sentence (to hark back to Geach's example) *He has been happier since his wife died* out of the blue, for example in an English language class to discuss its grammatical and semantic properties. I would make myself look ridiculous if I asked the students if this sentence is true or false. I can ask what the subject is, what the meaning is of the present perfect tense *has been*, etc. But I cannot reasonably ask whether the sentence is true or false. That is possible only if the sentence is properly anchored in discourse, so that it is known who is meant by *he* and in such a way that it is also understood that that person is a widower. Or, as Strawson has it, if the sentence is used as a statement.

[. . .]

Strawson, however, like Geach quoted above, goes further. It may be found that one of the anchoring points of a well-anchored occasion sentence is unsound, or false. If such falsity passes undetected nothing happens: the story goes on untrammelled, as when I spin a yarn about a non-existent duke of Lombardy, saying all sorts of things about him, and am believed by my gullible audience. But the moment I introduce the fictitious duke my story radically departs from reality in that subsequent sentences will fit into a context that has long lost its correspondence with the world as it is.

In Strawson's (and Geach's) view a sentence which is otherwise well-anchored but whose contextual anchoring is false in one or more respects, also lacks a truth value, no matter whether the falsity of the anchoring point or points in question is known or unknown to the discourse participants. [. . .]

[A] sentence, which is well-anchored but with a faulty context, is normally said to suffer from presupposition failure. For these sentences it is not obvious at all that they lack a truth value. They can be used to express a propositional commitment, and the question of their truth or falsity, therefore, most certainly does arise.

Now the Bivalence Principle is affected

Strawson's argument is [. . .] about sentences suffering from presupposition failure. He does recognize that they express a propositional commitment, and concludes that they must be taken into account in propositional logic, [. . .] Yet he also stresses repeatedly that 'the question of their truth or falsity simply does not arise', which is odd given the fact they do contain a real well-anchored proposition.

It seems that we must accept that the question of the truth or falsity of sentences suffering from presupposition failure does arise. The very history of presupposition theory, where this question keeps arising, proves the point. But if we disregard this detail and look at Strawson's analysis as it is, we see that he envisages a logic where propositions are allowed to lack a truth value, besides being either true or false. This idea makes perfect sense and is implementable as a system of propositional logic, known as a *gapped bivalent logic*. Now a gapped bivalent logic violates the Aristotelian Principle of the Excluded Third or Bivalence Principle. Geach's reassuring statement, quoted above, that this Principle is not at issue is therefore incorrect. The question of truth and falsity does arise, and the lack of a truth value is a third option, not admitted by the Aristotelian principle.

[. . .]

If Strawson's theory of presupposition is to cover not only cases of existential presupposition but all other cases as well, which is certainly what is intended, there are questions to answer. One serious question certainly arises if the other, non-existential presuppositions resist treatment in terms of a truth-value-gap. If for those cases it appears more fruitful to set up, for example, a three-valued logic, with the third value for sentences with presupposition failure, a way will have to be found to escape from the Fregean conclusion that failure of existential presupposition necessarily leads to the lack of a truth value.

Presupposition and negation in Strawson's analysis: Eubulides' paradox still unsolved. The Bivalence Principle is now seriously at risk

Quite apart from the logical aspects of non-bivalent logics, which must remain undiscussed here, let us consider Strawson's analysis of negation. Natural language negation, in Strawson's view, is presupposition-preserving. That is, if a sentence B presupposes, and therefore entails, A (that is, $B \gg A$ and $B \vdash A$), then *not-B* still presupposes, and therefore entails, A (*not-B* $\gg A$; *not-B* $\vdash A$). Thus, let B be the sentence *You have lost your horns*, which presupposes A: *You had horns before*, and asserts that the possession of horns by the addressee has come to an end. For Strawson, the negation of B, *You have not lost your horns*, still presupposes *You had horns before* but asserts that the possession of horns by the addressee has not come to an end: *not* negates only the assertive content of a sentence, but leaves the presuppositional entailment intact.

Since this goes for anything one may have lost or not lost, Strawson can say, with Eubulides, *What you have not lost you still have*. But the minor of Eubulides' Paradox of the Horns runs:

You have not lost your horns. If this preserves the same presupposition *You had horns before*, the paradoxical conclusion that the addressee still has horns will hold. In order to undo the paradox it is necessary to accept that the negation in *You have not lost your horns* is not presupposition-preserving. Hence the comment by Kneale and Kneale [. . .], that 'if a statement involves a presupposition . . . it may be negated either in a restricted way with acceptance of the same assumption or in an unrestricted way without acceptance of that presupposition'. In order to solve the paradox we must accept that the negation in *You have not lost your horns* is of the 'unrestricted' kind.

Strawson's presupposition theory is thus unable to solve the Paradox of the Horns. To solve that it seems necessary to assume a distinction between a 'restricted' and an 'unrestricted' negation, as proposed by Kneale and Kneale. If that distinction is incorporated into the logic any variety of bivalence, whether strict or gapped, must be given up.

Does the definite article induce an existential presupposition?

Another problem with Strawson's presupposition theory is the following. If the definite article *the* and the universal quantifier *all* (as is proposed in Strawson 1952: 174–6) carry with them an existential presupposition, then it should not be possible to deny the existence of a supposed entity by using a sentence of the form *The so-and-so does not exist*. Let us agree that there is nothing in this world that corresponds to the Monster of Loch Ness. It follows from Strawson's theory that the sentence *The Monster of Loch Ness exists* not only asserts but also presupposes the existence of that mysterious entity, and must be deemed to lack a truth value because *The monster of Loch Ness exists* is false! Likewise, the sentence *The Monster of Loch Ness does not exist* asserts its non-existence but presupposes its existence, ánd should suffer from a lack of truth value because it is true! But these sentences are simply false and true, respectively, if the Monster of Loch Ness does not exist, and the theory should account for that (see Atlas 1989: 91–119 for a perceptive discussion).[2]

[. . .]

6.2.3.2 The projection problem and the entailment analysis

[. . .]

Karttunen's treatment of the projection problem

Around 1970 the Finnish-American linguist Lauri Karttunen drew attention to what has since been called the 'projection problem' of presuppositions (see esp. Karttunen 1973, 1974). The problem consists in determining under what conditions, in what form and why a presupposition P carried by a carrier sentence C is 'projected' upwards when C is placed under a higher operator.

Some operators are 'holes': they preserve the presupposition P in an undiminished, fully entailing form. These operators generally preserve entailments, and hence also presuppositional entailments. The factive predicates, such as *know, realize, have forgotten, regrettable*, fall under this category. They induce the presupposition that the embedded *that*-clause if true. But other entailing operators, such as the conjunction *and*, belong to this group of operators as well.

Other operators are 'filters'. These generally let presuppositions of embedded clauses through but in a weakened form, no longer as full entailments but as more or less strong suggestions, invited inferences, or default assumptions (DAs). For example, a sentence like:

(32)   Joe believes that his son lives in Kentucky.

does not entail, but it strongly suggests that Joe has a son. This suggestion can be undone by preceding context, for example when (32) is uttered in a context where it has been established that Joe has no son. In such a case the listener will draw certain conclusions about Joe's mental soundness.

The predicate *believe* is thus a filter. So are *or, if, not*. The sentence:

(33)   Either Joe's son lives in Kentucky or Joe doesn't like travelling

does not entail but does suggest that Joe has a son. Yet the operator *or* does not always let presuppositions of its argument propositions through as DA's. In:

(34)   Either Joe's son lives in Kentucky or Joe has no son

no suggestion is left that Joe has a son. Similar phenomena occur with implications, and with *not* (as we shall see in an instant).

A third category of higher operators is called 'plugs': they stop all presuppositions of the embedded clause C, even in the weakened form of a DA. Examples are predicates like *try to convince, suggest* or *say*. A sentence like:

(35)   Joe says that his son lives in Kentucky

does not even suggest that Joe has a son, since he may spin any yarn he likes.

For about ten or fifteen years the projection problem of presuppositions dominated the literature on presupposition theory. No satisfactory solution, however, was presented. The 'filters', especially, proved resistant to all attempts at getting them under control. Nowadays it is felt that a solution to the projection problem will have to be an integral part of a general discourse-oriented theory of presupposition. Attempts at treating it in isolation have met with failure.

The entailment analysis of presupposition

Meanwhile, around 1975, an attempt was made to ban presupposition from semantics altogether and relegate it to pragmatics. The main authors were Wilson (1975) and Boër and Lycan (1976).

Taking Strawson's thesis that presuppositions are preserved under negation as their point of departure, they argued that this is not so, since negation is, in Karttunen's terms, a filter: it lets presuppositions through merely as a DA and not as a full entailment. This is shown by the consistency of sequences like:

(36)a. The King of France is NOT bald. There is no King of France!
    b. David is NOT divorced. He has never been married!

Admittedly, there is a suggestion or DA that France has a king and that David once entered matrimony, respectively, but these are not entailments.

Since suggestions or default assumptions are not the business of logic, logic has nothing to do with presuppositions and can carry on as before, unperturbed. Logically speaking, presuppositions are just entailments. Whatever is presuppositional is to be accounted for by pragmatics, one way or another. This analysis was dubbed the entailment analysis of presupposition.

[. . .] [A]lthough in most cases the negation word *not* can, apparently, override the DA whereby the presupposition is left intact, there are uses of sentence negation where the presupposition of the non-negated sentence cannot be overridden and is left intact as a full entailment. Consider, for example:

(37)a. Only Trevor was caught.   » Trevor was caught.
  b. Not only Trevor was caught.   » Trevor was caught.

The standardly accepted analysis is that (37a) presupposes, and thus entails, that Trevor was caught, and asserts that no-one else was. The normal negation of (37a) is (37b).[3] But (37b) still presupposes, and entails, that Trevor was caught. [. . .]

The same is found when sentence negation is morphologically incorporated (and not standing immediately over an existential quantifier, as in *nobody, never*). In such cases, too, presuppositions are preserved. Turkish, for example, normally incorporates negation, and such negations preserve presuppositions:

(39)   !Ben Kemal-ın araba-sı-nı   al- ma- dı- m.   Kemal-ın araba-sı yok
    I   Kemal's car-his-ACC buy-not-PAST-1sg. Kemal's car-his is-not
    'I didn't buy Kemal's car. Kemal has no car.'

The presupposition is that Kemal had a car. If he did not have one (39) cannot serve as a corrective answer to the inappropriate question (40), no matter how much emphasis is given to the negation morpheme *-ma-*:

(40)   Sen Kemal-ın araba-sı-nı   al-dı–n–mı?
    you Kemal's car-his-ACC buy-PAST-2sg-question particle
    'Did you buy Kemal's car?'

Turkish has no direct translation of *I did NOT buy Kemal's car: he hád no car*. The Horns Paradox, in other words, does not translate into Turkish.

Thirdly, factive clauses and nominalizations in subject position keep their presuppositions:

(41)a. That Trevor died did not surprise her » Trevor died.
  b. Trevor's death did not surprise her   » Trevor died.

The conclusion must, therefore, be that there are natural language sentences where the negation does preserve presuppositions as full entailments, without the presuppositions in question being necessary truths (which are entailed by any sentence). This conclusion is fatal for the entailment analysis, which claims the adequacy of standard logic for the logical analysis of natural language, and it necessitates a revision of standard ideas about the logic of natural language. Such a revision will have to bear on the very foundations of the logical system, as it involves a violation of the age-old Aristotelian Bivalence Principle.

6.2.3.3 *The discourse nature of presupposition*

  [. . .]

Presupposition is to be defined as a discourse phenomenon
The defining feature of presupposition seems to be the fact that a sentence B_A (i.e. B presupposing A) is fit for use only in a discourse that already contains the information carried

by A. A discourse or, more properly, a discourse domain is seen as a cognitive 'working space' for the interpretation of new incoming utterances. The information carried by each new utterance is added to the information already stored in the discourse domain. The technical term for this specific form of 'adding' information to a given discourse domain is *incrementation*. How exactly incrementation is best considered to take place is still very much a question of ongoing investigation: hypotheses and mechanisms are being tried out in various quarters. What counts here is that a sentence B_A is considered unusable in a discourse not allowing for the incrementation of A.

Negation is presupposition-preserving: the Negation Principle

When a sentence B_A is fit for a given discourse D, then not-B_A is likewise fit for incrementation in D, where *not* is the normal unmarked sentence negation of natural language and not the highly marked radical negation (see e.g. Seuren 1988) or Horn's (1985) metalinguistic negation. That is, we establish the Negation Principle:

Negation Principle: if B » A then also not-B » A

thereby matching the Logical Property just given. When not-B is incremented to D this means that B's papers, so to speak, are in order yet it is rejected because that is how the speaker chooses to tell his story. Given the defining property of presupposition, which says that a sentence B_A is fit for use only in a discourse that already contains the incrementation of A, and given the Negation Principle, which says that if B presupposes A then so does not-B, it follows that if A is disallowed in the discourse at hand, then both B and not-B must likewise be considered disallowed.

Criteria of usability of sentences in a discourse

As far as can be judged at the present state of the enquiry, there are two possible reasons for the incrementation of a sentence A, or of a sentence B entailing A, to be disallowed in a discourse D, a logical and a cognitive reason. A is blocked for logical reasons if D already contains information entailing the non-truth of A, in which case the incrementation of A would make D inconsistent. A is blocked for cognitive reasons if D fails to represent a recognizable state of affairs that makes functional sense in a given context. [. . .]

In any actual discourse where a sentence B is used, the presuppositions of B thus restrict the 'universe of interpretation' or 'setting' in terms of which B is to be interpreted. In this respect presupposition differs radically from ordinary entailment. For there is no requirement for ordinary entailments to precede their carrier sentences in discourse, whereas for presuppositions there is.

Accommodation or post hoc suppletion of presuppositions

The fact that presuppositions restrict the 'setting' in terms of which their carrier sentences are to be interpreted makes for a hugely important phenomenon in verbal communication. The point is that it is not necessary for A to be explicitly pronounced before B can be uttered. What happens normally is that a sentence B_A is uttered without A having occurred yet in the discourse. A is then quickly slipped in post hoc, so as to make B_A interpretable. This process is known as *accommodation* (Lewis 1970) or *post hoc suppletion* (Seuren 1985).

To use an example given in Karttunen (1974), a speaker may say:

(43)   We regret that pets are not allowed in the precinct.

He may do so without first having to actually utter the factive presupposition that goes with the verb *regret*, which would have resulted in the stilted:

(44)   Pets are not allowed in the precinct, and we regret that.

Post hoc suppletion is extremely common. It is made possible by the fact that presuppositions are systematically retrievable from the sentences that carry them. Although there is as yet no generally accepted analysis of the structural source of presuppositions in their carrier sentences, enough is known to trace them back to so-called presupposition inducers, which are often lexical verbs, sometimes expressions like *only* or *even*, and sometimes constructions like clefts or pseudoclefts. This means that anyone with a sufficient command of the language in question will grasp the presuppositions of a sentence on hearing or reading the sentence. If one or more of its presuppositions have not been actually uttered in preceding discourse the competent listener will simply supply them cognitively post hoc. This makes it unnecessary for a presupposition to be pronounced in full: owing to the fact that sentences carry presuppositions, a speaker may say things without actually saying them. Not only does this make for an enormous saving of energy in the verbal transmission of information, it also opens the way towards all kinds of communicative and literary devices, ranging from the coarse to the extremely subtle. This, however, is an aspect we must regrettably leave undiscussed in this context.
     [. . .]

Notes

*   Aristotle was a Macedonian by birth who tutored, and was later favoured by, Alexander the Great.
**   Orestes returns to Argos in disguise to avenge the murder of his father, Agamemnon. His sister, Electra, provides him with hospitality without recognizing him. Under these circumstances, is the sentence *Electra knows that her brother Orestes is in the kitchen* true or false?
†   The thirteenth century Portuguese philosopher, Peter of Spain, and Walter Burley, an English philosopher and logician who straddled the thirteenth and fourteenth centuries, explored the presupposition inducing properties of *only*. Thus, the sentence *Only Pragmatics is interesting* is held to presuppose that Pragmatics is interesting and to assert that nothing is interesting except Pragmatics.

1   The expression 'the largest real fraction', for example, has no content because the definite article has a claim to the possibility of pointing at a unique object. . . . If one were to determine, by means of this concept, an object that falls under it, two things would no doubt have to be shown first:

   1. that there is an object falling under this concept;
   2. that there is no more than one object falling under it.

   Since the first of these assertions is already false, the expression 'the largest real fraction' makes no sense.

                                                                (Frege 1884: 87–8)

2   A solution to this problem is given if it is assumed that the definite article does not induce a presupposition of existence but requires uniqueness of the discourse address to be selected by the definite description at issue. Then real existence does not follow from the word *the* but from the extensional character of the predicate in question with regard to the term in question.

3   Note that *Only Trevor was not caught* is not the negation of (37a): it presupposes that Trevor was not caught, and asserts that every-one else was. Curiously, Peter of Spain and Walter Burley deny the validity of (37b), no doubt because they saw trouble ahead.

■ ■ ■

POST-READING

1 To what extent is each of the following amenable to (a) formalist and (b) ecolinguistic explanation: *existential presupposition, the projection problem, negation and presupposition*? If you are unsure, reread the appropriate part of the text and then try to make your mind up.

2 Do you think it makes sense to argue that presupposition is an entailment, either from the formalist position or from the ecolinguistic position?

3 'A speaker may say things without actually saying them'. How do you react to Seuren's stating about presupposition what we are accustomed to claiming of implicature?

ROBERT C. STALNAKER

PRAGMATIC PRESUPPOSITIONS

PRE-READING

Write your own definition of presupposition, treating it as a pragmatic phenomenon. You may want to include words such as *addressee, assume/assumption, belief/believe, context, proposition, speaker*.

IN-READING

Each time you come across a sentence containing 'presupposition' or 'presuppositions' accompanied by the marginal mark | you should include this sentence in a concordance. (You should ignore sentences containing 'presupposition' or 'presuppositions' where there is no marginal mark and where there are two instances of 'presupposition/presuppositions' on a single line, only include the instance closest to the margin marked.) To make your concordance, you will need three columns. In the left-hand column, record any words that occur before *presupposition/s* that you deem relevant; in the central column, write 'presupposition' or 'presuppositions', as appropriate; in the right-hand column, record any words that occur after *presupposition/s* that you deem relevant. As you add each new sentence to the concordance, decide whether you think Stalnaker agrees with or is arguing against the point it makes.

■ ■ ■

PRAGMATIC PRESUPPOSITIONS
ROBERT C. STALNAKER

There is a familiar intuitive distinction between what is *asserted* and what is *presupposed* in the making of a statement. If I say that the Queen of England is bald, I presuppose that England has a unique queen, and assert that she is bald. If I say that Sam regrets that he voted for Nixon, I presuppose that Sam voted for Nixon, and assert that he feels bad about it. If I say that Ted Kennedy is the only person who could have defeated Nixon in 1972, I presuppose that Ted Kennedy could have defeated Nixon in 1972, and assert that no one else could have done so. Philosophers have discussed this distinction mainly in the context of problems of ·

reference. Linguists have discussed it in many other contexts as well. They have argued that the phenomenon of presupposition is a pervasive feature of the use of natural language, one that must play a role in the semantic analysis of many words and phrases.

The principal criterion that has been used to identify presuppositions can be stated in the following way: Q is presupposed by an assertion that P just in case under normal conditions one can reasonably infer that a speaker believes that Q from either his assertion or his denial that P. One who denies the example statements listed above—who says that the Queen of England is *not* bald, that Sam does *not* regret that he voted for Nixon, or that Ted Kennedy is *not* the only person who could have defeated Nixon in 1972, normally makes the same presuppositions as the person who makes the affirmative statements. Linguists have used this criterion to identify many examples of the phenomenon. The criterion, and many of the examples, are relatively clear and uncontroversial; it is clear that there is a phenomenon to be explained. But it is much less clear what kind of explanation of it should be given. Granted that either the statement that the Queen of England is bald, or the speaker who makes it, presupposes that England has a unique queen. But what is it about the statement, or the speaker, which constitutes this fact? There are two very different kinds of answers to this question.

The first answer is that presupposition is a semantic relation holding between sentences or propositions. This kind of account draws the distinction between presupposition and assertion in terms of the content or truth-conditions of the sentence uttered or the proposition expressed. Here is an example of such a definition: a proposition that P presupposes that Q if and only if Q must be true in order that P have a truth-value at all. The presuppositions of a proposition, according to this definition, are necessitated by the truth, and by the falsity, of the proposition. When any presupposition is false, the assertion lacks a truth-value.

The second answer is that presupposition should be given a pragmatic analysis. The distinction between presupposition and assertion should be drawn, not in terms of the content of the propositions expressed, but in terms of the situations in which the statement is made—the attitudes and intentions of the speaker and his audience. Presuppositions, on this account, are something like the background beliefs of the speaker—propositions whose truth he takes for granted, or seems to take for granted, in making his statement.

The pragmatic account is closer to the ordinary notion of presupposition, but it has frequently been assumed that the semantic account is the one that is relevant to giving a rigorous theoretical explanation of the linguistic phenomena. I want to argue that this assumption is wrong. I will suggest that it is important for correctly understanding the phenomena identified by linguists to give the second kind of analysis rather than the first. In terms of the pragmatic account, one can give intuitively natural explanations of some facts that seem puzzling when presupposition is viewed as a semantic relation. The pragmatic account makes it possible to explain some particular facts about presuppositions in terms of general maxims of rational communication rather than in terms of complicated and ad hoc hypotheses about the semantics of particular words and particular kinds of constructions. To argue this, I will sketch an account of the kind I want to defend, and then discuss some of the facts identified by linguists in terms of it.

Let me begin by rehearsing some truisms about communication. Communication, whether linguistic or not, normally takes place against a background of beliefs or assumptions which are shared by the speaker and his audience, and which are recognized by them to be so shared. When I discuss politics with my barber, we each take the elementary facts of the current political situation for granted, and we each assume that the other does. We assume that Richard Nixon is the President, that he recently defeated George McGovern by a large margin, that the United States has recently been involved in a war in Vietnam, which is a small country in Southeast Asia, and so forth. That we can reasonably take these facts for granted obviously makes our communication more efficient. The more common ground we can take for granted, the more efficient our communication will be. And unless we could reasonably treat *some* facts in this way, we probably could not communicate at all.

Which facts or opinions we can reasonably take for granted in this way, as much as what further information either of us wants to convey, will guide the direction of our conversation—will determine what is said. I will not say things that are already taken for granted, since that would be redundant. Nor will I assert things incompatible with the common background, since that would be self-defeating. My aim in making assertions is to distinguish among the possible situations which are compatible with all the beliefs or assumptions that I assume that we share. Or it could be put the other way around: the common background is defined by the possible situations which I intend to distinguish among with my assertions, and other speech acts. Propositions true in all of them are propositions whose truth is taken for granted.

Although it is normally inappropriate because unnecessary for me to assert something that each of us assumes the other already believes, my assertions will of course always have consequences which are part of the common background. For example, in a context where we both know that my neighbor is an adult male, I say "My neighbor is a bachelor," which, let us suppose, entails that he is adult and male. I might just as well have said "my neighbor is unmarried." The same information would have been conveyed (although the nuances might not have been exactly the same). That is, the *increment of information*, or of content, conveyed by the first statement is the same as that conveyed by the second. If the asserted proposition were accepted, and added to the common background, the resulting situation would be the same as if the second assertion were accepted and added to the background.

This notion of common background belief is the first approximation to the notion of pragmatic presupposition that I want to use. A proposition P is a pragmatic presupposition of a speaker in a given context just in case the speaker assumes or believes that P, assumes or believes that his addressee assumes or believes that P, and assumes or believes that his addressee recognizes that he is making these assumptions, or has these beliefs.

I do not propose this as a definition or analysis, first, since it is far from clear what it is to believe or assume something, in the relevant way and second, since even assuming these notions to be clear, the definition would need further qualification. My aim is not to give an analysis but rather to point to a familiar feature of linguistic contexts which, I shall argue, is the feature in terms of which a certain range of linguistic phenomena should be explained. The notion has, I think, enough intuitive content to enable us to identify a lot of particular cases, and the general outlines of the definition are clear enough to justify some generalizations about presuppositions which help to explain the facts. [. . .]

[N]ote that it is persons rather than sentences, propositions or speech acts that have or make presuppositions. This goes against the prevailing technical use of the term, according to which presuppositions, whether semantic or pragmatic, are normally taken to relate two linguistic things. One might define such a relation in terms of the pragmatic notion in something like one of the following ways: (a) One might say that a sentence x presupposes that Q just in case the use of x to make a statement is appropriate (or normal, or conversationally acceptable) only in contexts where Q is presupposed by the speaker, or (b) one might say that the statement that P (made in a given context) presupposes that Q just in case one can reasonably infer that the speaker is presupposing that Q from the fact that the statement was made; or (c) one might say that the statement that P (made in a given context) presupposes that Q just in case it is necessary to assume that the speaker is presupposing that Q in order to understand or interpret correctly the statement. As stated, these suggested definitions are vague, and each is different from the other. But I do not think it would be fruitful to refine them, or to choose one over the others.

It is true that the linguistic facts to be explained by a theory of presupposition are for the most part relations between linguistic items, or between a linguistic expression and a proposition. They are, as I interpret them, facts about the constraints, of one kind or another, imposed by what is said on what is appropriately presupposed by the speaker, according to various different standards of appropriateness. But I think all the facts can be stated and explained directly in terms of the underlying notion of speaker presupposition, and without introducing an intermediate notion of presupposition as a relation holding between sentences (or statements) and propositions.

[. . .]

The presumed background information—the set of presuppositions which in part define a linguistic context—naturally imposes constraints on what can reasonably or appropriately be said in that context. Where the constraints relate to a particular kind of grammatical construction, or to a particular expression or category of expressions, one has a linguistic fact to be explained. This is the case with the sample sentences with which I began. One of the facts could be stated like this: it is inappropriate to say "The Queen of England is bald" (or to say "the Queen of England is not bald") except in a context in which it is part of the presumed background information that England has a queen. Compare this with a description that interprets the phenomena in terms of a semantic concept of presupposition: the proposition expressed by "the Queen of England is bald" has a truth-value only if England has a unique queen. The first description, in contrast to the second, makes no claim at all about the content of the statement—about the truth-conditions of what is said. The description in terms of the pragmatic notion does not rule out a semantic *explanation* for the fact that a certain presupposition is required when a certain statement is made, but neither does it demand such an explanation. That is, one *might* explain why it is appropriate for a speaker to say "the Queen of England is bald" only if he presupposes that England has a queen in terms of the following two assumptions: first, that the statement lacks a truth-value unless England has a queen, and second, that one normally presupposes that one's statements have a truth-value. But one also might explain the fact in a different way. The *facts* about presuppositions, I am suggesting, can be separated from a particular kind of semantic explaination of those facts. This separation of the account of presupposition from the account of the content of what is said will allow for more diversity among presupposition phenomena than would be possible if they all had to be forced into the semantic mold. Let me suggest, more specifically, four of the advantages of making this move.

First, if presupposition is defined independently of truth-conditions, then it is possible for the constraints on presuppositions to vary from context to context, or with changes in stress or shifts in word order, without those changes requiring variation in the semantic interpretation of what is said. This should make possible a simpler semantic theory; at the very least, it should allow for more flexibility in the construction of semantic theories. For example, D.T. Langendoen points out in a paper on presupposition and assertion that normally, if one said "my cousin isn't a boy anymore" he would be asserting that his cousin had grown up, presupposing that he is male. But one might, in a less common context, use the same sentence to assert that one's cousin had changed sexes, presupposing that she is young.[1] If a semantic account of presupposition is given of this case, then one must say that the sentence is therefore ambiguous. On the pragmatic account, one just points to two different kinds of situations in which a univocal sentence could be used.

Second, if presupposition is defined independently of truth-conditions, then one can separate the question of entailment relations from the question of presupposition. On the semantic account, presupposition and entailment are parallel and incompatible semantic relations. *A* presupposes that *B* if and only if *B* is necessitated by *both A* and its denial. *A* entails *B* if and only if *B* is necessitated by *A* but *not* by its denial. Thus the claim that the sentence, "Sam realizes that P" *entails* that P conflicts with the claim that that sentence presupposes, in the semantic sense, that P. But using the pragmatic account, one may say that sometimes when a presupposition is required by the making of a statement, what is presupposed is also entailed, and sometimes it is not. One can say that "Sam realizes that P" entails that P—the claim is false unless P is true. "Sam does not realize that P," however, does not entail that P. That proposition may be true even when P is false. All this is compatible with the claim that one is required to presuppose that P whenever one asserts or denies that Sam realizes it.

Third, the constraints imposed by a statement on what is presupposed seem to be a matter of degree, and this is hard to explain on the semantic account. Sometimes no sense at all can be made of a statement unless one assumes that the speaker is making a certain presupposition. In other cases, it is mildly suggested by a speech act that the speaker is taking a certain assumption for granted, but the suggestion is easily defeated by countervailing evidence. If a speaker says to me, "Sam was surprised that Nixon lost the election," then I have no choice but to assume that he takes it for granted that Nixon lost. But if he says, "If Eagleton hadn't been dropped from the Democratic ticket, Nixon would have won the election" (without an "even" before the "if" or a "still" after the "Nixon"), there is a suggestion that the speaker presupposes that Nixon in fact did not win, but if the statement is made in the right context, or with the right intonation, the suggestion is overruled. This difference in degree, and variation with context is to be expected on the pragmatic account, since it is a matter of the strength of an inductive inference from the fact that a statement was made to the existence of a background assumption or belief.

Fourth, and perhaps most important, the pragmatic analysis of presupposition, because it relates the phenomena to the general communication situation, may make it possible to explain some of the facts in terms of general assumptions about rational strategy in situations where people exchange information or conduct argument. One way to explain the fact that a particular assertion requires or suggests a certain presupposition is to hypothesize that it is simply a fact about some word or construction used in making the assertion. In such a case, the fact about the presupposition requirement must be written into the dictionary, or into the semantics. But since we have an account of the *function* of presuppositions in conversations, we may sometimes be able to explain facts about them without such hypotheses. The propositions that P and that Q may be related to each other, and to common beliefs and intentions, in such a way that it is hard to think of a reason that anyone would raise the question whether P, or care about its answer, unless he already believed that Q. More generally, it might be that one can make sense of a conversation as a sequence of rational actions only on the assumption that the speaker and his audience share certain presuppositions. If this kind of explanation can be given for the fact that a certain statement tends to require a certain presupposition, then there will be no need to complicate the semantics or the lexicon.

For example, consider the word "know." It is clear that "x knows that P" entails that P. It is also clear that in most cases when anyone asserts or denies that x knows that P, he presupposes that P. Can this latter fact be explained without building it into the semantics of the word? I think it can. Suppose a speaker were to assert that x knows that P in a context where the truth of P is in doubt or dispute. He would be saying in one breath something that could be challenged in two different ways. He would be leaving unclear whether his main point was to make a claim about the truth of P, or to make a claim about the epistemic situation of x (the knower), and thus leaving unclear what direction he intended or expected the conversation to take. Thus, given what "x knows that P" means, and given that people normally want to communicate in an orderly way, and normally have some purpose in mind, it would be unreasonable to assert that x knows that P in such a context. One could communicate more efficiently by saying something else. For similar reasons, it would normally be inappropriate to say that x does not know that P in a context where the truth of P was in question. If the speaker's reason for believing his assertion were that he thought that P was false, or that he thought that x didn't believe that P, or didn't have reason to believe that P, then his statement would be gratuitously weak. And it would be unusual for a speaker to be in a position to know that one of these situations obtained, without knowing which.

This is a tentative and incomplete sketch of an explanation. Much more would have to be said to make it convincing. My point is to make it plausible that, in some cases at least, such explanations might be given, and to argue that where they can be given, there is no reason to build specific rules about presuppositions into the semantics.

I want now to illustrate these advantages of the pragmatic account by looking at some linguistic facts in terms of it. The two sets of facts I will consider are taken from two papers by Lauri Karttunen.[2]

First, on a distinction between two kinds of factive verbs. It is well known that among verbs which take a nominalized sentence complement (for example *believe, know, intend, see*) one can distinguish a subclass known as factive verbs (*know, regret, discover, see*, as contrasted with *believe, intend, assert, claim*). A number of syntactic and semantic criteria are used to draw the distinction, but the distinguishing mark that is relevant here is the following: If V is a factive verb, then *x V's that P* presupposes (and, I would say, entails as well) that P. If I assert or deny that Jones regrets, realizes, or discovers that Nixon won the election, then I presuppose that Nixon did in fact win. Karttunen has drawn a further distinction among two kinds of factive verbs which, he argues, requires a distinction between two kinds of presupposition relations. One kind of factive verb (labeled the *full factives*) includes *regret, forget* and *resent*. The basis for the distinction is as follows: with full factives, it is not only an assertion or denial of the proposition *x V's that P* that requires the presupposition that P, but also the *supposition* that *x V's* that P in the antecedent of a conditional, or the claim that the proposition *might* be true. With semi-factives, it is only the assertion or denial that require the presupposition. For example, consider the two statements:

> *Sam may regret that he voted for Nixon.*

> *If Sam regrets that he voted for Nixon, then he is a fool.*

Because these two statements clearly require the presupposition that Sam voted for Nixon, *regret* is seen to be a full factive.

The following is Karttunen's example to illustrate the contrast between full factives and semi-factives. Compare:

> *If I* { *regret*
> { *realize later that I have not told the truth,*
> { *discover*
> *I will confess it to everyone.*

In the first statement, the speaker clearly presupposes that he has not told the truth. In the other two cases, he clearly does not presuppose this. Thus *realize* and *discover* are seen to be semi-factives.

To explain the difference, Karttunen postulates a distinction between a strong and a weak kind of semantic presupposition. If P is necessitated by *Possibly Q*, and by *Possibly not-Q*, then Q strongly presupposes that P. Weak semantic presuppositions are defined in the usual way.

In discussing this example, I want to dispute both the data, and the theoretical account of them. I agree that there is a sharp contrast in the particular example given, but the matter is less clear if one looks at other examples. Consider:

If Harry discovers that his wife is playing around, he will be upset.

If Harry had discovered that his wife was playing around, he would have been upset.
If Harry had realized that his wife was playing around, he would have been upset.

Harry may realize that his wife has been playing around.
Harry may never discover that his wife has been playing around.

There is, I think, in all these cases a presumption that the speaker presupposes that Harry's wife is, or has been, playing around. The presumption is stronger in some of the examples than in others, but it seems to me that in some of them it is as strong as with *regret*. Further, if we assume that with the so-called semi-factives like *discover* and *realize*, there is *always* a presumption that the speaker presupposes the truth of the proposition expressed in the complement, we can still explain why the presumption is defeated in Karttunen's particular example. The explanation goes like this: if a speaker explicitly supposes something, he thereby indicates that he is not *pre*supposing it, or taking it for granted. So when the speaker says "if I realize later that *P*," he indicates that he is not presupposing that he will realize later that *P*. But if it is an open question for a speaker whether or not he will at some future time have come to realize that *P*, he can't be assuming that he already knows that *P*. And if he is not assuming that he himself knows that *P*, he can't be assuming that *P*. Hence *P* cannot be presupposed. A roughly parallel explanation will work for *discover*, but not for *regret*.

One can explain another of Karttunen's examples in a similar way. Consider the three questions:

> Did you { regret
{ realize that you had not told the truth?
{ discover

Here *realize* seems to go with *regret* and not with *discover*. The first two questions seem to require that the speaker presuppose that the auditor did not tell the truth, while the third does not. Again, we can explain the difference, even while assuming that there is a presumption that the presupposition is made in all three cases. The reason that the presumption is defeated in the third case is that the speaker could not make that presupposition without assuming an affirmative answer to the question he is asking. But in general, by asking a question, one indicates that one is not presupposing a particular answer to it. This explanation depends on the particular semantic properties of *discover*, and will not work for *realize* or *regret*.[3] It also depends on the fact that the subject of the verb is the second-person pronoun. Hence if the explanation is right, one would expect the presupposition to reappear in the analogous third-person question, "Did Sam discover that he hadn't told the truth?" It seems that it does.

Since on the pragmatic account, the constraints on presuppositions can vary without the truth-conditions changing, we can allow presupposition differences between first- or second-person statements and questions and the corresponding third-person statements and questions without postulating separate semantic accounts of propositions expressed from different points of view. So, while we have noted differences in the presuppositions required or suggested by the following two statements:

If Harry discovers that his wife has been playing around, he will be upset.

If I discover that my wife has been playing around, I will be upset (said by Harry).

This difference does not prevent us from saying that the two statements both have the same semantic content—that the same proposition is expressed in both cases. It would not be possible to say this on a semantic account of presupposition.

If the explanations I have sketched are on the right track, then we can account for at least some of the differences between factive and semi-factive verbs without distinguishing between two different kinds of presupposition relations. We can also account for some differences among semi-factives, and differences between first- and third-person statements without complicating the semantics. The explanation depends on just two things: first, some simple and very general facts about the relation between pragmatic presuppositions and assertions, questions, and suppositions; second, on the ordinary semantic properties of the particular verbs involved.

The second set of facts that I will discuss concerns the presuppositions of compound sentences. How do the presuppositions required by a conditional or conjunctive statement relate to the presuppositions that would be required by the component parts, stated alone? In general, what is the relation between the presuppositions required by an assertion that *A* and the assertion that *B* on the one hand, and by an assertion that *A and B* or that *if A, then B* on the other? Karttunen defends the following answer to the question: Let *S* be a sentence of the form *A and B* or *If A, then B*. *S* presupposes that *C* if and only if either *A* presupposes that *C*, or *B* presupposes that *C* and *A* does not semantically entail that *C*. In other words, the presuppositions of a conjunction are the presuppositions required by either of the conjuncts, *minus any required by the second conjunct which are entailed by the first*. The presuppositions of a conditional are the presuppositions of either antecedent or consequent minus those required by the consequent and entailed by the antecedent. So if I say "Harry is married, and Harry's wife is a great cook," I assert, and do not presuppose, that Harry is married. But the second conjunct, stated alone *(Harry's wife is a great cook)*, would require the presupposition that Harry is married. The sentence with conjuncts in reverse order would be unacceptable in any normal context *(Harry's wife is a great cook, and Harry is married)*.

Now if we regard Karttunen's generalization as a generalization about *semantic* presuppositions, then we will interpret it as a hypothesis about the way the truth-value (or lack of it) of a conjunction or conditional relates to the truth-values of the parts. The hypothesis has the consequence that the conjunction *and* is not truth-functional, since the truth-value of a conjunctive statement will in some cases depend on entailment relation between the conjuncts. It has the consequence that *and* is not symmetric. *A and B* may be false while *B and A* lacks a truth-value. Finally, it has the consequence that the simple conjunction *and* is governed by mysteriously complicated rules.

On the other hand, if we regard Karttunen's generalization as a generalization about *pragmatic* presuppositions, then we can reconcile it with the standard truth-functional account of *and*, and we can explain the generalization without postulating any ad hoc semantic or pragmatic rules. The explanation goes like this: first, once a proposition has been asserted in a conversation, then (unless or until it is challenged) the speaker can reasonably take it for granted for the rest of the conversation. In particular, when a speaker says something of the form *A and B*, he may take it for granted that *A* (or at least that his audience recognizes that *he* accepts that *A*) after he has said it. The proposition that *A* will be added to the background of common assumptions before the speaker asserts that *B*. Now suppose that *B* expresses a proposition that would, for some reason, be inappropriate to assert except in a context where *A*, or something entailed by *A*, is presupposed. Even if *A* is *not* presupposed initially, one may still assert *A and B* since by the time one gets to saying that *B*, the context has shifted, and it is by then presupposed that *A*.

As with the explanation sketched in the earlier discussion, this explanation rests on just two things: first, a simple pragmatic assumption about the way presuppositions shift in the course of a conversation—an assumption that says, roughly, that a speaker may build on what has already been said; second, an uncontroversial assumption about the semantic properties of the word *and*—in particular, that when one asserts a conjunction, he asserts both conjuncts. If we interpret presupposition to mean *pragmatic* presupposition, then we can deduce Karttunen's generalization from these two almost trivial assumptions.

The analogous generalization about conditional statements is explainable on equally simple assumptions. Here we need first the assumption that what is explicitly *supposed* becomes (temporarily) a part of the background of common assumptions in subsequent conversation, and second that an *if* clause is an explicit supposition. Again, Karttunen's generalization can be derived from these obvious assumptions.

I have been arguing in this paper for the fruitfulness of separating semantic from pragmatic features of linguistic expressions and situations, and of explaining a certain range of phenomena in terms of pragmatic rather than semantic principles. This goes against the trend of the work of generative semanticists such as George Lakoff and John Ross, who have emphasized the difficulty of separating syntactic, semantic, and pragmatic problems, and who have sometimes suggested that such distinctions as between syntactic and semantic deviance or semantic and pragmatic regularities are of more use for avoiding problems than for solving them. Partly to respond to this concern, I will conclude with some general remarks about the distinction between semantics and pragmatics, and about what I am *not* recommending when I suggest that the distinction be taken seriously.

First remark: semantics, as contrasted with pragmatics, can mean either the study of *meaning* or the study of *context*. The contrast between semantic and pragmatic claims can be either of two things, depending on which notion of semantics one has in mind. First, it can be a contrast between claims about the particular conventional meaning of some word or phrase on the one hand, and claims about the general structure or strategy of conversation on the other. Grice's distinction between conventional implicatures and conversational implicatures is an instance of this contrast. Second, it can be a contrast between claims about the truth-conditions or *content* of what is said—the proposition expressed—on the one hand, and claims about the *context* in which a statement is made—the attitudes and interests of speaker and audience—on the other. It is the second contrast that I am using when I argue for a pragmatic rather than a semantic account of presuppositions. That is, my claim is that constraints on the presuppositions are constraints on the contexts in which statements can be made, and not constraints on the truth-conditions of propositions expressed in making the statements. I also made use of the other contrast in arguing for this claim. I conjectured that one can explain many presupposition constraints in terms of general conversational rules without building anything about presuppositions into the meanings of particular words or constructions. But I make no general claim here. In some cases, one may just have to write presupposition constraints into the dictionary entry for a particular word. This would make certain presupposition requirements a matter of *meaning*, but it would not thereby make them a matter of *content*. There may be facts about the meaning of a word which play no role at all in determining the truth-conditions of propositions expressed using the word.

Second remark: in recommending a separation of content and context I am not suggesting that there is no interaction between them. Far from it. The semantic rules which determine the content of a sentence may do so only relative to the context in which it is uttered. This is obviously the case with sentences using personal pronouns, demonstratives, quantifiers, definite descriptions, or proper names. I suspect it happens in less obvious cases as well. But this interaction does not prevent us from studying the features which define a linguistic context (such as a set of pragmatic presuppositions) in abstraction from the propositions expressed in such contexts, or from studying the relationships among propositions in abstraction from the contexts in which they might be expressed.

A final remark: in some cases, distinctions such as that between semantic and pragmatic features may be used as a way to set problems aside. Some linguists have accused other linguists of using the distinction between syntax and semantics in this way. Deviant sentences which seem to conflict with syntactic generalizations are not treated as counterexamples, but instead are thrown into a "semantic waste-basket" to be explained away by some future semantic theory. In the same way, some may be suspicious that I am setting up a pragmatic wastebasket, and recommending that all the interesting problems be thrown away.

I do not think that this is always a bad procedure, but it is not what I am suggesting here. I am recommending instead the development and application of a pragmatic theory in which detailed explanations of phenomena relating to linguistic contexts can be given. It is true that traditionally the more well-developed and the more rigorous linguistic theories have focused on questions of grammar and content, while the discussions which emphasized the role of conversational content have been more informal and less theoretical. But there is no necessity in this. Potentially at least, a theory of pragmatics, and the notion of pragmatic presupposition can be as precise as any of the concepts in syntax and semantics. Although the explanations I have sketched in this paper are informal and incomplete, I think they suggest a strategy for giving explanations of linguistic phenomena relating to contexts which are both rigorous and intuitively natural.

Notes

1   D. Terence Langendoen, "Presupposition and Assertion in the Semantic Analysis of Nouns and Verbs in English," in *Semantics: An Interdisciplinary Reader in Philosophy, Linguistics and Psychology*, ed. by Danny D. Steinberg and Leon A. Jakobovits (Cambridge, England: Cambridge University Press, 1971).

2   Lauri Karttunen, "Some Observations on Factivity," *Papers in Linguistics* 4 (1971) and "Presuppositions of Compound Sentences," *Linguistic Inquiry*, IV (1973).

3   The relevant difference between *realize* and *discover* is this: because *realize* is a stative verb, a past tense statement of the form *x didn't realize that P* must be about some particular time in the past (determined by the context), and not about *all* times in the past. This means that *x didn't realize that P* may be true, even though *x now* knows that *P*. Therefore, a speaker may assume that his addressee knows or assumes that *P* without prejudging the question whether or not he realized (at the relevant past time) that *P*. In contrast, because *discover* is an inchoative verb, *x didn't discover that P* may be about *all* times in the past. For this reason, normally, *x didn't discover that P* implies that x has not *yet* discovered that *P*, and so does not now know that *P*. Therefore, if a speaker presupposes that *P*, he assumes that *x has* discovered that *P*, and so assumes a particular answer to the question he is asking.

Before re-reading

You'll probably want to re-read this paper. Before re-reading it, turn to the following paragraphs in the reading and use the sentences we suggest as a way of checking that you've understood Stalnaker's arguments:

- Paragraph beginning 'For example, consider the word 'know' . . . '
  - How do the following sentences help to illustrate Stalnaker's argument: *Leslie knows / doesn't know / thinks / doesn't think God exists / we all grow older.*
- Paragraph beginning 'In discussing this example, I want to dispute . . . '
  - How does the following sentence help to illustrate Stalnaker's argument: *If Margaret discovers her grandfather was a liberal, her reaction will be interesting.*
- Paragraph beginning 'One can explain another . . . '
  - How do the following sentences help to illustrate Stalnaker's argument: *Did you/Margaret discover/realise her grandfather was a liberal?*
- Paragraphs beginning 'On the other hand, if we regard . . . ' and 'As with the explanation . . . '
  - How do the following sentences help to illustrate Stalnaker's argument: *Lesley is a caring mother and her daughter takes after her / If Lesley is a caring mother, her daughter will take after her.*

POST-READING

1   Return to the definition of pragmatic presupposition you wrote as a pre-reading activity and compare it with Stalnaker's tentative definition: 'A proposition *P* is a pragmatic presupposition of a speaker in a given context just in case the speaker assumes or believes that *P*, assumes or believes that his addressee assumes or believes that *P*, and assumes that his addressee recognizes that he is making these assumptions, or has these beliefs.' Which definition do you prefer, yours or Stalnaker's? Why?

2   Are you sufficiently convinced by Stalnaker's arguments to agree that there is 'no need to complicate the semantics or the lexicon' with a theory of presupposition?

SECTION 2 FURTHER READING

Speech acts – a number of pragmatics textbooks provide useful overviews and/or critiques of SA Theory (see, e.g., Levinson 1983; Verschueren 1999; Mey 2001; Grundy 2008). Also worthy of exploration are Vanderveken and Kubo's (2002) *Essays in Speech Act Theory*, and Bach and Harnish's (1979), Ballmer and Brennenstuhl's (1981) and Wierzbicka's (1987) proposals for alternate SA taxonomies to those of Austin (1962) and Searle (1969, 1975b).

Implicature – Horn (2004) and Huang (2010a) each provide useful overviews of 'Implicature', in their papers of the same name. Horn (2004) appears in Horn and Ward's (eds) *The Handbook of Pragmatics*, Oxford: Blackwell. Wang (2010) appears in Cummings' (2010b) (ed.) *The Pragmatics Encyclopedia*, London and New York: Routledge. For a sense of Grice's enormous contribution to Pragmatics, see, e.g., Chapman's (2005) *Paul Grice, Philosopher and Linguist*, published by Palgrave Macmillan, and Wharton's (2010a) entry 'H.P. Grice' in *The Pragmatics Encyclopaedia* (details as above).

These are two classic texts if you have a **historical interest**:

Frege, G. (1892) 'Über sinn und Bedeutung' ('On Sense and Reference'), *Zeitschrift für Philosophie und Philosophische Kritik* NF 100, trans. P. Geach and M. Black (eds) (1970) *Translations from the Philosophical Writings of Gottlob Frege*, pp. 25–50, Oxford: Blackwell.
Strawson, P. (1950). 'On referring', *Mind* 59, 320–44.

Presupposition – If you are interested in **the projection problem**, you should read Karttunen's two papers:

Karttunen, L. (1973) 'Presuppositions of compound sentences', *Linguistic Inquiry* IV (2): 169–93.
Karttunen, L. (1974) 'Presupposition and linguistic context', *Theoretical Linguistics* 1 (1–2): 184–94.

For **factivity**, you should read Kiparsky and Kiparsky's classic paper:

Kiparsky, P. and Kiparsky, C. (1970) 'Fact', in M. Bierwisch and K.E. Heidolph (eds) *Progress in Linguistics*, pp. 143–73, The Hague: Mouton; reprinted in D.D. Steinberg and L.A. Jakobovitz (eds) *Semantics: an interdisciplinary reader in philosophy, linguistics and psychology*, pp. 345–69, Cambridge: Cambridge University Press.

After reading Kiparsky and Kiparsky, you may want to read:

Karttunen, L. (1971) 'Some observations on factivity', *Papers in Linguistics* 4: 55–69.

Horn's classic paper is a must-read on **negation**:

Horn, L.R. (1985) 'Metalinguistic negation and pragmatic ambiguity', *Language* 61, 121–74.

To follow up the issues raised in Stalnaker's paper, read:

Atlas, J.D. (2004) 'Presupposition', in L.R. Horn and G. Ward (eds) *The Handbook of Pragmatics*, pp. 29–52, Oxford: Blackwell.

Atlas offers an overview of presupposition and critiques Stalnaker's position (pp. 46–50). He also comments on a short section of Stalnaker's paper which we have omitted and which deals with situations where the need to be tactful overrides the need to exchange information. If you want to read Stalnaker's paper in its entirety, you can find it in the original source, in Davis, S. (ed.) (1991) *Pragmatics: A Reader*, pp. 471–82, Oxford: Oxford University Press, and in Stalnaker, R.C. *Context and Content*, pp. 47–62, Oxford: Oxford University Press.

SECTION 3

Post-Gricean pragmatics

THE SIX READINGS IN THIS SECTION cover the two major lines of development of Grice's theory of conversational implicature, 'neo-Gricean' pragmatics and 'post-Gricean', or relevance theoretic, pragmatics. As the names suggest, neo-Gricean pragmatics is an attempt to develop theory broadly within the Gricean framework, whereas post-Gricean pragmatics, although inspired by Grice's theory, develops in a new direction. All six readings share, albeit to different degrees, the (non-Gricean) perspective that semantic determination requires pragmatic input, and thus all six refute the simple distinction between sentence meaning (semantics) and speaker meaning (pragmatics) implicit in Speech Act theory and Gricean pragmatics.

NEO-GRICEAN PRAGMATICS

Arguably the most important early work in the neo-Gricean tradition is Larry Horn's (1984) paper, 'Toward a new taxonomy for pragmatic inference: Q-based and R-based implicature'. Horn regrouped Grice's maxims under two principles, the Q Principle (subsuming Grice's Q1 maxim and two of the Manner maxims – 'Avoid obscurity' and 'Avoid ambiguity') and the R Principle (subsuming Grice's Q2 and Relation maxims and one of the Manner maxims – 'Be brief'). The Q Principle captures the need to provide sufficient information for the hearer – so if 'some' is as much as the speaker can say, the hearer can take it that the speaker implies *not all*. The R Principle captures the speaker's preference for minimal forms, which are then subject to pragmatic strengthening – so if a speaker offers a hearer 'a drink', it's likely to be *an alcoholic drink*.

The two readings in the first part of Section 3 take their cues from Horn's proposals. In the first reading, Stephen Levinson argues that three rather than two principles guide interpretation. In the second, Reinhard Blutner shows how the Q Principle underlies the hearer's search for optimal meaning and the R Principle underlies the speaker's search for optimal form.

In a seminal paper, Levinson (1995) distinguished 'three levels of meaning' – entailment, utterance-token meaning and utterance-type meaning. This three-level division refines Grice's distinction between what is 'said' and what is 'conveyed'. In dealing with conveyed meaning, Levinson differentiates utterance-token meaning and utterance-type meaning, essentially building on Grice's distinction between particularized and generalized conversational implicature. Both 'Three levels of meaning' (1995) and *Presumptive Meanings* (2000a), from which the reading that follows is taken, focus principally on utterance-type meaning, which Levinson describes as 'a level of systematic pragmatic inference based not on direct computations about speaker intentions but rather on general expectations about how language is normally used' (2000a: 22). Utterance-type meanings such as *not all*, inferred from 'some', are, for Levinson, preferred interpretations recovered as default inferences, i.e. 'interpretations that tend to go through in the absence of information to the contrary' (2000a: 59).

A useful way of thinking of utterance-type meaning is as a level between the familiar levels of sentence-meaning and speaker-meaning. Unlike speaker- or utterance-token meanings, which are context-sensitive interpretations prompted by the maxim of Relation, utterance-type meanings arise as a result of the way in which language is characteristically used to express meaning, and thus belong within a theory of generalized idiomaticity.

In order to show that utterance-type meanings are preferred interpretations, Levinson reformulates Grice's Q1, Q2 and M maxims as *heuristics*, with the intention of capturing the fundamental insight underlying each maxim (2000a: 31–3):

> Heuristic 1 (Q1 related): *What isn't said, isn't.*
>
> Heuristic 2 (Q2 related): *What is simply described is stereotypically exemplified.*
>
> Heuristic 3 (M related): *What's said in an abnormal way, isn't normal.*

These three heuristics capture the insights that guide speakers and hearers and that invite the recovery of preferred interpretations. The availability of these heuristics 'serves to multiply the information content of any message by a factor of perhaps a score' (2000a: 34). Levinson adds that the time required to process this twenty-fold increase in the information content of utterances accounts for 'the slow coding rate of human speech', slow in the sense that, if we spoke three or even four times more quickly than we characteristically do, those we address would still be able to follow us. This is because, when we are involved in the online processing of speech, we use roughly a third of the time available for decoding what we hear and the other two-thirds for inferring the additional information being communicated.

In a further step, Levinson uses these heuristics as the basis for three proposed principles, the Q-Principle (Quantity), the I-Principle (Informativeness) and the M-Principle (Manner). The Q and I Principles, being derived from Grice's Q1 and Q2 maxims respectively, broadly correspond to Horn's Q- and R-Principles. The motivation for the M-Principle is the third heuristic, *What's said in an abnormal way, isn't normal*, which associates marked forms with marked interpretations.

The reading that follows draws on the second and third chapters of *Presumptive Meanings*. In the first part of the reading, 'Exploring I-inferences' (pp. 112–18), Levinson discusses the relationship between the second Quantity maxim and the Principle of Informativeness. In particular, this section explores the quasi technical terms associated with I-inference, including *specificity, stereotype, informativeness* and *minimal*. The section concludes with a re-examination of several interpretations which have been extensively discussed in the literature in a piecemeal way and which Levinson regards as attributable to the proposed I-Principle. The second part of the reading (pp. 166–7, 170–3, 177–80) deals with 'pragmatic intrusion', or the claim that Generalized Conversational Implicatures contribute to propositional content and are thus part of the input to truth-conditions. Levinson first traces out the received view of semantics as input to pragmatics. Working mainly with Q-Principle examples, he then argues that deictic resolution cannot, as Grice and others believe, be entirely semantic and that the received view of the semantics/pragmatics interface therefore needs to be revised.

The second reading in this section, Reinhard Blutner's 'Some perspectives on lexical pragmatics' (2011) is published for the first time here. Whereas Grice's theory of conversational implicature explores the extent to which what is said does not fully determine what is conveyed in an *utterance*, Blutner takes as his starting point the view that 'the meaning expressed by a *lexical unit* [our italics] is underdetermined by its semantics'. Blutner's contribution to the development of pragmatics, both in this reading and elsewhere, lies in his exploration of the extent to which lexis (traditionally regarded as part of what is 'said') as well as utterances convey pragmatic meaning.

In attempting to formalize lexical pragmatics, Blutner appeals to the notion of an optimal match between an input and an output. Thus the minimal spoken form 'drink' and the hearer-inferred meaning *alcoholic drink* are a pair, such that *alcoholic drink* is the optimal meaning for the form 'drink', and 'drink' is the optimal form for the meaning *alcoholic drink*. With the benefit of hindsight, we can see that Grice's original proposals were also optimality oriented in the sense that Grice too set out to account for the link between forms and preferred interpretations, both in particularized contexts and also when generalized across many instances of use.

In this reading, Blutner first discusses the processes by which the formal linguistic meaning of lexical items is optimized to give propositional content. These processes imply a truth functional pragmatics, since the truth conditional content of lexical items is enriched in ways that are context-sensitive. We therefore need to acknowledge that pragmatic interpretation is crucial for determining both what is 'said' and what is meant. Blutner's position, like Levinson's argument for 'pragmatic intrusion' in the variable resolution of deictic reference, marks an important departure from Grice's position in which underdetermination, and hence optimization, applies only to what is 'conveyed' and not to what is 'said'.

Blutner shows how optimization is bi-directional, providing both form meaning optimization (following Horn's hearer-oriented Q Principle) and meaning form optimization (following Horn's speaker-oriented R Principle). He discusses the need for the theory to be formulated in such a way as to take account of the pairing of not only unmarked but also marked form/meaning pairs, as allowed for, although in a different way, in Levinson's Q-, I- and M-Principles. Optimality theory in pragmatics, as in other fields, proposes efficiency- and informativeness-optimizing constraints to prevent the generation of non-optimal pairs. Blutner's use of the specification of gender in animate nouns as an illustration of the use of constraints in the generation of optimal form/meaning and meaning/form pairs illustrates the principles of OT pragmatics in a simple, understandable way. As you work your way through this section of the paper, you may feel that this example is as much semantic as pragmatic. For this reason, as you study the tables Blutner provides, it may be useful to think about more obviously pragmatic areas, such as the deixis examples discussed by Levinson in the previous reading, and about how such data might be captured in the kind of OT framework proposed here.

In the latter part of the reading, Blutner discusses *fossilization* – the conventionalization of implicatures for certain interpretations, in a way that looks forward to Section 6 and the work of Traugott and others in historical pragmatics. In this respect, Blutner's proposals differ from Traugott's suggestions, which appeal to Levinson's utterance-type and utterance-token meanings, but accomplish the same effect, so you may want to return to this reading before reading the papers in Section 6.

STEPHEN C. LEVINSON

PRESUMPTIVE MEANINGS

PRE-READING

1   Levinson uses the heuristic *What is simply described is stereotypically exemplified* as a bridge between Grice's second Quantity maxim and a proposed Principle of Informativeness. Note down three or four examples of form/meaning pairs such as 'drink'/*alcoholic drink* where the simple description (form) has a stereotypical exemplification (meaning).

2   Jot down your own informal definitions of the following terms, which you are about to encounter in the reading: *specificity, stereotype, informativeness* and *minimal*.

IN-READING

Each time you come across a sentence in the text with the marginal mark |, stop and think carefully about what Levinson says. If you find it insightful, note it down, using the '11.2.3–4' notation system (i.e. page 11, paragraph 2, lines 3–4) followed by the insightful sentence. (If you haven't come across this system before, you may find it useful as a note-taking device in your future reading.)

■ ■ ■

PRESUMPTIVE MEANINGS
STEPHEN C. LEVINSON

2.3 Exploring I-inferences

2.3.1 Formulating the maxim or heuristic

Recollect that Grice (1975) proposed two maxims of Quantity:

> Q1: "Make your contribution as informative as is required (for the current purposes of the exchange)."

Q2: "Do not make your contribution more informative than is required."

Grice (1975)

Is the second maxim (which I abbreviate Q2) otiose? Grice (1975: 46) was unsure:

> It might be said that to be overinformative is not a transgression of the CP [Cooperative Principle] but merely a waste of time. However it might be answered that such overinformativeness may be confusing in that it is liable to raise side issues; and there may also be an indirect effect, in that hearers may be misled as a result of thinking that there is some particular POINT in the provision of the excess information.

Perhaps the maxims of Relevance or Manner would handle these "indirect effects." And Grice (1989: 372) later repeated his doubts.

But the doubts seem misplaced, even from a strictly Gricean point of view. Thus he found no trouble imagining the correlate of such a principle in a nonverbal activity such as passing too many screws when one was required (1975: 47). Zipf (1949) has provided statistical data from many kinds of human activity, including language, that seem to support it. Two observations seem to have worried Grice. One was that Relevance might secure the same effects because too much information would surely be irrelevant (indeed, an infringement of the second maxim of Quantity may also constitute an infringement of the maxim of Manner). The other was that the principle did not, it seemed to him, yield the rich set of inferences one would expect in the category of flouted or exploited maxims (only one clear example being provided in Grice 1975: 52). But that, as it turns out, is the wrong place to look. It is in the observance of the maxim that its effects are most apparent, for there is indeed strong evidence in favor of its interpretive corollary, which as a first approximation might be phrased "Don't provide unnecessary information, specifically don't say what would be obvious anyway" (for much crosslinguistic evidence in favor of such a heuristic, see Haiman 1985). Such a principle might account for our tendency to interpret utterances in line with our knowledge about what is normal or typical, as in (37a). It is clear that providing too much information defeats this kind of interpretation, as in (37b), where the excess information does indeed lead the recipient to think "that there is some particular POINT in the provision of the excess information" as Grice imagined:

(37) a. "He opened the door."
         +> in the normal way by turning the handle.
     b. "He opened the door by turning the handle quickly anti-clockwise."
         +> not in the normal way.

The evidence for such a tendency towards economy is overwhelming. As Haiman (1985: 150) puts it, "there is a powerful tendency in languages . . . to give reduced expression to the familiar and the predictable," a correlation that is "one of the most well-attested in human language." But a tendency of this Zipfian sort could have sources other than the speaker's orientation to some maxim or heuristic.

There is in fact a great deal of evidence for the existence of a speaker's preference for minimal specifications, and its interpretive corollary, to be found in the extensive literature on the empirical properties of conversation (reviewed in Levinson 1987a: 79–98). I will cite just one general observation here. Researchers have noted that there is a decided preference for reference to persons to be achieved by the shortest expression, with the least descriptive content, that will do the job. That this has the status of a maxim, or expected procedure, is shown by the fact that when a speaker is in doubt about whether a brief form will do, the form is often produced with a distinctive rising intonation, and only when lack of response indicates that the recipient has not understood, is a fuller specification given, also with rising intonation; and so on recursively, until recognition is achieved. For example (from Sacks and Schegloff 1979: 19, where the question mark indicates the rising intonation):

(38) A: . . . well I was the only one other than that that the uhm tch
         Fords?
         uh Mrs. Holmes Ford?
         You know uh the the cellist.
                              [
     B: Oh yes. She's she's the cellist.
     A: Yes.

Unless there is some kind of maxim in operation, it would be hard to understand why a speaker would not initially choose, or immediately escalate to, a descriptive phrase that he knew would be more than sufficient to achieve successful reference. Note that a parallel pattern can be observed in self-identifications on the telephone (Schegloff 1979), where (a) intimates expect their identity to be conveyed just by the sample of voice quality in their first "Hello", only escalating step by step, when overt recognition is withheld, with further examples of voice quality, then nicknames or firstnames: "Hello (.) It's me (.) Steve (.) Levinson"; (b) persons less intimate may escalate to self-descriptive phrases: "Hello. It's Les (.) Garston (.) the man who called about the plumbing." Those who doubt the existence of some maxim of minimization (e.g., Carston 1995: 223) must therefore find not only an account of the general tendencies for minimization but also an account of this apparent orientation of speakers to just such a principle.

I offer the following (after Levinson 1987b) as a first approximation to a characterization of the maxim involved (more elaborate formulations and discussions can be found in Atlas and Levinson 1981; Levinson 1987a, 1987b). Following the practice initiated by Atlas and Levinson (1981), I call this rendition of Grice's Q2 maxim the *Principle of Informativeness*, or the *I-Principle* for short:

(39) *I-Principle*
     Speaker's maxim: the maxim of Minimization. "Say as little as necessary"; that is, produce the minimal linguistic information sufficient to achieve your communicational ends (bearing Q in mind).
     Recipient's corollary: the Enrichment Rule. Amplify the informational content of the speaker's utterance, by finding the most specific interpretation, up to what you judge to be the speaker's m-intended point,[1] unless the speaker has broken the maxim of Minimization by using a marked or prolix expression. Specifically:
     a.   Assume the richest temporal, causal and referential connections between described situations or events, consistent with what is taken for granted.
     b.   Assume that stereotypical relations obtain between referents or events, unless this is inconsistent with (a).
     c.   Avoid interpretations that multiply entities referred to (assume referential parsimony); specifically, prefer coreferential readings of reduced NPs (pronouns or zeros).

    d.   Assume the existence or actuality of what a sentence is about if that is consistent with what is taken for granted.

This characterization contains a number of undefined terms. The direction in which one would hope for clarification is mostly clear enough, but none of these are trivial notions. For now, I can offer only the following glosses:

1. *Specificity: p is more specific than q* if (a) *p* is more informative than *q* (e.g., *p* entails *q*); and (b) *p* is isomorphic with *q* (i.e., each term or relation in p has a denotation that is a subset of the denotations of the corresponding expressions in *q*). (For further remarks, see below.)
2. *Stereotype:* As Putnam (1975: 249ff) notes, a stereotype needn't have a close relation to reality or statistical tendency (e.g., "as fierce as a gorilla" or "absent-minded professor"). On Putnam's view, meanings are stereotypes that may fail to determine correct extensions; on my view, stereotypes are connotations associated with meanings, but not part of them, which nevertheless play a role in interpretation.
3. *Informativeness: p is more informative than q* if the set of states of affairs that *q* rules out is a proper subset of the set that *p* rules out (Bar-Hillel and Carnap 1952; Popper 1959). This account makes a number of idealizations and thus can only be considered a first approximation (see discussion in Levinson 1987b: 404–6).
4. *Minimal:* One needs to distinguish *semantic generality* (crucial here; e.g., *building* vs. *hall*) from *expression brevity* (e.g., *hall* vs. *auditorium*). Zipf (1949) argues that these tend to conflate (e.g., a pronoun is both semantically general and brief). This follows from the conjunction of his Law of Abbreviation ('the more use, the shorter the expression') and his Principle of Economic Versatility ('the more semantically general, the more use'). Equally in the Prague School theory of markedness, the unmarked expression in an opposition is both formally less complex and semantically general, whereas the marked expression is formally more complex and semantically more specific (Jakobson 1939; see also discussion in Horn 1989: Chapter 3).

This characterization is compatible with the original proposal in Atlas and Levinson (1981). We sketched there a two-level account: first, all the competing interpretations are generated; then the most informative is selected. The principles generating the set of competing interpretations were left open in that account, but clearly they should delimit the set of possible interpretations. In the sketch just given, the relevant principles are given a bit more flesh: they include the search for maximal cohesion, or temporal, spatial, causal, and referential connectedness, and the presumption of stereotypical relations and the actuality of referents. Again, in the earlier account, it was claimed that I-inferences:

> enrich "what is said" by *reshaping* the range of possible states of affairs associated with "what is said" to a narrower range of possible states of affairs associated with "what is communicated." "What is communicated" is MORE PRECISE than "what is said". In contrast, Q-inferences were held to *shrink* the range of possible states of affairs . . . "What is communicated" is MORE DEFINITE than "what is said".
>
> Atlas and Levinson (1981: 35–6, italics added)

The contrast intended was the idea that I-inferences are not just more informative in the sense that they entail what is said (that is equally true of most Q-implicatures): they introduce semantic relations absent from what is said, and in that sense can be said to reshape the proposition expressed (whereas Q-implicatures of the scalar type only introduce a negative bound from within the same semantic field). I have tried to capture this notion by building into the concept of more specificity (replacing the earlier concept of more precision) the requirement that although the interpretation is (partially) isomorphic with the content of what is said, each constituent may have a more restricted sense and denotation. Thus the phrase *a spoon in the cup* may have the interpretation 'a metal spoon partially inside the ceramic teacup', *went and bought* may have the interpretation 'went and then bought', *took a drink* the interpretation 'imbibed an alcoholic drink', *she bit her nails* the interpretation she bit her own finger nails', and so on. The isomorphism holds of course not at the level of English phrases and glosses but at the abstract level of propositional representation: what is implicated is a specialization of one or more of each of the intensions of what is said. It corresponds to the fact, noted below, that it is usually difficult to express an I-implicature as an unrelated proposition conjoined to 'what is said'.

Now, under the I-Principle rubric, I want to collect a whole range of inferences that appear to go in just the reverse direction to that in which Q-implicatures tend. To emphasize the tension, we may say that I-implicatures are inferences from *the lack of further specification to the lack of need for it*, whereas *Q-implicatures are inferences from the lack of informational richness to the speaker's inability to provide it*. Under the rubric of the I-Principle, we can gather a range of well-known phenomena, as follows (+> stands for 'implicates'; ++> stands for 'communicates', i.e., the sum of what is 'said' and the I-implicature in question):

(40) *Conditional perfection* (Geis and Zwicky 1971)
"If you mow the lawn, I'll give you five dollars."
I +> 'If you don't mow the lawn, I will not give five dollars' or perhaps 'If I give you $5, you will have mown the lawn.'
++> '(If and) only if you mow the lawn, will I give you five dollars.'

(41) *Conjunction buttressing* (e.g., Atlas and Levinson 1981)
An utterance of the form "p and q" where p and q describe events, such as "John turned the key and the engine started."
++> 'p and then q' (temporal sequence)
'p therefore q' (causal connectedness)
'A did X in order to cause q' (teleology, intentionality).

(42) *Bridging* (Clark and Haviland 1977)
"John unpacked the picnic. The beer was warm."
+> 'The beer was part of the picnic.'

(43) *Inference to stereotype* (Atlas and Levinson 1981)
"John said 'Hello' to the secretary and then he smiled."
++> 'John said 'Hello' to the female secretary and then John smiled.'

(44) *Negative strengthening* (Horn 1989: Chapter 5)
"I don't like Alice."
+> 'I positively dislike Alice.'

(45) *Preferred local coreference*
"John came in and he sat down."
++> 'John₁ came in and he₁ sat down.'

(46) *Mirror maxim* (Harnish 1976: 359)
"Harry and Sue bought a piano."
+> 'They bought it together, not one each.'

(47) Noun-noun compounds (NN-relations) (Hobbs et al. 1993)
"The oil compressor gauge."
+> 'The gauge that measures the state of the compressor that compresses the oil.'

(48) Specializations of spatial terms (Herskovits 1986)
    a. "The nail is in the wood."
        +> 'The nail is buried in the wood.'
    b. "The spoon is in the cup."
        +> 'The spoon has its bowl-part in the cup.'

(49) *Possessive interpretations* (Sperber and Wilson 1986)
    a. "Wendy's children"
        +> 'those to whom she is parent.'
    b. "Wendy's house"
        +> 'the one she lives in.'
    c. "Wendy's responsibility"
        +> 'the one falling on her.'
    d. "Wendy's theory"
        +> 'the one she originated.'

It is immediately clear that by comparison to, say, scalar Q-implicatures, these inferences are heterogeneous, and the kinds of procedures involved in actually deriving the inferences in question may differ significantly. The claim therefore is not that the same mental algorithms compute this range of inferences but rather that there is a single overarching principle that licenses them, legitimating the application of any of the subprocesses involved, and that this by virtue of its overall relation to the Q- and M- Principles regulates the conditions under which the particular inferences are blocked or canceled. To belabor the point: the I-principle here operates as an instruction to find an interpretation that meets certain requirements (positive, stereotypical, highly specific interpretations).

Now a question that immediately arises is: in what sense are these I-inferences *generalized*? Most of these inferences interact with shared background presumptions, which might in principle vary, and thus the inferences might have none of the cross-context, even crosslinguistic, invariance that are the hallmarks of GCIs. But at a sufficient level of abstraction, it is quite clear that the kinds of inferences here collected—for example, conjunction-buttressing, negative-strengthening, preferred patterns of coreference—do hold as preferred interpretations across contexts and indeed across languages. And at a slightly higher level of abstraction, the different types collected can be seen to share the property of maximizing the informational load by narrowing the interpretation to a specific subcase of what has been said.

[. . .]

In this chapter, though, rather than develop the analysis of GCIs further, I wish instead to use the modest harvest gathered so far as a lever on the general theory of meaning. It turns out that GCIs have fundamental implications for the way in which we should construct an overall theory of meaning—in particular, for what we may call (somewhat grandiosely) its *architecture*. I shall assume that "meaning" is essentially composite—that is, that we need to carve up the semiotic pie much in the way that Grice envisaged, into the component entailments, conventional implicatures, presuppositions, felicity conditions, GCIs, and PCIs associated with particular expressions on particular occasions of use. To describe and analyze these different aspects of meaning, we will need distinct bodies of principles (each constituting a component in the overall theory); for example, semantic inference is based on monotonic principles, but many aspects of pragmatic meaning are defeasible and nonmonotonic in character. We then have to ask: How do these elements or components of meaning interact? That I take to be a question about the architecture of a theory of meaning. Chomsky (1965) introduced a highly influential way of thinking about this: he suggested that the traditional levels of linguistic analysis (syntax, phonology, semantics) should be thought of as independent *components* or modules, with the interaction between components being conceived of in terms of *logical priority*—that is, the interaction being determined by what kind of *input* each module needs. He was thus able to finesse the central interesting question of the control and flow of information between components by building a solution into the components themselves (each component transforming a specific type of input into a specific kind of output appropriate as input to another component, such that the logical ordering of components does not need to be stipulated). In the theory of meaning, we seem to have inherited this thinking: semantics is normally held to be *logically prior* to pragmatics, and thus semantics is *autonomous* with respect to pragmatics in just the way that Chomsky imagines syntax to be autonomous with respect to semantics. This chapter attempts to demonstrate that this is simply not a tenable way of thinking in the theory of meaning.

The crucial fact that I will try to establish is that generalized conversational implicatures seem to play a role in the assignment of truth-conditional content.[2] This may seem not only a distinctly odd idea but even definitionally impossible, because implicatures are often partially defined in opposition to truth-conditional content. Some scholars have therefore argued that any such inferences should be called something else (e.g., "explicatures" or "implicitures"), but calling them something else will not change the fact that they are the very same beasts. In the end, it will be seen, I think, to be an inevitable conclusion that GCIs play a role in truth-conditional content. Now if there is such a role for generalized implicatures, then it will have major implications for the architecture of the theory of meaning—we will need to drastically revise our understanding of the pragmatics/semantics interface and the flow of information between the components in a general theory of meaning.

[. . .]

3.2 The received view: semantics as input to pragmatics

Grice (1989: 25, 87f) made the distinction between saying and implicating, but his definition of what is *said* is complex and by no means clear (see Harnish 1976: 332ff; Bach 1994a). Roughly, though:

(1)   U said that *p* by uttering *x* iff:
    a.   *x* conventionally ("timelessly") means *p*
    b.   *U* speaker-meant *p* (this condition serves, e.g., to select one of a number of ambiguous readings)
    c.   *p* = the conventional meaning of x minus any conventional implicatures (i.e., any non-truth-conditional but conventional aspects of meaning that 'indicate' but do not contribute to 'what is said').

There is a philosophical literature on Grice's notion of "what is said" that I will refer to in passing (but see especially Bach 1994a; Recanati 1993). But linguistic commentators have on the whole been happy to take Grice's notion of "what is said" as mapping more or less onto truth-conditional content (an interpretation encouraged by Grice's treatment of the logical connectives). (Due allowance has to be made of course for the satisfaction conditions, rather than truth conditions, of nonassetoric speech acts, but here I abstract away from this additional problem.) However, as Atlas and Levinson (1981: 1ff) note, two utterances with the same truth conditions (e.g., *It's done* and *It's done and if it's done, it's done*) can have quite distinct implicatures (see also the discussion of litotes in Section 2.4.1.3 [see original publication], and why, in particular, $\sim\sim p$ does not have the same import as p). Atlas and Levinson (1981) proposed therefore that what is said, in Grice's sense, should be related to the level of semantic representation or logical form, and this is the position I take here. (Such a level is almost certainly much more abstract and underspecified than was previously thought, but more of that later.)

Grice (1975: 44) also notes some essential prerequisites for an identification of what is said, and these will prove crucial:

> for a full identification of what the speaker had said one would need to know (a) the identity of [the referents], (b) the time of utterance, (c) the meaning on the particular occasion of utterance, of the phrase [uttered].

In short, we need to have resolved reference, fixed indexicals, and disambiguated expressions before we can identify what a speaker has said on an occasion of utterance.

In contrast to what is said, and on the basis of what is said, a speaker may conversationally implicate further propositions. By saying p, utterer *U conversationally implicates q* if:

(a)   *U* is presumed to be following the maxims,
(b)   the supposition q is required to maintain (a), and
(c)   *U* thinks the recipient will realize (b).

"To work out . . . a particular conversational implicature the hearer will rely on . . . the conventional meaning of the words . . . together with the identity of any references involved." (1975: 50)

The central idea is simple and clear. What is *said* is the input to the pragmatic reasoning responsible for output of *implicatures*: what is implicated is calculated on the basis of what is said (together with aspects of *how* it was said, in the case of Manner implicatures). "What is said" seems to be designed to be equivalent to the proposition expressed by the use of a sentence or the truth-conditional content of the utterance, and is in turn dependent on reference resolution, indexical fixing, and disambiguation. Although it is impossible to provide a diagram that is neutral over all the different theoretical positions, I believe that the received view of an abstract (competence) model of meaning assignment is more or less accurately captured in Figure 3.1 (this picture clearly doesn't capture the view in Situation Semantics or DRT [more on this later] nor does it incorporate theory-specific components of grammar).

Here, there is a logical ordering of operations, so that the syntax provides strings with structural analyses, selected between by a disambiguation device of some sort (usually not directly addressed in linguistic theory). The disambiguated structure can then be associated with a semantic representation or logical form, which in turn can then be associated with a model-theoretic interpretation, but only after the "fixing" of indexicals with the aid of a highly

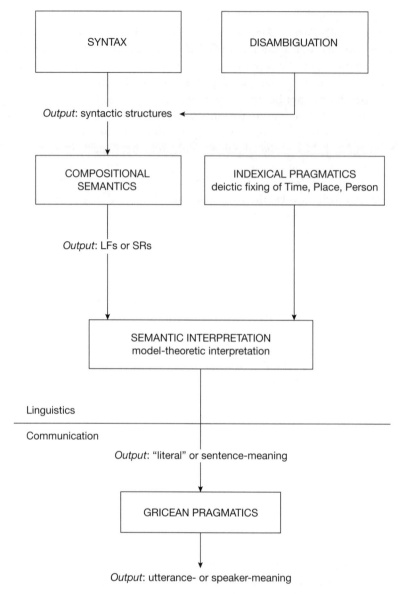

Figure 3.1 Received view of the semantics/pragmatics relation.

restricted kind of pragmatic input—namely, the values of the pragmatic indices obtaining in the speech situation. The interpretation is then taken to provide a proposition expressed by the utterance on an occasion of use. The output of the semantics is then the input to the pragmatics, where Gricean mechanisms provide augmented (and occasionally, as in "flouts," altered) interpretations.

In this chapter, I examine two major kinds of problem for the received view. The first problem, covered in Section 3.2.1 [see original publication], is that even if we accept Grice's rather restricted account of what is involved in fixing what is said, namely the factors already mentioned (reference identification, deixis, and disambiguation), implicatures can be seen paradoxically to play a role in the establishment of what is said. This leads to an interesting chicken-and-egg problem about the priority of what is said versus what is implicated. At this point, it will prove useful to pause to consider possible responses. The second problem, examined in Section 3.3 [see original publication], is that the content of generalized conversational implicatures can fall within the scope of logical operators and other higher level processes of semantic composition. In Section 3.4 [see original publication], I turn once again to reference fixing, now in detail, and show that GCIs interact with some of the crucial philosophical distinctions in reference. These three lines of evidence converge in requiring a rejection of the received view of the semantics/pragmatics interface and point in the direction of a new architecture for the theory of meaning.[*]

[. . .]

Indexical resolution

It is uncontroversial that certain pragmatic factors—namely, pragmatic indices or deictic parameters—are input to semantic interpretation. But it has been supposed that these indexical factors are of a limited kind and may be swept within a truth-conditional apparatus. There are a number of distinct assumptions here, each of which can be challenged:

1. *Indexical expressions are few in number and limited in kind.* (But in fact there are many different kinds of covertly indexical expressions; see Enç 1981; Barwise and Perry 1983; Mitchell 1986.)
2. *The indexical parameters or indices are a fixed, small set* for e.g., speakers, addressees, times of utterance, places of utterance, and indicated objects (see, e.g., Lewis 1972). (But crosslinguistic studies show that many more parameters may be required—for example, Kwakiutl forces a choice between "visible/nonvisible to participants" on most NPs in the same way that English forces a choice of tense on most verbs; see the catalogs of exotic deictic parameters in Fillmore (1975); Levinson (1983); Anderson and Keenan (1985).)
3. *The assignment of an indexical value to an indexical expression is a simple process of a direct mapping between context and expression.* There is a look-up table as it were, that assigns the expression I to the current speaker, the expression *here* to the place of utterance, *now* to the time of uttering, and so on.

It is this last assumption that I challenge here: that indexicals require no inferential resolution and, in particular, that the assignment of indexical values has nothing to do with pragmatic inference in general, and thus nothing to do with GCIs. The assumption is undermined by examples like the following, organized under the major traditional dimensions of deixis—namely, place, person, and time (Levinson 1983: Chapter 2):

(8)   *Place*
    a.   "Take *these three* drinks to the three people over there; take *these four* to the four people over there."
        Q ++> 'Take the drinks that are exactly three in number over there, take the drinks that are exactly four in number over there.'
    b.   "Some of those apples are ripe; *those ones are for you*, the other ones are for Bill."
        Q ++> 'Some but not all of those apples are ripe; just the ripe ones are for you . . .'

    c.   "This sofa is comfortable; come over *here*" vs. "California is beautiful; come over *here*."

        I-principle: delimits *here* by anaphoric resolution.

(9) *Person*

    a.   A: i. "He said you did it?"

            ii. "He confessed?" (alternative possible question).

        B: "He said *I* did it" (maxim of Relevance).

    b.   "*Some of you* know the news; I'm not talking to *you*; I'm talking to the rest of you."

        Q-principle: delimits *to you* to 'to some but not all of you'.

(10) *Time*

    a.   "I used to have a car like that."

        Q-implicates: 'I no longer have a car like that'.

    b.   "The meeting is on *Thursday*."

        Q-implicates: 'not tomorrow' when tomorrow is Thursday.

Consider the use of example (8a) in the absence of gestural indication (on the phrase *these three drinks*) and in a context where the speaker is pouring wine into two sets of glasses: one set has exactly three glasses, the other exactly four. Given that the numeral words in English can be argued to only implicate an upper bound, *three* glosses as 'at least three' at the level of semantic content, although it normally carries a GCI 'at most three'. Thus the expression *these three glasses* has the semantic content 'these glasses of cardinality no less than three'. It follows that, in the absence of gesture, the expression might equally designate either set of glasses. Yet the utterance would be perfectly felicitous in the circumstances sketched, because any interpreter would use the GCI 'at most three' to resolve the indexical reference. (Without such pragmatic resolution, the utterance ought to be anomalous; because it isn't, we must assume that GCIs play a role in fixing indexical reference.)[**]

    Consider now example (8b). The expression *some of those apples* is consistent with all of those apples but is delimited by a GCI to 'some but not all of those'. It is the pragmatically delimited set, a proper subset of the apples, that is introduced as a discourse referent by *some of those apples*. This is shown by the fact that the following demonstrative pronoun *those ones* must refer to a subset of the apples (cf. similar observations for nonindexicals by Kadmon 1987). If the phrase *those ones* is both anaphoric and deictic, which I believe is the right analysis, then the truth conditions for *those ones are for you* are dependent on the GCI that restricts the set of apples to less than all. The point may be sharpened by the subsequent contrastive referring phrase. without the pragmatic restriction on *those ones*, *the other ones* has no clear denotation.

    Example (8c) makes a simple but very general point. Indexical parameters are not alone sufficient, on the whole, to give one a reasonably circumscribed denotation (the one clear exception is the pronoun *I*, which is individuated by the speaker parameter alone; but see (9a)). For example, *here* denotes some region inclusive of some part of the speaker's immediate location; bring it here might mean 'bring it to my fingertips' (imagine the surgeon, in need of a scalpel, to the nurse) or 'bring it to Los Angeles' (perhaps we are talking about something that needs no exact location, like an advertising blimp). Suppose A is in Los Angeles and B is in New York and the following exchange takes place:

(11) A: "Where's the conference being held?"
     B: "It's being held here."

If *here* means 'some space inclusive of the speaker's location', then would B have told the truth if the conference is being held in Princeton? Surely not. But without further pragmatic restriction of the extent of *here*, what B said was true (a proper account of such restrictions can be found in Schegloff 1972). In the cases in (8c), it is clear that pragmatic restriction of the extent of *here* is made by anaphoric linkage to antecedents, a process that comes under the I-inferential category: *here* is essentially indexical but anaphorically restricted.

Person deixis might be thought to be immune from pragmatic resolution, but this is not the case. After all, even *I* can be interpreted as referring to the speaker of directly quoted speech (as in (9a), where a Relevance implicature would be instrumental in selecting interpretations according to alternate prior utterances). *You* clearly may refer to more than one addressee, or parties not addressed at all, or even some subset of the parties just previously addressed as in (9b). Here only if *some of you* implicates 'not all of you' will *the rest of you* have denotation.

Temporal deixis is in fact especially permeated by Gricean mechanisms, because temporal reference is normally made more precise by opposition to other temporal expressions that were not used—that is, by Q- and M-implicature. Thus *used to V* in (10a), where V is verb, will normally implicate 'no longer V' by opposition to the simple present (yet there's no inconsistency in "I used to love swimming, and in fact I still do"; see chap. 2). Or more simply, *Thursday* said on Wednesday will Q-implicate 'not tomorrow', because *tomorrow* would be the more informative expression and was not used (there are many Thursdays, but only one tomorrow, given a today!).

There can be little doubt then that GCIs, along with other pragmatic processes, are involved in the resolution of indexical expressions, without which, of course, no exact proposition will be expressed.

    [. . .]

Notes

*   For reasons of space, only the first 'problem' is covered in this reading.

**   Levinson's argument is that it is the GCI in (8a) and not the entailment that enables us to identify the set of glasses referred to in the way intended by the speaker. This is because *three glasses* entails 'not less than three' (*three glasses, in fact two* being a contradiction) and implies 'not more than three' by Q1. We know this is an implicature and not an entailment because *three glasses, in fact four* isn't a contradiction. Without this implicature and relying only on the entailment, we might take *these three glasses* to refer to either set. A similar argument underlies the interpretation of *some of those apples* in (8b): since *some, in fact all* isn't a contradiction, 'not all' is a Q1 implicature of *some*.

1   M-intention is Grice's (1989: 105) shorthand for the complex reflexive intention involved in speaker's meaning—namely, the speaker's intention to cause an effect in the recipient just by getting the recipient to recognize that that was his/her intention.

2   The truth-conditions of sentences or utterances? If utterances, so what? So asks Kent Bach. But on the views developed below (and indeed in Bach 1982, 1987, 1994a), sentences don't have truth-conditions, only utterances do. The interesting question then becomes: what kinds of inferential processes get us to the minimal proposition-bearing entity, and my claim is that these are just the same kinds of process, with the same kind of product, that elsewhere may take us from a proposition expressed to something else the speaker meant, which is more obviously an implicature.

■ ■ ■

POST-READING

1   Do you agree that pragmatic intrusion is unavoidable? What are the consequences of having to abandon the principle of logical priority, according to which each component provides input to the next component? Although Levinson suggests that we need 'to drastically revise our understanding of the pragmatics/semantics interface', he doesn't provide an updated version of Figure 3.1 to take account of this revision. Can you help him with this, by adapting the figure so that it takes account of Levinson's proposed changes?

2   Levinson asks, 'In what sense are these I-inferences generalized?' Either making use of your own knowledge of other languages/cultures or working with someone who speaks a language other than your own, try to come to some conclusions about this.

3   In Chapter 1 of *Presumptive Meanings*, Levinson distinguishes Q implicatures from M implicatures (2000: 41). He describes Q implicatures as 'informationally ordered sets'. This is because they are scalar – e.g. 'some' implies *not all* since, according to the Heuristic, *What isn't said* [in this case 'all'] *isn't*. M implicatures are 'sets of synonyms differing in markedness' following the Heuristic *What's said in an abnormal way, isn't normal*. How would you characterize I implicatures?

REINHARD BLUTNER

SOME PERSPECTIVES ON LEXICAL PRAGMATICS

PRE-READING

1   Make brief notes on what you think the distinctions might be between the following terms that you'll meet in the reading:
    *   *normative* and *naturalistic* approaches to the interpretation of lexical items;
    *   *literalism* and *contextualism*;
    *   *optimal interpretations* and *expressive optimization*;
    *   *unidirectional optimality theoretic semantics* and *unidirectional optimality theoretic syntax*, on the one hand, and *bidirectional optimality theory* on the other;
    *   *general* and *specific* interpretations of lexical items.
2   What do you think the following terms might mean: *truth functional pragmatics, constructional iconicity, recursive optimization*? Again, make brief notes.

IN-READING

The sentences in the table below are marked in the text with the marginal mark | . As you encounter each of them in the text, imagine that you are editing a summary of the reading and have to decide which you would want to include in your summary. Use the boxes in the table below to grade each according to how strongly you feel it should be included on the scale: A = essential, B = include if possible, C = can be omitted.

Lexical pragmatics starts from the hypothesis that the meaning expressed by a lexical unit is underdetermined by its semantics and provides a framework to study the processes involved in bridging the gap between the encoded and the communicated meaning of lexical units.	
... the view that a large range of adjectives behaves intersectively has been shown to be questionable.	
... both approaches [relevance theory and optimality theoretic pragmatics] take a naturalistic stance with regard to pragmatics and pursue the same main goal: developing a cognitive psychological model of lexical interpretation.	
... both relevance theory and optimality theoretic pragmatics claim that the linguistic semantics encoded by a natural language expression underdetermines what is communicated by an utterance of that expression.	
Radical literalism refers to an extreme literalism starting with a strict separation between semantics and pragmatics. It assumes that literal meaning can be determined in a purely linguistic way by looking at the semantic contributions made by the syntactic constituents of a sentence and their mode of composition.	
Radical literalism doubts the existence of unarticulated constituents.	
Radical contextualism doubts the existence of a level of sentence meaning which can be expressed by minimal propositions. It assumes underdetermination instead and it assumes the existence of unarticulated constituents.	
According to the syncretic view, sentences such as 'Cut the grass' express something very abstract, which is independent of the concrete background assumptions. This abstract propositional content is derived from the underspecified meaning of 'cut' and the meanings of the other context-independent constituents of the sentence.	
... radical contextualism can be seen as the methodological and philosophical foundation of lexical pragmatics.	
Radical literalism simply conflicts with the core idea of lexical pragmatics that lexical units are underdetermined by their semantics.	
Optimality theoretic pragmatics follows the neoGricean idea of assuming that two countervailing principles determine the interpretation mechanism ... : the Q principle and the R principle.	
The main idea [of a relevance theoretic approach to lexical pragmatics] is that the linguistically encoded meaning of a word is no more than an indication of the actual interpretation or utterance meaning.	
Bidirectional optimality theory falls within the family of linguistic models that are based on the optimization of linguistic output against a system of ranked constraints. This theory provides a general procedure of optimization of the relation between form and meaning, simultaneously optimizing in both directions, from meaning to form, and from form to meaning.	
Why is it the *male* reading that is associated with the 'short' (unmarked) term *osël* and the *female* reading that is associated with the other, 'longer' (marked) term?	
... unmarked forms preferentially correspond to unmarked meanings and marked forms preferentially correspond to marked meanings.	
The concept of fossilization refers to the transformation of a *weak* bidirectional optimization into a *strong* one ...	
Another main problem concerns a systematic exploration of the huge range of examples in terms of a unifying theory.	
In addition, we need theoretical explorations that are able to *predict* the phenomena rather describe them *post facto*.	

■ ■ ■

SOME PERSPECTIVES ON LEXICAL PRAGMATICS
REINHARD BLUTNER

1 Introduction

Lexical pragmatics starts from the hypothesis that the meaning expressed by a lexical unit is underdetermined by its semantics and provides a framework to study the processes involved in bridging the gap between the encoded and the communicated meaning of lexical units. The aim of this paper is to provide a concise introduction to lexical pragmatics, to explain some perspectives and problems in this research field, and to highlight some possible future developments.

The basic idea of lexical pragmatics was launched in a now classical paper (McCawley 1978). Discussing several examples – including the much quoted example in which *kill* and *cause to die* are distinguished, McCawley argued that 'a lexical item and a syntactically complex equivalent of it may make different contributions to the interpretation of a sentence without making different contributions to its semantic structure' (McCawley 1978: 257). Alluding to Grice's (1967) maxims of conversation, McCawley demonstrated that the difference between the linguistically encoded semantic structure and the suggested interpretation is a consequence of general principles of cooperative behaviour and as such is systematic and predictable. As a consequence, he claims, there is no need to formulate idiosyncratic restrictions that must be incorporated into the relevant lexical entries in order to restrict the system of interpretations. The suggested division of labour between semantics and pragmatics has important consequences for keeping semantics simple and for applying the semantic tool of decomposition.

In the next section, I will explain the basic phenomena that are discussed within lexical pragmatics. In Section 3, I will outline the philosophical and methodological background underlying lexical pragmatics, and the main proponents of this research field, relevance theory and optimality theory, are identified. Section 4 discusses the optimality theoretic approach to lexical pragmatics including a straightforward treatment of the idea of fossilization. Section 5 discusses some puzzles and open problems and draws some tentative conclusions.

2 Basic phenomena

Lexical pragmatics investigates the mechanisms by which linguistically-specified word meanings are modified in use. Following Wilson (2003) and Carston (2002a), we can distinguish three basic phenomena: narrowing, approximation and metaphorical extension.

2.1 Narrowing

Narrowing refers to the use of a lexical item to convey a more restricted interpretation than the semantically encoded one. Examples are the use of the word *drink* to mean 'alcoholic drink' or the use of *smoke* to mean 'smoke your joint' (at least in Amsterdam, where everybody knows the request 'please smoke inside').

Another example concerns the interpretation of reciprocals (Dalrymple et al. 1998). Consider for instance the following example:

(1a) The girls saw each other.
(1b) The girls are sitting alongside each other.

Sentence (1a) entails that every girl saw every other girl. This contrasts with sentence (1b) which obviously does not entail that each of the girls is sitting alongside each of the others (expressing a much weaker proposition, instead). The interpretation that is strongly preferred in these and similar cases is best described by the *strongest meaning hypothesis*: A reciprocal sentence is interpreted as expressing the logically strongest candidate truth conditions (given a lattice of propositions that structures the set of possible interpretations) which are not contradicted by known properties of the relation expressed by the reciprocal scope when restricted to the group argument. The starting point for this kind of strengthening is the minimal meaning that can be expressed by reciprocal sentences. Subsequent work has suggested extending the application of the strongest meaning hypothesis to the treatment of plurals (Winter 2001), prepositions (Zwarts 2003) and quantification (Blutner et al. 2003).

The interpretation of adjectival modification provides another example of narrowing (Lahav 1989). Normally, adjectives like *red*, *pregnant*, or *straight* are considered to be *intersective* adjectives, i.e. their meaning can be represented by one-place predicates and the combinatorial semantic operation that corresponds to adjectival modification is the intersection operation. Interestingly, Fodor and Pylyshyn (1988) conclude that these assumptions may explain the feature of systematicity in the case of adjectival modification. For example, when a person is able to understand the expressions *brown cow* and *black horse*, then she should understand the expressions *brown horse* and *black cow* as well.

Unfortunately, the view that a large range of adjectives behaves intersectively has been shown to be questionable. For example, Quine (1960) notes the contrast between *red apple* (red on the outside) and *pink grapefruit* (pink on the inside), and between the different colours denoted by *red* in *red apple* and *red hair*. In a similar vein, Lahav (1989, 1993) argues that an adjective such as *brown* doesn't make a simple and fixed contribution to any composite expression in which it appears:

> In order for a cow to be brown, most of its body's surface should be brown, though not its udders, eyes, or internal organs. A brown crystal, on the other hand, needs to be brown both inside and outside. A book is brown if its cover, but not necessarily its inner pages, is mostly brown, while a newspaper is brown only if all its pages are brown. For a potato to be brown it needs to be brown only outside. Furthermore, in order for a cow or a bird to be brown, the brown color should be the animal's natural color, since it is regarded as being 'really' brown even if it is painted white all over. A table, on the other hand, is brown even if it is only painted brown and its 'natural' color underneath the paint is, say, yellow. But while a table or a bird is not brown if covered with brown sugar, a cookie is. In short, what is to be brown is different for different types of objects. To be sure, brown objects do have something in common: a salient part that is wholly brownish. But this hardly suffices for an object to count as brown. A significant component of the applicability condition of the predicate 'brown' varies from one linguistic context to another.
>
> Lahav (1993: 76)

Polysemous nouns such as *opera*, *concert*, *school*, and *government* (Nunberg 1979) provide a third illustration of narrowing. For instance, we can identify three conceptual variants for the interpretation of *school* – the institution-, building-, and process-readings:

(2a) The school is part of a highly successful chain of language schools (institution-reading).

(2b) The school is situated in the centre of the city (building-reading).

(2c) The school takes place away from the mainland (process reading).

Bierwisch (1983) stresses that the semantic entry for these *institutional nouns* is underspecified with regard to the level of conceptually salient sense. He proposes a certain 'purpose' representing the core meaning of a given institutional noun. For instance, the purpose for 'school' is teaching and learning. It is this semantic condition which discriminates the core meanings from each other. Further, Bierwisch (1983) proposes several functions or 'templates' for specifying the particular interpretations of the noun under discussion. In the case of 'school', these functions refer to conceptual primes specifying institutions, buildings or processes related to the given purpose.[1]

2.2 Approximation

Approximation refers to the process of interpretive broadening where the interpretation of a word with a restricted core meaning is extended to a family of related interpretations. Cases in point are loose uses of numbers (e.g., *1000 students* used to mean 'about 1000 students'; cf. Krifka 2007a), geometric terms (e.g., *square* used to mean 'squarish'; cf. Wilson 2003), colour adjectives, where the precise colour value can deviate from the lexically addressed focal colour (e.g., *red* in *red nose*, *red bean*, and *red flag*). Recanati (2004a) introduced the term 'modulation' to describe the underlying mechanism of contextual modification. Providing a precise model of this mechanism is one of the big challenges facing lexical pragmatics.

2.3 Metaphorical extension

Metaphorical extension is a type of broadening that extends the space of possible interpretation much more radically than approximation. A good introductory example is English perception words (cf. Sweetser 1990). Following John Locke and Ferdinand de Saussure, Sweetser (1990) claims that the feature of arbitrariness could be taken as a sufficient condition for the presence of semantic information. It is certainly an arbitrary fact of English that *see* (rather than, say, *buy* or *smell*) refers to visual perception in an utterance such as 'I *see* the tree'. Given this arbitrary association between a phonological word and its meaning, however, it is by no means arbitrary that *see* can also have an epistemic reading, as in 'I *see* what you're getting at'. Moreover, it is not a coincidence that other sensory verbs such as *smell* or *taste* are not used to express an epistemic meaning. Sweetser (1990) sketches an explanation for such facts and insists that they have to do with conceptual organization. It is our *knowledge* about the inner world that accounts for vision and knowledge being highly related, in contrast to, say, smell and knowledge or taste and knowledge, which are only weakly related for normal human beings. If this claim is correct, then the information that *see* may have an epistemic meaning but *smell* and *taste* do not, no longer needs to be stipulated semantically. Instead, this information is pragmatic in nature, having to do with the utterance of words within a conceptual setting, and can be derived by means of some general mechanism of conceptual interpretation.

Another case of broadening that cannot be classified as approximation is the phenomenon of *predicate transfer* (Nunberg 1979; Sag 1981; Nunberg 1995), exemplified by the following:

(3a) The ham sandwich is sitting at table 9. (Preferred Interpretation: The one who ordered a ham sandwich is sitting at table 9.)

(3b) There are five ham sandwiches sitting at table 9. (Preferred Interpretation: There are five people who ordered ham sandwiches sitting at table 9.)

(3c) Every ham sandwich at the table is a woman. (Preferred Interpretation: Everyone who ordered a ham sandwich is a woman.)

Sag (1981) and Nunberg (1995) assume that the intension of the head noun (ham sandwich) has to be transferred to another property in order to get the intended (Nunbergian) interpretation (preferentially to the property of being the orderer of the ham sandwich).

Wilson (2003) discusses another variety of broadening, *category extension*. Typical examples are salient brand names (*Hoover, Kleenex*) which are used to denote a broader category ('vacuum cleaner', 'disposable tissue') including items from less salient brands. Further, certain prominent personal names lend themselves to category extension:

(4)   Stefan is the new *Hilbert*.

(5)   Federer is the new *Sampras*.

In (4), *Hilbert* evokes the category of gifted mathematicians, and *Sampras* in (5) evokes the category of gifted tennis players of a certain type. As Wilson (2003) stresses, these examples of category extension are not analyzable as approximations. The claim in (5) is not 'that Federer is a borderline case, close enough to being Sampras for it to be acceptable to *call* him Sampras, but merely that he belongs to a broader category of which Sampras is a salient member' (Wilson 2003: 345).

Other cases of metaphorical extension are more radical extensions of semantically specified interpretations, as illustrated by the following examples:

(6)   The president has been *under fire* for his veto.

(7)   My memory is a little foggy.

3 Theoretical prerequisites

Providing a categorization of different basic phenomena does not mean that we have to assume different computational mechanisms for explaining these phenomena. Rather, it is theoretically much more satisfying to look for a unified theory of lexical pragmatics. Presently, we find two main attempts at realizing such a unified approach. The first is based on *relevance theory* (Sperber and Wilson 1986/1995), the second on *optimality theoretic pragmatics* (Blutner 1998; Blutner and Zeevat 2004; Blutner et al. 2005). Both approaches agree on a number of important assumptions. For instance, both approaches take a naturalistic stance with regard to pragmatics and pursue the same main goal: developing a cognitive psychological model of lexical interpretation. This contrasts with the normative character that is generally attributed to the Gricean approach.

Further, both relevance theory and optimality theoretic pragmatics claim that the linguistic semantics encoded by a natural language expression underdetermines what is communicated by an utterance of that expression. Taking a lead from Atlas (e.g., Atlas 2005), both theories reject the doctrine of literal meaning, i.e. the idea that the *logical form* of a sentence conforms to its literal meaning. Instead, they assume *contextualism*, i.e. the claim that the mechanism of pragmatic interpretation is crucial both for determining what the speaker says and what he or she means (see Carston 2002a).

At this point, it seems appropriate to take a broader look at the variety of approaches to natural language interpretation. As Recanati has made clear in several publications (e.g., Recanati 1995, 2004a, 2005), most approaches to natural language interpretation can be classified along a range of attempts from radical literalism to radical contextualism. Radical literalism refers to an extreme literalism starting with a strict separation between semantics and pragmatics. It assumes that literal meaning can be determined in a purely linguistic way by looking at the semantic contributions made by the syntactic constituents of a sentence and their mode of composition. Hence, the contextual infiltration of semantics is very limited. Context-dependencies can only arise from indexical expressions, i.e. words such as 'I', 'you', and 'tomorrow' or demonstratives phrases such as 'this man' and 'that building'. No underdetermination of natural language expression is involved in these cases. Generally, the existence of underdetermination is rejected by radical literalism. A further hallmark concerns the existence of *unarticulated constituents*. This term refers to the idea of explaining the near equivalence of sentences such as 'it is raining' and 'it is raining here' by assuming an unarticulated constituent of place in the first sentence. It is a *constituent*, because there is no truth-evaluable proposition unless a place is supplied (since rain occurs at a time in a place). It is *unarticulated*, because there is no morpheme that designates that place (cf. Perry 1993). Radical literalism doubts the existence of unarticulated constituents.

The other extreme is radical contextualism. Radical contextualism doubts the existence of a level of sentence meaning which can be expressed by minimal propositions. It assumes underdetermination instead and it assumes the existence of unarticulated constituents. Relevance theorists, optimality theoretic pragmaticists and philosophers like Searle (1979) and Travis (1989) tend to the position of radical contextualism. Authors such as Bierwisch (1983), Cappelen and Lepore (2005a), Borg (2004), and Bosch (1995, 2009) are typical representatives of radical literalism.

There are two main positions between the radical poles: moderate literalism and the syncretic view (Recanati 2006). Moderate literalism (Stanley 2000; Taylor 2001)[2] accepts semantic underdetermination but rejects unarticulated constituents. It contrasts with radical literalism by allowing elements of underdetermination at the level of meaning (or logical form). Consider the following two sentences in order to make the point clear:

(8)   Robert is tall.
(9)   John weighs 80 kg.

A moderate literalist is likely to grant that (8) is genuinely context-sensitive. The adjective 'tall' seems to include a free variable that can be specified by some norm (for a what is Robert tall? Is he tall for an adult or for a young child?). Stanley (2000) assumes that this intuitive constituent is 'articulated' by a free variable (which is controlled by operators in the sentence). Interestingly, also the interpretation of (9) is affected by contextual factors, but in a much less direct way, and the moderate literalist is likely to deny that what is said by (9) is context-sensitive. Consider first the sentence (9) in a scenario where John has had a heart attack and the doctor is asking about his weight. The second scenario is when John is about to step on an elevator with a capacity of no more than an extra 80 kg. In scenario A, the speaker evidently communicates a proposition about the weight of John's naked body. In scenario B, the speaker communicates a different proposition about the combined weight of John's naked body, his clothing, his handbag, etc. A radical contextualist has to account for the context-sensitivity of (8) and (9) in a uniform way in expressing what is said by these sentences. The moderate literalist is likely to assume a minimal proposition in case of (9) capturing what is literally expressed by the different utterances of (9). It needs *secondary pragmatic processes* (Recanati 2004a, 2005, 2006) to express the additional interpretational differences since the moderate literalist would insist that the pragmatically enriched proposition is not *directly* asserted by the speaker.[3]

A second position between the two extremes, the *syncretic view*, accepts underdetermination and unarticulated constituents but it assumes a minimal proposition for expressing the meaning of a whole sentence. Recanati (2006) uses an example from Searle (1980) to explain this position. Searle considers the verb 'cut', which is not ambiguous in his view. However, in 'Bill cut the grass' and 'Sally cut the cake', it makes quite different contributions to the truth-conditional content of the utterance. This is because the background conditions (conceptual knowledge) underlying the verb 'cut' in connection with grass and cake are different, as described by Searle:

> The sort of thing that constitutes cutting the grass is quite different from, e.g., the sort of thing that constitutes cutting a cake. One way to see this is to imagine what constitutes obeying the order to cut something. If someone tells me to cut the grass and I rush out and stab it with a knife, or if I am ordered to cut the cake and I run over it with a lawnmower, in each case I will have failed to obey the order. That is not what the speaker meant by his literal and serious utterance of the sentence.
>
> Searle (1980: 222–3)

According to the syncretic view, sentences such as 'Cut the grass' express something very abstract, which is independent of the concrete background assumptions. This abstract propositional content is derived from the underspecified meaning of 'cut' and the meanings of the other context-independent constituents of the sentence. The calculated meaning of our sample sentence abstracts from particular uses – even generalizing over such strange uses as in Searle's example.

For other examples that make a similar point, we refer to the discussion of Quine's and Lahav's examples in Section 2.1. According to the syncretic view, a sentence like 'this apple is red' expresses a proposition that abstracts from the details of what part of the apple is red and to what extent. It simply means 'some part of the apple is red'.

There is a problem with the syncretic approach. In the apple example, for instance, conceptual knowledge about how apples are normally coloured is required in order to get something genuinely truth-evaluable. The sentence 'this apple is red' does not denote an apple whose inside is red and most of whose peel is green. Normally we call such an object a green apple, which is red inside. Hence, our intuitions about the truth-conditional content of this sentence are clearly context-sensitive. This example provides a vivid illustration of the need for *truth-functional pragmatics* (to use a term favoured by Recanati 2004a, see also Carston 2006).

All the examples discussed in Section 2 for motivating narrowing, approximation, and metaphorical extension demonstrate the view that the truth-conditional content of the corresponding sentence is context-sensitive and call for a truth-functional pragmatics. (For more discussion, see Blutner 2006). In this vein, radical contextualism can be seen as the methodological and philosophical foundation of lexical pragmatics. Moderate literalism and the syncretic view marginalize the idea of truth-functional pragmatics and radical literalism totally rejects this idea and the whole idea of lexical pragmatics. Radical literalism simply conflicts with the core idea of lexical pragmatics that lexical units are underdetermined by their semantics. All the other positions agree in admitting at least some elements of underdetermination.

Let us come back now to the main theoretical frameworks of implementing lexical pragmatics: relevance theory and optimality theoretic pragmatics. Besides the similarities I mentioned already, there are also important differences between the two approaches. Optimality theoretic pragmatics follows the neo-Gricean idea of assuming that two countervailing principles determine the interpretation mechanism (Atlas and Levinson 1981; Horn 1984; Blutner 1998; Atlas 2005; Horn 2005; Huang 2009): the Q principle and the R principle. The first principle is oriented toward the interests of the hearer and looks for optimal interpretations; the second principle is oriented to the interests of the speaker and looks for expressive optimization. In optimality theory, these principles correspond to different directions of optimization where the content of the optimization procedure is expressed by particular optimality theoretic constraints.

In contrast, relevance theory sees the communicative principle of relevance as the only effective principle. According to this principle, utterances convey a presumption of their own optimal relevance. That means that any given utterance can be presumed (i) to be at least relevant enough to warrant the addressee's processing effort and (ii) to be the most relevant one compatible with the speaker's current state of knowledge and her personal preferences and goals.

Obviously, both relevance theory and optimality theoretic pragmatics account for the resolution of the conflict between communicative effect and (processing) effort. This observation, and the fact that both approaches have a number of 'free parameters' for fitting the empirical data, makes a direct comparison relatively difficult. The notion of *blocking*, which is present in optimality theoretic pragmatics but missing in relevance theory, is presumably a substantial difference between the two approaches. The general idea is that a specialized item can block a general/regular process that would lead to the formation of an otherwise expected interpretation equivalent to it. For example, in English the specialized mass terms *pork, beef* and *wood* usually block the 'grinding' process which would otherwise give an uncountable reading for the countable nouns *pig, cow* and *tree*. This explains the following contrasts: 'I ate *pork/?pig*'; 'I like *beef/?cow*'; 'The table is made of *wood/?tree*'. It is important to note that blocking is not absolute, but may be cancelled under special contextual conditions (cf. Blutner 1998). This suggests that the blocking phenomenon is pragmatic in nature and may be explicable on the basis of Gricean principles.

A relevance theoretic approach to lexical pragmatics has been developed in Carston (2002a), Wilson (2003), and Wilson and Sperber (2002), *inter alia*. The main idea is that the linguistically encoded meaning of a word is no more than an indication of the actual interpretation or utterance meaning. Hence, the interpretation is not decoded but has to be inferred by a pragmatic mechanism. Furthermore, understanding any utterance, literal, loose or metaphorical, is a matter of seeing its intended relevance, as specified in the relevance-theoretic comprehension procedure. In other words, relevance theory 'suggests the following answers to the basic questions of lexical pragmatics: lexical-pragmatic processes are triggered by the search for relevance, they follow a path of least effort, they operate via mutual adjustment of explicit content, context and cognitive effects, and they stop when the expectations of relevance raised by the utterance are satisfied (or abandoned).' (Wilson 2003: 282).

4 The optimality theoretic approach to lexical pragmatics

Bidirectional optimality theory falls within the family of linguistic models that are based on the optimization of linguistic output against a system of ranked constraints (Blutner 2000; Blutner and Zeevat 2004; Blutner et al. 2005). This theory provides a general procedure of optimization of the relation between form and meaning, simultaneously optimizing in both directions, from meaning to form, and from form to meaning. This distinguishes bidirectional optimality theory from unidirectional optimality theoretic semantics (Hendriks and de Hoop 2001) – optimizing from form to meaning – and from unidirectional optimality theoretic syntax (Grimshaw 1997) – optimizing from meaning to form. To put it in a nutshell, bidirectional optimality theory evaluates form-meaning pairs. As described in Blutner (2000), there are two ways of defining optimality in a bidirectional setting, a strong way and a weak way. The strong version is based on the standard definition of optimality, applying this to candidate pairs instead of output elements.

The weak version uses a recursive definition of super-optimality of form-meaning pairs. A form-meaning pair is super-optimal if and only if there is no other super-optimal pair with a better form that expresses the same meaning, and there is no other super-optimal pair with a better interpretation of that same form. What counts as 'better' in this definition is determined by the constraints, and usually boils down to less marked. Usually, strong optimization gives only one optimal form-meaning pair, with the best form and meaning paired up. Weak optimization allows us to also pair up marked forms and meanings. As argued in Blutner (2000), this allows us to capture what is known as Horn's division of pragmatic labour: pairing unmarked forms with unmarked meanings, and marked forms with marked meanings. This way of associating forms and meanings is seen throughout many lexical and grammatical domains (McCawley 1978; Horn 1984; Levinson 2000a).

The idea of using optimality theory for formalizing lexical pragmatics was first proposed by Blutner (2000). There are now several case studies demonstrating the power of the formalism. Jäger and Blutner (2000, 2003) suggested an optimality theoretic analysis of the different readings of German *wieder* (again). Henriëtte de Swart (2004) provided an optimality theoretic approach to the pragmatics of negation and negative indefinites. Referring to the stage level/individual level contrast, Maienborn (2004, 2005) argued against the popular view that the distinction between stage level predicates and individual level predicates rests on a fundamental cognitive division of the world that is reflected in the grammar. Instead, she proposed a pragmatic explanation of the distinction, and gives, *inter alia*, a discourse-based account of Spanish *ser*/*estar*. Other applications include the pragmatics of dimensional adjectives (Blutner and Solstad 2000), the analysis of Dutch *om*/*rond* (Zwarts 2006), the pragmatics of negated antonyms (Blutner 2004; Krifka 2007b), the approximate interpretation of number words (Krifka 2007a), and several examples of semantic change (Eckardt 2002). Following Zwarts et al. (2009), I will explain the basic ideas of this approach by means of a simple example: the specification of gender in animate nouns.

4.1 The specification of gender in animate nouns

The gender opposition female – male embodies a contrast that led Roman Jakobson to formulate the concept of *markedness* first described in his work on the structure of the Russian verb (Jakobson 1984). Considering the difference between Russian *oslíca* 'she-ass' and Russian *osël* 'donkey', Jakobson notes that the feminine gender noun *oslíca* represents a marked category used only for a female animal of the species, where the corresponding masculine gender noun *osël* is used in a general sense for animals of both sexes. This latter reading we will call the 'kind reading' (referring to the animal as a 'kind' without specifying its sex). Jakobson observed further that in a specific context of contrast the female meaning may be cancelled, leaving only the male meaning: *èto oslíca?* 'Is it a she-ass?' – *nét, osël* 'no, a donkey'. Thus, depending on context, the unmarked (or neutral) form can be used either inclusively, subsuming the marked, or exclusively, in opposition to the marked.

The main approach to handling markedness in a formal way is what I will call the *default approach*. This approach starts with describing the marked term by specifying the relevant lexical features; in the case of *oslíca* it is 'female':

(10) *oslíca*: F.

However, no such specification is given in case of *osël*. In this case we can specify the relevant feature only by default, i.e. by a normative statement of a general preference, also called a markedness convention (Chomsky and Halle 1968; Kean 1995). In the case under discussion, the default is 'male' (M). Hence, we get the following specification by default:

(11) *osël*: M.

The default mechanism accounts for the observation that in certain contexts the default specification can be cancelled. However, this approach has the general problem that we always get a particular specification, either by default or from the context that overwrites the default. We never get the kind (K) interpretation. What we need is a mechanism that makes sure that the unmarked term can alternate between the general and specific interpretations:

(12) a. *osël*: M   b. *osël*: K   c. *oslíca*: F.

There is a series of other examples illustrating the asymmetric pattern of opposition; see the following examples in English where the first two exhibit male stereotypicality and the last two exhibit female stereotypicality:

(13) a. *actor*: M   b. *actor*: K   c. *actress*: F
(14) a. *dog*: M   b. *dog*: K   c. *bitch*: F
(15) a. *cow*: F   b. *cow*: K   c. *bull*: M
(16) a. *sheep*: F   b. *sheep*: K   c. *ram*: M.

Further problems for the classical markedness theory are discussed, among others by Haspelmath (2006) and Zwarts et al. (2009). For example, there are these puzzling examples of symmetric alternations:

(17) a. *widow*: F   b. *?* : K   c. *widower*: M
(18) a. *prince*: M   b. *?* : K   c. *princess*: F
(19) a. *mare*: F   b. *horse*: K   c. *stallion*: M
(20) a. *nurse*: F   b. *nurse*: K   (e.g., *male nurse*).

In (17) the male term is marked, in (18) it is the female term. However, there is no kind reading for either of these terms. Something similar happens in (19) where a special term (horse) is used for the kind reading.[4] Another exceptional term is *nurse* (20) which has a clear female stereotype but it allows for the kind reading in certain constructions.

As pointed out by Zwarts et al. (2009), bidirectional optimality theory provides a solution to the problems of semantic markedness in gender opposition. Consider first Jacobson's example with the terms *osël/oslíca*. In this case we have six possible form-meaning pairs that are in competition with each other. These six pairs are illustrated by the left column of Table 1.

Table 1 Optimality theoretic tableau demonstrating strong bidirectionality with two terms, three meanings and one constraint

		oslíca ⇔ F
☞	osël, M	
	osël, F	*
☞	osël, K	
	oslíca, M	*
☞	oslíca, F	
	oslíca, K	*

Source: Adapted from Zwarts (2009)

Following Zwarts (2009), we only have to introduce one lexical constraint for directing the mechanism of competition: *oslíca* ⇔ F. This constraint says 'use the word *oslíca* if and only if the meaning is female'. As indicated in Table 1, only those candidates that pair a female marker with a form other than *oslíca* and those candidates that pair up the form *oslíca* with a meaning other than 'F' violate this constraint (indicated by *). Hence, on the basis of this one constraint and by using the strong version of bidirectional optimization we get exactly the three pairs that were stipulated in (12).

It is not difficult to see how the examples of symmetric alternations can be analyzed: for example (17) we need two lexical constraints *widow* ⇔ F and *widower* ⇔ M; similarly, for example (18); for example (19) we have to add an extra lexical rule for the term 'horse': *horse* ⇔ K; for the nurse domain (20), we have to consider one term only and a competition between three meanings, which require one lexical rule: *nurse* ⇔ F.

I have already mentioned that depending on context, the unmarked (or neutral) form can be used either inclusively (subsuming the marked) or exclusively (in opposition to the marked). To describe the influence of context, Zwarts et al. (2009) introduce a constraint of gender relevance (GREL) which can be in one of two states, + or −, depending on the context: GREL (+) applies if gender distinction is relevant. It penalizes the 'K' value. GREL (−) applies if gender distinction is irrelevant. It penalizes the 'M' and 'F' values. Table 2 gives an example for a context where gender is important (cf. Jakobson's example, repeated here: *èto oslíca?* 'Is it a she-ass?' − *nét, osël* 'no, a donkey').

Table 2 Selecting strongly optimal pairs in a gender-relevant context

		oslíca ⇔ F	GREL (+)
☞	osël, M		
	osël, F	*	
	osël, K		*
	oslíca, M	*	
☞	oslíca, F		
	oslíca, K	*	*

Source: Adapted from Zwarts (2009)

What about the motivation of the lexical constraints introduced so far? This is one of the important research questions that cannot be answered by the present kind of analyses using strong bidirectionality. Why is it the *male* reading that is associated with the 'short' (unmarked) term *osël* and the *female* reading that is associated with the other, 'longer' (marked) term? Generally, these questions concern the *evolution* of lexical constraints. In the following subsection, I will discuss some factors that determine the formation of lexical constraints in domains with gender opposition.

4.2 Fossilization

The idea of fossilization refers to the mechanism of the conventionalization of implicatures, i.e. a mechanism for sanctioning certain interpretations. The idea was first developed in Geis and Zwicky's (1971) paper on 'invited inferences'. A closely related approach is Morgan's (1978) theory of short-circuited implicatures, where a fundamentally pragmatic mechanism has become partially grammaticalized. Using this idea, Horn and Bayer (1984) propose an elegant account of so-called neg-raising, i.e. the availability (with certain predicates) of lower clause understandings of higher clause negations. Here is an example:

(21) a. Surface form: Robert doesn't think Stefan left.
    b. Interpretation: Robert thinks Stefan didn't leave.

The principal difficulty for pragmatic treatments of these neg-raising interpretations is the existence of lexical exceptions to the process, i.e. we find pairs of virtual synonyms where one member allows the lower clause understanding and the other blocks it. One of Horn and Bayer's (1984) examples concerns opinion verbs. For instance, Hebrew *xogev* 'think' permits neg-raising readings while *maamin* 'believe' does not. Interestingly, the opposite pattern obtains in Malagasy. In French, *souhaiter* 'hope, wish' exhibits neg-raising, but its near-synonym *espérer* does not – although its Latin etymon *sperare* did. Horn and Bayer (1984) argue that conversational implicatures may become conventionalized ('pragmatic conventions') and this conventionalization sanctions neg-raising.

 The short-circuiting of implicatures as a matter of convention has important empirical consequences for lexical pragmatics. *Inter alia*, these consequences were discussed in connection with the classical pattern of constructional iconicity (or Horn's (1984) division of pragmatic labour) which holds that unmarked forms preferentially correspond to unmarked meanings and marked forms preferentially correspond to marked meanings. McCawley (1978) listed numerous cases of constructional iconicity in the lexicon, the most famous of which was mentioned earlier in connection with *kill* (denoting direct causation) and *cause to die* (denoting indirect causation). Krifka (2007a) observed that the phenomenon is the decisive factor in determining the precise/vague interpretation of measure expressions.

 In optimality theoretic pragmatics, the notion of weak bidirectionality (super-optimality) was introduced as a solution to account for the kind of recursive optimization that takes place during language change (Blutner 1998, 2000). The concept of fossilization refers to the transformation of a *weak* bidirectional optimization into a *strong* one (Blutner 2006, 2007a). For example, the weak system describes the phenomenon of constructional iconicity (linking unmarked forms with unmarked meanings and marked forms with marked meanings) through a recursive optimization process. This is a costly process that does not work in this way in online processing (Blutner 2007b). Instead, the effect of super-optimization will be fossilized into a psychologically more realistic model of strong optimization.

I will illustrate the idea of fossilization with Jakobson's example of gender opposition in animate nouns. Following Zwarts et. al (2009), I will argue that lexical constraints are fossilized from a system of semantic and morphological asymmetries. In many languages, there is a general bias for the *male* interpretation. This is expressed by a constraint *F (see Table 3) which penalizes female interpretations. Considering different forms, there is a general bias for (morphologically) simple forms. *STRUC(TURE) is a well-known constraint penalizing any (morphological) structure (e.g., Grimshaw 1997). Obviously, *STRUC prefers the term *osël* over the term *oslíca*. Table 3 shows the competition between the six possible pairs in a context where gender is important.

Table 3 Weak bidirectionality and two super-optimal solution pairs

		GREL (+)	*STRUC	*F
✌	*osël*, M			
	osël, F			*
	osël, K	*		
	oslíca, M		*	
✌	*oslíca*, F		*	*
	oslíca, K	*	*	

Source: Adapted from Zwarts et al. (2009)

The solution concept of weak bidirectionality provides two optimal pairs indicated by ✌. The first solution is the pair [*osël*, M]. It does not violate any of the constraints and it is the only pair that comes out as the winner if the strong mode of bidirectionality is used. According to the definition of weak bidirectionality at the beginning of Section 4, there is another solution, the pair [*oslíca*, F], which has a marked form and a marked content. It is a solution since it differs in both components, form and content, from the first solution pair and thus cannot be blocked by it. All other pairs are blocked by one of the two solutions: [*osël*, F], [*osël*, K] and [*oslíca*, M] are blocked by the first solution, and [*oslíca*, K] is blocked by the second solution pair [*oslíca*, F] since the violation of the context constraint GREL(+) outweighs the violation of *F. This is because of the ranking of the constraints that goes from left (highest) to right (lowest) in the tableau.

It is evident that Table 3 and Table 2 show the same set of solutions, Table 3 by using the weak solution concept and Table 2 by using the strong solution concept. Hence, we can see Table 2 as a fossilized variant of Table 3; in other words, the two markedness constraints *STRUC and *F fossilize in one lexical constraint *oslíca* ↔ F. Hence, in the domain of gender opposition, which was studied by Zwarts (2009), the process of fossilization provides the missing link between a psychologically realistic online system with lexical constraints and the more complex processing system with recursive bidirectional optimization.

5 Open problems

Although the problem of gender specification for animate nouns is possibly not at the centre of lexical pragmatics, it gives a fairly simple illustration of the observation that the borderline between semantics and pragmatics is transparent in at least one direction: tendencies predicted from pragmatics (conversational implicatures modeled by weak bidirectionality) may become *frozen* or fossilized in the semantic component of knowledge representation. The details of the fossilization process are an open problem. There are proposals (Van Rooy 2004) that model the process as a kind of signaling game using Darwinian evolutionary mechanisms (see also Steels 1998). Other proposals use the alternative framework of (bidirectional) iterated learning (Kirby and Hurford 1997, 2002; Jäger 2004). Iterated learning is oriented to the self-organizing dynamics of language as an observationally learned and culturally-transmitted communication system.

Another main problem concerns a systematic exploration of the huge range of examples in terms of a unifying theory. Both relevance theory and optimality theoretic pragmatics are possible starting points for this project. However, much more has to be done than substantiate some of the basic claims of lexical pragmatics. In addition, we need theoretical explorations that are able to *predict* the phenomena rather describe them *post facto*. An interesting area where this could be possible is the field of language change (Traugott and Dasher 2005) where the idea of fossilization may find powerful application.

In Section 2.2 the example of adjectival modification was mentioned, where the colour value of a construction can deviate from the lexically addressed focal colour (what is the colour of a *red nose, red bean, red flag*?). There are fully compositional geometrical (vector) models that can handle this problem (Mitchell and Lapata 2008; Blutner 2009), models which have their origin in connectionist modelling (Plate 2000). What is the relation between these geometrical models and the present symbolic approach? This question is important since its answer can shed new light on the mechanisms underlying blending theory (Fauconnier and Turner 2002).

In this paper, the phenomenon of constructional *iconicity* has been an important issue. Interestingly, there are also examples of *anti-iconicity*. They are found in connection with semantic broadening. A good example can be found in Dutch, where besides the preposition *om* (= Engl. 'round'; German 'um') the French loanword word *rond* is used to refer to the ideal shape of a circle. From this original use, the form *rond* comes into competition with the original (and unmarked) form *om*. The result is a division of labour, as demonstrated in the work of Zwarts (2003, 2006). Interestingly, the linguistically marked form *rond* is semantically close to the ideal shape of a circle (unmarked meaning) whereas the unmarked form *om* is semantically close to the detour interpretation (marked interpretation). Hence, unmarked forms are associated with marked interpretations and marked forms with unmarked interpretations. How to account for this puzzling phenomenon of anti-iconicity? Is there a theoretical solution that accounts for iconicity and anti-iconicity in terms of a mechanism of cultural evolution – a mechanism that simulates the process of conventionalization?

Obviously, lexical pragmatics is an emerging field of research, both empirically and theoretically. At the moment most researchers are concerned with empirical work, mainly concentrating on listing the puzzles and giving a fairly precise description of them. I think there are several reasons why we need more theoretical work that endeavours to explain the phenomena rather than being satisfied to describe them. The theoretical work should also establish connections to neuronal underpinning and to the diachronic dimension of language use.

Notes

1   For a more detailed discussion of Bierwisch (1983) and related approaches, the reader is referred to Blutner (2002).

2   *Moderate literalism* is Recanati's term (e.g., Recanati 2006). Others (including Taylor 2001) call it *moderate contextualism*.

3   The position of the moderate literalist is slightly different from the position taken by researchers who avoid speaking of underdetermination and introduce instead hidden indexicals or quasi-deictic elements (e.g., Sag 1981; Bierwisch 1983; Bartsch 1987; Bosch 2009).

4   The horse terminology is much more complex than shown in (18). For instance, there is the term 'colt' referring to a young, uncastrated male horse between the age of birth and 4 years. In contrast, the term 'filly' refers to a young female horse which has not yet had a foal between the age of birth and 4 years. Further, the term 'gelding' is used for a castrated male horse and the term 'stallion' is used for an uncastrated adult male horse over 4 years of age. The problem of markedness is related to the problem of categorization as discussed within the framework of cognitive linguistics (e.g., Taylor 2002).

■ ■ ■

POST-READING

1   Bad news: Your publisher is counting words and says you can only include ⅔ of the items you'd graded A in the in-reading activity so you need to return to the table and decide which ⅔ are the most crucial.

2   Discuss with a colleague/think through the following issues

   • 'Unarticulated constituents' are rejected by radical literalism because they would be structure-building. Do you think contextualists are justified in arguing that they are entirely pragmatic? If so, why? If not, why not?

   • Where would you place the Levinson reading in this section on the radical literalism ↔ radical contextualism cline?

   • How psychologically plausible do you find such a theory of constraints on pragmatic interpretation?

   • Blutner concludes by looking forward to a situation in which models are able to predict rather than simply describe data. Do you think such an approach is justified in pragmatics, where context and particularity are central concepts?

RELEVANCE THEORETIC PRAGMATICS

Although Relevance Theory had been informally discussed for some years, especially following the publication in 1981 of Wilson and Sperber's important paper, 'On Grice's theory of conversational implicature', the theory was not fully elaborated until the publication of Sperber and Wilson's *Relevance: Communication and Cognition* in 1986. A second edition, identical to the first apart from a 25 page 'postface' (as opposed to 'preface') proposing a number of changes in the theory, was published in 1995.

Given the influence of relevance theory and the wide range of approaches to the study of language and mind it has inspired, it's important at the outset to understand the theory and its motivation. For this reason, the two readings that open this sub-section provide a definitive account of relevance theory and its application. Diane Blakemore's paper was first published as the 'Relevance theory' entry in Verschueren et al.'s *Handbook of Pragmatics* (1995). Published here for the first time, Billy Clark's 'Recent developments in relevance theory' (2011), deals with the period from 1995 to 2011, and hence should be read as an addendum to Blakemore's work. Taken together, these readings provide a comprehensive and accessible background to Relevance Theory and to the ongoing work it has inspired. The two readings that follow, Carston's discussion of explicit meaning and Sperber and Wilson's exploration of the relationship between the public language we use and our private thoughts, demonstrate ways in which relevance theory has contributed to our understanding of pragmatics in particular, as well as language and cognition more generally.

Much of the metalanguage of relevance theoretic pragmatics is similar to that used by Grice and by the neo-Griceans. Grice's use of 'principle' (as in *Cooperative Principle*) finds an echo not only in Horn and Levinson's work but also in relevance theory with its two *Principles of Relevance*. Similarly, Levinson's view of a category of meaning as 'presumptive' and Blutner's appeal to 'optimality' as a metric of the relationship of meaning and form has a parallel in Sperber and Wilson's claim that an act of communication such as an utterance conveys 'a presumption of its own optimal relevance' (1986/1995). However, the extent to which neo-Gricean and relevance theoretic approaches share meta-theoretic constructs should not blind us to the differences between them. Levinson's default inferences and Blutner's search for a predictive system of constraints on form/meaning pairs are readily relatable to the linguistic pragmatics of Section 2 and the philosophy of language framework within which accounts of presupposition, speech act theory and conversational implicature were developed. Relevance theory, on the other hand, provides an account of the cognitive processes involved in understanding utterances which matches the commitment of processing resources to the 'cognitive effects' obtained in optimizing relevance. Relevance theoretic pragmatics thus explores the mental capacity (decoding, inferring, etc.) required to interpret communicative behaviour within a philosophy of mind framework. Indeed, relevance theory's contribution isn't principally to the philosophy of language but to the theory of mind and the nature of cognition, frequently going so far as to propose domain-specific modular accounts of pragmatic processing (e.g. Sperber and Wilson 2002).

A theory of mind approach to pragmatics implies that representations do not stop at representations of states of affairs in the world, but include the ability to construct 'metarepresentations' of our own beliefs and attitudes and of the beliefs and attitudes of others. In processing the relevance of an utterance, we need to identify what we take to be the speaker's communicative intention. Because an utterance signals a communicative intention, we cannot fully understand that intention without constructing what we hope will be an accurate metarepresentation of it. A consistent inability to construct such metarepresentations may constitute an impairing pathological condition investigatable within a clinical pragmatics framework (see Section 10).

In 'Relevance theory', Blakemore introduces and explains the key concepts of the theory, in particular:

- The guarantee that 'every act of ostensive communication communicates a presumption of its own optimal relevance', as postulated by Sperber and Wilson (1986), so that the most relevant interpretation, implicature or 'contextual effect' is obtained by the least effort. Conversely, the more effort required to obtain a contextual effect, the less relevant that effect will be.[1]
- The role of inference in fleshing out linguistically encoded semantic representation, to give otherwise underdetermined propositions a fully explicit propositional meaning. Such effects are termed *explicatures*.
- The involvement of contextual assumptions in the identification of *higher level explicatures* which convey the speaker's attitude towards explicatures and implicatures.
- Interpretive resemblance, or the extent to which a proposition is a faithful representation of a thought, so that a metaphor is a weak implicature which loosely represents a speaker's thought and an ironical utterance is a representation of a thought from which a speaker is understood to disassociate herself.
- Procedural constraints on interpretation. For example, while *Are we going to town* might, in a given context, be optimally understood as a question requiring a *yes/no* answer, *Are we going to town then* might, in its context, be optimally understood as an invitation to confirm that speaker and hearer have agreed to go to town. In this case 'then' acts as a constraint limiting the interpretation of the utterance.

Blakemore also draws attention to the ways in which Sperber and Wilson's and Grice's theories differ, and in particular to Sperber and Wilson's view of pragmatic inference, not as inductive or probabilistic as in Grice, but as deductive, i.e. the outcome of a device which blindly computes propositions and the most accessible contextual assumptions so as to produce the most relevant contextual effects. Relatedly, Sperber and Wilson's theory also differs from

Grice's in proposing the *Communicative Principle of Relevance* ('Every act of ostensive communication communicates a presumption of its own optimal relevance') as an exceptionless generalization about human behaviour rather than as a maxim that may be followed or violated.

Blakemore's 'Relevance theory' was published in 1995 and serves as a commentary on the 1986 edition of Sperber and Wilson's *Relevance: Communication and Cognition.* Clark's 'Recent developments in relevance theory' begins at the point where Blakemore leaves off. Clark first explains Sperber and Wilson's 1995 'postface' modifications to the original theory and then discusses the heuristic for interpreting communicative acts and the metarepresentational ability implicit in relevance theory within a theory of mind framework. In the second part of his paper, Clark outlines recent work in several central areas and provides an invaluable list of state-of-the-art research relating to the semantics/pragmatics interface, conceptual and procedural meaning, lexical pragmatics, metaphor and irony, and the many areas in which empirical testing of the predictions of relevance theory have been pursued.

Robyn Carston's *Thoughts and Utterances* (2002a) is a detailed study of what she terms 'explicit communication'. Her thesis is that linguistic meaning – the meaning encoded in the linguistic expressions used – underdetermines what is said, so that a hearer makes use of inference to work out not only what is implicated but also what is expressed. Thus the propositional content of what we say has to be enriched by inference for its *explicit* content to be communicated. *Thoughts and Utterances* is about how this process is accomplished, and explores the nature and scope of explicature as a preliminary to re-analysing two much debated areas, 'and'-conjunction and negation. Carston argues that the wide range of pragmatically inferred temporal and causal relations between propositions conjoined by 'and' demonstrates its underdetermined linguistic meaning (on the perhaps challengeable assumption that it has a linguistic meaning at all). These inferred relations are explicatures according to Carston, rather than implicatures recovered as I-inferences as in Levinson's *Presumptive Meanings.* Similarly, the naturalness of explicature as an enrichment process capable of accounting for 'metalinguistic', 'constituent' and other forms of negation makes the (in any case, undesirable) concept of a series of different encodings difficult to sustain. Finally, Carston suggests that processes such as narrowing and broadening suggest that 'enrichment' may be one type of concept adjustment in a larger set in which linguistic codes are treated as pointers to the thought being communicated in a constrained, mind-reading process.

Thoughts and Utterances is an exceptionally stimulating book, which deals with notoriously challenging problems. Even the title is wonderfully clever, hinting as it does at the problematic nature of the relationship of thoughts and utterances, linked as they are by the underdetermined conjunction 'and'.

The reading we have chosen from Chapter 2 is a relatively straightforward illustration of the careful way in which Carston proceeds. She argues that Sperber and Wilson's definition of explicature needs to be modified to take account of the effect of sentential adverbs in embedded clauses ('subparts of the logical form'). So if someone says, 'Frankly, I've reached the limit of my understanding', we treat 'frankly' as modifying the speech-act description, which we recover as a higher-level explicature (*she tells me frankly that she's reached* ...). But if someone says 'Although, frankly, I've reached the limit of my understanding, I'm not giving up yet', things aren't so simple. In this utterance, 'frankly' isn't a communicated entailment (?*although she tells me frankly that she's reached* ...). Rather, it constitutes evidence of commitment to the embedded proposition that she's reached the limit of her understanding. In other words, the motivation for explicatures (of this kind) is that they reflect speaker commitment to the communication of a proposition and cannot be captured in the form of a straightforward higher-level speech act description.

The final reading in this section, Sperber and Wilson's paper, 'The mapping between the mental and the public lexicon', is reprinted here in full. In it, the authors discuss the mapping between words and concepts. They argue that words act as pointers to 'indefinitely many notions or concepts' so that when we hear a word we typically construct an ad hoc concept that will rarely be the same as the concept communicated. In this respect, words function as we would expect them to in an inferential theory of communication in which 'all a communicator has to do in order to convey a thought is to give her audience appropriate evidence of her intention to convey it'. Sperber and Wilson argue that by uttering 'I'm tired' in response to an invitation to go to the cinema, the speaker communicates a notion that is not encoded in English and that at the same time is more specific than the notion encoded by the public word 'tired'. This paper illustrates the importance of relevance theory as a cognitive account of meaning construction and leads us to consider the nature of mental representation in a way undreamt of in Grice's original proposals.

Taken together, the six readings in Section 3 represent a remarkable journey from the study of pragmatics within a philosophy of language framework to the study of the role of pragmatics in cognition.

Note

1   The term 'contextual effect' was replaced by 'cognitive effect' in the 1995 modification of relevance theory, as discussed by Clark in the second reading in this sub-section.

DIANE BLAKEMORE

RELEVANCE THEORY

PRE-READING

Work through the three extracts below, which you will encounter in the reading. Try to complete the blank spaces in the way you expect Blakemore to do:

- . . the linguistic properties of an utterance do not .... which the speaker intends to express: reference assignment, disambiguation, the restoration of ellipsed material, the resolution of vagueness are all .... and are all, according to relevance theory, part of the domain of pragmatics.
- Why do we pay attention to information? And the answer to this question, it is argued, is that we pay attention to information which ....
- Utterance interpretation is not exhausted by the recovery of explicatures and implicatures. Contextual assumptions are also involved in the identification of ....

IN-READING

Unless you are happy to write on this book, make an A4 photocopy of the line drawing of the human brain below. As you work through the reading, whenever you come across a term italicized by Blakemore, write a brief note explaining it wherever on your photocopy you feel is most appropriate.

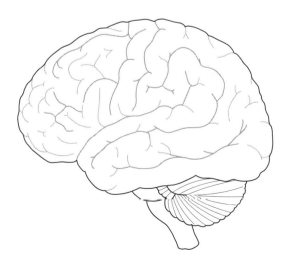

■ ■ ■

RELEVANCE THEORY
DIANE BLAKEMORE

Sperber and Wilson's relevance theory, presented most fully in Sperber and Wilson (1986), is an approach to communication and utterance understanding based on a general view of cognition. In contrast with formal approaches to pragmatics (e.g. Gazdar 1979) and socio-cultural approaches (e.g. Leech 1983), relevance theory views pragmatic interpretation as a psychological matter involving inferential computations performed over mental representations, governed by a single cognitive principle. The assumption underlying this approach is that the mind is modular, and, in particular, that there is a distinction between linguistic computations and representations on the one hand, and non-linguistic computations and representations on the other. It is this psychological distinction which, according to relevance theory, underlies the distinction between semantics and pragmatics.

The domain of pragmatics, as it is defined by this distinction, is not co-extensive with its domain as it is defined by those (e.g. Gazdar 1979) who take the basic distinction to be the one between truth-conditional and non-truth-conditional meaning. Consider, for example, the following utterances made by someone pointing to a packet of breakfast cereal:

(1)   This is made with 80% recycled board.
(2)   This is vitamin fortified.

While the speaker of (1) will be taken to be referring to the packet, in (2) *this* will be understood as referring to its contents. Since these interpretations cannot be recovered solely on the basis of the linguistic properties of the utterance, their recovery, according to relevance theory, is a matter for pragmatics. However, according to Gazdar's criterion, the question of how *this* is interpreted is a question for semantics, since it is about the identification of the truth conditions of the utterances.

This is only one of a whole range of respects in which the linguistic properties of an utterance do not fully determine the proposition which the speaker intends to express: reference assignment, disambiguation, the restoration of ellipsed material, the resolution of vagueness are all dependent on non-linguistic or contextual assumptions, and are all, according to relevance theory, part of the domain of pragmatics.

Although the proposition expressed by an utterance is not encoded by its linguistic form, it is directly dependent on the meanings of the words uttered. It is obtained by fleshing out a linguistically encoded semantic representation. Sperber and Wilson call the result of fleshing out a linguistically encoded representation in the intended way the *proposition expressed* by the utterance. However, an utterance may communicate assumptions which are not so directly connected to the meaning of the words uttered. For example, both (1) and (2) could be produced with the intention of implying (3):

(3)   You should buy this cereal.

Such intended contextual assumptions and conclusions are *implicatures*. The proposition expressed is one of several propositions which may be explicitly communicated. Sperber and Wilson call such explicitly communicated propositions *explicatures*.

This distinction does not correspond to any other distinctions that have been made in pragmatics. In particular, it does not correspond to Grice's (1975, 1989) distinction between *saying* and *implicating*, a distinction which many would say lies at the heart of modern pragmatics.

For Grice, what is implicated is distinguished from what is said by the fact that its derivation depends crucially on the assumption that certain standards of communication have been met. Thus while Grice recognized that contextual assumptions play a role in the recovery of what is said, he did not recognize that the use of these assumptions is constrained by the same principles that are involved in the recovery of what is implicated. The insight underlying Grice's notion of implicature, that the act of communication creates expectations which it then exploits, was of fundamental importance in the development of relevance theory. However, Sperber and Wilson have taken it much further so that not only the recovery of intended contextual assumptions and conclusions, but also the identification of explicitly communicated propositions all involve inferences which are governed by the same pragmatic principle. This idea is explored by Carston (1988b) in her discussion of the explicature/implicature distinction.

According to relevance theory, to say that a hearer uses contextual assumptions to infer the speaker's intended interpretation is to say that they are used as premises in a deductive inference. This is not, however, to say that a hearer may have *proof* of the speaker's intentions. Since there is always the possibility that the set of contextual assumptions brought to bear on the interpretation of an utterance is different from the one envisaged by the speaker, there is always the possibility that communication may fail. Some authors (e.g. Levinson 1983; Leech 1983) take the fact that the processes involved in utterance interpretation are non-demonstrative to mean that deduction plays little or no role. Sperber and Wilson argue that, on the contrary, deductive inference plays a vital role in utterance interpretation. Although there is no rule or algorithm for computing the correct (or intended) contextual premises, the hearer's choice of contextual premises is constrained by a cognitive principle. The assumptions chosen in accordance with this principle are used in a deductive inference. Consider, for example, (4b) interpreted as a response to (4a):

(4) (a) Is Jane coming to the party?
     (b) Her exams start tomorrow.

Intuitively, a plausible interpretation for (4b) is that yielded by the assumptions in (5):

(5) (a) Jane gets very nervous about exams.
     (b) If Jane is nervous about her exams, she will not be going to any parties.

However, from a logical point of view, there is no reason why a hearer might not instead be led to access the assumptions in (6a) and (b) and derive the conclusion in (6c):

(6) (a) Jane gets very nervous about exams.
     (b) When Jane gets nervous she always bites her fingernails.
     (c) Jane will be biting her fingernails.

Indeed, in principle, there is no reason why the hearer should not be led to access still further assumptions and derive still further conclusions. For example, in principle, the hearer might access the assumptions in (7a) and derive the conclusion in (7b):

(7) (a) When Jane bites her fingernails she wears gloves when she goes out.
     (b) Jane will be wearing gloves when she goes out.

In fact, from a logical point of view, there is nothing to stop the hearer adding more and more contextual assumptions and deriving more and more implications.

This suggests two central questions for pragmatics: (i) Why do hearers not assume that the speaker intended them to keep on expanding the context indefinitely deriving more and more implications? (ii) Why do hearers assume that the first satisfactory interpretation they do derive is the one that is intended? According to relevance theory the answer to both of these questions lies in the answer to another: why do we pay attention to information? And the answer to this question, it is argued, is that we pay attention to information which seems *relevant*.

Relevance is defined in terms of *contextual effect* and *processing effort*. There are three ways in which a newly presented piece of information may interact with the context to yield a contextual effect: (i) it may combine with contextual assumptions to yield a *contextual implication* (that is, a logical implication derivable neither from the contextual assumptions nor from the new information alone); (ii) it might strengthen an existing assumption; (iii) it may contradict and lead to the elimination of an existing assumption.

Suppose that you open your wallet and find that it contains $28. How might this information be relevant to you? First consider a situation in which you need to pay back your friend the $50 he lent you and you have decided to go to the bank if you do not have enough. In this situation the information will be relevant by combining with your existing assumptions to yield the contextual implication that you need to go to the bank. Next consider a situation in which you believe that you have enough money to pay back your friend the $50 you owe. Here the information will be relevant by virtue of contradicting and hence eliminating an existing assumption. Finally, consider the situation in which you believe that you do not have enough money to reimburse your friend. Here the information achieves relevance by virtue of confirming or strengthening an existing assumption.

But surely, any assumption that you care to make would have some contextual effect in these situations. Why is it, for example, that in the circumstances just described you are more likely to form the assumption that you have $28 in your wallet when you look in it than the assumption, say, that one of the bank notes has been written on? Provided that you are prepared to spend enough time and effort accessing contextual assumptions you are bound to derive some contextual effect.

The point is that hearers are not prepared to spend any amount of time and effort in the recovery of contextual effects. If they were, there would be nothing to stop them from continuing to process new information bringing more and more contextual assumptions to bear on its interpretation. Processing information yields rewards (contextual effects) only at a cost. Although each expansion of the context yields more contextual effects, as the size of the context grows so does the cost of using the assumptions it contains. The greater the contextual effects, the greater the relevance, but the greater the processing effort entailed, the lower the relevance.

The fundamental assumption of relevance theory is that all information processing is relevance oriented. However, whereas in the case of information that is simply discovered, people may have just hopes of relevance; in the case of information that is communicated, a hearer may have expectations of relevance. By *communication*, Sperber and Wilson mean specifically ostensive or, in other words, intentional, overt communication in which a speaker not only intends to convey a particular message but is also actively helping the hearer recognize this.

It is clear that thus defined, communication cannot succeed unless the audience pays attention to the act of communicative behaviour (ostensive stimulus). Equally, it is clear that an audience will pay attention to a phenomenon only it if seems relevant to them. This suggests that an act of ostensive communication automatically communicates a *presumption of relevance*. Sperber and Wilson argue that the presumption of relevance carried by every act of ostensive communication has two aspects: on the one hand it creates a presumption of adequate effect, while on the other, it creates a presumption that no gratuitous processing effort is required for the recovery of those effects. Taken together these presumptions define a level of *optimal relevance*.

The principle of relevance is simply the thesis that every act of ostensive communication communicates a presumption of its own optimal relevance. This principle, in contrast with Grice's maxims of conversation, is not a norm which may be followed or violated, but an exceptionless generalisation about human cognition. This is not to say that every act of ostensive communication is in fact optimally relevant. Suppose, for example, that as you enter a lecture hall I gesture towards the empty seat beside me without realizing that you have seen it. In this situation the proposition that there is an empty seat beside me will have no contextual effects and hence be irrelevant to you. However, although this interpretation of my gesture is inconsistent with the presumption of relevance, it is consistent with the principle of relevance inasmuch as it is not difficult for you to see how I might have *thought* it was optimally relevant to you. I would not have attempted to communicate at all unless I intended you to believe that I had achieved optimal relevance. In other words, it is the fact that the presumption of optimal relevance was communicated by my gesture that is crucial in the explanation of how its intended interpretation is recovered.

This is not to say that the intended interpretation is always recovered. The principle of relevance does not guarantee that communication will succeed. It justifies the selection of the first accessible interpretation which a rational communicator might have believed to be optimally relevant. Communication will succeed only to the extent that there is such an interpretation and it is the one intended.

Recall, for example, utterance (1) as it is interpreted by someone choosing a breakfast cereal:

(1)   This is made with 80% recycled board.

This utterance will give the hearer access to the stereotypical and hence accessible contextual assumption that packets are made from cardboard. If the resulting interpretation yields adequate contextual effects (including, for example, the one in (3)), and puts the hearer to no unjustifiable effort in achieving those effects, and if, furthermore, the assumption that this was the intended interpretation does not conflict with other assumption that the hearer is entertaining, this is the only interpretation the hearer is justified in choosing. It is always possible to imagine a situation in which a cereal is made from cardboard, but this requires some effort. If the speaker had intended this (rather unlikely) interpretation, then s/he would have spared the hearer the unjustifiable effort of first recovering and accepting the more accessible interpretation by formulating the utterance in another way.

It follows from this that if the speaker does put the hearer to extra effort, then the hearer is entitled to expect that this will be offset by extra or different contextual effects. Recall the example in (4b) where the speaker does not say explicitly that Jane is not coming to the party, but expects the hearer to derive it on the basis of an assumption such as the one in (8):

(4)   (a)   Is Jane coming to the party?
      (b)   Her exams start tomorrow.

(8)   If Jane's exams start tomorrow, she won't want to go to any parties.

Since the assumption in (8) forms part of the smallest and most accessible context which yields adequate contextual effects, it must have been the one intended by the speaker. But accessing and using this context involves effort which would not have been required had the speaker answered directly. How might this effort be justified?

There are various possibilities. For example, the speaker might want to explain that there is a good reason for Jane's not coming. Or s/he may want to remind the hearer that the examinations are imminent. Or s/he may want to convey something about Jane's state of mind. None of these are specifically intended by the speaker in the way that the implicature that Jane is not coming is. They are simply lines of interpretation suggested by the utterance. Or, as Sperber and Wilson put it, they are *weakly implicated*.

This suggests that speakers make decisions not only about whether what they want to communicate is to be implicated or explicated, but also about the extent to which they will constrain the recovery of implicatures. The tighter the constraint, the stronger the implicature. As with any decision about style, this will be governed by the aim of optimising relevance and cannot help but reveal the speaker's assumptions about the hearer's contextual and processing resources, and hence something about his/her assessment of their relationship. Consider, for example, the use of the construction in (9) (from Sperber and Wilson 1986):

(9)   Mary came with Peter, Joan with Bob, and Lily with a sad smile on her face.

The use of gapping encourages hearers to find matching parallelisms in interpretation. They are encouraged to find a set of contextual assumptions in which the facts that Mary came with Peter, Joan with Bob and Lily with a sad smile have identical or directly contrasting implications. But there is a whole range of ways in which the required parallelisms could be recovered, and the hearer is left with a great deal of responsibility in the interpretation process. For example, is Lily sad because, in contrast with the others, she has no-one to accompany her? Does Lily make a point of appearing alone and sad? Is Lily's sad smile as familiar as the sight of the other couples? Do the others have anything to do with Lily's sad smile? In other words, this utterance achieves most of its relevance through a range of *weak* implicatures. Sperber and Wilson call the effect achieved by such an utterance a *poetic effect*, which is not to suggest that it can be achieved only by poets. As they show in their analysis of figurative utterances (see below) and in their briefer discussion of repetition (1986: 219–22), this approach to style applies to everyday examples of communication as well as to more poetic-creative examples.

Utterance interpretation is not exhausted by the recovery of explicatures and implicatures. Contextual assumptions are also involved in the identification of the speaker's attitude towards these explicatures and implicatures. For example, the speaker of (10) might be understood to be asserting that the hearer is leaving, or guessing that hearer is leaving, or wondering whether the hearer is leaving, or telling the hearer to leave:

(10)   You are leaving.

To a certain extent the speaker's intended attitude can be linguistically encoded, for example, by the imperative syntax in (11):

(11)   Leave.

However, as (10) shows, the syntactic structure of the utterance is at best a clue as to the intended interpretation. Moreover, in some cases the hearer must identify the hearer's attitude entirely on the basis of the context. Consider, for example, how the hearer decides whether the speaker's attitude to the proposition expressed is one of endorsement in (12):

(12) [Tom has just left the room wearing a gloomy expression]
     He looked cheerful.

In speech-act theory the question here would not be what attitude the speaker intended to communicate, but rather what speech act s/he intended to perform. This suggests a view of language in which it is a vehicle for action rather than a vehicle for thought. And, indeed, Austin's (1962) speech act theory grew out of the recognition that language is used not just to say things, but also to do things. He argued that a better understanding of language depended on a better understanding of how language is embedded in social institutions, and of how it can be used not just to describe the world, but also to change it. The fundamental assumption here is that the classification of speech acts plays an essential role in communication so that the prerequisite for successful communication is the identification of the speech act that the speaker intended to perform.

It might seem that we could reformulate this claim in Sperber and Wilson's framework simply by saying that in each of the following the hearer of the (a) utterance is intended to recover the *higher-level explicature* in (b), or more generally, that the hearer of an utterance intended as an act of a particular type is intended to develop its logical form into a higher-level explicature which describes the speaker as performing that act:

(13) (a) I promise you that Tom will be there.
     (b) The speaker is promising the hearer that Tom will be there.

(14) (a) I warn you that Tom will be there.
     (b) The speaker is warning the hearer that Tom will be there.

(15) (a) I guess that Tom will be there.
     (b) The speaker is guessing that Tom will be there.

(16) (a) I assert that Tom will be there.
     (b) The speaker is asserting that Tom will be there.

However, there are some important respects in which Sperber and Wilson's approach diverges from the speech act theory approach. In the first place, Sperber and Wilson would not describe the speaker of either (15) or (16) as performing a particular kind of speech *act*. The higher-level explicatures in (15b) and (16b) are descriptions of the speaker's *attitude* towards the proposition his/her utterance expresses, and the role of the so-called performative in (15a) and (16a) is to guide the hearer in the identification of the speaker's attitude.

This is not to say that the explicit performatives in (13a) and (14a) should be analysed as indicators of the speech act the speaker is performing, as they would be in speech act theory. Rather their role is to guide the hearer in the interpretation process so that the relevance of the higher-level proposition lies in the way it helps the hearer derive the right kind of contextual implications from the embedded proposition.

According to speech act theory, communication succeeds only if the hearer identifies the type of speech act being performed. Thus for example, a speaker who intends (17) as a promise must communicate the proposition in (13b), while a speaker who intends it as a warning must communicate the proposition in (14b):

(17) Tom will be there.

However, as Sperber and Wilson (1986) have demonstrated, this assumption cannot be maintained. The identification of (17) as a warning is not a prerequisite for understanding the utterance, but it is rather a consequence of understanding it. More particularly, it is a consequence of recognizing that the speaker intends that certain sorts of contextual implications should be derived. Similarly, a hearer does not have to recover the proposition in (16b) in order to understand (17) as a guess. To intend an utterance as a guess is to intend that the hearer recognizes that the speaker does not have conclusive evidence for the truth of the proposition it expresses, and hence that s/he cannot be strongly committed to its factuality. If the hearer does recover the proposition in (15b), it is as a result of understanding the utterance, and in particular of identifying the speaker's attitude towards the proposition it expresses. A similar point can be made about assertions.

In contrast with warnings and guesses and assertions, promises can only be understood if they are recognized as such. However, this simply follows from the fact that promising, in contrast with guessing, asserting and warning, exists only within a particular moral framework, and the fact that some institutional knowledge is necessary for the interpretation of promises is of no more interest to pragmatics than the fact that a certain amount of culinary knowledge is necessary for understanding a recipe.

If this is right, then the interpretation of promises, warnings, guesses and assertions does not require any extra special pragmatic machinery. In contrast, it does seem that the differences between the following require some sort of special speech act theoretic machinery:

(18a)   Tom will jump over the rope.

(19a)   Will Tom jump over the rope.

(20a)   Tom, jump over the rope.

For it seems that the differences in syntactic mood can be correlated with differences in speech act type so that whereas the declarative in (18a) indicates that the hearer is intended to recover the description in (18b), the interrogative in (19a) indicates the speaker's intention to communicate the description in (19b), and the imperative in (20a) indicates the speaker's intention to communicate the description in (20b):

(18b)   The speaker is saying that Tom will jump over the rope.

(19b)   The speaker is asking whether Tom will jump over the rope.

(20b)   The speaker is telling Tom to jump over the rope.

As Sperber and Wilson show, not only is the recovery of such descriptions an essential part of the comprehension process, but also saying, telling and asking, in contrast with, for example, promising, are not institutional and culture-dependent, but genuinely universal. At the same time, however, they show that if the correlation between sentence type and speech act type is to be maintained, then the standard speech act theoretic definition of 'saying that' as a general type of assertive act, 'telling to' as a general form of action-requesting directive, and 'asking whether' as a general kind of information-requesting directive must be abandoned. An assertive is a speech act which commits the speaker to the truth of the proposition expressed by his/her utterance. But as the ironic example in (12) and the metaphorical utterance in (21) show, not every declarative utterance is assertive in this sense:

(21)   My neighbour is a dragon.

According to relevance theory, the key to the interpretation of figurative utterances lies in the notion of representation by resemblance, or, *interpretive resemblance*. It is argued that an utterance can be used to represent any representation which it resembles whether public (another utterance) or private (a thought). In fact, it is claimed that every utterance is an interpretive representation of a thought – namely, the thought that the speaker wishes to communicate.

An utterance interpretively resembles another representation to the extent that it shares logical and contextual implications with it. In some cases the optimally relevant utterance may be one which very closely resembles the speaker's thought. In other cases, for example, metaphors, the optimally relevant utterance may be one which involves a *looser* resemblance, and the hearer's task is to identify the degree of faithfulness attempted. Thus metaphors are not regarded as deviations from a norm of truthful speaking (cf. Grice 1978), but are a consequence of the search for relevance.

Even in very standardised cases the interpretation of a metaphor will entail processing effort which would not have been required by a fully literal utterance. In relevance theory extra effort entails extra effect. However, the extra rewards achieved by a metaphorical utterance are to a considerable extent the sole responsibility of the hearer. That is, they are weakly communicated. It is this range of weak implicatures which explains why metaphors (even standardized ones) cannot be paraphrased without loss.

In the case of an ironic utterance like (12) the thought communicated is presented as a representation of another speaker's thought. There are quite ordinary examples of utterances used to interpret someone else's thought or speech, for example, reported speech or summaries. Ironic utterances are distinguished by the fact that their relevance lies not in the information they give about the content of the attributed thought, but rather in the attitude of the speaker towards this thought. In particular, an ironic utterance conveys an attitude of dissociation or ridicule. Although the assumption that the speaker thinks that the attributed thought is ridiculous is strongly communicated, it is left to the hearer to decide just how ridiculous the thought is. Thus an ironic utterance involves a mixture of strong and weak communication. As Wilson and Sperber (1992a) show, this analysis accounts for a range of examples which cannot be accommodated in the traditional analysis of irony in which the speaker means the opposite of what is said.

As we have seen, relevance theory assumes that there is a distinction between linguistic and non-linguistic communication. An assumption is *linguistically* communicated only if the linguistic properties of an utterance help with its recovery. However, we have also seen that not everything that is linguistically communicated is linguistically encoded. For example, the recovery of (22) as the proposition expressed by the utterance in (1) is partly an inferential process constrained by pragmatic principles:

(1)   This is made with 80% recycled board.

(22) The cereal packet is made with 80% recycled cardboard.

The borderline between linguistic and non-linguistic communication has been a major area of pragmatic research. For example, Carston (1988a, 1993) has argued that the claim that inference is involved in the identification of the proposition expressed has important implications for Grice's (1975, 1989) analysis of conjoined utterances.

As Wilson and Sperber (1993) have shown, the role of the linguistic properties of utterances is not restricted to the recovery of the proposition expressed by utterances. They argue that although sentence adverbs like the one in (23) do not contribute to the proposition expressed, they do contribute to a higher-level explicature like the one in (24):

(23)   Seriously, I cannot help you.

(24)   The speaker told the hearer seriously that she could not help him.

Blakemore's (1990) analysis of performatives follows along similar lines.

Wilson and Sperber argue that while sentence adverbs and performatives may not contribute to the truth conditions of the utterances which contain them, they do encode *conceptual* information–information which is a constituent of (higher-level) explicatures. However, recent work suggests that not all linguistic meaning encodes conceptual information. For example, Wilson and Sperber (1993) argue that linguistic mood encodes *procedural* information – that is, constraints on the construction of explicatures. This idea is explored further by Clark (1991) in his analysis of non-declarative sentences, and is applied by Blass (1990) to the analysis of the Sissala 'hearsay' particle *re*. Kempson (1988) has also been developing a procedural approach to anaphora in the sense that they impose constraints on the proposition expressed.

According to Wilson and Sperber (1993), the distinction between conceptual and procedural linguistic meaning follows from the view that utterance understanding involves the construction of mental representations which undergo inferential computations. It is generally accepted that linguistic meaning can partially encode the constituents of these representations. However, given that their construction and manipulation involves mental computations, it is possible that linguistic meaning should also play a role in constraining those computations.

This idea was explored by Blakemore (1987, 1988) in the analysis of a range of expressions which had resisted analysis in truth-conditional terms – for example, the so-called discourse connectives *after all, moreover, but*, and *so*. These expressions were analysed in procedural terms as semantic constraints on implicatures, an analysis which contrasts with Grice's (1989) conceptual analysis. However, the fact that these phenomena are non-truth-conditional should not be taken to suggest that the distinction between conceptual and procedural meaning coincides with the distinction between truth-conditional and non-truth-conditional linguistic meaning. As the analysis of sentence adverbs and performatives has shown, linguistic meaning may encode conceptual information which is not part of the proposition expressed. And as the analysis of non-declarative utterances and attitudinal particles has shown, linguistic meaning may encode information which either constrains or contributes to the construction of explicatures. As Wilson and Sperber (1990) suggest, this might mean that the linguistic distinction between truth-conditional and non-truth-conditional meaning should be abandoned, leaving just the cognitive distinction between the conceptual and the procedural and the pragmatic distinction between the explicit and the implicit. At the very least, relevance theory shows that the relationship between linguistic form and pragmatic interpretation requires closer scrutiny.

■ ■ ■

POST-READING

There are joint post-reading activities for Blakemore and the reading that follows.

BILLY CLARK

RECENT DEVELOPMENTS IN RELEVANCE THEORY

PRE-READING

Work through the two extracts below, which you will encounter in the reading. Try to complete the blank spaces in the way you expect Clark's text to do:

*   In one paper discussing this, they [Wilson and Sperber] suggest that 'verbal communication is governed not by expectations of .... but by expectations of ....
*   Robyn Carston has consistently defended the view that linguistic semantics concerns the relationship between ...., while pragmatics concerns ....

■ ■ ■

RECENT DEVELOPMENTS IN RELEVANCE THEORY
BILLY CLARK

There have been many significant developments in Relevance Theory, and in pragmatics more generally, since Diane Blakemore's 1995 handbook entry. Debates about the nature and goals of pragmatic theory have been explored within individual frameworks and across different ones. There has also been considerable development within Relevance Theory. These include adjustments to the theory itself, new and adapted accounts of particular linguistic and non-linguistic phenomena, new ways of testing and new ways of applying the theory. A small selection of these are mentioned here.

1 Developing the theory

In 1995, a 'postface' in the second edition of the book *Relevance* (Sperber and Wilson 1986, 2nd edition 1995) proposed three modifications to the theory. One of these was terminological. Two were adjustments to the substance of the theory. The terminological change was to refer to two principles of relevance rather than one. The more substantial changes were to the definition of relevance (specifically to the kinds of effects which contribute to relevance) and to the presumption of optimal relevance.

1.1 Two principles of relevance

The classic source for the theory (Sperber and Wilson 1986), and other earlier versions, suggested two law-like generalisations which are central to Relevance Theory. One is about human cognition in general and one about (ostensive-inferential) communication in particular. The second generalisation was termed 'The Principle of Relevance'. In the postface to the second edition of *Relevance*, Sperber and Wilson (1995: 255–279) suggested that some readers had been confused by the fact that only one of the two generalisations was described as a 'Principle'. In an attempt to make things clearer, they decided to present both generalisations as 'Principles'. Since 1995, then, there are two Principles of Relevance. The First, or Cognitive, Principle of Relevance says:

(1) First, or Cognitive, Principle of Relevance:
     Human cognition tends to be geared to the maximisation of relevance.

This says that our cognitive system in general tends to allocate attention and processing resources so as to produce as many cognitive effects as possible for as little effort as possible (see Sperber 2005 for discussion of how such a cognitive system might be implemented).
   The Second, or Communicative, Principle of Relevance says:

(2) Second, or Communicative, Principle of Relevance:
     Every ostensive stimulus conveys a presumption of its own optimal relevance.

Now that both generalisations have equal status as Principles, one about maximising relevance in cognition in general and the other about optimising relevance in communication, the hope is that it will be less likely for readers to assume wrongly that communication involves a presumption of maximal relevance. Some commentators made this mistake, pointing out correctly that it is too strong to expect communicative acts to provide 'as many effects as possible for as little effort as possible' and suggesting incorrectly that this was a claim of the theory.

1.2 Definition of relevance

The second change was a small but significant alteration to the definition of relevance to an individual or relevance within a cognitive system. In the earlier framework, these were defined in terms of contextual effects and processing effort. In the new framework, contextual effects produced by a cognitive system are renamed 'cognitive effects' and the definition of relevance to an individual or cognitive system now refers not merely to cognitive effects but to 'positive cognitive effects'. While this change might seem small, the motivation for it is significant. Specifically, the new definition recognises that contextual effects which are treated by a cognitive system as true or well-evidenced, and hence as contributing to relevance, may in fact be false, and therefore detrimental to the cognitive system. A positive cognitive effect is one that actually does contribute to relevance (e.g., by actually being true or well-evidenced) rather than merely seeming to the individual to do so. As Sperber and Wilson (1995: 265) put it, 'for an input to be relevant, its processing must lead to cognitive gains'. A 'positive cognitive effect' is defined as 'a cognitive effect that contributes positively to the fulfilment of cognitive functions or goals'. While one idea behind this is that cognitive effects which are true, or well evidenced, are more worthwhile than those effects which merely seem so, Sperber and Wilson stop short of including a notion of truth, or knowledge increase, in the definition of 'positive cognitive effects'. The reason they give for this is that 'we want to leave open the possibility of taking into account, in the full picture, other possible contributions to cognitive functioning, involving, for instance, the reorganisation of existing knowledge, or the elaboration of rational desires' (Sperber and Wilson 1995: 266). One effect of this reformulation is that it helps to make clear the role of the notion of truth in relevance-theoretic pragmatics. Sperber and Wilson have consistently argued against the idea that there is an expectation that utterances will be literally true. In one paper discussing this, they suggest that 'verbal communication is governed not by expectations of truthfulness but by expectations of relevance' (Wilson and Sperber 2002: 215). While utterances need not express true propositions, the truthfulness of the inferential conclusions they lead to is an important factor in determining their overall relevance.

1.3 Presumption of optimal relevance

The third change in 1995 was to the Presumption of Optimal Relevance. The new version says that:

(3)   Presumption of optimal relevance
   a.   the ostensive stimulus is relevant enough for it to be worth the addressee's effort to process it.
   b.   the ostensive stimulus is the most relevant one compatible with the communicator's abilities and preferences.

To some extent, this is a straightforward simplification. The first clause no longer makes explicit reference to the set of assumptions the speaker intends to make manifest by producing the stimulus. The idea that the stimulus 'is relevant enough' does this job on its own. To satisfy the presumption in clause (a), enough positive cognitive effects must be derivable from the stimulus to justify the effort involved in deriving them (the stimulus may not in fact lead to enough effects to justify the effort spent, but the act of communicating makes manifest that the communicator believes that it will). In the case of clause (b), the change involves more than simplification. The earlier formulation said that the stimulus was 'the most relevant one the communicator could have used' (Sperber and Wilson 1986: 164) to communicate the set of assumptions intended. The new formulation says that it is the most relevant one 'compatible with the communicator's abilities and preferences'. Why this change? Sperber and Wilson (1995: 268) suggest that the original formulation of clause (b) was 'at best too vague and at worst too strong'. The reference to preferences allows for the possibility that the communicator avoids the utterance which would be easiest for the audience to process because of other considerations, for example considerations of politeness, ideological correctness or stylistic preference, factors affecting the communicator's willingness to divulge certain information, or even considerations of the communicator's own effort. The reference to abilities allows for the possibility that the communicator might not have access to some relevant information at the time of speaking, or might not know which formulation would be most relevant to the addressee at that time.

1.4 Relevance-guided comprehension heuristic

The central claims of Relevance Theory (the definition of relevance and the two principles of relevance) lead to predictions about what interpreters will do in working out a communicator's intention. This has been made more salient in recent discussion (e.g., Sperber and Wilson 2002; Wilson and Sperber 2002, 2004) by the presentation of a comprehension heuristic for interpreting communicative acts:

(4)   Relevance-guided comprehension heuristic
    a.   Follow a path of least effort in deriving cognitive effects: test interpretations (e.g., disambiguations, reference resolutions, implicatures, etc.) in order of accessibility.
    b.   Stop when your expectations of relevance are satisfied.

This says that, in working through all of the inferential processes involved in utterance-interpretation, addressees should follow a path of least effort in looking for cognitive effects, and stop at the first interpretation which makes the utterance relevant in the expected way. This was always a prediction of the theory but its presentation in this form makes clearer what is involved in developing an overall interpretation.

1.5 Modularity

Relevance theory was initially developed on the assumption that it would be compatible with a broadly Chomskyan notion of language/grammar and Fodorian assumptions about the modularity of mind (Fodor 1983). As Blakemore points out above, the assumption was that a language module, understood as an input system linking phonological or graphological input with semantic representations, provided the input to pragmatic inference, and that pragmatic inference involved unencapsulated central cognitive processes. More recently, Sperber and Wilson and others have suggested a rethink of the nature of the modular systems involved in pragmatics (see discussion in Sperber 2001; Sperber 2005; Sperber and Wilson 2002; Wilson 2005). This rethink has been influenced by work on cognition from an evolutionary perspective and by developing ideas about the nature of modules and the domain-specificity of pragmatic inference. On this view, modules are understood as 'dedicated mechanisms . . . which cannot be seen as special cases of more general mechanisms operating in broader domains' (Wilson 2005: 1131). Pragmatic inferences seem to be modular in this broader sense. Recent work in Relevance Theory assumes that pragmatic inference may be carried out by a domain-specific comprehension mechanism, which is one of a number of sub-modules or mechanisms which together account for our ability to attribute mental states to others, usually referred to as 'theory of mind' (a term coined by Premack and Woodruff 1978; see also Astington et al. 1988; Baron-Cohen 1995; Carruthers and Smith 1996; Davies and Stone 1995a, 1995b; Leslie 1987; Scholl and Leslie 1999). A central component of this comprehension sub-module would be the relevance-guided comprehension heuristic in (4) above.

1.6 Metarepresentation

Related to consideration of the relationship between pragmatics and theory of mind, there has been ongoing exploration of both the nature of the metarepresentational abilities involved in pragmatic inference and how children develop these abilities (for discussion, see Wilson 2000). Sperber (1994) proposes three possible strategies which might be used in pragmatic interpretation and which vary in terms of how much metarepresentational ability they require. These are 'naïve optimism', 'cautious optimism' and 'sophisticated understanding'. An interpreter who follows the 'naïve optimist' strategy will interpret communicative acts on the assumption that the communicator is both 'competent' enough to achieve optimal relevance and 'benevolent' enough not to lead the interpreter astray. As soon as a naïve optimist finds an interpretation which makes the utterance relevant in the expected way, he will assume that this is the one the communicator intended. A 'cautious optimist' will be able to consider the possibility that the communicator is 'benevolent' but not 'competent', and so may be able to arrive at an interpretation which, while not actually relevant, is one which a communicator aiming at optimal relevance might have intended. A 'sophisticated understander' will be aware not only that communicators might be mistaken but also that they might be intentionally deceitful. This means that they may be able to arrive at interpretations which are not relevant in the expected way, but which a deceitful interpreter might have intended them to accept as such. These strategies correspond to different levels of metarepresentational ability. A naïve optimist need not represent the communicator's thoughts at all in arriving at a hypothesis about the communicator's meaning. A cautious optimist can think about what the communicator might have thought would be an appropriate interpretation. A sophisticated understander can go even further and think about what the communicator might have intended the interpreter to think would be an appropriate interpretation. Understanding these strategies might shed light on aspects of pragmatic development and on the pragmatic performance of people with conditions which affect pragmatic performance, such as autism or Asperger's syndrome. (Work in these areas includes Bezuidenhout and Sroda 1998; Happé 1993; Leslie and Happé 1989. Recent work on mind-reading and metarepresentational abilities includes Ifantidou 2005a, 2005b, 2005c; Mascaro and Sperber 2009; Mercier and Sperber 2009; Sperber 2000, 2001; Sperber and Wilson 2002.)

2 Developing accounts of linguistic and non-linguistic phenomena

As well as developments to the foundational and core assumptions of the theory, a wide range of work has continued to explore specific linguistic and non-linguistic phenomena. Semantic analyses have been proposed for a wide range of expressions in a wide range of languages. There has also been considerable debate on general questions about meaning and pragmatic phenomena.

2.1 Explicature, implicature and the semantics-pragmatics distinction

There has been considerable ongoing discussion of how to draw the semantics-pragmatics distinction and the distinction between explicit and implicit communication. In a number of studies (including Carston 2002a, 2004, 2008, 2009a, 2010), Robyn Carston has consistently defended the view that linguistic semantics concerns the relationship between linguistic expressions and what they encode, i.e. fragmentary or underspecified semantic representations, while pragmatics concerns all of the other things which are inferred when understanding ostensively communicative acts. On this view, the explicit/implicit distinction cross-cuts the semantics/pragmatics distinction: on one hand, pragmatic inference is involved in recovering explicatures; on the other, linguistically encoded meanings contribute to the recovery of implicatures. One particular area of debate has concerned the claim that the recovery of explicatures involves 'free enrichment', i.e. that some of the pragmatically processes involved in recovering explicit content do not depend on any linguistic feature of the utterances which give rise to them (for recent discussion of this issue, see Carston 2010; Hall 2008). Proponents of other views, some further removed from the Relevance Theory position than others, include Bach (1994b, 1997, 2001, 2010), Borg (2004, 2007), Cappelen and Lepore (2005b), Horn (1992, 1996), Jaszczolt (2005), Levinson (2000a) and Recanati (2001, 2004a, 2010).

2.2 Conceptual and procedural meaning

The conceptual-procedural distinction, originally developed by Diane Blakemore (1987), has been explored in a number of areas and applied to a wide range of phenomena. Blakemore initially considered expressions with procedural meanings which affect the possible implicatures of utterances. More recent work has extended the scope of procedural meaning to various kinds of explicatures. Wilson and Sperber (1993) sketch a range of possible kinds of conceptual and procedural meaning and accounts have been developed of a wide range of linguistic expressions in a wide range of languages. The approach has also been extended to prosody (Clark 2007; Clark and Lindsey 1990; Escandell-Vidal 1998, 2002; Fretheim 1998; House 1990, 2006; Imai 1998; Vandepitte 1989; Wilson and Wharton 2006) and to nonverbal communication (de Brabanter 2010; Wharton 2009). Blakemore herself has continued to develop her account of procedural meaning, extending this approach to a wider range of expressions and applying it in analysing particular kinds of literary and non-literary style (Blakemore 2002, 2007a, 2007b, 2008, 2009).

2.3 Lexical pragmatics

Understanding of the nature of conceptual meaning has also changed. An important development in relevance-theoretic lexical pragmatics is the assumption that words, whether or not they encode fully specified concepts which are stable across contexts, function as pointers or clues to the concept the speaker intends to convey, which may differ from context to context. The interpretation process thus involves the creation of 'ad hoc' concepts constructed and used for the specific purpose of interpreting specific utterances. The concept communicated by a specific word in a specific context may be narrower than the lexical meaning generally understood. For example, in a context where a singing teacher is talking to a singer during a rehearsal:

(5)   Breathe!

would usually be intended to refer to a particular kind of breathing, i.e. to something narrower than the lexically encoded concept.
      In another context, the intended sense of a word may be broader than the encoded concept:

(6)   The room was silent at the start of the lecture.

Absolute silence is not possible and it is likely that some noises are perceived by the speaker here. So the notion of 'silence' intended is broader than the encoded concept.
      In some cases, the sense intended may be simultaneously narrower and broader than the encoded concept:

(7)   I like Jane but she is a prima donna.

Assuming that (7) is not referring to someone who is literally a prima donna, the sense understood may be both broader in that it now includes someone who is not a member of an opera company and narrower in that it refers to the subset of prima donnas who are bossy, demanding, and so on. (For further discussion, see Sperber and Wilson 1998; Carston 2002a, 2002b; Wilson 2003; Wilson and Carston 2007.)

2.4 *Metaphor*

This approach has particularly significant implications for the relevance-theoretic account of metaphor. The earlier account (Sperber and Wilson 1986, 1990) assumed that metaphorical interpretation could be explained with reference to the interpreter's task of distinguishing the set of implicatures intentionally communicated by an utterance from its broader range of implications. An utterance of (7) would provide access to the implication that Jane is a member of an opera company but the hearer would know not to attribute an intention to communicate this. On this view, the proposition expressed is not communicated in cases of metaphor. On the new account, the proposition expressed by the second clause is (8), where the asterisk indicates a pragmatically adjusted concept:

(8)   Jane is a PRIMA DONNA*.

The proposition containing the ~~adju~~   d and the interpreter's task is
                                                                      stent across the two accounts
                                                                      communicative norm.
                                                                      ry account of metaphor with
                                                                      s tradition (e.g., Fauconnier
                                                                      s included discussion of how
                                                                      the question of whether it
                                                                      from both kinds of approach
                                                                      09a). Some of this discussion
                                                                      ese are properties which are
                                                                      which seem to 'emerge' as

on some properties which
nsitivity, and so on. There
se features, with relevance
etic account can deal with
r and Wilson 2008; Vega

alysis of irony, with the
heory (Clark and Gerrig
and Wilson's attributive/
rie 2006, 2008; Kumon-
he extent, the debate can

between approaches, such as those proposed by Currie and Recanati, which see an element of pretence as essential to cases of irony, and the Relevance Theory account which proposes that the essential features of irony are a dissociative attitude to, and the attribution to one or more others of, the thought represented by the ironic utterance. In a recent paper, Wilson (2009b) argues that 'although certain "parodic" forms of irony can indeed be seen as involving pretence or simulation, pretence is not a necessary feature of irony, and prototypical cases of irony . . . involve echoic use without any element of pretence' (Wilson 2009b: 210).

3 Testing the theory

One final area where there have been significant developments in recent years is in the range of methods used to test predictions of the theory. Alongside applications in areas such as stylistics (e.g., Bursey and Furlong 2006; Clark 1996, 2009; Furlong 1996, 2001; MacMahon 1996, 2001a, 2001b, 2007, 2009a, 2009b; Pilkington 1996, 2000), politeness and phatic communication (e.g. Attardo 1997; Bonnefon et al. 2009; Christie 2007; Escandell-Vidal 1996; Haicun 2005; Haugh 2003; Jary 1998; Padilla Cruz 2008, 2009; Ruhi 2007, 2008; Ruhi and Dogan 2001; Watts 2003; Yongping 2002; Zegarac and Clark 1999) the analysis of multimodal and visual communication (e.g., Forceville 1996, 1999, 2000, 2002, 2005; Mateo Martínez and Yus 2006; Yus 1998) and applications in translation (e.g., Boase-Beier 2004a, 2004b; Gutt 1998, 2004; Rosales Sequeiros 2005; Setton 1999, 2005a, 2005b, 2006), there have been developmental studies (e.g., Bezuidenhout and Sroda 1998; Blaye et al. 1999; Breheny 2006; Foster-Cohen 2004a, 2004b; Ifanfidou 2005a, 2005b; Noveck 2001; Papafragou 1997, 1998a, 2002, 2003; Pouscoulous and Noveck 2009; Pouscoulous et al. 2007), increased use of corpora (Andersen 1999; Jary 2008; de Klerk 2005; Navarro 2006; Zajac 2004) and, perhaps most significantly, the emergence of a new field of experimental pragmatics. Experimental work has focused on a number of areas, including intuitions about the explicit-implicit distinction (Gibbs and Moise 1997, Nicolle and Clark 1999) and developmental studies (Noveck 2001; Papafragou 1997, 2002, 2003; Pouscoulous and Noveck 2009; Pouscoulous et al. 2007). A significant amount of research has focused on scalar implicature and the question of whether inferences such as (11) are generated by default (i.e. automatically) when interpreting utterances such as (10):

(10) Some of the students enjoyed the lecture.

(11) Not all of the students enjoyed the lecture.

(see, for example, Bott and Noveck 2004; Breheny et al. 2006; Noveck 2001; Papafragou and Musolino 2003; Pouscoulous et al. 2007). There has also been significant work testing central notions of the theory (Girotto et al. 2001; Van der Henst et al. 2002a; Van der Henst et al. 2002b; Van der Henst and Sperber 2004; Sperber, Cara and Girotto 1995). For overviews on experimental pragmatics, see Noveck and Sperber (2007) and Sperber and Noveck (2004).

4 Conclusion

These are a few of the important developments in work involving Relevance Theory since 1995. Of course, there have been many more. Other useful sources include a summary of recent developments by Carston and Powell (2006) and more general summaries by Wilson and Sperber (2004), Sperber and Wilson (2005) and Yus (2006, 2010). Blakemore's (1992) introductory textbook is still relevant and Clark (2011) offers a fuller introduction. For fuller theoretical discussion, two particularly useful sources are Blakemore (2002) and Carston (2002a). The most frequently updated resources are the websites of individual authors and the Relevance Theory Online Bibliographic Service, which is maintained by Francisco Yus at the Universitat d'Alacant (www.ua.es/personal/francisco.yus/rt.html).

2.4 Metaphor

This approach has particularly significant implications for the relevance-theoretic account of metaphor. The earlier account (Sperber and Wilson 1986, 1990) assumed that metaphorical interpretation could be explained with reference to the interpreter's task of distinguishing the set of implicatures intentionally communicated by an utterance from its broader range of implications. An utterance of (7) would provide access to the implication that Jane is a member of an opera company but the hearer would know not to attribute an intention to communicate this. On this view, the proposition expressed is not communicated in cases of metaphor. On the new account, the proposition expressed by the second clause is (8), where the asterisk indicates a pragmatically adjusted concept:

(8) Jane is a PRIMA DONNA*.

The proposition containing the adjusted concept is communicated and the interpreter's task is to work out which implicatures follow from this. What is consistent across the two accounts is the assumption that non-literalness is not a departure from a communicative norm.

There has been ongoing comparison of the Relevance Theory account of metaphor with other approaches, including those within the Cognitive Linguistics tradition (e.g., Fauconnier and Turner 2002, 2008; Lakoff and Johnson 1980, 1987). This has included discussion of how well each approach accounts for metaphor and, more recently, the question of whether it might be possible to develop an approach which combines elements from both kinds of approach (see Gibbs and Tendahl 2006; Tendahl and Gibbs 2008; Wilson 2009a). Some of this discussion has focused around so-called 'emergent features' of metaphor. These are properties which are not associated with the original concept used metaphorically but which seem to 'emerge' as part of the process of interpretation:

(9) My surgeon is a butcher.

A metaphorical interpretation of (9) would attribute to the surgeon some properties which are not properties of butchers, e.g., a disregard for human life, insensitivity, and so on. There has been discussion of how well each approach can account for these features, with relevance theorists suggesting a way in which the inferential, relevance-theoretic account can deal with them. (For further discussion, see Carston 2002a, 2002b; Sperber and Wilson 2008; Vega Moreno 2007; Wilson and Carston 2006, 2008.)

2.6 Irony and metarepresentation

There has been continuing discussion of the relevance-theoretic analysis of irony, with the main competitors in this area being seen as varieties of pretence theory (Clark and Gerrig 1984), or approaches which propose to combine aspects of Sperber and Wilson's attributive/echoic account with aspects of pretence accounts (Csibra 2010; Currie 2006, 2008; Kumon-Nakamura et al. 1995; Recanati 2007; Southgate et al. 2009). To some extent, the debate can be seen as dividing between approaches, such as those proposed by Currie and Recanati, which see an element of pretence as essential to cases of irony, and the Relevance Theory account which proposes that the essential features of irony are a dissociative attitude to, and the attribution to one or more others of, the thought represented by the ironic utterance. In a recent paper, Wilson (2009b) argues that 'although certain "parodic" forms of irony can indeed be seen as involving pretence or simulation, pretence is not a necessary feature of irony, and prototypical cases of irony . . . involve echoic use without any element of pretence' (Wilson 2009b: 210).

3 Testing the theory

One final area where there have been significant developments in recent years is in the range of methods used to test predictions of the theory. Alongside applications in areas such as stylistics (e.g., Bursey and Furlong 2006; Clark 1996, 2009; Furlong 1996, 2001; MacMahon 1996, 2001a, 2001b, 2007, 2009a, 2009b; Pilkington 1996, 2000), politeness and phatic communication (e.g. Attardo 1997; Bonnefon et al. 2009; Christie 2007; Escandell-Vidal 1996; Haicun 2005; Haugh 2003; Jary 1998; Padilla Cruz 2008, 2009; Ruhi 2007, 2008; Ruhi and Dogan 2001; Watts 2003; Yongping 2002; Zegarac and Clark 1999) the analysis of multimodal and visual communication (e.g., Forceville 1996, 1999, 2000, 2002, 2005; Mateo Martínez and Yus 2006; Yus 1998) and applications in translation (e.g., Boase-Beier 2004a, 2004b; Gutt 1998, 2004; Rosales Sequeiros 2005; Setton 1999, 2005a, 2005b, 2006), there have been developmental studies (e.g., Bezuidenhout and Sroda 1998; Blaye et al. 1999; Breheny 2006; Foster-Cohen 2004a, 2004b; Ifanfidou 2005a, 2005b; Noveck 2001; Papafragou 1997, 1998a, 2002, 2003; Pouscoulous and Noveck 2009; Pouscoulous et al. 2007), increased use of corpora (Andersen 1999; Jary 2008; de Klerk 2005; Navarro 2006; Zajac 2004) and, perhaps most significantly, the emergence of a new field of experimental pragmatics. Experimental work has focused on a number of areas, including intuitions about the explicit-implicit distinction (Gibbs and Moise 1997, Nicolle and Clark 1999) and developmental studies (Noveck 2001; Papafragou 1997, 2002, 2003; Pouscoulous and Noveck 2009; Pouscoulous et al. 2007). A significant amount of research has focused on scalar implicature and the question of whether inferences such as (11) are generated by default (i.e. automatically) when interpreting utterances such as (10):

(10) Some of the students enjoyed the lecture.

(11) Not all of the students enjoyed the lecture.

(see, for example, Bott and Noveck 2004; Breheny et al. 2006; Noveck 2001; Papafragou and Musolino 2003; Pouscoulous et al. 2007). There has also been significant work testing central notions of the theory (Girotto et al. 2001; Van der Henst et al. 2002a; Van der Henst et al. 2002b; Van der Henst and Sperber 2004; Sperber, Cara and Girotto 1995). For overviews on experimental pragmatics, see Noveck and Sperber (2007) and Sperber and Noveck (2004).

4 Conclusion

These are a few of the important developments in work involving Relevance Theory since 1995. Of course, there have been many more. Other useful sources include a summary of recent developments by Carston and Powell (2006) and more general summaries by Wilson and Sperber (2004), Sperber and Wilson (2005) and Yus (2006, 2010). Blakemore's (1992) introductory textbook is still relevant and Clark (2011) offers a fuller introduction. For fuller theoretical discussion, two particularly useful sources are Blakemore (2002) and Carston (2002a). The most frequently updated resources are the websites of individual authors and the Relevance Theory Online Bibliographic Service, which is maintained by Francisco Yus at the Universitat d'Alacant (www.ua.es/personal/francisco.yus/rt.html).

■ ■ ■

POST-READING

1 How do you react to the suggestion with which Blakemore concludes the reading, that 'the linguistic distinction between truth-conditional and non-truth-conditional meaning should be abandoned, leaving just the cognitive distinction between the conceptual and the procedural and the pragmatic distinction between the explicit and the implicit'?

2 Are you persuaded that Speech Act theory has got it wrong and that language is actually a vehicle for thought rather than for action?

3 Write two short paragraphs, one in favour of retaining Sperber and Wilson's original concept, 'contextual effect', and one in favour of replacing it by 'cognitive effect'. Do you think the modification serves any useful purpose?

ROBYN CARSTON

THOUGHTS AND UTTERANCES

PRE-READING

In this extract from *Thoughts and Utterances*, Carston argues for a series of amendments to Sperber and Wilson's original definition of explicature: 'An assumption communicated by an utterance U is *explicit* if and only if it is a development of a logical form encoded by U.' Her revised definition reads: 'An assumption (proposition) communicated by an utterance is an 'explicature' of the utterance if and only if it is a development of (a) a linguistically encoded logical form of the utterance, or of (b) a sentential subpart of the logical form.' Crucial in proposing her modification to the original definition is the use of 'frankly' in the utterance 'Kim shouldn't pass the course, because she, frankly, has not done the work'. Can you work out why this use motivates Carston's modification?

IN-READING

At several points in the reading, the text is accompanied by a marginal mark | . Pause at each of these places, and think about whether you agree with Carston's argument. Sometimes it'll be easy to agree, sometimes you'll have to think long and hard about it. Do not continue reading until you're sure either that you agree or that you have a very good reason for disagreeing.

■ ■ ■

THOUGHTS AND UTTERANCES
ROBYN CARSTON

2.3.1 Explicature

The assumptions communicated by a speaker fall into two classes: 'explicature' and 'implicature'. Sperber and Wilson's (1986, 1995: 182) definitions are as follows:

(I)   An assumption communicated by an utterance U is *explicit* [hence an 'explicature']
      if and only if it is a development of a logical form encoded by U. [*Note*: in cases
      of ambiguity, a surface form encodes more than one logical form, hence the use
      of the indefinite here, '*a* logical form encoded by U'.]

(II) An assumption communicated by U which is not explicit is implicit [hence an
      'implicature'].

[. . .] There are two points worth emphasizing here. The first is that the explicature/
implicature distinction applies only to those assumptions that fall within the speaker's
communicative intention. This opens up the possibility of a difference between the proposition
expressed by the speaker and her explicature(s): the proposition expressed may or may not
be communicated; only when it is communicated is it an explicature of the utterance. This
distinction is essential to the standard relevance-theoretic account of non-literalness, [. . .]; in
cases of metaphorical or ironical use, it seems that the proposition expressed is not explicated.
It is also essential to the account of non-declarative utterances, such as imperatives, interrogatives,
hortatives and others, since, if we follow the standard speech-act line on these, all of the
following have the same propositional content, but the only case where that proposition is
communicated (hence explicated) is (18a), the declarative:

(18) a.   Billy is going home.
     b.   Go home, Billy!
     c.   Is Billy going home?
     d.   Would that Billy would go home.

I'll consider the imperative in a little more detail later in this section.

Second, clearly the content of explicatures comes from two distinct sources, the linguistic
expressions used and the context, and it is derived in two distinct ways depending on its
source, by linguistic decoding or by pragmatic inference. As discussed at length in the previous
chapter, the logical form, which is the output of the decoding phase, virtually never constitutes
a fully propositional entity, but is rather a schema for the inferential construction of fully
propositional assumptions. Several utterances with one and the same propositional content
may differ with regard to the relative contributions of decoding and inference to that content.
So, although the explicatures of such (declarative) utterances may be the same, they will vary
in their degree of explicitness:

(19) a.   Mary Jones put the book by Chomsky on the table in the downstairs sitting-
          room.
     b.   Mary put the book on the table.
     c.   She put it there.
     d.   On the table.

An utterance of any one of (19a)–(19d) could be used, in different contexts, to communicate
explicitly one and the same proposition (or thought or assumption). Clearly (19c) and (19d)
leave a great deal more to pragmatic inference than does (19b), which in turn is less explicit
than (19a). Given the essential nature of the underdeterminacy thesis, as argued in the previous
chapter, no linguistic expression will achieve full explicitness; that is, will fully encode the
propositional form communicated. [. . .]

As discussed in some detail in the preceding chapter, there is a range of processes, which can be loosely called cases of pragmatic enrichment (or development), that are required in the recovery of the proposition the speaker intended to express (an explicature, if she communicated it). An early discussion of this phenomenon appears in Wilson and Sperber (1981), who look at the example in (21a). Let us suppose that the outcome of the two processes of disambiguation and reference assignment (in a particular context) is as given in (21b), which is fully propositional (so truth-evaluable):

(21) a.   John plays very well.
     b.   John Murray plays some musical instrument very well.
     c.   John Murray plays the violin very well.
     d.   John Murray should be admitted to the National Youth Orchestra.

As they say, in most instances a hearer would interpret (21a) as expressing something more specific than (21b), say (21c), in circumstances of John Murray playing the violin in front of the speaker and hearer. They note a couple of important features of (21c): it entails (hence is more informative than) (21b), and it is on the basis of (21c) rather than (21b) that the implicatures of the utterance would be worked out, for instance (21d) in an appropriate context. An important question arises here that did not arise for the Gricean approach, according to which (21b) would be 'what is said'. The question is how far the process of pragmatically developing the logical form goes and what constraints there are on it, or, in other words, how it can be determined, for any given instance of a pragmatic inference, whether it is a contribution to the proposition expressed or an independent implicated assumption. Various criteria for distinguishing the proposition expressed (or basic explicature) from implicature have been proposed (see, for instance, Carston 1988b and Recanati 1989, 1993), some of which are discussed in Section 2.6 [see original publication], and the outline of some actual derivations of explicatures and implicatures in Subsection 2.3.4 [see original publication] is intended to show that the ultimate arbiter is the relevance-based comprehension strategy itself.

So far I've considered only the explicature that an utterance has when the proposition the utterance expresses is communicated (overtly endorsed) by the speaker, but in fact Sperber and Wilson's idea is that utterances typically have several explicatures. A development of the logical form may be such that the propositional form (proposition expressed) is embedded in a range of different sorts of higher-level descriptions, including (weak) speech-act and propositional-attitude descriptions (Wilson and Sperber 1993: 5–6). For instance, Mary's reply to Bill's question in (22) might have the explicatures given in (23):

(22) a.   Bill: Did your son visit you at the weekend?
     b.   Mary (visibly happy): He did.

(23) a.   Mary's son visited her at the weekend.
     b.   Mary says that her son visited her at the weekend.[1]
     c.   Mary believes that her son visited her at the weekend.
     d.   Mary is happy that her son visited her at the weekend.

The hearer may actually represent only some subset of these (though the speaker has made manifest her intention to make the others manifest as well). In a situation in which, for instance, Bill knows that Mary has been worrying about a growing rift between her son and herself, he may represent just (23a) (the base-level, we could say, explicature) and the higher-level explicature (23d). These are the explicitly communicated assumptions most likely to give rise to contextual effects (that is, to be relevant). In some other case, a higher-level explicature describing the speaker's belief might be the major contributor to the relevance of the utterance; for instance, in a context in which this representation could overturn or modify the hearer's existing representation of the speaker's beliefs. The importance of higher-level explicatures (in which the proposition expressed is embedded) is most apparent when we look at cases of non-literalness, on the one hand, and at cases of non-declarative utterances, on the other.

On the relevance-theoretic account, an utterance of a sentence in the imperative mood communicates an explicature which describes a certain state of affairs as both achievable (or, 'potential') and desirable (to some degree *x*), to the speaker or the hearer or, perhaps, a salient third person; these indeterminacies have to be pragmatically resolved. For example, in an appropriate context, an utterance of (24a) could communicate the higher-level explicatures in (24b)–(24d) (S for the speaker, H for the hearer):

(24) a.   Buy some milk.
     b.   S is telling H to buy some milk.
     c.   It is moderately desirable to S (and achievable) that H buy some milk.
     d.   S is requesting H to buy some milk.

As on certain speech-act accounts, the idea here is that the proposition expressed is the same as that expressed by the corresponding declarative; here it would be 'the hearer buy(s) some milk'. This propositional form of an imperative is subject to the various enrichment processes already discussed with regard to declarative cases: disambiguation, reference assignment, propositional completion and propositional strengthening. The italicized forms beneath the following examples are rough indications of the sorts of enrichments that might have to be made:

(25) a.   Stop him!
          [*(You) stop Bruce from getting into a fight with Sid!*]
     b.   Have a bath!
          [*(You) bath your body very soon!*]
     c.   Give this decision some thought!
          [*(You) give this decision an appreciable amount of thought!*]

These propositional forms are clearly not explicatures of the imperative utterance, however, since they are not communicated (they are not presented as actual but merely as potential and desirable). It is the higher-level representations which are explicitly communicated, so for an utterance of (24a) it is (24b)–(24d). (See Wilson and Sperber 1988; Wilson 1991; Clark 1991, 1993, for fuller accounts of this analysis of imperatives and of other non-declarative utterances.)

The distinction between higher-level explicatures and the explicated propositional form of the utterance is interesting from another point of view too. Several classes of sentential adverbial have been analysed by theorists as not being part of the propositional form of the utterance:

(26) a.   Frankly, I'm unimpressed.
     b.   Confidentially, she won't pass the exam.
     c.   Happily, Mary's son visited her this weekend.
     d.   Unfortunately, I missed the train.

   e.   Obviously, I'm going to miss the deadline.

   f.   Possibly, we're too late.

'Frankly' and 'seriously' are cases of illocutionary adverbials; 'happily' and 'unfortunately' are cases of evaluative (attitudinal) adverbials and 'obviously' and 'perhaps' are evidential adverbials. It seems that the propositional form (and hence the truth-conditional content) of these utterances does not include the contribution made by the adverbial.[2] Where, then, do these elements make their contribution? They each decode into a mentally represented concept, which must feature in some representation derived by the hearer. There is a neat answer to this in the system Sperber and Wilson have developed: they contribute to a higher-level explicature. This is most easily seen in the case of the illocutionary adverbials, which slot straightforwardly into the role of modifier of a speech-act verb in the higher-level speech-act description:

(27) a.   I tell you frankly that I'm unimpressed.

     b.   I inform you confidentially that she won't pass the exam.

Evidentials comment on what the speaker sees as the degree of evidential support for the proposition expressed, which may in turn affect the degree of conviction she represents herself as having in the truth of the proposition expressed (that is, the propositional attitude explicature):

(28) a.   It is obvious (obviously true) that the speaker is going to miss the deadline.

     b.   The speaker strongly believes that she is going to miss the deadline.

     c.   It is possible that the speaker and X are too late [for . . .].

     d.   The speaker weakly believes that she and X are too late [for . . .].

And, in similar vein, for the evaluative adverbials:

(29) a.   It is a happy eventually that Mary's son visited her this weekend.

     b.   It is unfortunate that the speaker missed the train.

There is probably a further range of indeterminacies to be pragmatically resolved here: 'obvious to whom?', 'happy for whom?', 'unfortunate in whose opinion?', etc.

    So far so (relatively) good, but this brings us to a problem with the definition of explicature as given above. Let's look at some more complex cases involving sentence adverbials:

(30) a.   Kim shouldn't pass the course, because she, frankly, hasn't done the work.

     b.   Kim might pass the course, although, confidentially, she hasn't done the work.

     c.   She has missed a lot of lectures and she, obviously, hates linguistics.

The argument has been that sentential adverbials contribute to higher-level explicatures, but in (30a) and (30b) they are modifying an embedded clause, which is certainly not a development of the logical form of the utterance, but is rather a constituent (a proper subpart) of the logical form of the utterance, and hence of the propositional form into which it is developed. It seems that either we are wrong about the role of these adverbials, or the propositional constituents into which the subordinate clauses are developed must be explicatures in their own right (or perhaps both).

In fact, the problem arises independently of the issue of the correct treatment of sentence adverbials. The simplest illustration is the case of an 'and'-conjunction:

(31) a.   Sam went to a party and Jane watched a video.
     b.   Sam went to a party.
     c.   Jane watched a video.

Intuitions seem to be unequivocal that an utterance of (31a) communicates not only the conjunctive proposition but also the two constituent propositions, (31b) and (31c). So, again, these are explicatures which are embedded within the proposition expressed by the utterance. The point carries over to examples like those in (30) but without the sentence adverbials, so (32a) communicates explicitly both (32b) and (32c), as well as the more complex proposition of which they are constituents:

(32) a.   Kim shouldn't pass the course because she hasn't done the work.
     b.   Kim shouldn't pass the course.
     c.   Kim hasn't done the work.

What all these examples show is that the definition of explicature given above is too restrictive. On the basis of the cases considered so far, (30)–(32), it looks as if it should be amended so as to include communicated entailments of the proposition expressed. However, there are other cases where the intuition of explicitness of communication applies to subpropositions which are not entailed by the proposition expressed. The following examples are based on one from Sperber and Wilson (1995: 294, footnote a), who acknowledge the problem that this sort of case raises for the definition of explicature:

(33) a.   I'm telling you that it's not possible.
     b.   It's not possible.

(34) a.   I'm totally certain that Emily will come.
     b.   Emily will come.

A speaker of the utterances in (33a) and (34a) who explicates the proposition expressed in each case, also explicitly communicates (33b) and (34b) respectively, though these are not entailments of the proposition expressed (the truth of P does not follow from the truth of my telling you that P or from the truth of my being totally certain that P).
    As well as not being a necessary feature of an explicature, the property of being entailed (and communicated) may not be sufficient either. Consider the following, in which an utterance of the sentence in (a) communicates the proposition in (b):

(35) a.   (Confidentially) the judge is my father.
     b.   The judge is a man.

(36) a.   (Unfortunately) I bought some pork.
     b.   I bought some meat.

Intuitions seem to vary across individuals as to whether the propositions in (b) in each case are explicatures or implicatures, so in these cases we need to look to more theoretical considerations. Notice that while examples (30)–(34) involve clauses within clauses and so propositions within propositions (once the proposition expressed has been pragmatically constructed), examples (35) and (36) are single clauses and the proposition they express contains no propositional subparts. It is the multi-clausal nature of (30)–(34) which has, so far, been the essential property in motivating the need for a broader definition of explicature, since in each case it is the possibility of explicating a subproposition contained within their propositional form that is not met by the current definition. This cannot arise for examples (35) and (36) because they are single-clause cases, so they should comply with the current definition; according to that definition, the communicated proposition shown in (b) in each case is not an explicature because it is not a development (an inferential enrichment) of any element of encoded meaning. On the assumption that the notion of a development of an encoded semantic representation is central to the account of explicature and should remain so, these cases fall outside its range. In the next section [see original publication], I will suggest that they are indeed implicatures, since they are derived entirely inferentially (in fact, deductively) as are implicated conclusions quite generally.

So it seems that being a communicated entailment of the proposition expressed may be neither necessary nor sufficient for qualification as an explicature. At the least, it is not necessary, as the examples in (33) and (34) attest. It is worth noting that the intuition that the embedded propositional form is communicated, hence explicated, does not go through if the person of the main clause subject is changed or if the main verb semantics is altered in certain ways:

(37) a.   John is telling us that it's not possible.
     b.   The child is quite certain that Emily will come.
     c.   I hope that it's not possible.
     d.   I doubt that Jane will come.

The speaker of these utterances is not explicitly communicating the proposition expressed by the embedded clauses, 'it's not possible', 'Emily will come' (and is probably not communicating them at all). The relevant difference between the two cases is plain to see: in uttering (33) or (34), the speaker is expressing her commitment to the truth of the embedded proposition, while, in uttering any of (37a)–(37d), she is not. The point is that if the proposition expressed by an utterance itself expresses speaker commitment to a subproposition contained within it, then if the proposition expressed is communicated so must be the subproposition. A similar point can be made about the cases involving the factive-type entailments, such as (30)–(32); in communicating (overtly endorsing) the proposition expressed by the utterance, the speaker cannot but communicate (endorse) the contained propositions that are entailed.

So what we are after in a modified definition of explicature is a characterization that encompasses the following *communicated* assumptions/propositions: (a) the proposition expressed, (b) embeddings of the proposition expressed in higher-level descriptions, and (c) propositional subparts of the proposition expressed. I suggest that the following quite minor amendment of the original definition does the job:

(III) An assumption (proposition) communicated by an utterance is an 'explicature' of the utterance if and only if it is a development of (a) a linguistically encoded logical form of the utterance, or of (b) a sentential subpart of a logical form.

Ideally, this would be made a little more precise (for instance, what exactly is meant by a 'sentential subpart' of the logical form?), and perhaps streamlined by a single characterization of 'development of a logical form' and 'development of a sentential subpart', so as to eliminate the disjunctive element of the definition, which might suggest we are not dealing with a unified phenomenon. However, as it stands, I think it is descriptively adequate and relatively clear. Note that, as with the original definition, the main work is done by the two central concepts: '(ostensively) communicated' and 'development (pragmatic enrichment)'.

Let's return to the example which first prompted the revision, (30a) (repeated here for convenience), and look at its explicatures:

(30) a.   Kim shouldn't pass the course, because she, frankly, hasn't done the work.

Assuming that the proposition expressed by this utterance is (38a) and that it is communicated, the utterance may have the following explicatures, in accordance with clause (a) of the definition:

(38) a   Kim shouldn't pass the course because she hasn't done the work.
   b.   S is saying that Kim shouldn't pass the course because she hasn't done the work.
   c.   S believes that Kim shouldn't pass the course because she hasn't done the work.
   d.   S is sad that Kim shouldn't pass the course because she hasn't done the work.

In addition, it will have the explicatures in (39) and (40), in accordance with clause (b) of the definition:

(39) a.   Kim shouldn't pass the course.
   b.   S believes Kim shouldn't pass the course.
   c.   S is saying that Kim shouldn't pass the course.

(40) a.   Kim hasn't done the work.
   b.   S believes that Kim hasn't done the work.
   c.   S is telling H frankly that Kim hasn't done the work.

While these may be communicated (that is, the speaker's intention to make them manifest to the hearer is itself made mutually manifest), this is not to say that the hearer will represent all of them; it is almost certain that he will not. He is likely to represent (40c) because the use of 'frankly' in this utterance makes it highly manifest and so, given the Principle of Relevance, likely to have cognitive effects.

Note that, according to this amended definition, as with the original one, the entailment cases in (35) and (36) do not qualify as explicatures, because, although they may be communicated, they are not developments of any sentential part of the decoded semantic representation of the utterance. It seems that only those entailments which are 'visible' in, and detachable from, the propositional form of the utterance are candidates for explicaturehood, and there may be an interesting complementarity with those entailments that can be implicated, a point touched on again in section 2.3.3 [see original publication] on implicature. This is backed up by differences in the functioning of the sentence adverbials in the clear cases of explicated entailments, on the one hand, and in these non-transparent cases, on the other. While the adverbials can play their standard role in higher-level descriptions involving the former (as in (40c)), this is just not possible with this second set of cases:

(41) a.   Confidentially, the judge is my father.
      b.   ?S is telling H confidentially that the judge is a man.
      c.   Unfortunately, I bought some pork.
      d.   ?It is unfortunate that S bought some meat.

An utterance of (41a) does not explicitly communicate (41b) and an utterance of (41c) does not explicitly communicate (41d).

Notes

1   Declarative indicators, such as the indicative mood in this example, encode the information that the clause represents an actual or possible state of affairs, or, equivalently, that the clause comes with a belief attitude attached; this applies to all clauses, main or embedded. When actually *uttered*, declarative indicators in the main clause ensure that the *utterance* counts as a case of 'saying that', or 'telling H that', but since there is an array of uses of declarative sentences on which the speaker is not endorsing the propositional content (non-literal cases such as ironical uses, jokes and various (tacitly) attributive uses), this notion does not entail speaker commitment (that is, the belief attitude may or may not be held by her).

2   It turns out that the facts are rather more subtle than this: illocutionary (e.g. 'frankly') and attitudinal (e.g. 'sadly') adverbials do not contribute to the truth conditions of the utterance, while evidentials (e.g. 'clearly', 'possibly') and, much more obviously, hearsay adverbials (e.g. 'allegedly', 'reportedly') do contribute to truth conditions. See Ifantidou-Trouki (1993), Ifantidou (1994, 2001) for detailed discussion of these differences and how they might be accounted for. Bach (1999) also looks at a range of these adverbials but divides them up differently from Ifantidou. He makes a distinction between 'utterance modifiers', which include illocutionary adverbials, and 'content modifiers', which include attitudinal and evidential adverbials, and he suggests rather different analyses for the two types of case.

■ ■ ■

POST-READING

1   Carston discusses borderline explicature/implicature enrichments and appeals to 'the notion of a development of an encoded semantic representation' as being central in explicature. Return to examples (40)–(49) in the Levinson reading from *Presumptive Meanings*. Which of these examples would Carston treat as explicatures and which as implicatures? What do you learn about explicature and implicature from this? Do you think that Levinson fails to make a distinction that seems well motivated?

2   How do you react to Levinson's view that 'GCIs pose a special problem for any deductive account because they so plainly arise as a preferred interpretation only to be cancelled or annulled later at some distance without any sense of selfcontradiction by the speaker' (2000: 57)?

3   Think back to Levinson's Q-inference: Do you think that *not all* could be a pragmatic enrichment of 'some' and therefore ought to be regarded as an explicature?

4   Think back to Levinson's M-inference: Given that M-inferences provide marked meanings, would you expect these to be implicatures more often than not?

5   Levinson uses 'pragmatic intrusion' to argue that pragmatic inference contributes to truth-conditions and hence that we should think of pragmatics as truth-conditional or truth functional. Now that you have read the extract from *Thoughts and Utterances*, do you feel that truth is relevant to our understanding of propositional meaning?

DAN SPERBER AND DEIRDRE WILSON

THE MAPPING BETWEEN THE MENTAL AND THE PUBLIC LEXICON

PRE-READING

1 Do you think either of the following positions mentioned by Sperber and Wilson is supportable:
   - 'languages such as English or Swahili are the sole medium of thought. There is a genuine one-to-one correspondence between public words and mental concepts'?
   - 'there are no such things as individual mental concepts'?
2 Which of the three following positions mentioned by Sperber and Wilson do you find most persuasive:
   - 'nearly all individual concepts are lexicalised, but many words encode complex conceptual structures rather than individual concepts. So there are fewer concepts than words, and the mapping is partial mostly because many words do not map onto individual concepts';
   - 'genuine synonyms, genuine homonyms, nonlexicalised concepts and words that do not encode concepts are all relatively rare, so there is roughly a one-to-one mapping between words and concepts';
   - 'the mapping is partial, and the main reason for this is that only a fraction of the conceptual repertoire is lexicalised. Most mental concepts do not map onto words'.

IN-READING

1 When you reach examples (1) and (2) in the reading, replace each of Sperber and Wilson's examples with three or four examples of your own.
2 When you've read to the end of Section 2 (page 152), stop and make a list (using periphrastic formulas of course) of several ineffable concepts that seem to exist in your own 'mentalese'.
3 When you've read through examples (11)–(15), think up and note down another Peter/Mary exchange using a predicate other than 'tired' to illustrate the point that Sperber and Wilson make.
4 When you reach examples (16) and (17), consider whether you could provide similar examples of your own, making use of the Peter/Mary exchange you invented in relation to (11)–(15).

5   When you've read example (18) and the two following paragraphs, think up two or three examples of your own to show 'how a word which encodes a given concept can be used to convey (as a component of a speaker's meaning) another concept that neither it nor any other expression in the language actually encodes'.

■ ■ ■

THE MAPPING BETWEEN THE MENTAL AND THE PUBLIC LEXICON
DAN SPERBER AND DEIRDRE WILSON

1   Introduction

There are words in the language we speak and concepts in our minds. For present purposes, we can use a relatively common-sense, unsophisticated notion of a linguistic word. A bit more needs to be said, now and later, about what we mean by a concept. We assume that mental representations have a structure not wholly unlike that of a sentence, and combine elements from a mental repertoire not wholly unlike a lexicon. These elements are mental concepts: so to speak, 'words of mentalese'. Mental concepts are relatively stable and distinct structures in the mind, comparable to entries in an encyclopaedia or to permanent files in a data-base. Their occurrence in a mental representation may determine matching causal and formal (semantic or logical) relationships. On the one hand, there are relationships between the mind and the world. The activation of a concept may play a major role in causal interactions between the organism and external objects that fall under that concept. On the other hand, there are relationships among representations within the mind. The occurrence of a concept in a mental representation may play a causal role in the derivation of further representations, and may also contribute to the justification of this derivation.

2   Three types of mapping

What kind of mapping is there (if any) between mental concepts and public words? One extreme view is that natural languages such as English or Swahili are the sole medium of thought. In this case, obviously, there is a genuine one-to-one correspondence between public words and mental concepts. An opposite extreme view is that there are no such things as individual mental concepts at all, and therefore no conceptual counterparts to public words. We will ignore these extreme views. We assume that there are mental concepts, and that they are not just internalisations of public words, so that the kind and degree of correspondence between concepts and words is a genuine and interesting empirical issue.

In principle, the mapping between mental concepts and public words might be exhaustive (so that every concept corresponds to a word and conversely), or partial. If it is partial, this may be because some concepts lack a corresponding word, because some words lack a corresponding concept, or both. The mapping between words and concepts may be one-to-one, one-to-many, many-to-one, or a mixture of these. However, the idea that there is an exhaustive, one-to-one mapping between concepts and words is quite implausible.

Some words (for instance the third person pronoun 'it') are more like placeholders and do not encode concepts at all. Many words seem to encode not a full-fledged concept but what might be called a pro-concept (for example 'my', 'have', 'near', 'long' – while each of these examples may be contentious, the existence of the general category should not be). Unlike pronouns, these words have some conceptual content. As with pronouns, their semantic contribution *must* be contextually specified for the associated utterance to have a truth-value. For instance, 'this is my book' may be true if 'my book' is interpreted as meaning *the book I am thinking of*, and false if it means *the book I wrote* (and since there are indefinitely many possible interpretations, finding the right one involves more than merely disambiguation). Similarly, whether 'the school is near the house' is true or false depends on a contextually specified criterion or scale; and so on. We believe that pro-concepts are quite common, but the argument of this chapter does not depend on that assumption (or even on the existence of pro-concepts). What we will argue is that, quite commonly, all words behave *as if* they encoded pro-concepts: that is, whether or not a word encodes a full concept, the concept it is used to convey in a given utterance has to be contextually worked out.

Some concepts have no corresponding word, and can be encoded only by a phrase. For instance, it is arguable that most of us have a non-lexicalised concept of *uncle-or-aunt*. We have many beliefs and expectations about uncles-or-aunts (i.e. siblings of parents, and, by extension, their spouses). It makes sense to assume that these beliefs and expectations are mentally stored together in a non-lexicalised mental concept, which has the lexicalised concepts of *uncle* and *aunt* as sub-categories. Similarly, people who do not have the word 'sibling' in their public lexicon (or speakers of French, where no such word exists) may nonetheless have the concept of *sibling* characterised as child of same parents, and object of many beliefs and expectations, a concept which has *brother* and *sister* as sub-categories. So it seems plausible that not all words map onto concepts, nor all concepts onto words.

The phenomenon of polysemy is worth considering here. Suppose Mary says to Peter:

(1)   Open the bottle.

In most situations, she would be understood as asking him to uncork or uncap the bottle. One way of accounting for this would be to suggest that the general meaning of the verb 'open' gets specified by the properties of its direct object: thus, opening a corked bottle means uncorking it, and so on. However, this cannot be the whole story. Uncorking a bottle may be the standard way of opening it, but another way is to saw off the bottom, and on some occasion, this might be what Mary was asking Peter to do. Or suppose Mary says to Peter:

(2)   Open the washing machine.

In most situations, she will probably be asking him to open the lid of the machine. However, if Peter is a plumber, she might be asking him to unscrew the back; in other situations, she might be asking him to blow the machine open, or whatever.

The general point of these examples is that a word like 'open' can be used to convey indefinitely many concepts. It is impossible for all of these to be listed in the lexicon. Nor can they be generated at a purely linguistic level by taking the linguistic context, and in particular the direct object, into account. It seems reasonable to conclude that a word like 'open' is often used to convey a concept that is encoded neither by the word itself nor by the verb phrase 'open X' (For discussion of similar examples from alternative perspectives, see Caramazza and Grober 1976; Lyons 1977; Searle 1980, 1983; Lehrer 1990; Pinkal 1995; Pustejovsky 1995; Fodor and Lepore 1996; Pustejovsky and Boguraev 1996.)

So far, we have argued that there are words which do not encode concepts and concepts which are not encoded by words. More trivially, the existence of synonyms (e.g. 'snake' and 'serpent') shows that several words may correspond to a single concept, and the existence of homonyms (e.g. 'cat' or 'bank') shows that several concepts may correspond to a single word. So the mapping between concepts and words is neither exhaustive nor one-to-one.

Although the mapping between words and concepts is imperfect, it is not haphazard. Here are three contrasting claims about what this imperfect mapping might be like:

(3)   Nearly all individual concepts are lexicalised, but many words encode complex conceptual structures rather than individual concepts. So there are fewer concepts than words, and the mapping is partial mostly because many words do not map onto individual concepts.

(4)   Genuine synonyms, genuine homonyms, non-lexicalised concepts and words that do not encode concepts are all relatively rare, so there is roughly a one-to-one mapping between words and concepts.

(5)   The mapping is partial, and the main reason for this is that only a fraction of the conceptual repertoire is lexicalised. Most mental concepts do not map onto words.

In the *Language of Thought* (1975), Jerry Fodor famously argued against (3) and in favour of (4). According to the version of claim (3) he criticised, words correspond in the mind to definitions couched in terms of a relatively compact repertoire of primitive concepts: for example, the word 'bachelor' might have as its conceptual counterpart the complex mental expression *unmarried man*; the word 'kill' might have as its conceptual counterpart the complex mental expression *cause to die*, and so on. Many words – perhaps most – would be abbreviations for complex conceptual expressions, rather than encoding individual concepts. Against this view, Fodor argued that most words have no plausible definitions and must therefore correspond to mental primitives. There are psycholinguistic reasons for thinking that even a word like 'bachelor', which seems to have a definition, is best treated as encoding a single concept *bachelor*, which would itself be a (mental rather than public) abbreviation for a complex mental expression (Fodor 1975: 152).

As Fodor points out, verbal comprehension is fast, and unaffected by the alleged semantic complexity of lexical items. 'Kill' is no harder to process than 'die', and 'bachelor' is no harder than 'unmarried', even though it might be argued that the meaning of 'die' is included in the meaning of 'kill', and the meaning of 'unmarried' is included in meaning of 'bachelor'. All this suggests to Fodor that the structure of mental messages is very close to that of the public sentences standardly used to communicate them. 'It may be that the resources of the inner code are rather directly represented in the resources we use for communication' (Fodor 1975: 156).

Fodor's argument against (3), combined with a rather traditional view of linguistic communication, seems to weigh in favour of (4). Fodor does, as he says himself, view language 'the good old way':

A speaker is, above all, someone with something he intends to communicate. For want of a better term, I shall call what he has in mind a message. If he is to communicate by using a language, his problem is to construct a wave form which is a token of the (or a) type standardly used for expressing that message in that language

(Fodor 1975: 106)

Here, Fodor is adopting an updated version of what we have called the code theory of verbal communication (Sperber and Wilson 1986/1995). The classical code theory was based on the following assumptions:

(6)   For every thought that can be linguistically communicated, there is a sentence identical to it in content.

(7)   The communication of a thought is achieved by uttering a sentence identical to it in content.

Assumption (7) is clearly too strong. Sentences with pronouns are obvious counter-examples: they are used to communicate different thoughts on different occasions, and are not identical in content to any of these thoughts.

The updated code theory accepts (6), but rejects (7) in favour of the weaker assumption (8):

(8)   The communication of any thought *can be* achieved by uttering a sentence identical to it in content.

For the classical code theory, the only way to communicate thoughts is to encode them. For the updated code theory, this is still the basic way, but there are also inferential short-cuts. The updated theory admits that the basic coding-decoding process can be speeded up, supplemented, or even by-passed by use of contextually informed inferential routines. Though full encoding is possible, the theory goes, it is often unnecessary. By exploiting shared contextual information and inferential abilities, communication can succeed even when a name or description is replaced by a pronoun, a phrase is ellipsed, or a whole thought is indirectly suggested rather than directly encoded.

Still, on both classical and updated versions of the code theory, the semantic resources of a language must be rich enough to encode all communicable thoughts. Every concept that can be communicated must be linguistically encodable. There may be a few non-lexicalised concepts (e.g. *uncle-or-aunt*) which are encodable only by a phrase; but it is reasonable to think that, in general, the recurrent use of a concept in communication would favour the introduction and stabilisation of a corresponding word in the public language.

Because Fodor uncritically accepts the code theory of communication, and because he does not even consider claim (5), let alone argue against it, his excellent arguments against claim (3) do not unequivocally point to the conclusion in (4). Claim (5) might still be correct. We want to argue that it is, and hence that most mental concepts do not map onto words.

There are two interpretations of claim (5) on which it would be trivially true, or at least easily acceptable. First, it is clear that the number of perceptual stimuli that humans can discriminate is vastly greater than the number of words available to name them: for instance, it has been claimed that we can discriminate anything up to millions of colours, while English has a colour vocabulary of a few hundred non-synonymous terms, only a dozen of which are in frequent use (Hardin 1988: 182–3). If we have a concept for every colour that we can discriminate (or even for every colour that we have had the opportunity to discriminate), it is clear that we have many more concepts than words. However, a discrimination is not the same as a conceptualisation of the items discriminated. Someone may discriminate two shades of vermilion, and even think, *here are two shades of vermilion*, without forming a distinct mental structure, let alone a stable one, for each of these two shades.

A concept, as we understand the term, is an enduring elementary mental structure, which is capable of playing different discriminatory or inferential roles on different occasions in an individual's mental life. We are not considering ephemeral representations of particulars (e.g. an individual tree, an individual person, a particular taste), attended to for a brief moment and then forgotten. Nor are we considering complex conceptual structures, built from more elementary mental concepts, which correspond to phrases rather than words, and are not stored in long-term memory. Even so, it might be argued that people do form many idiosyncratic, non-lexicalised concepts on the basis of private and unshareable experience. For example, you may have a proper concept of a certain kind of pain, or a certain kind of smell, which allows you to recognise new occurrences, and draw inferences on the basis of this recognition, even though you cannot linguistically express this concept, or bring others to grasp and share it. More generally, it is arguable that each of us has ineffable concepts – perhaps a great many of them. This would again make claim (5) trivially true.

We will return to this point later, and argue that effability is a matter of degree. For the time being, we will restrict ourselves to effable concepts: concepts that can be part of the content of a communicable thought. We want to argue that, even on this interpretation, claim (5) is true: there are a great many *stable* and *effable* mental concepts that do not map onto words.

3 Inference and relevance

The alternative to a code theory of verbal communication is an inferential theory. The basic idea for this comes from the work of Paul Grice (1989); we have developed such a theory in detail in our book *Relevance: Communication and cognition* (1986/95). According to the inferential theory, all a communicator has to do in order to convey a thought is to give her audience appropriate evidence of her intention to convey it. More generally, a mental state may be revealed by a behaviour (or by the trace a behaviour leaves in the environment). Behaviour capable of revealing the content of a mental state may also succeed in *communicating* this content to an audience. For this to happen, it must be used ostensively: that is, it must be displayed so as to make manifest an intention to inform the audience of this content.

Peter asks Mary if she wants to go to the cinema. Mary half-closes her eyes and mimes a yawn. This is a piece of ostensive behaviour. Peter recognises it as such and infers, non-demonstratively, that Mary is tired, that she wants to rest, and that she therefore does not want to go to the cinema. Mary has communicated a refusal to go to the cinema, and a reason for this refusal, by giving Peter some evidence of her thoughts. The evidence was her mimed yawning, which she could expect to activate in Peter's mind the idea of her being tired. The ostensive nature of her behaviour could be expected to suggest to Peter that she *intended* to activate this idea in his mind. Mary thought that the idea activated, and the manifestly intentional nature of its activation, would act as the starting point for an inferential process that would lead to the discovery of her meaning. She might have achieved roughly the same effect by saying 'I'm tired.' This would also have automatically activated the idea of her being tired (this time by linguistic decoding). It would have done so in a manifestly intentional way, thus providing Peter with strong evidence of Mary's full meaning.

In general, inferential communication involves a communicator ostensively engaging in some behaviour (e.g. a piece of miming or the production of a coded signal) likely to activate in the addressee (via recognition or decoding) some specific conceptual structure or idea. The addressee takes this deliberately induced effect, together with contextual information, as the starting point for an inferential process which should lead to the discovery of the message (in the sense of proposition plus propositional attitude) that the communicator intended to convey.

The idea activated and the message inferred are normally very different. The idea is merely a trigger for discovery of the message. Often, the triggering idea is a fragment, or an incomplete schematic version, of the message to be communicated. The inferential process then consists in complementing or fleshing out the triggering idea.

It is possible, at least in principle, for the idea activated by the communicator's behaviour to consist of a proposition and a propositional attitude (i.e. a full thought) which is just the message she intended to convey. In this limiting case, the inferential process will simply amount to realising that this is all the communicator meant. The classical code theory treats this limiting case as the only one. Every act of communication is seen as involving the production of a coded signal (e.g. a token of a sentence) which encodes exactly the intended message. No inferential process is needed. The sentence meaning (or, more generally, the signal meaning) is supposed to be identical to the speaker's meaning. The updated code theory treats this limiting case as the basic and paradigmatic one. Hearers should assume by default that the sentence meaning is the speaker's message, but be prepared to revise this assumption on the basis of linguistic evidence (the sentence does not encode a full message) or contextual evidence (the speaker could not plausibly have meant what the sentence means).

Since the classical code theory is patently wrong, the updated code theory might seem more attractive. However, the classical theory had the advantage of offering a simple, powerful and self-contained account of how communication is possible at all. The updated theory loses this advantage by invoking an inferential mechanism to explain how more can be communicated than is actually encoded. The updated theory offers two distinct mechanisms – coding-decoding and inference – which may be singly or jointly invoked to explain how a given message is communicated. Why should the first of these be fundamental and necessary to human linguistic communication, while the second is peripheral and dispensable? The classical theory, which treats coding-decoding as the *only* explanation of communication, entails as a core theoretical claim that every communicable message is fully encodable. In the updated theory, this is a contingent empirical claim, with little empirical support and no explanatory purchase.

What is the role of inference in communication? Is it merely to provide short-cuts along the normal paths of coding-decoding (in which case any inferentially communicated message could have been fully encoded)? Or does inference open up new paths, to otherwise inaccessible end-points, making it possible to communicate meanings that were not linguistically encodable? (By 'not linguistically encodable' we mean not encodable in the public language actually being used, rather than not encodable in any possible language.) In the absence of any plausible account of the inferential processes involved in comprehension, the reasonable, conservative option might be to assume that inference does not enrich the repertoire of communicable meanings. For example, if all we had to go on was Grice's ground-breaking but very sketchy original account (in his 1967 William James lectures, reprinted in Grice 1989), we would have very little idea of how inferential comprehension processes actually work, how powerful they are, and whether and how they might extend the range of communicable concepts.

Relevance theory (Sperber and Wilson 1986/95; see also references therein) offers a more explicit account of comprehension processes, which claims that what can be communicated goes well beyond what can be encoded. Here, we will give a brief, intuitive outline of relevant aspects of the theory.

The basic ideas of the theory are contained in a definition of relevance and two principles. Relevance is defined as a property of inputs to cognitive processes. The processing of an input (e.g. an utterance) may yield some cognitive effects (e.g. revisions of beliefs). Everything else being equal, the greater the effects, the greater the relevance of the input. The processing of the input (and the derivation of these effects) involves some cognitive effort. Everything else being equal, the greater the effort, the lower the relevance. On the basis of this definition, two principles are proposed:

(9)   *Cognitive principle of relevance*: Human cognition tends to be geared to the maximisation of relevance.

(10)   *Communicative principle of relevance*: Every act of ostensive communication communicates a presumption of its own relevance.

More specifically, we claim that the speaker, by the very act of addressing someone, communicates that her utterance is the most relevant one compatible with her abilities and preferences, and is at least relevant enough to be worth his processing effort.

As noted above, ostensive behaviour automatically activates in the addressee some conceptual structure or idea: for example, the automatic decoding of an utterance leads to the construction of a logical form. This initial step in the comprehension process involves some cognitive effort. According to the communicative principle of relevance, the effort required gives some indication of the effect to expect. The effect should be enough to justify the effort (or at least enough for it to have seemed to the speaker that it would seem to the hearer to justify the effort – but we will ignore this qualification, which plays a role only when the speaker deliberately or accidentally fails to provide the hearer with sufficiently relevant information; see Sperber 1994).

4 Relevance and meaning

The communicative principle of relevance provides the motivation for the following comprehension procedure, which we claim is automatically applied to the on-line processing of attended verbal inputs. The hearer takes the conceptual structure constructed by linguistic decoding; following a path of least effort, he enriches this at the explicit level and complements it at the implicit level, until the resulting interpretation meets his expectations of relevance; at which point, he stops.

We will illustrate this procedure by considering the interpretation of Mary's utterance in (11):

(11)   *Peter*: Do you want to go to the cinema?
       Mary: I'm tired.

Let's assume (though we will soon qualify this) that Peter decodes Mary's utterance as asserting that Mary is tired. By itself, the information that Mary is tired does not answer Peter's question. However, he is justified in trying to use it to draw inferences that would answer his question and thus satisfy his expectations of relevance. If the first assumption to occur to him is that Mary's being tired is a good enough reason for her not to want to go to the cinema, he will assume she meant him to use this assumption as an implicit premise and derive the implicit conclusion that she doesn't want to go to the cinema because she is tired. Peter's interpretation of Mary's utterance contains the following assumptions:

(12)   (a)   Mary is tired
       (b)   Mary's being tired is a sufficient reason for her not to want to go to the cinema
       (c)   Mary doesn't to want to go to the cinema because she is tired.

Mary could have answered Peter's question directly by telling him she didn't want to go to the cinema. Notice, though, that the extra (inferential) effort required by her indirect reply is offset by extra effect: she conveys not just a refusal to go, but a reason for this refusal. There may, of course, be many other conclusions that Peter could derive from her utterance, for example those in (13):

(13) (a) Mary had a busy day
      (b) Mary wouldn't want to do a series of press-ups.

But even if these conclusions were highly relevant to Peter, they would not help to satisfy the specific expectations of relevance created by Mary's utterance. The fact that she was replying to his question made it reasonable for him to expect the kind and degree of relevance that he himself had suggested he was looking for by asking this question, and no more.

However, there is a problem. How plausible is it that the fact that Mary is tired is a good enough reason for her not to want to go to the cinema? Why should Peter accept this as an implicit premise of her utterance? Does Mary never want to go to the cinema when she is tired, even if she is just a little tired, tired enough for it not to be false to say that she is strictly speaking tired? Surely, in these or other circumstances, Peter might have been aware that Mary was somewhat tired, without treating it as evidence that she didn't want to go to the cinema.

As noted above, a hearer using the relevance-theoretic comprehension procedure should follow a path of least effort, enriching and complementing the decoded conceptual structure until the resulting interpretation meets his expectations of relevance. We have shown how this procedure would apply to Mary's utterance in (11) to yield the implicatures (12b) and (12c). This is a case where the explicit content is complemented at the implicit level. However, for this complementation to make sense, some enrichment must also take place at the level of what is explicitly communicated.

If comprehension is to be treated as a properly inferential process, the inferences must be sound (in a sense that applies to non-demonstrative inference). From the mere fact that Mary is tired, Peter cannot soundly infer that she doesn't want to go to the cinema. For the implicatures (12b) and (12c) to be soundly derived, Mary must be understood as saying something stronger than that she is tired *tout court*: her meaning must be enriched to the point where it warrants the intended inferences. The process is one of parallel adjustment: expectations of relevance warrant the derivation of specific implicatures, for which the explicit content must be adequately enriched.

Mary is therefore conveying something more than simply the proposition that she is tired, which would be satisfied by whatever is the minimal degree of tiredness: she is conveying that she is tired enough not to want to go to the cinema. If she were 'technically' tired, but not tired enough for it to matter, her utterance would be misleading, not just by suggesting a wrong reason for her not wanting to go to the cinema, but also by giving a wrong indication of her degree of tiredness. Suppose Peter thought that she was being disingenuous in using her tiredness as an excuse for not going to the cinema. He might answer:

(14) Come on, you're not *that* tired!

He would not be denying that she is tired: merely that she is tired to the degree conveyed by her utterance.

How tired is that? Well, there is no absolute scale of tiredness (and if there were, no specific value would be indicated here). Mary is communicating that she is tired enough for it to be reasonable for her not to want to go to the cinema on that occasion. This is an ad hoc, circumstantial notion of tiredness. It is the degree of tiredness that has this consequence.

In saying (11), Mary thus communicates a notion more specific than the one encoded by the English word 'tired'. This notion is not lexicalised in English. It may be that Mary will never find another use for it, in which case it will not have the kind of stability in her mental life that we took to be a condition for mental concepthood. Alternatively, she may recognise this particular sort of tiredness, and have a permanent mental 'entry' or 'file' for it, in which case it is a proper concept. In the same way, Peter's grasp of the notion of tiredness Mary is invoking may be ephemeral, or he may recognise it as something that applies to Mary, and perhaps others, on different occasions, in which case he has the concept too.

It might be argued that the word 'tired' in Mary's utterance, when properly enriched, just means *too tired to want to go to the cinema*. This is a meaning which is perfectly encodable in English, even though it is not lexicalised. Suppose this were so, and that Mary has a stable concept of this kind of tiredness: her utterance would still illustrate our point that there may be many non-lexicalised mental concepts. The fact that this concept is encodable by a complex phrase would be no reason to think Mary does not have it as an elementary concept, any more than the fact that 'bachelor' can be defined is any reason to think we have no elementary mental concept of *bachelor*.

In any case, it is unlikely that Mary's answer in (11) is really synonymous with her answer in (15):

(15) *Peter*: Do you want to go to the cinema?
      Mary: I'm too tired to want to go to the cinema.

Mary's answer in (11) has a degree of indeterminacy that is lost in (15). Quite apart from this, the apparent paraphrasability of her answer in (11) is linked to the fact that she is answering a yes-no question, which drastically narrows down the range of potential implicatures and the enrichment needed to warrant them. Yet the enrichment mechanism is itself quite general, and applies in contexts where the range of implicatures is much vaguer, as we will show with two further examples.

Imagine that Peter and Mary, on holiday in Italy, are visiting a museum. Mary says:

(16) *Mary*: I'm tired!

As before, if her utterance is to be relevant to Peter, she must mean more than just that she is strictly speaking tired. This time, though, the implications that might make her utterance relevant are only loosely suggested. They might include:

(17) (a) Mary's enjoyment of this visit is diminishing.
      (b) Mary would like to cut short their visit to the museum.
      (c) Mary is encouraging Peter to admit that he is also tired and wants to cut short the visit.
      (d) Mary would like them to go back to their hotel after this visit to the museum, rather than visiting the Duomo, as they had planned.

If these and other such conclusions are implicatures of her utterance, they are only weak implicatures: implications that Peter is encouraged to derive and accept, but for which he has to take some of the responsibility himself (for the notion of 'weak implicature', see Sperber and Wilson 1986/95: Chapter 4). Whatever implicatures he ends up treating as intended (or suggested) by Mary, he will have to adjust his understanding of her explicit meaning so as to warrant their derivation. Mary will be understood as having conveyed that she is tired to such a degree or in such a way as to warrant the derivation of these implicatures. This overall interpretation is itself justified by the expectation of relevance created by Mary's utterance (i.e. by this particular instantiation of the communicative principle of relevance).

That evening, at a trattoria, Mary says to Peter:

(18)   I love Italian food!

She does not, of course, mean that she loves all Italian food, nor does she merely mean that there is some Italian food she loves. So what does she mean? It is often suggested that in a case like this, the expression 'Italian food' denotes a prototype, here *prototypical Italian food*. This presupposes that there is a readily available and relatively context-independent prototype. In the situation described above, it so happens that Mary is a vegetarian. Moreover, her understanding of Italian food is largely based on what she finds in an 'Italian' vegetarian restaurant in her own country where she sometimes goes with Peter, which serves several dishes such as 'tofu pizza' that are definitely not Italian. Mary's utterance achieves relevance for Peter by implicating that she is enjoying her food, and sees it as belonging to a distinct category which the expression 'Italian food' suggests but does not describe.

Even if Mary's use of the term 'Italian food' were less idiosyncratic, it would not follow that all Peter has to do to understand it is recover a prototype. Much recent research has cast doubt on the view that word meanings can be analysed in terms of context-independent prototypes, and suggests instead that ad hoc meanings are constructed in context (see e.g. Barsalou 1987; Franks and Braisby 1990; Franks 1995; Butler 1995). We would add that this contextual construction is a by-product of the relevance-guided comprehension process. The explicit content of an utterance, and in particular the meaning of specific expressions, is adjusted so as to warrant the derivation of implicatures which themselves justify the expectations of relevance created by the utterance act. These occasional meanings may stabilise into concepts, for the speaker, the hearer, or both.

These examples are designed to show how a word which encodes a given concept can be used to convey (as a component of a speaker's meaning) another concept that neither it nor any other expression in the language actually encodes. There is nothing exceptional about such uses: almost any word can be used in this way. Quite generally, the occurrence of a word in an utterance provides a piece of evidence, a pointer to a concept involved in the speaker's meaning. It may so happen that the intended concept is the very one encoded by the word, which is therefore used in its strictly literal sense. However, we would argue that this is no more than a possibility, not a preferred or default interpretation. Any interpretation, whether literal or not, results from mutual adjustment of the explicit and implicit content of the utterance. This adjustment process stabilises when the hypothesised implicit content is warranted by the hypothesised explicit content together with the context, and when the overall interpretation is warranted by (the particular instantiation of) the communicative principle of relevance.

This approach sheds some light on the phenomenon of polysemy illustrated by the example of 'open' above. A verb like 'open' acts as a pointer to indefinitely many notions or concepts. In some cases, the intended concept is jointly indicated by the verb and its direct object (as with the ordinary sense of 'open the washing machine'), so that the inferential route is short and obvious. There may be cases where such routinely reachable senses become lexicalised.

In general, though, polysemy is the outcome of a pragmatic process whereby intended senses are inferred on the basis of encoded concepts and contextual information. These inferred senses may be ephemeral notions or stable concepts; they may be shared by few or many speakers, or by whole communities; the inference pattern may be a first-time affair or a routine pattern – and it may be a first-time affair for one interlocutor and a routine affair for another, who, despite these differences, manage to communicate successfully. (For relevance-theoretic accounts of polysemy, see Carston 1996, 1998; Deane 1988; Groefsema 1995; Papafragou 1998b; Wilson and Sperber 1998.)

5 Implications

Our argument so far has been that, given the inferential nature of comprehension, the words in a language can be used to convey not only the concepts they encode, but also indefinitely many other related concepts to which they might point in a given context. We see this not as a mere theoretical possibility, but as a universal practice, suggesting that there are many times more concepts in our minds than words in our language.

Despite their different theoretical perspectives, many other researchers in philosophy, psychology and linguistics have converged on the idea that new senses are constantly being constructed in context (e.g. Franks and Braisby 1990; Goshke and Koppelberg 1992; Barsalou 1987; Gibbs 1994; Franks 1995; Recanati 1995; Nunberg 1996; Carston 1996, 1998). However, it is possible to believe that new senses can be contextually constructed, without accepting that there are more mental concepts than public words.

Someone might argue, for example, that the only stable concepts are linguistically encodable ones. Unless a new sense constructed in context is linguistically encodable, it cannot be a stable concept of the speaker's, and will never stabilise as a mental concept in the hearer. When Mary says at the museum that she is tired, the understanding that she and Peter have of her kind and degree of tiredness cannot be divorced from their understanding of the whole situation. They do not construct or use an ad hoc concept of tiredness. Rather, they have a global representation of the situation, which gives its particular contextual import to the ordinary concept of tiredness.

We would reply as follows. We do not deny – indeed, we insist – that most occasional representations of a property (or an object, event or state) do not stabilise into a concept. Most contextually represented properties are not recognised as having been previously encountered, and are not remembered when the situation in which they were represented is itself forgotten. However, some properties are recognised and/or remembered even when many or all of the contextual elements of their initial identification are lost. For example, you look at your friend and recognise the symptoms of a mood for which you have no word, which you might be unable to describe exactly, and whose previous occurrences you only dimly remember; but you know that mood, and you know how it is likely to affect her and you. Similarly, you look at the landscape and the sky, and you recognise the weather, you know how it will feel, but you have no word for it. Or you feel a pain, you recognise it and know what to expect, but have no word for it; and so on. You are capable not just of recognising these phenomena but also of anticipating them, imagining them, regretting or rejoicing that they are not actual. You can communicate thoughts about them to interlocutors who are capable of recognising them, if not spontaneously, at least with the help of your communication. Your ability to recognise and think about the mood, the weather, the pain, is evidence that you have a corresponding stable mental file or entry, i.e. a mental concept. The evidence is not, of course, conclusive, and there could be a better hypothesis. However the suggestion that what has been contextually grasped can only be remembered with all the relevant particulars of the initial context is not that better hypothesis.

There is a more general reason for believing that we have many more concepts than words. The stabilisation of a word in a language is a social and historical affair. It is a slow and relatively rare process, involving co-ordination among many individuals over time. A plausible guess is that, in most relatively homogenous speech communities in human history, less than a dozen new words (including homonyms of older words and excluding proper names) would stabilise in a year. On the other hand, the addition of new concepts to an individual's mind is comparatively unconstrained. It is not a matter of co-ordinating with others, but of internal memory management. There is no question that we are capable of acquiring a huge amount of new information every day. Do we store it all in pre-existing files, or do we sometimes – perhaps a few times a day – open a new file, i.e. stabilise a new concept? Notice that this would not involve adding extra information to long term memory but merely organising information that we are going to add anyhow in a different, and arguably more efficient way.

Information filed together tends to be accessed together, and efficient memory management involves not only filing together what is generally best accessed together, but also filing separately what is generally best accessed separately. Thus, you may be able to recognise a certain type of food (which the public linguistic expression 'Italian food' may hint at in an appropriate context but does not describe), and this ability may play a role in your mental life: say in deciding what to eat or cook on a given occasion. Where is information about this kind of food stored in your memory? Does it have its own address, or does it have to be reassembled from information filed elsewhere every time it is used?

How and how often we open new files, and thus stabilise new mental concepts, is an empirical question, to be investigated with the methods of psychology. However, the hypothesis that we can open a new file only when we have a public word that corresponds to it is a costly one, with no obvious merit. It amounts to imposing an arbitrary and counter-productive constraint on memory management. (This is not, of course, to deny the converse point that on encountering a new word you may stabilise a new concept, and that many of our concepts originate partly or wholly from linguistic communication – a point for which there is much evidence, in particular developmental, e.g. Gelman and Markman 1986.)

While the kind of collective co-ordination needed to stabilise a word in a speech community is an elaborate affair, the typically pairwise co-ordination involved in any given communicative act is a relatively simpler achievement – the kind of achievement that a pragmatic theory such as relevance theory aims to explain. This co-ordination may be somewhat loose. When Mary says at the museum that she is tired, her utterance gets its explicit meaning through adjustment to a set of weak implicatures: that is, implicatures whose exact content is not wholly determined by the utterance. The ad hoc concept of tiredness that Peter constructs (i.e. the concept of tiredness which warrants the derivation of these weak implicatures) is unlikely to be exactly the same as the one Mary had in mind (since she did not foresee or intend exactly these implicatures). This is not a failure of communication. It is an illusion of the code theory that communication aims at duplication of meanings. Sometime it does, but quite ordinarily a looser kind of understanding is intended and achieved. The type of co-ordination aimed at in most verbal exchanges is best compared to the co-ordination between people taking a stroll together rather than to that between people marching in step.

Returning to the question of effability, we would maintain that this is a matter of degree. Some concepts are properly shared, and can be unequivocally expressed: a mathematical discussion would provide good examples. Other concepts are idiosyncratic, but as a result of common experience or communication, are close enough to the idiosyncratic concepts of others to play a role in the co-ordination of behaviour. Still other concepts may be too idiosyncratic to be even loosely communicated. The fact that a public word exists, and is successfully used in communication, does not make it safe to assume that it encodes the same concept for all successful users; and in any case, the concept communicated will only occasionally be the same as the one encoded. Communication can succeed, despite possible semantic discrepancies, as long as the word used in a given situation points the hearer in the direction intended by the speaker. Thus, Peter and Mary might differ as to the exact extension of 'tired': Peter might regard as genuine though minimal tiredness a state that Mary would not regard as tiredness at all. Mary's successful use of the term in no way depends on their meaning exactly the same thing by it. Similarly, their concepts of Italy might pick out different entities in space or time (for example, is Ancient Roman History part of Italian History? That depends on what you mean by 'Italy'). Mary's successful use of the term 'Italian' should be unaffected by these discrepancies.

More generally, it does not much matter whether or not a word linguistically encodes a fullfledged concept, and, if so, whether it encodes the same concept for both speaker and hearer. Even if it does, comprehension is not guaranteed. Even if it does not, comprehension need not be impaired. Whether they encode concepts or pro-concepts, words are used as pointers to contextually intended senses. Utterances are merely pieces of evidence of the speaker's intention, and this has far-reaching implications, a few of which we have tried to outline here.

■ ■ ■

POST-READING

1   Do you agree that 'all words behave *as if* they encoded pro-concepts'?
2   Do you think that 'inference open[s] up new paths, to otherwise inaccessible end-points, making it possible to communicate meanings that were not linguistically encodable'?
3   Do you incline to the prototype view of the meaning of a superordinate category term such as *food*, or are you persuaded that the ad hoc position makes more sense?

SECTION 3 FURTHER READING

Neo-Gricean pragmatics

The place to begin is with Horn's paper:

Horn, L.R. (1984) 'Toward a new taxonomy for pragmatic inference: Q-based and R-based implicature', in D. Shiffrin (ed.) *Meaning, Form, and Use in Context*, Washington, District of Columbia: Georgetown University Press.

Given that the first reading represents only a tiny part of a very important book, you might want to read the entire monograph:

Levinson, S.C. (2000a) *Presumptive Meanings*, Cambridge, Massachusetts: The MIT Press.

Alternatively, the essential arguments, but without the rich array of supporting data, can be found in a more condensed form in:

Levinson, S.C. (1995) 'Three levels of meaning', in F. Palmer (ed.) *Grammar and Meaning*, pp. 90–115, Cambridge: Cambridge University Press.

Lexical pragmatics

For an early paper which shows how Blutner moves from Lexical Semantics to Lexical Pragmatics and which refers extensively to Gricean and neoGricean pragmatics, read:

Blutner, R. (1998) 'Lexical pragmatics', *Journal of Semantics* 15: 115–62.

For elaborations of the OT approach to lexical pragmatics and the formulation of constraints, including some challenging reading, read:

Blutner, R. and Zeevat, H. (eds) (2004) *Optimality Theory and Pragmatics*, Basingstoke: Palgrave/Macmillan (especially the editors' introduction and papers by Mattausch, Beaver and Lee, and van Rooy).

For an attempt at bridging gaps with relevance theory, read:

Blutner, R. (2007a) 'Optimality theoretic pragmatics and the explicature/implicature distinction', in N. Burton-Roberts (ed.) *Pragmatics*, pp. 67–89, Basingstoke: Palgrave.

For a useful, recent discussion of lexical pragmatics in the relevance theoretic framework, read:

Wilson, D. and Carston, R. (2007) 'A unitary approach to lexical pragmatics: relevance, inference and ad hoc concepts', in N. Burton-Roberts (ed.) *Pragmatics*, pp. 203–59, Basingstoke: Palgrave Macmillan.

Relevance theory

Many of the principles of relevance theory are discussed in Wilson and Sperber's earlier paper:

Wilson, D. and Sperber, D. (1981) 'On Grice's theory of conversational implicature', in P. Werth (ed.) *Conversation and Discourse*, pp. 155–78, London: Croom Helm. Reprinted in A. Kasher (ed.) (1998) *Pragmatics: Critical Concepts* Vol.II, London: Routledge.

The full theory was published in:

Sperber, D. and Wilson, D. (1986) *Relevance: Communication and Cognition*. Oxford: Blackwell.

A second edition of *Relevance: Communication and Cognition* appeared in 1995 containing the original 254-page text of the 1986 edition together with a 25-page 'postface' proposing a number of changes in the theory.

Deirdre Wilson's entry in *The Pragmatics Encyclopedia* provides a concise, up-to-date summary of the essential principles of Relevance Theory and the various fields in which it has been applied:

'Relevance Theory', in L. Cummings (ed.) (2010a) *The Pragmatics Encyclopedia*, pp. 393–8, London: Routledge.

Given that the reading from *Thoughts and Utterances* represents only a tiny part of a very important book, you might want to read the entire monograph. If you can't read all of it, at least read Chapter 1, which locates pragmatics in what Chomskyans would call a Knowledge of Language framework:

Carston, R. (2002a) *Thoughts and Utterances*, Oxford: Blackwell Publishing.

For the place of relevance theory in cognitive science, read:

Sperber, D. and Wilson, D. (2002) 'Pragmatics, modularity and mindreading', *Mind and Language* 17, 2–23.

Over the years, many important, relevance theoretic articles have been published in *Lingua*, including those in three special editions, 87/1–2 (1990), 90/1–2 (1993) and 116/10 (2006).

SECTION 4

Indexicality

Introduction

ANYONE WHO READS ACADEMIC BOOKS knows that an *index* is prepared by the writer and contains entries that point the reader to places in a text where something (hopefully something worth knowing) can be identified. Peirce was the first to use the term *indexical* to describe linguistic items which similarly point the addressee to aspects of the utterance context in search of an intended referent. This is how Hookway explains *index* and *indexical* in his entry under 'Peirce' in the *Oxford Companion to Philosophy*:

> an index denotes an object to which it stands in a direct existential relation: the conventions governing the use of ordinary indexical expressions such as 'this' do not fix the reference unaided but rather guide us in interpreting it as an index.
>
> (Hookway 1995: 650)

Pragmatic textbooks have tended to take a narrow view of indexicality, focusing principally on the closed-class items we call *deictics,* which retain a non-variable form but which point to different referents in different contexts of use. Two of the three papers reprinted in this section also focus on deictics. The third takes a broader view of the way 'indexical expressions guide us in interpreting'.

One thorny issue in the study of indexicality is the difficulty of separating the semantic or invariable meaning properties of deictics from their pragmatic or variable ones. As Verschueren puts it in one of the readings, 'even though a theoretical distinction can be made between those aspects of the meaningfulness of signs that are constant across different specific contexts and those that are connected with ongoing usage, they are hard to identify in practice'. Since human language is neither entirely symbolic on the one hand nor purely indexical on the other, as Rubba puts it in another of the readings, 'deictic semantics as well as pragmatic and cultural knowledge are intimately intertwined'.

It's probably because of the way in which indexicals have both semantic properties and pragmatic character and because they necessarily point to the context in which utterances occur that most Pragmatics textbooks that discuss deixis place that chapter before the chapters on speech acts, presupposition and implicature. You may be surprised, therefore, that we have not followed this tradition. From a historical, and, we think, methodological point of view, there are good reasons to begin, as we do here, with *Linguistic Pragmatics* and, in particular, the work of those linguistic philosophers like Austin and Grice who first shaped our discipline, and then to move on to the work of post-Gricean contemporary pragmaticians who develop the insights of these earlier linguistic philosophers. This means that it's only in this section, when we turn to indexicality, that we make the transition from theories of language usage, typically exemplified with invented examples or with examples abstracted from real contexts of use, to explanations of contextualized language. For example, when you read Verschueren's paper, you will see that he takes issue with the approach to the study of Pragmatics considered in the earlier sections of this Reader, and asserts that the 'proper domain of linguistic pragmatics' is 'usage phenomena'.

In choosing the three papers in this section, we have tried to be as representative as possible and to show ways in which the study of indexicality has developed. Thus, the first paper focuses principally on the utterance context as the default origo for deictic reference. The second paper focuses on discourse processing and in particular on how place deictics which index referents not present in the immediate spatial domain are interpreted. The final paper focuses on the role of indexicals as a metapragmatic means of guiding interpretation in an ideologically conditioned way.

Stephen Levinson's paper, 'Deixis', originally appeared in Horn and Ward's *The Handbook of Pragmatics* and is perhaps the most authoritative short account of the phenomenon of deixis, or 'linguistic expressions that require indexical resolution'. Apart from the opening paragraphs, Section 1 and one paragraph from Section 3, the paper is reprinted in full here.

In the reading, as it is reproduced here, Levinson first discusses indexicality as a link between a semantically impoverished sign and an object of reference, and then traces out some of the approaches to deixis explored by both semanticists and linguistic philosophers. He draws attention to the closed-class of 'pure deictics' such as *I*, whose meanings don't extend beyond that which they index, and to open-class expressions such as *today* which have an evident semantic content but which, like pure deictics, refer variously depending on the context of the utterance in which they occur. As well as setting out a taxonomy of the uses of demonstrative expressions, he also explores cross-linguistic variation in the realization of indexicality. Finally, he concludes that 'Indexicality probably played a crucial part in the evolution of language, prior to the full-scale recursive, symbolic system characteristic of modern human language.'

Jo Rubba's paper, 'Alternate grounds in the interpretation of deictic expressions', is about what is sometimes called 'decentering' – the use of deictics to index referents identified in relation to a ground which isn't immediate to the speaker or the addressee. In particular, Rubba is interested in how we are able to identify referents successfully in a situation where the relevant indexical ground does not coincide with the immediate location, current time and speaker reference point of the utterance. In order to resolve this problem, Rubba appeals to Fauconnier's mental space account of discourse processing. This allows us to model the viewpoint needed to render a deictic like *here* proximal to a location in a ground which we construct as a cognitive representation. Thus it's possible for the indexical ground constituted by immediate location, current time and speaker origo to be substituted by an alternate ground, a temporary knowledge-base constructed as a mental representation.

Rubba's paper is situated firmly in the cognitive linguistic tradition, not only in its appeal to mental space theory, but also in the way that what she calls 'utterance ground' is understood. The central tenet of Langacker's two-volume *Foundations of Cognitive Grammar* is the principle of *profiling*, according to which we conceptualize *figures* such as 'the beginning' in the phrase 'the beginning of term' against a *base*, in this case 'term'. This approach to conceptualization can be traced back to Rubin's (1915) pioneering work on figure and ground in visual perception, thus demonstrating the cognitive linguists' contention that our fundamental knowledge of language is a transparent reflection of our sentient experience of reality (rather than the product of the black-box or dedicated module-in-the-mind, as in generative linguistics). Thus, Rubba's view of indexicality as a figure/ground phenomenon appeals to the fundamental *gestalt* on which visual perception too is based.

One of the strengths of this paper is that the author makes many of the key concepts of cognitive linguistics accessible to readers unfamiliar with this approach. As well as explaining mental space theory and profiling, Rubba also shows how schemata (termed *Idealized Cognitive Models* or ICMs in the cognitive tradition) provide generalized grounds. This paper also makes a convincing case for the possibility of treating as a further alternate ground the enduring representations of encyclopedic knowledge that we store in ICMs, and store in ways that demonstrate our own orientation to such knowledge. In this way, Rubba significantly extends our understanding of the semantics of deixis.

In order to reduce the reading to an appropriate length, we have omitted the sections towards the end of the paper which deal with personal pronouns and in particular with the generic use of *you*. In its edited form, the reading therefore presents a coherent account from a cognitive linguistics perspective of how spatial deictics may be used to index phenomena not present in the here-and-now of the utterance event. To the extent that it helps to explain the absence in many utterances of prototypical deictic effects such as gesture, Rubba's is a truly important paper.

For Verschueren ('Notes on the role of metapragmatic awareness in language use'), deixis is an implicitly metalingual phenomenon in which an element in the code makes 'compulsory reference to the given message.' Understood properly, indexicality is a property not only of deictics but also of a very wide range of phenomena that index, guide or constrain the desired pragmatic interpretation of utterances and link code and message overtly. These include self-referential expressions and descriptions of talk activity, discourse markers and procedurals, sentence adverbs, hedges, and contextualization cues, as well as several other categories.

An important and persuasive argument in Verschueren's paper is that the traditional treatment of these items as discrete *objects* 'that happen to have language within their referential scope' and get tacked on to utterances to assist in their interpretation fails to recognize the role of indexicality in every utterance. For this reason, Verschueren encourages us to view indexicality as a *dimension* of language whose self-reflexive function is inevitable, pervasive and inescapably metapragmatic.

Verschueren works with naturally occurring data which are neither invented nor elicited but arise naturally and are made use of opportunistically. The different views of what constitute appropriate data for the study of pragmatics taken by the authors of the three papers in this section should prompt us to consider both what kind of pragmaticians we intend to be ourselves, and also how we view the relationship of data and theory.

Another theme that Verschueren explores is the inevitability of ideological mediation and our tendency to be least consciously aware of just this dimension of the language we use. He argues that identities are not given but constructed, a perspective also associated with the 'macro-micro debate' in Conversation Analysis and discussed earlier in the Introduction. In the way that he approaches context, Verschueren implicitly allies himself with the Scheglovian position that there are no distal or presumptive contexts since such contexts are made relevant only as proximal effects of talk (the 'micro' position). Again, we need to consider our own identity as pragmaticians as we make up our minds about where we stand in this debate: do our utterances reflect presumptive contexts or do we create contexts through our use of language?

In terms of disciplinary alignment, Verschueren makes reference to the work of Jakobson and, in particular, Silverstein, and distances himself from the work of Grice and Searle, which, for him, fails to recognize the importance of 'observable, situated linguistic practice'. This approach is later taken up trenchantly by Pressman and Briggs in Section 9, *Pragmaticians on Pragmatics*.

Verschueren's paper is reprinted in full here apart from the omission of the original abstract, one figure, a couple of consequential sentences, and three of the original footnotes. It's not until you have reached the mid-point in his paper that you come across the following observation, which we share with you now so as to put you on your guard as you read: 'finally, the entire stretch of discourse (and whatever follows it in this text) is about properties of language use, formulated at the metalevel of linguistic theory and analysis, and hence it is one long marker of metapragmatic awareness, abounding with categorizations, suggestions, claims, etc.'

STEPHEN C. LEVINSON

DEIXIS

PRE-READING

In a single sentence, write down the most essential information about deixis that you would want to convey to someone unfamiliar with the concept.

IN-READING

Before you start to read, make a photocopy of the quotations from Levinson's paper below, and then cut the copy into separate quotations following the dotted lines:

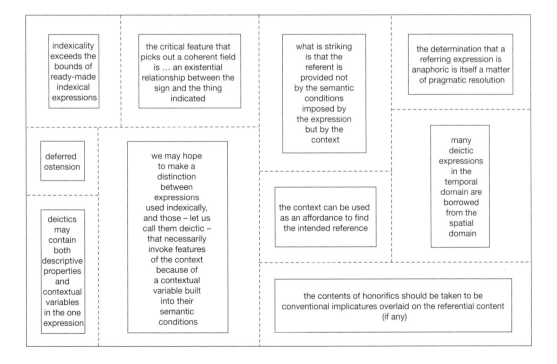

Make an A3 photocopy of the cityscape below. Alternatively, you can download a landscape or seascape from the internet and make an A3 copy of that.

↑

YOU ARE HERE

Now imagine yourself at the bottom the cityscape. The cityscape features that are close to you represent ideas that are clear; the features that are further away represent ideas that are less clear. As you read the paper, stop at each quotation, which you'll find marked with | and study the quotation and the surrounding text carefully, making sure that you understand the concept as fully as possible. Then take the relevant photocopied quotation and use glue to stick it on the cityscape – stick it close to you if you're confident that you fully understand the concept and further away if it's still relatively hazy. If you think it's a central concept in the theory of deixis, stick it directly in front of you, and if you think it's a peripheral concept, stick it to the left or right of centre. If you and one or more classmates are reading Levinson at the same time, we would encourage you to compare your cityscapes once you have completed the in-reading task.

■ ■ ■

DEIXIS
STEPHEN C. LEVINSON

[In Section 1 (which we omit), Levinson notes that, among animals, only human beings are able to communicate messages that are independent of the context in which they arise and that therefore lack an indexical dimension. This prompts him to ask whether 'in studying indexicality in natural languages we are studying archaic, perhaps primitive aspects of human communication' that might have preceded our ability to express symbolic meaning. He notes, however, that the apparently simple distinction between indexicality and symbolic meaning is blurred by the typicality of utterances that relate symbolic meaning to time, place and speaker.]

2 The challenge of indexicality

Deixis is the study of deictic or indexical expressions in language, like *you, now, today*. It can be regarded as a special kind of grammatical property instantiated in the familiar categories of person, tense, place, etc. In what follows, I adhere to this conservative division of the deictic field, because there is much to be said about how linguistic expressions build in properties for contextual resolution. But it is important to realize that the property of indexicality is not exhausted by the study of inherently indexical expressions. For just about any referring expression can be used deictically:

(3) *He* is my father (said of man entering the room)
(4) *Someone* is coming (said ear cocked to a slamming door)
(5) *The funny noise* is our antiquated dishwashing machine (said pointing chin to kitchen)
(6) What *a great picture*! (said looking at a picture).

For most such cases, some gesture or pointed gaze is required, and we may be tempted to think that a demonstration is the magic ingredient, as in the following cases where the demonstration replaces a linguistic expression:

(7) The editor's sign for "delete" is [followed by written demonstration]
(8) He is a bit [index finger to forehead, indicating "mad"].

But this is not a necessary feature:

(9) *The chairman* hereby resigns (said by the chairman)
(10) *He* obviously had plenty of money (said walking through the Taj Mahal). (after Nunberg 1993).

So what is the property of indexicality? With inherently deictic expressions like the demonstrative pronoun *this*, what is striking is that the referent is provided not by the semantic conditions imposed by the expression but by the context; for example, the speaker may be holding up a pen. It is the obvious semantic deficiency of *this* that directs the addressee's attention to the speaker's gesture. In a similar way, the semantic generality of *he* without prior discourse context (as in (3) or (10)) forces a contextual resolution in the circumstances of the speech event. In this respect, there is a close relation between exophora and anaphora. In both cases we have contextual resolution of semantically general expressions – in the physical space–time context of the speech event and in the ongoing discourse respectively (Levinson 2000a: 268ff) Third-person referring expressions which are semantically deficient, in the sense that their descriptive content does not suffice to identify a referent, invite pragmatic resolution, perhaps by default in the discourse, and failing that in the physical context.

But semantic deficiency can't be the only defining characteristic of indexicality. After all, there is a cline of referring expressions like *he, the man, the short man, George, the President, the second President to be the son of a President* (see Abbott 2004), and unambiguously identifying descriptions are the exception rather than the rule in natural language. Semantic deficiency or vacuity is resolved through the kind of mutual windowing of attention in which the speaker says *I just saw what's-his-name*, expecting the addressee to be able to guess who (for the mechanism see Schelling 1960 and H.H. Clark 1996). Although such a narrowing of possibilities relies on mutual attention to mutual knowledge in the context, to call such phenomena "deictic" or "indexical" would be to render the label too broad to be useful. Rather, the critical feature that picks out a coherent field is precisely the one that C. S. Peirce outlined, namely an existential relationship between the sign and the thing indicated – so that when *he* is said in the Taj Mahal, or *this* is said when holding a pen, the sign is connected to the context as smoke is to fire (although non-causally). How? The key is the direction of the addressee's attention to some feature of the spatio-temporal physical context (as in the case of *this*, said holding the pen), or the presumption of the prior existence of that attention (as in the *he*, said in the Taj Mahal). Indexicality is both an **intentional** and **attentional** phenomenon, concentrated around the spatial–temporal center of verbal interaction, what Bühler (1934b) called the deictic *origo*.

This brings us to gesture, one obvious way of securing the addressee's attention. In philo- sophical approaches to language, ostension or gestural presentation has been thought crucial for acquisition (try teaching the word *ball* to a two-year-old with no ball in sight), but as both Wittgenstein and Quine have observed, pointing is hardly as self-explanatory as Mill imagined – when I point at a river and say *This is the Thames*, I could be pointing to one square kilometer of map-grid, or just the left bank, the sun sparkling on the ripples, or even the cubic meter of water just then flowing past my index finger on its way to the sea (Quine 1961: Chapter 4; Wettstein 1984). Pointing works like inadequate descriptions, through the exercise of a Schelling coordination problem – I plan to pick out with a gesture just what I think you'll think I plan to pick out, given where we are and what we are doing. The reflexive phrasing here recalls Grice's (1957) theory of meaning, in which when I point and say *I mean that* I intend to invoke in you a referent-isolating thought by virtue of your recognizing that that is my intention.

In this way gesture – and arguably deixis in general – is crucially intentional: you cannot say "False!" to my utterance "I am referring to *that*." Deictic gestures do seem to be special; for example, they are made further from the body than other kinds of gesture (McNeill 1992: 91), and we now know something about their universal bases and cross-cultural variation (Kita 2003). But the role of gesture is a much more complicated business than suggested by the philosophers, who imagine, for example, that demonstratives always require gestures (see e.g. Lewis's 1972: 175 coordinate for "indicated objects"). Not only can gestures be reduced to directed gaze or a nod (or in some cultures to a pursing of the lips – see Enfield 2002), they may be rendered unnecessary by the circumstances (consider "What was that?" said of a noise, or "This is wonderful" said of a room). As Fillmore (1997) points out, demonstratives typically have two uses – *this city* resists a gesture (symbolic usage), just as *this finger* requires one (gestural usage), while there are specific expressions (like presentatives or American *yea* in *yea big*) that always require gestures.

To sum up so far: indexicality involves Peirce's "dynamical coexistence" of an indexical sign with its object of reference. It is normally associated with linguistic expressions that are semantically insufficient to achieve reference without contextual support. That support is provided by the mutual attention of the interlocutors and their ability to reconstruct the speaker's referential intentions given clues in the environment.

This does not, however, suffice to establish clear boundaries to the phenomena. One problem is what Bühler (1934b) called *Deixis am Phantasma* ("deixis in the imagination"), in which one imagines oneself somewhere else, and shifts the deictic origo by a series of transpositions. Suppose I try to describe to you where I left a book, and I say, "Imagine this room were my office. The book would be right here [pointing to the edge of my desk]." As Fillmore (1975) observes, much deixis is relativized to text, as in reported speech or in the opening line of a Hemingway short story: "The door of Henry's lunchroom opened and two men came in," where, as Fillmore notes, the inside of Henry's lunchroom has become the deictic origo.

Then there is anaphora, which is so closely linked to deixis that it is not always separable, as in *I've been living in San Francisco for five years and I love it here* (where *here* is both anaphoric and deictic), bridged by the intermediate area of textual deixis (as in *Harry said "I didn't do that" but he said it in a funny way*, where *it* does not refer to the proposition expressed but to Harry's utterance itself). An additional boundary problem is posed by the fact that the class of indexical expressions is not so clearly demarcated. For example, in *Let's go to a nearby restaurant*, *nearby* is used deictically, but in *Churchill took De Gaulle to a nearby restaurant* it is not – is this deixis relativized to text, or does *nearby* simply presume some point of measurement? Suppose we yield *nearby* up to deixis, then what about *enemy* in *The enemy are coming*? *Enemy* seems to presume an implicit agonistic counterpart, which may be filled deictically but may not (as in *Hannibal prepared for the onslaught of the enemy*; see Mitchell 1986). There is no clear boundary here. Even more difficult, of course, is the point made above: indexicality exceeds the bounds of ready-made indexical expressions, i.e. deictics with in-built contextual parameters, as shown by the indexical use of third person pronouns and referring expressions.

3 Deictic expressions in semantic theory

Let's return to relative terra firma, namely special-purpose deictic expressions – that is, linguistic expressions that require indexical resolution. The special semantic character of such expressions is an abiding puzzle in the philosophy of language. Expressions like *today* have a constant meaning but systematically varying reference. In some ways they resemble proper names, since they often have little descriptive content (and hence resist good paraphrase), but in their constantly changing reference they could hardly be more different (Kaplan 1989: 562). Above all, they resist eliminative paraphrase into non-indexical objective description – *I am Stephen Levinson* cannot be paraphrased as *Stephen Levinson is Stephen Levinson*. *The speaker of this utterance is Stephen Levinson* gets closer, but fails to eliminate the indexical component now shifted to *this* and introduces token-reflexivity.

So how should we think about the meaning of indexicals? What is clear is that any sentence with indexicals (and given person, tense, and spatial deixis, that means nearly every natural language sentence) cannot directly express a proposition, for a proposition is an abstract entity whose truth value is independent of the times, places, and persons in the speech event. If we think of propositions as mappings from worlds to truth values, then whereas we might be able to characterize the meanings of non-indexical expressions in terms of the part they play in such a mapping, there seems no such prospect for indexical expressions.

In philosophical approaches to semantics a consensus has now arisen for handling indexical expressions as a two-stage affair, a mapping from contexts into propositional contents, which are then a mapping from, say, worlds to truth values. In Montague's (1970) early theory the content of deictic expressions was captured by mapping contexts (a set of indices for speakers, addressees, indicated objects, times, and places) into intensions. In Kaplan's (1989) theory, all expressions have this characteristic mapping (their CHARACTER) from contexts into intensions (their proposition-relevant content). The meaning of *I* is its character, a function or rule that variably assigns an individual concept, namely the speaker, in each context (Kaplan 1978; cf. Carlson 2004). Non-indexical expressions have constant character, but may (rigid designators) or may not (other referring expressions) have constant content.

Another influential version of the two-stage theory can be found in Situation Semantics (Barwise and Perry 1983). There, utterances are interpreted with respect to three situations (or states of affairs): the UTTERANCE SITUATION (corresponding to Montague's indices), the RESOURCE SITUATION (which handles other contextually determined reference like anaphora), and the DESCRIBED SITUATION (corresponding to the propositional content). Indexicals and other contextually parameterized expressions get their variables fixed in the utterance and/or resource situations, which are then effectively discarded – it is just the value of the variables, e.g. the referent of *I* or *that*, that is transferred to the described situation (e.g. *I gave him that* has the described content of "Stephen Levinson gave him that book"). Meaning is relational, the meaning of an indexical characterized as the relation between utterance/resource situations and described situations. This large improvement over the Montague theory no longer requires a complete pre-specification of relevant aspects of the context as in Montague's indices – other ad hoc factors can be picked up in the resource situation.

The central property of two-stage theories is that indexicals do not contribute directly to the proposition expressed, the content of what is said, or the situation described. Instead, they take us to an individual, a referent, which is then slotted into the proposition expressed or the situation described, or, as Nunberg (1993: 159) puts it: "The meanings of indexicals are composite functions that take us from an element of the context to an element of a contextually restricted domain, and then drop away."

This kind of treatment of indexicality falls far short of descriptive adequacy. First, the indexicals which have been the target of most philosophical approaches (sometimes called "pure indexicals" – expressions like *I, now,* or *here*), seem to have their semantico-pragmatic content exhausted by a specification of the relevant index (speaker, time, and place of speaking respectively; see Wettstein 1984). But closely related indexicals like *we, today, nearby* may also express additional semantic conditions (at least one person in addition to the speaker, the diurnal span which contains the coding time, a place distinct from here but close to here, respectively). So deictics may contain both descriptive properties and contextual variables in the one expression. Perhaps a more difficult problem for the view that deictics just deliver referents to the proposition expressed is the fact that they can in fact express quantified variables. For example, in *Every time a visiting soprano comes, we sing duets* the pronoun *we* denotes a set consisting of the speaker and a variable (Nunberg 1993). In addition, nearly all deictics are heavily dependent on pragmatic resolution – *Come here* may mean come to this sofa or come to this city according to context (see Levinson 2000a: 177ff.).

Secondly, the idea that the relevant contextual features can be fixed in advance (as is required by the Montague-style solution) is problematic. Suppose I say, "This is the largest walnut tree on the planet": I could be pointing to a tree some distance away, or we could just be standing underneath it, or I could be touching a picture in a book, or if you were blind I could be running your hand over the bark, or I could be telling you what we are about to see as we walk over the hill. The mode of demonstration just does not seem to be determined in advance (see Cresswell 1973: 111ff.). Thirdly, there are many aspects of the meaning of demonstratives that exceed any such specification by predetermined index. When Sheila says, "We have better sex lives than men," *we* doesn't just mean "speaker plus some other"; it denotes the set of women, including the speaker. Such usages exploit indexicality in the Peircean sense, that is, the direct connections between the situation of speaking (here, the fact that the speaker is female) and the content of what is communicated. Fourth, there is the problem that Quine called "deferred ostension," now familiar through the work of Nunberg (1977, 1993, 2004). Suppose we are listening to a program on a radio station and I say "CNN has just bought this" – I don't refer to the current jingle but the radio station. Or I point at a Coca-Cola bottle and say "That used to be a different shape" – what I refer to is not the current bottle, but the type of container of the holy liquid, and I assert that tokens used to be of a different shape. In these cases, the indicated thing is not the thing referred to, and the Montagovian or Creswellian mechanism will get us the wrong proposition. Fifth, these treatments of indexicality presuppose that there is a clear class of indexical expressions with a built-in variable whose value is instantiated in the context. But third-person, non-deictic expressions can have indexical uses, as when I say, pointing to a man in a purple turban, "He is Colonel Gaddafi's nephew."

There are then a formidable set of obstacles to the treatment of indexicals as simply a rule-governed mapping from contextual indices to intensions, or utterance-situations into individuals which can then play a role in described situations. [. . .]

A final aspect of the semantic character of indexical expressions that should be mentioned is their special PROJECTION PROPERTIES, which follow from the fact that demonstratives and many other deictics have no substantial descriptive content, so that once the contextual parameters have been fixed they are "directly referential" (Kaplan 1989). A true demonstrative remains transparent in an intensional context – in "Ralph said he broke that" *that* can only be the thing the speaker is now pointing at, not the thing Ralph pointed at – the speaker cannot withhold a gesture on the grounds that Ralph made it. Further, deictics do not generally fall under the scope of negation or modal operators: *That is not a planet* cannot be understood as "I am not indicating x and x is a planet" (Enç 1981). Deictics resist attributive or "semantic" readings; thus whereas *The man who can lift this sword is our king* has both a referential and attributive reading ("whoever can . . . "), *That man who can lift this sword is our king* has only a referential reading. In addition to the paradoxes of self-reference, there are sentences with indexicals which have the curious property of being at the same time contingently true or false, yet upon being uttered are automatically true or self-verifying, as in *I am here now* or *I am now pointing at that* (said pointing at something).

4 The role of pragmatics in the resolution of deictic expressions: a close look at demonstrative systems

We have seen that indexicality exceeds the bounds of the built-in indexical expressions in any language. Moreover, the field of indexical expressions is not clearly delimited, because insofar as most referring expressions do not fully individuate solely by virtue of their semantic content but rather depend for success on states of mutual knowledge holding between discourse participants, the great majority of successful acts of reference depend on indexical conditions. Still, we may hope to make a distinction between expressions used indexically, and those – let us call them deictic – that necessarily invoke features of the context because of a contextual variable built into their semantic conditions. This distinction will also be plagued by borderline examples, as exemplified above by expressions like *nearby* or even *enemy*. Even if we decide that *local* as in *the local pub* is an expression with an unfilled variable that is preferentially filled by spatial parameters of the context of speaking, we would be loath to think that all quality adjectives are deictic just because they have a suppressed comparator as argument (as in *John is tall*, implying taller than the average reference population, as supplied by the context). Fuzzy borders to a phenomenon do not make categories useless (otherwise color terms would not exist), so in what follows we will proceed by focusing on deictic expressions which clearly involve inherent contextual variables.

The pragmatic character of indexicality is not the only central issue for a pragmatic theory of deictic expressions, for the organization of the semantic field of contrastive deictic expressions is often itself determined by pragmatic factors. As an illustration of this, we concentrate here on the cross-linguistic comparison of demonstrative systems, which have played a central role in philosophical and linguistic thinking about deixis. The analysis of demonstratives is much complicated by their multi-functional role in language – they are often used not only to point things out, but to track referents in discourse and more generally to contrast with other referring expressions. It has become traditional to distinguish amongst at least some of the uses (Levinson 1983, Diessel 1999) shown in Figure 5.1.

The relations between these uses are probably more complex than this taxonomy suggests, but it is clearly not sufficient to distinguish simply between exophoric (deictic) and endophoric (non-deictic) at the highest branch as in Levinson (1983: 68) and Diessel (1999: 6), since discourse deixis is intra-text but deictic, and empathetic and recognitional uses are extra-text but non-deictic. The following examples illustrate the distinctions involved:

(11) "Give me **that** book" (exophoric: book available in the physical context)
(12) "I hurt **this** finger" (exophoric gestural: requires gesture or presentation of finger)
(13) "I like **this** city" (exophoric symbolic: does not require gesture)
(14) "I broke **this** tooth first and then **that** one next" (gestural contrastive)
(15) "He looked down and saw the gun: **this** was the murder weapon, he realized" (transposed)
(16) " 'You are wrong'. **That's** exactly what she said" (discourse deictic)
(17) "It sounded like **this**: whoosh" (discourse deictic)
(18) "The cowboy entered. **This** man was not someone to mess with" (anaphoric)
(19) "He went and hit **that** bastard" (emphathetic)
(20) "Do you remember **that** holiday we spent in the rain in Devon?" (recognitional).

Exophoric, gestural, non-transposed uses of demonstratives have usually been considered basic. Diessel (1999) points out that exophoric gestural uses are the earliest in acquisition, the least marked in form, and the source of grammaticalization chains that run through the other uses. In what follows we shall concentrate on the exophoric gestural uses. Less well supported

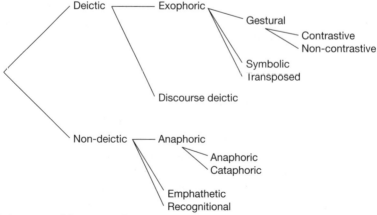

Figure 5.1 Distinct uses of demonstratives.

is the supposition that the basic semantic contrasts between sets of exophoric demonstratives are spatial in nature, encoding degrees of distance from speaker or addressee (cf. Anderson and Keenan 1985). There is no a priori reason why this should be the case, yet grammars of languages almost invariably describe demonstrative systems in this spatial way. There are two major kinds of paradigm: speaker-anchored distance systems, and speaker/addressee-anchored systems, as illustrated by Spanish and Quileute (Anderson and Keenan 1985):

(21) **Spanish** *Distance from speaker*

—	(proximal)	*este*
+	(medial)	*ese*
++	(distal)	*acquel*

(22) **Quileute** *Close to speaker*   *Close to addressee*

+	—	*xo′ʔo*
—	+	*so′ʔo*
+	+	*sa′ʔa*
—	—	*á:ǧa′ʔa*

Although a few languages may have only one demonstrative pronoun or adjective, this is supplemented in probably most (Diessel 1999: 36 claims all) cases by a proximal/distal contrast in deictic adverbs ("here" vs. "there"). Three-term systems may be speaker-anchored (like two-term systems), speaker/addressee-anchored, or both. Systems with more than four terms combine other semantic dimensions, like visibility or vertical distance relative to the speaker, or shape of the referent.

A speaker-anchored distance system with three terms is often organized in terms of a binary opposition between proximal and distal, with the distal category permitting finer discrimination (McGregor argues for such an analysis for Warrwa, where the medial is the most marked form; see van Geenhoven and Warner 1999: 60). Some systems combine both speaker- and addressee-anchored systems, as with the Yélî Dnye demonstrative determiners:[1]

(23)

	Speaker-based	Addressee-based
Proximal	**ala**	**ye**
Medial	**kî**	—
Distal	**mu** (far from Speaker, can apply to objects close to Addressee)	

Kî is the unmarked term here – it can refer freely, but if the speaker or addressee is actually holding something, the speaker- or addressee-centered term pre-empts it. Thus the medial interpretation is due entirely to pragmatic pre-emption from the more semantically specified forms. In this semantic generality, the Yélî Dnye medial contrasts with the marked Warrwa medial.

Yélî Dnye shows that there are actually at least three kinds of multi-term systems, not just the two posited in the literature – speaker-centered distance systems (with no addressee-centered forms) vs. person-based systems (with no medial-from-speaker forms, and where distal is interpreted as distal from both S[peaker] and A[ddressee]).

So far we have taken demonstratives to code spatial discriminations. But this may not always be so (cf. Hanks 1996; Himmelmann 1997). Two systems that have traditionally been treated as addressee-anchored distance systems have on close analysis proved to be less spatial than thought. Here is a typical analysis of Turkish and Japanese demonstratives:

(24)		Turkish	Japanese
	"Near Speaker"	*bu*	*ko*
	"Near Addressee"	*şu*	*so*
	"Near neither Speaker nor Addressee"	*o*	*a*

Close analysis of video-taped task-oriented communication shows that these glosses do not reflect real usage conditions (Özyürek and Kita 2002). For Turkish the correct analysis seems to be that *şu* presumes lack of joint attention and is used to draw the attention of the addressee to a referent in the context, while *bu* and *o* presume that the referents are already in the addressee's attentional focus, in which case *bu* is used for objects closer to the speaker and *o* for those distant from the speaker. A similar story can be told for Japanese: *so* has two functions – one simply to indicate that the referent is close to addressee, the other (as with Turkish *şu*) to draw the addressee's attention to a new referent. This latter usage is pre-empted by *ko* when the referent is very close to speaker, and by *a* when far from both speaker and addressee. A primary oppositions here involves not proximity to speaker vs. addressee, but rather shared vs. non-shared attentional focus.

This finding fits with the pre-theoretical ruminations above: indexicality crucially involves some link between utterance and context so that the context can be used as an affordance to find the intended reference. As noted, deictic expressions and gestures both do this by drawing the addressee's attention to some feature of the spatio-temporal environment (or of adjacent utterance). Also highlighted is the crucial role gesture plays in deixis, for gesture serves to direct the addressee's attention. The prototypical occurrence of demonstratives with gestures seems crucial to how children learn demonstratives, which are always amongst the first fifty words learned and often the first closed-class set acquired; the acquisition of the pointing gesture precedes that of the words (Clark 1978; Tanz 1980).

Finally, it is often suggested that definite articles are simply demonstratives unmarked for distance (Lyons 1977: 653–4; Anderson and Keenan 1985: 280), but this does not fit the fact, noted above, that many demonstrative systems themselves have unmarked members (like *that* in English), nor the fact that a number of languages (like German) have only one demonstrative that contrasts with a definite article. There certainly is close kinship between definite determiners and demonstratives, as shown by the frequent grammaticalization of the former from the latter. Both contrast with indefinites (see Diessel 1999), and both share a presumption of uniqueness within a contextually given set of entities (Hawkins 1991; Abbott 2004). It is the focusing of attention on the physical context that is the special character of demonstratives in their basic use.

5 The fields of deixis

I turn now to a brief survey of deictic expressions in language. Linguists normally treat deixis as falling into a number of distinct semantic fields: person, place, time, etc. Since Bühler (1934b), the deictic field has been organized around an **origo** or "ground zero" consisting of the speaker at the time and place of speaking. Actually, many systems utilize two distinct centers – speaker and addressee. Further, as Bühler noted, many deictic expressions can be transposed or relativized to some other origo, most often the person of the protagonist at the relevant time and place in a narrative (see Fillmore 1997).

We can make a number of distinctions between different ways in which deictic expressions may be used. First, many deictic expressions may be used non-deictically – anaphorically, as in *We went to Verdi's Requiem last weekend and really enjoyed <u>that</u>*, or non-anaphorically, as in *Last* *weekend we just did this and <u>that</u>*. Second, when used deictically, we need to distinguish between those used at the normal origo and those transposed to some other origo. It might be thought that the latter are not strictly speaking deictic (since they have been displaced from the time and place of speaking), but consider *He came right up to her and hit her like this here on the arm*, in which the speaker pantomimes the protagonists, so licensing the use of *come, this*, and *here*. Third, as noted, deictic expressions may be used gesturally or non-gesturally (*this arm* versus *this room*), while some like tense inflections may not occur with gestures at all. "Gesture" here must be understood in the widest sense, since pointing in some cultures (like the Cunha) is primarily with lips and eyes and not hands and since even vocal intonation can function in a "gestural" way (*Now hold your fire; wait; shoot NOW*, or *I'm over HERE*). Similarly, many languages have presentatives (like French *voila!*) requiring the presentation of something simultaneous with the expression, or greetings requiring the presentation of the right hand, or terms like *thus* requiring a demonstration of a mode of action.

The deictic categories of person, place, and time are widely instantiated in grammatical distinctions made by languages around the world (see Fillmore 1975; Weissenborn and Klein 1982; Anderson and Keenan 1985; Levinson 1983: Chapter 2; Diessel 1999). Bühler's origo, the speaker and the place and time of her utterance, along with the role of recipient or addressee, recurs at the core of deictic distinctions in grammar after grammar. These are the crucial reference points upon which complex deictic concepts are constructed, whether honorifics, complex tenses, or systems of discourse deixis. They constitute strong universals of language at a conceptual level, although their manifestation is anything but uniform: not all languages have pronouns, tense, contrasting demonstratives, or any other type of deictic expression that one might enumerate.

Unfortunately, cross-linguistic data on deictic categories are not ideal. One problem is that the **meaning** of deictic expressions is usually treated as self-evident in grammatical descriptions and rarely properly investigated, and a second problem is that major typological surveys are scarce (but see Diessel 1999; Cysouw 2001). But despite the universality of deictic categories like person, place, and time, their expression in grammatical categories is anything but universal. For example, despite claims to the contrary, not all languages have first and second person pronouns (cf. "The first and second person pronouns are universal": Hockett 1961: 21), not all languages have spatially contrastive demonstrative pronouns or determiners (contra Diessel 1999, who suggests universality for such a contrast in demonstrative adverbs), not all languages have tense, not all languages have verbs of coming and going, bringing and taking, etc. Rather, deictic categories have a universality independent of their grammatical expression – they will all be reflected somewhere in grammar or lexis.

5.1 *Person deixis*

The grammatical category of person directly reflects the different roles that individuals play in the speech event: speaker, addressee, and other. When these roles shift in the course of conversational turn-taking the origo shifts with them (hence Jespersen's 1922 term SHIFTERS for deictic expressions): A's *I* becomes B's *you*, A's *here* becomes B's *there* and so forth.

The traditional person paradigm can be captured by the two semantic features of speaker inclusion (S) and addressee inclusion (A): first person (+S), second person (+A, -S), and third person (-S, -A), hence a residual, non-deictic category. Most languages directly encode the +S and +A roles in pronouns and/or verb agreement, and the majority explicitly mark third person (-S, -A). But there are clear exceptions to the alleged universality of first and second person marking; in Southeast Asian languages like Thai there are titles (on the pattern of "servant" for first person, "master" for second person) used in place of pronouns and there is no verb agreement (Cooke 1968). Many languages have no third person pronouns, often indirectly marking third person by zero agreement. Thus Yélî Dnye has the following pronoun paradigm (with different paradigms in possessive and oblique cases):

(25) **Yélî Dnye nominative pronouns**

	Singular	Dual	Plural
1	*nê*	*nyo*	*nmo*
2	*nyi*	*dp:o*	*nmyo*
3	φ	φ	φ

The paradigmatic analysis of person marking, whether in pronouns or agreement, is a more complex area than one might at first suppose. Although the traditional notions first, second and third persons hold up remarkably well, there are many kinds of homophony, or different patterns of syncretism, across person paradigms (Cysouw 2001). Much of this complexity is due to the distinctive notions of plurality appropriate to this special paradigm: first person plural clearly does not entail more than one person in +S role, amounting to a chorus. "We" notions are especially troubling, since many languages distinguish such groups as: +S+A vs. +S+A+O (where O is Other, i.e. one or more third persons), vs. +S-A, vs. +S-A+O. In some pronominal systems "plural" can be neatly analyzed as augmenting a minimal deictic specification with "plus one or more additional individuals" (AUG). Thus the distinction between *I* and *we* might be analyzed as (+S, -AUG), (+S, +AUG). Additional motivation for such an analysis is the fact that a number of languages treat "I + you" – i.e. speech-act participants – as a singular pronominal package, which is then augmented to form a "I + you + other" pronoun. The following is the paradigm from Rembarrnga (Dixon 1980: 352):

(26) **Rembarrnga dative pronouns (after Dixon 1980)**

	Minimal	Unit augmented	Augmented
+S	ŋənə	yarrpparraʔ	yarrə
+S+A	yəkkə	ŋakorrpparraʔ	ŋakorrə
+A	kə	nakorrparraʔ	nakorrə
-S-A masc	nawə	parrpparraʔ	parrə
-S-A fem	ŋatə	parrpparraʔ	parrə

Tamil, Fijian, and other languages distinguish INCLUSIVE from EXCLUSIVE *we*, i.e. (+S, +A) from (+S, -A, +AUG). A few languages (like Pirahã) do not mark plurality in the person paradigms at all (Cysouw 2001: 78–9).

One much studied phenomenon in person deixis is in the effect of reported speech on speakers' self-reference – where we say *John said he would come* many languages permit only in effect "John said 'I will come'." In Yélî Dnye thoughts and desires must also retain the correct subjective person: *John wants to come* must be rendered "John wants 'I come'." Then there is the phenomenon of honorifics, which typically make reference to speaking and recipient roles, dealt with separately below under the rubric of social deixis (Section 5.5). Yet another important area is the special role that speaker and addressee roles play in typologically significant grammatical hierarchies; many languages have no dedicated reflexives in first and second person, and many treat first and second person as the topmost categories on an animacy hierarchy, governing case-marking, passivization, and other syntactic processes (see Comrie 1989). In addition, although in the Bühlerian and the philosophical traditions the speaking role is given centrality, the importance of the addressee role is reflected in a number of special grammatical phenomena, e.g. vocative case and special forms for titles, kin-terms and proper names used in address.

Apart from its grammatical importance, person has a special significance because of its omnipresence – it is a grammatical category marked or implicit in every utterance, which inevitably indicates first, second or third person in nominal or verbal paradigms, either explicitly or by contrastive omission.

5.2 Time deixis

In Bühler's origo, the temporal "ground zero" is the moment at which the utterance is issued ("coding time" of Fillmore 1997). Hence *now* means some span of time including the moment of utterance, *today* means that diurnal span in which the speaking event takes place, and *is* predicates a property that holds at the time of speaking. Similarly we count backwards from coding time in calendrical units in such expressions as *yesterday* or *three years ago*, or forwards in *tomorrow* or *next Thursday*. In written or recorded uses of language, we can distinguish coding time from receiving time, and in particular languages there are often conventions about whether one writes "I am writing this today so you will receive it tomorrow" or something more like "I have written this yesterday so that you receive it today."

The nature of calendrical units varies across cultures. Yélî Dnye recognizes the day as a diurnal unit, has words for "yesterday" and "the day before," and special monomorphemic words for tomorrow, the day after tomorrow and so forth for ten days into the future, and thereafter a generative system for specifying days beyond that. It needs such a system because there is no concept of week, or any larger clockwork system of calendrical units that can be tied to coding time as in English *next March*. But most languages exhibit a complex interaction between systems of time measurement, e.g. calendrical units, and deictic anchorage through demonstratives or special modifiers like *next* or *ago*. In English, units of time measurement may either be fixed by reference to the calendar or not: thus *I'll do it this week* is ambiguous between guaranteeing achievement within seven days from utterance time, or within the calendar unit beginning on Sunday (or Monday) including utterance time. *This year* means the calendar year including the time of utterance (or in some circumstances the 365-day unit beginning at the time of utterance) but *this November* tends to mean the next monthly unit so named (or alternatively, the November of this year, even if past), while *this morning* refers to the first half of the diurnal unit including coding time, even if that is in the afternoon (see Fillmore 1975).

However, the most pervasive aspect of temporal deixis is tense. The grammatical categories called tenses usually encode a mixture of deictic time distinctions and aspectual distinctions, which are often hard to distinguish. Analysts tend to set up a series of pure temporal distinctions that correspond roughly to the temporal aspects of natural language tenses, and then catalogue the discrepancies (cf. Comrie 1985: 18ff.). For example, one might gloss the English present tense as specifying that the state or event holds or is occurring during a temporal span including the coding time, the past tense as specifying that the relevant span held before coding time, the future as specifying that the relevant span succeeds coding time, the pluperfect (as in *He had gone*) as specifying that the event happened at a time before an event described in the past tense, and so on. Obviously, such a system fails to capture much English usage (*The soccer match is tomorrow* (see Green 2004), *John will be sleeping now, I wanted to ask you if you could possibly lend me your car*, etc.), but it is clear that there is a deictic temporal element in most tenses. Tenses are traditionally categorized as ABSOLUTE (deictic) versus RELATIVE (anterior or posterior to a textually specified time), so that the simple English past (*He went*) is absolute and the pluperfect (*He had gone*) is relative (anterior to some other, deictically specified point).

Absolute tenses may mark just, for example, past vs. non-past, or up to nine distinct spans of time counted out from coding time (Comrie 1985: Chapter 4). Yélî Dnye has six such tenses, which – as in other Papuan and some Bantu languages – are interpreted precisely in terms of diurnal units. So counting back from the present, there is (in the continuous aspect) a tense specific to events that happened earlier today, another tense for yesterday, and yet another for any time before yesterday. In the other direction, there is a tense for later today, and a separate tense for tomorrow or later. Interestingly, the tense particles for tomorrow incorporate those for yesterday (and the word for "the day before yesterday" incorporates the word for "the day after tomorrow"), indicating a partial symmetry around coding time. Yélî Dnye, like a number of Amerindian languages (see Mithun 1999: 153–4), also has tensed imperatives, distinguishing "Do it now" from "Do it sometime later."

The interpretation of tenses often involves implicatures, so that e.g. *Believe it or not, Steve used to teach syntax* implicates that he no longer does so, but this is clearly defeasible as one can add *and in fact he still has to do so* (see Levinson 2000a: 95 for a relevant analytic framework and Comrie 1985 for the role of implicature in the grammaticalization of tense). Many languages in fact have no absolute deictic tenses (e.g. Classical Arabic; see Comrie 1985: 63), although they may pick up deictic interpretations by implicature. Yet other languages, e.g. Malay or Chinese, have no tenses at all. A specially interesting case in point is Yucatec, which not only lacks tenses but also lacks relative time adverbials of the "before" and "after" kind (cf. Bohnemeyer 1998). How on earth do speakers indicate absolute and relative time? By implicature of course. Bohnemeyer sketches how this can be done: for example, by the use of phasal verbs, so that *Pedro stopped beating his donkey and began walking home* implicates that he first stopped donkey-beating and then after that proceeded homewards.

However, for languages that have tense, this grammatical category is normally obligatory, and ensures that nearly all sentences (with the exception of tenseless sentences like *Two times two is four*) are deictically anchored with interpretations relativized to context. Although we tend to think of tenses as a grammatical category instantiated in predicates, some languages like Yup'ik tense their nouns as well, so one can say in effect "my FUTURE-sled" pointing at a piece of wood (Mithun 1999: 154–6). Note that even in English many nominals are interpreted through Gricean mechanisms as tensed; "John's piano teacher was a karate black-belt in his youth" suggests that the person referred to is currently John's piano teacher (Enç 1981). All of these factors conspire to hook utterances firmly to coding time.

It is clear that many deictic expressions in the temporal domain are borrowed from the spatial domain. In English, temporal prepositions and connectives like *in (the afternoon), on (Monday), at (5.00 p.m.), before* and *after* are all derived from spatial descriptions. The demonstratives in English follow the same pattern (cf. *this week*) and in many languages (like Wik Mungan, as described in Anderson and Keenan 1985: 298) "here" and "there" are the sources for "now" and "then." Many languages work with a "moving time" metaphor, so that we talk about *the coming week* and *the past year* – which is natural since motion involves both space and time. In general, the ways in which the spatial domain is mapped onto the temporal domain are quite intriguing, for as Comrie (1985: 15) notes, the temporal domain has discontinuities that the spatial one lacks (as in the discontinuity between past and future, unlike the continuity of places other than "here"), while space has discontinuities (like near speaker vs. near addressee) which the temporal one lacks (at least in the spoken medium, when "now" is effectively both coding and receiving time).

5.3 Spatial deixis

We have already examined two of the central kinds of place-deictic expressions, namely demonstrative pronouns and adjectives. But as we noted, there are one-term demonstrative (ad/pro)nominal systems unmarked for distance (German *dies* or *das* being a case in point, see Himmelmann 1997). Thus *here* and *there* may be the most direct and most universal examples of spatial deixis (Diessel 1999: 38). As a first approximation, English *here* denotes a region including the speaker, *there* a distal region more remote from the speaker. Languages with a speaker-anchored distance series of demonstrative pronouns will also have a speaker-centered series of demonstrative adverbs. It is clear that there is no necessary connection between the number of pronominal or adnominal demonstratives and demonstrative adverbs – German for example has one demonstrative pronoun (or rather no spatial distinction between *dies* and *das*) but two contrastive demonstrative adverbs. Malagasy has seven demonstrative adverbs, but only six demonstrative pronouns, apparently encoding increasing distance from speaker (Anderson and Keenan 1985: 292–4, although many commentators have suspected other features besides sheer distance). Speaker-centered degrees of distance are usually (more) fully represented in the adverbs than the pronominals, and it may be that no language has a person-based system in the demonstrative adverbs if it lacks one in the pronominal or adnominal demonstratives.

Very large paradigms of demonstratives usually involve many ancillary features, not all of them deictic. Yup'ik has three sets of demonstratives (31 in all) conventionally labeled "extended" (for large horizontal objects or areas or moving referents), "restricted" (for small, visible, or stationary objects), and "obscured" (for objects not in sight); cf. Anderson and Keenan (1985: 295), after Reed et al. (1977). Here the restricted condition is an additional non-deictic condition, but the other two sets involve a visibility feature that is deictic in nature (visible by the speaker from the place of speaking). Visibility is a feature reported for many North American Indian languages, and not only in demonstratives – in Kwakwa'la every noun phrase is marked for this deictic feature by a pair of flanking clitics (Anderson and Keenan 1985, citing Boas). But caution is in order with a gloss like "visibility"; Henderson (1995: 46) glosses the Yélî Dnye demonstratives *kî* and *wu* as "visible" and "invisible" respectively, but *wu* is more accurately "indirectly ascertained, not directly perceivable or not clearly identifiable to addressee," while *kî* is the unmarked deictic, pragmatically opposed to *wu* in one dimension and to the proximal/distal deictics in another.

Apart from visibility, deictics often contain information in an absolute frame of reference, that is, an allocentric frame of reference hooked to geographical features or abstract cardinal directions. Thus the large Yup'ik series of demonstratives has "upstream"/"downstream"/"across river" oppositions, West Greenlandic has "north"/"south" (Fortescue 1984), and languages used by peoples in mountainous areas of Australia, New Guinea, or the Himalayas often contain "uphill"/"downhill" oppositions (see Diessel 1999: 44–5 for references). Such languages are likely to use absolute coordinates unhooked from the deictic center (as in "north of the tree" (see Levinson 1996 for exposition)). In a cross-linguistic survey of demonstratives in 85 languages, Diessel (1999) attests, in addition to these deictic factors, such non-deictic properties of the referent as animacy, humanness, gender, number, and the boundedness of Eskimo languages mentioned above.

In many kinds of deictic expressions the deictic conditions are indeed backgrounded, and other semantic properties foregrounded. Thus if I say "He didn't come home," you are unlikely (absent contrastive emphasis on *come*) to read what I said as "He went home, but not toward the deictic center." Verbs of "coming" and "going" are not universal. In the first place, many languages do not have verbs encoding motion to or from the deictic center – they make do instead with "hither"/"thither" particles. Secondly, explicit verbs of "coming" and "going" vary in what they encode (Wilkins and Hill 1995; Wilkins et al. 1995). If someone comes toward me but stops short before he arrives at the tree over there, I can say "He came to the tree" in English, but not in Longgu or Italian, where we must say "He went to the tree." In fact we can distinguish at least four distinct kinds of "come" verbs, according to whether they are marked for telicity or require the goal to be the place of speaking, as exemplified below (Wilkins et al. 1995):

(27) **Varieties of COME verbs**

	+telic	-telic (i.e. unmarked)
Goal is place of speaking	*Longgu*	*Italian*
Goal need not be place of speaking	*Ewe*	*Tamil*

Thus, it turns out there is no universal lexicalized notion of "come," although alignment with the place of speaking is a candidate for a universal feature. The notions underlying "go" may be somewhat more uniform because on close examination they generally do *not* encode anything about alignment of vectors with the deictic center (contra to, for example, Miller and Johnson-Laird 1976). Rather, "come" and "go" verbs tend to be in privative opposition, with "come" marked as having such an alignment, and "go" unmarked. Scalar implicature can then do the rest: saying "go" where "come" might have been used but wasn't implicates that the speaker is not in a position to use the stronger, more informative "come" because its conditions have not been met, and thus that the motion in question is not toward the deictic center.[2] Variants in "go" semantics should then be the mirror image of variants in "come" semantics, illustrating the point stressed in Levinson (2000a) that many Saussurean oppositions may be as much in the pragmatics as in the semantics.

Not all languages lexicalize the "toward the deictic center" feature in their verbs. Consider Yélî Dnye, which has a "hither" feature that can be encoded in variant forms of the verbal inflectional particles. Now there are irregular verbs that obligatorily take this feature, including a motion verb *pwiyé*. So it is tempting to gloss *pwiyé* "come," but in fact it is perfectly usable to encode motion away from the deictic center (one can say "He *pwiyé*-d off in that direction"), because it is just an irregular verb with meaning somewhat unrelated to its obligatory inflectional properties. So to say "Come here!" one can either use *pwiyé* or the unmarked "go" verb *lê*, but now marked with the "hither" particle. Note that Yélî Dnye has no "thither" particle – because by privative opposition it is not necessary: any motion verb unmarked for "hither" will be presumed to have a "thither" (or at least not-"hither") interpretation. Once again implicature provides the opposition.

5.4 Discourse deixis

In both spoken and written discourse, there is frequently occasion to refer to earlier or forthcoming segments of the discourse: *As mentioned before, In the next chapter*, or *I bet you haven't heard this joke*. Since a discourse unfolds in time, it is natural to use temporal deictic terms (*before, next*) to indicate the relation of the referred-to segment to the temporal locus of the moment of speaking or the currently read sentence. But spatial terms are also sometimes employed, as with *in this article* or *two paragraphs below*. Clearly, references to parts of a discourse that can only be interpreted by knowing where the current coding point or current reading/ recording point is are quintessentially deictic in character.

A distinction is often made between textual deixis and general anaphora along the following lines. Whereas textual deixis refers to portions of the text itself (as in *See the discussion above* or *The pewit sounds like this: pee-r-weet*), anaphoric expressions refer outside the discourse to other entities by connecting to a prior referring expression (anaphora) or a later one (cataphora, as in *In front of him, Pilate saw a beaten man*). Insofar as the distinction between anaphoric and cataphoric expressions is conventionalized, such expressions have a clear conventional deictic component, since reference is relative to the point in the discourse. Thus Yélî Dnye has an anaphoric pronoun *yi*, which cannot be used exophorically and contrasts with the demonstratives that can be used cataphorically, looking backwards in the text from the point of reading like the English legalese *aforementioned*. These expressions, with their directional specification from the current point in the text, demonstrate the underlyingly deictic nature of anaphora.

Many expressions used anaphorically, like third person pronouns in English, are general-purpose referring expressions – there is nothing intrinsically anaphoric about them, and they can be used deictically as noted above, or non-deictically but exophorically, when the situation or discourse context makes it clear (as in *He's died*, said of a colleague known to be in critical condition). The determination that a referring expression is anaphoric is itself a matter of pragmatic resolution, since it has to do with relative semantic generality. For this reason, *the ship* can be understood anaphorically in *The giant Shell tanker hit a rock, and the ship went down*, while resisting such an interpretation in *The ship hit a rock, and the giant Shell tanker went down* (see Levinson 2000a for a detailed Gricean analysis, and Huang 2000, 2004 for surveys of pragmatic approaches to anaphora).

An important area of discourse deixis concerns discourse markers, like *anyway, but, however*, or *in conclusion* (see Schiffrin 1987; Blakemore 2004). These relate a current contribution to the prior utterance or text, and typically resist truth-conditional characterization. For this reason, Grice introduced the notion of conventional implicature, noting that *but* has the truth-conditional content of *and*, with an additional contrastive meaning which is non-truth conditional but conventional.

5.5 Social deixis

Social deixis involves the marking of social relationships in linguistic expressions, with direct or oblique reference to the social status or role of participants in the speech event. Special expressions exist in many languages, including the honorifics well known in the languages of Southeast Asia, such as Thai, Japanese, Korean, and Javanese. We can distinguish a number of axes on which such relations are defined (Levinson 1983; Brown and Levinson 1987):

(28) **Parameters of social deixis**

Axis		Honorific types	Other encodings
(1)	Speaker to referent	Referent honorifics	Titles
(2)	Speaker to addressee	Addressee honorifics	Address forms
(3)	Speaker to non-addressed participant	Bystander honorifics	Taboo vocabularies
(4)	Speaker to setting	Formality levels	Register

The distinction between (1) and (2) is fundamental in that in (1) "honor" (or a related attitude) can only be expressed by referring to the entity to be honored, while in (2) the same attitude may be expressed while talking about unrelated matters. In this scheme, respectful pronouns like *vous* or *Sie* used to singular addressees are referent honorifics that happen to refer to the addressee, while the Tamil particle *nka* or Japanese verbal affix *-mas* are addressee honorifics that can be adjoined by the relevant rules to any proposition. The elaborate honorifics systems of Southeast Asia are built up from a mixture of (1) and (2) – for example, there are likely to be humiliative forms replacing the first person pronoun (on the principle that lowering the self raises the other) together with honorific forms for referring to the addressee or third parties (both referent honorifics), and in addition suppletive forms for such verbs as "eat" or "go," giving respect to the addressee regardless of who is the subject of the verb (see Brown and Levinson 1987; Errington 1988; Shibatani 1999).

The third axis is encoded in BYSTANDER HONORIFICS, signaling respect to non-addressed but present party. In Pohnpei, in addition to referent and addressee honorifics, there are special suppletive verbs and nouns to be used in the presence of a chief (Keating 1998). Many Australian languages had taboo vocabularies used in the presence of real or potential in-laws, or those who fell in a marriagable section for ego but were too close to marry (Dixon 1980: 58–65; Haviland 1979). Yélî Dnye has a similar, if more limited, taboo vocabulary for in-laws, especially parents and siblings of the spouse. The fourth axis involves respect conveyed to the setting or event. Most Germans use a system of address with *Du* vs. *Sie* and First Name vs. *Herr/Frau* + Last Name which is unwavering across formal or informal contexts; they find surprising the ease with which English speakers can switch from First Name to Title + Last Name according to the formality of the situation (Brown and Gilman 1960; Lambert and Tucker 1976). Many European languages have distinct registers used on formal occasions, where *eat* becomes *dine*, *home* becomes *residence*, etc., while Tamil has diglossic variants, with distinct morphology for formal and literary uses.

Systems of address of any kind – pronouns, titles, kin-terms – are guided by the social-deictic contrasts made by alternate forms. The contents of honorifics (see Shibatani 1999) should be taken to be conventional implicatures overlaid on the referential content (if any), for the deictic content is not cancelable and does not fall under the scope of logical operators (see Levinson 1979a).

6 Conclusions

This chapter has touched on a number of topics that establish deixis as a central subject in the theory of language. Indexicality probably played a crucial part in the evolution of language, prior to the full-scale recursive, symbolic system characteristic of modern human language. The intersection of indexicality and the symbolic system engenders a hybrid with complexities beyond the two contributing systems. These complexities are evident in the paradoxes of token-reflexivity and in the puzzles of the psychological content of indexical utterances. Deictic categories like person are universal (although variably expressed), demonstrating their importance to the fundamental design of language. Their special role in language learning and differential elaboration in the languages of the world makes a typology of the major deictic categories an important item on the agenda for future research.

Notes

1   Yélî Dnye is an isolate of the Papuan linguistic area spoken on Rossel Island (Henderson 1995; Levinson 2000b).

2   There is evidence suggesting a similar privative relation between *this* and *that*, with the former marked as [+proximal] and the latter unmarked for proximity, picking up its distal meaning by the Quantity maxim.

■ ■ ■

POST-READING

1   Give yourself a score out of 10 for the extent to which you could now talk in an informed way about each of the following: *deictic origo, gesture, plurality, direct reference, absolute and relative tense, absolute spatial coordinates.* Return to the paper and re-read the relevant paragraphs if you need to improve your score.

2   What changes would you now make to the sentence you wrote before reading the paper?

JO RUBBA

ALTERNATE GROUNDS IN THE INTERPRETATION OF DEICTIC EXPRESSIONS

PRE-READING

Rubba begins her paper with the following extract from interview data:

> JF16: There's a part of southeast San Diego where *you* do go down, *you* see all these Vietnamese theaters and everything in Vietnamese and when I see that I just kind of feel, well, *I* don't belong in *this* place, *this* is where the Vietnamese people are, I don't belong *here*.

She points out that the immediate discourse situation cannot be taken as the domain for finding referents for the italicized deictics although we can all find referents without difficulty. Have you any preliminary thoughts about how we do it?

IN-READING

As you read the paper, you'll come across five passages with | symbols in the margin. Stop reading at each and work out which, if any, of the following four randomly ordered comments might plausibly be discussed in relation to the marked text:

- It's not clear that space-building is always prompted by the overt content of an utterance.
- Without ground there can be no figure.
- Pragmaticians ought to be cautious about distinguishing between the inherent grammaticality of a sentence and its acceptability as an utterance.
- Deixis ought to be amenable to relevance theoretic treatment.

As you think about the relation of a comment to the text, try also to come to a conclusion about whether you agree with the comment per se.

■ ■ ■

ALTERNATE GROUNDS IN THE INTERPRETATION OF DEICTIC EXPRESSIONS
JO RUBBA

[. . .] This paper addresses the problem of finding referents for locational deictic expressions such as *this place*, *that place*, *here*, *there*, and personal pronouns.

Finding referents for such expressions is far from simple. Deictic expressions are usually thought of as referring to entities in the immediate utterance situation—*I* refers to the speaker, *you* to the hearer, *here* to a location construed as proximal to the discourse participants in some sense, and so forth. In actual usage, however, deictic elements are not always used to refer to elements of the immediate utterance situation. This paper addresses usages of this type. Consider the examples in (1), taken from interview data:

> (1)   JF16: There's a part of southeast San Diego where *you* do go down, *you* see all these Vietnamese theaters and everything in Vietnamese and when I see that I just kind of feel, well, *I* don't belong in *this* place, *this* is where the Vietnamese people are, I don't belong *here*. (italics added)

It is clear to speakers of English that the pronoun *you* in this utterance does not refer to the listener in the discourse situation. Rather, it is a generic, and could felicitously be replaced by generic *one*. In addition, the locative deictic expressions—*this place, here*—refer not to a location perceived as proximal to the participants in the interview, but to a distant neighborhood. This is clear from substitution tests: replacing the locational deictics with a proximal location, such as *your office* (where the interview took place) or *La Jolla* (the neighborhood where the interview was set) renders quite a different, and seemingly wrong, interpretation, while substituting a nominal such as *a Vietnamese neighborhood* preserves what we believe to be the speaker's intended meaning. Thus the immediate discourse situation cannot be taken as the domain for finding referents for these deictic expressions; nonetheless, we have no trouble finding referents and hence understanding the speaker. How do we accomplish this? In this paper, I bring to bear on this question devices from complementary theories within cognitive linguistics: the theories of cognitive grammar (Langacker 1987, 1991), mental spaces (Fauconnier 1985), and cognitive models (Lakoff 1987).

Factors in the interpretation of deictics

There are numerous factors that must enter into the interpretation of deictics in discourse processing. The first is the inherent semantic content or value of deictic expressions (cf. Rauh 1981); I refer here to their basic or default values, e.g., *I* as speaker, *you* as hearer, *this* (nominal) as a proximally construed entity, etc. The meanings of deictics are highly *schematic*. That is, they are only partially specified, and therefore may apply across a large number of actual discourse situations: all speakers in a discourse, on their turns, can refer to themselves using the pronoun *I*, and no confusion will result. The pronoun *I* is applicable to any person who is currently taking the role of speaker; no further features of that individual are specified. This schematicity can be problematic, however. In some cases the listener must work to find a referent for a deictic expression. Suppose two graduate students are strolling across campus on a fine day. There has been a lull in the conversation when one of them suddenly utters the sentence in (2):

(2) I'm tired of this place.

Several candidate locations suggest themselves as referents for the expression *this place:* the campus as a physical location; the university as an abstract location; the town in which the university is situated; or perhaps even the state or country in which the campus is situated. Without further context, the hearer will not be able to definitively settle on one of these candidates. It is typical that, in the absence of further clarification on the part of the speaker, the hearer may utter a request for clarification, such as the sentence in (3):

(3) What do you mean, this campus, or this university, or what?

In many, if not most, cases, the discourse topic or domain serves to narrow the field of candidates enough so that the hearer can assume one of the candidates. Thus a second factor in the interpretation of deictics is the limitation of candidate referents by the discourse topic or domain. So, for example, if the utterance in (2) is uttered toward the end of a long diatribe against the students' department, the rigors of the graduate program, the indignities of graduate student labor, etc., the hearer would feel satisfied in concluding that the university as an abstract location is the referent that the speaker had in mind. If, however, the preceding conversation concerned the hot weather, traffic jams, general lack of events of cultural interest, and so on, of the university town, the hearer may feel that the town is the most suitable referent. With sufficient context, the hearer is spared a good deal of work in finding a referent, because one of the candidates has been primed by the foregoing conversation.

A third resource available for the determination of suitable referents is the extended use of deictics that are conventional for the language in question. So, for example, if (4) is the response to a request for clarification on how to make *crêpes à la française*, the listener is hardly likely to object with sentence (5):

(4) Well, you take half a cup of flour; you beat an egg together with some milk, and then you mix this fluid in with the flour in small quantities until . . .

(5) Hey, why do you say *you?* I've never done this before. If I had, I wouldn't be asking for the recipe!

Speakers of English know that a sanctioned use of the second-person pronoun *you* is as a generic; that is, its use to stand for "any person" in such utterances. Numerous extended uses of deictics are allowed in English, and in this paper I shall examine (i) deictics in utterances that may be characterized as quotes or as free indirect speech; and (ii) uses such as generic *you* which do not appear to exploit an utterance context at all.

I will concern myself primarily with the first and third factors in this paper, assuming the second and leaving the investigation of its complexities for future research. Cognitive grammar (Langacker 1987, 1991) will be used to depict the semantic value of deictic expressions as referring to some aspect of the utterance *ground*, i.e., the utterance context. I will then explore how we get extended uses which do not exploit this context (or at least do not obviously or solely exploit it)—uses which involve *alternate grounds* to the actual discourse context, with reference to which we may find referents for deictic expressions. As sources of such alternate grounds I will consider mental spaces (Fauconnier 1985), which provide alternate utterance contexts within which deictics may be used, and cognitive models (Lakoff 1987), which provide frames with roles or relationships which deictics may refer to. I will examine how mental space construction, as discourse proceeds, provides access to contexts permitting interpretation of deictics that are inappropriate if we take the actual discourse context as ground; and how cognitive models provide a viewpoint which is in accord with deictic semantics.

[. . .]

The semantics of deictics

Among the factors used in interpreting deictic expressions is their inherent semantic content (Rauh 1981). Crucial to the cognitive grammar view, as laid out by Langacker (1985), is the notion of the *ground*, a technical term referring to "the speech event, its setting, and its participants" (Langacker 1985: 113). The setting includes the time and place of the speech event. A deictic expression is "one that includes the ground—or some facet of the ground— in its scope of predication [i.e., its meaning]" (Langacker 1985: 113). Specifically, a deictic expression designates some entity—a person, object, time, or location—and specifies a relation between that entity and a reference point within the ground. Figure 1 is a composite diagram which may be used to illustrate the meaning of numerous deictics.

The oval in the diagram represents the speech situation. *S* stands for the speaker, *H* for the hearer; *t* labels the arrow representing time, and *t'* is the time of the speech event; *LOC* represents the location of the speech event. One of the elements within the ground serves as a reference point relative to which other elements are judged proximal or distal—let us take the speaker *S* as reference point, as both Langacker (1978) and Talmy (1988) point out that it is the default reference point for deictic expressions. The dot labeled *x* signifies an object that is construed as proximal to the reference point; the dot labeled *y* signifies an object that is construed as distal to the reference point. A particular deictic expression would designate one of the elements represented in Figure 1; and its relation to the reference point would feature prominently in the semantics of the expression. For English deictics, only two relations are coded, proximal and distal. Talmy characterizes these relations as being, respectively, "on the speaker side or non-speaker side of a conceptual partition drawn through space, time, or some other qualitative dimension" (1988: 168). [. . .]

Adopting the spatial and temporal boundaries of the speech event as the partition determining proximal vs. distal relations, we may use Figure 1 to illustrate the semantics of various deictics in their most basic senses. In cognitive grammar, an expression derives its semantic value by virtue of the elements contained within its base, plus the *profiling* of one of these elements. Profiling is equivalent to designation—the profiled elements of the base are the elements which the expression designates or names. For example, profiling *S* in Figure 1 creates a linguistic expression which designates the speaker in a speech event—the pronoun *I*. Profiling *H*, on the other hand, creates an expression designating the hearer or addressee— the pronoun *you*. Profiling *LOC* would give the meaning of *here*, profiling *t'* would give *now*. Profiling *x* would give the meaning of *this* in its nominal sense. Shifting to entities construed

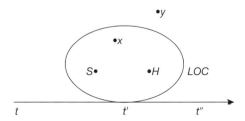

Figure 1

as distal to the reference point, profiling *y* would give the meaning of nominal *that* if *y* is a thing, or *there* if *y* is a location; supposing we were to profile t″, we would have the semantics of *then*.

Thus, according to the cognitive-grammar view of deictic semantics, in order to interpret deictics in discourse we must have in our representation of the import of the discourse a conception of the ground, as well as entities, one or more of which is a reference point for assessing the others; and relations between the entities and the reference point within the ground. But as we saw in (1), the actual discourse setting cannot be taken as the ground in every case. It is at best the default ground, as Fillmore suggests (1971: 41–2), and hence my characterization of the meanings of deictics in the discussion of Figure 1 as their basic or central (default) senses. In support of this characterization, Hanks writes, "the concept of decentering is tied inevitably to the idea of a normal, automatic, nondecentered usage, in which the indexical ground is right where it should be, so to speak. We recognize cases of decentering by their failure to correspond to the normal cases. It is relevant to the plausability of this view that speakers make basic-level assumptions and routinize their indexical usage so as to privilege the corporeal frame [= actual utterance ground] as the one that is available until further notice. This is significant, since it weighs the actual frame more heavily than the other possible ones" (1990: 228). Thus the actual utterance ground is the prototypical base for deictics, since it is "privileged"—it serves as automatic ground and as a standard against which decentered uses are measured; and it is the default in the sense that it is assumed to be "available until further notice."

Mental space theory gives us other important aspects of basic deictic semantics. Pronouns have in their semantics *connectors* [. . .] between the discourse ground—i.e., the actual utterance ground, which is a mental space, insofar as it is mentally comprehended by the discourse participants and it is the subject of language within the discourse—and other spaces constructed in ongoing conversation. Because of these connectors, pronouns may function as *triggers*, which are expressions used to identify a *target* element in a mental space. Consider example (6):

(6)   In this picture, I'm wearing a gorilla suit.

The expression *in this picture* builds a mental space. The connector and other semantic features inherent in the pronoun *I* allow a listener to use the pronoun as a trigger to identify the person wearing the gorilla suit in the picture (the target) with the speaker of the sentence in the actual discourse context (in spite of the obscuring function of the gorilla suit). This role of pronouns as triggers is basic in both aspects of my analysis—in the role of mental spaces as alternate grounds and in the role of cognitive models as alternate grounds. This will become apparent in following sections.

Analysis

Mental spaces as alternate grounds

In this section I explore the role of mental spaces in providing alternate grounds for the interpretation of deictic expressions. I discuss how a mental space provides a new domain peopled with entities in relation to each other, accessible to deictic reference, and how a viewpoint or reference point different from that of the actual discourse participants may be set up.

The mental space structure of even a short segment of discourse, such as a single entry in my interview data, is an extraordinarily complex affair: mental spaces are constructed and sometimes multiple embeddings of spaces occur; each space is peopled with objects and relations by the language following space-building expressions; the focus or currently active space may switch several times in a multiclausal sequence; and background knowledge is imported into constructed spaces. To make the explication of mental spaces as alternate grounds manageable, I simplify the description to a large extent. Thus my diagrams and descriptions of mental space structure in the data are radically simplified.

The examples analyzed in this section illustrate how mental spaces provide grounds for interpreting deictics in quoted speech and in free indirect speech. The role of mental spaces in providing such alternate grounds is to provide the discourse participants with alternative domains to the actual discourse situation; they may people these domains with entities, predicate attributes of them, and compute relations among them. One state of affairs which can occur within a constructed space is an utterance event—i.e., an individual within a space speaks or has thoughts similar to internal speech; the space then serves as the ground for that utterance. The relations between the speaker in the space and other elements in it may sanction uses of deictics that conflict with what we would expect if the actual discourse situation were taken as the ground. An example from the interview data that illustrates this is given in (7):

(7)   JF16: . . . or the same with when I go to, like, a Spanish part of town, you know, see everything in Spanish, and I say, well, you know, *this* is not where I belong. (italics added)

The italicized proximal deictic *this* in example (7) cannot be felicitously read as referring to the location of the actual speech event where this sentence was uttered, the interview site. But if we substitute the phrase *a Spanish neighborhood* for *this*, a felicitous reading within the context of the utterance is maintained. We must find an alternate ground for interpreting *this*—an alternate domain wherein proximal relations hold between the reference point (the speaker) and other elements, such as the location of the speech event. A simplified mental space diagram for this segment is shown in Figure 2.

Note the multiple embedding of spaces. The space marked *R* is the origin space, the speaker's conception of reality (reality is mentally comprehended by speakers and is thus just

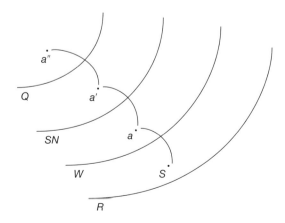

Figure 2

another mental space; see Fauconnier 1985: 14–16). This space would include the interview situation and hence the default ground for the speaker's utterances. *S*, the speaker, is the only element shown in this space, although of course many others would be present, for instance, myself as her interlocutor.

The word *when* is a space builder, instructing the listener to construct a time space, marked *W*. The pronoun *I*, a nominal, sets up an element, marked *a*, in *W*. Relations in *R* can be used to find a reading for *I*. Without explicit blockage by certain linguistic expressions, relations in *R* are available for interpretation of deictics in later spaces; recall also the discussion above of pronouns as triggers. Thus we understand that it is the speaker in *R* who goes to the Spanish part of town on some occasions. Within *W*, the location nominal *a Spanish neighborhood* sets up another space, a location space, marked *SN*. The relation *go to*, which has as its subject the pronoun *I*, places the speaker in *SN*, hence the element *a′*, which corresponds to *a* in *W* and to *S* in *R*. Then within *SN* we have yet another space, a quote space built by the verb *say*—this is marked *Q* in the diagram. By virtue of the meaning of the verb, this space portrays an utterance and hence all the appurtenances of an utterance event, namely, a ground, including a speaker, a location of the speech event, etc. This speaker is explicitly set up by the pronoun *I* of *this is not where I belong*, and is shown as element *a″* in the diagram. We can connect this element with *a′* of *SN*, by virtue of *a*'s subject relation to *say*, and thence with *a* of *W* and *S* of *R*.

Note that a different interpretation for *I* could be available in a different discourse situation. Suppose, for example, that JF had been describing not her own feelings but her brother's. She could easily utter the statement in (8), and the listener could easily read *I* as the brother, not the speaker JF:

(8)   . . . when he goes to a Spanish part of town . . . and he says, this is not where
       I belong.

Because a quoting verb like *say* sets up an utterance event and therefore a ground, an alternate ground is easily available for the interpretation of deictics in the quoted utterance.

A location for the utterance event portrayed by the words following *say* is available from among the spaces constructed so far, namely, *SN*, the Spanish neighborhood. The quote space is situated within this space, i.e., the speaker of the quoted clause has been placed in *SN* by preceding language. This sets the Spanish neighborhood up as a location which can be construed as proximal to the speaker (the subject of *say* in *SN*). Therefore taking the Spanish neighborhood as a referent for *this* gives a felicitous reading, indeed the only felicitous reading in context.

A more complex example illustrates the crucial role of mental spaces in these extended uses of deictics. Consider the segment of JF16 cited above in (1), and repeated here as (9):

(9)   JF16: There's a part of southeast San Diego where you do go down, you see all
       these Vietnamese theaters and everything in Vietnamese and when I see that I
       just kind of feel, well, I don't belong in *this place, this* is where the Vietnamese
       people are, I don't belong *here*. (italics added)

Again we find that a suitable paraphrase for the italicized proximal deictic expressions in this segment is a phrase like *a Vietnamese neighborhood*, and not phrases indicative of locations truly proximal to the interview event such as *La Jolla* or *your office*. What sanctions proximal deictics in this example? Figure 3 gives a partial diagram of the spaces constructed in this segment.

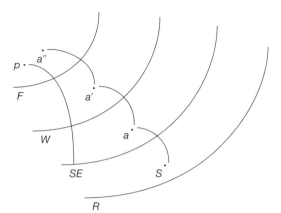

Figure 3

To simplify the discussion somewhat, let us say that the first sentence, beginning with *There's*, sets up a locational space, *SE* (southeast San Diego) within *R*. This space is the setting for the segment I wish to focus on, which begins with the word *when*. As we saw above, *when* is a space-building expression and creates a time space in which events may be postulated. The event postulated is *I see that*, where *that* refers to the previously mentioned Vietnamese theaters and shop signs and such in Vietnamese. Another event is postulated within the *when* space, namely, *I feel*. Now *feel*, as a propositional-attitude verb, sets up a space *F* in *W*. In *F* we find the feelings and responses of the speaker. Three expressions of her feelings follow. These expressions set up elements and predicate relations among them: a speaker a'' (*I*) and a location *p* (*this place, this, here*). The relations *not belong in p* of a'' and the equation of *p* with yet another space, *where the Vietnamese people are* are set up (these are, for simplicity's sake, not shown in the diagram). We have already seen how we may find a reading of the actual discourse speaker for *I* in such a space construction by virtue of the connector semantics of pronouns; of greater interest is the presence of the proximal locational deictics *this place, this*, and *here*, for which we unproblematically identify the Vietnamese neighborhood as referent. [. . .]

   The verb *feel* introduces language about the internal responses of the speaker to a given situation; these responses may be given in the form of a quote, exploiting proximal relations between the experiencer (the subject of *feel*) and the location; but it is not the verb *feel* alone which supplies all the specifics of an utterance situation and therefore sanctions the proximal deictics, as I argued was the case with the quotative verb *say* in the previous example. Rather it is the collective contribution of several space-building expressions which, taken together, supply all the necessary specifications of an utterance ground (location from *where;* time from *when*, and a reference point from the subject of *feel*). Taken together, these expressions build a scenario in which proximal deictics are sanctioned and allow us to read the language after *well* as a quote (even if as a quote of internal speech or thought to oneself). This is clear when we remove some of the space-building expressions (and their subsequent clauses): use of proximal deictics becomes marginal or disallowed under these circumstances. Removing both the *when* clause and the *feel* clause has the result of making proximal deictics bad, as in (10); note, however, that distal deictics, exploiting the distal relations between the speaker and the Vietnamese neighborhood in *R* (reality), are fine, as in (11):

(10)   ???There's a part of southeast San Diego where you do go down, you see all these
        Vietnamese theaters and everything in Vietnamese; and I just don't belong in
        this place, this is where the Vietnamese people are, I don't belong here.

(11)   There's a part of southeast San Diego where you do go down, you see all these Vietnamese theaters and everything in Vietnamese; and I just don't belong in that place, that is where the Vietnamese people are, I don't belong there.

My intuitions tell me that (10), without the space-building *when I see that* and *I just kind of feel*, is far less acceptable than (11), which lacks the space builders but uses distal deictics, in accord with the actual relations between the reference point (the interviewee) and the topic location (the Vietnamese neighborhood). It is especially clear that the language after *and* cannot be read as a quote. Some readers may believe that the switch from generic *you* to *I* influences these judgments, but the reader is invited to substitute *I* for *you* across the board in both versions; it does not change the judgments.

Just what is needed to sanction the proximal locational deictics? Let us try the segment with one or the other of the two space-building expressions which are missing from (10) and (11):

(12)   a.   ???There's a part of southeast San Diego where you do go down, you see all these Vietnamese theaters and everything in Vietnamese; and when I see that, well, I don't belong in this place, this is where the Vietnamese people are, I don't belong here.
       b.   ??There's a part of southeast San Diego where you do go down, you see all these Vietnamese theaters and everything in Vietnamese; and I just kind of feel, well, I don't belong in this place, this is where the Vietnamese people are, I don't belong here.

(12a) is quite bad, in my judgment; it seems that supplying an utterance location and an utterance time is still not enough to get a quote reading on the clauses with the proximal deictics. (12b), in which the verb *feel* supplies a viewpoint, is better, but still marginal. In (12b), the reading for *I* is not the conceptualizer that the discourse participants are imagining as located in the Vietnamese neighborhood, but rather the speaker in the interview situation,[1] i.e., the interviewee is describing her feelings in general about such ethnic neighborhoods, not her feelings on particular occasions when she finds herself actually located in such a neighborhood. Because we use relations in R to compute a reading for the *I* of *I feel*, and because no space builder intervenes between it and the following clauses to introduce an alternate utterance ground, we expect deictics in those clauses to exploit relations in R also; hence the acceptability of distal deictics in those clauses, as seen in (13):

(13)   There's a part of southeast San Diego where you do go down, you see all these Vietnamese theaters and everything in Vietnamese; and I just kind of feel, well, I don't belong in that place, that is where the Vietnamese people are, I don't belong there.

It seems that neither space-building expression alone is sufficient to sanction the proximal deictics. Both are needed: *where* provides an utterance location, *when* provides an utterance time, and *feel* provides a viewpoint; both are crucial aspects of an utterance ground. In order to set up an alternative world within which a speech event is to be situated, we must have all ground elements present: location, time, and reference point (speaker). These are given by three space-building expressions in this segment: *where, when,* and *feel*.

These judgments are complicated by the fact that the mere presence of the proximal deictics, with intonation and stress typical of a quotation (acting out the utterance), as well as elements whose contribution I am neglecting, such as *well*, can force the quotation reading and make the segment without space builders or with only one space builder sound better (albeit still marginal). It is important to test the putative quotation with and without real-speech intonation in order to evaluate the various versions accurately. This fact underscores the importance of the inherent semantic content of deictics and their contribution to the interpretation of utterances such as (9).

To sum up, this section has demonstrated how space-building language provides alternate utterance grounds for interpreting deictics. In cases where an explicit quotative verb such as *say* is used, the semantics of the quotative verb set up a space which is an utterance event. In other cases, such as with the verb *feel*, space-building expressions can contribute the necessary features of an utterance ground—time, place, and reference point—and sanction the use of proximal deictics which would otherwise conflict with the specifications found in the actual discourse situation.

Cognitive models as alternate grounds

A cognitive model is another sort of mental representation proposed by cognitive linguistics (see especially G. Lakoff 1982 and 1987). Unlike a mental space, which is a temporary knowledge base constructed in the course of a particular discourse, a cognitive model is an enduring representation which stores our knowledge of a domain. The term *cognitive model*, especially the term *Idealized Cognitive Model*, or *ICM*, originates with G. Lakoff (1982), but the notion arises from numerous sources in linguistics and artificial intelligence, such as the notion of a *script* (Schank and Abelson 1977), a *frame* (Fillmore 1982), or a *schema* (Bobrow and Norman 1975; Rumelhart et al. 1986). Cognitive models are built up on the basis of experience as well as innate properties of the mind (G. Lakoff 1982). The information in cognitive models may be stored in the form of propositions or of images of various sorts, including visual images or images in other sensory modes.

Cognitive models not only store but also organize our knowledge of a given domain. Thus some elements within a cognitive model may be privileged in some psychological sense; or the whole domain stored in a given cognitive model may have the structure of a radial category (G. Lakoff 1987). It is important to note that cognitive models do not store our knowledge of how things happen in actuality. Rather, they are *idealized*; that is, they are simplified and adjusted in various ways. One important aspect of cognitive models is that they often provide norms for situations or behavior; that is, they store our expectations and perhaps desires as to how particular scenarios should play out, rather than the noisy reality we actually encounter from day to day. Quinn (1987) examines one example, the American cultural model of marriage: how Americans conceive of marriage and what they expect to happen in a marriage, how they expect the partners in a marriage to behave, and so forth. Cognitive models can thus provide us with default assumptions about the world and specifically about the behavior of ourselves and of others (Fauconnier, p.c.).

In this section, I show how cognitive models, which are assumed by the speaker to be shared with her interlocutor and therefore remain implicit, function in alternate-ground phenomena. I discuss examples in which cognitive models provide conceptual connections which sanction metonymic language use; how they provide alternative viewpoints, without explicit space building or explicit appeal to the assumed model; and how they provide normative and antinormative scripts or frames with roles that are referred to with pronouns, assuming viewpoints provided by the model.

Given the cognitive-model construct, we would expect idealized models to be entertained regarding such behavior as immigration. One conclusion I reached in the study from which the data in this paper are drawn (Rubba 1988) was that my informants, and probably many other Americans, maintain several idealized cognitive models pertaining to culture and to immigration. I propose three specific models pertinent to the present topic: (i) an ICM of territoriality, or the relation between a culture (an abstract object) and physical space; (ii) a cultural map of San Diego, a particular application of the ICM of territoriality by residents of San Diego; and (iii) an immigration script or scenario, which prescribes the ideal(ized) way in which immigrants to this country should behave, what aspirations they should have, etc. [. . .] We can find evidence for such models in language use, not only in the overt propositional content of statements, but also in the use of a number of linguistic expressions, such as *but* or *still*, that indicate that a given situation corresponds to or conflicts with such a model. [. . .]

The association of culture with space in this territoriality ICM is a pragmatic function, or connector, [. . .]—a conceptual link between subfacets of a cognitive model, in this case a cultural group and the physical territory it occupies. This connector, like others, sanctions metonymic language use. JF speaks on several occasions of *belonging in a place*. This is such common language that it is hard to see the metonymy. However, one must acknowledge that two domains are being mixed: the notion of *belonging*, which has to do with abstract identification or affiliation with an abstract entity such as a group or culture, and physical space, which, apart from impositions upon it by human conceptualizers, has no boundaries or inherent affiliations. When JF makes statements like the one in (15), she is invoking the deeply held association between culture and territory, and using the spatial expression *here* to identify the culture that occupies the space:

(15)   JF16: This is where the Vietnamese people are, I don't belong here. . . . When I go to, like, a Spanish part of town, you know, see everything in Spanish, and I say, well, you know, this is not where I belong.

It is clear that JF is not talking literally about her physical location, but rather its cultural affiliation; for, if all of the Vietnamese people were to move to other areas, and folk of JF's own ethnic identity were to move into the neighborhood in question, we would not then expect statements reflecting feelings of not belonging from her about this location.

JF also illustrates a default assumption given by reasoning according to the territoriality ICM: if a person is observed in a particular physical location, and that location is recognized as being the territory of a particular culture, then that individual is assumed to be a member of that culture. Hence the *but* of JF16: "I can *be* there, but I don't belong." The default assumption is that being in a physical location entails belonging to the culture occupying that territory; JF's statement here asserts a violation of the default (one of the uses of the word *but* in English), a case in which physical presence does not entail cultural membership.

The second proposed cognitive model is a cultural map of San Diego, i.e., a stored mental representation of the locations of various neighborhoods in San Diego, including information about the ethnicity of the residents there. Obviously, the details and accuracy of such a map will vary from individual to individual depending on factors such as length of time residing in the area, how much the individual knows about San Diego, etc. Importantly, this map is likely to be *oriented*, that is, a given individual will perceive some area of San Diego as her "home" territory, or will perceive certain neighborhoods as being potential homes or not in accordance with her ethnic and cultural affiliation. Areas considered not to be potential home territories will be accorded a different status by the conceptualizer, and this status may be reflected in language use (see the discussion of inheritance of the cultural map below).

The third cultural model is a script or scenario for immigration to one country from another. Since presence in a physical space entails membership in the associated culture, individuals who commit themselves to leaving one physical space and taking up permanent residence in another are expected to change their cultural affiliation also, bringing it in line with the culture associated with the new physical location. Leaving one territory permanently entails abandoning the culture associated with that space; entering another territory with the intention to stay entails adopting the culture of that territory (assimilating to the new culture). [. . .]

"Recalcitrant" immigrants who do not rapidly assimilate violate this scenario, and JF indicates this with the expression *still*, which, in one of its senses, indicates conflict with a normative model, as in (17):

(17)   JF16: These people, they've come to America and still, they wanna be back [in the home country], you know, they don't want—they wanna be here for the advantages, but they don't wanna give up what they've . . . where they have come from. . . . And I just don't think you can do that in this country.

To summarize, several cognitive models which are interrelated and pertain to the domain of cultural affiliation—including physical location, immigration, and the ethnic makeup of a particular place (San Diego)—supply the necessary entities and relationships for comprehending linguistic expressions in the data. I now turn to the analysis of how these apply in the interpretation of deictic expressions.

In the discussion of mental spaces, I implied that the use of a deictic entails the presence in the awareness of the speakers of an utterance ground, and that the use of a deictic invariably invokes this ground. The discussion of deictic semantics also assumed that an utterance event invariably forms the base of the semantics of a deictic. I propose here an extension of the semantics of deictics which does not involve an utterance event as a ground; rather, some other oriented domain serves as the base set of entities and relations for interpreting a deictic. It is crucial that the domain is *oriented*, that is, that it contains a reference point of some sort from the vantage point of which other entities are evaluated. This will become clear presently. The domains I have in mind are the cognitive models about culture, territory, and immigration discussed above. I will examine two examples from the interview data. The first involves the use of a distal deictic to pick out a proximal location. The second involves the use of the personal pronouns *you* and *they* to identify not participants in the actual discourse situation, but roles in cognitive models and individuals in mental spaces.[*]

Inheritance of the cultural map

Consider a statement by JF at the beginning of the segment JF16, given in (18b):

(18)   a.   JR: I have kind of, kind of mixed feelings about different things, like I, I react in certain ways when I'm, like when I'm on the bus and I see an ad all in Spanish or you know, you walk down certain streets in a city, 'n you see most of the shop signs in Asian characters or something. I wonder, how do you feel when you encounter things like that? You know, what are your own, your own personal gut reactions? When you see a shop sign in Spanish or . . .

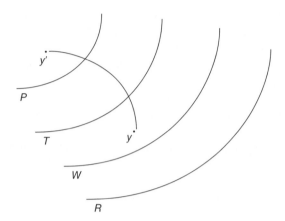

Figure 4

b. JF16: [starting over my finish] Well, well the fir, I guess the firs, the first
thing you think is, um, you know, that you're in *that* part of the city, and
I, I think usually you see that kind of stuff usually in the older part of the
city, and um, I know, um, you can go out to like sorta there's a part of
southeast San Diego where you do go down, you see all these Vietnamese
theaters and everything in Vietnamese . . . (emphasis is JF's)

The point of interest in this example is the use of the distal deictic *that* in the phrase *that part
of the city*. Note that the word was pronounced with heavy emphasis. Figure 4 gives a mental
space diagram of this portion of the segment. With my question *how do you feel when you
encounter things like that?* I set up a *when* space *W* within the origin space *R* (reality). JF's response
remains in the *when* space, where she sets up the element *y* with the word *you*; this invokes a
role paraphrasable as *one* or *someone*. She cues us to remain in this space by using the present
tense on the verb *think*. This verb then sets up another space, a thought space (*T*) which
contains the thoughts of the generic individual set up by *you*. These thoughts comprise the
clause *that you're in **that** part of the city*. The nominal *that part of the city* sets up another space,
a location space, marked *P*. The word *you* and the relation *be in* of *you're in* set up the element
y′ in *P*. The identity of the elements *y* and *y′* is established by retention of the second person
and by the trigger function of pronouns as discussed above.

Thus the space-building process in this discourse segment places a generic individual *you*
in an ethnic neighborhood; *you*, the generic individual, has thoughts there, including something
like "self is in *that* part of the city." We can identify the part of the city as the ethnic neighborhood
by virtue of the space building—the neighborhood has been set up by me in the question, and
the element *y′* placed there by virtue of JF's remaining in the space I set up. We saw in the
discussion of the quotative verb example above that just such space building can provide the
relations needed to sanction a proximal deictic; and we can imagine the use of one, if *y*'s
thoughts were to be portrayed as a quote of internal speech. So what grounds the use of the
distal deictic *that* in this segment?

As I have mentioned previously, relations in *R* are always available for the grounding of
deictics, unless explicitly blocked by, for instance, a quotative verb, and one possible analysis
of *that* is that it exploits the actual distal relation of the neighborhood in question to the
interview site. However, several factors militate against this interpretation. One is the change

in interpretation we get if we imagine an alternative scenario. Many neighborhoods are located distantly enough from the one where the interview took place to sanction distal deictics. We could have been discussing a distant mainstream, "non-ethnic" neighborhood, and an expression like *There's no shopping mall (tram stop/library branch) in that part of the city* would be unremarkable, with the distal deictic simply referring to a spatially distant location. Another factor is the heavy intonational emphasis on the demonstrative. I would class this usage not as taking the actual discourse context as ground, but as being an example of a special use of highly stressed definite determiners to attribute to the modified nominal some special significance, often already known to both speaker and hearer (at least, the speaker assumes that the hearer shares the knowledge necessary to appreciate the special status of the nominal's referent). Consider the examples in (19):

(19) a. My Dad always used to go on and on about how he had met *the* Bob Jones, the famous golfer, on his honeymoon.
 b. Upon entering the house I realized that this wasn't just any house. It was *the* house—the house where it had all happened, so many years ago.
 c. I tossed and turned and couldn't sleep because I couldn't shake the knowledge that I was lying in *that* bed—the bed where the old man had died.
 d. The first thing you think is . . . you're in *that* part of the city.

Emphatically stressed definite determiners in these sentences indicate a special significance of each nominal's referent; in these examples, I have provided appositive phrases which give a clue as to the nature of this significance. The *that* in (18b) is a special definite determiner like the ones in (19). The special significance of the nominal *part of the city* is computed by virtue of importation of knowledge structures held by individuals in *R* and imputed to the generic conceptualizer in *P*. Recall what is going on by virtue of the space construction in this discourse segment: we are imagining the generic person's thoughts and it is this generic person who uses *that* in her thoughts. What is invoked with the deictic is a subpart of the generic individual's encyclopedic knowledge—I suggest the cultural map of San Diego. The emphatic determiner points to an item of encyclopedic knowledge that is shared by the discourse participants (here, generic *you*, plus the interviewer and interviewee). Use of the deictic activates the model or scenario within which the item is relevant, as well as the item itself. In this case, the generic individual is in the ethnic neighborhood, and is at the same time invoking her model of how that part of town fits into her cultural map of San Diego; the deictic *that* indicates that it has marked status.

Note that the speaker—the interviewee—assumes that the hearer will understand what is special about that part of the city with little specification of the factors that underlie its significance. She assumes that the foregoing description in my question is sufficient to establish the markedness of the neighborhood; in other words, she assumes that her interlocutor (as well as the generic individual in space *P!*) shares her classification of that part of the city as an ethnic neighborhood, and that its status as such is sufficiently marked to be deserving of a special definite determiner. This is implicit, background knowledge which is nevertheless necessary to comprehend the use of *that*: a case of semantic freeloading, in which cultural knowledge is available for the interpretation of a linguistic expression by being imported into constructed spaces. [. . .]

The relevant question for this study is: What is the ground for the use of the deictic *that* in this segment? I suggest that the ground is the shared (or presumed shared) model of San Diego's neighborhoods and their cultural affiliation. The usage is similar to, possibly an extension of, the discourse deictic use of *that* to "point" to previously mentioned entities. An example is given in (21):

> (21)   A: Do you think the doctor made a mistake in your treatment?
>   B: You bet. And I'm hiring an attorney for *that* reason.

Discourse deictics take the text of the discourse as ground; definite deictics such as *that* point to material that has been mentioned already and is therefore known and accessible to all participants in the discourse. In similar fashion, a usage such as that in (18) relies on knowledge presumed by the speaker to be shared by the discourse partipants. However, the knowledge in question is not a text constructed in discourse (in fact, as we have seen, the discourse is rather impoverished in providing a referent for *that*), but the knowledge stored in a cognitive model. Thus the ground for this kind of usage is the cognitive model in which a classification of San Diego's neighborhoods is given.

[. . .]

Conclusion

In this paper, I have analyzed some of the extended uses of deictic expressions in English. I first gave a general outline of the problem—the task of finding referents for deictics in ongoing discourse; factors that enter into solving this problem; and the central notion of the account, alternate grounds. I then reviewed a concept of deictic semantics which offers enough detail to examine specifically which aspects of deictic semantics are exploited in alternate-ground phenomena. These semantic features were shown to be imported into other domains or onto other bases or grounds—alternate utterances, as in quotes and free indirect speech; or, in further extensions, into non-utterance bases, including shared models, such as the cultural map of San Diego; shared norms for behavior; and scripts or scenarios that are typical without necessarily being normative or prescriptive.

The analysis presented here demonstrates how deictic semantics as well as pragmatic and cultural knowledge are intimately intertwined in a particular access problem: accessing the intended referents of deictics in discourse. It also deals with some important viewpoint phenomena, showing how space-building language provides speakers the opportunity to displace the viewpoint relevant for deictic expressions in the discourse, and how the orientedness of some cultural models provides a viewpoint which can be adopted in interpreting deictics such as special *that* [. . .]. Also illustrated is metaphor, the importation of semantic structure into new domains: deictic semantics are transferred into domains which are not interpretable as utterance or indexical grounds, such as the domain for [. . .] special definite determiners such as *that* in the example considered here. Another aspect of the importation of structure is semantic freeloading: the automatic inheritance, into constructed spaces, of models from the origin space (such as the cultural map of San Diego), without explicit language invoking the model; The speaker assumes, when she says "*that* part of the city," that her interlocutor shares the cultural map *and* has access to it within the constructed space. [. . .]

Overall, I hope to have relayed the complexity of the task language users face when they encounter a deictic expression in discourse and must find a referent for it. I have explored only a small number of cases of what is no doubt a very widespread phenomenon, and have shown that constructs from various branches of cognitive linguistics are useful in explicating this phenomenon. This work is but a beginning to what promises to be a large and fertile area for applications of cognitive linguistics to discourse research.

Notes

* The second example is omitted from the paper as reprinted here.

1 We cannot allow the fact that these two individuals—the actual discourse speaker (the interviewee) and the conceptualizer in the Vietnamese neighborhood—are the same person to confuse this discussion. In mental-space terms, these are two distinct entities in distinct spaces; their identity is established by means of connectors, as discussed above, as well as by other aspects of the utterance, such as elements or spaces which would lead us to connect the last *I* to a person other than the speaker.

■ ■ ■

POST-READING

Order the following list of terms used by Rubba according to which you think come closest to describing the essential content of her paper: *alternate grounds, candidate locations, cognitive models, the conception of ground, decentering, finding referents, interpreting deictics, mental representation, the semantics of deictics, space-building, utterance ground, viewpoint.*

JEF VERSCHUEREN

NOTES ON THE ROLE OF METAPRAGMATIC AWARENESS IN LANGUAGE USE

PRE-READING

Write down the heading *The role of indexicality in the generation and negotiation of meaning*. Now write the opening sentence of a paragraph on this topic.

IN-READING

1   At the end of each page of the text, pause and, if appropriate, add to and/or revise the paragraph you began to write before you started to read.

2   As you reach the points in the text marked with |, stop reading and provide an example of the phenomenon under discussion. In those cases where Verschueren provides an example, provide an additional example of your own.

■ ■ ■

NOTES ON THE ROLE OF METAPRAGMATIC AWARENESS IN LANGUAGE USE
JEF VERSCHUEREN

[. . .]

This paper argues that metalanguage is an important topic for linguistic research because it reflects metapragmatic awareness, a crucial force behind the meaning-generating capacity of language in use. The reflexive awareness in question is no less than the single most important prerequisite for communication as we know it. It is part of what Tomasello (1999) describes as people's ability to identify with others and thus to work collaboratively towards common goals.[1]

In a first section, the notions of metalanguage and metapragmatics will be briefly introduced and clarified. Section 2 goes into the relevance of metalinguistic or metapragmatic phenomena as reflections of metapragmatic awareness, a notion that will be situated in relation to an overall theory of pragmatics. A third section elaborates on some aspects of the functioning of metapragmatic awareness in actual language use. Finally, some of the social implications of this functioning will be reviewed, in particular in relation to language ideologies and identity construction.

1 Metalanguage and metapragmatics

Let's start out by establishing an intertextual link – and thereby engaging in the conscious use of metalanguage. During a meeting of which this article is a side product, the issue was raised repeatedly of how useful the notion of METALANGUAGE was, more often than not with the implication that its usefulness was very limited. Yet, depending on the perspective one takes, the significance of the notion may range from useful and interesting to absolutely necessary. First one may regard 'metalanguage' as an identifiable **object**, separable from other manifestations of 'language.' Applied to the text you have just started to read, the term would cover the use of lexical items such as 'intertextual,' phrases such as "the text you have just started to read" and "thereby engaging in the conscious use of metalanguage", or utterances such as "[. . .] the issue was raised repeatedly of how useful the notion of 'metalanguage' was" or "what Tomasello (1999) describes as [. . .]." It would cover conversational interventions such as "What do you mean by that?" or "That's not what I said". Such occurrences are pervasive in most types of discourse. Hence, because of its obvious correspondence with a range of empirical facts, the notion is necessarily a useful and interesting one. Yet its usefulness, from this perspective, remains limited. One might object, for instance, that what we are concerned with is simply language about language, i.e. manifestations of language in general which happen to have language within their referential scope. We would still have to demonstrate what is so special about it – if anything. We would have to demonstrate that the reflexivity involved is neither fortuitous nor trivial.

A second way of approaching 'metalanguage' is to look at it as a **dimension** of language – to be found in **all** language use – rather than a collection of instances of metalinguistic language use. While a discussion of this dimension would have to refer to all metalinguistic phenomena covered by the object notion of 'metalanguage', it moves beyond such phenomena into the realm of basic properties of any stretch of discourse, thus significantly expanding the relevance of the notion. This approach has a reasonably long history in linguistics, where the influences of pragmatist semiotics (in particular Peirce's theory of indexicality) combined with Prague School structuralism in the person of Roman Jakobson, who may have provided the single most forceful and influential introduction of 'metalanguage' as a linguistic topic. In his "Shifters, verbal categories, and the Russian verb" (1971), Jakobson points out that the two basic ingredients of linguistic communication, the message (M) and the code (C), may both be 'utilized' (used) and 'referred to' (pointed at, mentioned). 'Referring to' is a metalinguistic activity as soon as it has ingredients of linguistic communication within its scope. This activity may take place either within or across message and code, thus yielding four types of metalinguistic usage: Messages referring to messages (M/M) are to be found in various forms of quoted and reported speech (for an authoritative treatment of which, in terms of speech about speech, Jakobson refers to Vološinov 1930); an instance of code referring to code (C/C) is the proper name, which cannot be defined without circular reference to the code itself (i.e. a name means anyone or anything to whom or to which the name is assigned); messages referring to the code (M/C) are found whenever a word is 'mentioned' rather than 'used', as in " 'Pup' means a young dog" or " 'Pup' is a monosyllable" (a topic which has been commonly debated in philosophy at least since Carnap 1937); finally, a case where code and message overlap or where an element of the code makes "compulsory reference to the given message" (C/M) is provided by the category of 'shifters' (a term borrowed from Jespersen 1921), i.e. indexical symbols such as personal pronouns, aspect, tense, mood and evidentials, which necessarily 'shift' in relation to changes in the context of use and hence in relation to the content of the message. In more general terms, Jakobson (1960, 1985) presented the 'metalingual function' as one of his six basic functions of language. Clearly, only Jakobson's M/M and M/C categories of metalinguistic functioning fit into the object notion of 'metalanguage', while C/C and C/M can only be conceived in terms of a metalinguistic dimension. This observation gives rise to a rough classification of metalinguistic phenomena into two categories, as visualized in Table 1, one included in the dimension view of metalanguage only (say 'implicit metalanguage'), the other included in both the dimension and the object view ('explicit metalanguage').

Because of its necessary relation to usage phenomena (the proper domain of linguistic pragmatics), *the study of the metalinguistic dimension of language* could be called META-PRAGMATICS. In fact, the term has been used in this way, e.g. by Michael Silverstein (1976b, 1979, 1993). In Silverstein's view, strongly inspired by Jakobson but taking an interdisciplinary (primarily anthropological-linguistic) point of view, pragmatics encompasses "the totality of indexical relationships between occurrent signal forms and their contexts of occurrence, regardless of whether such contexts are other occurrent signal forms [. . .] or not specifically such [. . .]" (1993: 36). Whatever pragmatic functioning there may be, there is always the possibility of metapragmatic functioning, conceived in terms of *reflexivity*. He goes on to emphasize the importance of reflexivity more strongly still, taking away all suspicion that the phenomenon we are confronted with would be fortuitous or trivial:

> Without a metapragmatic function simultaneously in play with whatever pragmatic function(s) there may be in discursive interaction, there is no possibility of interactional coherence, since there is no framework of structure — here, interactional text structure — in which indexical origins or centerings are relatable one to another as aggregated contributions to some segmentable, accomplishable event(s).
>
> (Silverstein 1993: 36–37)

And, "metapragmatic function serves to regiment indexicals into interpretable event(s) of such-and-such type that the use of language in interaction constitutes (consists of)" (1993: 37). In other words, there is a constant interaction between pragmatic and metapragmatic functioning. This observation definitely lifts metapragmatics or metalanguage (seen as a dimension rather than an object) from the merely interesting and useful to the absolutely necessary if we want to understand language use.

In order to make the vast field of inquiry opened up by this view more manageable, Silverstein identifies three dimensions of contrast along which metapragmatic phenomena can be usefully situated. First, he distinguishes metafunctions according to their object of *meta-semiosis*. Along this dimension, metapragmatics—bearing on a reflexive relation to the pragmatic or indexical dimension of language—is opposed to (while at the same time incorporating) metasemantics, which deals with the reflexivity related to the semiotic realm of sense, i.e. an

Table 1 Metalinguistic phenomena

	metalanguage as a **dimension** of language use
metalanguage as an **object**	
[Jakobson's M/M + M/C]	[Jakobson's C/C + C/M]
explicit metalanguage	**implicit metalanguage**

"abstractable constancy in denotational capacity of grammatically constructed expressions" (1993: 41). A second dimension is formed by degrees and kinds of *denotational explicitness*. Most natural languages have (partially) explicit metapragmatic forms of expression, e.g. in the form of metapragmatic lexical items (such as performative verbs). There are also inherently (hence relatively explicitly) metapragmatic semantico-referential forms such as deictic expressions. At the implicit end of the scale we find metapragmatic indexicality, i.e. indexical signaling of something about indexical signaling. It is here that one may, e.g., situate the theoretical contribution of Gumperz's (1982a) 'contextualization cues', the linguistic means (often prosodic) that speakers use (usually with a very low degree of awareness) to signal how (forms occurring in) utterances are to be appropriately interpreted. Third, types of metapragmatic functioning differ in terms of the *mutual calibration* of the metapragmatic signaling event and the signaled pragmatic event-structure. Put simply, there is a difference, for instance, between cases in which the relationship between the two events is a 'reporting on' rather than a 'coincidence'. It is with reference to this dimension that the double communicative layering inherent in the pragmatic-metapragmatic relationship can be fully accounted for.

It is important to keep such possible distinctions in mind, while it is not necessary to adhere strictly to the associated terminology. For one thing, this author has trouble distinguishing between metapragmatics and metasemantics; even though a theoretical distinction can be made between those aspects of the meaningfulness of signs that are constant across different specific contexts and those that are connected with ongoing usage, they are hard to identify in practice. Aspects of denotational explicitness and mutual calibration between the pragmatic and the metapragmatic, on the other hand, will help to structure the following exposition. At the same time, they should function as a frame of interpretation for what follows; for instance, when we use the contrast explicit-implicit, it should be clear that this is a scale rather than a dichotomy, though because of the difficulty in giving all phenomena a specific place on the scale, the presentation will still look dichotomous.

As already mentioned, a dimension approach to metalanguage, exemplified in the Silversteinian formulation, implies a necessary or crucial link between the study of metalanguage or metapragmatics and pragmatics in general. The following section will be an attempt to define that link. Before doing so, however, let me specify two ways of using the term 'metapragmatics' which I want to distance myself from in what follows. Neither of them bears on the 'reflexivity' of language itself. The first is 'metapragmatics' in the sense of critical discussions of pragmatics; this belongs to the order of endeavors which any self-respecting scientific discipline has to engage in. According to the second, "Metapragmatics studies the conditions under which pragmatic, i.e. users', rules are supposed to hold" (Mey 1993: 277)— a topic which would generally be regarded as the province of pragmatics itself. There is a reason why such confusion could arise, but we can only explain that later. First we have to go deeper into the fundamental relationship between pragmatics and metapragmatics. In the following section we will introduce the notion of 'metapragmatic awareness' in relation to a general theory of pragmatics, arguing for the central role it plays in any type of language use, thus strengthening the view of metalanguage as a dimension rather than an object in its own right and demonstrating the relevance – indeed, necessity – of taking metalinguistic or metapragmatic functioning into account when approaching instances of language use.

2 Pragmatics and the central role of metapragmatic awareness

This paper is formulated against the background of a theory of linguistic pragmatics which defines language use as the adaptable and negotiable making of linguistic choices, both in production and in interpretation, from a variable (and constantly varying) range of options in an interactive effort at generating meaning (see Verschueren 1999).[2] The highly dynamic processes that are involved take place in a medium of adaptability which, rejecting any strict dichotomy between society and cognition, could be labeled 'mind in society' (following Vygotsky 1978). The mental phenomena characterizing this medium of adaptability that are most visibly at work in the meaningful functioning of language are perception and representation, planning, and memory. In addition to their being determined by the workings of such mechanisms, all meaning-generating processes occupy a specific *status* in relation to the medium of adaptability. In other words, not everything that happens in linguistic behavior occupies the same place in consciousness. Various *manners of processing or degrees of salience* (a term originally inspired by Errington 1988) may be involved. Just consider the opening sentences of this section:

(1)   This paper is formulated against the background of a theory of linguistic pragmatics which defines language use as the adaptable and negotiable making of linguistic choices, both in production and in interpretation, from a variable (and constantly varying) range of options in an interactive effort at generating meaning (see Verschueren 1999). The highly dynamic processes that are involved take place in a medium of adaptability which, rejecting any strict dichotomy between society and cognition, could be labeled 'mind in society'.

following Vygotsky (1978)

Though writing is a verbal activity involving a generally high degree of consciousness in the making of linguistic choices (in comparison to more spontaneous oral interaction), much in (1) is the product of quite automatic processing. Thus for someone with a reasonable command of English the verb *to be* quite naturally transforms into *is* when a correspondence with *this paper* is required in the present, and into *are* when the subject is the plural *processes*. Similarly, following the basic English word order subject-verb-object is hardly a matter of conscious decision-making. Even a conventionalized violation of the 'standard' rule requiring implicit subjects of non-finite clauses to be coreferential with the explicit subject of the main clause, resulting in the dangling participle *rejecting*, is not really the product of intentional design. On the other hand, as in most academic writing, word choice and the development of an argumentational structure are (expected to be) highly salient activities, the product of conscious effort. What happens on the interpreter side is roughly analogous.

   Being a crucial aspect of what goes on when language is used (whether in uttering or in interpreting), pragmatic analyses have to come to terms with the role of consciousness, awareness, or salience – whatever the preferred term may be—in order to understand linguistic behavior. [. . .] [S]alience has within its scope all the processes operating on structural choices anchored in context that contribute to the meaningful functioning of language. In other words, language users know more or less what they are doing when using language. Self-monitoring, at whatever level of salience, is always going on.

   It is this general aspect of language use in relation to the medium of adaptability that I call *reflexive* or *metapragmatic awareness* (a usage that is in line with the terminology anthropologists use, as reflected in Lucy 1993). Studying this type of awareness is crucial to an understanding of verbal *behavior* because, like any other form of social action, language use is always *interpreted*, in the sense that the actors involved attach meaning to it, so that the actors' interpretations become part and parcel of what needs to be described and explained. We will return to this point in Section 3.

On the basis of these observations we may be able to understand Mey's confusion (referred to at the end of Section 1) about metapragmatics in relation to pragmatics: 'The conditions under which pragmatic rules are supposed to hold' suggests a distance between conditions and rules; the conditions, however, necessarily belong to the rules (disregarding for the moment the question whether we want to talk about rules rather than principles at all); they form a normative package as it were; but of course there is no normativity without awareness, and the norms involved are constantly negotiated and manipulated; it is at this metalevel of awareness, which is necessarily at work whenever language is used, that the proper domain of metapragmatics is situated, inseparable from but still beyond the 'rules-cum-conditions' (which cannot really be broken up into 'rules' and 'conditions').

Awareness is not measurable, and the notion lends itself to easy speculation. Hence the centrality of metapragmatic awareness could easily mean the end of pragmatics as an empirical enterprise. Fortunately, the self-monitoring in question, at various levels of consciousness or salience, leaves identifiable linguistic traces. Returning to (1), just consider the following features:

- the **self-referential use** of *this paper*, which does not only refer to the overall activity of which the chosen phrase is itself a constitutive part, but which also **categorizes** that overall activity as a specific genre of language use, thus providing it with a specific frame of interpretation
- the explicit **intertextual links** that are introduced by *see . . .*, *following . . .*, and *formulated against the background of*, where the first two are mainly informative while the last one also instructs the addressees how to interpret what is about to follow
- the **metapragmatic description** of a verbal activity carried out elsewhere, as with the linguistic action verb *defines*
- the introduction of a **modality** in *could be*, which draws explicit attention to the status of the choice in the author's conceptualization of the ideational state of affairs referred to
- other **metapragmatic markers** such as the quotation marks in '*mind in society*', which draw attention to the lexical choice-making itself, as a kind of warning against unreflective interpretation
- finally, the entire stretch of discourse (and whatever follows it in this text) is about properties of language use, formulated at the metalevel of linguistic theory and analysis, and hence it is one long marker of metapragmatic awareness, abounding with categorizations, suggestions, claims, etc.

Thus, while all linguistic choice-making implies some degree of consciousness (which is not always equally observable), some choices openly reflect upon themselves or upon other choices. Reflexive awareness is so central that all verbal communication is self-referential to a certain degree, or that there is no language use without a constant calibration (to use Silverstein's term) between pragmatic and metapragmatic functioning. This phenomenon forms the proper domain of *metapragmatics*.

The range of indicators of metapragmatic awareness is not restricted to those exemplified with reference to (1) above. It includes all of Jakobson's 'shifters', Gumperz's 'contextualization cues' (such as instances of code switching), anything ever discussed under the labels 'discourse markers/ particles' or 'pragmatic markers/ particles' (such as *anyway, actually, undoubtedly, I guess, you know,* etc.), 'sentence adverbs' (such as *frankly, regrettably*), hedges (such as *sort of, in a sense*), instances of 'mention' vs. 'use' (again as already suggested by Jakobson), as well as direct quotations, reported speech, and more implicitly embedded 'voices.'[3] Independently of the Silversteinian tradition, though fully compatible with it, the label 'metapragmatics' has been used to describe specifically the linguistic study of one category of indicators of metapragmatic awareness, namely 'metapragmatic terms' or—more specifically still—'linguistic action verbs' (Verschueren 1985a, 1987, 1989b; Kiefer and Verschueren 1988). This more restricted form of metapragmatics was motivated as an empirical-conceptual approach to linguistic action, i.e. an attempt to come to grips with the varying ways in which linguistic behavior is conceptualized by those engaged in it, by way of scrutinizing empirically observable linguistic reflections of those conceptualizations (such as the verbs and verb-like expressions used, in natural language, to talk about the conceptualized behavior in question). This approach to language on language could be regarded, in a Silversteinian perspective, as a form of 'folk-metapragmatics', to be approached with due caution.[4] As Silverstein (1981b) pointed out, speakers' awareness of pragmatic phenomena (an interesting cross-linguistic study of which is provided by Lucy 1993) does not have to match the linguist's metapragmatic descriptions. Naïvely confusing these two may contribute to the furthering of a specific kind of folk meta-pragmatics inherent in Western linguistics itself. Assuming that such naïve confusion can be avoided, at least some of my further comments will be based on results obtained in this line of research.

Using the dichotomy introduced in Table 1 (which was declared to be scalar rather than dichotomous), let us assign, for the sake of easy reference in what follows, a 'place' to the different indicators of metapragmatic awareness, as reviewed briefly in Table 2.

Returning briefly to the scalarity of the distinction, it may be useful to point at a property of (1). The fact that deictic expressions, and in particular personal pronouns, are absent from the example does not mean that there is no person deixis. Clearly, the deictic center is the author and his own work. The degree of implicitness is higher than if there would have been personal pronouns. This is a function of the genre of academic writing to which the example

Table 2 Indicators of metapragmatics awareness

explicit metalanguage	implicit metalanguage

• metapragmatic descriptions (e.g. by means of metapragmatic lexical items such as speech act verbs or performative verbs)
• self-referential expressions
• discourse markers/particles or pragmatic markers/particles
• sentence adverbs
• hedges
• explicit intertextual links
• quoted and reported speech
• 'mention' (vs. 'use')
• some 'shifters' e.g. (some) evidentials
• some 'contextualization cues' (many of the above can be included in this category)
	• most 'shifters'
	   • deictic expressions (pronouns, tense, etc.)
	   • aspect
	   • mood and modality
	   • some evidentials
	• many 'contextualization cues' (e.g. prosodic patterns, code switching, etc.)
	• implicit 'voices'
	[• proper names, i.e. Jakobson's C/C, which may not be fully treatable on a par with the other metalinguistic phenomena]

belongs. But genre is only one parameter that corresponds to degrees of explicitness. Developmental research (e.g. Hickmann 1993) suggests that there are also age differences in the relative use of more explicit vs. more implicit forms of metalanguage.

3 The functioning of metapragmatic awareness

Metapragmatic awareness (of which we should remember that it may be present at any level of salience) functions in at least two crucial ways, related to—though not coinciding with—the categories of explicit and implicit metalanguage (see Table 4.3.2 [see original publication]).

3.1 Anchoring

First of all, forms of more implicit metalanguage such as deictic expressions[5] reflect an awareness of the ways in which utterances or sets of structural choices are situated or anchored in a temporal, spatial, social or discourse context. [. . .] Without such anchoring, any cognitive processing or interpretation is impossible or, as Silverstein puts it, "there is no possibility of interactional coherence" (1993: 36). This kind of function is also performed by some types of explicit metalanguage, in particular those that establish discourse deixis. In this domain, a special place is occupied by instances of self-reference, and in particular the full self-reference manifested in the performative use of speech act verbs (such as *promise* in *I promise that I will come tomorrow*), requiring the kind of calibration between the metapragmatic signaling event and the signaled pragmatic event-structure that Silverstein would call 'coincidence' (a label which corresponds directly with a term used by early 20th-century German specialists in Slavic linguistics for exactly this type of construction: *Koinzidenzfall*). The relation to problems of cognitive processibility is clear from a close study of the constraints on performativity of this kind: Only speech act verbs which do not require separate reference to properties of the describing act involved in the use of an explicitly metapragmatic verb (i.e. properties of the metapragmatic signaling event) for an adequate description of their meanings, and can be fully accounted for in terms of properties of the described act (i.e. of the signaled pragmatic event-structure) lend themselves to performative use; if this condition is not satisfied, a conceptual distance is involved which blocks complete self-referentiality (see Verschueren 1995a).

3.2 Reflexive conceptualization

A second type of functioning relates primarily to forms of explicit metalanguage, though its effects are often far from salient or only with difficulty accessible to consciousness. As already suggested, linguistic behavior—as a form of social behavior—cannot be understood without an understanding of the notions in terms of which the behavior is conceptualized by those engaged in it, whether as utterer or interpreter, i.e. without an understanding of the reflexive conceptualization that accompanies production and interpretation choices. [. . .] Let us illustrate this with reference to (2), distributed by the United States Information Service on 11 February 1999 (numbers in square brackets added for easy reference; boldface, italics, and underlining added):

b.
[1] **TEXT:** ALBRIGHT *THANKS* MONTENEGRIN LEADER FOR *SUPPORT* ON KOSOVO
[2] (SecState *calls* President Djukanovic Feb. 9)
[3] <u>Washington</u> – Secretary of State Madeleine Albright *expressed U.S. thanks* to the president of Montenegro for *supporting* international *efforts to resolve* the crisis in Kosovo.

[4] In *a call* to President Miklo Djukanovic February 9, Albright *assured* him that "Montenegro's concerns would be kept in mind at the Kosovo *settlement talks* in Rambouillet, France," <u>according to State Department spokesman James Rubin</u>.

[5] **Following is the text** of the *statement*:

[6] **(Begin text)**

[7] <u>U.S. Department of State</u>

[8] <u>Office of the Spokesman</u>

[9] **Press statement** by <u>James P. Rubin, Spokesman</u>

[10] February 9, 1999

[11] Secretary's *Call* to Montenegrin President Djukanovic

[12] On February 9 Secretary Albright *called* Montenegrin President Djukanovic to *thank* him for his government's *continued support* for international *efforts to resolve* the Kosovo crisis.

[13] The Secretary *noted* the constructive role Montenegro had played throughout the crisis and *praised* Montenegro for leading the way on democratization and economic reform in the Federal Republic of Yugoslavia (FRY).

[14] The Secretary *took this opportunity to assure* President Djukanovic that Montenegro's concerns would be kept in mind at the Kosovo *settlement talks* in Rambouillet, France.

[15] In his February 5 *letter* to the secretary, President Djukanovic had *stressed his government's support* for *any political settlement* reached by the two parties that did not affect Montenegro's constitutional position in the FRY.

[16] Finally, the Secretary *assured* President Djukanovic that *world attention on* the Kosovo situation **does not mean** FRY President Milosevic has a free hand to cause problems elsewhere in the FRY or the region.

[17] **(End text)**

[18] NNNN

Looking at the stretches of explicit metalanguage, we find illustrations for the above claim on two levels, the level of reporting on verbal behavior as well as the self-referential level. First, with the exception of "calls" in [2], "a call" in [4], "Call" in [11], "called" in [12], and "letter" in [15]—which focus on a channel of communication – all *italicized* portions of text show that reporting on verbal behavior is inevitably interpretive. Within the context of this article it is not even possible to begin spelling out all implications of social and institutional meaning carried along by "expressed thanks" in [3], "assured" in [4] or even "statement" in [5]. All of these descriptive metapragmatic choices reflect assessments of the communicative status and meaning of the described speech events. The quality of the descriptions, then, depends crucially on the degree to which the reflected assessments match frames of meaning that inform the described events. In contexts of communicative controversy, therefore, the incidence of opposing interpretations, emerging from the descriptive choices, is extremely high. And as with all linguistic choice-making, even without the surfacing of oppositions any choice that is made carries along its contrast sets implicitly.

Second, on the self-referential level, **boldface** portions of text demonstrate clearly the importance that is generally attached to the interpretive status accorded to any speech event and the efforts that are often made to protect such status against contaminating reframings. It is the function of "TEXT" in [1], "Following is the text . . . " in [5], "Begin text" in [6], and "End text" in [17] to define the status of the communication as precisely as possible in order to avoid the imposition of unintended frames of meaning. The same can be said of "Press statement" in [9], even though the speech event covered by this term is technically one layer removed from the superordinate structure of (2); I say 'technically' because the source of the two layers is the same. Communicative status protection is further accomplished by means of explicit source indications (<u>underlined</u> in [3], [4], [7], [8], and [9]).

Furthermore, there is a cyclic presence of these two levels (indicated here in ***bold italic***). Thus "does not mean" in [16] is an attempt to freeze the interpretability of a communicative complex descriptively captured as "world attention". In this case, the form of autoreferentiality that is involved hinges on the fact that the U.S. is one of the main engineers of this "world attention" in spite of the descriptive distancing. (For an interesting study of how all the above metapragmatically shapes the communicative status of specific genres such as press releases, see Jacobs 1999.)

4 Social implications of the functioning of metapragmatic awareness

4.1 Metapragmatic awareness and language ideologies

Language use, just like other forms of social behavior, is interpreted by the actors involved. In the realm of social life in general, more or less coherent patterns of meaning which are felt to be so commonsensical that they are no longer questioned, thus feeding into taken-for-granted interpretations of activities and events, are usually called ideologies.[6] Similarly, when elements of metapragmatic awareness can be seen to form persistent frames of interpretation related to the nature and social functioning of language which are no longer subject to doubt or questioning, it becomes possible to talk about ideologies of language.[7] The latter become relevant topics of investigation in a variety of ways.

First of all, indeed, there is the inseparability of (local) linguistic practice and (systemic) metalinguistic conceptualization whenever language is used. As could already be concluded from example (2), much of the meaning negotiation that forms the dynamics of linguistic interaction is a struggle over the communicative status of utterances, involving norms (generally accepted or hegemonically imposed even if not generally adhered to) against which the ongoing (or past, or future) behavior can be evaluated. Though this is most clearly the case in institutional settings (witness the acceptability rating of different types of questions and answers during a trial), it is an integral part of what goes on in everyday conversations as well (at any level of choice-making, even at the level of language choice in a multilingual context—see e.g. Meeuwis 1997), so that understanding these processes is necessary for any adequate pragmatic analysis.

Second, under certain circumstances the 'struggle' may be suspended in favor of facile judgment. This is most typically the case when interpretations informed by habitual conceptualizations are not subject to further negotiation. This may be a purely personal or occasion-specific occurrence. But it may also result from the incompatibility of aspects of communicative style (a notion which would not make sense without the metapragmatic level) as documented in the literature on intercultural communication (e.g. Gumperz 1982a) or on international news reporting (e.g. Verschueren 1985b, 1989a). What happens in such cases is that the experience of the naturalness of the invoked normativity, resulting directly from interpretation and conceptualization habits rooted in or related to ideologies of language, interferes with further meaning negotiation (a process which may be greatly enhanced by the absence of any direct interaction). Insight into the ingredients of language ideologies may therefore help us to understand what goes on in such specific settings.

By way of illustration, in order to show that none of this is innocent, take example (3), which is an extract from an official report following interviews with an asylum seeker as part of the procedure to determine eligibility for refugee status in Belgium. (The example is borrowed from Blommaert 1999a):

(3)   It has to be noted that the concerned *remains very vague* at certain points. Thus he is *unable to provide details* about the precise content of his job as 'political informant'. Furthermore, the account of his escape *lacks credibility*. Thus *it is unlikely* that the concerned could steal military clothes and weapons without being noticed and that he could consequently climb over the prison wall.

It is also unlikely that the concerned and his wife could pass the passport control at Zaventem bearing a passport lacking their names and their pictures.

Furthermore, the itinerary of the concerned *is impossible to verify* due to a lack of travel documents.

The statements of the concerned *contain contradictions* when compared to his wife's account. Thus he declares that the passports which they received from the priest were already completely in order at the time they left Angola. His wife claims that they still had to apply for visa in Zaïre.

The phrases in italics are clearly not value-free descriptions. They focus on (i) commonsense plausibility and hence the trustworthiness of the applicants, (ii) the need for documentary evidence, and (iii) the nature of the communicative activities that make up the summarized narrative. The interpretations are characterized by automatic applications of specific types of normativity, the validity of which is not questioned. As to (i), the inability to produce a convincing story is seen as a sign of lying—a judgment that is probably extended beyond the 'doubtful' stretches to the very grounds for seeking asylum. As to (ii), the norms of administrative records are imposed on the telling of part of a life story. As to (iii), a notion such as *contradiction* is applied across different narratives as if such an application would not require the careful comparison of entire discourse contexts.

Third, the workings of language ideologies can not only be observed in forms of everyday interaction, institutional discourse, education, political rhetoric, mass communication, and the like, but also linguistic theories and analyses themselves do not escape from their influence. Silverstein (1979) may have been the first to point this out convincingly. Others, mostly linguistic anthropologists, followed suit in their criticisms of the Gricean and Searlean paradigms in pragmatics, confronting what linguists took for granted with observable, situated linguistic practice. That the history of linguistics itself (or pragmatics in particular) is not free from 'ideological' fluctuations is easy to observe; just think of the notion of linguistic relativity, proposed as a principle by Whorf, elevated to the level of dogma by his followers, turned into a dirty word among linguists in the sixties and seventies, and resurrected during the last ten to fifteen years (witness Gumperz and Levinson 1996). From such observations we should learn that a constant monitoring of linguistic rhetoric in view of the ideological underpinnings of theories and analyses is not a luxury but a prerequisite for the advancement of linguistic pragmatics. (For an excellent example of such a critical approach to some of the linguistic literature, see Eelen's (1999) study of politeness research.)

4.2 Metapragmatic awareness and identity construction

Example (2) illustrates (in the underlined segments) how explicit attempts may be made to define the identity of the utterer or of the source of a message. The functioning of aspects of 'identity' would be hard to understand without reference to metapragmatiuc awareness. Most of the time it does not take the explicit form exemplified in (2), but it hinges on the subtle signaling involved in category-specific linguistic choices. Typical examples are forms of code switching (Gumperz 1982a; Auer 1998) which become symbolic for specific social groups or formations of which membership is typically required for an utterer to be able to use a certain code; similarly, switching to a code one assumes the interpreter to be more familiar with accomplishes a process of other-categorization (see e.g. Hinnenkamp 1991). In conversation analysis, the entire literature on participation frameworks and membership categorization devices (see e.g. Antaki and Widdicombe (eds) 1998) is fundamentally concerned with the meta-pragmatics of identity construction. That identities are not 'given' but dynamically constructed in discourse—which further strengthens the assumption that metapragmatic awareness must be fundamentally involved—should be clear from a small example such as (4). This example (borrowed from D'hondt 1999) is a fragment from an ordinary conversation in the streets of Dar es Salaam (from which I have eliminated the original Kiswahili and the transcription conventions):

(4) [N & G talking about a soccer game they want to watch]
    N: If it is granted to us.
    G: Inshallah, inshallah, inshallah.
    N: Eh? But in the mosque I do not see you?
    G: That's where I am going right now.

As D'hondt points out, reference to a future course of events (the watching of a soccer game)—which should not simply be taken for granted by humans who cannot themselves control the future—is followed by the formulaic "If it is granted to us," which is then acknowledged and upgraded by G's series of "Inshallah's" ('If God wishes'). Though there is a categorial relationship between G's utterance and being a muslim, the value of G's linguistic choices as identity markers is variable. The signaling of identity could have been left entirely implicit, and its contextual relevance might have been nil. But then N taps into his metapragmatic awareness of the identity-signaling value or potential of the linguistic choices made by G to topicalize it explicitly in "But in the mosque I do not see you?", a topicalization which is accepted by G in his next response.

5 Conclusion

There is a reason why the title of this article is simply "Notes on . . . ". The task of completing the picture is far beyond its scope. By way of conclusion, I would simply like to draw the attention once more to the fact that metapragmatic awareness—and hence all of its linguistic manifestations—contributes crucially to the generation and negotiation of meaning which, in a pragmatic theory, is the core process of what language use is all about. This is not only the case at the obvious levels of conscious self-monitoring and audience design, but also at much lower levels of salience where it underlies and contributes to the meaning of most aspects of linguistic choice-making. Singling the metalinguistic dimension of language out for separate scientific attention is therefore a valuable heuristic strategy in order not to forget its fundamental contribution to all pragmatic functioning.

    [. . .]

Notes

1   According to Tomasello, this ability to identify with others is the source of cultural learning, the cognitive switch that separates homo sapiens from primates and that explains the complex development of industries and institutions within historical (rather than evolutionary) time.

2   The theory in question views pragmatics as a general functional perspective on (any aspect of) language, i.e. as an approach to language which takes into account the full complexity of its cognitive, social, and cultural (i.e. 'meaningful') functioning in the lives of human beings.

3   For a more detailed overview of indicators of metapragmatic awareness, see Verschueren (1999: 189–195).

4   A recent plea for the study of folk linguistics (Preston 2000), linked to earlier proposals such as one by Hoenigswald (1966), is entirely in line with this interest, though formulated outside the context of a theory of pragmatics.

5   In his theory of 'pragmatics as implicitness' Östman (1986) excludes deixis from the realm of pragmatics (and includes it in semantics) because it represents a form of explicit rather than implicit meaning. Leaving aside the issue of the line that is drawn between semantics and pragmatics, there is no contradiction between that stance and the treatment of deictic expressions as types of *implicit metalanguage*: Saying that their metalinguistic functioning is more implicit (even though it leaves a 'trace') does not amount to saying that their meaning, in general, is implicit.

6   For remarks on the pragmatics of ideology research, see Verschueren (1995b) and (1996); for an extensive exercise, see Blommaert and Verschueren (1998).

7   For an overview of research on language ideology, see Woolard and Schieffelin (1994); for some recent contributions to this topic area, see Schieffelin et al. (1998) and Blommaert (1999b).

■   ■   ■

POST-READING

1   Make a mind-map based on what you have read, with *metapragmatics* in the centre.

2   Write clues for the entries in the crossword below following the usual practice of listing first *Across* and then *Down* clues by number. If you and one or more classmates have been reading Verschueren at the same time, you can either work together or work separately and then compare clues.

		¹N																

A crossword grid with the following filled answers:

Across:
- 2 (14) INTERPRETATION
- 4 (10) MEMBERSHIP
- 6 (8) SALIENCE
- 7 (5) SENSE
- 8 (6) CHOICE
- 9 (12) ADAPTABILITY
- 11 (see 23) REFERENTIALITY
- 14 (11) REFLETXIVITY
- 15 (14) METAPRAGMATICS
- 17 (6) DEIXIS
- 18 (9) AWARENESS
- 21 (11) CALIBRATION
- 22 (4) FOLK
- 23 and 11 (4–14) SELF
- 24 (8) IDENTITY

Down:
- 1 (11) NORMATIVITY
- 3 (9) ANCHORING
- 5 (12) METALANGUAGE
- 10 (12) PERFORMATIVITY
- 12 (9) REFERENCE
- 13 (9) DIMENSION
- 16 (8) INDEXING
- 19 (6) SCALAR
- 20 (4) COND

Across

2	(14)
4	(10)
6	(8)
7	(5)
8	(6)
9	(12)
11	(see 23)
14	(11)
15	(14)
17	(6)
18	(9)
21	(11)
22	(4)
23 and 11	(4–14)
24	(8)

Down

1	(11)
3	(9)
5	(12)
10	(12)
12	(9)
13	(9)
16	(8)
19	(6)
20	(4)

SECTION 4 FURTHER READING

Philosophical approaches to indexicality

Evans, G. (1981) 'Understanding demonstratives', in H. Parret and J. Bouveresse (eds) *Meaning and Understanding*, Berlin: Walter de Gruyter; reprinted in P. Ludlow (ed.) (1997) *Readings in the Philosophy of Language*, pp. 717–44, Cambridge, Massachusetts: MIT Press.

Frege, G. (1918) 'Der Gedanke: eine logische Untersuchung' ('The thought: a logical inquiry'), trans. A.M. and Marcelle Quinton (1956) in *Mind* 65: 289–311; reprinted in P. Ludlow (ed.) (1997) *Readings in the Philosophy of Language*, Cambridge, Massachusetts: MIT Press.

Kaplan, D. (1989) 'Demonstratives', in J. Almog, J. Perry and H.K. Wettstein (eds) *Themes from Kaplan*, pp. 481–563, Oxford: Oxford University Press.

Perry, J. (1977) 'Frege on demonstratives', *Philosophical Review* 86: 474–97; reprinted in P. Ludlow (ed.) (1997) *Readings in the Philosophy of Language*, pp. 693–714, Cambridge, Massachusetts: MIT Press.

Deixis

Anderson, S.R. and Keenan, E.L. (1985) 'Deixis', in T. Schopen (ed.) *Language Typology and Syntactic Description: grammatical categories and the lexicon*, vol. 3, pp. 259–308, Cambridge: Cambridge University Press.

Diessel, H. (1999). *Demonstratives: Form, Function and Grammaticalization*, Amsterdam: John Benjamins.

Spatial frames of reference

Levinson, S.C. (1996) 'Frames of reference and Molyneux's question: crosslinguistic evidence', in P. Bloom, M. A. Peterson, L. Nadel and M. F. Garrett (eds) *Language and Space,* Cambridge, Massachusetts: MIT Press, 109–69.

Cognitive linguistics background

Fauconnier, G. (1997) *Mappings in Thought and Language*, Cambridge: Cambridge University Press.

Lakoff, G. (1982) 'Categories: An essay in cognitive linguistics' in Linguistics Society of Korea (ed.) *Linguistics in the Morning Calm*, Seoul: Hanshin.

Lakoff, G. (1987) *Women, Fire, and Dangerous Things*, pp. 68–76, Chicago, Illinois: Chicago University Press.

Langacker, R.W. (1987) *Foundations of Cognitive Grammar: Theoretical Prerequisites*, Stanford, California: Stanford University Press.

Langacker, R.W. (1991) *Foundations of Cognitive Grammar: Descriptive Application*, Stanford, California: Stanford University Press.

Metapragmatics in the sociocultural tradition

Lucy, J.A. (ed.) (1993) *Reflexive Language: Reported Speech and Metapragmatics*, Cambridge: Cambridge University Press. (Esp. Chapter 1.)

Indexicality and the sign

Silverstein, M. (1976b) 'Shifters, linguistic categories, and cultural description', in K. Basso and H. Selby (eds) *Meaning in Anthropology*, pp. 11–55, Albuquerque, New Mexico: University of New Mexico Press.

SECTION 5

Historical pragmatics

Introduction

T**HERE ARE TWO MAIN TYPES** of historical pragmatic studies: those which seek to account for the pragmatic features of texts at a particular point in time and those, like the readings in this section, which seek to determine how particular pragmatic features have changed over time. Diachronic studies share certain similarities with contemporary contrastive studies in that they seek to specify those elements that remain constant when different stages of the same language are compared. That said, researchers who undertake diachronic pragmatic studies are as interested in *pragmatic equivalence* as they are semantic equivalence, i.e. in capturing and comparing not only the linguistic inventory but also 'its communicative use across different historical stages of the same language' (Jacobs and Jucker 1995: 13). In our first reading, for example, Elizabeth Traugott traces the development of *as/so long as* in English, and demonstrates how its conditional meaning ('provided that', 'if') has become semanticized over time, having initially been an invited inference derived from the temporal meaning ('for as long as'), which was derived, in turn, from the spatial meaning ('the same length as').

Traugott's reading is also interesting because of her argument that 'there would be no semantic change of interest to linguists if it were not for the central role of pragmatic inferencing and implied meaning that goes on in the flow of speech (and writing)'. Traugott's paper appears here in the form in which it was originally published in Jef Verschueren's (1999) *Pragmatics in 1998. Selected Papers from the 6th International Pragmatics Conference* (Vol. 2). Traugott begins by asking 'what kinds of pragmatic meanings are relevant' to semantic change and how these should be modelled. Traugott's suggestions for suitable models include: (i) a Cognitive Linguistics approach, which might focus on the processes by which one conceptual domain is metaphorically mapped onto another, 'and the role of prototypes in such mappings . . .'; (ii) an approach that is directly linked with Verschueren (1999), and which also sounds remarkably similar to that of Historical Sociopragmatics in that it seeks to investigate examples of local language use from a specific time in the past in a way that takes account of the cognitive, social and cultural contexts influencing the interaction; and (iii) her own approach, aptly named 'the Invited Inferencing Theory of Semantic Changes (or IITSC)' (emboldening as in original).

Traugott's (1999) IITSC model is a speaker-based approach, which builds on both Grice (1975) and also Levinson's (1995) neo-Gricean proposals outlined in the introduction to Section 3: in particular, the notions of *coded meaning* (semantics), *utterance-token meaning* (invited inferences, which are approximately equivalent to conversational implicature[s]) and *utterance-type meaning* (generalized invited inferences, which are well established in the community). The 'speaker' focus is deliberate, as Traugott is seeking to demonstrate that it is speakers/writers who primarily motivate 'the strong tendency in semantic change toward subjectification', that is, do 'most of the work of innovation'. But she is aware of 'the importance of guiding addressees to an interpretation', and has argued elsewhere that the notion of *invited inference* allows for 'the possibility of alluding to *both* the speaker's strategic action (inviting) and the hearer's response (inferencing)' (Traugott 2002: 29). Traugott's neo-Gricean approach, as exemplified in this particular reading, also argues for polysemy: for example, the co-existence of the conditional meaning of *as/so long as* alongside the (more traditional) temporal and spatial meanings from which it is derived ('equal in length' > 'equal in time' > 'provided that').

Particularly common in historical pragmatics are studies of the diachronic development of speech acts, address terms, pragmatic markers, and discourse strategies (including im/politeness strategies). The second and third readings in this section discuss two of the above in detail – the study of pragmatic markers and the study of speech acts over time – and also touch upon im/politeness (albeit to a more limited extent).

Pragmatic markers – termed 'procedural encodings' and treated as constraints on interpretation by Blakemore (see Section 3) – serve discursive (or textual) and cognitive (or interpersonal) functions. More specifically, they help to hold a sequence of utterances together, whilst also signaling the speaker's epistemic attitudes and feelings (towards the hearer and/or message). In addition, they can provide signals as to speaker role, identity, etc. Modern examples include items such as *I know, I mean, well*, etc. In this reading taken from Laurel Brinton's (1996) monograph, *Pragmatic Markers in English*, we primarily focus on Middle English *I gesse.* That said, we have included extracts from earlier (more generic) sections of the monograph, so that we can provide an inventory of the functions of pragmatic markers (as Brinton sees them) and explain the process by which particular lexical constructions undergo grammaticalization over time, that is, come to serve more of a grammatical function (or functions) and lose some or all of their lexical meaning. In regard to *I gesse*, itself, we include the bulk of Brinton's discussion of the different uses of this pragmatic marker in Chaucer's *Canterbury Tales*. For example, in Chaucer's dialogic mode, 'they are generally attached to propositions expressing matters about which the speaker, for a variety of reasons, cannot be entirely certain, such as personal evaluations, opinions said to be generally held, deductions based on appearances, and so on. In contrast, in narrative they are often used tongue-in-cheek and attached to propositions expressing inexactness concerning time, space, and even plot details, to the narrator's external evaluations, and to metacomments on the telling of the tale'. This mimetic quality is particularly worthy of note, because it allows Chaucer (as narrator) to profess ignorance or inadequacy 'for humorous or artistic reasons' (see Bronson 1940: 33), and to leave open the possibility of the addressees responding as they see fit – or, at least, 'to inveigle or seduce the addressee into believing' they have this freedom (see Corum 1975: 139) – something that Brinton links to negative politeness, following Brown and Levinson (1978/87).

According to Brinton, epistemic parentheticals such as *I gesse* 'can be considered a case of grammaticalization', but they are not "textbook cases": following a semantic development of 'act of cognition > mode of knowing (evidential) > (un)certainty (epistemic)', the first stage highlighted by Brinton represents the process by which verbs denoting a mental act ('think', 'believe', 'guess') come to be used to denote a state of mind, whilst the second stage, 'from evidential to epistemic, seems to be an extremely clear example of the conventionalization of a conversational implicature' of knowing. As you read Brinton's extract, we hope that you will gain a sense of (some of) the processes involved in – and the processes that lead to – the (apparently, unidirectional) grammaticalization of pragmatic markers.

The final paper in this section, by Andreas Jucker and Irma Taavitsainen, 'Diachronic speech act analysis: Insults from flyting to flaming', provides an account of insults/insulting over thirteen/fourteen centuries, and thus touches upon 'verbal aggression'. However, given our focus here on historical pragmatics, we have opted to omit Jucker and Taavitsainen's discussion of flaming (the term used to denote hostile/insulting interaction between internet users). There is a wealth of diachronic speech act studies from which we might have drawn: we decided upon Jucker and Taavitsainen's article (which was originally published in the first edition of the *Journal of Historical Pragmatics*) for two main reasons. First, the authors advocate a prototype approach to diachronic speech act analysis, which means rejecting an application of speech act theory in its most conservative Searlean sense, in favour of seeing speech acts as 'fuzzy concepts which show both diachronic and synchronic variation in a [multidimensional] "pragmatic space"' – in this case, of face threatening acts, which includes 'slanders and slurs, oaths, swearing, disparaging remarks about non-present third parties and of course agonistic or ritual insults'. The primary 'shared' characteristic of the above is their *disparaging* 'predication about the target' – but this feature can be signalled on a number of levels, according to Jucker and Taavitsainen, and thus be used to differentiate between different realizations of insults. For example, they use the semantic level to distinguish truth-conditional insults from 'perfomative' insults (i.e. utterances that are blatantly untrue); they use the formal level to distinguish creative insults from ritual, 'rule governed' insults; they use the level they label 'context dependence' to distinguish conventional from particularised insults; they use the speaker level to distinguish aggressive insults from ludic insults; and use the perlocutionary level to distinguish 'reactions in kind' from 'denial, violence, silence', etc. The Unferth episode in Beowulf, with its 'Claim, Defense, and Counterclaim' pattern, thus constitutes an example of highly stylised ritual insulting. In contrast, the extended insult that the Host of the *Canterbury Tales* makes to the Cook in regard to food poisoning is creative, whilst the insult he himself receives from the Pardoner ('And thou shalt kisse the relikes . . . ') is 'a particularized and non-truth-conditional or performative insult'.

Our second reason for opting for Jucker and Taavitsainen relates to their claim – in later work (see, e.g., Taavitsainen and Jucker 2008) – that this proposed framework can also be applied to other (English) speech acts/speech act categories – as long as we are sensitive to the fact that the salience of particular components will be dependent on the speech act/speech act category under investigation: for example, in Taavitsainen and Jucker (2008: 7), they predict that, with (English) apologies, the *form* category is likely to be most prominent, as apologies tend to be 'expressed in routinised, perhaps even ritual and rule-governed forms'; and that the dimension of 'irony versus sincerity' (the third aspect of *speaker attitude*) will become 'prominent with compliments'.

ELIZABETH CLOSE TRAUGOTT

THE ROLE OF PRAGMATICS IN SEMANTIC CHANGE[1]

PRE-READING

Semantic change involves a change in meaning, over time, to a particular lexical item or construction, which - in cases like *as/so long as* - can also lead to polysemy (i.e. the same construction having multiple possible meanings), as, in this paper, where Traugott demonstrates how *as/so long as* has developed the conditional meaning via an extension of its temporal meaning, which was derived, in turn, via an extension of its length meaning. Before reading Traugott's explanation of this pragmatically-influenced process, jot down some examples of lexical items or constructions you are aware of that are polysemous. If you find it difficult to come up with your own examples initially, we would suggest that you might begin by listing three or four discourse particles like 'as long as'. Using a dictionary, such as the Online OED, trace the various senses of these polysemous items or constructions as a means of determining: which sense was the original one, whether they can still *mean* this today (in appropriate circumstances) and also what additional *meanings* they now have, and the order in which these additional meanings first came into use.

IN-READING

We have identified the following, in the Traugott text, using the marker, | : 'coded meaning', 'utterance-token meaning', 'utterance-type meaning', 'speaker/writer-negotiated meaning'. As you come to each entry, write down a definition for them *in your own words*.

■ ■ ■

THE ROLE OF PRAGMATICS IN SEMANTIC CHANGE
ELIZABETH CLOSE TRAUGOTT

Introduction

At the end of "Logic and conversation" Grice ventured "it may not be impossible for what starts life, so to speak, as a conversational implicature to become conventionalized" (1989 [1975]: 39), in other words, pragmatic meaning may become semantic meaning. It is widely agreed that much semantic change has pragmatic, conversational origins (e.g., Levinson 1983, 1995; Horn 1984; König 1991; Ariel 1994). In my view there would be no semantic change of interest to linguists if it were not for the central role of pragmatic inferencing and implied meaning that goes on in the flow of speech (and writing). But what kinds of pragmatic meanings are relevant, and how should they be modeled?

I start with an outline of the objectives of work on semantic change, and move on to a sketch of three approaches to semantic change, including my own, the Invited Inferencing Theory of Semantic Changes (or IITSC). The approach and the model of IITSC are illustrated with the example of the development of *as/so long as* in English. I end with some remarks on the kind of pragmatics needed to account for semantic change.

Objectives of work on semantic change

Meaning change is often thought to be haphazard. However, it is in fact highly regular, most especially in domains other than nominals. Current research seeks to identify regularities in paths of meaning change, and the motivations that lead to these changes.

There are three central questions:

Question 1: "Given the form-meaning pair L (lexeme) what changes did meaning M undergo?"—here the focus is on the development of polysemies (semasiology, e.g., *as long as* 'equal in length' > 'equal in time' > 'provided that'; *even* 'evenly' > 'unexpected member of set of alternatives' [the focus particle use as in *Even Samantha has left*]; or *sanction* 'approve, authorize' > 'impose penalty').

Question 2: "Given the concept C, what lexemes can it be expressed by?"—here the focus is on the development of (near)synonyms in lexical fields (onomasiology, e.g., CONDITIONAL expressed by *if, when, as long as, suppose, provided that*, etc.; CONCESSIVE by *although, while, however*, etc.; PENALIZE has recently had *sanction* added to older *penalize*, etc.)).

Question 3: "Given the concept C, what other conceptual domain is it likely to develop into?" (e.g., SANCTITY > AUTHORIZATION; TEMPORAL > CONDITIONAL; TEMPORAL > CONCESSIVE).

What kinds of approaches to these questions are at the forefront of current work and that involve historical pragmatics?

One approach is connected with Cognitive Linguistics and focuses on metaphoric processes. Cognitive Linguistics highlights conceptual structure, and the nature of conventionalized semantics. It privileges metaphorical mapping from one conceptual domain to another; also iconic, analogical relationships, and the role of prototypes in such mappings (see e.g., Sweetser

1990; Blank 1997; Geeraerts 1997; and, with attention to semantic change in grammaticalization, Langacker 1990). Understanding metaphors requires pragmatic inferencing to relevant meanings (see e.g., Lakoff 1993; Morgan 1993; Sperber and Wilson 1995), but pragmatics has not been the main focus of historical work in the Cognitive Linguistics tradition.

Another approach is connected with work by Verschueren (e.g., 1999) and others that combines certain aspects of sociolinguistics with formal pragmatics and theories of action. It is centrally concerned with communicative acts in speech events and highlights the contexts in which communication takes place (Jucker 1995). Jucker framed the field as follows for the Historical Pragmatics panel at this Congress:

> Historical pragmatics . . . studies historical language data by asking explicitly and systematically what the specific situation was in which the data was produced, who the writer was, and to what audience it was addressed . . . It studies the development of specific linguistic elements which can only be described by reference to their pragmatic function in specific communicative situations.

The research methodology is aimed primarily at accounting for language in use, and for the effect of language-external factors such as situations, participants in them, and text types.

A third approach is the Invited Inferencing Theory of Semantic Change (IITSC) (see e.g., Traugott 1997). According to this theory, the key motivations for change are associative, metonymic, indexical meanings that arise in the process of speech and writing. Particular attention is paid to ways in which they lead to changes in the linguistic system, that is, in the semantics of the lexicon, constructions, and in grammatical markers.

IITSC combines cognitive linguistics with communication-based historical discourse analysis/historical pragmatics (Schwenter and Traugott 1995; Traugott and Dasher 2002). IITSC arose in the context of thinking about cross-linguistic regularities in grammaticalization (see e.g., work by Givón 1979; Traugott 1989; Brinton 1988; Traugott and König 1991; Bybee et al. 1994), but currently ranges over any domain in which semantic change occurs. The basic hypothesis is that a Lexeme L may gain semantic properties from the context in which they are typically used.

To answer the fundamental questions posed at the beginning: "What kinds of pragmatic meanings are relevant to semantic change, and how should they be modeled?" we need to consider assumptions concerning levels of meaning.

Assumptions concerning levels of meaning in IITSC

Building on Levinson's (1995) three levels of meaning, I assume we need to distinguish:

Coded meaning (semantics): this is a convention of language. English *as long as* has the polysemies 'of same length as', 'during the time that', 'provided that'; by contrast, Fr. *tandis que* from Lat. *tam diu quam* 'as long (temporally) as' has the polysemies 'during the time that', 'although'.

Utterance-token meaning: meanings that arise ad hoc; these are invited inferences [IINs] (approximately equivalent to conversational implicatures [CIs]) and defeasible. They may be based on encyclopedic knowledge, or (in a nonce-situation) on the situation at hand, including linguistic context.

Utterance-type meaning: generalized invited inferences [GIINs] (approximately equivalent to generalized conversational implicatures [GCIs]). These are preferred meanings, conventions of use which are defeasible, such as *post hoc ergo propter hoc* (a causal relationship between p and q in *after p, q* is frequently understood, but can be canceled). These GIINs are linguistically based.

I prefer the term "invited inferences" (which originates with Geis and Zwicky 1971) over "implicatures" because it invokes interaction (however, I do not restrict it to generalized implicatures like they do). Speakers/writers can invite hearers/readers to let implicatures go through—in historical data such invitations are often reinforced by similar meanings in surrounding discourse. Addressees infer (correctly, or incorrectly), but in ways common to the community.

IITSC is a speaker-based approach, with emphasis on strategic negotiation in the flow of speech/writing. Although it recognizes the importance of guiding addressees to an interpretation (as proposed by Relevance Theory, see e.g., Sperber and Wilson 1995, and Blakemore 1987), nevertheless the assumption of IITSC is that the speaker/writer does most of the work of innovation, not the hearer/reader. The idea is that the speaker/writer tries out a new use exploiting available implicatures. If the innovative use succeeds, the hearer/reader will interpret the intention correctly, and possibly experiment in similar ways in producing speech/writing. But rarely does the act of interpretation itself lead directly to innovation.

The emphasis on speaker/writer-negotiated meaning (as opposed to imperfect processing) motivates the strong tendency in semantic change toward subjectification, in the sense of the preemption of meaning to speaker's attitudes, beliefs, and metatextual, rhetorical, argumentative intent (see Traugott 1995; contrast Langacker 1990).

Assumptions concerning the role of pragmatic heuristics in IITSC

Levinson (1995) interprets Grice's maxims as heuristics: guidelines governing language use. Of these the most important for historical pragmatics are (in my characterization):

a) The *Q-heuristic* (roughly, Grice's Quantity$_1$, Horn's Q-Principle): "Make your contribution as informative as required, and imply no more thereby".

b) The *R-heuristic* (roughly, Grice's Quantity$_2$, Horn's R-Principle): "Say no more than you must, and mean more thereby"; this warrants enriched interpretations relevant to context, and invites inferences to specific subcases.

c) The *M-heuristic* (roughly, Grice's Manner): "periphrastic expression warns 'marked/pragmatically special situation'".

As a working methodology and empirically testable hypothesis, we can assume that the heuristics and linguistically based IINs are roughly equivalent across languages, times, and the modalities of speech and writing. By contrast, GIINs are language-specific as they involve conventionalized uses.

Hypotheses for change

The hypotheses concerning relevant heuristics for change, are as follows:

1. The Q-heuristic ("Make your contribution as informative as required, and imply no more thereby") invokes "literal meaning" and impedes change (contra Horn 1984).

2. The R-heuristic ("Say no more than you must, and mean more thereby") leads to change, as it induces enrichment of what is said/written.

3. The M-heuristic ("Special expression warns 'marked situation'"), when it reinforces the R-heuristic, is especially likely to lead to semantic change in grammaticalization.
4. There is the potential for change when the R-heuristic is exploited innovatively by inducement of ad hoc invited inferences or IINs (especially in redundant linguistic context). An enriched IIN may then become a GIIN if it acquires saliency in the community.

Horn (1984, 1998) has suggested that Q-based implicatures can lead to certain types of semantic narrowing, e.g., of a "hyponym to the complement of a named subject"; thus *rectangle* (any four-sided shapes with right angles, including squares) is allegedly narrowed to all such shapes excluding squares. This kind of analysis is, however, in my view the result of looking at lexical items out of context. According to the OED *rectangle* is "Usually limited to figures whose adjacent sides are unequal, and is contrasted with square". More importantly, the first example of *rectangle* cited is as in (1), which suggests that the meaning was narrow to start with:

(1) If one side containing the right Angle, be longer than the other containing side, then is that figure called a Rectangle.

OED rectangle

The Q-heuristic may impede change, but that does not mean it plays no role at all in change. Standardization often exploits the Q-heuristic, as is manifested in the search for unambiguous, literal meaning, and the resistance to change typically associated with it.

The IITSC model of semantic change

The IITSC model of semantic change is as follows (based on Traugott 1997: 6):

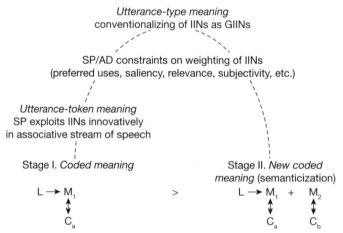

Figure 5.1 Model of invited inferencing theory of semantic change.

Note this is a model of increase in polysemy. "A becomes B" is entirely misleading. There is always variation between old and new as in (2):

$$(2) \quad A > \{ \begin{matrix} A \\ B \end{matrix} \}$$

Over time, the semantic link between older and newer meaning may become severed so that speakers would not intuit a connection. This can result in homonymy. Few, if any, people would now connect *even* 'smooth' with the scalar focus particle *even*; or *still* 'quietly' with the scalar temporal particle *still* 'in continuation', but in the short term, and sometimes even over several centuries polysemies coexist, as characterized in (3):

(3) A > { A / B } > B

An example: The development of **as/so long as** in English

As an example, consider the development of *as/so long as*. In Modern English *as long as* can be a subordinator of spatial measure ('the same length as') or of temporal measure ('for as long as') or a conditional ('provided that, if'). *So long as* can be a subordinator of temporal measure or a conditional. Both derive from Old English *swa lange swa*.

In Old and Middle English the spatial and temporal meanings coexisted, and the temporal is presumably derived from the spatial. All examples that can be interpreted as conditional also have temporal meaning, in other words, the temporal is salient, and the conditional can be construed as an IIN. The conditional reading involves the inference that the time-frame is a contingent (and imaginary) frame for the applicability of the main clause proposition. Nevertheless Kortmann (1997) lists *swa lange swa* from Old English under "conditional subordinators"— apparently he interprets the conditional reading as semantically polysemous.

My claim is that the conditional reading is induced in certain contexts. These include generic and stative contexts, the latter especially when the time-reference of the *as/so long as* clause is later than or extends beyond that of the main clause as in (4):

(4) wring þurh linenne claö on þæt eage **swa lange swa**
     wring through linen cloth on that eye as long as
     him ðearf sy.
     him need be:SUBJ
     'squeeze (the medication) through a linen cloth onto the eye as long as he needs.'
     (850–950 Lacnunga (Magic Medicine), p. 100)

Here temporal coextension of administering the medicine with stative need invites the inference of conditional 'provided that'. This is because the main clause is imperative, part of a set of procedures to be followed in imaginary situations; in such imaginary situations, the need is construed as contingent and temporary (signaled by the subjunctive). There is even an IIN of "conditional perfection" (see e.g., Geis and Zwicky 1971; Van der Auwera 1997), which derives from the projected temporariness of the need together with the generic distributive aspect ('on all occasions that').

The conditional reading is also available if the time-reference of the temporal clause is later than the main clause. In (5) we find a past tense form but the time reference of the subordinate clause (being in the ship) is later than that of the main clause (ordering food):

(5) he ordeynd for hir mete & drynke & al þat was necessary vnto hir
     as long as sche was wythinne þe schip.
     'He ordered for her food and drink and all that was necessary for her as long as she was on the ship.'
     (c. 1438 Kempe, I. 231)

This can be paraphrased as "For as long as she was in the ship/until such time as she was no longer in the ship."

In Early Modern English, however, the conditional IIN begins to be generalized to contexts in which the conditional appears to be more salient; that is, the temporal meaning, though present, is not predominant. The contexts have been extended to event structures involving patterns of reasoning and cognition that are unlikely to change. However, the general context suggests that a change is not only possible but would be valued, as in (6):

> (6) a. But, be the tradition ever so well attested, and the books ever so genuine, yet I cannot suppose them wrote by persons divinely inspired, ***so long as*** I see in them certain characters inconsistent with such a supposition.
>
> (1732 Berkeley, Alciphron, p. 227)
>
> b. The only particular in which any one can differ from me is, either that perhaps he will refuse to call this necessity; but ***as long as*** the meaning is understood, I hope the word can do no harm.
>
> (1739–40 Hume, Treatise Human Nature Bk. 2, p. 409)

(6) a. can be paraphrased as "For as long as I see certain characteristics in them/until such time as I no longer see certain characteristics in them". At this stage we can say the conditional reading has become a GIIN of temporal *as/so long as*.

By the mid nineteenth century the conditional GIIN has clearly been semanticized as a conditional polysemy of temporal *as/so long as*. Temporality is absent, except that now temporality can itself be an invited inference of contingency. In other words, the original relationship between core meaning and invited inference has been reversed:

> (7) a. This [classification as member of species] may be safely done, and is often done, ***as long as*** a sufficient number of characters, let them be ever so unimportant, betrays the hidden bond of community of descent.
>
> (1865 Darwin, Origin of the Species, p. 409)

This does not mean *'This classification is often done for the length of time that a sufficient number of characters betrays the hidden bond' or *'until such time as a sufficient number no longer betrays a common bond'. Similarly, *so long as I get somewhere* in:

> (7) b. "Would you tell me, please, which way I ought to go from here?"
> "That depends a good deal on where you want to get to," said the Cat.
> "I don't much care where——" said Alice.
> "Then it doesn't matter which way you go," said the Cat.
> "——***so long as*** I get *somewhere*," Alice added as an explanation.
>
> (1865 Carroll, Alice in Wonderland, Chap. 6)

does not mean *'until such time as I don't get there'. This is an entirely different situation from Old, Middle and indeed Early Modern English, where the 'for the length of time that/until X no longer holds' interpretations are always possible.

The new polysemous conditional now shows syntactic properties typical of conditionals, e.g., adverbial fronting is permitted within the subordinate clause as in (8):

(8) He added, "They can keep this equipment *as long as* by keeping it they don't exceed the limits of the treaty that we signed."

(May 1991, United Press International)

The expression 'They can keep this equipment if by keeping it they . . . ' is acceptable, but not *'They can keep this equipment for the length of time that by keeping it they . . . '

Finally, temporal overlap with the main clause or later time reference is no longer required, as the constructed example in (9) shows:

(9) You can leave, *as long as* noone was hurt.

This can be paraphrased as 'It's all right for you to leave provided noone was hurt', and could plausibly be said over the phone to the witness of an accident.

Note the development of this new polysemy is an instance of subjectification in the sense of preemption to the speaker/writer's rhetorical purposes.

Particularly interesting is the fact that there appear to be no examples in which an *as/so long as* clause in English has been saliently associated with an implicature that it is both a) presupposed true and b) adversative. That is, there are no instances of a concessive reading meaning *although*. By contrast, Fr. *tandis que*: 'aussi longtemps que' > 'pendant que' is attested with the GIIN (or polysemy?) of concessivity from about 1623 ('au lieu que' according to Wartburg 1996). The *Dictionnaire Robert* says:

"d'abord, avec le sens du latin «aussi longtemps que», aujourd'hui archaïque . . ., puis avec une nuance ancienne de simultanéité (XIIIᵉ s.) et une nuance accessoire d'opposition dans la simultanéité au début du XVIIᵉ s. (1623)"[2]

(Dictionnaire Robert *tandis que*).

From similar semantic beginnings, with similar IINs, different GIINs developed in different contexts (presumably temporal), hence different polysemies.

Conclusion

A close look at the discourse (and particularly the textual) contexts of semantic change suggests that:

a) Pragmatics plays a crucial bridging role between stages in the semantic development of a lexeme or construction.
b) The changes are local, and associative; they require a pragmatics that privileges process, not end-product and result.
c) The changes require a pragmatics that allows meanings to be added over time.
d) The changes require a pragmatics in which speaker/writer plays a central innovative role.
e) The changes require a pragmatics that allows for polysemy (not one that argues for monosemy or homonymy wherever possible).
f) The relevant heuristics are the R-heuristic and the M-heuristic.

On the widely-held assumption that a theory which accounts for both synchronic and diachronic variation is preferable to one that accounts for only one of these, a modified neo-Gricean perspective seems to be the most adequate. This is because it is speaker based (rather than hearer-based, as in the case of Relevance Theory). It is process-oriented (rather than product-oriented, as is the case in some metaphor theory, e.g., Heine et al. 1991). It allows for polysemy and multiple heuristics (contra Relevance Theory which argues for one heuristic: Relevance, only). IITSC is just such a modified neo-Gricean theory.

It must of course be acknowledged that not all aspects of regular semantic change are explicable in terms of invited inferencing in the sense adopted here. The data need to be investigated from different perspectives. These include an action-oriented pragmatics that privileges the role of interlocutors in situations (and is especially important for understanding the actuation or starting point of a change). The varying perspectives also include a cognitively oriented pragmatics based in work on metaphor and prototypicality. This is especially important for constraints on likelihood of IINs becoming GIINs and of GIINs being semanticized. Furthermore, different semantic domains may be subject to different processes, given their different cognitive and communicative functions. Which domains these are is still subject to empirical investigation. But in the process of this investigation we will continue to find that much semantic change is regular, and that the regularity cannot be accounted for without paying attention to the implicatures and inferences that arise in language use.

Notes

1   Data are from the Helsinki Corpus (see Rissanen et al. 1993) and from other computerized corpora made available by Academic Text Services, Stanford University.
      The following abbreviations are used: C = (universal) conceptual structure, GIIN = generalized utterance-type invited inference, IIN = utterance-token invited inference, L = lexeme, M = meaning; SP/AD = speaker/writer-hearer/reader.
2   "First with the sense of Latin 'for the length of time that', now archaic . . ., then with a ancient nuance of simultaneity (13thC) and an additional nuance of opposition in the simultaneity at the beginning of the 17thC (1623)." This particular formulation is problematic; presumably it means an old nuance (implicature) of simultaneity was semanticized (or at least became a GIIN) in the 13thC, and a later one arising out of simultaneity was semanticized (or became a GIIN) in the 17thC.

■   ■   ■

POST-READING

1   Traugott's main finding in regard to *as/so long as* is that its meaning of *length* became extended so that it could also be applied to, first, *time*, and then, *conditionality*. This extension was initially an 'innovative' one, on the part of the speaker, which was recognized by the hearer in particular contexts. This 'new use' then became 'conventionalized', i.e. part of the possible (recognized) linguistic meanings of *as/so long as*.
   •   Use the Online OED (or similar historical dictionary) to confirm that *as/so long as* did develop in this way (*length > time > conditionality*).
   •   Drawing from Traugott's examples, explain why it is possible that a *length* meaning can become extended so that it also represents *time* and *conditionality*.
   •   If you have access to English corpora, historical and modern, find examples of *as/so long as*, and determine which meaning they represent in context (*spatial, temporal* or *conditional*), remembering to make a note of their dates of use.
2   Traugott believes speakers/writers do 'most of the work of [meaning] innovation', not least because the speaker/writer can try out 'a new use', which exploits 'available implicatures.

If the innovative use succeeds, the hearer/reader will interpret the intention correctly, and possibly experiment in similar ways in producing speech/writing', at which point, invited inferences might become enriched and, subsequently, conventionalized/generalized. Do you find Traugott's argument convincing in this regard? Why/why not? If you're not convinced, are there other explanations that you can offer for meaning innovation? To help you formulate a response to this question, you might consider drawing from the ideas regarding 'intention' and 'perception', discussed in, e.g., Sections 2, 3, 4 and 7.

3   Which heuristic or heuristics aid semantic change, according to Traugott, and which impede semantic change? As well as naming the heuristics, summarize the reasons Traugott gives for her aiding/impeding argument, and say whether you find Traugott's argument convincing. Again, where possible, try to draw from other readings in this Reader when formulating your response.

4   In what way is the conditional meaning of 'as long as' more 'subjective' than the spatial or temporal meaning? Find out as much as you can about the development of modal auxiliaries in English and consider the extent to which historical change in this area is also in the direction of subjectification. When undertaking this exercise, you might find it useful to make reference to Jenny Coates' (1983) *The Semantics of the Modal Auxilaries*, published as part of the Croom Helm Linguistic Series.

LAUREL J. BRINTON

PRAGMATIC MARKERS IN ENGLISH
Grammaticalization and discourse functions

PRE-READING

We include two versions of the same transcript below, which we've taken from Anne Barron's (2001: 164) *Acquisition in Interlanguage Pragmatics: Learning How To Do Things With Words in a Study Abroad Context*, published by John Benjamins. The transcript relates to a native Irish English speaker learning German who's been asked to comment upon whether 'a German NS would have acted any differently to the way they . . . had acted in offering help . . . in [a] roleplay'. The first version includes pragmatic markers. In the second, some of the pragmatic markers have been removed:

Learner	. . . I think if they weren't really that friendly with you, they'd say, okay, well, I offered.
Researcher	*Do you think it'd be the same in Ireland?*
Learner	No, I think, I think in Ireland, they'd be more, you know what I mean, they're more, em, they wouldn't want anyone thinking they wouldn't offer, whereas here, you know, they offer, you both know you've offered, so you don't think any more about it, sort of thing . . . in Ireland, well, unless they don't like you, they're going to be kind of say 'go on'.
Learner	. . . I think if they weren't really that friendly with you, they'd say, okay, I offered.
Researcher	*Do you think it'd be the same in Ireland?*
Learner	No, I think, I think in Ireland, they'd be more, they're more, em, they wouldn't want anyone thinking they wouldn't offer, whereas here, they offer, you both know you've offered, so you don't think any more about it . . . in Ireland, unless they don't like you, they're going to be say 'go on'.

1 Make a list of the pragmatic markers we have removed on a separate sheet of paper, and state whether you think each of these linguistic elements serves an interpersonal function (i.e. signals something about the speaker or the speaker's relationship with the hearer), a textual function (i.e. acts as a cohesive device) or both (i.e. signals an interactive

relationship between speaker, hearer, and message). If you can, explain why you believe the different pragmatic markers have the function(s) that they do.

2   Is there an argument for seeing the *think* examples we have kept in (' ... I think ... ', 'Do you think ... ' / ' ... I think, I think ... ') as pragmatic markers? Why/why not? What about the filler 'em'? Does it serve a similar interpersonal or textual function to a pragmatic marker? Why/why not? What about the final 'say' (see last line)? Is 'say' functioning as a pragmatic marker here or a repair? Why? Can you find any pragmatic markers in the second version that we have not mentioned here? If so, what function(s) are they serving?

IN-READING

Make a photocopy of the text below, which we've taken from the Brinton reading:

The "_____" mode is the expression of the _____'s attitudes, _____, judgments, _____, and demands, as well as of the nature of the _____ exchange, the role of the _____ and the role assigned to the _____. The _____ mode consists in the _____'s intrusion into the speech event. Halliday considers the _____ mode to be expressed "_____", distributed throughout the discourse, rather than discretely, in features such as _____, modality, tone, _____, and intensity. It is clear that both the "subjective" (h) and the "interpersonal" (i) functions of pragmatic markers belong within Halliday's _____ component.

In the "_____" mode, the _____ structures meaning as _____, creating cohesive passages of discourse; it is "language as _____", using language in a way that is relevant to _____. Halliday considers the _____ mode to be manifest cumulatively and "periodically" in the theme-focus structure of discourse, in the distribution of given and new information, and in _____ relations. [...] The need to initiate and close discourse (a), to mark topic shifts (d), to indicate _____ information (e), and to constrain the relevance of adjoining utterances (f) are all part of the structuring of utterances as a _____ on a _____ level; they are equally important in _____ and _____ discourse. The turn-taking system of conversation (b, c), which organizes it as a _____ discourse, has as its analogue in written or monologic discourse the organization of chunks of information in paragraphs and episodes [...]; as Redeker (1991: 1163–4) notes, turn-taking is simply "a special case of discourse segment transitions". Repair-marking (g), which is also important for _____ in oral discourse, is not generally an issue in written discourse, in which planning time eliminates mistakes and hence the need for _____. Thus, we can understand functions (a–g) as part of the _____ component of language.

When you reach the section of the reading highlighted by the marginal mark '|' you will recognize the complete version of the text you have photocopied. Use this as a source to close the gaps in your photocopied text. Once you have added the missing words, and before you continue reading, simplify the information given in this extract so that you are left with clear, succinct definitions for Halliday's 'interpersonal' and 'textual' modes of language.

■ ■ ■

PRAGMATIC MARKERS IN ENGLISH GRAMMATICALIZATION AND DISCOURSE FUNCTIONS
LAUREL J. BRINTON

[. . .]

Inventory of functions

Determining the inventory of functions of pragmatic markers is a difficult task. First, taxonomies of pragmatic markers, which are generally functionally based, differ significantly [. . .] Second, studies of individual pragmatic markers often attribute a wide variety of meanings to a single marker, some of which may overlap with the meanings attributed to other markers. For example, *well*, the most frequent of the discourse particles, is said to serve as a "channelholding" device (Brown 1977: 121) or "dispreferred response" signal (Levinson 1983: 366); to function as a general introductory or disjunctive marker (Stubbs 1983: 69–70); to be either a qualifier (expressing agreement or positive reaction, reinforcement, exclamatory surprise, and answer prefix) or a frame (denoting new topic, clarification of topic, or partial shift in topic, marking direct speech, or self-editing) (Svartvik 1979); to express reservation or doubt, abruptness or impatience, or hesitation or indecision (Crystal and Davy 1975: 101–2); to indicate the incompleteness of one's own response or the inadequacy or insufficiency of another's response (Lakoff 1973); to signal that what follows is not exactly what the speaker assumes the asker wants to be told (Murray 1979); to preface responses which are "face-threatening" (Owen 1981); to indicate that the speaker accepts the situation but that acceptance is problematic in some way (Carlson 1984); to show that the content of the response "is not fully consonant with prior coherence options" (Schiffrin 1987: 103; also 1985); to give explicit acknowledgment while indicating that the content does not meet expectations (Hines 1978); to give the speaker a device to minimize a possible face-threatening situation resulting from a failure to abide by the axiom of relevance (Watts 1986: 58); to indicate that the most immediately accessible context may not be the most relevant one for interpretations of the following utterance (Jucker 1993: 435); and to make clear that the speaker is now examining the contents of private thought but to leave the particulars of the thought to the hearer's deduction (Schourup 1985).

   Although there is apparently no consistency among the taxonomies, and studies of individual pragmatic markers yield conflicting and confusing results, it is nonetheless possible to glean a fundamental set of functions from general studies of pragmatic markers (omitting, for the most part, studies of single markers):

(a) to initiate discourse, including claiming the attention of the hearer, and to close discourse;
(b) to aid the speaker in acquiring or relinquishing the floor;
(c) to serve as a filler or delaying tactic used to sustain discourse or hold the floor;

(d) to mark a boundary in discourse, that is, to indicate a new topic, a partial shift in topic (correction, elaboration, specification, expansion), or the resumption of an earlier topic (after an interruption);

(e) to denote either new information (Erman 1987: 201; Schiffrin 1987) or old information (Quirk et al. 1985: 1482; Schiffrin 1987);

(f) to mark "sequential dependence", to constrain the relevance of one clause to the preceding clause by making explicit the conversational implicatures relating the two clauses, or to indicate by means of conventional implicatures how an utterance matches cooperative principles of conversation (Levinson 1983: 128–9, 162–3, what he calls a "maxim hedge");

(g) to repair one's own or others' discourse;

(h) subjectively, to express a response or a reaction to the preceding discourse or attitude towards the following discourse, including also "back-channel" signals of understanding and continued attention spoken while another speaker is having his or her turn and perhaps "hedges" expressing speaker tentativeness; and

(i) interpersonally, to effect cooperation, sharing, or intimacy between speaker and hearer, including confirming shared assumptions, checking or expressing understanding, requesting confirmation, expressing deference, or saving face (politeness).

Textual and interpersonal functions

While the functions listed above seem quite heterogeneous, I believe that they fall into two categories, the first set (a–g) belonging to the "textual" mode of language and the second set (h–i) belonging to the "interpersonal" mode, two of the three modes or functions of language identified by Halliday (1970, 1979). Halliday's third mode, the "ideational" mode, which, following Traugott (1982), I will call the "propositional" mode, is the expression of content, of the speaker's experience of both the outside and the inside world, including happenings, participants, and circumstances. It is realized in elemental structures in the constituent structure of language. Given the relative lack of semantic or propositional content in pragmatic markers, they generally fall outside the propositional component, though [. . .] they derive diachronically from it.

The "interpersonal" mode is the expression of the speaker's attitudes, evaluations, judgments, expectations, and demands, as well as of the nature of the social exchange, the role of the speaker and the role assigned to the hearer. The interactive mode consists in the speaker's intrusion into the speech event. Halliday considers the interpersonal mode to be expressed "prosodically", distributed throughout the discourse, rather than discretely, in features such as mood, modality, tone, key, and intensity. It is clear that both the "subjective" (h) and the "interpersonal" (i) functions of pragmatic markers belong within Halliday's interpersonal component.

In the "textual" mode, the speaker structures meaning as text, creating cohesive passages of discourse; it is "language as relevance", using language in a way that is relevant to context. Halliday considers the textual mode to be manifest cumulatively and "periodically" in the theme-focus structure of discourse, in the distribution of given and new information, and in cohesive relations. To understand functions (a–g) above as "textual" one needs a more global conception of the textual component than Halliday uses, one which moves beyond the level of the sentence to the structure of the entire discourse; one requires as well a recognition of the different text-structuring requirements of oral conversation and written discourse, particularly narrative. The need to initiate and close discourse (a), to mark topic shifts (d), to indicate new and old information (e), and to constrain the relevance of adjoining utterances (f) are all part of the structuring of utterances as a text on a global level; they are equally important in oral and written discourse. The turn-taking system of conversation (b, c), which organizes it as a cohesive discourse, has as its analogue in written or monologic discourse the organization of chunks of information in paragraphs and episodes [. . .]; as Redeker (1991: 1163–4) notes, turn-taking is simply "a special case of discourse segment transitions". Repair-marking (g), which is also important for coherence in oral discourse, is not generally an issue in written discourse, in which planning time eliminates mistakes and hence the need for repair. Thus, we can understand functions (a–g) as part of the textual component of language.

[. . .]

Leech (1983: 57, 59–62) argues that Halliday is wrong in integrating the propositional, interpersonal, and textual modes all within the "grammar" of language. He argues that the interpersonal component is an "input constraint" and the textual component an "output constraint" on the grammar, or propositional component. Both components have the characteristics of pragmatic components; for example, they are principle-controlled rather than rule-governed (p. 21), they are nonconventional (i.e., motivated by the goals of communication) rather than arbitrary (p. 24), they are expressed continuously and indeterminately rather than discretely (p. 70), they depend on problem solving rather than mapping (p. 36), and they require functional rather than formal explanations (p. 47). For these reasons, he terms them "pragmatic", and it is for this reason that I prefer to call discourse markers "pragmatic", since they have both textual and interpersonal functions.

[. . .]

Grammaticalization of pragmatic markers

[. . .] Traugott cites the "conversational routines" *well* and *right* as examples of the semantic shift in the process of grammaticalization from propositional to interpersonal meaning, and *why* as an example of the shift from propositional to textual to interpersonal, in that it changes from a mark of interrogation to a complementizer to a "hearer-engaging" form (1982: 251, 252, 255). Romaine and Lange (1991: 272) point to a parallel development in northern varieties of British English with *but*, from preposition to conjunction to pragmatic marker (as in *I really don't want it but*). Finell (1989) proposes a similar historical development for the pragmatic marker *well* from a predicate adjective (in structures such as *it is well with me, that is very well* occurring in the fourteenth to sixteenth centuries) to a more independent element. If the discourse use of *well* is understood as 'the speaker accepts a situation', then the change from 'find good' to 'accept' is transparent (Carlson 1984: 27). [. . .] *well* moves from the propositional to the interpersonal component, and it changes in meaning from less to more personal: "expressive *well* shows the attitude of the speaker towards the topic spoken of, or towards the interlocutor" (Finell 1989: 655). In a more detailed study, Finell (1986) shows that *however* begins in Old English as an adverbial in the propositional component, occupying a set position and modifying a single word or phrase, moves into the textual component as a conjunctive adverb in the sixteenth to seventeenth centuries, and ends in the interpersonal component in the nineteenth century as an interrogative or exclamatory form. While *however* always serves as a means of conveying speaker attitude, Finell believes that it is closest to a pragmatic marker in its second stage. Finell (1992) argues that pragmatic markers such as *well*, *however*, *anyhow*, and *besides*, which function as "topic changers", start out in the propositional component as expressions of time, space, manner, or concession, and in the process of grammaticalization acquire more subjective meanings; in fact, she sees this process as being motivated by the speakers' desire to express their attitudes toward the ongoing discourse, wishes for interaction, and politeness. Finally, Traugott (1995) briefly discusses the grammaticalization of *let's* and *let alone* as pragmatic markers. *Let's* has developed from a second-person imperative in Old English to a first-person hortative in Middle English to a pragmatic marker in Modern English indicating "that the speaker is cognizant of the presence of the hearer and will take a turn, respond, etc." (as in *Let's see now, what was I going to say?*); it has "the textual and metalinguistic function of bracketing a unit of discourse". *Let alone* has developed from an imperative in Middle English to a pragmatic marker in the nineteenth century which expresses "speaker's attitude regarding possible alternatives on a scale of inclusion". Both developments, she believes, show an increase in subjectification.

Romaine and Lange's (1991) study of the quotative function of *(be) like* (as in *And I'm like, "Great"*) is most interesting in this respect. They argue that *be like*, as opposed to forms such as *say* or *go*, is used in cases of reduced speaker commitment; the speaker is not committed to the exact words of the quotation since the material quoted need not have been explicitly lexicalized (pp. 232, 243, 263); it is "what might have been said/thought" (p. 247) (also Blyth et al. 1990: 222–3). *Be like* is a form which allows the speaker to retain the vividness and emotiveness of direct speech while preserving the pragmatic force of indirect speech (Romaine and Lange 1991: 228, 263, 264, 268). Furthermore, it possesses a quality of speaker subjectivity since it is often used for self-presentation (pp. 237, 238, 242, 243). *Like* has not acquired the status of a verb of saying, but functions rather as a "quotative complementizer" (p. 248). It has many, but not all, of the characteristics of a pragmatic marker (pp. 246–51), though Romaine and Lange reserve the term "discourse marker" for the focusing function of *like* (as in *And there were like people blocking, you know?*; see Underhill 1988). While they treat the development of this pragmatic marker in detail, they point out that their discussion lacks historical depth because of the recency of the form. Nonetheless, they propose the development shown in Figure 5.2.1, which, while not strictly sequential, recognizes an increase in grammaticality and a change in category membership (p. 262) from preposition (as in *nectarines are like peaches*) to conjunction (as in *It looks like we'll finish on time*) to quotative and focuser. They believe that both the original semantic and syntactic properties lead to the discourse functions which develop (pp. 246, 265–6)

> In our view, both semantic and grammatical properties of markers can affect the kind of grammaticalization process that takes place and contribute to the communicative force of the marker. Semantically, it is because *like* has the referential meanings of 'comparison', 'for example', 'as if', and so on, that it is suitable for use in a construction reporting hypothetical discourse or thought. Syntactically, it is because it can occupy a slot immediately preceeding the comparison . . . that it can function as an anaphor whose scope is forward or backward.
>
> (p. 259)

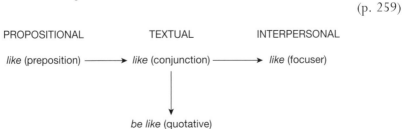

Figure 5.2.1 The development of like.

Adapted from Romaine and Lange (1991: 261).

The quotative complementizer results from specialization within the textual component (p. 261) from conjunction to complementizer: "This happens when the speaker presents the clause created for comparison or exemplification so that it can be construed as a report of speech or thought" (p. 262). This change involves a shift from less to more personal (p. 260), comes about through metonymic association (p. 262), and results in an increase in pragmatic significance (p. 266), all expected by Traugott's Tendencies.

Thompson and Mulac (1991) discuss the grammaticalization of *I think* and *I guess* from grammatical phrases consisting of subject + main verb (+ complement) to syntactically free "epistemic parentheticals", comparable to adverbs (as in *It's just your point of view you know what you like to do in your spare time I think*). They argue that epistemic parentheticals, though not prototypical examples of grammaticalization, show the expected shift in categorial status (pp. 318, 325) and follow recognized principles of grammaticalization (pp. 323–5; see above). However, for some unspecified reason, they distinguish epistemic parentheticals from "pragmatic expressions" such as *you know* or *I know* (p. 316) and suggest that the forms are attested only synchronically (p. 324), but, as will be shown below, *I guess* goes back to Middle English, where it serves as a common pragmatic marker.

[. . .]

First-person epistemic parentheticals in Middle English

Middle English possesses quite a large inventory of KNOW-verbs occurring in first-person epistemic parentheticals, and although these parentheticals are to some extent stereotyped, there is still a fair amount of syntactic flexibility. At least three major variants are found: what Quirk et al. (1985: 1112) call type (i) comment clauses (i.e., like matrix clauses usually requiring *that*-complements) and type (ii) comment clauses (i.e., like finite adverbial clauses introduced by *as*), as well as an additional matrix clause type beginning with a coordinating conjunction *and*, *but*, or *for*. Additionally, the order of subject and verb may be reversed, modal auxiliaries may occur, or there may be accompanying adverbials or prepositional phrases [. . .]:

[. . .]

First-person epistemic parentheticals in Chaucer

[. . .]

[*The Canterbury Tales*, henceforth] *CT* is a particularly fruitful text for examination because of its several different modes of discourse. I first categorized the first-person epistemic parentheticals in *CT* in respect to their occurrence in the prologues to and links between tales and in the tales themselves; of the total number of first-person parentheticals, 27 occur in the prologues/ epilogues and 60 in the tales. While this distribution might seem significant, a more important criterion proves to be whether the parentheticals occur in narration or in discourse (i.e., dialogue/ monologue). Because of the complex narrative structure of *CT*, five textual modes can be distinguished:

(a) External Narration: Chaucer's narration of the external frame story of the journey to Canterbury;
(b) Primary Internal Discourse: the dialogue of the pilgrims on the journey, including the prologues to tales;
(c) Primary Internal Narration: the pilgrims' narrations of their tales;
(d) Secondary Internal Discourse: the dialogue of characters within the tales; and
(e) Secondary Internal Narration: the narration of stories by characters within the tales.

Ness and Duncan-Rose (1982: 306–7) identify these five categories of discourse and narration in CT, plus an additional two categories. One of their categories, Tertiary Internal Discourse (the dialogue of characters within a secondary internal narration), can be ignored here since no parentheticals are found in this mode of discourse. Ness and Duncan-Rose give no linguistic evidence for the other category, which they call External Direct Discourse and which they define as Chaucer the poet addressing the audience outside the narrative; we shall see below that there is in fact justification for establishing this category.

[. . .]

Contexts of occurrence

One finds that first-person epistemic parentheticals in Chaucer's dialogic mode are used in quite different contexts than in his narrative mode. In discourse, first-person epistemic parentheticals are generally attached to propositions expressing matters about which the speaker, for a variety of reasons, cannot be entirely certain, such as personal evaluations, opinions said to be generally held, deductions based on appearances, and so on. In contrast, in narrative they are attached to propositions expressing inexactness concerning time, space, and even plot details, to the narrator's external evaluations, and to metacomments on the telling of the tale.

[. . .]

A summary of the contexts of occurrence of first-person epistemic parentheticals can be found in Table 5.2.1.

Functions in discourse

While there is some overlap in contexts of occurrence—particularly in the expression of speaker judgment—first-person epistemic parentheticals seem to function quite differently in Chaucer's

Table 5.2.1 Contxts of occurence for first-person epsitemic parentheticals in Chaucer

---

DISCOURSE
Internal (Primary or Secondary)
* personal opinion, evaluation, or interpretation
* general opinion or truth
* expected consequence or result of an action
* presumed cause of an event
* judgment based on appearances
* belief or feeling attributed to another
  (emphatic) promise or assertion

NARRATIVE
Internal (Primary or Secondary)
* metacomment on the telling of the tale
* inexact or imprecise measurement of time or space
* (emphatic) description of plot detail
* narrator's comment, evaluaton, or judgment
External (see categories of DISCOURSE above) = External Discourse

---

discourse than in his (internal) narration. In discourse, their uses can be broadly seen as subjectively epistemic and evidential, functions associated with comparable forms in Modern English.

Epistemic meaning

It is well recognized that Modern English has a set of "modal lexical verbs" (Perkins 1983; Coates 1987), such as *believe*, *think*, *suppose*, and *know*, which are used not to denote acts of cognition or to give a "psychological history" (Benveniste 1971: 228; R. Lakoff 1972: 241; Lyons 1977: 739, 799) but rather to report mental states or attitudes (Urmson 1952: 482–3, 484–5, 490, 491; also Perkins 1983: 97; Palmer 1986: 136) [. . .]. These expressions serve primarily to modify the force of an utterance, as "hedges", or as markers of modality. They can be understood as markers of epistemic modality, which can be defined briefly as "the degree of commitment by the speaker to what he says" (Palmer 1986: 51) or "the speaker's assumptions, or assessment of possibilities, and, in most cases, . . . the speaker's confidence or lack of confidence in the truth of the proposition expressed" (Coates 1987: 112). Epistemic modal verbs are used to "signal what degree of reliability is claimed for, and should be accorded to, the statement to which they are conjoined" (Urmson 1952: 485). They can express certainty or confidence and hence function emphatically to strengthen the force of an utterance (e.g., *know*), or, more often, they express uncertainty, lack of confidence, or tentativeness and hence weaken or soften the force of an utterance (e.g., *think*) (Corum 1975: 136; Quirk et al. 1985: 1114; Coates 1987: 115–16).

While there is no consensus about the inventory of verbs serving as epistemic markers in Modern English, the most commonly listed verbs are *assume, believe, estimate, expect, feel, guess, know, presume, suppose, suspect, think,* and *understand* (see Urmson 1952: 482; Givón 1982: 45; Perkins 1983: 97; Quirk et al. 1985: 1114; Biber and Finegan 1989: 98, 119–20). Modal verbs normally function as main verbs taking *that* sentential complements but also occur frequently as parentheticals without the required complementation. As such, they generally occur with first-person subjects in the simple present tense or as impersonal constructions such as *it seems* or *it appears* (Perkins 1983: 98; Quirk et al. 1985: 1114). These parentheticals may appear sentence initially, medially, or finally, in which cases the modality can be said to be "thematized", "interpolated", or "adjoined" (Perkins 1983: 104). Modal verbs can be compared with modal auxiliaries, for example *may* with *I think* or *must* with *I conclude*; however, there is not an absolute equivalence between the two forms, because modal verbs, while functioning grammatically as modal predicators, express more lexical meaning than the corresponding modals (Palmer 1986: 129, 130, 137; cf. Quirk et al. 1985: 1113). Modal verbs compare even more closely with modal adverbs, for example, *I know* with certainly or *I believe* with *probably/ maybe* (Urmson 1952: 487; Perkins 1983: 98; Quirk et al. 1985: 1114).

[. . .]

[. . .] [M]any of the same verbs identified as modal lexical verbs in Modern English— namely, *believe, guess, know, suppose, think,* and *understand*—are used parenthetically in Middle English as well. A number of other verbs, now archaic or obsolete, are used in a similar way. Furthermore, these parentheticals occur consistently in Middle English in contexts which express the speaker's uncertainty or lack of confidence and, less often, certainty. Thus, it seems clear that forms identified as first-person epistemic parentheticals in Modern English function already in Middle English as markers of epistemic modality. In fact, Kivimaa (1968: 13, 48) observes that expressions such as as *I gesse, as it thoughte me, as I was war, as I trowe*, and so on in Middle English are "comments concerning the reliability of something stated" or assure the listener of the truthfulness of a statement.

Subjective meaning

First-person epistemic parentheticals of Modern English are also said to contribute a subjective element to an utterance. Thus, Benveniste remarks that "By saying I *believe* (*that* . . .), I convert into a subjective utterance the fact asserted impersonally"; a personal form such as *I believe* is an "indicator of subjectivity" (1971: 224). In fact, a distinction is often made between "objective" and "subjective" epistemic modality (see Lyons 1977: 797–801), the latter being defined as "a conclusion drawn by the speaker from his own knowledge of the state of the world at the time of speaking" and the former as "a logical conclusion drawn by others on the basis of their observation' (Watts 1984: 131). Modal verbs such as *think* and *believe* are considered markers of subjective epistemic modality (Lyons 1977: 797; Coates 1987: 115). Perkins (1983: 101, 103) points out that if a speaker "wishes to make the modality of his utterance explicitly subjective, he may use a modal lexical verb with a first person subject, although he is obliged here to specify further the nature of the subjective epistemic state". In their parenthetical use, the modal verbs of Middle English occur predominately with first-person subjects, and we can conclude that the first-person epistemic parentheticals of Middle English, like those of Modern English, have an epistemic function that is explicitly subjective.

[. . .] [I]n addition to the variety of epistemic parentheticals expressing subjective epistemicity, Middle English provides a range of means for expressing objective epistemicity. In Modern English, most modal adverbs, such as *possibly, evidently, seemingly, supposedly, certainly,* and *clearly*, express objective epistemic modality, as do many nominal/ adjectival/ participial impersonal constructions, such as *it is {likely, possible, certain, alleged, conjectured, inferred} that* or *there's a possibility that*, while modal auxiliaries and some modal adverbs, such as *maybe* and *perhaps*, are neutral. Though most of these forms are French borrowings and acquire epistemic meaning only in the Early Modern English period (see Hanson 1987), there exist other adverbs and adverbial phrases in Middle English that express objective epistemic modality, both certainty (e.g., *iwis, certes, certeyn, pardee*) and doubt (e.g., *paraventure, parchaunce*).

[. . .]

Evidential meaning

While (un)certainty seems to be the primary meaning of first-person epistemic parentheticals, in origin they are transparently markers of evidentiality. [. . .]

First-person epistemic parentheticals meet two of the three criteria of evidentials recognized by Anderson (1986: 274–5). First, "evidentials are not themselves the main predication of the clause, but are rather a specification added to a factual claim ABOUT SOMETHING ELSE"; we saw above that this was the case with first-person epistemic parentheticals since they do not denote an act a cognition but merely serve to mitigate or intensify the utterance to which they are attached. Second, first-person epistemic parentheticals are "free syntactic forms" and thus belong to the class of structures Anderson associates with evidentials. However, Anderson's third criterion, that evidentials have evidential meaning "as their primary meaning, not only as a pragmatic inference" raises two questions in respect to first-person epistemic parentheticals: (a) to what extent are epistemicity and evidentiality separate categories, and (b) is the meaning of (un)certainty or that of mode of knowing primary in the first-person epistemic parentheticals?

The separation of epistemicity, which concerns matters of certainty and confidence, and evidentiality, which concerns sources of knowledge and modes of knowing, is a matter of scholarly dispute. For Palmer (1986: 51) epistemicity encompasses evidentiality: "the speaker's understanding or knowledge . . . clearly includes both his own judgments and the kind of warrant he has for what he says"; he sees "inference" and "confidence", for example, as two types of epistemic modality (p. 64). In defining evidentiality as the means used to "qualify the reliability of information communicated" in respect to source of evidence, degree of precision, probability of truth, and expectations concerning probability, Mithun (1986: 89–90) seems to subsume epistemicity into evidentiality, as does Chafe (1986: 263) when he includes source of knowledge (evidence, language, or hypothesis) and mode of knowing (belief, induction, hearsay, or deduction), as well as the range from reliable to unreliable, in the domain of evidentiality (also Biber and Finegan 1989: 93–4). Anderson (1986: 310), too, includes epistemic modals within the category of evidentiality. However, many see the two categories as distinct, while admitting that evidentiality impinges on epistemicity. Hardman (1986: 114) believes that "truth and certainty are byproducts of data-source marking, rather than primary ingredients, although source and certainty may be interwoven", and Willett (1988: 86) concludes that "the **source** of a speaker's information can skew the relation between his/her **conception** of the truth of a situation and the strength of his/her **assertion** about that situation". Even Chafe (1986: 266) admits that "mode of knowing implies something about reliability but not vice versa". The difficulty in distinguishing evidentiality and epistemicity arises in part because, as Chung and Timberlake point out (1985: 245), the same morphological forms can encode both.

The second question, whether evidential or epistemic meaning is primary in the first-person epistemic parentheticals, is more difficult to answer. For reasons that will become clearer in the discussion of the development of first-person epistemic parentheticals [. . .], I believe that it is the epistemic rather than the evidential meaning which is primary in these forms at least by Middle English. [. . .]

Functions in narrative

[. . .] Chaucer's use of first-person epistemic parentheticals in the narrative of the Canterbury pilgrims is mimetic of their use in oral discourse and serves interpersonal purposes.

Intimacy signal

[. . .]
The first-person epistemic parentheticals in Chaucer have been recognized as a "colloquialism" used to establish a rapport between narrator and audience. For example, [. . .] Bronson (1940: 21–2) recognizes expressions such as *I gesse, I trowe, I woot, I undertake, I seyde* 'I said', *I seigh* 'I say', and *I dorste swere* 'I dare swear' in "The general prologue" as contributing to the tone of "an easy and intimate conversation". Citing the same expressions, Malone (1951: 146–8) sees them as part of Chaucer's easy, informal, chatty, conversational style, since by means of them he both speaks of himself and addresses his audience directly; they are "a springboard from which he plunges into what amounts to a *tête-à-tête* with his readers", as he takes them into his confidence. Mehl (1974), speaking not only of minor imprecisions marked by first-person epistemic parentheticals but also of larger omissions in Chaucer's texts, observes that these are rhetorical devices to involve the audience. In underscoring imperfections and limitations, they have a mimetic quality: "the poet wants to present us with the same kind of uncertainty, pleasure and provocation that we meet in our daily relationship with complex and unpredictable human beings" (p. 178). And they call upon the audience to become involved in the construction of the story: "by directing the attention of the audience to gaps in his account at the most critical points in the story, he makes sure that our imagination becomes active in the right direction" (p. 183).

In the case of internal narration, the audience addressed consists of the pilgrims on the journey to Canterbury, while in the case of external narration, the audience could be either an actual audience which might have listened to an oral recitation of Chaucer's work, as Bronson (1940) seems to assume, or solitary readers of the text, as Mehl (1974) assumes. But the difference is not significant to the point being made here. In the first case this linguistic device of oral conversation is used unselfconsciously and is a reflection of the oral storytelling context in which the teller interacts with the listeners, while in the second case it is used selfconsciously as "a literary motif" introduced to create "the illusion of a lively and mutual relationship between the fictional narrator . . . and the fictional audience with which we are asked to identify ourselves" (Mehl 1974: 174, 175).

Politeness marker

While the function of involving the audience in the construction of the discourse serves purposes of intimacy and is hence interpersonal, an even more significant interpersonal function of first-person epistemic parentheticals is for purposes of politeness. Considering pragmatic markers in general, Östman (1982: 161, 170) argues that while forms such as *I guess* are used in writing primarily for indirectness, they are used in speech primarily for planning (which is speaker-oriented) and politeness (which is interaction-oriented).

It has been suggested that first-person epistemic parentheticals in Modern English "have an important role to play in mediating interpersonal meaning" and in "expressing addressee-oriented meaning" (Coates 1987: 120). First-person epistemic parentheticals can be used for purposes of "positive politeness" (Brown and Levinson 1978: 124), which is understood as the speaker's orientation toward the hearer's positive face, that is, the wish for his or her wants to be desirable to others. In cases of positive politeness, the speaker acts as if she or he wants what the hearer wants, considers the hearer important, and likes the hearer (Brown and Levinson 1978: 67, 75). Coates (1987: 127) observes that in reducing the force of utterances, first-person epistemic parentheticals serve to diminish speakers' claims for themselves and express their need to be liked and admired. They blur speakers' intents and avoid precise communication of speakers' attitudes (Brown and Levinson 1978: 121–2). They thus serve as a modesty device. Bronson (1940: 33) has argued that the Chaucerian persona expresses "a genuine and unaffected modesty", but this modesty would certainly seem to be a literary pose; even Bronson admits that "when [Chaucer] professes ignorance or inadequacy, he does so usually for humorous or artistic reasons."

More importantly, it has been argued that first-person epistemic parentheticals serve the purposes of what has been called "negative politeness" (Brown and Levinson 1978: 154, 159, 169; Coates 1987: 121, 126). Negative politeness is understood as the speaker's recognition of and respect for the hearer's negative face, that is, the hearer's desire not to be impeded or imposed upon. Negative politeness consists in deference, self-effacement, restraint, and avoidance (Brown and Levinson 1978: 67, 75, 77). First-person epistemic parentheticals, though they are subjective in nature, are in fact oriented towards the hearer. By not taking full responsibility for the reliability of information (see Brown and Levinson 1978: 159, 169), the speaker leaves open the possibility of the hearer's responding to that information as he or she sees fit. First-person epistemic parentheticals can be used if the speaker is not certain about how the hearer will respond and does not want to offend or impose by assuming a certain response. For example, R. Lakoff (1972: 241) suggests that the pragmatic meaning of *I guess it's raining* is 'It is my opinion that it's raining, but I might be mistaken. I hope you agree, but I can't demand it'. And Coates (1987: 122, 129) argues that *It's quite bitter Guinness, I think* is "a strategy for facilitating open discussion" and avoiding disagreement; she sees such forms as a means "to express the speaker's sensitivity to the addressee".

The two interpersonal uses of first-person epistemic parentheticals are closely related: as an intimacy signal first-person epistemic parentheticals call upon the hearer to participate in the discourse, and as a negative politeness marker they allow the hearer freedom to respond in different ways. We can see these two interrelated functions in the use of first-person epistemic parentheticals in Chaucer's narrative, especially in their use for the expression of the speaker's or narrator's judgments or evaluation; first-person epistemic parentheticals call on hearers or readers to come to their own conclusions, which may differ from those of the speaker/ narrator. However, as Corum (1975: 134–5, 139) observes in the use of first-person epistemic parentheticals in Modern English, this may be a kind of "devious", "manipulative", "deceptive", or "sneaky" use "to inveigle or seduce the addressee into believing the content of the proposition". That is, they may be used to "elicit [the] addressee's explicit agreement" (p. 138). In Chaucer's use of first-person epistemic parentheticals, especially in the external narration, there appears merely to be the pose of modesty and only an apparent freedom for the audience to respond in a way other than that intended by the narrator. Also, as Brown and Levinson (1978: 160) observe of Tzeltal *mak* 'perhaps, I guess, I suppose', such forms are useful for understatement and irony (see A. Prol. 288, for example).

Development of first-person epistemic parentheticals

First-person epistemic parentheticals seem to arise, more or less fully developed, in the Middle English period. According to Goossens (1982: 84), Old English is generally deficient in markers of epistemic modality. He finds that nothing "grammaticalizes" the epistemic function in Old English. He believes that the modal auxiliaries contribute in a "real, but also very restricted" way to the expression of epistemicity, though later scholars (Denison 1990; Warner 1990) have found somewhat more evidence for epistemic meaning in the modals in Old English. Goossens also finds that while some adverbs express (objective) possibility (*wenunga* 'possibly, perhaps', *gewene* 'perhaps', *eaþe* + *magan* 'may easily, perhaps') and certainty (*œfœstla* 'certainly', *forsoþ* 'indeed', *forgeare* 'very certainly', *hwœt* 'indeed', *huru* 'surely, truly', *butan tweon* 'undoubtedly') as do certain periphrastic constructions (*wen is þœt* literally 'opinion is that' but glossed 'perhaps' [see Gorrell 1895: 386], *nid/neod is þœt* 'the necessity is that'), these are "not clearly epistemic", or they merely show "epistemic potential". He sees the matrix clause *ic wene þœt* 'I suppose that' as a "(potential) performative marker of epistemic meaning" and believes that *ic teohhi(g)e þœt* 'I consider that' may express probability.

In fact, Old English possess a large variety of KNOW-verbs, classified by Gorrell (1895: 384–404) as verbs of thinking, believing, etc. and verbs of direct perception ([1]a.), as well as some periphrastic nominal and adjectival forms with *be* ([1]b.), which take nominal *þœt*-complements:

[1]   a.   *gelifan* 'to believe, trust', *hogian* 'to think, consider', *hycgan* 'to think, consider', *oncnawan* 'to know', *ongitan/undergitan* 'to recognize', *smeagan* 'to consider', *teohhian* 'to suppose, consider', *þencan* 'to think', *þyncan* 'to seem', *tweogan* + negative 'to doubt not', *understandan* 'to understand', *wenan* 'to think, suppose', *witan* 'to know'
      b.   *geleaflic* 'probable, credible', *cuð* 'known', *gesyne* 'seen, evident', *sweotol* 'evident, manifest', *tweo* + negative 'no doubt', *wen* 'supposition, opinion'

While *þæt* may be omitted with KNOW-verbs, the contexts in which omission occurs are quite limited (see Mitchell 1985, 2: 29–36; Traugott 1992: 236; cf. Gorrell 1895: 346–50), and, even when it is omitted, the tense, mood, or pronominal form of the attached clause often indicates its continued syntactic dependency. There are some examples, however, where the attached clause seems to be direct speech, i.e., syntactically independent; noting that this occurs when the verb is present tense, Mitchell (1985, 2: 33) gives examples with *ic wat*, *ic wene*, and *þæt is her swa cuð* 'this is here so known'. The following are typical:

[2]   a.   Ic wat, *inc waldend god / abolgen wyrð* . . .
           'I know, god the ruler becomes angry with you two . . . '
                                          (ASPR 1, Genesis 551–2)

      b.   *þa andswarode simon. ic wene. se ðe he mare forgef. Ða cwæð he rihte. þu demdest*
           'then answered Simon, I think, he who forgave more; then he [Jesus] said you judge rightly'
                           (*Anglo-Saxon Bible* [Luke] 7.43; cited in Venezky and Healey 1980)

      c.   ic wene *wit syn oferswiþede*
           'I know we (two) are overcome'
                           (*Blickling homilies* 189.29–30; cited in Venezky and Healey 1980)

In these cases, *ic wene* and *ic wat* approximate parentheticals. Gorrell (1895: 396) argues that *witan þeah* should be translated 'very probably' and *ic wat þeah þu wene* as 'probably you think'. Based on Venezky and Healey (1980) and the HCET, however, it seems that constructions without *þæt* are quite rare and that Gorrell (1895: 396–7) overstates the case when he claims that deletion of *þæt* is "very frequent" with *witan* and concludes that "all things tend to show that the subordinating power of *witan* is considerably weaker than that of verbs of saying and thinking, and that there is a constant tendency to use this verb as a simple introductory expression like the Modern English 'you know'". Moreover, there are clearly no examples of medial or final parentheticals with KNOW-verbs in Old English.

The only construction in Old English resembling parenthetical KNOW-verbs is syntactically complete clauses with an anaphoric demonstrative referring back to the preceding clause, that is, relative clauses:

[3]   a.   "*Habbað we to þæm mæran micel ærende, / Deniga frean, ne sceal þær dyrne sum / wesan, þæs ic wene.*"
           'We have for the famous lord of the Danes a great errand; nor shall anything there be secret, of this I think'
                                          (ASPR 4, *Beowulf* 270–2)

      b.   *se hæfde ænne sunu nu for þrym 3ærum, & se wæs, þæs þe ic wene, V wintre*
           'he had one son now for three years, and he was, of this which I know, five winters old'
                           (Waerferth, *Dialogues of Gregory the Great* 19.289.3–4;
                                          cited in Venezky and Healey 1980)

[. . .]
These might be better glossed 'as I think' or 'as I know'.

Keeping the Old English situation in mind, in the sections that follow I will consider both semantic and syntactic aspects of the development of epistemic parentheticals, arguing that their development can be considered a case of grammaticalization, albeit not a "textbook case" (see Thompson and Mulac 1991: 324–5).

Semantic development: from evidential to epistemic

The diachronic sources identified for evidentials include perfects, verbs of perception, verbs of communication, and expressions of logical necessity, i.e., deontics (Anderson 1986; Willett 1988: 61; Matlock 1989; Traugott 1989: 47–8). While it is well known that epistemics typically evolve from deontics, as in the case of the English modals, their origin in evidentials has not before been recognized for English, though Traugott (1989: 33, 48) notes that "epistemics and evidentials share a great number of similarities in their semantic development" and suggests that it would be fruitful "to investigate the extent to which [epistemics] intersect with evidentials" in their development. In the case of first-person epistemic parentheticals, the route of semantic development that I propose is the following:

act of cognition > mode of knowing (evidential) > (un)certainty (epistemic)

In the first stage, verbs meaning 'think', 'believe', and 'guess', used to denote a mental act, come to be used to denote a state of mind. This development of mental construct evidential markers from verbs of cognition would seem to be analogous to the development of hearsay, sensory, and inferential evidentials from verbs of perception meaning 'hear', 'see', and 'feel' (see Anderson 1986: 278–86). While Anderson (1986: 286) sees "weakening and generalization" of meaning in this shift, Matlock (1989: 219–21; see also Willett 1988: 80) considers it metaphorical, based on the underlying metaphor "knowing is seeing" and involving an increase in "speaker situatedness", or what could be better called subjectivity. While the development of mental construct evidentials does not seem to involve a comparable metaphorical transfer from concrete sensory to abstract mental domain, there is both the development of metalinguistic meaning, following Traugott's second Tendency, and an increase in subjectivity, following Traugott's third Tendency, as meaning shifts from the speaker's mental act to his or her belief state ([. . .] Traugott 1989: 48). Traugott (1995) notes further that in expressions such as *I think*, "the subject is losing referential (objective) properties, and becoming simply the starting point of a perspective", a shift from subject of proposition to subject of utterance.

The second stage in the process, from evidential to epistemic, seems to be an extremely clear example of the conventionalization of a conversational implicature. [. . .] [I]t is probably best to define evidentiality in a narrow sense, encompassing modes of knowing and sources of evidence, but excluding matters of reliability and confidence, since these seem to be implicatures. That is, whereas many evidentials imply uncertainty, they do not necessitate it. Like all implicatures, these expressions of uncertainty are defeasible (Levinson 1983. 114). For example, although a hearsay evidential would normally imply some degree of uncertainty (*I hear he's coming, but I'm not certain*), the implication of uncertainty can be canceled (*I hear he's coming, and I'm certain he is*); such cancelations are also possible for the implicatures of mental construct evidentials, e.g., *I {guess, am guessing} that he's coming to the party, and I'm quite sure he will*. If, as I have argued above, the primary—and conventional—meaning of the first-person epistemic parentheticals in Middle English is epistemic uncertainty, not evidential nonactuality, then there has been a meaning shift in which the conversational implicature of uncertainty stemming from the mental mode of knowing has been conventionalized or semanticized as the conventional meaning of the expression. [. . .]

Syntactic development: from main clause to parenthetical

It has been noted that for the first-person KNOW—parentheticals in Modern English, the expected hierarchical relationship is reversed, with the original subordinate clause being the "real utterance" or the "assertion proper" and the original matrix clause having a subsidiary role (Urmson 1952: 495; Benveniste 1971: 228–9). Quirk et al. (1985: 1113) suggest that a sentence such as *I believe that there were no other applicants for that job* can be converted into *There were no other applicants, I believe, for the job* by a "reversal of syntactic roles", though they note that the two sentences are not entirely equivalent. [. . .]

This reversal of the relationship of subordination, with the original subordinate clause (the *that*-clause) assuming main clause status and the original main clause assuming parenthetical, or adjunct, status has been seen as a synchronic process of development. Ross (1973) gives detailed semantic and syntactic arguments for the synchronic derivation of sentences such as *Max is a Martian, I feel* from *I feel that Max is a Martian* by a process of "slifting", or sentence lifting, which moves the *that*-clause from under the domination of *I feel* and adjoins it to the left of the erstwhile superordinate clause; a further rule of "niching", he postulates, moves the parenthetical into clause-medial position. Thompson and Mulac (1991:313) suggest a reverse development from subject + main verb + complement constructions (with and then without *that*) to parenthetical:

[4] a. I think that *we're definitely moving towards being more technological*.
 b. I think Ø *exercise is really beneficial, to anybody*.
 c. *It's just your point of view you know what you like to do in your spare time* I think.

Thompson and Mulac's evidence for the evolution of first-person epistemic parentheticals from matrix clause structures is quantitative; they believe that there is a direct correlation between the frequency of the "target" construction, the *that*-less construction [4]b., and the epistemic parenthetical [4]c.: "those subjects and verbs occurring most frequently without *that* are precisely those which occur most frequently as [epistemic parentheticals]" (p. 317, p. 314). In a corpus of conversational Modern English, they found that *think* and *suppose* constituted 65% of all nominal-complement-taking verbs and that *think* and *suppose* accounted for 85% of the verbs in epistemic parentheticals (p. 319). More importantly, *think* occurred 91% of the time without *that* and *guess* 99% of the time, compared with a rate of 75% *that*-less complements with all other verbs (p. 320); in fact, *I think* occurred 92% of the time without *that* (p. 323). Furthermore, *I* was the subject 83% of the time with nominal-complement-taking verbs and 95% of the time with epistemic parentheticals. Thompson and Mulac conclude that the quantitative results argue for the sequence of development shown in [4] and that it is the "blurring of the distinction between 'main' and 'complement' clause" seen in [4]b. which gives rise to the epistemic parentheticals (p. 316).

Thompson and Mulac suggest that the process they describe "is largely attested only synchronically" (1991: 324), yet we find all three structures shown in [4], as well as medial parentheticals, occurring in Middle English:

[5] a. I woot right wel that *swich was my biheste*.
 'I know quite well that such was my promise'

(Chaucer, *CT* D.WB 1059)

 b. "I woot right wel *I nam but deed* . . ."
 'I know full well I am not dead . . .'

(Chaucer, *CT* A.Mil. 3296)

c.   *That Grekis ben of heigh condicioun/* I woot ek wel"
'That Greeks are of high character I know also well'

(Chaucer, TC V 967–8)

d.   *"I have no cause,* I woot wel, *for to sore . . . "*
'I have no cause, I know well, to soar . . . '

(Chaucer, TC I 670)

While one may safely presume a synchronic correspondence (though not complete synonymity) among the four structures shown in [5], one must question whether there is a diachronic correspondence, that is, whether [5]c. or [5]d. derive diachronically from [5]b. Moreover, one must investigate whether the Middle English data show the quantitative correlation Thompson and Mulac found in Modern English between *that*-less forms and epistemic parentheticals.

[. . .] [M]y findings for a corpus of Chaucerian English [. . .] do not show the clear correlation that Thompson and Mulac found in Modern English. Some verbs (BELIEVE and DOUBT) are used too rarely to be significant; for others (DEEM and THINK), the subject and complement types are quite evenly distributed, while for SEEMETH, forms without personal experiencer are more common than forms with. Still other verbs (GUESS, LEVE, and UNDERTAKE) are used almost exclusively as parentheticals, and thus seem to be fully developed as parentheticals by the Middle English period. Only GUESS, SUPPOSE, TROW, WOOT, and THYNKETH occur more often with first-person subjects or experiencers than with second- or third-person ones, and of these, only TROW and WOOT are followed more often by *that*-less complements than by *that*-complements. It is significant, however, that TROW and WOOT are the most common parentheticals after GUESS. The data on WOOT are confused by the fact that WOOT, as well as UNDERSTAND and KNOW, is used quite often in the second person; again, it is probably significant that these same verbs occur frequently in a variety of 'you know' parentheticals (29 times in my corpus) [. . .].

Therefore, although the development that Thompson and Mulac (1991) suggest for Modern English is intuitively appealing, there seems to be fairly restricted quantitative evidence in Middle English for it. Furthermore, the fact that first-person epistemic parentheticals of the type found in Middle and Modern English do not occur in Old English also argues against their account. Two aspects of epistemic parentheticals in Middle English point to quite a different syntactic development. First is the existence of relative structures where the main clause is pronominalized within the parenthetical with the demonstrative pronoun *that/this*, the personal pronoun *it*, or a form such as *therof*, all of which are anaphoric.

[. . .]

Given that comparable parentheticals occur in Old English [. . .] with an anaphoric demonstrative, this syntactic type should probably be considered a remnant form.

A second piece of evidence concerning the development of epistemic parentheticals is provided by the existence of parentheticals beginning with *as* and *so*. As Quirk et al. (1985: 1116) point out, *as/ so* can function either as a relative pronoun (e.g., *I live a long way from work, as you know* = 'which you know') or as a subordinator with the meaning 'in so far as' (e.g., *He is the best candidate, as it seems*). While in Middle English, *as* generally functions as a relative (Kivimaa 1968: 11), *as*-parentheticals in final position [6]a.–b. seem to be most naturally interpreted as the relative-type and those in initial or medial position [6]c.–e. as the subordinator-type. Note especially [6]f., where the latter interpretation is explicit:

[6] a. "*For thrittene is a convent, as I gesse.*"
         'For thirteen is a convent, as I guess [= 'which I guess']'
                                        (Chaucer, *CT* D.Sum. 2259)

     b. "*She hath ynough to doone, hardyly, / To wynnen from hire fader*, so trowe I."
         'She has enough to do, assuredly, to get away from her father, so I believe
         [= 'which I believe']'
                                        (Chaucer, *TC* V 1124–5)

     c. *But, as I gesse, Alla was not so nyce . . .*
         'but, as I guess [= 'in so far as I can guess'], Alla was not so foolish . . . '
                                        (Chaucer, *CT* B.ML 1088)

     d. *He was that tyme in Geminis, as I gesse, / But litel fro his declynacion . . .*
         'He was at that time in Gemini, as I guess [= 'in so far as I can guess'], but
         little from his declination . . . '
                                        (Chaucer, *CT* E.Mch. 2222–3)

     e. "*Ther is no wight that woot*, I trowe so, / *Where it bycometh*"
         'There is no person who knows, as I believe [= 'as far as I know'], what
         happens to it'
                                        (Chaucer, *TC* II 796–7)

     f. *Of which to telle in short is myn entente / Th'effect*, as fer as I kan understonde.
         'Of which to tell in short is my intent the effect, as far as I can understand'
                                        (Chaucer, *TC* II 1219–20)

Quirk et al. (1985: 1116) also note the existence of "merged" forms in Modern English with
optional *it*, e.g., *as (it) often happens, as I understand (it)*. While a pronoun may occur in *as*-
parentheticals in Middle English, it is generally a dummy subject with an impersonal verb
[7]a.–b. Though [7]c. might appear to be an example of Quirk et al.'s merged type, it would
seem that *that* here is not an anaphoric pronoun but a "free conjugational affix" (Phillipps 1966)
or pleonasm:

[7] a. "*I may wel maken*, as it semeth me, / *My reasonyng of Goddes purveyaunce . . .*'
         'I may well make, as it seems to me, my reasoning of God's foresight . . .'
                                        (Chaucer, *TC* IV 1045–6)

     b. "*Swich thyng is gladsom*, as it thynketh me."
         'Such a thing is pleasing, as it seems to me'
                                        (Chaucer, *CT* B.NP 2778)

     c. "*Thyne eyen daswen eek*, as that me thynketh . . . "
         'Your eyes daze also, as it seems to me . . . '
                                        (Chaucer, *CT* H.Mcp. 31)

Kivimaa (1968: 14) finds that pleonastic *as that* is rare in Chaucer, but occurs primarily in
"turns of speech" such as that cited in [7]c.

In any case, parentheticals with relative *as*, especially in final position, appear to be equivalent to parentheticals with demonstrative *that/this* or pronominal *it*, since all contain relative pronouns referring anaphorically to the attached clause. Seeing both types of parentheticals as part of the same development, therefore, I argue for the syntactic development set out in [8] below (in place of that postulated in [4]). In Old English, an appositional relative clause, or "sentential relative clause" (see Quirk et al. 1985: 1244–5), with *this/ that* relative pronoun existed; given its occurrence at the clause margin, generally postposed, the relative clause was probably only loosely subordinated to the matrix clause. In Middle English the inventory of relative pronouns in this structure increases to include *it*, *thereof*, as, and *so*. Then, in Middle English, the relative construction begins to undergo changes. Either the anaphoric form is deleted, giving parentheticals such as *I gesse*, *I trowe*, *I suppose*, and *I woot*, or *as* is grammaticalized as a pure subordinator introducing an adverbial clause. Once grammaticalization occurs, the parentheticals can move to other positions in the sentence:

[8]   Stage I: *They are poisonous.* That I think.
      Stage II: *They are poisonous,* {that I think, I think that/ it, as/ so I think}. =
                 'which I think'
      Stage III: *They are poisonous,* I think. OR
                 They are poisonous, as I think. = 'as far as I think, probably'
      Stage IV: I think, *they are poisonous. They are,* I think, *poisonous.*

In initial position, as noted earlier, *I think* is ambiguous between the parenthetical and the (nonparenthetical) matrix clause without following complementizer (*I think they are poisonous*). It is interesting to note that *that* complement structures are standardly understood as deriving from an appositional relative clause in which the relative pronoun later grammaticalizes as the complementizer, i.e., *I think that*, *that they are poisonous* > *I think that they are poisonous* (see Traugott 1992: 237–8; Hopper and Traugott 1993: 185–9). Evidence for this derivation is an Old English example such as the following with both *þæt*s still present:

[9]   *ic þæt hicge nu, þæt ic ðine bebodu bliðe gehealde.*
      'I now think that, that I your command happily fulfill'
                 (ASPR 5, *Paris Psalter* 118.146; cited in Venezky and Healey 1980)

The first *þæt* is object of the verb *hicge* and points to the clause which follows, while the second *þæt* is a relative pronoun copy of it. Thus, the matrix clause—parenthetical and matrix clause—complement constructions have analogous derivations in that both originate in relative clauses; however, in the latter the demonstrative is "anticipatory" and cataphoric, referring to the clause that follows, while in the former the demonstrative is "resumptive" and anaphoric, referring to the clause that precedes.

The relation of syntactic to semantic change is somewhat difficult to establish. However, I would suggest that in Stage I, the form *that I think* denotes the cognitive act, with the act and the content of the act (the proposition *they are poisonous*) being equivalent. In Stage II, as the form *that I think* is more fully subordinated to the matrix clause, it takes on an evidential meaning, denoting the means of knowing rather than the cognitive act. The shift from evidential to epistemic meaning in Stage III perhaps correlates with the loss of anaphoric connectives since the form *I think*, being appositionally rather than anaphorically connected to the matrix clause, now expresses the degree of (un)certainty underlying the proposition rather than the source of knowledge for that proposition. Likewise, the form *as I think* with the explicit conjunction *as* expressing degree ("as far as") denotes degree of (un)certainty rather than source of knowledge. Finally, the extension in Stage IV provides evidence that the shifts, both syntactic and semantic, have occurred. Note that it is possible from Stage II onwards to express the cognitive act only by means of the regular main verb–complement structure (*I think* [*that*] *they are poisonous*).

Grammaticalization

While it must be acknowledged from the outset that epistemic parentheticals are not typical of the grammaticalization process in certain respects—for example, in beginning the process as clauses or phrases rather than as individual words (see Thompson and Mulac 1991: 318), in not undergoing either phonological or morphological bonding, and in becoming syntactically more free rather than more fixed—I believe that the diachronic evidence offers support for considering their development a case of grammaticalization. [. . .] *I gesse* forms undergo an increase in morphological fixation (generally as first-person present tense forms). More importantly, they suffer "decategorialization" from a subject-full verb construction to a particle-like parenthetical; Thompson and Mulac (1991: 318, 324) note that the category status of epistemic parentheticals is difficult to determine, but propose that they are best considered a subcategory of adverb. They argue as well that an epistemic parenthetical functions as a "unitary epistemic morpheme" (p. 315) or a "single element" (p. 318), which suggests a kind of "coalescence", though morphological fusion does not seem to occur. Thompson and Mulac further observe (pp. 324–5) that epistemic parentheticals exhibit "divergence" or "form/meaning asymmetry" in that while they are grammaticalized in certain contexts, in other contexts they continue to be used as ordinary subject-full verb constructions, available for negation and questioning, for example. Epistemic parentheticals also adhere to Hopper's principle of "persistence" (1991: 28 [. . .]) in that the evidential meaning (indeed the core cognitive meaning) is preserved to some extent, even in the grammaticalized epistemic expression. The original meaning accounts for the varying modal strengths of the different first-person epistemic parentheticals, for example, with *I guess* expressing more tentativeness than *I think*, since guessing is less certain than thinking (Thompson and Mulac 1991: 325), and with *I know* more often expressing certainty rather than uncertainty, since knowledge is more secure than belief.

Semantically, in shifting from propositional to expressive or interpersonal meaning, epistemic parentheticals follow the direction of change observed in grammaticalization. Furthermore, the development of epistemic parentheticals involves a well-recognized principle of semantic change in grammaticalization, that is, pragmatic strengthening, as the implicature of uncertainty arising from the mental mode of knowing is conventionalized.

[. . .]

■ ■ ■

POST-READING

Now that you have had time to reflect on the Brinton Reading, give yourself a score out of 10 for the extent to which you could now talk in an informed way about:

1 Grammaticalization.
2 The functions of pragmatic markers.

3   Epistemic meaning.
4   The evolution of the English pragmatic marker, *I guess*.

Make a note of your scores for 1–4, adding a date. Then commit to a date in the not-too-distant future, when you will return to this exercise: we would suggest that, at the 'second sitting' (and, if relevant, subsequent sittings), you seek to add to your earlier notes both *before re-reading and after re-reading* Brinton, so that you can gain a better sense of (i) how your knowledge/reading comprehension is improving overall, and (ii) the sections that still require more detailed attention on your part.

ANDREAS H. JUCKER AND IRMA TAAVITSAINEN

DIACHRONIC SPEECH ACT ANALYSIS
Insults from flyting to flaming

PRE-READING

1 The opening paragraph on the sleeve of Nancy McPhee's (1982) *The Complete Book of Insults* reads:

> Through the centuries, men and women have exercised their highest powers of invention and wit in speaking ill of one another. And in most of us there is a streak of malice which secretly delights in the pointed put-down, and relishes the audacious phrase we would hardly dare to use overselves!

Like *The Complete Book of Insults* generally, the quotation indicates that insulting requires a certain level of linguistic prowess and creativity. Indeed, in the *Forward* (p. 7), McPhee likens insulting to 'verbal warfare' and intimates that, at its best, it constitutes 'an art'. Do you agree with McPhee's assessment that insulting is a creative activity, if not 'an art', requiring linguistic prowess? Why/why not?

2 As a 'first approximation' towards a definition of insults/insulting, Jucker and Taavitsainen provide three dictionary definitions. We have reproduced them below for you:

> To assail with offensively dishonouring or contemptuous speech or action; to treat with scornful abuse or offensive disrespect; to offer indignity to; to affront, outrage. (*OED* 'insult' v.)

> An act, or the action, of insulting (...); injuriously contemptuous speech or behaviour; scornful utterance or action intended to wound self-respect; an affront, indignity, outrage. (*OED* 'insult' n.)

> To treat, mention, or speak rudely; offend, affront. An offensive or contemptuous remark or action; affront; slight. A person or thing producing the effect of an affront. (*Collins English Dictionary and Thesaurus* 1993 (based on the Bank of English) 'insult' vb.)

Photocopy these definitions so that you can use arrows and/or highlighting to demonstrate where these definitions overlap/differ.

IN-READING

1   Jucker and Taavitsainen distinguish conventionalized insults from particularized insults. When you reach the first marginal mark (|) note down the way(s) in which they are said to differ.

2   As you read the section on 'Anglo-Saxon warriors: Boasts and rituals', note down the labels Jucker and Taavitsainen use to identify both historical and 'modern forms of ritual insult'.

3   At the end of the section on '. . . Boasts and rituals', pause for a moment so that you can note down the typical characteristics of a 'flyting' incident.

4   Stop at the second marginal mark (|) and make sure that you understand why the *Romeo and Juliet* example involving a non-verbal gesture 'show[s] how polite behavior and its violations are culture-specific'.

■ ■ ■

DIACHRONIC SPEECH ACT ANALYSIS INSULTS FROM FLYTING TO FLAMING
ANDREAS H. JUCKER AND IRMA TAAVITSAINEN

[. . .] There is a wide range of contrastive analyses of speech acts across different cultures (e.g. Blum-Kulka et al. 1989; Blum-Kulka 1997; Oleksy 1988; Wierzbicka 1991; Trosborg 1995) [. . .] These approaches are methodologically important for a diachronic speech act analysis, since in both cases the realization of a particular speech act is compared in different linguistic and cultural contexts, that is to say historical distance and geographical or indeed social distance pose very similar [. . .] methodological problems [. . .] The Cross-Cultural Speech Act Realization Project (CCSARP) (Blum-Kulka et al. 1989) for instance analyzes requests and apologies in different cultures. This is based on the assumption that requests and apologies exist as language functions in all the languages under investigation but that they may be realized differently in these languages. That is to say, the function (in this case more precisely the illocutionary force of a particular speech act) stays stable while its actual form (i.e. its realization) may differ and is the object of investigation. However, it has been recognized for quite some time now that different cultures may in fact use a different range of speech functions, so that there is no easy correlation, let alone any identity of speech functions across languages. An apology in Japanese, for instance, may not only be a realization of a universal language function that differs from the corresponding realization in English, but it may be a significantly different social act.

In the history of a language, the range of speech functions changes in the same way as the range of genres and text types changes as a result of social changes, changes in political institutions, advances in technology, language contact and so on (Görlach 1992; Fritz 1995, 1997; Taavitsainen 1997). Thus it is imperative to be very careful in the identification of specific speech acts for a diachronic investigation. The different realizations across time may well reflect, at least partly, differences in function.

[A] second problem concerns the fuzziness of speech acts. Utterances can be vague or even ambiguous as to their illocutionary force. An utterance like *Do I hear a noise?* may be used by a teacher as a reprimand, by somebody listening to a violinist practicing on her instrument as an insult, by somebody caught in the deafening roar of an airplane taking off as an ironic statement, or it may be used as a genuine request for information. Even in one given situation the illocutionary force may be deliberately vague. The utterance *I wouldn't do this*, for instance, can be used as a statement, a piece of advice and a warning all at the same time. In some cases explicit performatives can be used to realize a particular speech act, especially in the case of illocutionary speech act verbs (*I hereby ask you . . . , I hereby promise to you that I will . . . , I hereby tell you . . .* , etc.), but only some speech act verbs may be used in this way, and some speech act verbs may be used to perform other speech acts (indirect speech acts), as for instance in *I promise that you will fail the exam if you do not study more diligently*. Thus speech acts as functional units do not correspond directly to speech act verbs of a particular language.

[A] third problem concerns the inventory of speech acts. A precise description of a speech act cannot be achieved without reference to neighboring speech acts (semantic field theory here conceptualized as pragmatic space). As we will see, a careful description of insults must also take into account such neighboring speech acts as slanders and slurs, oaths, swearing, disparaging remarks about non-present third parties and of course agonistic or ritual insults.

Data in historical pragmatics

The material [for] our analysis [of insults] can be divided into [. . .] fictional and non-fictional, i.e. reports on real-life verbal aggression. In fiction the instances [. . .] need not reflect actual ways of insulting people. Instead, these speech acts may show generic developments that can be conventionalized and typicalized. The advantage of fictional material is that the speech events are often given *verbatim* in direct quotations and described in their context, from the situation that gave rise to the exchange to the perlocutionary effects of the words used and the possibly ensuing actions.

Examples of insults from the Old English period are limited: there is a predominance of heroic poetry and total lack of, [. . .] e.g. [. . .] nonliterary materials. [. . .] These ritual insults reflect the Old English literary tradition, but the trend runs through time up to the present day so that it is still recognizable [. . .]. Middle English literature shows more variety, and fictional insults from this period seem to have two extreme poles. A specific generic development is found in the genre of saints' lives in which the use of verbal aggression acquired a functional role. [. . .] The other end of the scale consists of personal and particularized insults that abound in Chaucer's *Canterbury Tales*.

Real-life materials emerge for the first time in the Late Middle English period [in the form of] private letters [. . .] ([see, e.g.] the Paston letters from the fifteenth century). Our assumption was that we would find many more examples of personal insults in Early Modern English letters [. . .], but this was not the case. Letters may contain accounts of impolite behavior and people's reactions, but they do not usually contain the events that caused them. [That is, d]escriptions of insults are rare. [. . .] Reports on courtroom trials [do] contain insults, but [as will become clear] the power relations of the participants are extremely biased. [. . .].

Insults are frequent in Early Modern English fiction and drama. Shakespeare is a particularly rich source and examples of insults and adjacent speech acts can be found in his works. In Present-day English the data is far more varied. The researcher has no longer to rely on written sources, but can use all the data-gathering techniques developed by sociolinguists and pragmatists. Among the many possibilities [   ] [are r]itual insults of black adolescents [. . .] (an oral form of interaction), and flaming [. . .] (a type of insulting behavior that is germane to the medium of electronic communication).

The nature of insults

A first approximation

[. . .]. In the *Oxford English Dictionary* [insult/insulting is] [. . .] defined as follows:

> To assail with offensively dishonouring or contemptuous speech or action; to treat
> with scornful abuse or offensive disrespect; to offer indignity to; to affront, outrage.
> (*OED* 'insult' v.)
> An act, or the action, of insulting (. . .); injuriously contemptuous speech or behaviour;
> scornful utterance or action intended to wound self-respect; an affront, indignity,
> outrage. (*OED* 'insult' n.)
> To treat, mention, or speak rudely; offend, affront. An offensive or contemptuous
> remark or action; affront; slight. A person or thing producing the effect of an affront.
> (*Collins English Dictionary and Thesaurus* 1993 (based on the Bank of English) 'insult'
> vb.)

The most important feature that derives from these definitions is the fact that insults describe
to a large extent the effect on the addressee, that is to say a perlocutionary effect. This makes
insults a difficult unit for investigation, [. . .] [not least] [. . .] because the same utterance may
achieve different effects for different addressees. One particular insult may be insulting for
one particular addressee while it might not be insulting for another. [. . .] It is even possible
to insult unintentionally. An addressee may feel deeply offended by an utterance that was
meant as a statement. In the following section, we develop the distinction between the
illocutionary and the perlocutionary aspects of insults.

Illocutionary force and perlocutionary effect of insults

[. . .] Speech act theorists distinguish between three aspects of utterances: the locutionary act,
the illocutionary force and the perlocutionary effect (see Austin 1962: 98–117; or for a recent
summary Sbisà 1995: 498–9). The locutionary act pertains to the physical act of producing an
utterance. In everyday language this aspect is described by such speech act verbs as "say" or
"utter". The illocutionary force of an utterance can be described by verbs such as "order",
"advise", "promise", "state", "ask", "thank" and so on. It focuses on the act that is performed
by the speaker in issuing an utterance. The perlocutionary effect, finally, describes the effect
the utterance has on a particular hearer, that is the feelings, thoughts or actions that the
utterance stirs in the hearer. These are three aspects that co-occur in a single utterance. Thus
a speaker may utter a number of words (locutionary act) in order to ask a question (illocutionary
force), which may have the unintended effect of annoying the target (perlocutionary effect).

In this sense, then, the illocutionary force of an insult describes the primary act the speaker
performs such as attack, assault, contemptuous remark, nasty comment and so on. Hill and
Öttchen (1995) have this aspect in mind when they classify Shakespearean insults into name-
calling, general abuse, knavery and villainy, and expletives. These are forms of insults, whatever
the reaction of the target. The perlocutionary effect, on the other hand, consists of offence,
wounded feelings, affront, or outrage.

Thus an insult in spite of all the variety can be reduced to the following three essential
elements: First, a predication about the target (or about some part of his/her social identity,

e.g. his/her profession). That is to say the speaker utters something about the target or uses words to characterize him/her, or uses an epithet to address him/her. Second, this predication is perceived as inappropriate and demeaning by the target. And third, the target experiences this predication as a face-threatening speaker intention, that is to say he or she believes that the speaker made the predication with the intention to hurt or demean him or her.

The first two of these three are obligatory defining criteria. If there is no predication about a target, we do not want to define it as an insult. Similarly if the predication is not seen as disparaging, we do not include this speech act in our analysis. The last feature tends to be present in the speech acts that we are interested in, but we would also allow for situations in which a person feels insulted even though he/she is aware that an insult was not intended. We are well aware that other researchers might draw the line differently, but we wish to introduce this terminological convention as a means of delimiting our object of investigation.

A disparaging remark about an absent third party on this analysis cannot be an insult unless the third party is closely connected to somebody in the audience, in which case this latter person becomes the target. Thus a rude remark about the present government would not count as an insult unless a member of the government is present or somebody who feels personally close to the government (for political or personal reasons). In this case the target of the insult would be this person and not the government.

Personal insults in the pragmatic space of face threatening acts

Hill and Öttchen (1995: 22) in their collection of Shakespearean insults use a broad definition: "We define insults broadly. Some sit smug at the center of the definition, clearly intended to cast aspersion. Others come from around the edges — like disparaging insinuations, self-judgements or cynical observations." This suggests a prototype approach, the insults varying in their degree of conformity to prototypical insults. We would like to develop this idea and argue that speech acts are fuzzy concepts which show both diachronic and synchronic variation in a "pragmatic space". We use the term "space" in analogy to the concept of semantic fields in which expressions are analyzed in relation to neighboring expressions (Lyons 1977: 583; Hofmann 1993: 298; Welte 1993: 158–79). We prefer the term "space" to "field" because it indicates the multidimensionality of criteria that are relevant in the description of specific speech acts.

We suggest that at least the dimensions shown in Table 5.3.1 (see page 258) are important for the pragmatic space of insults.

The first two dimensions concern the formal level of the insults. In the literature on insults there is usually a distinction between ritual and personal insults. However, the ritual should not be seen in direct opposition to the personal. There are two dimensions involved: the ritual as rule-governed versus the creative as not following conventionalized patterns, and the ludic versus aggressive, which we will introduce below. The insults reported in the *Canterbury Tales*, in court proceedings or in private letters are creative in the sense that they do not follow any conventionalized patterns. The structure of courtroom insults is cumulative and goal-driven as it aims at influencing the target's behavior in a planned and premeditated way. On the same formal level we distinguish between typified and *ad hoc* insults. In some fictional genres insults have developed into speech acts in which a brief discourse has a typicalized form so that it schematically represents an entire speech event (see Fludernik 1993: 411). Such speech acts may serve as functional *loci* in the plot (see page 261 in the section on insults in saints' lives).

Table 5.3.1 Pragmatic space of insults

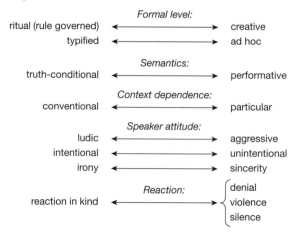

On the semantic level, we distinguish between truth-conditional and performative insults. This distinction is useful in order to distinguish between slanders and slurs, on the one hand, and name-calling and expletives, on the other. The former category includes utterances that would be testable in a law-court (according to Lindahl 1987 such law-suits were common in the Middle Ages). The latter category comprises utterances that are face-threatening without predicating any testable description about the target. This distinction is important for various forms of verbal dueling. The insults that the contestants hurl at each other must be perceived to be blatantly untrue. Abuse which has some basis in truth is likely to turn the verbal dueling from playful to serious (see Edwards and Sienkewicz 1990: 130; Labov 1972a, 1972b; Arnovick 1995). Oaths and swearing are not in themselves insults since they do not encode a predication about a target, but they may be perceived as insults if the addressee perceives them as disrespectful. This may be an intrusion into the addressee's personal territory to the extent that swearing in the presence of the addressee suggests that the speaker deems this to be appropriate in the presence of the addressee.

The dimensions on the next level are concerned with the attitude of the speaker. The sounding of African-American adolescents (Abrahams 1962; Labov 1972a, 1972b) as well as the flyting of Anglo-Saxon warriors and medieval knights (Arnovick 1995; Bax 1981) follow strict patterns and in this sense are rule-governed. However, the former is mostly ludic, that is to say a mere contest of verbal prowess, while the latter may lead to physical violence in the form of a duel or a battle. Banter as a form of playful insults between intimates is another and probably widespread form of ludic insults (Leech 1983: 144–5).

Insults may also be unintentional. As we have outlined above, insults are primarily perlocutionary. An utterance may have the effect of wounding the addressee even if the speaker did not mean to offend him/her. To cite a real-life example, at an international conference a speaker severely overstepping his time limit was interrupted and felt to be offensive by one member of the audience, but not by all. This means, of course, that unintentional insults can only be recognized for the analyst of historical data if a reaction by the target is recorded.

Furthermore, we distinguish between conventionalized insults and particularized insults (on the analogy of conventionalized and particularized implicatures). Conventionalized insults are those which in normal circumstances are understood as insults by all members of a speech community, e.g. slanderous remarks, contemptuous remarks, name calling, and demeaning expletives. In this area the analyst is on fairly safe ground since the illocutionary force of the utterance encodes the intention to have a particular perlocutionary effect. The identification of such conventionalized insult illocutions becomes more difficult of course the further removed the analyst is from the speech community under investigation.

Particularized insults, on the other hand, are those which do not have this conventional force. They are more difficult to identify for the analyst because they depend on the reaction of the target to an utterance that does not have this conventional force. And it is in this category that unintentional insults may occur. The target (who was not targeted by the speaker) perceives a predication about himself/herself as face-threatening and as having been made with the intention to demean, wound or outrage him/her.

The last dimension concerns the reaction of the target. A personal insult requires a denial or an excuse, while a ritual insult requires a response in kind (Labov 1972a: 153; Arnovick 1995: 604). Flytings may either end in actual violence or in silence, with which one of the contenders admits his inferiority. The Canterbury pilgrims react by counter-abuse, physical violence or silence. Reactions in courtrooms reflect the power relations of the participants, and in letters we often have the reactions only (see *ME Letters: Real-life aggression*).

Insults in the history of English

In the following we shall give an outline of a partial history of insults in English by drawing from a variety of sources from Old English to Modern English, though such a description cannot even attempt to be comprehensive. We shall try to assess the position of specific insults within the dimensions of the pragmatic space of verbal aggression and apply the analytical grid outlined above. The examples we have used when developing our theory highlight spots in the pragmatic space of antagonistic behavior. It is not possible to draw an evolutionary line of development, but the examples serve to illustrate various types of insults. We shall also give the sociohistorical context of the speech event as accurately as possible and we also pay attention to the generic developments when relevant.

Anglo-Saxon warriors: boasts and rituals

In the Old English heroic tradition insults occur in the pragmatic space of boasts and challenges. The flyting of the Anglo-Saxon warriors follows strict rules. The standard sequence consists of Claim, Defense, and Counterclaim, where the Claim and the Counterclaim consist of boasts and insults, which relate to the past deeds of the contenders, and threats, vows and curses, which relate to the future (Clover 1980: 452). The setting is outdoors, where the contenders meet face-to-face, a body of water often separating them, or it is indoors in the drinking hall.

Clover (1980: 453) lists the typical insults and reduces the topics to a few major categories that focus on cowardice, failure of honor, and irresponsible behavior; crimes of kinship emerge as a central theme. He also argues that Germanic flyting cannot be analyzed as ritual insults in Labov's terms because they provoke very strong responses. The preliminary incident is never disputed even by the offended partner. "This is perhaps the most striking characteristic of flytings: they argue interpretations, not facts" (Clover 1980: 458). As we mentioned before, flytings may either end in actual violence or in silence. In our terms both Germanic flyting and sounding can be described as ritual since both are rule-governed, but the former lacks the ludic quality of the latter.

A well-known example is the Unferth episode in Beowulf, which is related to Norse flyting combining both the "senna" tradition (i.e. the formal exchange of insults and threats) and the "mannjafnaðr" tradition (i.e. the formal exchange of boasts) (Clover 1980: 445–6). The flyting thus consists of an exchange of verbal provocations between hostile speakers in a predictable and highly stylized way. The scene takes place shortly after Beowulf's arrival, after Hrothgar has greeted him in the drinking hall [. . .] Beowulf is invited to sit and tell of his famous victories. But first Unferth addresses Beowulf with a speech that is both heavily ironic and insulting to Beowulf. He accuses Beowulf of having risked his life for a foolish contest with Breca and for having lost the contest. He concludes his speech by saying that he does not expect Beowulf to be successful in an encounter with Grendel. In the words of Clover (1980: 461) "the Claim thus amounts to a double charge of frivolous behavior and heroic inadequacy." Beowulf counters in the appropriate style by accusing Unferth of being drunk:

(1) Ðonne wene ic to þe wyrsan geþingea, ðeah þu heaðoræsa gehwær dohte, grimre guðe, gif þu Grendles dearst nihtlongne fyrst nean bidan.'
Beowulf maþelode, bearn Ecgþeowes: 'Hwæt, þu worn fela, wine min Unferð, beore druncen ymb Brecan spræce, sægdest from his siðe.'
["Therefore I expect the worse result for you — though you have prevailed everywhere in battles, in grim war — if you dare wait near Grendel a night-long space." Beowulf spoke, the son of Ecgtheow: "Well, my friend Unferth, drunk with beer you have spoken a great many things about Breca — told about his adventures."]

(*Beowulf* 525–32a)

Beowulf recounts the events of his contest with Breca in an entirely different light. Breca was not stronger, and moreover he, Beowulf, destroyed a mighty sea-beast. And he continues, if Breca's people, the Scyldings, were any match for him, they would not have had to suffer the humiliation at the hands of Grendel. Through this speech Beowulf successfully silences Unferth. Hrothgar, the king, is delighted because Beowulf's performance suggests that he might succeed against Grendel (on the Unferth episode see also Arnovick 1995: 608–9).
[. . .]
Ritual insults continue beyond the period of heroic poetry. Bax (1981, 1999) reports such behavior in the ritual challenges between later medieval knights, [and] Sounding or playing the dozens by African-American adolescents are modern forms of ritual insults [. . .].
The patterns are so well recognized even now that a parody works as a source of humor in a block-busting film from the 1970's (*Monty Python and the Holy Grail*, 1974):

[2] *Arthur* (shouting to Guard on the castle wall): If you will not show us the grail, we shall take your castle by force.
Guard (shouting back in a French accent): You don't frighten us, English peacocks. Go and boil your bottoms sundry silly persons. I blow my nose at you so-called Arthur person. You and your silly English k-nigets. (rude noises and gestures)
Sir Gallahad (to Arthur): What a strange person!
Arthur (to Guard): Now look here my good man . . .
Guard: I don't wanna talk to you no more you empty-headed animal food trough vapors. I fart in your general direction. Your mother was a hamster and your father smelled of elderberries.

[. . .]

Saints and tyrants: typified speech acts

In saints' lives insults have developed special functions and achieved a typicalized form [. . .]. This is a strictly generic development that took place in late Middle English, and culminated in the late developments of the genre. Insults are regularly found in the saints' bold and insulting speeches to the tyrant. In the course of time they acquired a pattern in which heavenly and worldly power, Christ and the tyrant, are put in contrast. Abusive metaphors like "foul, deadly dunghill" are used of the latter. The perlocutionary effect on the tyrant is anger which ultimately leads to the death of the saint. The saint remains intact and firm in her faith. [For example, in] Chaucer's *The Second Nun's Tale* Cecile mocks the judge "Lo, he dissymuleth heere in audience; He stareth, and woodeth in his advertence!" (SNT VIII (G) 466–7). This is a personal insult, a predication about the judge's looks and behavior. The perlocutionary effect on the tyrant leads to the [. . .] martyrdom of the saint. It may be that Chaucer's narrative skill served to shape this literary tradition which seems to have culminated in the late ME prose version of the legend of St Katherine in MS Southwell Minster 7 (c. 1500; eds. Nevanlinna and Taavitsainen 1993). The confrontation scene shows the use of typicalized phrases and metaphors:

> [3] "Now vndyrstond, I pray the, juge /whi/che of these I ou3t to cheose: a feyr euerlastyng kyng and a gloriose, or ellys a fowle dedly donghyll?" And then themperour, full of dispyte and woodnes, seyde to hur, "Cheose þe oon of þese .ij.: do sacrifice, or ellys suffre deþe."
>
> (lines 874–8)

A cumulative sequence of insults is used in another scene between the tyrant and fifty rhetoricians who have become converted to the Christian faith. The saint has overcome them in a debate: they admit Katherine's superiority, but the tyrant mocks them. The insult consists of a predication *overcomyn by a mayde* with a demeaning illocution, an attack on the rhetoricians' renown as learned scholars. The reaction is in kind, but realized by more subtle means: the illocution of contempt is achieved by a shift of pronoun, from respectful address with 3e to the second person singular *thou*, an address to an inferior. This marks a change of attitude in the speaker, and the target realizes the change. The perlocutionary effect of this insult is anger and madness *woo and wood*, leading to the grim action of killing. This is a common pattern in confrontations between the tyrant and the saint or people who have become converted into the Christian faith [. . .].
   [. . .]

Chaucer's Canterbury pilgrims: truth-conditional and creative

Chaucer's *Canterbury Tales* offer a panoply of characters from almost all social ranks and from all three estates of Chaucer's England. These fictional characters interact on various levels in a wide range of situations, in a wide range of genres (cf. Taavitsainen 1995), and in a wide range of styles ranging from the polite and refined to the rustic, lewd and insulting.
   The insults in the *Canterbury Tales* are personal and not ritual in the sense that every single insult is highly original ([. . .] see Jucker 2000). There is no general pattern, and many of the reactions clearly indicate the highly charged perlocutionary effect achieved by the insults [. . .].
   In the first example the Host, Harry Baily, talks to the Cook and describes his cooking in terms that sound like food-poisoning:

[4] Now telle on, Roger; looke that it be good,   4345
     For many a pastee hastow laten blood,
     And many a Jakke of Dovere hastow soold
     That hath been twies hoot and twies coold.
     Of many a pilgrym hastow Cristes curs,
     For of thy percely yet they fare the wors,   4350
     That they han eten with thy stubbel goos,
     For in thy shoppe is many a flye loos.

(CkPro, I 4345–52)

This extended insult is creative because it is not rule-governed but it is also what we have termed conventional. Even without a reaction from the Cook it can be classified as an insult, because of the seriousness of the accusation. In this case the Cook reacts in a good-humored way, but promises to repay Harry Bailly later by telling a story of an inn-keeper in turn.

In the second example, the Pardoner asks Harry Bailly to kiss his bogus relics. Such a request is neither true nor false, but it infuriates Harry Bailly:

[5] I rede that oure Hoost heere shal bigynne,
     For he is moost envoluped in synne.
     Com forth, sire Hoost, and offre first anon,
     And thou shalt kisse the relikes everychon,
     Ye, for a grote! Unbokele anon thy purs.

(PardT, VI 941–5)

In speech act terms, this utterance might be classified as a polite invitation or an offer if it were not for the Host's violent reaction. It is the perlocutionary effect, that is to say the reaction of the target, which turns the utterance into an insult. Thus, this is an example of a particularized and non-truth-conditional or performative insult.

Chaucer does not always tell us the effect of insults on their targets, but those that he does relate are just as varied as the forms of verbal aggression themselves. Very often the targets react in kind, that is to say with counterabuse. The Miller insults the Reeve by telling a story of a duped and cuckolded carpenter, and the Reeve retorts with a story of a miller who fares even worse. [. . .] Other reactions to insults in the *Canterbury Tales* comprise stunned silence, physical violence [. . .] or the intervention of the Host [. . .].
     [. . .]

ME letters: real-life aggression

The earliest example of a non-fictional insult is perhaps the letter from Margaret Paston to John Paston I, written in 1448. It gives a detailed account of how a situation with personal insults could develop. It started with non-verbal disrespectful behavior, a violation of the polite code. This served as a provocation to verbal assaults, name-calling with derogative terms and accusations, accompanied by the violent action of throwing stones. The aggression was extended to other people associated with the target, the narrator and her mother. Unfortunately the writer has censored the word-for-word account of the outburst of verbal aggression, the "large langage", because she considered it taboo in written language:

[6] And whanne Gloys was a-yenst Wymondham he seid þus, 'Couere thy heed!'
     And Gloys seid ageyn, 'So I shall for the.' And whanne Gloys was forther passed

by þe space of iij or iiij strede, Wymondham drew owt his dagger and seid, 'Shalt þow so, knave?' And þerwith Gloys turned hym and drewe owt his dagger and defendet hym, fleyng in-to my moderis place; and Wymondham and his man Hawys kest stonys and dreve Gloys into my moderis place. And Hawys folwyd into my moderis place and kest a ston as meche as a forthyng lof into þe halle after Gloys; and þan ran owt of þe place ageyn. And Gloys folwyd owt and stod with-owt þe gate, and þanne Wymondham called Gloys thef and seid he shuld dye, and Gloys seid he lyed and called hym charl, and bad hym come hym-self or ell þe best man he hadde, and Gloys wold answere hym on for on. And þanne Haweys ran into Wymondhams place and feched a spere and a swerd, and toke his maister his swerd. And with þe noise of þis a-saut and affray my modir and I come owt of þe chirche from þe sakeryng; and I bad Gloys go in to my moderis place ageyn, and so he dede. And thanne Wymondham called my moder and me strong hores, and seid þe Pastons and alle her kyn were (. . .) Myngham (. . .)e seid he lyed, knave and charl as he was. And he had meche large langage, as ye shall knowe her-after by mowthe.

(p. 224, italics removed)

Such a detailed account is, however, rare.

[. . .]

Shakespeare's courtiers: verbal aggression and perlocutionary effects

Shakespeare's plays are full of name-calling and insults; Hill and Öttchen (1995) list over 4,000 individual instances from Shakespeare's plays, unfortunately decontextualised. Most of them combine two adjectives (or participles) and a noun epithet after *thou* e.g. *Thou loggerheaded pale-hearted hugger-mugger!*, *Thou roynish knotty-pated horn-beast!*, *Thou infectious unchinsnouted barnacle!*. In these phrases, the second person singular seems to be a marked form of address, and in some cases the use of the pronoun could itself be an insult, as it may contain a predication about the social status of the target. Its use as a sociolinguistic marker was not, however, constant (see Calvo 1992).

Insults by name-calling are amply illustrated in the opening scene of *The Tempest* when the courtiers are introduced. The scene is contrary to audience expectations: instead of courtesy, impolite and insulting language with curses follows (cf. Caliban below). The boatswain is superior to the noblemen in this situation, and the scene serves to point out that human social hierarchies do not apply when nature enforces equality. The arrogant behavior of the courtiers towards their social inferiors is typified by name-calling. The boatswain's reply *Work you, then* is a typical reaction to misjudged criticism, that of responding in kind. The boatswain swears as an outburst of emotions in his toil, and when the courtiers interrupt him again, he makes sarcastic remarks. These are answered by insults:

[7] *Boats.* A plague upon this howling! they are louder than the weather, or our office.
Enter Sebastian, Antonio, *and* Gonzalo
Yet again? What do you here? Shall we give o'er and drown? Have you a mind to sink?
Seb. A pox o' your throat! you bawling, blasphemous, incharitable dog!
Boats. Work you then.

> *Ant.*   Hang, cur! hang, you whoreson, insolent noisemaker! We are less afraid
> to be drown'd than thou art.
>
> (*The Tempest*, I.i.36–45)

[In *Romeo and Juliet*, a] [. . .] non-verbal gesture [. . .] [is] perceived as an insult, [and] leads
to derogative words (cf. the Paston letter mentioned above). [. . .] The opposite sides are
introduced in a confrontational situation and the expectations of the audience are aroused; thus
the scene has a thematic function in the play and is typified in that sense (cf. saints' lives).
Non-verbal provocation leads to verbal dueling that constitutes a negotiation whether the biting
of a thumb is an insult or not. This scene also shows how polite behavior and its violations
are culture-specific: the significance of the gesture itself may be lost to the modern audience:

> [8] *Gre.*   I will frown as I pass by, and let them take it as they list.
> *Sam.*   Nay, as they dare. I will bite my thumb at them, which is disgrace to
> them if they bear it.
> *Abr.*   Do you bite your thumb at us, sir?
> *Sam.*   I do bite my thumb, sir.
> *Abr.*   Do you bite your thumb at us, sir?
> *Sam.*   [*Aside to Gregory*] Is the law of our side if I say ay?
> *Gre.*   [*Aside to Sampson*] No.
> *Sam.*   No, sir, I do not bite my thumb at you, sir, but I bite my thumb, sir.
> *Gre.*   Do you quarrel, sir?
> *Abr.*   Quarrel, sir? No, sir.
> *Sam.*   But if you do, sir, I am for you.
>
> (*Romeo and Juliet* I.i.40–54)

[. . .]

Magic in language: insults and curses

Swearing and cursing are speech acts that are adjacent to insulting but both the illocutions and
the assumed perlocutionary effects distinguish them. The scene with Caliban's first entry has
them both. Prospero entices Caliban to come forth by using rude language with name-calling
and derogatory predications about his generation. This is Caliban's own kind of language, and
perceived as rude and intentionally insulting even by him. His reaction is worse than in kind:
it is a curse. Cursing as a speech act had a strong illocutionary force as cursing was connected
with magical use of language. and believed to have an effect: what was said would come true.
This is the speaker intention in cursing; there is no predication about the target. Prospero, in
turn, reacts to the curse in kind and uses his magic, which in this case is not much different
from Caliban's, to inflict cramps and itches upon him:

> [9] *Pros.*   Come, thou tortoise, when?
>   . . .
> *Pros.*   Thou poisonous slave, got by the devil himself
>   Upon thy wicked dam, come forth!
> *Enter* CALIBAN.
> *Cal.*   As wicked dew as e'er my mother brush'd
>   With raven's feather from unwholesome fen

> Drop on you both! A south-west blow on ye,
> And blister you all o'er.
> *Pros.*   For this, be sure, to-night thou shalt have cramps,
> Side-stitches, that shall pen thy breath up; . . .
>
> (*The Tempest*, I.ii.316, 318–26)

Another speech act adjacent to insulting is taunting. It uses insults as provocation to an action; thus the illocutions and perlocutions are different from insults, though predications about the target are included. For example, after Macbeth has announced his resolution to abstain from murder, Lady Macbeth taunts him by accusations of cowardice in a long, rhetorical speech (I.vii. 35–58). [. . .]

17th century court officials

[Some] court proceedings from the 17th century record very aggressive real-life insults, including [. . .] name-calling and demeaning predications about the honesty and character of the target. [. . .] [Take, for example, the 1685 trial of] Lady Alice Lisle, [who] was tried on charges of high treason [. . .]. A witness was heard by the name of Dunne, a baker, who was involved as a messenger in the activities of which Lady Lisle was accused. In the course of the interrogation he keeps contradicting himself and gives a very confused account of the events. As a result the Lord Chief Justice, who asks the questions, grows increasingly impatient. He keeps admonishing Dunne to say the truth and he repeatedly accuses him of lying, and he does this in terms which can only be described as insulting. This can be seen in affective features like exclamations and a cumulative list of abusive terms, aggressive questioning, irony and mocking, accusations and strong threats which all reflect speaker attitude. The pattern in name-calling is exactly the same as in the examples found in Shakespeare's plays. [. . .]

[10]   L.C.J. Why, thou vile Wretch didst not thou tell me just now that thou pluck'd up the Latch? Dost thou take the God of Heaven not to be a God of Truth, and that he is not a Witness of all thou say'st? Dost thou think because thou prevaricatest with the Court here, thou can'st do so with God above, who knows thy Thoughts, and it is infinite Mercy, that for those Falshoods of thine, he does not immediately strike thee into Hell? Jesus God! there is no sort of Conversation nor human Society to be kept with such People as these are, who have no other Religion but only Pretence, and no way to uphold themselves but by countenancing Lying and Villany: Did not you tell me that you opened the Latch your self, and that you saw no body else but a Girl? How durst you offer to tell such horrid Lyes in the presence of God and of a Court of Justice? Answer me one Question more: Did he pull down the Hay or you?
Dunne: I did not pull down any Hay at all.

(p. 114)

[11]   *L.C.J.* Thou art a strange prevaricating, shuffling, sniveling, lying Rascal. Mr *Pollexsen*. We will set him by for the present, and call Barler, that is the other Fellow.

(p. 115)

[12]   *L.C.J.* And why did'st thou tell so many Lyes then? Jesu God! that we should live to see anysuch Creatures among Mankind, nay, and among us too, to the

> Shame and Reproach be it spoken of our Nation and Religion: Is this that that
> is called the Protestant Religion, a thing so much boasted of, and pretended
> to? We have heard a great deal of Clamour against Property and Dispensations,
> what Dispensations pray does the Protestant Religion give for such Practices as
> these? I pity thee with all my Soul, and pray for thee, but it cannot but make
> all Mankind to tremble and be filled with Horror, that such a wretched Creature
> should live upon the Earth: Prithee be free, and tell us what Discourse there
> was?
>
> *Dunne.* My Lord, they did talk of Fighting, but I cannot remember what it was.
>
> (p. 122)

Several elements are striking about these examples. First, insults are only used by the Lord
Chief Justice to this one witness. There is a very big power differential between him and
Dunne. The court transcripts do not betray any reaction by Dunne at all. He keeps answering
in the same fashion in short sentences, addressing the Lord Chief Justice with the phrase *my
Lord* in virtually every utterance. The outbursts quoted above do not provoke any defensive
or even counter-attacking reactions.

The insults recorded in extracts [10] to [12] can also be classified as accusations, warnings
or intimidations. This pragmatic space is of course genre specific. The Lord Chief Justice tries
to intimidate Dunne to such an extent that he tell the truth. The strategy seems to work since
Dunne eventually tells the events in a way which corresponds more closely and in a more
plausible way with the events told by Lady Lisle and by the other witnesses.

In the global structure of these court transcriptions, these passages appear at crucial points,
when Dunne admits to something that he denied earlier. In the case of [10] he had earlier
claimed that he himself had opened the stable door. Upon persistent questioning, he admits
that Carpenter had done it for him, which causes the Lord Chief Justice's outburst recorded
in [10]. This gives the proceeding a new turn. It is now clear that there were more people
on the scene than Dunne had at first admitted, and Dunne proceeds to tell a quite different
version of the events of that particular night.

In [11] the Lord Chief Justice is exasperated by Dunne's answers which he clearly does
not believe. He decides to call another witness. In [12] it again turns out that earlier claims
by Dunne that a girl had shown him the way to a room in the house was wrong and he admits
that this too was Carpenter. After the Lord Chief Justice's outburst recorded in extract [12],
Dunne remembers more of the events and even some details of a conversation that he must
have overheard on that evening but which so far he had claimed to know nothing about.

[. . .]

20th century adolescents: sounding [. . .]

[. . .] The ritual insults of urban black adolescents and other subcultures in the English-speaking
world have attracted the attention of researchers for a long time (e.g. Abrahams 1962; Labov
1972a and 1972b; Smitherman 1977; Eder 1990; Edwards and Sienkewicz 1990: Chapter 6;
Arnovick 1995; Bronner 1996; and Murray 1996). These practices are variously known as
"playing the dozens", "sounding", "screaming", "joining" or "signifying".

The purpose of playing the dozens is to better one's opponent with caustic and humorous
insults that are seen as patently untrue. Thus the practice is fundamentally ludic but with the
inherent danger of seriousness as soon as insults are perceived to be too close to reality. As
Arnovick (1995: 604) states, "personal, individualized statements work best as insults, but they

also have the greatest potential to incite violence. Ritualized or formulaic insults are the more conventional weapon in the sounding game."

The appropriate response to a ritual insult is a response in kind. If the target of a ritual insult reacts with defensive action such as a denial, the ritual insult is redefined as a personal insult. Arnovick (1995: 611): "sounding is rooted in game. It is essentially ludic in its mode of reference." [. . .]

Similar data have recently been collected from London teenage culture. Unlike [. . .] Afro-American adolescents, [the] girls participated in ritual insulting exchanges with face-threatening, unmitigated strategies. They were used to express intimacy and closeness in friendship rather than to negotiate status or rank (Hasund and Stenström 1997: 127, 129). There seems to be a clear pattern: swearing and demeaning predications about the target form the core, the tone is ludic, and the reaction is in kind. Ritual insults of this kind should perhaps be seen as part of the learning process on how to respond to insults in a non-serious manner (cf. teasing children and banter).

[. . .]

Conclusion

[In this paper, we have argued that the speech act of insulting should be seen as sharing] a multidimensional pragmatic space with neighboring speech acts. Specific realizations are context-specific, culture-specific and time-specific. Moreover it is not only the realization that changes over time but the underlying speech function may change too. Quite clearly, medieval flyting, Shakespearean name-calling and present-day [sounding] are not realizations of one and the same speech function of insult: [. . .] they are different speech functions located in the pragmatic space of antagonistic behavior.

■ ■ ■

POST-READING

1   Does Jucker and Taavitsainen's discussion of insults and insulting tally with McPhee's description of insulting and, if so, in what ways? What do Jucker and Taavitsainen discuss in regard to insulting, which is not picked up by the McPhee quotation in the pre-reading activity?

2   After listing dictionary definitions of *insult,* Jucker and Taavitsainen state that 'the most important feature that derives from the[m] is the fact that insults describe to a large extent the effect on the addressee, that is to say a perlocutionary effect'. Do they keep to this view themselves throughout the rest of the reading? Why/why not?

3   'A precise description of a speech act cannot be achieved without reference to neighboring speech acts (semantic field theory here conceptualized as pragmatic space)'. Provide an account of Jucker and Taavitsainen's theory, stating how it allows for 'fuzzy boundaries' between speech acts.

4   According to Jucker and Taavitsainen:

> An utterance like *Do I hear a noise*? may be used by a teacher as a reprimand, by somebody listening to a violinist practicing on her instrument as an insult, by somebody caught in the deafening roar of an airplane taking off as an ironic

statement, or it may be used as a genuine request for information. Even in one given situation the illocutionary force may be deliberately vague. The utterance *I wouldn't do this*, for instance, can be used as a statement, a piece of advice and a warning all at the same time.

Develop Jucker and Taavitsainen's argument, by providing contexts in which *Do I hear a noise* functions as (a) a reprimand, (b) an insult, and (c) another speech act of your own choosing, and *I wouldn't do this* functions as (a) advice, (b) a warning, (c) both advice and a warning, and (d) another speech act of your own choosing. Finally, consider what kinds of speech act *Do I hear a rumour* and *I wouldn't do that* might function as.

5   Using Jucker and Taavitsainen's examples from different historical periods as supporting evidence, state which, if any, is more important – the illocutionary force of insults, or their perlocutionary effect(s).

6   Has the 'art' of insulting changed at all, over time? If so, how?

SECTION 5 FURTHER READING

Situating historical pragmatics

Andreas H. Jucker's (1995) edited collection, *Historical Pragmatics*, is an important landmark in the development of the field. A second edited collection of the same name, edited by Jucker and Taavitsaineen (2010), is also likely to become a landmark publication. A comparison of Brinton (2001), Culpeper (2010a), Jucker et al. (1999) and Traugott (2004) – in conjunction with the articles within *Historical Pragmatics* (1995) – will help you to gain a sense of the relationship between Historical Pragmatics, Historical Dialogue Analysis and Historical Discourse Analysis, and the extent to which the disciplines overlap. Many of the above will also help you to gain a better sense of the difference(s) between the form-to-function approach and function-to-form approach adopted within these disciplines. In addition, we would suggest that you read Archer (2005) and Culpeper (2009) to gain an understanding of the historical sociopragmatic approach.

Speech act studies

A classic work in this area is Arnovick (1999): Arnovick traces a number of culturally/socially important speech acts over time, including the agonistic insult, *Bless you!*, the promise and the common curse. Jucker and Taavitsainen's (2008) edited collection also contains a number of valuable studies. For non-English studies, see, e.g., Schlieben-Lange (1976, 1979), Schlieben-Lange and Weydt (1979, 1983), Fritz and Muckenhaupt (1981), Weigand (1988), Bax (1991), Lebsanft (1988) and Schrott (2000). For a summary of the evolution of English speech acts over time, which picks up on the use of im/politeness approaches, a prototype approach and/or the idea of a shared pragmatic space to explain speech acts and their development over time, see Archer (2010).

Grammaticalization studies

There are a proliferation of grammaticalization studies: see, e.g., the work of Brinton (2006), Traugott and Dasher (2002), Hopper (2010) and Hopper and Traugott (2003). In addition, see Love (2001) for arguments that the grammaticalization process, in general, may not always be unidirectional; and also Erman and Kotsinas (1993), who argue that items such as pragmatic markers can be seen as lying outside the grammar and not having grammatical functions. As such, the process they undergo is more akin to pragmaticalization than grammaticalization.

Journals

The most relevant journal in this area is the *Journal of Historical Pragmatics*.

General books

Some general books on the history of the English language also include sections on historical pragmatics: see, for example, *The Handbook of the History of English* (van Kemenade and Los 2006) and Watts and Trudgill's (2002) *Alternative Histories of English*.

SECTION 6

Politeness, face and impoliteness

Introduction

ERVING GOFFMAN HAS BEEN influencing Western conceptions of 'face' and 'facework' for some thirty years now. An extract from his pioneering work, 'On facework: an analysis of ritual elements in social interaction', thus makes up our first reading in this section on **Politeness, face and impoliteness**. Although this work was originally published in 1955 in the *Psychiatry Journal for the Study of Interpersonal Processes*, we have opted to include the 1967 version as reprinted in *Interaction Ritual: Essays on Face-to-Face Behaviour* – in particular, pages 5–25 (with some omissions).

The edited reading includes Goffman's detailed discussions of 'face' and 'facework'. He defines 'face', as 'the positive social value a person effectively claims for himself by the line others assume he is taking during a particular contact', and defines 'facework' as a discursively-constructed endeavour, which involves a temporary 'mutual acceptance' of the 'line', according to established social and/or situational standards. Goffman sums up this 'mutual acceptance' as follows:

> Just as the member of any group is expected to have self-respect, so also he is expected to sustain a standard of considerateness; he is expected to go to certain lengths to save the feelings and the face of others present, and he is expected to do this willingly and spontaneously.

As this reading reveals, however, Goffman is very aware that interlocutors will occasionally engage in facework 'for what can be safely gained from it' and, as such, he's also careful to stress that the adoption of a mutually-accepting line should not be taken to mean interlocutors are always 'candidly' expressing 'heart-felt evaluations'. To illustrate this, he points to those who 'fish for compliments' by being overtly modest in the presence of others who (they hope) are likely to lavish praise upon them in return.

As will become clear, Goffman also allows for the fact that, in some cases, interlocutors may actually engage in (verbal and non-verbal) activities that *intentionally threaten* the face of others. *Intentional* face threats constitute one of three possible face threats, according to Goffman, the others being *incidental* face threats and *accidental* face threats. Very briefly, the three face threats represent differing levels of speaker intent: in the case of *incidental* face threats, the speaker is aware that an 'unplanned by-product' of her actions might be that of face damage, but this is not her primary intent (cf. *intentional* face threats); in the case of *accidental* face threats, any resulting face damage is completely unintentional on the part of the speaker.

Goffman's (albeit) subsidiary focus on 'the aggressive use of facework' helps to explain why researchers interested in linguistic impoliteness have drawn from his work as much as researchers interested in linguistic politeness. Indeed, both the Politeness reading and the two Impoliteness readings which follow the Goffman reading all draw upon his ideas in some way.

The Politeness reading we include here is taken from pages 57–85 of Penelope Brown and Stephen Levinson's (1987) *Politeness: Some Universals in Language Usage*, the section that details how we, as interlocutors, attempt to minimise threats to face, using one of five 'superstrategies':

- The first superstrategy, *bald on record*, is used when we deem a given face threatening act (also known as an FTA) to be minimal and, as such, to require no redressive action, or when we deem the relationships between the interlocutors to be such that no redressive action is required: for example, Brown and Levinson argue that we would not expect to attend to face issues in an emergency situation, where people's lives may be at risk (such as when we need others to quickly vacate a burning building).
- The second superstrategy, *positive politeness*, is used when we deem that an on-record strategy is still appropriate, but that the FTA is such that it requires our explicitly attending to our interlocutor's positive face: positive face is defined, by Brown and Levinson, as the 'want' of every 'competent adult member' to be approved of in their actions. We might attend to our interlocutor's positive face by 'treating him as a member of an in-group, a friend, [and/or] a person whose wants and personality traits are known and liked'.
- The third superstrategy, *negative politeness*, is used when we deem the FTA to be such that it requires our explicitly attending to our interlocutor's negative face: negative face is the want of every individual to be unimpeded in their actions. We attend to our interlocutor's negative face by respecting – or acknowledging – their 'freedom to act' without imposition: for example, we are likely to redress our requests 'with apologies for interfering or transgressing, with linguistic and non-linguistic deference, with hedges on the illocutionary force of the act, with impersonalizing mechanisms (such as passives) that distance' us 'from the act, and with other softening mechanisms that give' our 'addressee on 'out', a face-saving line of escape, permitting him' or her 'to feel that his' or her 'response is not coerced'. Of course, how much of this mitigation we engage in will depend upon the social, familial and/or power relationship between us and our interlocutors. To this end, Brown and Levinson identify a calculation by which we might compute the 'weightiness' of a given FTA: $W_x = D(S,H) + P(H,S) + R_x$ (see reading for details).
- The fourth superstrategy, *off record*, comes into play when we deem an FTA to be such that an on record strategy would be inappropriate. The off record superstrategy involves using indirectness, as a means of allowing a given utterance to have 'more than one . . . attributable intention', thus preventing the utterer from being 'held to have committed himself to one particular intent'. Brown and Levinson provide the example, 'Damn, I'm

out of cash, I forgot to go to the bank today', which can be interpreted as both a statement and a request for a (small) cash loan. However, the utterer cannot be said for certain to have made a request, as s/he can easily claim that s/he was merely pointing out that s/he had forgotten 'to go to the bank'.

- When we deem the risk to face to be too great, Brown and Levinson suggest we are likely to use their fifth superstrategy, which is to not do the FTA at all.

One of the most controversial claims made by Brown and Levinson is that the 'want' of every individual to be approved of in their actions (positive face) and the 'want' of every individual to be unimpeded in their actions (negative face) are both universal. This claim has been hotly contested by researchers interested in Pacific Rim cultures, not least because such cultures tend to prioritise in-group interests over individual wants. Some researchers are also troubled by 'the reduction of face to wants' (positive or negative), because they believe that – no matter which culture is under investigation - 'face is more than just want: it is also (or perhaps primarily) a social value and norm' (see, e.g., Kopytko's critique of Brown and Levinson in Section 9). Our third reading in this section on **Politeness, face and impoliteness** – Miriam Locher and Richard Watts' (2008) 'Relational work and impoliteness: negotiating norms of linguistic behaviour' – represents one possible 'social norm' approach.

Crucial to Locher and Watts' approach is the primacy they give to first-order im/politeness (or im/politeness$_1$): put simply, Locher and Watts believe that, when seeking to identify im/politeness, we should be led by the perceptions of the participants involved and not by any academic view of what is and is not im/polite (i.e. what they call second-order im/politeness or im/politeness$_2$). As such, their approach – and, in particular, their emphasis on what the interlocutors do rather than on what theorists might expect interlocutors to do – shares certain similarities with Conversation Analysis (see, e.g., Section 8). Locher and Watts also highlight the importance of recognizing that interlocutors will be assigned different *faces* on different occasions and, as such, will negotiate face (their own and others') via the use of context-specific 'expectation frames'. Their interpretation of Goffmanian facework is therefore more dynamic than Brown and Levinson's. Indeed, whereas Brown and Levinson prioritize the 'FTA-minimizing' politeness strategies available to rational agents in a given situation, Locher and Watts adhere to the view that both supportive and aggressive facework can be *politic* (i.e. be considered by participants to be appropriate to the ongoing social interaction), and that what makes any verbal or non-verbal behaviour *im/polite* is the extent to which that behaviour exceeds participants' expectations of what is politic within a given situation and/or for a given community of practice.

To demonstrate this, they analyse a political interview dating from 1984, between UK presenter Fred Emery and the then-president of the National Union of Mineworkers, Arthur Scargill. In their analysis, they specifically focus on the ways in which Emery and Scargill *breached* the expectation frames that we tend to associate with political interviewing, and by so doing produced *salient* behaviour. For example, British political programmes like Panorama tend to exhibit an 'increased level of aggressiveness and a supposed concomitant loss of "respect" on the part of the interviewer towards political interviewees'. What is at issue, according to Locher and Watts, is whether Emery was outside the 'frame of normality' for interviewing in seeking to restrict Scargill's action environment by asking him questions and not allowing him the *interactional space* to answer those questions. Are interruptions – especially ones you 'apologize' for ('sorry if I interrupt you . . . ') – acceptable practices for an interviewer or not? Locher and Watts further problematize the issue for us by providing evidence to suggest that Scargill opted to *frame* Emery as someone who was being overtly rude and aggressive, that is, he was acting in a way that was beyond the 'sanctioned' aggression which typifies 'this public form of social practice' in Britain. It's worth our reiterating that Locher and Watts's focus on Scargill's perception of Emery's 'rude' behaviour is a very important feature of their analysis as, as we have already highlighted, 'in a first order approach to impoliteness, it is the interactants' *perceptions* of communicators' intentions rather than the intentions themselves that determine whether a communicative act is taken to be impolite or not. In other words, the uptake of a message' by H and others 'is as important as if not more important than the utterer's original intention'. Note our mention of both 'H and others' above: in the case of political interviews, especially, the audience's perceptions as to whether interviewers' behaviour sits outside the 'frame of normality' for interviewing is also extremely important, of course.

The audience factor is also evident in our final paper in this section, Jonathan Culpeper's 'Impoliteness and entertainment in the television quiz show: *The Weakest Link*'. The Culpeper reading is particularly interesting, not least because he is one of a number of researchers to draw on Goffman's distinction between *accidental, intentional* and *incidental* face threat as a means of emphasizing that, prototypically, impolite behaviour tends to be *intentional* on the part of the aggressor, and understood as such by the target. Yet, he has also sought to mirror Brown and Levinson's superstrategies for politeness, to some extent, so that he can explain the various types of *im*politeness. For example, he includes the categories, 'bald-on-record impoliteness', 'positive impoliteness', 'negative impoliteness' and 'off-record impoliteness', as well as 'sarcasm or mock politeness' and 'withhold politeness'. The off-record category constitutes a development to his original 'anatomy of impoliteness' model (Culpeper 1996), and it is this and other developments, which Culpeper details here, that provide readers with a useful complement to the Locher and Watts reading. For example, like Locher and Watts, Culpeper emphasizes the importance of considering the context of one's data, which in his case is taken from the UK-version of *The Weakest Link* quiz show, hosted by Anne Robinson. Rather than drawing on the notion of expectation frames, however, Culpeper draws on Levinson's (1992) notion of 'activity type'. The aim remains the same, of course: determining how what one says will be 'taken — that is, what kinds of inferences will be made from what is said'. Again like Locher and Watts, Culpeper is particularly interested in the extent to which a given activity type can serve to 'sanction' and, by so doing, 'neutralize' any potential impoliteness. Rather than focussing upon the participants' potential use of framing strategies, however, he focuses on the fact that, even when activity types like entertainment quiz shows *sanction* the use of aggression, FTAs are not always (or completely) 'neutralized' for the targets of the aggression themselves. He suggests that this is especially the case when the maxim of Quality has not been (sufficiently) suspended for the targets, since it seems to affect their ability to reconstitute sanctioned aggression like that exhibited on *The Weakest Link* as, for example, banter. Culpeper's response is to offer a revised definition of impoliteness, which is able to capture both occasions when 'the speaker communicates face-attack intentionally' (cf. Goffman's definition for *intentional* face threat) and also occasions when 'the hearer perceives and/or constructs behavior as intentionally face-attacking' whether or not the speaker meant his/her utterances to be taken in this way (cf. Goffman's definition for *accidental* face threat).

ERVING GOFFMAN

ON FACE-WORK
An analysis of ritual elements in social interaction

PRE-READING

If someone were to say *Get out of my face!* to you, how might you interpret it? And how would you interpret *You really lost face when you did that!*? Provide a scenario where you might expect to hear each utterance and also your likely response to them. Finally – before you begin your reading of Goffman – write down your (personal) understanding of 'face' and 'facework'.

IN-READING

1   When you reach Goffman's definition of 'losing face' and 'saving face' (marked by the first | in the margin), stop reading and compare them to your own. How similar are the definitions, and to what extent do they differ?

2   Explain, in your own words, the significance of 'the rule of self respect' and the 'rule of considerateness'. You may find it helpful to quickly re-read the section immediately prior to our second | in the margin when answering this particular question.

3   Stop reading at the third | in the margin. In discussing 'the traffic rules of social interaction', Goffman seems to suggest that face-saving work equates to demonstrating the *how* of interaction; that is to say, 'one learns about the code the person adheres to . . . but not why he is ready to follow the code'. In your own words, summarize some of the 'motives' Goffman gives for engaging in face-saving work.

■ ■ ■

ON FACE-WORK
AN ANALYLSIS OF RITUAL ELEMENTS IN SOCIAL INTERACTION
ERVING GOFFMAN

Every person lives in a world of social encounters, involving him either in face-to-face or mediated contact with other participants. In each of these contacts, he tends to act out what is sometimes called a *line*—that is, a pattern of verbal and nonverbal acts by which he expresses his view of the situation and through this his evaluation of the participants, especially himself. Regardless of whether a person intends to take a line, he will find that he has done so in effect. The other participants will assume that he has more or less willfully taken a stand, so that if he is to deal with their response to him he must take into consideration the impression they have possibly formed of him.

The term *face* may be defined as the positive social value a person effectively claims for himself by the line others assume he has taken during a particular contact. Face is an image of self delineated in terms of approved social attributes [. . .]

[. . .] One's own face and the face of others are constructs of the same order; it is the rules of the group and the definition of the situation which determine how much feeling one is to have for face and how this feeling is to be distributed among the faces involved.

A person may be said to *have*, or *be in*, or *maintain* face when the line he effectively takes presents an image of him that is internally consistent, that is supported by judgments and evidence conveyed by other participants, and that is confirmed by evidence conveyed through impersonal agencies in the situation. At such times the person's face clearly is something that is not lodged in or on his body, but rather something that is diffusely located in the flow of events in the encounter and becomes manifest only when these events are read and interpreted for the appraisals expressed in them.

[. . .]

[. . .] [W]hile concern for face focuses the attention of the person on the current activity, he must, to maintain face in this activity, take into consideration his place in the social world beyond it. A person who can maintain face in the current situation is someone who abstained from certain actions in the past that would have been difficult to face up to later. In addition, he fears loss of face now partly because the others may take this as a sign that consideration for his feelings need not be shown in the future. There is nevertheless a limitation to this inter-dependence between the current situation and the wider social world: an encounter with people whom he will not have dealings with again leaves him free to take a high line that the future will discredit, or free to suffer humiliations that would make future dealings with them an embarrassing thing to have to face.

[. . .]

In our Anglo-American society, as in some others, the phrase "to lose face" seems to mean to be in wrong face, to be out of face, or to be shamefaced. The phrase "to save one's face" appears to refer to the process by which the person sustains an impression for others that he has not lost face. Following Chinese usage, one can say that "to give face" is to arrange for another to take a better line than he might otherwise have been able to take,[1] the other thereby gets face given him, this being one way in which he can gain face.

[. . .] Once [a person] takes on a self-image expressed through face he will be expected to live up to it. [. . .] His social face [. . .] is only on loan to him from society; it will be withdrawn unless he conducts himself in a way that is worthy of it. [. . .]

Just as the member of any group is expected to have self-respect, so also he is expected to sustain a standard of considerateness; he is expected to go to certain lengths to save the feelings and the face of others present, and he is expected to do this willingly and spontaneously because of emotional identification with the others and with their feelings.[2] In consequence, he is disinclined to witness the defacement of others.[3] [. . .]

The combined effect of the rule of self-respect and the rule of considerateness is that the person tends to conduct himself during an encounter so as to maintain both his own face and the face of the other participants. This means that the line taken by each participant is usually allowed to prevail, and each participant is allowed to carry off the role he appears to have chosen for himself. A state where everyone temporarily accepts everyone else's line is established.[4] This kind of mutual acceptance seems to be a basic structural feature of interaction, especially the interaction of face-to-face talk. It is typically a "working" acceptance, not a "real" one, since it tends to be based not on agreement of candidly expressed heart-felt evaluations, but upon a willingness to give temporary lip service to judgments with which the participants do not really agree.

[. . .]

Ordinarily, maintenance of face is a condition of interaction, not its objective. Usual objectives, such as gaining face for oneself, giving free expression to one's true beliefs, introducing depreciating information about the others, or solving problems and performing tasks, are typically pursued in such a way as to be consistent with the maintenance of face. To study face-saving is to study the traffic rules of social interaction; one learns about the code the person adheres to in his movement across the paths and designs of others, but not where he is going, or why he wants to get there. One does not even learn why he is ready to follow the code, for a large number of different motives can equally lead him to do so. He may want to save his own face because of his emotional attachment to the image of self which it expresses, because of his pride or honor, because of the power his presumed status allows him to exert over the other participants, and so on. He may want to save the others' face because of his emotional attachment to an image of them, or because he feels that his coparticipants have a moral right to this protection, or because he wants to avoid the hostility that may be directed toward him if they lose their face. He may feel that an assumption has been made that he is the sort of person who shows compassion and sympathy toward others, so that to retain his own face, he may feel obliged to be considerate of the line taken by the other participants.

By *face-work* I mean to designate the actions taken by a person to make whatever he is doing consistent with face. Face-work serves to counteract "incidents"—that is, events whose effective symbolic implications threaten face. [. . .] Whether or not the full consequences of face-saving actions are known to the person who employs them, they often become habitual and standardized practices; they are like traditional plays in a game or traditional steps in a dance. Each person, subculture, and society seems to have its own characteristic repertoire of face-saving practices. It is to this repertoire that people partly refer when they ask what a person or culture is "really" like. And yet the particular set of practices stressed by particular persons or groups seems to be drawn from a single logically coherent framework of possible practices. It is as if face, by its very nature, can be saved only in a certain number of ways, and as if each social grouping must make its selections from this single matrix of possibilities.

The members of every social circle may be expected to have some knowledge of face-work and some experience in its use. In our society, this kind of capacity is sometimes called tact, *savoir-faire*, diplomacy, or social skill. Variation in social skill pertains more to the efficacy of face-work than to the frequency of its application, for almost all acts involving others are modified, prescriptively or proscriptively, by considerations of face.

If a person is to employ his repertoire of face-saving practices, obviously he must first become aware of the interpretations that others may have placed upon his acts and the interpretations that he ought perhaps to place upon theirs. In other words, he must exercise perceptiveness. But even if he is properly alive to symbolically conveyed judgments and is socially skilled, he must yet be willing to exercise his perceptiveness and his skill; he must, in short, be prideful and considerate. Admittedly, of course, the possession of perceptiveness and social skill so often leads to their application that in our society terms such as politeness or tact fail to distinguish between the inclination to exercise such capacities and the capacities themselves.

I have already said that the person will have two points of view—a defensive orientation toward saving his own face and a protective orientation toward saving the others' face. Some practices will be primarily defensive and others primarily protective, although in general one may expect these two perspectives to be taken at the same time. In trying to save the face of others, the person must choose a tack that will not lead to loss of his own; in trying to save his own face, he must consider the loss of face that his action may entail for others.

In many societies there is a tendency to distinguish three levels of responsibility that a person may have for a threat to face that his actions have created. First, he may appear to have acted innocently; his offense seems to be unintended and unwitting, and those who perceive his act can feel that he would have attempted to avoid it had he foreseen its offensive consequences. In our society one calls such threats to face *faux pas, gaffes*, boners, or bricks. Secondly, the offending person may appear to have acted maliciously and spitefully, with the intention of causing open insult. Thirdly, there are incidental offenses; these arise as an unplanned but sometimes anticipated by-product of action—action the offender performs in spite of its offensive consequences, although not out of spite.

From the point of view of a particular participant, these three types of threat can be introduced by the participant himself against his own face, by himself against the face of the others, by the others against their own face, or by the others against himself. Thus the person may find himself in many different relations to a threat to face. If he is to handle himself and others well in all contingencies, he will have to have a repertoire of face-saving practices for each of these possible relations to threat.

The basic kinds of face-work

The avoidance process—The surest way for a person to prevent threats to his face is to avoid contacts in which these threats are likely to occur. [. . .]

Once the person does chance an encounter, other kinds of avoidance practices come into play. As defensive measures, he keeps off topics and away from activities that would lead to the expression of information that is inconsistent with the line he is maintaining. At opportune moments he will change the topic of conversation or the direction of activity. He will often present initially a front of diffidence and composure, suppressing any show of feeling until he has found out what kind of line the others will be ready to support for him. Any claims regarding self may be made with belittling modesty, with strong qualifications, or with a note of unseriousness; by hedging in these ways he will have prepared a self for himself that will not be discredited by exposure, personal failure, or the unanticipated acts of others. And if he does not hedge his claims about self, he will at least attempt to be realistic about them, knowing that otherwise events may discredit him and make him lose face.

Certain protective maneuvers are as common as these defensive ones. The person shows respect and politeness, making sure to extend to others any ceremonial treatment that might be their due. He employs discretion; he leaves unstated facts that might implicitly or explicitly contradict and embarrass the positive claims made by others.[5] He employs circumlocutions and deceptions, phrasing his replies with careful ambiguity so that the others' face is preserved even if their welfare is not. He employs courtesies, making slight modifications of his demands on or appraisals of the others so that they will be able to define the situation as one in which their self-respect is not threatened. In making a belittling demand upon the others, or in imputing uncomplimentary attributes to them, he may employ a joking manner, allowing them to take the line that they are good sports, able to relax from their ordinary standards of pride and honor. And before engaging in a potentially offensive act, he may provide explanations as to why the others ought not to be affronted by it. For example, if he knows that it will be necessary to withdraw from the encounter before it has terminated, he may tell the others in advance that it is necessary for him to leave, so that they will have faces that are prepared for it. But neutralizing the potentially offensive act need not be done verbally; he may wait for a propitious moment or natural break—for example, in conversation, a momentary lull when no one speaker can be affronted—and then leave, in this way using the context instead of his words as a guarantee of inoffensiveness.

When a person fails to prevent an incident, he can still attempt to maintain the fiction that no threat to face has occurred. The most blatant example of this is found where the person acts as if an event that contains a threatening expression has not occurred at all. He may apply this studied nonobservance to his own acts—as when he does not by any outward sign admit that his stomach is rumbling—or to the acts of others, as when he does not "see" that another has stumbled. Social life in mental hospitals owes much to this process; patients employ it in regard to their own peculiarities, and visitors employ it, often with tenuous desperation, in regard to patients. [. . .]

[. . .]

Another kind of avoidance occurs when a person loses control of his expressions during an encounter. At such times he may try not so much to overlook the incident as to hide or conceal his activity in some way, thus making it possible for the others to avoid some of the difficulties created by a participant who has not maintained face. Correspondingly, when a person is caught out of face because he had not expected to be thrust into interaction, or because strong feelings have disrupted his expressive mask, the others may protectively turn away from him or his activity for a moment, to give him time to assemble himself.

The corrective process—When the participants in an undertaking or encounter fail to prevent the occurrence of an event that is expressively incompatible with the judgments of social worth that are being maintained, and when the event is of the kind that is difficult to overlook, then the participants are likely to give it accredited status as an incident—to ratify it as a threat that deserves direct official attention [. . .]

The sequence of acts set in motion by an acknowledged threat to face, and terminating in the re-establishment of ritual equilibrium, I shall call an *interchange*.[6] [. . .]. The interchange seems to be a basic concrete unit of social activity and provides one natural empirical way to study interaction of all kinds. Face-saving practices can be usefully classified according to their position in the natural sequence of moves that comprise this unit. Aside from the event which introduces the need for a corrective interchange, four classic moves seem to be involved.

There is, first, the challenge, by which participants take on the responsibility of calling attention to the misconduct; by implication they suggest that the threatened claims are to stand firm and that the threatening event itself will have to be brought back into line.

The second move consists of the offering, whereby a participant, typically the offender, is given a chance to correct for the offense and re-establish the expressive order. Some classic ways of making this move are available. On the one hand, an attempt can be made to show that what admittedly appeared to be a threatening expression is really a meaningless event, or an unintentional act, or a joke not meant to be taken seriously, or an unavoidable, "understandable" product of extenuating circumstances. On the other hand, the meaning of the event may be granted and effort concentrated on the creator of it. Information may be provided to show that the creator was under the influence of something and not himself, or that he was under the command of somebody else and not acting for himself. When a person claims that an act was meant in jest, he may go on and claim that the self that seemed to lie behind the act was also projected as a joke. When a person suddenly finds that he has demonstrably failed in capacities that the others assumed him to have and to claim for himself—such as the capacity to spell, to perform minor tasks, to talk without malapropisms, and so on—he may quickly add, in a serious or unserious way, that he claims these incapacities as part of his self. The meaning of the threatening incident thus stands, but it can now be incorporated smoothly into the flow of expressive events.

As a supplement to or substitute for the strategy of redefining the offensive act or himself, the offender can follow two other procedures: he can provide compensations to the injured—when it is not his own face that he has threatened; or he can provide punishment, penance, and expiation for himself. These are important moves or phases in the ritual interchange. Even though the offender may fail to prove his innocence, he can suggest through these means that he is now a renewed person, a person who has paid for his sin against the expressive order and is once more to be trusted in the judgmental scene. Further, he can show that he does not treat the feelings of the others lightly, and that if their feelings have been injured by him, however innocently, he is prepared to pay a price for his action. Thus he assures the others that they can accept his explanations without this acceptance constituting a sign of weakness and a lack of pride on their part. Also, by his treatment of himself, by his self-castigation, he shows that he is clearly aware of the kind of crime he would have committed had the incident been what it first appeared to be, and that he knows the kind of punishment that ought to be accorded to one who would commit such a crime. The suspected person thus shows that he is thoroughly capable of taking the role of the others toward his own activity, that he can still be used as a responsible participant in the ritual process, and that the rules of conduct which he appears to have broken are still sacred, real, and unweakened. An offensive act may arouse anxiety about the ritual code; the offender allays this anxiety by showing that both the code and he as an upholder of it are still in working order.

After the challenge and the offering have been made, the third move can occur: the persons to whom the offering is made can accept it as a satisfactory means of re-establishing the expressive order and the faces supported by this order. Only then can the offender cease the major part of his ritual offering.

In the terminal move of the interchange, the forgiven person conveys a sign of gratitude to those who have given him the indulgence of forgiveness.

The phases of the corrective process—challenge, offering, acceptance, and thanks—provide a model for interpersonal ritual behavior, but a model that may be departed from in significant ways. For example, the offended parties may give the offender a chance to initiate the offering on his own before a challenge is made and before they ratify the offense as an incident. This is a common courtesy, extended on the assumption that the recipient will introduce a self-challenge. Further, when the offended persons accept the corrective offering, the offender may suspect that this has been grudgingly done from tact, and so he may volunteer additional corrective offerings, not allowing the matter to rest until he has received a second or third acceptance of his repeated apology. Or the offended persons may tactfully take over the role of the offender and volunteer excuses for him that will, perforce, be acceptable to the offended persons.

An important departure from the standard corrective cycle occurs when a challenged offender patently refuses to heed the warning and continues with his offending behavior, instead of setting the activity to rights. This move shifts the play back to the challengers. [. . .]

[. . .]

Making points—the aggressive use of face-work

Every face-saving practice which is allowed to neutralize a particular threat opens up the possibility that the threat will be willfully introduced for what can be safely gained by it. If a person knows that his modesty will be answered by others' praise of him, he can fish for compliments. [. . .] If others are prepared to overlook an affront to them and act forbearantly, or to accept apologies, then he can rely on this as a basis for safely offending them. [. . .] Finally, at some expense to himself, he can arrange for the others to hurt his feelings, thus forcing them to feel guilt, remorse, and sustained ritual disequilibrium.

When a person treats face-work not as something he need be prepared to perform, but rather as something that others can be counted on to perform or to accept, then an encounter or an undertaking becomes less a scene of mutual considerateness than an arena in which a contest or match is held. [. . .] The general method is for the person to introduce favorable facts about himself and unfavorable facts about the others in such a way that the only reply the others will be able to think up will be one that terminates the interchange in a grumble, a meager excuse, a face-saving I-can-take-a-joke laugh, or an empty stereotyped comeback of the "Oh yeah?" or "That's what you think" variety. The losers in such cases will have to cut their losses, tacitly grant the loss of a point, and attempt to do better in the next interchange. [. . .]

In aggressive interchanges the winner not only succeeds in introducing information favorable to himself and unfavorable to the others, but also demonstrates that as interactant he can handle himself better than his adversaries. Evidence of this capacity is often more important than all the other information the person conveys in the interchange, so that the introduction of a "crack" in verbal interaction tends to imply that the initiator is better at footwork than those who must suffer his remarks. However, if they succeed in making a successful parry of the thrust and then a successful riposte, the instigator of the play must not only face the disparagement with which the others have answered him but also accept the fact that his assumption of superiority in footwork has proven false. He is made to look foolish; he loses face.

[. . .]

Notes

1   See, e.g., Smith (1984: 17, *n*1).
2   Of course, the more power and prestige the others have, the more a person is likely to show consideration for their feelings, as Dale (1941: 126*n*) suggests. [. . .]
3   Salesmen, especially street "stemmers," know that if they take a line that will be discredited unless the reluctant customer buys, the customer may be trapped by considerateness and buy in order to save the face of the salesman [. . .].
4   Surface agreement in the assessment of social worth does not, of course, imply equality; the evaluation consensually sustained of one participant may be quite different from the one consensually sustained of another. Such agreement is also compatible with expression of differences of opinion between two participants, provided each of the disputants shows "respect" for the other, guiding the expression of disagreement so that it will convey an evaluation of the other that the other will be willing to convey about himself. [. . .]
5   When the person knows the others well, he will know what issues ought not to be raised and what situations the others ought not to be placed in [. . .]. When the others are strangers to him, he will often restrict himself to specific areas he knows are safe. On these occasions, as Simmel suggests (1950: 320–1), " . . . discretion consists by no means only in the respect for the secret of the other, for his specific will to conceal this or that from us, but in staying away from the knowledge of all that the other does not expressly reveal to us.".
6   The notion of interchange is drawn in part from Chapple (1940: 26–30), and Horsfall and Arensberg (1949: 19). For further material on the interchange as a unit see Goffman (1953: Chapters 12–13, pp. 165–95). [. . .]

POST-READING

As highlighted in the introduction, although Goffman defines 'facework' as being primarily geared towards counteracting events that threaten face, he is very much aware that interactants will occasionally engage in facework 'for what can be safely gained from it' and, in some cases, may even engage in (verbal and non-verbal) activities that *intentionally* threaten the face of others. How useful, in your view, are Goffman's different levels of face threat, i.e. *accidental*, *incidental* and *intentional*? Which, if any, seems to be the most relevant to your own understanding of facework? Finally, do you agree with Goffman that facework is primarily geared towards *counteracting* events that threaten face, but can also be used to deliberately threaten face?

PENELOPE BROWN AND STEPHEN C. LEVINSON

POLITENESS
Some universals in language usage

PRE-READING

If you had to prioritize your 'desire to be approved of' and 'your desire for freedom of action', which would you say was most important to you? Why?

IN-READING

1   Brown and Levinson construct a 'model person' (MP) to help them explain their approach to politeness (see first | in margin). What do they say the MP allows them to do? How useful is this concept, in your view?
2   Stop reading at the point at which Brown and Levinson begin to discuss the factors that 'MPs' employ when deciding which politeness strategy to use (marked by a second | in the margin): 'social distance' of S and H (D), 'relative power' of S and H (P), and the 'absolute ranking of imposition' (R). Summarize *in your own words* what D, P and R are intended to capture about the '*actors*' concerned, and what Brown and Levinson stress they do not represent or capture.

■ ■ ■

POLITENESS:
SOME UNIVERSALS IN LANGUAGE USAGE
PENELOPE BROWN AND STEPHEN C. LEVINSON

Introduction

[. . .]

The problem

[. . .] it is observable that in many languages (in circumstances where social structures permit such distinctions), when formulating a small request one will tend to use language that stresses in-group membership and social similarity (as in the inclusive 'we' of 'Let's have another cookie then' or 'Give us a dime'). When making a request that is somewhat bigger, one uses the language of formal politeness (the conventionalized indirect speech acts, hedges, apologies for intrusion, etc.). And finally, when making the sort of request that it is doubtful one should make at all, one tends to use indirect expressions (implicatures). The same holds, *mutatis mutandis*, for criticisms, offers, complaints, and many other types of verbal act. What these related problems seem to share is a strategic orientation to participants' 'face', the kernel element in folk notions of politeness.

Our overall problem, then, is this: What sort of assumptions and what sort of reasoning are utilized by participants to produce such universal strategies of verbal interaction? We want to account for the observed cross-cultural similarities in the abstract principles which underlie polite usage. We hope, further, that a formal model that accounts for these cross-cultural similarities will also provide a reference model for culturally specific usages: that is, it promises to provide us with an ethnographic tool of great precision for investigating the quality of social relations in any society.

Method

[. . .] We attempt to account for some systematic aspects of language usage by constructing, tongue in cheek, a Model Person (MP) [. . .]: a wilful fluent speaker of a natural language, further endowed with two special properties – rationality and face. By 'rationality' we mean something very specific – the availability to our MP of a precisely definable mode of reasoning from ends to the means that will achieve those ends. By 'face' we mean something quite specific again: our MP is endowed with two particular wants – roughly, the want to be unimpeded and the want to be approved of in certain respects.

With this cardboard figure we then begin to play: How would such a being use language? In particular, caught between the want to satisfy another MP's face wants and the want to say things that infringe those wants, what would our rational face-endowed being do? By a strange coincidence we find that a dyadic model of two cooperating MPs (potentially with an audience) accounts for just those peculiar cross-cultural regularities in language usage that we have introduced above as our problem. We can show this by deriving linguistic strategies as *means* satisfying communicative and face-oriented *ends*, in a strictly formal system of rational 'practical reasoning'.

In carrying out this programme we lay ourselves open to the attack that we are here inappropriately reviving the economic homunculus, since our predictive model is essentially built on the assumption of rational agents with certain properties. However, there is intended no claim that 'rational face-bearing agents' are all or always what actual humans are, but simply that these are assumptions that make the most sense of the data, and are assumptions that all interacting humans know that they will be expected to orient to. A stronger point is this: it can be demonstrated that in order to derive the kind of inferences from what is said that speakers can be shown to draw, such assumptions simply have to be made. This is a technical point first made by Grice (1967, 1975) when discussing 'conversational implicature' and substantiated by work in linguistics since. If A says 'What time is it?', and B replies '(Well) the postman's been already', then A assumes that what B said was rationally oriented to what A said, and hence A derives from B's utterance the inference that it is, say, past 11 a.m. This kind of inference is what we refer to throughout as 'conversational implicature' (c.i.). The whole exchange is heard as coherent only on the assumption that B intended to cooperate, and rationally chose a means that would achieve his cooperative end. So in language usage, at any rate, it is demonstrable that such rational assumptions are in fact made.

[. . .] We hope that our MP will provide a reference model for the description of culture-specific styles of verbal interaction; we hope [. . .] by this means to be able to characterize to some extent the 'ethos' of a culture or subculture, and that most ephemeral of ethnographic observations, the affective quality of social relationships.

Note that we shall be attempting here a reduction of some good, solid, Durkheimian social facts – some norms of language usage – to the outcome of the rational choices of individuals. The chances are that if you actually ask a speaker why he said 'You couldn't by any chance tell me the time, could you?' rather than 'Tell me the time', he'll say he is conforming to conventional expectations of politeness [. . .]. [A]lthough, as Lewis has argued (1969), conventions can themselves be overwhelming reasons for doing things (as anthropologists have usually assumed), there can be, and perhaps often are, rational bases for conventions. The observations below include, we claim, examples of such rationally based conventions.

We consider that if the predictions made by our model are borne out by the data drawn from usage in a small sample of unrelated cultures and languages, strong support may be inferred for the original assumptions. Our data consist in first-hand tape-recorded usage for three languages: English (from both sides of the Atlantic); Tzeltal, a Mayan language spoken in the community of Tenejapa in Chiapas, Mexico; and South Indian Tamil from a village in the Coimbatore District of Tamilnadu. This is supplemented by examples drawn from our native-speaker intuitions for English, and by elicited data for Tzeltal and Tamil. Occasional examples are drawn from secondhand sources for Malagasy, Japanese, and other languages. We believe it is legitimate to project from a careful three-way experiment in three unrelated cultures to hypotheses about universals in verbal interaction because, as will become evident, the degree of detail in convergence lies far beyond the realm of chance.

Summarized argument

We outline the argument here, to keep it from getting lost in the detailed explanations and definitions that follow. Concepts defined in the next section are in **bold** type. 'S' stands for 'speaker' and 'H' for 'addressee' throughout the paper; in this outline, S and H are MPs. Among MPs, it is mutual knowledge[1] that for all MPs:

(i) All MPs have **positive face** and **negative face**, and all MPs are **rational agents** – i.e. choose means that will satisfy their ends.

(ii) Given that face consists in a set of wants satisfiable only by the actions (including expressions of wants) of others, it will in general be to the mutual interest of two MPs to maintain each other's face. So S will want to maintain H's face, unless he can get H to maintain S's without recompense, by coercion, trickery, etc.

(iii) Some acts intrinsically threaten face; these 'face-threatening acts' will be referred to henceforth as **FTAs**.

(iv) Unless S's want to do an FTA with maximum efficiency (defined as **bald on record**) is greater than S's want to preserve H's (or S's) face to any degree, then S will want to minimize the face threat of the FTA.

(v) Given the following set of strategies, the more an act threatens S's or H's face, the more S will want to choose a higher-numbered-strategy; this by virtue of the fact that these strategies afford payoffs of increasingly minimized risk:

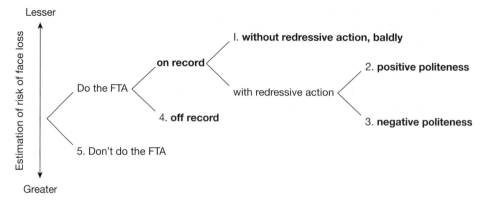

Figure 6.2.1

(vi) Since i–v are mutually known to all MPs, our MP will not choose a strategy less risky than necessary, as this may be seen as an indication that the FTA is more threatening than it actually is.

The argument: intuitive bases and derivative definitions

Assumptions: properties of interactants

We make the following assumptions: that all competent adult members of a society[2] have (and know each other to have):

(i)   'face', the public self-image that every member wants to claim for himself, consisting in two related aspects:

(a)   negative face:[3] the basic claim to territories, personal preserves, rights to non-distraction – i.e. to freedom of action and freedom from imposition

(b)   positive face: the positive consistent self-image or 'personality' (crucially including the desire that this self-image be appreciated and approved of) claimed by interactants

(ii)   certain rational capacities, in particular consistent modes of reasoning from ends to the means that will achieve those ends.

Face. Our notion of 'face' is derived from that of Goffman (1967) and from the English folk term, which ties face up with notions of being embarrassed or humiliated, or 'losing face'. Thus face is something that is emotionally invested, and that can be lost, maintained, or enhanced, and must be constantly attended to in interaction. In general, people cooperate (and assume each other's cooperation) in maintaining face in interaction, such cooperation being based on the mutual vulnerability of face. That is, normally everyone's face depends on everyone else's being maintained, and since people can be expected to defend their faces if threatened, and in defending their own to threaten others' faces, it is in general in every participant's best interest to maintain each others' face, that is to act in ways that assure the other participants that the agent is heedful of the assumptions concerning face given under (i) above. (Just what this heedfulness consists in is the subject of this paper.)

Furthermore, while the content of face will differ in different cultures (what the exact limits are to personal territories, and what the publicly relevant content of personality consist in), we are assuming that the mutual knowledge of members' public self-image or face, and the social necessity to orient oneself to it in interaction, are universal.

Face as wants. [. . .] [W]e treat the aspects of face as basic wants, which every member knows every other member desires, and which in general it is in the interests of every member to partially satisfy. In other words, we take in Weberian terms the more strongly rational *zweckrational* model of individual action, because the *wertrational* model (which would treat face respect as an unquestionable value or norm) fails to account for the fact that face respect is not an unequivocal right.* In particular, a mere bow to face acts like a diplomatic declaration of good intentions; it is not in general required that an actor fully satisfy another's face wants. Secondly, face can be, and routinely is, ignored, not just in cases of social breakdown (affrontery) but also in cases of urgent cooperation, or in the interests of efficiency.[4]

Therefore, the components of face given above [. . .] may be restated as follows. We define:

> **negative face:** the want of every 'competent adult member' that his actions be unimpeded by others.
> **positive face:** the want of every member that his wants be desirable to at least some others.

Negative face, with its derivative politeness of non-imposition, is familiar as the formal politeness that the notion 'politeness' immediately conjures up. But positive face, and its derivative forms of positive politeness, are less obvious. The reduction of a person's public self-image or personality to a want that one's wants be desirable to at least some others can be justified in this way. The most salient aspect of a person's personality in interaction is what that personality requires of other interactants – in particular, it includes the desire to be ratified, understood, approved of, liked or admired. The next step is to represent this desire as the want to have one's goals thought of as desirable. In the special sense of 'wanting' that we develop, we can then arrive at positive face as here defined. To give this some intuitive flesh, consider an example. Mrs B is a fervent gardener. Much of her time and effort are expended on her roses. She is proud of her roses, and she likes others to admire them. She is gratified when visitors say 'What lovely roses; I wish ours looked like that! How do you do it?', implying that they want just what she has wanted and achieved.

Our definition of positive face is adequate only if certain interpretations are borne in mind. First of all, the wants that a member wants others to find desirable may actually have been satisfied; that is, they may now be past wants represented by present achievements or possessions. Also, the wants may be for non-material as well as material things: for values (love, liberty, piety), or for actions (like going to the opera or to the races, or playing tennis).

In addition, on the view that the objects of desire are propositions like 'I have beautiful roses', natural-language expressions of wanting often leave the subject and predicate unspecified, as in 'I want an ice cream cone.' This leaves an ambiguity in our formula for some agent A's face want: A wants some B to want his wants, but is B desired to want 'B has an ice cream cone' or 'A has an ice cream cone' or 'Everyone eats ice cream cones'? The answer seems to be that in different circumstances each of the different interpretations may be reasonable. For instance, if a male admires a female's apparel it would be a natural interpretation that he wanted her apparel for her, rather than for himself.

A third point is that, in general, persons want their goals, possessions, and achievements to be thought desirable not just by anyone, but by some particular others especially relevant to the particular goals, etc. (For instance, I may want my literary style to be admired by writers, my roses by gardeners, my clothes by friends, my hair by a lover.) These others constitute a collection of sets (extensionally or intensionally defined) each linked to a set of goals.

So our formula is to be interpreted in the light of this (grossly over-simplified) example:

> H wants some persons (namely a_1, a_2, a_3 . . .) to want the corresponding set of H's wants (w_1, w_2, w_3 . . .).

> Let a_1 = set of all the classes of persons in H's social world.
> a_2 = set of all the persons in H's social strata.
> a_3 = H's spouse.

> Let w_1 = H has a beautiful front garden; H is responsible and law-abiding.
> w_2 = H has a powerful motorbike and a leather jacket.
> w_3 = H is happy, healthy, wealthy, and wise.

These particular facts are obviously highly culture-specific, group-specific, and ultimately idiosyncratic. Nevertheless there do exist (in general) well-defined areas of common ground between any two persons of a society. If they are strangers it may be reduced to an assumption of common interest in good weather or other such safe topics; if they are close friends it may extend to a close identity of interests and desires. Still, however well-defined these areas are, to *assume* that (say) I am in the set of persons who will please you by commenting on your clothes is to make an extremely vulnerable assumption, one that may cause affront. It is largely because of this that attention to positive face in a society is often highly restricted.

Rationality. We here define 'rationality' as the application of a specific mode of reasoning – what Aristotle (1969) called 'practical reasoning' – which guarantees inferences from ends or goals to means that will satisfy those ends. Just as standard logics have a consequence relation that will take us from one proposition to another while preserving truth, a system of practical reasoning must allow one to pass from ends to means and further means while preserving the 'satisfactoriness' of those means (Kenny 1966).

The sorts of inferences one wants a system of practical reasoning to capture are things like:

(1)   Vote!
      (Vote for Wilson!) or (Vote for Heath!)

That is, if I want to, or ought to, or have been ordered to, vote, then to satisfy that want or command, I ought to vote for Wilson, or Heath, or anybody for that matter.

[. . .] Aristotle's 'practical syllogism', which in standard logic would follow the fallacious form of 'affirming the consequent' [. . .] ha[s] a curious relation to standard logical inferences, for:

[2]   John voted
      John voted for Wilson

is certainly not necessarily true, but the inverse:

[3] John voted for Wilson
     John voted

is certainly true. This prompted a suggestion of Kenny's that a *means* to an *end* should be considered satisfactory only if, when the proposition describing the means is true, the proposition describing the end is true. It turns out that based on this interpretation of practical-reasoning consequence, a decidable formal system with a semantic interpretation can be constructed, and Aristotle's intuitions can be cast into a rigorous mould which we dub 'Kenny logic'. ([. . .] see Atlas and Levinson 1973.)

A further aspect of rational behaviour seems to be the ability to weigh up different means to an end, and choose the one that most satisfies the desired goals. This can be captured by a 'fuzzy' version of Kenny logic, with an added preference operator [. . .]. This will treat all preferences as rational ones, and exclude extrinsically weighted wants or Kantian imperatives – for our purposes a perfectly feasible move.

While our formal system accounts for much of the content of the intuitive notion of rationality, the latter does seem to include some notion of maximization, or minimum-cost assessment in the choice of means to an end. For example, if I want a drink of water, and I could use the tap in this room or the tap in the bathroom or the tap in the garden, it would surely be 'irrational' to trot out into the garden unnecessarily (provided that I have no secret want to be in the garden, etc.). If this is so, we can capture it by defining a perennial desire of MPs, in general, not to waste effort to no avail.

Intrinsic FTAs

Given these assumptions of the universality of face and rationality, it is intuitively the case that certain kinds of acts intrinsically threaten face, namely those acts that by their nature run contrary to the face wants of the addressee and/or of the speaker. By 'act' we have in mind what is intended to be done by a verbal or non-verbal communication, just as one or more 'speech acts' can be assigned to an utterance.[5]

First distinction: Kinds of face threatened. We may make a first distinction between acts that threaten negative face and those that threaten positive face.

Those acts that primarily threaten the addressee's (H's) negative-face want, by indicating (potentially) that the speaker (S) does not intend to avoid impeding H's freedom of action, include:

(i)   Those acts that predicate some future act A of H, and in so doing put some pressure on H to do (or refrain from doing) the act A:
      (a) orders and requests (S indicates that he wants H to do, or refrain from doing, some act A)
      (b) suggestions, advice (S indicates that he thinks H ought to (perhaps) do some act A)
      (c) remindings (S indicates that H should remember to do some A)
      (d) threats, warnings, dares (S indicates that he – or someone, or something – will instigate sanctions against H unless he does A).
(ii) Those acts that predicate some positive future act of S toward H, and in so doing put some pressure on H to accept or reject them, and possibly to incur a debt:
      (a) offers (S indicates that he wants H to commit himself to whether or not he wants S to do some act for H, with H thereby incurring a possible debt)
      (b) promises (S commits himself to a future act for H's benefit)

(iii) Those acts that predicate some desire of S toward H or H's goods, giving H reason to think that he may have to take action to protect the object of S's desire, or give it to S:
   (a) compliments, expressions of envy or admiration (S indicates that he likes or would like something of H's)
   (b) expressions of strong (negative) emotions toward H – e.g. hatred, anger, lust (S indicates possible motivation for harming H or H's goods).

Those acts that threaten the positive-face want, by indicating (potentially) that the speaker does not care about the addressee's feelings, wants, etc. – that in some important respect he doesn't want H's wants – include:

(i)   Those that show that S has a negative evaluation of some aspect of H's positive face:
   (a) expressions of disapproval, criticism, contempt or ridicule, complaints and reprimands, accusations, insults (S indicates that he doesn't like/want one or more of H's wants, acts, personal characteristics, goods, beliefs or values)
   (b) contradictions or disagreements, challenges (S indicates that he thinks H is wrong or misguided or unreasonable about some issue, such wrongness being associated with disapproval).
(ii) Those that show that S doesn't care about (or is indifferent to) H's positive face:
   (a) expressions of violent (out-of-control) emotions (S gives H possible reason to fear him or be embarrassed by him)
   (b) irreverence, mention of taboo topics, including those that are inappropriate in the context (S indicates that he doesn't value H's values and doesn't fear H's fears)
   (c) bringing of bad news about H, or good news (boasting) about S (S indicates that he is willing to cause distress to H, and/or doesn't care about H's feelings)
   (d) raising of dangerously emotional or divisive topics, e.g. politics, race, religion, women's liberation (S raises the possibility or likelihood of face-threatening acts (such as the above) occurring; i.e., S creates a dangerous-to-face atmosphere)
   (e) blatant non-cooperation in an activity – e.g. disruptively interrupting H's talk, making non-sequiturs or showing non-attention (S indicates that he doesn't care about H's negative-or positive-face wants)
   (f) use of address terms and other status-marked identifications in initial encounters (S may misidentify H in an offensive or embarrassing way, intentionally or accidentally).

Note that there is an overlap in this classification of FTAs, because some FTAs intrinsically threaten both negative and positive face (e.g. complaints, interruptions, threats, strong expressions of emotion, requests for personal information).

Second distinction: Threats to H's face versus threats to S's. Secondly, we may distinguish between acts that primarily threaten *H's* face (as in the above list) and those that threaten primarily *S's* face. To the extent that S and H are cooperating to maintain face, the latter FTAs also potentially threaten H's face. FTAs that are threatening to S include:[6]

(i)   Those that offend S's negative face:
   (a) expressing thanks (S accepts a debt, humbles his own face)
   (b) acceptance of H's thanks or H's apology (S may feel constrained to minimize H's debt or transgression, as in 'It was nothing, don't mention it.')
   (c) excuses (S indicates that he thinks he had good reason to do, or fail to do, an act which H has just criticized; this may constitute in turn a criticism of H, or at least cause a confrontation between H's view of things and S's view)

    (d) acceptance of offers (S is constrained to accept a debt, and to encroach upon H's negative face)

    (e) responses to H's *faux pas* (if S visibly notices a prior *faux pas*, he may cause embarrassment to H; if he pretends not to, he may be discomfited himself)

    (f) unwilling promises and offers (S commits himself to some future action although he doesn't want to; therefore, if his unwillingness shows, he may also offend H's positive face).

(ii) Those that directly damage S's positive face:[7]

    (a) apologies (S indicates that he regrets doing a prior FTA, thereby damaging his own face to some degree – especially if the apology is at the same time a confession with H learning about the transgression through it, and the FTA thus conveys bad news)

    (b) acceptance of a compliment (S may feel constrained to denigrate the object of H's prior compliment, thus damaging his own face; or he may feel constrained to compliment H in turn)

    (c) breakdown of physical control over body, bodily leakage, stumbling or falling down, etc.

    (d) self-humiliation, shuffling or cowering, acting stupid, self-contradicting

    (e) confessions, admissions of guilt or responsibility – e.g. for having done or not done an act, or for ignorance of something that S is expected to know

    (f) emotion leakage, non-control of laughter or tears.

These two ways of classifying FTAs (by whether S's face or H's face is mainly threatened, or by whether it is mainly positive face or negative face that is at stake) give rise to a four-way grid which offers the possibility of cross-classifying at least some of the above FTAs. However, such a cross-classification has a complex relation to the ways in which FTAs are handled.

Strategies for doing FTAs

In the context of the mutual vulnerability of face, any rational agent will seek to avoid these face-threatening acts, or will employ certain strategies to minimize the threat. In other words, he will take into consideration the relative weightings of (at least) three wants: (a) the want to communicate the content of the FTA x, (b) the want to be efficient or urgent,[8] and (c) the want to maintain H's face to any degree. Unless (b) is greater than (c), S will want to minimize the threat of his FTA.

    The possible sets of strategies may be schematized exhaustively as in Figure 6.2.2. In this schema, we have in mind the following definitions:

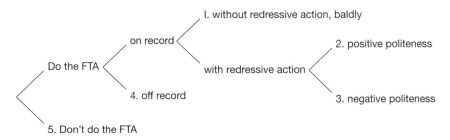

Figure 6.2.2 Possible strategies for doing FTAs.

An actor goes **on record** in doing an act A if it is clear to participants what communicative intention led the actor to do A (i.e., there is just one unambiguously attributable intention with which witnesses would concur). For instance, if I say 'I (hereby) promise to come tomorrow' and if participants would concur that, in saying that, I did unambiguously express the intention of committing myself to that future act, then in our terminology I went 'on record' as promising to do so.

In contrast, if an actor goes **off record** in doing A, then there is more than one unambiguously attributable intention so that the actor cannot be held to have committed himself to one particular intent. So, for instance, if I say 'Damn, I'm out of cash, I forgot to go to the bank today', I may be intending to get you to lend me some cash, but I cannot be held to have committed myself to that intent (as you would discover were you to challenge me with 'This is the seventeenth time you've asked me to lend you money'). Linguistic realizations of off-record strategies include metaphor and irony, rhetorical questions, understatement, tautologies, all kinds of hints as to what a speaker wants or means to communicate, without doing so directly, so that the meaning is to some degree negotiable.

Doing an act **baldly, without redress**, involves doing it in the most direct, clear, unambiguous and concise way possible (for example, for a request, saying 'Do X!') [. . .] following the specifications of Grice's Maxims of Cooperation (Grice 1967, 1975). Normally, an FTA will be done in this way only if the speaker does not fear retribution from the addressee, for example in circumstances where (a) S and H both tacitly agree that the relevance of face demands may be suspended in the interests of urgency or efficiency; (b) where the danger to H's face is *very* small, as in offers, requests, suggestions that are clearly in H's interest and do not require great sacrifices of S (e.g., 'Come in' or 'Do sit down'); and (c) where S is vastly superior in power to H, or can enlist audience support to destroy H's face without losing his own.

By **redressive action** we mean action that 'gives face' to the addressee, that is, that attempts to counteract the potential face damage of the FTA by doing it in such a way, or with such modifications or additions, that indicate clearly that no such face threat is intended or desired, and that S in general recognizes H's face wants and himself wants them to be achieved. Such redressive action takes one of two forms, depending on which aspect of face (negative or positive) is being stressed.

Positive politeness is oriented toward the positive face of H, the positive self-image that he claims for himself. Positive politeness is approach-based; it 'anoints' the face of the addressee by indicating that in some respects, S wants H's wants (e.g. by treating him as a member of an in-group, a friend, a person whose wants and personality traits are known and liked). The potential face threat of an act is minimized in this case by the assurance that in general S wants at least some of H's wants; for example, that S considers H to be in important respects 'the same' as he, with in-group rights and duties and expectations of reciprocity, or by the implication that S likes H so that the FTA doesn't mean a negative evaluation in general of H's face.

Negative politeness, on the other hand, is oriented mainly toward partially satisfying (redressing) H's negative face, his basic want to maintain claims of territory and self-determination. Negative politeness, thus, is essentially avoidance-based, and realizations of negative-politeness strategies consist in assurances that the speaker recognizes and respects the addressee's negative-face wants and will not (or will only minimally) interfere with the addressee's freedom of action. Hence negative politeness is characterized by self-effacement, formality and restraint, with attention to very restricted aspects of H's self-image, centring on his want to be unimpeded. Face-threatening acts are redressed with apologies for interfering or transgressing, with linguistic and non-linguistic deference, with hedges on the illocutionary force of the act, with impersonalizing mechanisms (such as passives) that distance S and H from the act, and with other softening mechanisms that give the addressee on 'out', a face-saving line of escape, permitting him to feel that his response is not coerced.

There is a natural tension in negative politeness, however, between (a) the desire to go on record as a prerequisite to being seen to pay face, and (b) the desire to go off record to avoid imposing. A compromise is reached in **conventionalized indirectness**, for whatever the indirect mechanism used to do an FTA, once fully conventionalized as a way of doing that FTA it is no longer off record. Thus many indirect requests, for example, are fully conventionalized in English so that they are on record (e.g., 'Can you pass the salt?' would be read as a request by all participants; there is no longer a viable alternative interpretation of the utterance except in very special circumstances). And between any two (or more) individuals, any utterance may become conventionalized and therefore on record, as is the case with passwords and codes.

A purely conventional 'out' works as redressive action in negative politeness because it pays a token bow to the negative-face wants of the addressee. That is, the fact that the speaker bothers to phrase his FTA in a conventionally indirect way shows that he is aware of and honours the negative-face wants of H.

Factors influencing the choice of strategies

[. . .] [A]ny rational agent will tend to choose the same genus of strategy under the same conditions – that is, make the same moves as any other would make under the circumstances. This is by virtue of the fact that the particular strategies intrinsically afford certain payoffs or advantages, and the relevant circumstances are those in which one of these payoffs would be more advantageous than any other.

We consider these in turn – first the intrinsic payoffs and then the relevant circumstances – and then relate the two.

The payoffs: *a priori* considerations. Here we present a fairly complete list of the payoffs associated with each of the strategies, derived on *a priori* grounds.

By going *on record*, a speaker can potentially get any of the following advantages: he can enlist public pressure against the addressee or in support of himself; he can get credit for honesty, for indicating that he trusts the addressee; he can get credit for outspokenness, avoiding the danger of being seen to be a manipulator; he can avoid the danger of being misunderstood; and he can have the opportunity to pay back in face whatever he potentially takes away by the FTA.

By going *off record*, on the other hand, a speaker can profit in the following ways: he can get credit for being tactful, non-coercive; he can run less risk of his act entering the 'gossip biography' that others keep of him; and he can avoid responsibility for the potentially face-damaging interpretation. Furthermore, he can give (non-overtly) the addressee an opportunity to be seen to care for S (and thus he can test H's feelings towards him). In this latter case, if H chooses to pick up and respond to the potentially threatening interpretation of the act, he can give a 'gift' to the original speaker. Thus, if I say 'It's hot in here' and you say 'Oh, I'll open the window then!', you may get credit for being generous and cooperative, and I avoid the potential threat of ordering you around.

For going on record with *positive politeness*, a speaker can minimize the face-threatening aspects of an act by assuring the addressee that S considers himself to be 'of the same kind', that he likes him and wants his wants. Thus a criticism, with the assertion of mutual friendship, may lose much of its sting – indeed, in the assumption of a friendly context it often becomes a game (cf. Labov 1972a) and possibly even a compliment (as between opposite-sexed teenagers). Another possible payoff is that S can avoid or minimize the debt implications of FTAs such as requests and offers, either by referring (indirectly) to the reciprocity and on-going relationship between the addressee and himself (as in the reference to a pseudo prior agreement with *then* in 'How about a cookie, then') or by including the addressee and himself equally as participants in or as benefitors from the request or offer (for example, with an inclusive 'we', as in 'Let's get on with dinner' from the husband glued to the TV).

For going on record with *negative politeness*, a speaker can benefit in the following ways: he can pay respect, deference, to the addressee in return for the FTA, and can thereby avoid incurring (or can thereby lessen) a future debt; he can maintain social distance, and avoid the threat (or the potential face loss) of advancing familiarity towards the addressee; he can give a real 'out' to the addressee (for example, with a request or an offer, by making it clear that he doesn't really expect H to say 'Yes' unless he wants to, thereby minimizing the mutual face loss incurred if H has to say 'No'); and he can give conventional 'outs' to the addressee as opposed to real 'outs', that is, pretend to offer an escape route without really doing so, thereby indicating that he has the other person's face wants in mind.

Finally, the payoff for the fifth strategic choice, 'Don't do the FTA', is simply that S avoids offending H at all with this particular FTA. Of course S also fails to achieve his desired communication, and as there are naturally no interesting linguistic reflexes of this last-ditch strategy, we will ignore it in our discussion henceforth.

For our purposes, these payoffs may be simplified to the following summary:

On-record payoffs:
(a)   clarity, perspicuousness
(b)   demonstrable non-manipulativeness

Bald-on-record (non-redressed) payoff:
    efficiency (S can claim that other things are more important than face, or that the act is not an FTA at all)

Plus-redress payoff: S has the opportunity to give face
(a)   positive politeness – to satisfy H's positive face, in some respect
(b)   negative politeness – to satisfy H's negative face, to some degree

Off-record payoffs:
(a)   S can satisfy negative face to a degree greater than that afforded by the negative-politeness strategy
(b)   S can avoid the inescapable accountability, the responsibility for his action, that on record strategies entail.

When they are considered in this order, we can already see that on *a priori* grounds there is a pattern of circumstances in which the payoffs would be most advantageous: roughly, the more dangerous the particular FTA *x* is, in S's assessment, the more he will tend to choose the higher-numbered strategy. Running through the individual payoffs we see why this would be so.

The use of the first strategy (on record, minus redress) leaves S responsible without any means to minimize the FTA *x*. The use of redressive action affords S the opportunity to placate H by partially satisfying some of his perennial desires. The use of the second strategy (positive redressive action) allows S to satisfy a wide range of these perennial desires of H's (not necessarily directly related to *x*), while the use of the third (negative redressive action) allows S to satisfy to some extent H's want to be left unimpeded – the want that is directly infringed by *x*. By indicating reluctance to impinge on H, S implies that if the matter had been less pressing S would never have disturbed H (and will not do so for future matters that are not so pressing). Finally, the fourth strategy (off record) affords S the opportunity of evading responsibility altogether (by claiming, if challenged, that the interpretation of *x* as an FTA is wrong), and simultaneously allows S to avoid actually *imposing* the FTA *x* on H, since H himself must choose to interpret *x* as an FTA rather than as some more trivial remark.

Note that positive politeness precedes negative politeness in the continuum of FTA 'danger' for the following reasons. Positive politeness redresses by means of fulfilling H's want that some others should want some particular desires of his. To pursue this strategy S must make the assumption that he is a member of the set of these others; the efficacy of his redress is totally vulnerable to H's concurrence in this assumption. Negative politeness, on the other hand, is addressed to a generalized desire for freedom of action; in paying H in this currency, S makes no vulnerable assumptions and does no redressive action that is not immediately *relevant* to the imposition that *x* imposes (thus leaving himself invulnerable to charges of irrelevant flattery, etc.).[9]

Why then, given the danger associated with FTAs, do actors not take out the maximum insurance policy and always choose the off-record strategy? There must be some factors in the circumstances or the payoffs that cause a tension in the opposite direction from the pull that FTA danger exerts. One of these is a purely practical functional pressure: the off-record strategy leads to ambiguities and unclarities, while redressive action takes time, foresight, and effort. But another seems to be the inherent tension between an actor's negative-face wants and his positive-face wants, for the latter include both the former and (typically) contrary wants. Thus I can want simultaneously both to be undisturbed and to be shown tokens of admiration, care, regard, etc. – opposing wants that I will resolve (say) by in general wanting to be not imposed upon, but in some circumstances wanting some particular persons' expressions of regard, care, etc. For reasons discussed above it is safer to assume that H prefers his peace and self-determination than that he prefers your expressions of regard, unless you are certain of the contrary. But most importantly, since the availability of the strategies and the nature of face and practical reasoning are mutual knowledge to participants, they will have expectations of certain estimates of face risk for particular FTAs in particular circumstances. If an actor uses a strategy appropriate to a high risk for an FTA of less risk, others will assume the FTA was greater than in fact it was, while it is S's intention to *minimize* rather than overestimate the threat to H's face. Hence in general no actor will use a strategy for an FTA that affords more opportunity for face-risk minimization than is actually required to retain H's cooperation.

Thus the set of discrete payoffs can be lined up against a continuum of opposing forces that describes the circumstances in which each strategy would be most advantageous. We can sum up this section diagrammatically, as in Figure 6.2.3.

The circumstances: Sociological variables. [. . .] [T]he assessment of the seriousness of an FTA (that is, the calculations that members actually seem to make) involves the following factors in many and perhaps all cultures:

(i)   the 'social distance' (D) of S and H (a symmetric relation)
(ii) the relative 'power' (P) of S and H (an asymmetric relation)
(iii) the absolute ranking (R) of impositions in the particular culture.

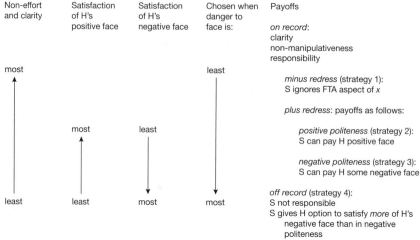

Figure 6.2.3 A priori factors influencing strategy selection.

An immediate clarification is in order. We are interested in D, P, and R only to the extent that the actors think it is mutual knowledge between them that these variables have some particular values. Thus these are not intended as *sociologists'* ratings of *actual* power, distance, etc., but only as *actors'* assumptions of such ratings, assumed to be mutually assumed, at least within certain limits.

Our argument here has an empirical basis, and we make the argument in as strong a form as our ethnographic data will allow.[10]

Computing the weightiness of an FTA. For each FTA, the seriousness or weightiness of a particular FTA *x* is compounded of both risk to S's face and risk to H's face, in a proportion relative to the nature of the FTA. Thus apologies and confessions are essentially threats to S's face (as we have seen), and advice and orders are basically threats to H's face, while requests and offers are likely to threaten the face of both participants. However, the way in which the seriousness of a particular FTA is weighed seems to be neutral as to whether it is S's or H's face that is threatened, or in what proportion. So let us say that the weightiness of an FTA is calculated thus:

$$W_x = D(S,H) + P(H,S) + R_x$$

where W_x is the numerical value that measures the weightiness of the FTA *x*, $D(S,H)$ is the value that measures the social distance between S and H, $P(H,S)$ is a measure of the power that H has over S, and R_x is a value that measures the degree to which the FTA *x* is rated an imposition in that culture. We assume that each of these values can be measured on a scale of 1 to *n*, where *n* is some small number. Our formula assumes that the function that assigns a value to W_x on the basis of the three social parameters does so on a simple summative basis. Such an assumption seems to work surprisingly well, but we allow that in fact some more complex composition of values may be involved. In any case, the function must capture the fact that all three dimensions P, D, and R contribute to the seriousness of an FTA, and thus to a determination of the level of politeness with which, other things being equal, an FTA will be communicated.

First, we must clarify our intent. By D and P we intend very general pan-cultural social dimensions which nevertheless probably have 'emic' correlates.[11] We are not here interested in what factors are compounded to estimate these complex parameters; such factors are certainly culture-specific. For instance, P(H,S) may be assessed as being great because H is eloquent and influential, or is a prince, a witch, a thug, or a priest; D(S,H) as great because H speaks another dialect or language, or lives in the next valley, or is not a kinsman. More specifically, we can describe these factors as follows.

D is a symmetric social dimension of similarity/difference within which S and H stand for the purposes of this act. In many cases (but not all), it is based on an assessment of the frequency of interaction and the kinds of material or non-material goods (including face) exchanged between S and H (or parties representing S or H, or for whom S and H are representatives). An important part of the assessment of D will usually be measures of social distance based on stable social attributes. The reflex of social closeness is, generally, the reciprocal giving and receiving of positive face.

P is an asymmetric social dimension of relative power, roughly in Weber's sense. That is, P(H,S) is the degree to which H can impose his own plans and his own self-evaluation (face) at the expense of S's plans and self-evaluation. In general there are two sources of P, either of which may be authorized or unauthorized – material control (over economic distribution and physical force) and metaphysical control (over the actions of others, by virtue of metaphysical forces subscribed to by those others). In most cases an individual's power is drawn from both these sources, or is thought to overlap them. The reflex of a great P differential is perhaps archetypally 'deference', as discussed below.

R is a culturally and situationally defined ranking of impositions by the degree to which they are considered to interfere with an agent's wants of self-determination or of approval (his negative- and positive-face wants). In general there are probably two such scales or ranks that are emically identifiable for negative-face FTAs: a ranking of impositions in proportion to the expenditure (a) of *services* (including the provision of time) and (b) of *goods* (including non-material goods like information, as well as the expression of regard and other face payments). These intra-culturally defined costings of impositions on an individual's preserve are in general constant only in their rank order from one situation to another. However, even the rank order is subject to a set of operations that shuffles the impositions according to whether actors have specific rights or obligations to perform the act, whether they have specific reasons (ritual or physical) for not performing them, and whether actors are known to actually *enjoy* being imposed upon in some way.[12]

So an outline of the rankings of negative-face impositions for a particular domain of FTAs in a particular culture involves a complex description like the following:

(i) (a) rank order of impositions requiring services
    (b) rank order of impositions requiring goods.
(ii) Functions on (i):
    (a) the lessening of certain impositions on a given actor determined by the obligation (legally, morally, by virtue of employment, etc.) to do the act A; and also by the enjoyment that the actor gets out of performing the required act
    (b) the increasing of certain impositions determined by reasons why the actor *shouldn't* do them, and reasons why the actor *couldn't* (easily) do them.

For FTAs against positive face, the ranking involves an assessment of the amount of 'pain' given to H's face, based on the discrepancy between H's own desired self-image and that presented (blatantly or tacitly) in the FTA. There will be cultural rankings of aspects of positive face (for example, 'success', 'niceness', 'beauty', 'generosity'), which can be re-ranked in particular circumstances, just as can negative-face rankings. And there are personal (idiosyncratic) functions on these rankings; some people object to certain kinds of FTAs more than others. A person who is skilled at assessing such rankings, and the circumstances in which they vary, is considered to be graced with 'tact', 'charm', or 'poise'.

In the argument below we associate with each of these variables, D, P, and R, a value from 1 to n assigned by an actor in particular circumstances. No special substantial claim is intended; the valuation simply represents the way in which (for instance) as S's power over H increases, the weightiness of the FTA diminishes.[13] One interesting side effect of this numerical representation is that it can describe these intuitive facts: the threshold value of risk which triggers the choice of another strategy is a constant, independent of the way in which the value is composed and assessed. Thus one goes off record where an imposition is small but relative S–H distance and H's power are great, and also where H is an intimate equal of S's but the imposition is very great.

Context-dependence of P, D, and R. Our social dimensions P, D and R can be viewed in various ways. Taking P as an extended example, we could argue that individuals are assigned an absolute value on this dimension that measures the power that each individual has relative to all others. Thus a bank manager might be given a high rating, and a lowly worker a low one. But when the worker pulls a gun, or sits on a jury trying the manager, or represents his union, the power may be reversed. To save the view that there are absolute (context-free) assignments to P, we would then have to allow for contextual reclassifications that adjust the assignments in certain circumstances.

A more plausible view would be that P is a value attached not to individuals at all, but to roles or role-sets. Thus in the role-set manager/employee, or parent/child, asymmetrical power is built in. Then we would have to allow that there are role-sets like gangster/victim, in order to handle the way in which individuals can find the relative P values that they normally expect inverted by circumstances. But do all kinds of naked power come clothed in role-sets? If so, the notion of social role must be watered down. There is, moreover, another problem with this view. Individuals acquire sets of roles, and high P values in one role do carry over into the conduct of another. When a new President is elected, his old friends may still be friends, but they are unlikely to retain the old equality.

A third view would be that stable social valuations, whether of individuals or of roles, are only one element that enters into the assessment of P. Other situational sources of power may contribute to or adjust or entirely override such stable social valuations. Momentary weaknesses in bargaining power, strength of character, or alliances may all play a role in the assessment of P.

It is the last view that seems to us most adequate, even if it is the least definite suggestion. And we shall assume that situational factors enter into the values for P, D, and R, so that the values assessed hold only for S and H in a particular context, and for a particular FTA. Let us just illustrate the kinds of ways in which each of our social dimensions is context-relative in this sense.

Taking first the distance variable, note that two American strangers who would treat one another with great circumspection and formality in a chance encounter in the streets of New York City might well embrace each other with all the excesses of positive politeness if they were to meet in the Hindu Kush. A possible explanation of this familiar phenomenon is that wherever one is, all members of the local social universe must be assigned places across the entire scale of social distance. So in New York the strangers are assigned high D values, but in the Hindu Kush the even stranger natives displace the American visitors towards each other on the dimension of social distance.

The context-relativeness of relative power P is demonstrable in the following case. A man from a lowly caste in South India who approaches a Brahman requiring ritual services will treat him with great deference. When the Brahman comes to visit the low-caste man in the latter's capacity as a government official, it will be the Brahman who adopts the deferent or even servile attitude (Beck 1972: 159, nn. 34, 35). Compare too the switch in deference in Europe when one speaker passes from his own field of expertise into the other speaker's field. In these cases, P values seem to change as the roles of supplicant/specialist and expert/learner are switched.

Some of the special ways in which the ranking of impositions can be contextually inverted have been mentioned. But even where the rank order is maintained, impositions can still situationally vary in value; to ask for a dollar is generally to ask for more than to ask for a dime, yet to ask for a dime just outside a telephone booth is less than to ask for a dime for no apparent reason in the middle of the street. Thus the perceived situational reasonableness of the request enters into an assessment of its R value.

P, D, and R as independent variables. It might be appropriate to be able to demonstrate that our P, D, and R factors are all relevant and independent, and are the only relevant ones used by actors to assess the danger of FTAs. But our claim is not that they are the *only* relevant factors, but simply that they *subsume* all others (status, authority, occupation, ethnic identity, friendship, situational factors, etc.) that have a principled effect on such assessments. However, we can illustrate their independence and relevance by the following examples, with reference to our formula and to the claim that W_x provides the speaker with the major reason for choosing among the five sets of politeness strategies.

Considering first the D variable, we can take two cases where P and R are constant and have small values in the estimate of S – in other words, where the relative power of S and H is more or less equal, and the imposition is not great. Such small impositions are found, for example, in requests for 'free goods', those things and services (like a match, or telling the time, or giving directions) which all members of the public may reasonably demand from one another. With P and R held constant and small, only the expression of D varies in the following two sentences:

(1) Excuse me, would you by any chance have the time?
(2) Got the time, mate?

Our intuitions are that (1) would be used where (in S's perception) S and H were distant (strangers from different parts, say), and (2) where S and H were close (either known to each other, or perceptibly 'similar' in social terms). D, then, is the only variable in our formula that changes from (1) to (2), and in doing so lessens W_x which provides the motive for the particular linguistic encoding of the FTA.

Turning to the P variable, suppose D and R are held constant and have small values (e.g. if S and H know each other by sight, and the imposition is a request for free goods):

(3) Excuse me sir, would it be all right if I smoke?
(4) Mind if I smoke?

Our intuitions are that (3) might be said by an employee to his boss, while (4) might be said by the boss to the employee in the same situation. Here, then, P is the only variable that changes from (3) to (4) (more exactly, P of H over S), and this again lessens W_x which provides S with the reasons for his choice between (3) and (4) for his linguistic encoding.

That R is also independently variable can be similarly demonstrated. Suppose P is small and D is great (S and H are strangers, for example), and P and D are held constant. Then compare:

(5)   Look, I'm terribly sorry to bother you but would there be any chance of your lending me just enough money to get a railway ticket to get home? I must have dropped my purse and I just don't know what to do.

(6)   Hey, got change for a quarter?

Both might be said at a railway station by a frustrated traveller to a stranger, but our intuitions are that S in saying (5) considers the FTA to be much more serious than the FTA done in (6). The only variable is R, and it must be because R_x is lower in (6) that the language appropriate to a low W_x is employed there. Our conclusion is that in the ranking of impositions in Anglo-American culture, asking for a substantial amount of money without recompense is much more of an imposition than a request to search in one's pockets for change. In each case above, the first option (examples 1, 3, and 5) is a linguistic realization of the negative-politeness strategy, and the second (2, 4, and 6) is a realization of the positive-politeness strategy.

Ambiguity and disambiguation as evidence for P, D, and R. [. . .] Our formula is a means of compounding the factors that make an FTA dangerous into a single index of risk, *Wx*. *Wx* is then a motive for the choice of one of the strategies 1–5 in Figure 6.2.1 (see page 286) [. . .] Hence the choice of strategy will in general 'encode' the estimated danger of the FTA; this is why one receives with considerable apprehension phrases like:

(7)   I'm awfully sorry to bother you, and I wouldn't but I'm in an awful fix, so I wondered if by any chance . . .

But if our representation of the factors underlying the assessment of W_x is correct, such phrases do not display *which* variable (D, relative P, or R) is primarily responsible for the weight of *x*. In other words, the formula, in compounding the variables into a single index, makes the sources of the final assessment ambiguous. [. . .]

Taking deference to be the humbling of the self or the 'raising' of the other – that is, claims about the value of P(H,S) – we can see that it may perform the function of disambiguating which factor was most important in the assessment of W_x. For suppose the choice of negative politeness (strategy 3) or off record (strategy 4) 'encodes' a weighty W_x: then if S asserts that H is relatively much more powerful than S, he indicates that W_x was assessed crucially on values of P, hence that R_x is probably small (since a bigger value would send S to strategy 5, 'Don't do the FTA at all'). Some markers of deference, then, ought to ease the apprehension of the addressee when he hears a sentence like example (7) above.

In terms of our first observation that *Wx* is compounded of the risk of *x* to H's face and the risk of *x* to S's face, if S indicates that H's relative power is greater than his, he claims that W_x is primarily a risk to himself rather than to H. Note then that phrases like (7) above are likely to be prologues to awful impositions only where D and relative P are mutually known to be fairly small, leaving only R_x to account for the high *Wx*. The low D and P values may be assumed, or in the case of D may be claimed by means of familiar usages like:

(8)   {Look,   }
      {Hey,   }, Harry, I'm awfully sorry to bother you . . .
      {My God, }

(9)   Look, Harry, you're a friend, so . . .

while high P values and low R values can be claimed by usages like:

(10) Excuse me, {Sir,   } I'm sorry to bother you but I wonder if you could just
                  {Officer,   }
                  {Your Excellency,}
        possibly do me a small favour . . .

These examples show that factors like P, D, and R are involved in the calculation of W_x, and since that calculation compounds them and the chosen strategy does not directly reflect them, there would be motivation for their values to be directly claimed.

Again, consider threatening suggestions or warnings like (11), (12), and (13) below, in the light of our claim that W_x is compounded of risk to H's face and risk to S's face:

(11) It's no skin off my teeth, but I think you might want to take a look at what
        your son is up to in the gooseberry patch.
(12) I don't care, but I think maybe you ought to be more careful when you park
        your car next to mine in future.

Since the initial phrases deny any risk to the speaker's face, and the strategy chosen is off record, W_x is high but can only be due to risk to H. Hence this sort of FTA may be designed to cause considerable consternation to the addressee. And a threat like (13) again refers to the factors D, P, and R, claiming small D with an initial address phrase, and small R with words like *little* and *just*, and thus leaving only a very high relative P of S over H – and not vice versa – to account for the choice of an off-record strategy:

(13) Look sonny, it might not be advisable to just go pushing your little fingers into
        this little pie.

The integration of assessment of payoffs and weighting of risk in the choice of strategies. We here explain why, as W_x increases, a rational agent would tend to choose to use the higher-numbered strategies. Figure 6.2.3 (see page 296) [. . .] summarizes the circumstances in which each strategy would be most appropriately employed on *a priori* grounds. As the FTA danger increases, the higher-numbered strategies serve best to minimize face risk. Immediately we can see why the observed factor W_x would correlate with the choice of strategies, for W_x is an estimate of risk.

We can now relate the *a priori* and the sociological facts. Any MP with the properties we have attributed to him (the ability to use practical reasoning from wants to means that will satisfy those wants, and the retention of the specific wants called 'face') would employ the strategies in the circumstances in which the payoffs of each one were most appropriate (i.e. would most satisfy his face wants) – in fact, as in Figure 6.2.3.

Now, if it is empirically the case that FTA danger is assessed by estimating P, D, and R values, then our MP would take the least possible risk with 'strangers' (high D values) and 'dominant members' (high P(H,S) values) when making serious impositions (high R_x values).

Our MP would not do all FTAs with the strategy of *least* risk because it costs more in effort and loss of clarity, because he may wish to satisfy the other perennial desire of H's – for positive face – but most importantly because choice of the least risky strategy may indicate to H that the FTA is more threatening than it actually is, since it would imply an excessively high rating of P or D or R, or some combination.

In short, our original assumptions that define our MP as a 'rational agent with face' *predict* that rational face-bearing agents will choose ways of doing face-threatening acts that minimize those threats, hence will choose a higher-numbered strategy as the threat increases. This neatly fits the observational ethnographic fact that as risk estimated in terms of *social* variables increases, a similar choice of strategies can be observed.

Because some such weak universal sociological generalizations appear to be viable (that the danger of an FTA is assessed in terms of factors like P, D, R), and because our MP is a reasonable approximation to universal assumptions, we can account for the fact that an observer in a foreign culture, on seeing a speaker and addressee interact, feels that S is (say) not a close friend of H's (or thinks that H is more powerful than S, or thinks x is a big imposition) purely from observing the linguistics of S's FTA. This observation may be made in Chiapas, in Tamilnad, or in California.

[. . .]

A short note is in order on our use of the word 'strategy'. We do not mean to imply that what we dub 'strategies' are necessarily conscious. For the most part they do not seem to be, but when interactional mistakes occur, or actors try to manipulate others, they may very well emerge into awareness. And they are open to introspection, at least in part. But the general unconscious nature of such strategies raises fundamental methodological problems that we simply skirt. We cannot pretend to have any special insight into what is probably the biggest single stumbling block to theory throughout the social sciences: the nature of the unconscious and preconscious where all the most important determinants of action seem to lie. We continue to use the word 'strategy', despite its connotations of conscious deliberation, because we can think of no other word that will imply a rational element while covering both (a) innovative plans of action, which may still be (but need not be) unconscious, and (b) routines – that is, previously constructed plans whose original rational origin is still preserved in their construction, despite their present automatic application as ready-made programmes.

[. . .]

Notes

*   *Zweckrational*, or purpose driven rationality, calculates the effect of our actions on other people as we think through the means required to achieve particular ends, *wertrational*, or value-driven rationality, is motivated by personal belief, so that we act as we think appropriate, irrespective of the extent to which it enables us to achieve particular ends.

1   We follow Schiffer (1972): if it is mutual knowledge between A and B that C, then A knows that B knows that A knows . . . that C.

2   Juvenile, mad, incapacitated persons partially excepted.

3   The notions and labels for positive and negative face derive ultimately from Durkheim's 'positive and negative rites' (in *The Elementary Forms of the Religious Life*, 1915), partially via Goffman.

4   A third argument in favour of a model based on 'wants' rather than 'norms' was pointed out to us by Gillian Sankoff: that it allows a dynamic to be introduced into the analysis. For particular levels of face redress characterize particular social relations (as we shall argue), and such relations have histories – are constituted, worked on, negotiated. A norm-based analysis requiring a static level of face redress could not account for this.

5   Following Grice (1957): a communicative act is a chunk of behaviour B which is produced by S with a specific intention, which S intends H to recognize, this recognition being the communicative point of S's doing B.

6   Readers may note that many of these are responses to prior H-originated FTAs. This is because if H has made a prior FTA threatening the present S's face, whatever S now chooses to do is likely to be

dealing with his own threatened face. (He could of course choose to redress his own face loss by attacking H's face, rather than by protecting his own.)

7 These acts are damaging to S's face because of his basic positive-face wants of self-control and self-respect. In evidencing failure to achieve these wants he makes it unlikely that H will approve of him, as well as threatening H's face (potentially) with embarrassment *for* S. The existence of these kinds of acts as face threats is exploited in the conventionalized self-face-humbling of extreme deference [. . .]

8 This want has a number of origins: (a) It may be considered to be part of rationality: minimize effort. (b) It may be a derivative want from wanting something that can only be achieved by efficiency or urgency [. . .].

9 We draw encouragement for the importance of the three factors P, D, and R from Grimshaw's independent identification of very similar dimensions (Grimshaw 1980).

10 The numerical values are here intended only as a model of relative measures of proportions of P, D, and R, and not of course as absolute values of some sort. [. . .]

11 The significance of these dimensions in language usage was initially explored by Brown and Gilman (1960) in their work on the T/V distinction in pronouns. That emic correlates exist can be seen in the way that informants actually talk in terms of social distance, both vertically and horizontally. Thus in Tamil one talks of *tuuram contam* (literally 'distant own-kind', i.e. distant kin) on the horizontal social dimension; and of *uyira jaati* (literally 'high kind' or 'high caste') and *kiiRe jaati* ('low kind' or 'low caste') on the vertical social dimension.

12 Gillian Sankoff points out (personal comm.) that assessments like this (whether an actor is known to enjoy being imposed upon) raise a very complex problem, that of assessing the status of 'mutual knowledge' in a given interaction. How do we know what is mutually known, and how do we know we know? While recognizing the difficulties with this notion, we consider that it is one with which a theory of interaction will have to come to grips.

13 However, there is perhaps one implicit claim, and that is that a variable like 'social distance' on at least one psychological level is not a binary choice between, say, 'in-group' and 'out-group', although it may be so conceptualized on another level. There is some psychological evidence (Rosch 1977) and some linguistic evidence (G. Lakoff 1972) that supports us in this view; it suggests that categorization is a secondary process that follows complex estimations of *degrees* of membership of an object in a set. Here we attach no great importance to the claim, but it is worth noticing that our R factor has a similar binary categorization into 'free goods' and 'non-free goods' (at least in Western society: see Goffman 1967, 1971).

■ ■ ■

POST-READING

1 Although Brown and Levinson acknowledge that their P, D and R factors are *not* 'the *only* relevant factors' shaping FTAs, they contend that their descriptions of P, D and R are sufficiently broad to be able to '*subsume* ... status, authority, occupation, ethnic identity, friendship, situational factors, etc. ... '. Do you agree? Why/why not?

2 Off-record politeness strategies involve saying things in such a way that 'there is more than one unambiguously attributable intention', and, as such, 'the actor cannot be held to have committed himself to a particular intent'. Construct your own off-record example of a request for a small-ish amount of money that you'd be prepared to ask a work colleague you don't know very well. Then answer the following:

• Would you use the same construction to request money from your boss? If not, why not?

• Would you ask such a request differently, if your interlocutor was someone you know well (whether your colleague or your boss)? If yes, how? If not, why not?

• Would you ask the request differently, if your interlocutor was a family member? Would you still use off-record strategies? Why/why not?

- Would you ask the request differently, if you were asking for quite a large amount of money. If yes, how? Is this the case, regardless of the social/familiar/power relationship between you and your interlocutor?

3   Brown and Levinson suggest that **conventionalized indirectness** should be considered an *on*-record (as opposed to an *off*-record) strategy, because requests like 'Can you pass the salt?' will always 'be read as a request by all participants', not least because 'there is no longer a viable alternative interpretation except in very special circumstances'. Does their argument in regard to conventionalized indirectness contradict or support what they say earlier about off-record politeness strategies? Why/why not?

4   Some researchers believe that Brown and Levinson's emphasis on EITHER positive face OR negative face is unhelpful *(see*, e.g., Harris 1984; O'Driscoll 1996; Bousfield 2008). Can you think of situations in which a request affects both the target's negative and positive face (i.e. their freedom of action and their desire for approval)? If so, note them down.

MIRIAM A. LOCHER AND RICHARD J. WATTS

RELATIONAL WORK AND IMPOLITENESS
Negotiating norms of linguistic behaviour

PRE-READING

As we explained in our introduction to this reading (see page 273), Locher and Watts contend that we negotiate face (our own and others') via the use of context-specific 'expectation frames'. Before beginning the reading, draw on your experience of the extent to which/how you amend your behaviour in the following contexts: the office, the classroom, an interview, a family meal, a lunch date with friends, when shopping, etc. How conscious of face issues are you in these different environments – very conscious, intermittently conscious, not conscious at all? Why/why not?

IN-READING

1   Locher and Watts provide two definitions of power (Wartenberg 1990; Watts 1991) and a checklist summarizing 'the nature and exercise of power' before beginning their analysis of the Emery-Scargill interview proper. When you reach this point in the reading, which we've marked for you (see first | in margin):
   •   Write out each definition and also Locher's checklist on a separate piece of paper and, using arrows, begin to identify points at which Locher's bullet points on her checklist directly link to Wartenberg's and/or Watts' definitions.
   •   If you find that some of the Locher bullet points don't seem to link directly to Wartenberg's and/or Watts' definitions, consider whether they might be implicit in Wartenberg's and/or Watt' definitions.
   •   Make a list of any of Locher's bullet points which (in your view) do not link to Wartenberg's and/or Watts' definitions either directly or implicitly.
2   Locher and Watts seem to identify an interesting conundrum in their reading – that, in spite of Emery's behaviour being 'sanctioned by a redefinition of the norms of appropriateness in this public form of social practice', Scargill can nevertheless attempt to 'frame Emery's behaviour' in such a way so as 'to present himself (and by extension the NUM) as the butt of unjustified criticism at the hands of the media' (see second | in margin):
   •   What evidence of impoliteness having taken place do Locher and Watts suggest we will be *unlikely* to find, given Emery is allowed to ask 'the kinds of questions that audiences might reasonably be expected to hear' as part of his interviewer role?

- What activities/behaviour do they point to as evidence that Scargill is 'framing' Emery's behaviour as 'impolite'?
- In what way(s) are Scargill's activities said to be an 'exercise of power'?

■ ■ ■

RELATIONAL WORK AND IMPOLITENESS: NEGOTIATING NORMS OF LINGUISTIC BEHAVIOUR
MIRIAM A. LOCHER AND RICHARD J. WATTS

[. . .]

Relational work and frames of expectations

Relational work is defined as the work people invest in negotiating their relationships in interaction (Locher 2004; Locher and Watts 2005; Locher 2006). It is based on the idea that any communicative act has both an informational as well as an interpersonal aspect (cf. Watzlawick et al. 1967; Halliday 1978). In other words, communicative acts always embody some form of relational work. Taking this approach means that we are not restricted to studying merely the polite variant of the interpersonal aspect of a communication, as Brown and Levinson ([1978] 1987) have predominantly done, but can equally focus on impolite, or rude aspects of social behaviour. Relational work, in other words, comprises the entire spectrum of the interpersonal side of social practice.

In our earlier work (e.g. Locher and Watts 2005), we argued that whether interactants perceive or intend a message to be polite, impolite or merely appropriate (among many other labels) depends on *judgements* that they make at the level of relational work *in situ*, i.e. during an ongoing interaction in a particular setting. These judgements are made on the basis of norms and expectations that individuals have constructed and acquired through categorising the experiences of similar past situations, or conclusions that one draws from other people's experiences. [. . .] The notion of 'frame', as used, for example, by Tannen (1993b) or Escandell-Vidal (1996), is what we are evoking here. [. . .]

[. . .] While individuals of the same social group, interacting in the same situation may have developed similar frames of expectations and may indeed judge the level of relational work similarly, there can still be disagreement within any social group about judgements on social behaviour. This is because the norms themselves are constantly renegotiated, and because the cognitive domains against which a lexeme such as *polite* is profiled change conceptually over time as well (cf. Sell 1992; Ehlich 1992; Watts 2006). We have called this flexibility the 'discursive' nature of im/politeness (Watts 2003; Locher and Watts 2005). There is, in other words, no linguistic behaviour that is inherently polite or impolite.

[. . .]

The notions of 'impolite' or 'polite' should thus be understood as judgements by participants in the interaction in question. They are, in other words, first order concepts rather than second order, theoretical ones. In this way our approach differs considerably from that of other researchers who have worked on politeness and impoliteness. Kienpointner (1997: 252), for example, states quite clearly that his approach to rudeness (rather than impoliteness) is of a second order type. This is most manifest when he talks of linguistic strategies employed to achieve rudeness analogous to Brown and Levinson's ([1978] 1987) linguistic strategies for polite behaviour. The same can be said for Lachenicht (1980), Culpeper (1996), Culpeper et al. (2003) and Culpeper (2005).

Another aspect of difference linked to the distinction between a first order and second order approach to impoliteness has to do with the notion of *intentionality*. Kienpointner (1997: 259) defines rudeness as "non-cooperative or competitive communicative behaviour". We certainly agree that non-cooperativeness may play a role in the definition of rudeness. On the other hand, if we interpret Kienpointner's 'or' as being an exclusive, logical operator (either P or Q, rather than P and/or Q), we wish to dispute that competitiveness is equal to rudeness. Competitive communicative behaviour may be cooperative and positively valued in certain contexts (cf. Tannen 1981; Schiffrin 1984b; Watts 2003). Non-cooperativeness is important in behaviour that intentionally aims at hurting the addressee. Culpeper (2005: 37), Lachenicht (1980) and Bousfield (2007a, 2007b [. . .]) deal explicitly with intentional impoliteness/rudeness. Lachenicht (1980: 619), in mirroring Brown and Levinson's ([1978] 1987) politeness strategies, postulates the following:

> Aggravation strategies are also sensitive to social factors. A very powerful person will probably be attacked only by off record means. Friends and intimates would probably be attacked by means of positive aggravation whereas socially distant persons would be attacked by means of negative aggravation.
>
> (Lachenicht 1980: 619)

He goes on to say that "[i]f the purpose of aggravation is to hurt, then means must be chosen that *will* hurt" (1980: 619–620, emphasis in original). This comment points to the interlocutors' awareness of the norms of the interaction in question. If this were not the case, they could not play with the level of relational work and adjust it to their own ends. Taking a first order approach to impoliteness means that we are able to recognise this, whilst at the same time stressing the point that both the speaker's and the hearer's judgements have to be considered. A speaker may wish to be aggressive and hurtful, but still not come across as such to the hearer. Alternatively, a hearer may interpret the speaker's utterance as negatively marked with respect to appropriate behaviour, while the speaker did not intentionally wish to appear as such. In a first order approach to impoliteness, it is the interactants' *perceptions* of communicators' intentions rather than the intentions themselves that determine whether a communicative act is taken to be impolite or not. In other words, the uptake of a message is as important [as] if not more important than the utterer's original intention.

There are also a number of important overlaps in our understanding of the phenomenon with previous work on impoliteness. Kienpointner (1997: 255), for example, states that "rudeness could be termed inappropriateness of communicative behaviour *relative to* a particular context" (emphasis added) and is a matter of degree.[1] Mills (2005: 268) argues that "[i]mpoliteness can be considered as any type of linguistic behaviour which is *assessed as* intending to threaten the hearer's face or social identity, or as transgressing the hypothesized Community of Practice's norms of appropriacy" (emphasis added). Both Kienpointner's and Mills' perspective on rudeness here match our understanding of impoliteness as breaches of norms that are negatively evaluated by interactants according to their expectation frames.

Finally, the notion of power cannot be ignored when dealing with relational work in all its facets. Since relational work is defined as the work people invest in negotiating their relationships in interaction, power issues always play a crucial role in negotiating identities. In Watts (1991) and Locher (2004), we have dealt with the notion of power in interaction. Our understanding of power is that it is not a static concept, but is constantly renegotiated and exercised in social practice. All interlocutors enter social practice with an understanding of a differential distribution of social status amongst the co-participants, but the actual exercise of power is something that we can only witness in the interaction itself. [. . .]

Breaching norms in a political interview

[. . .]

The stretch of social interaction we wish to analyse [. . .] is a political interview on the BBC television current affairs programme *Panorama* which lasted for roughly ten minutes. [. . .] The programme was broadcast towards the end of the miner's strike in 1984 and the topic dealing with the miners' strike consists of a documentary film (purportedly giving evidence of violence on the picket lines, the hardship experienced by miners' families and the increasing number of miners trickling back to work) and the subsequent interview with Arthur Scargill, then president of the National Union of Mineworkers. The interviewer is the programme moderator, Fred Emery. [. . .] [W]e shall focus on selected passages from the interview and, from a digitalised version of the original videotape, will also present visual markers of exasperation and frustration on the part of Scargill.

Political interviews and the problem of power

The main purpose in analysing the interview is to show how our interpretation of inappropriate social behaviour – which could have been metapragmatically commented on by either of the two participants but wasn't – is intimately tied to issues of power and the exercise of power in the interview situation. Work on news interviews and political interviews (Beattie 1982; Jucker 1986, 2005; Greatbatch 1986; Clayman and Heritage 2002) gives evidence of an increased level of aggressiveness and a supposed concomitant loss of "respect" on the part of the interviewer towards political interviewees in the British media, although it is not entirely clear when this trend began. At all events, it was certainly in place at the beginning of the 1980s and was (and has remained) relatively prominent in the BBC's *Panorama* programme.

We define a "political interview" as a subgenre of the "news interview" as defined by Clayman and Heritage (2002: 7–8) since it is clear that not all news interviews involve politicians. The term "political interview" itself is used to define media interviews with politicians held with the intention of providing the wider audience with an idea of the interviewee's political views, policy statements and, obviously, media presence.

The development of a more conflictual, aggressive mode of conducting political interviews helps to counterbalance the status that politicians are institutionally endowed with when they appear as public figures in the media. In an extract from the BBC Editorial Guidelines[2] addressed to programme producers the following advice is given:

> **We should be clear when making requests for political interviews about the nature of the programme and context for which they are intended**. Our arrangements must stand up to public scrutiny and must not prevent the programme asking questions that our audiences would reasonably expect to hear. (emphasis in original)

The statement that the programme arrangements should not prevent questions "that our audiences would reasonably expect to hear" can be interpreted as a justification for these new interviewing techniques. Given the documentary shown at the beginning of the programme and the exasperation that the majority of *Panorama* viewers must have felt after almost eleven months of strike, interviewing Scargill certainly did "fit the nature of the programme". So most of Emery's questions can be interpreted, without exaggeration, as those that the audience would have expected to hear.

Research work on interviewing assumes that the power relations between interviewer and interviewee are skewed in favour of the interviewer, since s/he has the right to choose which questions to ask, even though the interviewee is still at liberty to refuse to answer a question (e.g. Jucker 1986, 2005). However, what normally occurs in political interviews is that the interviewee hedges proper answers to questions or uses the question as a means to expatiate at length on other issues (cf. the analysis of the interview between David Dimbleby and Tony Blair in Watts 2003: Chapter 9). We would prefer to consider power as playing a role in *all* social interaction, including any form of interviewing (Watts 1991; Locher 2004). Locher (2004: 38) uses both Watts' and Wartenberg's definitions of the exercise of power, which we present here as follows:

> *A* exercises power over *B* when *A* affects *B* in a manner contrary to *B*'s initially perceived interests, regardless of whether *B* later comes to accept the desirability of *A*'s actions.
>
> (Watts 1991: 62)

> A social agent *A* has *power over* another social agent *B* if and only if *A* strategically constraints B's action-environment.
>
> (Wartenberg 1990: 85, emphasis added)

The checklist Locher gives to summarise the nature and exercise of power contains the following propositions, which fit neatly into our way of viewing power in social practice:

- Power is (often) expressed through language.
- Power cannot be explained without contextualization.
- Power is relational, dynamic and contestable.
- The interconnectedness of language and society can also be seen in the display of power.
- Freedom of action is needed to exercise power.
- The restriction of an interactant's action-environment often leads to the exercise of power.
- The exercise of power involves a latent conflict and clash of interests, which can be obscured because of a society's ideologies.

(Locher 2004: 39–40)

Power, like impoliteness, is discursively negotiated and is always latently present in every instantiation of social practice. Indeed, power is intimately linked to individuals' perceptions of impolite behaviour, as we shall see in the analysis of the political interview.

Contextualising the interview

Before proceeding to our analysis, we need to give some important background information in order to place the interview into its proper socio-historical context. The 1984 miners' strike began in the South Yorkshire coalfield as a protest against the National Coal Board's (NCB) decision to close five pits in the area. The National Union of Mineworkers (NUM), whose president at the time was Arthur Scargill, officially supported the strike action but omitted to hold a national ballot among the union's members as to whether the union as a whole wanted to continue the strike. When challenged on this issue by Emery, Scargill states the following (the transcription conventions are given in the Appendix):

> [1]   I carried out the wishes and instructions of my members\and those instructions were/that we should not have a (.) national ballot under rule 43 \ (..) but that we should support the action that had already been taken by miners \ prior to me making any statement on the matter under national rule 41 \ (..) if I had have ignored that instruction \ I would have been guilty (..) of defying the conference of my union \

The "conference" of the NUM, however, is not to be equated with a democratic, rank and file vote, as Emery suggests to Scargill at a later point in the interview. In the documentary film preceding the interview, one of the miners had commented on the fact that, had Scargill chosen to ballot the union members' views earlier in the strike, he would probably have won, thus implying that support of the rank and file of union members has now dwindled considerably.

The strike openly played into the hands of the Conservative government of the time under Margaret Thatcher, who were determined not to give way. In fact, the NCB's closure plans went much further than the original five pits, as Scargill explicitly notes during the interview. Whether the Thatcher government *were* "guilty" of intervention with the Coal Board to prevent an agreement remains an allegation made by Scargill,[3] but close analysis of the interview appears to indicate the strength of Scargill's argument. The waste of large sums of taxpayers' money after 11 months of strike will not have disposed the television audience favourably to Scargill's attempted evasive tactics in answering Emery's first question: "Are you now willing to discuss uneconomic pits?"

[. . .]

The physical set-up of the interview in the studio is that of an oval table with Emery at one end and Scargill at the other. The camera switches from one participant to the other.[4] The only time when we have a frontal view of the whole table showing both the interviewer and the interviewee is in example [3] below when they indulge in a veritable 20-second tirade of incomprehensible simultaneous speech, which took one of the authors of this chapter at least two hours to transcribe.

Analysing the struggle for power

Given our comments on the conflictual nature of political interviews in the media and the BBC's own guidelines on the kinds of questions that audiences might reasonably be expected to hear, Emery's behaviour would appear to be sanctioned by a redefinition of the norms of appropriateness in this public form of social practice. The viewing audience are not likely to evaluate his utterances with adjectives such as *impolite, rude, insulting*, or *aggressive*, although the incomprehensible simultaneous speech in example [3] below might indeed be open to this kind of interpretation, as we shall argue later. Scargill, on the other hand, can frame[5] Emery's behaviour as having any of these qualities in order to present himself (and by extension the NUM) as the butt of unjustified criticism at the hands of the media. The problem is that

Scargill, as a public figure, must be aware of the norms of appropriateness in operation during the interview, and for this reason could hardly allow himself to use any of the adjectives listed above. The analysts' question, therefore, is how we can interpret Scargill's attempt to frame Emery as being impolite by other means.

The first evidence of such an attempt occurs shortly after the beginning of the interview in example [2]. The significant section of the sequence for our analysis is highlighted in grey:

[2]

---

1   E: peter taylor reporting \ well with me in the studio watching the film \ is mr arthur scargill \ president of the national union of mineworkers \ mr scargill \ (. .) the issue causing (. .) the breakdown (.) was all last week/the issue (. .) at the front of the news \ and in everybody's minds \ was the union's refusal to accept the closure of uneconomic pits \ are you now willing to discuss uneconomic pits \

    S: (. . .) we're not prepared to go along to the national coal board\ and

---

2   E: you're not \ sorry if I interrupt you (.) there \ y/ I-I/ let me just remind you that—

    S: start—   [er::] [er::] are you- are you going to let

---

3   E: you- you said you're not \ let's

    S: me answer the question \ you put a question \ for god's sake let me answer\

---

4   E: – let's have the (.) question again \ and see of we (..) get it right clear \ are you now willing to discuss uneconomic pits \   go ahead \

    S: (..) can I answer \

After introducing Scargill in stave 1, Emery goes on to contextualise the question he intends to put as being the issue "at the front of the news and in everybody's minds", thereby including the television audience through the pronoun *everybody*. The question concerns Scargill's and the NUM's willingness (or unwillingness) to discuss uneconomic pits. Scargill begins his answer in stave 1 but is stopped in his tracks by an intervention in stave 2, which Emery himself admits is an interruption. On being interrupted Scargill looks down and away from his interlocutor and compresses his lips with a down-turned corner of his mouth (Stillshot 1, overleaf). The posture shows him as having leaned back slightly from the force of the interruption. In other words, Scargill's facial expression and posture at this point in the interaction reveal what could be interpreted as resigned exasperation.

Emery's "you're not" (stave 2) is a pre-empted answer to his question, even though it is as yet unclear how Scargill would have answered had he been allowed to continue. His way out of the face-threatening situation is to apologise for the interruption, but the brief bout of stammering following the apology is evidence of a certain amount of insecurity. Scargill realises this and immediately intervenes with two filled pauses "[er::]" at the same time as Emery is producing the somewhat highminded moralistic utterance "let me just remind you that—" (stave 2).

Stillshot 1: Scargill's reaction to Emery's first interruption.

How does power play a role in the interpretation of this sequence? Emery has given the floor to Scargill but promptly restricts his freedom of action to answer in the way that he wants and not as Emery imagines he will. Restriction of Scargill's action-environment as the interviewee in a political interview is an exercise of power by Emery, and it is expressed through language. At the same time the restriction of an interviewee's action-environment is sanctioned to a certain extent in this interactional context.

In order to counter the exercise of power by Emery, it is essential that Scargill represents him as having acted rudely and aggressively without actually using either of these lexemes himself. His reassertion of the right to answer the question is accompanied by the emotional utterance "For God's sake let me answer!" indicating a negative evaluation of Emery's behaviour as violating the norms of appropriateness, as he frames them in this interaction, along the parameter of impoliteness. This is played upon in stave 4 when he mockingly asks for permission to answer the question when it is put the second time ("can I answer").

After example [2], Scargill is given the time to make a lengthy answer. Throughout, he avoids explicitly answering the question, although Emery (and presumably the television audience with him) infers that the preconditions that Scargill talks about at such great length are indeed preconditions placed on talks by the National Coal Board to the effect that uneconomic pits are indeed the issue. He changes tack in example [3], stave 2, by referring to BBC's Michael Eaton having "blown the gaff" the previous evening, only to be stopped once more by Emery:

[3]

---

1   E:
    S: those two points alone could resolve this dispute \ but you see \ michael eaton on bbc television

---

2   E: yes but bef-before we go on talking about what mr eaton said/ no \
    S: yesterday \ blew the gaff \ but you see/listen \ no no \ no no \ no no \ you've stopped me

---

3   E: you can take it up with Mr Eaton \ I interrupted you because you said \ (.) you were not
    S: once \ he/ no \ you interrupted me once \ (. . .) well we can go on like this—

---

4   E: prepared to discuss uneconomic pits \ right \ can I remind you what mr orme said in commons
    S: I'm sorry \ I did not say that \ no \ you- you can listen to me\

---

5   E: today \ (. .) no \ (. .) let me remind you what mr orme said \ he said that – yes \ but you take
    S: and I will give an answer first of all \ (. .) what happened was \ that mr eaton said yesterday on

---

6   E: that up with mr eaton \   yes \
    S: television \ that the twelve percent as capacity of this industry \ was going to be closed \ by the

---

7   E:
    S: national coal board \ twelve percent capacity equals sixty pit closures \ and sixty thousand jobs

---

8   E: yes \ the point is \ when I asked you whether you were prepared to discuss uneconomic pits \ and
    S: lost \

---

9   E: you said \ "no we're not" \ I interrupted then \ because mr orme said in the commons today/ let
       me remind you\ in the debate \ that the num's offer of unconditional talks means \ and I quote \
       that anyaspect can be discussed \ including . . .
    S:

Emery's initial interruption just after the beginning of the interview has put Scargill on his guard and this results in a 20-second free-for-all in which each of the two participants tries to restrict the other's freedom of action to take or retain the floor. The consequence is incomprehensibility on the part of anybody listening to the programme. The discursive struggle for power here is again linked to the notion of the norms of appropriacy in relational work. It is also at this point in the programme that we get a diagonal camera sequence, which means that both participants are visible to the audience (Stillshot 2). Throughout this 20-second sequence, Emery's manual gestures are evidence of an aggressive attempt to take over the floor, whereas Scargill uses his hands defensively to retain it.

We interpret the change of camera perspective as resulting from the necessity faced by the programme editor of deciding which of the two co-participants to focus on at that moment.

Stillshot 2: The camera angle during the 20-seconds overlap.

The diagonal shot is evidence of his/her dilemma. One of the possible conclusions that members of the audience may have made at this point in the interview is that the two co-participants are not only inconsiderate to one another but also towards the wider audience.

The co-participants' utterances during this 20–second sequence may or may not have been understood by members of the wider audience, but when we look at the transcript, we realise after the event that both participants were closely monitoring what the other was saying. For example, Emery makes the following statement in stave 3: "I interrupted you because you said you were not prepared to discuss uneconomic pits". He then uses the discourse marker "right" to induce Scargill to corroborate this fact and is immediately countered by Scargill's "I'm sorry. I did not say that" (stave 4). Once again, Emery is trying to restrict Scargill's freedom of action by framing him as not being prepared to discuss this issue.

Now, the problem here is to decide whether the implicature Emery has inferred from Scargill's unwillingness to discuss preconditions set by the NCB is valid. Let us return to the socio-historical contextualisation of the interview itself. The audience and both Emery and Scargill are aware that by this time in the strike (after 11 months) the "preconditions" that Scargill mentions concern the need to discuss the issue of uneconomic pits. So when Scargill talks about those preconditions for negotiation with the NCB he can only mean the need to discuss those pits. We conclude from this that Emery's implicature is indeed valid. On the other hand, Scargill is still perfectly justified in claiming that he did not *say* anything about uneconomic pits. At all events, Emery's framing of Scargill appears to have been successful when he repeats his accusation once more without being contradicted this time by Scargill: "When I asked you whether you were prepared to discuss uneconomic pits, and you said, 'No, we're not' . . . " (staves 8–9, example [3]).

Three further sequences will now be looked at briefly in which Emery comes very close to insulting Scargill. The first of these concerns the list of promises which Scargill originally made to the miners, their failure to have taken effect and Emery's accusation that Scargill doesn't have "any clout" in example [4]. Example [5] concerns the dispute over whether or not Scargill allowed the NUM to ballot the opinion of its members. Example [6] is the open accusation made by Emery but thinly disguised as being an opinion voiced by other trade union leaders and left wingers that Scargill is "a disaster" when it comes to negotiating:

[4]

1   E: but if-if-if that is a victory \ as you claim \
S: as it does to keep him at work \ producing coal \ (..) it doesn't make sense\

2   E: (..) and you promised them \ let me remind you \ all last summer \ that coal stocks were running
down \ that power cuts would soon come in august \ and by christmas \ and they wouldn't and so
on \ the fact is \ (..) you've got no clout \ have you \ to deliver on those promises you made to
S:

3   E: them \ how much longer are you going to ask your miners to suffer \
S: let me make two points first

4   E:
S: first of all \

[5]

1   E: look \ whatever the merits of your case \ let's look \ if we may \ at your tactics \ not having a
ballot \ when many of your own people/ ronnie mott we heard there in that film \ believed that
you might have won \ (.) had a ballot been held in favour of a strike \ not condemning picketing
violence was another thing which he also mentioned \ which alienated a lot of opinion from
your case\ making misleading promises \ as I mentioned \ having your funds sequestered\
S:

2   E: haven't you in fact let your members down \
S: (..) no \ I haven't \ I would let my members down if

3   E:
S: I betrayed them \ and I'd never do that \ first of all \ (..) don't say that I didn't have a ballot \ (. .) I

4   E: well you didn't \ did you \
S: carried out the wishes on the instruction—if you're going to keep interrupting when you

5   E: no \ I/ you said \ "don't say that I didn't have a ballot" \ and you didn't \ (..) go ahead \ (..) you
    S: ask me a question \

---

6   E: didn't have a ballot \
    S: (. . .) I carried out the wishes and instructions of my members \

[6]

---

1   E: do you know what they say about you \ (. .) other union leaders I've spoken to \ other left
       wingers \ they say that [er::] you make a marvellous advocate for your case \ but as a negotiator \
    S:

---

2   E: (..)you're a disaster \ (..) it's true \ isn't it \
    S: oh \ (. .) well of course \ it means that you're [er::] talking as

---

3   E:
    S: silly as they [er::] are \

The major issue in each of these three sequences is whether or not Emery can be considered to have gone beyond the bounds of the redefined norms of appropriate behaviour for a political interview. If any of these three sequences contains a blatant face attack directed at Scargill with an attempt to malign Scargill's character, both Scargill and the television audience would be justified in evaluating his behaviour as at least *impolite*, if not *aggressive* or downright *insulting*.

To say that a co-participant does not have clout and cannot deliver on promises made in example [4] is, admittedly, a weak form of insult, but it is the kind of statement that one might expect in present-day political interviews. It is, in other words, sanctioned[6] behaviour, and it is highly likely to have been expectable in the early 1980s. Scargill's response does not display a show of indignation; he simply goes on with the utterance "Let me make two points first of all." We would therefore suggest that Scargill does in fact accept the redefined norms of appropriate behaviour for televised political interviews, which strengthens our interpretation that he has tried to frame Emergy as being aggressive in example [2].

Accusing an interviewee of making misleading promises, implying that he has been undemocratic in not allowing the union to ballot the opinion of its members and is responsible for having the funds of his trade union sequestered in [5] are a little less severe, since, apart from Emery's personal evaluation of the promises having been misleading, it is true to say that the funds were sequestered and that the NUM did not have a ballot amongst its members. However, it is precisely these facts which are likely to damage Scargill's (and also the National Union of Mineworkers') public image if they are admitted. It is interesting to see that it is the accusation of not having held a ballot which causes the altercation which follows and not the accusation of being misleading or the sequestration of the union funds. Scargill chooses to challenge the one accusation which is a crystal-clear fact in the eyes of the general public (including Emery), and he resorts to the same strategy as at the beginning of the interview, viz. the framing of Emery as restricting his freedom of action to explain the matter by interrupting him.

By far the most damaging insult is the one put forward by Emery in [6], viz. that Scargill is a disaster when it comes to negotiating. The visual sequence of Scargill's reaction to this veiled insult shows an increased rate of blinking and a movement of the tongue across the lips possibly indicating a dry mouth at this point. This is the one point in the whole interaction, with the possible exception of Emery's initial interruptive sequence, at which Scargill might have been able to frame Emery as indulging in insulting behaviour. He is prevented from doing so by Emery's skilful embedding of the insult into alleged statements by third parties ("Do you know what they say about you, other union leaders I've spoken to, other left wingers? They say that . . . "; stave 1) and by inviting Scargill himself to comment on the truth of the proposition that he is a disaster ("It's true, isn't it?"; stave 2). Scargill's response is to frame both those who Emery claims have made this statement and Emery himself as "talking silly" (staves 2–3) and to launch into a self-righteous appraisal of his own past achievements as a negotiator in the Yorkshire coalfield.

In the absence of explicitly expressed evaluations of the co-participants' behaviour as going beyond the sanctioned norms of appropriate behaviour in a televised political interview, i.e. lexemes such as *impolite*, *rude*, *insulting*, *aggressive*, etc., we are forced to fall back on other utterances by the co-participant in the defensive position in a political interview, who is almost always the interviewee. What we have tried to do in this section is to demonstrate that we have to keep a close check on affective linguistic reactions such as "for God's sake let me answer" (example [2], stave 3), accusations of illicit behaviour such as "you interrupted me once" (example [3], stave 3), "don't say that I didn't have a ballot" (example [5], stave 3), "if you're going to keep interrupting when you ask me a question" (example [5], stave 4), or countering a perceived insult with another such as "it means that you're as silly as they are" (example [6], stave 2–3). We have suggested that a further rich source of evidence is to interpret the defensive co-participant's gestures, body posture and facial expressions as displaying frustration, indignation, shock, etc. Beyond that, one other method would be to record the reactions of the participants after the event, or in the case of the television audience to gather a set of verbalised reactions to what the viewers observed, which would be similar to collecting the various responses from an Internet discussion board [. . .]. While there is a danger that there might be a discrepancy between the *in situ* reaction and reaction after the event, there must be some kind of overlap to give the researcher interpretative clues.

One point should have emerged from our analys[is] [. . .], and that concerns the desirability of working from genuine data collected in instances of social practice and working from first-order notions of what participants in social practice categorise as impolite behaviour rather than working from an idealised theory of what impoliteness is. We shall investigate the consequences of this approach to impoliteness in the final section.

Implications and conclusions

Relational work refers to all aspects of the work invested by individuals in the construction, maintenance, reproduction and transformation of interpersonal relationships among those engaged in social practice. In this sense it is equivalent to facework, but only if we accept that facework is always present in any form of socio-communicative verbal interaction. If facework is only taken to refer to rationally motivated means of mitigating face-threatening acts, which is implicit in the Brown and Levinson understanding of facework, then it cannot always be taken to be present in social practice.

Goffman (1955) conceptualises face as "a socially attributed aspect of self that is on loan for the duration of the interaction in accordance with the line or lines that the individual has adopted for the purposes of [the] interaction" (Watts 2003: 105). He tends to look at the social side of face, whereas Brown and Levinson focus on its cognitive nature. Relational work understands face as combining the two, in that what an individual develops as his/her continual construction of self depends on social interaction, and social interaction takes place between individuals.

Relational work is always inherent in all forms of social practice, and it involves every individual's conceptualisation of the behaviour appropriate to the forms of social practice in which s/he is engaged. At the same time different conceptualisations depend crucially on the conceptualisations made by others, i.e. the work invested in constructing, maintaining, reproducing and transforming ongoing interpersonal relationships is at one and the same time both social and individual. It is, in other words, intersubjective.

We cannot therefore expect that the relational work that we carry out in every instance of social interaction that involves us as participants is always at a level of personal consciousness, and where it is not (which we would take to be the default situation), we suggest that it is socially unmarked. It is simply social behaviour which goes unnoticed, a part of what Bourdieu (1990) calls our "feel for the game", or, to use the notion of frames of expectation once again, part of what we are used to and expect to occur.

At any point in ongoing social interaction, however, something might occur which lies outside this frame of normality and which demands our attention as a co-participant since it doesn't fit the frame, and at such junctures in the overall social practice it demands that we make some kind of moral judgement. Marked behaviour of this kind might elicit positive evaluations, one of which would be to judge the behaviour as *polite*. Negatively marked behaviour, on the other hand, will evoke judgements of impoliteness, but it is also likely to evoke a wide range of possible responses ranging from the relatively neutral *impolite*, through *rude* to *boorish*, *aggressive, insulting, inconsiderate*, as well as a host of other negative judgements.

Our understanding of relational work entails an understanding of these judgements, whether positive or negative, as being discursively constructed and as being individual evaluations of the social behaviour of others. In this sense, both "politeness" and "impoliteness" are what we call first-order constructs and are not second-order terms in a rational, universal theory of politeness.

In this chapter we have focused on the negatively marked side of relational work in an attempt to tease out how those involved in ongoing social interaction evaluate the verbal behaviour of their co-participants. We have noted that, while making judgements about the behaviour of others *after the event* could easily entail the metapragmatic use of lexemes such as those given above, they are far less likely to be used metapragmatically during the course of an interaction. This makes it much more difficult for a researcher (also after the event) to make interpretations of negatively marked behaviour. In the Emery–Scargill interview we thus needed to pay close attention to comments made by either of the two participants during the interview, to study closely the visual signals revealing negative evaluations, to consider the wider implications of what is involved in producing a television broadcast of this type (the significance of the documentary film shown immediately prior to the interview, the physical set-up in the television studio, the editing being carried out live with camera shots, etc.) and, above all, to contextualise the sequence of social practice within a wider socio-political, socio-historical context. If the researcher is prepared to do all this (and probably much more than we have indicated in this chapter), then it is indeed possible to tease out negative evaluations of co-participants' behaviour which would lie within the range of impoliteness in the relational work being carried out.

It is also possible to see how forms of impoliteness (just like forms of politeness), even though they may be discursively disputed terms, are intimately involved in the exercise of power. It would not be possible to attribute attempts to gain and exercise power if relational work were not seen as a continually flexible, continually changing attempt to negotiate meaning in social practice, and it is for that reason that impoliteness, like politeness, is only a human universal if we are prepared to see it as the product of individual instances of social interaction.

Appendix

[. . .]
The transcript has been made with an adaptation of the Hiat transcription conventions (cf. Ehlich 1993) in which turns are represented horizontally in the form of musical staves rather than vertically as in a drama script. This takes up a little more space but is particularly useful to represent concurrent speech by two or more interactants.

Simplified transcription conventions:

\   end of a tone unit
/   "self-interruption" leading to a recycling of the turn
the- the repetition
——   unfinished utterance
::   lengthened syllables (only apparent here in the filled pause [er::])
[er::]   material included within square brackets refers to non-lexical utterances
(.)   unfilled pause of under 0.5 seconds
(..)   unfilled pause of between 0.5 and 1 second in length
(. . .)   unfilled pause of more than 1 second.

Notes

1   While Kienpointner (1997) uses the 'term' rudeness as an umbrella term, i.e. as a second order term, he still recognises that rudeness as well as politeness are not absolute terms.
2   Available at www.bbc.co.uk/guidelines/edguide/politics/politicalinterv.shtml [2006]. Although we don't have access to instructions given to editorial staff in the 1980s, we can assume that similar guidelines would have been issued at that time.
3   Scargill says "the fact is there was government intervention to stop it" and later "I condemn the f/ police brutality that I saw \ and massive state interference and intervention".
4   Our personal impression was that the physical set-up frames notions such as *distance* and *unreachability* and effectively turns the metaphor of the table as the locus of conciliation via negotiation into a metaphor of an unbridgeable gap between two irreconcilable points of view. In this way the sense of a gulf between interviewer and interviewee is heightened.
5   The term "frame" in this context should be understood slightly differently from expectation frames [. . .], but nevertheless as being related to them. We use "frame" in the present analysis to refer to ways in which individuals engaged in social practice *represent* others (including co-participants) through the various semiotic codes at their disposal. The difference between the two uses of "frame" is this: whereas frames of expectation are formed through earlier experience of social practice, representational frames are constructed in ongoing instances of social practice to represent the character traits, ideas and opinions of and even statements made by others. They are used as a means of creating in third persons (here the television audience) expectations as to how the represented others are likely to behave.

In the present sequence of social practice, the desired representation is one of inappropriate behaviour on the part of the other, i.e. Emery attempting to frame Scargill as behaving inappropriately, and vice versa.

6   Sanctioned behaviour does not automatically mean that it is normalised in its effect, i.e. that it does not hurt the recipient (cf. Culpeper 2005).

■ ■ ■

POST-READING

1   Locher and Watts suggest that 'politeness' and 'impoliteness' constitute evaluative judgements, and that these evaluative judgements are made at the point when behaviour is perceived as sitting outside the 'frame of normality' for a given activity (i.e. when behaviour doesn't 'fit the frame'). How useful is it, in your view, to view im/politeness in this way?

2   There are three occasions when, according to Locher and Watts, 'Emery comes very close to insulting Scargill'.
   •   What strategies does Emery use, which serve to allow Locher and Watts to claim these are 'close to' insults rather than constituting explicit insults?
   •   Are these strategies *role-specific*? Why/why not?
   •   In your view, does Emery ever go 'beyond the bounds of the redefined norms of appropriate behaviour for a political interview?' If so, when – and why?

3   The concept of power and impoliteness are closely linked, according to Locher and Watts – not just in 'any form of interviewing' but 'in *all* social interaction'. Do you agree? Why/why not?

4   Locher and Watts argue that their relational approach combines an interest in both the 'cognitive nature' of face (cf. Brown and Levinson) and also 'the social side of face' (see, e.g., Goffman's interest in the 'socially attributed aspect of self that is on loan for the duration of the interaction in accordance with the line or lines that the individual has adopted for the purposes of the interaction').
   •   Do you think that Locher and Watts' approach is a development of Brown and Levinson's 'face-saving' approach – or a reaction against it? Identify extracts from Locher and Watts which support your view.
   •   Where is Goffman's influence evident (if at all)? Again, provide extracts from the Locher and Watts reading as supporting evidence.

JONATHAN CULPEPER

IMPOLITENESS AND ENTERTAINMENT IN THE TELEVISION QUIZ SHOW
The Weakest Link

PRE-READING

As the title of this reading indicates, Culpeper explores impoliteness within a television quiz show. This suggests that impoliteness can be *entertaining*, under certain circumstances. Identify what circumstances need to be in place for you in order for you to find impoliteness entertaining. To what extent are the reasons you have highlighted *personal* to you, and to what extent do they reflect *cultural tendencies*, in your view?

IN-READING

1 *Off-record impoliteness* is not the same as 'insincere off-record politeness' (such as *mock politeness/sarcasm*) according to Culpeper (see first | in margin). Why is this?
2 Culpeper suggests the activity of answering (on quiz shows such as *The Weakest Link*) risks the face of contestants in at least five ways (see second | in margin). Note these down and then try to add one more of your own.

■ ■ ■

IMPOLITENESS AND ENTERTAINMENT IN THE TELEVISION QUIZ SHOW: *THE WEAKEST LINK*
JONATHAN CULPEPER

[. . .]
    [. . .] In my most recent work on impoliteness (2003), a collaboration with Derek Bousfield and Anne Wichmann, attention was drawn to a number of deficits in the original politeness model I proposed in 1996. We emphasized the need to go beyond the single speaker's utterance, lexically and grammatically defined. However, my original definition of impoliteness was not revised, simply restated in a slightly more succinct form as: "communicative strategies designed to attack face, and thereby cause social conflict and disharmony" (Culpeper et al. 2003: 1546). [. . .] [T]he assumption that face-attack will "cause social conflict and disharmony" [. . .] had

evolved by way of contrast to how researchers had defined politeness, for example: [The role of the Politeness Principle is] "to maintain the social equilibrium and the friendly relations which enable us to assume that our interlocutors are being cooperative in the first place" (Leech 1983: 82). But there are two problems here: it is not clear what this social conflict and disharmony consists of, and it is not a necessary condition of impoliteness having taken place. In fact, looking ahead to our discussion of *The Weakest Link*, it is not at all clear in what sense there is social conflict and disharmony here. Moreover, the definition fails to take adequately into account what the hearer is doing. This speaker bias is another legacy from politeness work, particularly that of Brown and Levinson (1987).

A better definition is proposed by Tracy and Tracy: "we define face-attacks as communicative acts perceived by members of a social community (and often intended by speakers) to be purposefully offensive" (1998: 227). [. . .] [T]he authors also refer to Goffman (1967), who relates such face-threat to cases where "the offending person may appear to have acted maliciously and spitefully, with the intention of causing open insult" (Goffman 1967: 14). However, their definition still needs some unpacking (e.g., in what ways might these attacks be unintended?), and the roles of the speaker and hearer are not very transparent. I thus propose a revised definition:

> Impoliteness comes about when: (1) the speaker communicates face-attack intentionally, or (2) the hearer perceives and/or constructs behaviour as intentionally face-attacking, or a combination of (1) and (2).

The key aspect of this definition is that it makes clear that impoliteness, as indeed politeness, is constructed in the interaction between speaker and hearer. [. . .] [T]he prototypical instance of impoliteness involves both (1) and (2), the speaker communicating face-attack intentionally and the hearer perceiving/constructing it as such. For example, a potentially impolite act such as an interruption may seem just to involve activity on the part of the speaker, but, as Bilmes (1997) convincingly argues, interruptions are a reciprocal activity, involving both "doing interrupting" and "doing being interrupted" (1997: 514–50). [. . .] [O]ther permutations of (1) and (2) are [also] possible. Face-attack may be intentionally communicated but fail to find its mark in any way, or, conversely, the hearer may perceive or construct intentional face-attack on the part of the speaker, when none was intended. Consider this example of the latter:

> [Context: An extended family is eating a meal at a Pizza Hut. There is a tense relationship between participants A and B.]
> A: Pass me a piece of garlic bread, will you?
> B: That'll be 50p
> [A opens purse and proceeds to give B 50p].

In this context, B's request for payment was intended as a joke – as banter. A, however, reconstructs it as a genuinely impolite act, thereby, attacking B herself by constructing him as mean. [. . .]

Two other aspects of my definition are noteworthy. Firstly, the notion of intention is of central importance, and it will be clear from [. . .] my references to Goffman why this is so (i.e., it helps us exclude by-product, accidental and mock types of face-threat). This can be related to Grice's distinction between "natural meaning" and "non-natural meaning": for an utterance to have non-natural meaning it must not merely have been uttered "with the intention of inducing a certain belief but also the utterer must have intended the "audience" to recognize the intention behind the utterance" (Grice [1957] 1989: 217). Impoliteness, then, has two layers: the offensive information being expressed by the utterance and the information that that information is being expressed intentionally.[1] Of course, recognizing intentions is highly problematic: they have to be inferred in communication. A corollary of this is that recognizing categories like "by-product", "accidental" and "mock" is a matter of inferencing not just signaling. Secondly, it will be clear that I am not abandoning the concept of "face", despite criticisms in the literature, particularly with regard to Brown and Levinson's notion of negative face having a "Western" bias in focusing on individual autonomy (e.g., Matsumoto 1988; Gu 1990; for a more general critique of "face", see Bargiela-Chiappini 2003). Impoliteness concerns offense, and face, in my view, still represents the best way of understanding offense. Of course, face should be more adequately conceptualized and contextually sensitive. Helen Spencer-Oatey (e.g., 2002) is one of the few researchers to [. . .] propose definitions based on solid empirical work. Space precludes a full outline of her proposals, but I offer a brief summary in Table 6.4.1.

The notion of face is split into two components. Quality face is clearly present in Brown and Levinson's (1987) notion of positive face, and there are hints of social identity face. Spencer-Oatey explicitly splits two very different components: the former being an individual or personal aspect, and the latter being a matter of one's identity in the group. Already, one can see how we are moving away from Brown and Levinson's (1987) emphasis on individual autonomy. Interestingly, "sociality rights" are not considered face issues, "in that an infringement of sociality rights may simply lead to annoyance or irritation, rather than to a sense of face-threat or loss

Table 6.4.1 Revising the notion of face: components of "rapport management"

Face (defined with reference to Goffman (1972: 5): "the positive social *value* a person effectively claims for himself [sic] by the line others assume he has taken during a particular contact" [Spencer-Oatey's emphasis])	*Quality face:* "We have a fundamental desire for people to evaluate us positively in terms of our personal qualities, e.g., our confidence, abilities, appearance etc." *Social identity face:* "We have a fundamental desire for people to acknowledge and uphold our social identities or roles, e.g., as group leader, valued customer, close friend."
Sociality rights (defined as "fundamental personal/social *entitlements* that a person effectively claims for him/herself in his/her interactions with others" [Spencer-Oatey's emphasis])	*Equity rights:* "We have a fundamental belief that we are entitled to personal consideration from others, so that we are treated fairly, that we are not unduly imposed upon or unfairly ordered about, that we are not taken advantage of or exploited, and that we receive the benefits to which we are entitled." *Association rights:* "We have a fundamental belief that we are entitled to association with others that is in keeping with the type of relationship that we have with them."

Source: Spencer-Oatey (2002: 540–2)[2]

(although it is possible, of course, that both will occur)" (Spencer-Oatey 2002: 541). Brown and Levinson's (1987) notion of negative face overlaps primarily with the notion of equity rights, in as far as they relate to matters of imposition and costs/benefits, but it also overlaps to a degree with association rights. I will refer to all these components in my analyses of impoliteness in *The Weakest Link*, but the most relevant components are Quality face (e.g., attacks on the inadequacy of the contestant in answering the questions) and Social Identity face (e.g., attacks on the contestant's regional accent and job).

A model of impoliteness

[. . .] In so far as theories have predictive power, the model of impoliteness I have been developing is not yet a theory. Two areas in particular need attention. Firstly, impoliteness is not inherent in particular linguistic and non-linguistic signals. The same argument for politeness is made repeatedly by Watts (2003). This is not to refute the fact that some linguistic items are very heavily biased towards an impolite interpretation (one has to work quite hard to imagine contexts in which "you fucking cunt" would not be considered impolite). Nevertheless, this instability means that impoliteness comes about in the interaction between linguistic and non-linguistic signals and the context, and so context must be fully factored in. Some work on the co-text was undertaken in Culpeper et al. (2003), but we still know little about the effect of particular social relations (e.g., power) and of the activity type in which the impoliteness takes place. This paper has as one of its aims an examination of a particular genre or activity type. Secondly, descriptions of politeness and impoliteness tend to over-emphasize lexical and grammatical resources, and hence they have a limited view of the communicative signal. Work on prosody undertaken in Culpeper et al. (2003) by Anne Wichmann made a start in improving this situation. A particular aim of the present study is to emphasize the importance of prosody in descriptions of impoliteness, and in *The Weakest Link* in particular.

It is appropriate at this point to re-state my impoliteness model in brief, because I will refer to it in this paper and because I wish to develop it further:

> *Bald on record impoliteness*: the FTA is performed in a direct, clear, unambiguous and concise way in circumstances where face is not irrelevant or minimized.

> *Positive impoliteness*: the use of strategies designed to damage the addressee's positive face wants, e.g., ignore the other, exclude the other from an activity, be disinterested, unconcerned, unsympathetic, use inappropriate identity markers, use obscure or secretive language, seek disagreement, use taboo words, call the other names.

> *Negative impoliteness*: the use of strategies designed to damage the addressee's negative face wants, e.g., frighten, condescend, scorn or ridicule, be contemptuous, do not treat the other seriously, belittle the other, invade the other's space (literally or metaphorically), explicitly associate the other with a negative aspect (personalize, use the pronouns "I" and "You"), put the other's indebtedness on record.

> *Sarcasm or mock politeness*: the FTA is performed with the use of politeness strategies that are obviously insincere, and thus remain surface realisations.

> *Withhold politeness*: the absence of politeness work where it would be expected. For example, failing to thank somebody for a present may be taken as deliberate impoliteness.
> (Summarized from Culpeper 1996: 356–7)

[. . .]

Each of the super strategies was originally modeled on a politeness counterpart in Brown and Levinson's (1987) politeness framework, with one apparent exception – "sarcasm or mock politeness" – which [was] [. . .] inspired by Leech's (1983) conception of irony [(i.e.).] [. . .] using politeness for impoliteness. [. . .]

[. . .] [C]onsider this example:

[Context: From the television program *Pop Idol*, hosted by Ant and Dec. The aim of the show is to select the best contestant from numerous would-be pop stars. This extract occurs in one of the later programs in a series, when the number of contestants is down to 10. It occurs at the beginning of the program. The judges sit in front of the studio audience and can hear all that is said.]

Ant: Our judges have been accused of being ill-informed, opinionated and rude.
Dec: We'd like to set the record straight: our judges are not ill-in-formed.

In some ways, this appears to fit the notion of off-record politeness. [. . .] [A]n "impolite" belief that they are "opinionated and rude" is not stated – an ostensibly polite maneuver. Moreover, setting "the record straight" raises expectations of a polite defense. However, they very obviously fail to set the whole record straight, thus flouting the maxim of quantity and generating the strong implicature that the accusation that the judges are "opinionated and rude" is true. The blatant way in which this happens would make it very difficult for Ant and Dec to deny the implicature. In sum, what we have here is insincere off-record politeness: it is not a genuine attempt to avoid causing offense. As such, it falls within my category of sarcasm.

However, there is a further kind of off-recordness or indirectness that is not covered by any of my categories. Consider the following example, specifically, the emboldened part:[3]

[Context: From the film *Scent of a Woman*. Charlie (CH) is a student at a prestigious private school, but he is not rich and is supported by student aid. In order to make ends meet, rather than go home for Thanksgiving, he responds to an advertisement asking for somebody to act as a carer for a blind relative – the Colonel (COL). The dialogue below occurs a few turns into their first encounter.]

COL: Simms Charles, senior. You on student aid, Simms?
CH: Ah, yes I am.
COL: For student aid read crook. Your father peddles car telephones at a 300% mark-up; your mother works on heavy commission in a camera store, graduated to it from expresso machines. Ha, ha! **What are you . . . dying of some wasting disease?**
CH: No . . . I'm right here.

This is not at all cooperative in Grice's (1975) sense, and, as with off-record politeness, the "impolite" belief is conveyed by implication. It is a rhetorical question that implicates, via the maxim of quality, the impolite belief that there is evidence that Charlie is dying of a wasting disease. However, this is not like the sarcasm examples that have as one of their defining features some claim, no matter how superficial, to be polite. The Colonel's utterance has no such claim. What we have here is the off-record (in the sense that it flouts a maxim) expression of impoliteness. I thus propose an additional category for my impoliteness model:

Off-record impoliteness: the FTA is performed by means of an implicature but in such a way that one attributable intention clearly out-weighs any others.

[. . .] I shall illustrate off-record impoliteness further in my analyses of *The Weakest Link*.

Impoliteness as entertainment

[. . .]

Quiz shows are a specific type of game show [. . .] based on a competition: identifying either a winner through the elimination of participants from the game, or the amount of money an individual is to be rewarded with. [. . .] Quiz shows vary according to (amongst other things) the amount and kind of "chat" that is allowed. The term "chat" is used by Tolson (1991: 179) to refer to:

> a clear shift of *register* within the program format where it occurs, such that the primary business of the format is temporarily delayed or suspended. Thus in the context of the game show, chat between participants delays the actual playing of the game [. . .]

[. . .] With quiz shows, the "primary business of the format" is clearly the question-answer sequences comprising the quiz. But this format does not offer much scope for humiliating participants. Chat reflecting on the proceedings has much more to offer, not least of all because it can involve a shift towards personal/private matters. In *The Weakest Link*, chat occurs after a round of questions and answers, and has the following structure:

1. The host evaluates the round in general and initiates the discovery of the "weakest link" (i.e., the person who got most answers wrong).
2. Contestants nominate who they think is the "weakest link".
3. The host interacts with each contestant in turn, ostensibly in order to reveal their performance in the quiz.
4. The contestant with the most nominations leaves (a voice-over reveals to the TV audience whether they had in fact got the most questions wrong).

[. . .] [I]mportantly, this chat [. . .] is non-supportive. In fact, the program is structured to maximize the potential for face-damage. The reasons why *The Weakest Link* has great potential for face-damage include:

- Answers are given in public. Face is fundamentally related to what others think – "the positive social value a person effectively claims for himself [sic] by the line others assume he [sic] has taken during a particular contact" (Goffman 1967: 5). Greater public exposure means that more face is at stake.
- Answers are given by individuals, and thus they have complete responsibility for them. Contrast this with *University Challenge*, where some answers are given by the team.
- The easier the question is thought to be, the more foolish the contestant may feel if the answer is wrong. The questions on *The Weakest Link* are considerably easier than those on *University Challenge*. The fact that contestants still get them wrong probably has more to do with the high-pressure situation.

- There is no pre-answer sympathizing chat to reduce the impact of an incorrect answer. On *Who Wants to Be a Millionaire*, Chris Tarrant's frequent supportive comment is "the questions are only easy if you know the answer".
- The chat allows reflection on the inadequacy of the answers, and thus the answers. On *University Challenge* chat is minimal, and on *Who Wants to Be a Millionaire* chat occurs before the answer is given.
- The chat allows a shift towards personal aspects, and thus aspects which may be more face-sensitive.

ANNE ROBINSON

Central to the success of *The Weakest Link* has been the host, Anne Robinson. [. . .] She came to be more generally known to the British public through her caustic articles for various tabloid newspapers. She has developed this caustic style for the purposes of the persona she presents on *The Weakest Link*, as these quotations from the BBC website make clear:

> A cross between Cruella de Vil, a dominatrix and a bossy school ma'am . . . all names given to the flame-haired presenter of the Weakest Link. It has also earned her the title of the Rudest Woman on Television.

> The program has attracted up to fifteen million viewers, and Anne's contemptuous and dismissive phrase **"You are the Weakest Link, good-bye"**, has become something of a national catchphrase.

> Anne Robinson's acid delivery and her verbal put-downs have given her a reputation as the rudest person on television. *"You're a coward, aren't you?"; "We're not fainting with admiration here"; "pathetic"; "appalling"; "shameful"; "stupid."* – just some of Anne's choicer phrases!

> www.bbc.co.uk/weakestlink.shtml

WHO-QUESTIONS AND YES-NO QUESTIONS

> Who should sling their hook? Who isn't performing? Who is a waste of rations? Who should go and lock themselves in a darkened room? Who's tripped up just once too often? Who is several sandwiches short of a picnic? Who's not coming up with the goods? Whose time is up? Whose lights will be turned out? Whose train fare could have been better spent? Did you go to school? Lost the plot? Running on empty?

All these who-questions and yes-no questions achieve their impoliteness by implication. They are rhetorical questions implicating impolite beliefs that there is somebody who should sling their hook, who isn't performing, or who didn't go to school, is lost, etc. Note also that several are metaphorical: people don't have hooks or lights, and are not rations, picnics or cars. Rhetorical questions and metaphors both flout the maxim of quality. These are off-record strategies expressing impolite beliefs – they are off-record impoliteness.

(PSEUDO) APHORISMS

He who stumbles should not survive; He who hesitates deserves a hard time

Both of these instances are intertextual: the first is from Apostles, the second is modeled on the age-old adage "he who hesitates is lost". Because they are not straightforward expressions, they flout the maxim of manner. Again, we have off-record impoliteness.

SOUND PATTERNS

Despatch the deadwood; Sack the culprit; Give the heave-ho to the hopeless; Root out the rubbish; Dazed and confused; Waste of space.

All these instances contain obvious sound pattering. They flout the maxim of manner, implicating particular impolite beliefs. Again, we have off-record impoliteness.

One important aspect of all of the above examples is that they have a degree of creativity. But also note that they are nearly all based-on or incorporate a formula of some kind. The first group, with the exception of "Did you go to school?" and possibly "Whose lights will be turned out?", incorporate the following formulaic expressions:[4]

sling [possessive determiner] hook; waste of rations; lock [reflexive pronoun] in a darkened room; once too often; several [plural noun phrase] short of a [noun phrase]; coming up with the goods; time is up; could have been better spent; lost the plot; running on empty.

Furthermore, the second group, the (pseudo) aphorisms, is clearly based on a formulaic expression drawn from the original text, and the third group, the sound patterns, is mostly based on a semi-fixed grammatical frame: "[verb, usually imperative] the [noun]" (perhaps a frame evolved from "give the heave-ho"). However, note also that the use of some of these formulae is somewhat creative. For example, "he who hesitates deserves a hard time" adopts a creatively original predicate "deserves a hard time" instead of "is lost"; "give the heave-ho" becomes part of a creative alliterative pattern with the addition of "to the hopeless". These characteristics, the use of formulae and the creative or "clever" use of language, raise a serious issue, for these are amongst the characteristics of ritualized banter (Labov 1972b). According to the definition of impoliteness outlined [previously], this is mock impoliteness not genuine impoliteness. [. . .]

PROSODIC ASPECTS OF SOME CATCHPHRASES

[. . .] The catchphrase "you are the weakest link goodbye" is [. . .] cited on the BBC website as being one of Anne Robinson's particular "contemptuous and dismissive" phrases [. . .]. "You are the weakest link" does [. . .] express a negative belief, but it is not at all obvious that this alone qualifies it as being "contemptuous and dismissive". For this, we must look to the prosody.[5] Figure 6.4.1 displays the results of an instrumental analysis of this phrase, which can be heard at: www.bbc.co.uk/weakestlink/clips/classic/ index.shtml.[6]

The figure consists of three tiers. The first at the top is a spectogram, representing fluctuations in air pressure. It provides indications of relative loudness (intensity) and duration. The second is a fundamental frequency graph, representing changes in pitch (fundamental

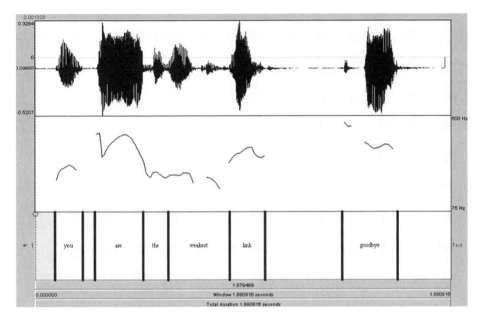

Figure 6.4.1 Instrumental analysis of "you are the weakest link goodbye".

frequency expressed in Hertz) over time. It provides an indication of the intonation contour of the utterance. The third contains the words that were spoken. Note that there is no direct relationship between these figures and meaning. The acoustic features represented in these figures are cues that may trigger the perception of phonological features, and then those features may in turn be used in an inference process to generate particular meanings.

As Figure 6.4.1 makes clear, the catchphrase is made up of two distinct tone units, "you are the weakest link" and "goodbye". Regarding the first, heavy stress falls on "are". This can be seen from the pitch prominence, and the loudness and duration. Notice also that there is a brief pause immediately before "are", giving the stress even greater perceptual prominence. In terms of Sperber and Wilson's (1986) relevance theory, such heavy stress makes a claim on our attention, and thus guarantees some informational reward. That information might be an interpretation such as: "the suspicion was that you were the weakest link; I am now confirming that you *really are* the weakest link". This implication exacerbates the attack on Quality Face. Turning to the second distinct tone group, "goodbye", this utterance fits the vocal characteristics of "anger/frustration", such as slightly faster tempo, tense articulation, and – as is transparent from the figure – much higher pitch average (cf. Murray and Arnott 1993: 1103–4, and refs therein). Furthermore, note the intonation contour is that of a fall with a very high starting point – a pattern that is likely to suggest finality to the hearer (cf. Wichmann 2000: 69–71). This rapid dismissal of the contestant primarily attacks Equity Rights (e.g., the belief that we are [e]ntitled to "fair dismissal"), but also has important secondary implications for Quality Face, as it implies their lack of value. [. . .]

The second catchphrase I will consider is "you leave with nothing", which can be heard at: www.bbc.co.uk/weakestlink/clips/classic/ index.shtml. Figure 6.4.2 displays the results of instrument of analysis.

An important feature of this catchphrase is that it forms two distinct tone units, "you leave with" and "nothing". Unlike the tone units "you are the weakest link" and "goodbye", the break

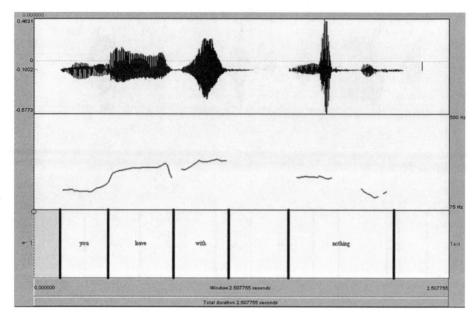

Figure 6.4.2 Instrumental analysis of "you leave with nothing".

here occurs between the preposition "with" and its complement "nothing": it is a salient disruption. To understand this break, one needs to remember what happens in standard game shows. When a contestant must leave, they leave with a prize, even if it is only a consolation prize, and the host announces the prize as a surprise: hence, rising intonation on "you leave with" and then a dramatic pause before the prize is revealed. Anne Robinson's impoliteness here feeds off this strategy: instead of the expected prize, the contestant gets "nothing". Also, note that the second tone unit does not contain the kind of prosody one might expect of jubilation. "Nothing" steps down the pitch range, relative to the preceding discourse, and contains a falling tone, thereby adding an air of deflation and a sense of finality (cf. Wichmann 2000: 69–71). The explicit withholding or frustration of reward can be seen as Equity rights impoliteness, as it works by reminding the contestant that a "benefit" has been withheld (it also has secondary implications for Quality Face, as withholding the benefit implies that the contestant was not good enough to merit it).

THE WEAKEST LINK: AN EXTRACT FROM A STANDARD EPISODE

I will now analyze an extract from a standard (i.e., not a celebrity special) episode of *The Weakest Link* screened on BBC2 (March 6, 2003). I supply a broad orthographic transcription below, the emboldened parts being the ones to which my phonetic and prosodic analyses will pay particular attention (AR = Anne Robinson):

```
1    AR:       so Danny what do you do
2    Danny:    I'm a sales consultant Anne but I'm also a part-time football referee
[. . .]
5    AR:       is that different from a salesman
6    Danny:    it's a posh word Anne
```

7	AR:	well you don't come from a posh place do you
8	Danny:	a little bit harsh Anne, I live in Solihull now so I've moved up.
9	AR:	what was wrong with Liverpool
10	Danny:	**eer**
11	AR:	**eeh**
12	Danny:	[*laughter*] it's quite a rough place so I wanted to better myself so I moved to the Midlands to er give the Brummies a bit of humour . .
13	AR:	why Chris
14	Danny:	she was unlucky to get a question on football and I've er postponed a few matches myself so that question stuck in my mind
[. . .]		
23	AR:	so you're a fitness instructor [Jay
24	Jay:	[I am Anne
25	AR:	who trained you
26	Jay:	**the Australian army trained me**
27	AR:	oh. **is that why you go up in all your sentences**
28	Jay:	**yes.**

MIMICRY

[. . .]

Danny's pause-filler "er" is articulated further to the front of the mouth than would be the case in RP (Anne Robinson's accent, broadly speaking), which would be closer to [ə]. This is a characteristic of his Liverpool accent. The position of Danny's "er" relative to other vowel sounds is represented by star in the upper chart of Figure 6.4.3.[7] Anne Robinson provides an echo of Danny which is even more to the front than would be normal for a Liverpool accent. This is shown in the lower chart of Figure 6.4.3.

Mimicry, here, consists of a caricatured re-presentation. As Goffman (1974: 539) points out, mimicry involves quoting someone, and a quotation will involve features of the original accent and gestural behavior as well. But if one quotes "too much" (e.g., all the original speaker's prosodic features) the quoter becomes "suspect". This is the kind of mimicry that interests me. But what exactly counts as "too much"? To recognize a "quotation" as such and to infer the speaker's meaning, requires inferential work. One can conceive impolite mimicry as a special case of Sperber and Wilson's (1986) echoic irony, where the "echo" is of somebody's behavior (typically, a characteristic behavior), rather than their verbal utterance or thoughts. According to Sperber and Wilson (1986: 240), the recovery of the relevant implicatures depends:

> first, on a recognition of the utterance as an echo; second, on an identification of the source of the opinion echoed; and third, on a recognition that the speaker's attitude to the opinion echoed is one of rejection or disapproval.

Mimicry requires broadening of the term "utterance" by replacing it with "behavior", the replacement of the abstract term "opinion" with "behavior", and an extra element (the third item):

> first, on a recognition of the behaviour as an echo; second, on an identification of the source of the behaviour echoed; third, the recognition that the source behaviour is a characteristic of the speaker who gave rise to it, and fourthly, on a recognition that the speaker's attitude to the behaviour echoed is one of rejection or disapproval.

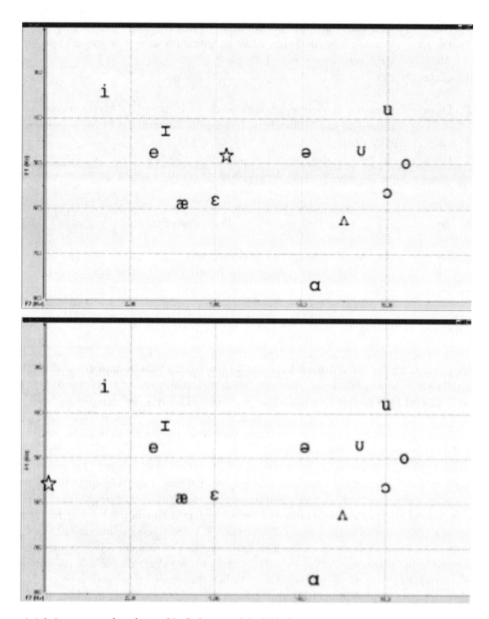

Figure 6.4.3 Insturmental analysis of "er" above and "eeh" below.

So, the hearer must recognize Anne Robinson's "eh" as an echo, Danny's "er" as the source of the echo, Danny's particular articulation of "er" as one of his characteristics (i.e., of his Liverpool accent), and then must work out Anne Robinson's attitude. Regarding the final point, Sperber and Wilson (1986: 241) state: "[g]enuine irony is echoic, and is primarily designed to ridicule the opinion echoed". Whilst I am not convinced that their sweeping statement applies to all types of irony, it does fit mimicry. [. . .]

[. . .] In terms of my impoliteness model, mimicry best fits Equity Rights impoliteness, since it casts judgment downwards from a position of power. But, as with many other politeness and impoliteness strategies, there are other social implications. Importantly, mimicry also attacks

Social Identity Face, since it implies that an identity characteristic of the speaker, such as regional accent, is odd or unpleasant. Note that Danny's laughter seems to be a counter strategy – an attempt to "laugh off" the attack. But note also that the laughter is some evidence of the fact that Danny might have perceived Anne Robinson as being impolite in the first place. How genuine that impoliteness is, of course, an issue, not least of all because, paradoxically, Anne Robinson herself originally comes from Liverpool.

[The extract contains a second example of mimicry involving the accent of Jay, the Australian: see lines 26–8]. [. . .] As is clear from the orthographic transcription, Anne Robinson draws attention to a feature of Jay's pronunciation. The high rising tone (or Australian question intonation) is a well-known feature of Australian English (e.g., Guy and Vonwiller 1989), not just in academic circles but also more generally through its discussion in the media. It refers to the use of rising contours, which one might expect to correlate with questions, for statements. Although Anne Robinson's *words* draw attention to a characteristic of Jay's speech, there are no obvious implications of unpleasantness, because the mimicry is conveyed by the prosody. Let us first look at Jay's immediately preceding discourse, as represented in Figure 6.4.4.

Rising intonation is not transparent here. There is a slight rise on "army" and more clearly on "me". But the fact that there are not clear rises is not important for Anne Robinson, since there are other features that are characteristic of the Australian accent. For example, Australian English speakers tend to have a narrower range of pitch, and this is quite noticeable in the figure. Also, various segmental features are marked. For example, the first vowel in "army" is closer to the [a:] of broad Australian English than the [ɑ:] of RP (and of Anne Robinson). In sum, Jay sounds Australian, and this affords Anne Robinson the grounds for strongly implying that he has the stereotypical Australian feature of the high rising tone. Anne Robinson's echo is represented in Figure 6.4.5.

Anne Robinson produces an echoic acoustic caricature of a purported feature of Jay's prosody. She attacks his Social Identity Face. Interestingly, Anne Robinson utters a yes/no

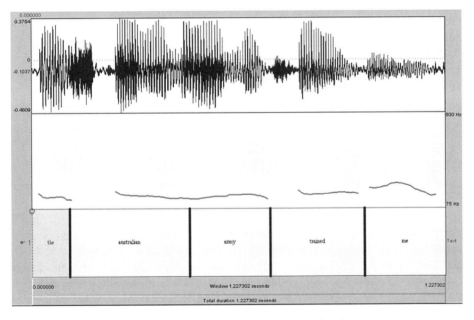

Figure 6.4.4 An instrumental analysis of "the Australian army trained me".

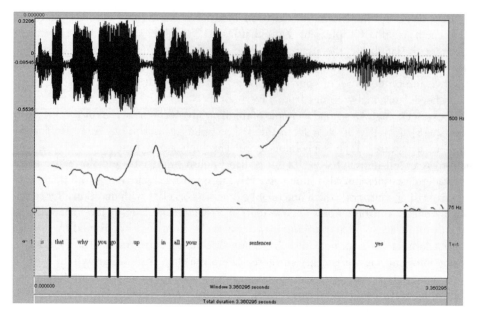

Figure 6.4.5 An instrumental analysis of "is that why you go up in all your sentences" and "yes".

question, which would normally carry a rising tone (e.g., Quirk et al. 1985: 807). In order to carry-off the mimicry of the high rise, she produces two exaggerated rises: one on "up" and one at the end of her utterance on "sentences". The fact that Jay's original prosody bears only the faintest relation to her caricature is not an issue: mimicry can work by attributing a behavior to the target, regardless of how apparent or real that behavior is.

With the above discussions in mind, I can state that impolite mimicry involves the following elements:

The echo. The production and recognition of a behavior as not only an echo, but also a distortion of the echoed behavior.

The echoed behavior. An identification (or attribution to the target) of the behavior which was echoed (typically, an identity characteristic of the person who gave rise to it).

The echoer. A recognition that the attitude of the person who produced the echo is one of ridicule towards the person identified as (or attributed with being) the source of the echoed behavior.

Finally, note that Jay's response, "yes", apparently accepts the face-damage. However, as shown in Figure 6.4.4, it is much lower in pitch. As Wichmann (2000: 139ff.) points out, speakers can do conflicting things by simultaneously signaling "disaffiliation" through a marked shift in pitch and loudness, whilst uttering cooperative words. This is an impoliteness counter-strategy that hovers between accepting and blocking the face-attack. It has the advantage that it is difficult to counter, since disaffiliation could be denied.

[. . .]

Is offense really communicated and taken by participants in the context of *The Weakest Link*? [. . .]

As a preliminary to addressing this question, it is instructive to consider Watts' (2003) distinction between "politic behaviour" and "politeness". In doing so, we will see that Watts alludes to three different types of "impoliteness". Politic behavior is "perceived to be appropriate to the social constraints of the ongoing interaction", whereas politeness is "perceived to go beyond what is expectable, i.e., salient behaviour" (Watts 2003: 19). Some researchers see politeness as a matter of doing what is appropriate, but Watts is clearly right in allowing for the fact that people frequently do more than what is appropriate. The distinction Watts makes, in my view, is not absolute but a matter of degree. It captures the difference between highly routinized behaviors, such as greetings and leave-takings, and behaviors which are more elaborate, inviting, as Watts sees it, "potential classification" as politeness. This politeness, he argues, can be evaluated positively or negatively (e.g., it could include "potential irony, aggressiveness, abuse, etc.") (Watts 2003: 161). Given Watts' concerns with people's actual usage and understanding of terms like "politeness", it seems a little odd to talk of negatively evaluated politeness. This, the first type of "impoliteness", seems to be what I would understand by my impoliteness superstrategy of "sarcasm". Watts goes on to say that if politic behavior is "missing", it "tend[s] to lead to an evaluation of a participant's behavior as 'impolite', 'brash', 'inconsiderate', 'abrupt', 'rude', etc." (Watts 2003: 169; see also 131, 182). If the politic behavior is intentionally missed out, then this, the second type of "impoliteness", would equate with my impoliteness superstrategy of "withhold politeness". For cases where the absence of politic behavior is unintentional, I have reserved the term "rudeness". Watts also refers to a third kind of "impoliteness": "sanctioned aggressive facework" (Watts 2003: 260). According to Watts (2003: 131–2):

> certain social interaction types have interaction orders with lines [in Goffman's facework sense] that *sanction or neutralise face-threatening* or *face-damaging acts*, e.g., interaction between family members or among close friends, competitive forms of interaction such as political debate, rigidly hierarchised forms of interaction, e.g., in the military services.

This type of behavior is pertinent to my discussion of *The Weakest Link*: is it the case that here we have one of those social interaction types that sanction or neutralize face-threat or damage?

In one sense Anne Robinson's behavior is non-politic: [. . .] exploitative quiz shows run counter to the generic "polite" norms – the politic behavior – of standard shows. However, the issue is whether the exploitative quiz show *The Weakest Link* constitutes its own social interaction type [or activity type] which sanctions or neutralizes "impolite" behaviors. [. . .] [. . .]
[. . .]
According to Levinson, the notion of activity type:

> refers to any culturally recognized activity, whether or not that activity is coextensive with a period of speech or indeed whether any talk takes place in it at all [. . .] In particular, I take the notion of an activity type to refer to a fuzzy category whose focal members are goal-defined, socially constituted, bounded events with *constraints* on participants, setting, and so on, but above all on the kinds of allowable contributions. Paradigm examples would be teaching, a job interview, a jural interrogation, a football game, a task in a workshop, a dinner party, and so on.
>
> (1992: 69)

Levinson goes on to say that:

> Because of the strict constraints on contributions to any particular activity, there are corresponding strong expectations about the functions that any utterances at a certain point in the proceedings can be fulfilling.
>
> (1992: 79)

And this has the important consequence that: "[activity types] help to determine how what one says will be 'taken' – that is, what kinds of inferences will be made from what is said" (1992: 97). The (im)politeness value of an utterance is partly determined by the activity of which it is a part. A good example is ritualized banter (or "sounding", "playing the dozens") (see Labov 1972b). In brief, this activity type takes place between friends (or members of an "in-group") and involves the trading of formulaic insults, the suspension of the maxim of quality (typically, insults cannot be literally true), and the demonstration of cleverness (e.g., the use of poetic effects such as metrical rhythm and rhyme). Within this activity type, insults are not to be taken as impolite, but act socially to reinforce the group.

How might this work in relation to *The Weakest Link*? *The Weakest Link* is a game show, constituted by a certain structure and certain conversational acts, as I have already elaborated in this paper. Moreover, it has formulaic elements (e.g., the catchphrases and one-liners discussed above) and verbal cleverness (e.g., the one-liners). Rather like ritualized banter, all this might suggest that the "impoliteness" is not being taken seriously. Moreover, the participant responsible for producing most of the potentially "impolite" utterances is a persona Anne Robinson created for the show – it is a fiction. This means that one cannot straight-forwardly attribute face-attacking intentions to Anne Robinson. A similar point is made by Montgomery (1999: 144) in his discussion of the chat show host Mrs Merton:

> In order for a guest to take issue with a threat to face in the moment by moment conduct of the discourse, would require them to treat Mrs Merton seriously as if she were indeed a real person issuing a real FTA. Instead the rather elaborately contrived persona of Mrs Merton gives a mock or playful quality to the performance of the discourse.

All this means that *theoretically* it is difficult for a hearer to "take" what the host says as intentionally face-attacking, since the face-attack can be seen as a function of the game and not a personal goal. One might argue then that the "impoliteness" is not only sanctioned by the dominant group (e.g., the people who create, produce and host the show), but neutralized by the nature of the activity type.

However, *in practice* things are less straightforward. What concerns me is that people can and do still take offense in such situations [. . .] [For example, a]fter Danny's pause-filler is mimicked, he produces a nervous laugh and looks down; [. . .] after Jay's high-rising tone is mimicked, he produces a prosodically disaffiliating "yes" and a smile. These actions suggest that they have taken Anne Robinson's words as an attack. Moreover, these non-verbal features suggest emotional reactions such as embarrassment. [. . .] There is also occasional evidence of embarrassment, humiliation and distress in the comments made to the camera by the contestants themselves after they have been voted off. But if the "impoliteness" is supposedly neutralized by the context of the activity type, where game-driven impoliteness is expected, why do the participants' actions suggest that personal offense is taken? I would argue that targets of impoliteness tend not to pay sufficient attention to the context. The tendency for people to underestimate the impact of situational factors is a well-established finding in social psychology (e.g., Ross 1977; Tversky and Kahneman 1974; Gilbert and Jones 1986). One reason for this is that behavior tends to be more salient than situational factors [. . .]

As far as *The Weakest Link* is concerned, we are left with a situation where there can be different perspectives on the same event: some people – perhaps including the real Anne Robinson – may see it all as a game and the "impoliteness" as unreal; some others – perhaps the contestants *in situ* – may not pay adequate attention to the context and view the "impoliteness" as real. Such dual perspectives are fully accommodated within my definition of impoliteness, which explicitly allows any combination of speaker and hearer perspectives. [. . .]

Notes

1   In fact, though there is not space to elaborate the argument, Sperber and Wilson's (1986) notion of 'ostensive communication' suits my purposes rather better, because it is a broader notion than Grice's non-natural meaning, and consequently better able to accommodate non-linguistic communication.

2   Goffman (1972) cited here is simply a different edition of Goffman (1967). The page numbers are the same.

3   This is part of a longer extract analyzed in Culpeper (1998).

4   I searched various corpora and the web (via WebCorp at http://www.webcorp.org.uk/) to establish the fact that these all occur with a certain regularity in the language. However, some expressions are restricted to particular registers. 'Waste of rations', for example, seems to be largely restricted to army jokes.

5   For a useful brief introduction to prosodic resources and their 'attitudinal' functions, as well as insights into prosody and impoliteness, see Anne Wichmann's work in Culpeper et al. (2003: 1568–75). More generally, Knowles (1987: Chapters 9 and 10) offers an accessible survey of prosody in conversation, and Couper-Kuhlen (1996) is a key collection of papers on this topic.

6   I used *Praat 4.2* (Boersma and Weenik 2004) for all analyses of intonation (i.e., all figures except 6.4.3 and 6.4.4).

7   Figures 6.4.3 and 6.4.4 were produced with *Speech Analyzer 2.4* (2001). A vowel sound is comprised of various formants (resonances) produced in the vocal tract. F1, on the vertical axis of the figure, can provide an indication of vowel height, such that the lower the F1 value the higher the vowel. F2, on the horizontal axis of the figure, can provide an indication of tongue advancement, such that the higher the F2 value the further to the front the vowel. The algorithms used to capture formant values are complex and not always reliable. To ensure that Figures 6.4.3 and 6.4.4 represent a true picture, I also sampled individual formant values for confirmation.

■   ■   ■

POST-READING

1   According to Culpeper, 'impoliteness . . . has two layers: the offensive information being expressed by the utterance and the information that that information is being expressed intentionally'. To unpack this, Culpeper alludes to both Goffman, and his distinctions between *intentional*, *incidental* and *accidental* levels of face threat, and Grice, and, in particular, his 'distinction between "natural meaning" and "non-natural meaning"'. How does Culpeper specifically link Goffman and Grice in order to explain his 'two layers' of impoliteness idea?

2   Culpeper suggests that 'face-attack may be intentionally communicated but fail to find its mark in any way, or, conversely, the hearer may perceive or construct intentional face-attack on the part of the speaker, when none was intended'.

- Explain the difference between an act that H *perceives* S has committed intentionally, and an act that H *constructs* as being intentional on the part of S, drawing – if possible – on illustrative examples (your own and/or Culpeper's).
- Describe a 'face-attack' which 'fail[s] to find its mark in any way', again drawing on an illustrative example (from your own experiences or from TV/radio).

3   The diagram below seeks to capture the way in which Culpeper's impoliteness superstrategies *mirror* Brown and Levinson's superstrategies:

FACE	Bald-on-Record	
ENHANCING	Positive	
STRATEGIES	Negative	
	Off-record	
	With-hold FTA	
----	----	----
	Sarcasm	
	Off-record	*FACE*
	Negative	*AGGRAVATING*
	Positive	*/ ATTACKING*
	Bald-on-Record	*STRATEGIES*

In your own words, explain why 'bald-on-record' politeness and 'bald-on-record' impoliteness are situated furthest away from one another in the above diagram.

4   'In some circumstances, remaining silent/not saying anything can be *an attempt to aggravate face* as opposed to being *an attempt to save face, by with-holding an FTA*'. Do you agree with our statement? Why/why not? Provide illustrative examples to justify your answer.

SECTION 6 FURTHER READING

Politeness

For extensive overviews of politeness, see the monographs by Eelen (2001), Watts (2003) and Bargiela-Chiappini (2003). We also recommend the paper by Fraser (1990), which provides a useful distinction between the 'social-norm' view, the 'conversational-maxim' view, the 'face-saving' view and the 'conversational-contract' view of politeness. Fraser, himself, describes the conversational-contract view in detail, and we have included two readings, here, that represent the social-norm view and the face-saving view (but see also Locher 2004 and Mills 2003). Groundbreaking studies relating to the conversational maxim view include Lakoff (1973) and Leech (1983). In addition, we recommend the 'pragmatic scales' approach of Spencer-Oatey (see, e.g., 1993, 2000, 2002, 2008), which is briefly discussed in the Culpeper reading.

Impoliteness

Impoliteness has been an important research area in its own right from the 1990s onwards. However, two important works – Lachenict (1980) and Lakoff (1989) – predate much of the later work. The monographs by Bousfield (2008) and Culpeper (2010b) deal extensively with impoliteness, and highlight the influence of both Brown and Levinson (1987) and Goffman (1967). Additional Brown and Levinson and/or Goffman-inspired im/politeness approaches include: Austin (1990), Penman (1990), Culpeper (1996, 2005), Tracy and Tracy (1998) and Culpeper et al (2003). In addition, Archer (2008) and Tracy (2008) seek to demonstrate how face-work can be verbally aggressive without necessarily being deemed to be impolite. Their work can thus be seen to be complimentary to both the Locher and Watts and the Culpeper reading.

Non-Western conceptions of face

For non-Western critiques of Brown and Levinson's work, see, e.g., Matsumoto (1989), Gu (1990), Mao (1994) and Lim (1994).

Relevant Journals

There are a wealth of im/politeness-related articles within the *Journal of Pragmatics*, the *Journal of Intercultural Pragmatics* and the *Journal of Politeness Research*.

SECTION 7

Cross-cultural and intercultural pragmatics

I N T H I S S E C T I O N W E F O C U S on two entirely different, although frequently confused, concepts. The first, cross-cultural pragmatics, explores culturally determined uses of language across cultures, and, in particular, variation in the realization of speech acts and politeness phenomena. The second, intercultural pragmatics, explores communication between second language users with different first language and native culture backgrounds.

From a practical point of view, i.e. as this distinction affects language users, consider the case of Mary. She lives in a 'foreign' country and frequently interacts with members of the 'host' culture in their own language. She is eager to learn about local pragmatic norms, particularly where they contrast with her own. Her developing expertise is in cross-cultural pragmatics. Her case contrasts with that of Hideki and Roberto, neither of whom speaks the other's first language. They use English as a lingua franca when collaborating on their research project and need to find ways of exchanging pragmatic meanings that they can both recover in that lingua franca. Their developing expertise is in intercultural pragmatics. Mary's focus is on culture-specific pragmatic formulas, Hideki and Roberto's is on universal features of communication. In this respect, this section is something of a mirror image of the previous one. As we saw when we studied politeness, the early theories tended to set out from the premise that politeness was a universal phenomenon, and it was left to later accounts to draw attention to culture-specific phenomena. In contrast, the earlier work in the field explored in this section typically focuses on the specific ways in which particular cultures convey pragmatic meanings, whilst the universalist position associated with intercultural pragmatics has come late to the table.

The most carefully conceived, comprehensive study in cross-cultural pragmatics is the *Cross-Cultural Speech Act Realization Project* (CCSARP). This project involved a team of ten researchers collaborating in the collection and analysis of data across seven languages and language varieties. In order to ensure strict comparability, the data were elicited from both native and non-native speaker participants by means of a common instrument of measurement. Specifically, the CCSARP researchers set out to determine the extent of any cross-cultural variation in the realization of two speech acts, *requests* and *apologies*. The team were especially interested in the extent to which requests were realized directly or indirectly, and in the categories and strategies used for apologies. The project also investigated the extent to which apparently identical social situations were differentially evaluated in the different cultural settings studied.

The first substantial set of CCSARP findings were published in 1989 in *Cross-Cultural Pragmatics: Requests and Apologies* edited by three of the research team, Shoshana Blum-Kulka, Juliane House and Gabriele Kasper. CCSARP studies have since been conducted in many different contexts, and the CCSARP instrument of measurement has been adopted in countless masters, doctoral and other research studies. The reading we have chosen is from the introductory section of this seminal volume, in which the editors describe the design of the instrument of measurement employed in the project and the coding methods applied to the resulting data. As this reading is methodological, we strongly recommend that you also read at least one study reporting on the CCSARP findings from the same volume (see 'Further reading' page 385).

Despite the carefully conceived nature of the study, the CCSARP methodology has not been immune from criticism. In particular, the Discourse Completion Tests (DCTs) used to elicit data necessarily reduce complex and extensive social contexts to simple frames, and then require participants to self-report their supposed utterances in such contexts. Expectably enough, the validity of the resulting data as a representation of actual talk has been called into question.

Blum-Kulka *et al.* note that 'most of the studies in interlanguage pragmatics to date [i.e. up until 1989, DEA & PG] focus on communication rather than learning'. This predominant focus is also reflected in the majority of the studies included in *Cross-Cultural Pragmatics: Requests and Apologies.* In contrast, the second reading in this section focuses on learning. Cook's small-scale study 'Why can't learners of JFL distinguish polite from impolite speech styles?' focuses, not on speech acts, but on indexicality, and specifically the contextualization cues that distinguish polite from impolite utterances in Japanese.

The particular focus of Cook's paper is on the extent to which learners of Japanese as a foreign language are able to distinguish a speech style as impolite when the referential content of the containing utterances is contextually appropriate. Cook shows that utterances where content and speech style are in conflict are problematic not only for learners, whose politeness expectations tend to reflect their own cultural norms, but also for teachers. They are problematic for teachers because contextualization cues such as hedging and the appropriate context for the assertive sentence-final particle *yo* seem so obvious as to be below the radar of instructors, who then fail to provide the kind of explicit instruction that learners require. Cook's findings strongly echo Verschueren's view of indexicality in Section 4 as a reflection of a user's ideology to which that user is frequently blind.

Cook's paper is reproduced in its entirety apart from a single example and two very short sub-sections. If you are a student reader, we hope you will feel that this is the kind of project that you might hope to replicate in your own work, albeit on a more modest scale.

In her paper, Cook draws attention to the limited opportunities for what she calls 'language socialization' in the foreign language classroom. Blum-Kulka *et al.* also address this issue and suggest that their work has implications for foreign language teaching, including the possibility of more accurate target-culture, paper-based and electronic materials, the inclusion of cross-cultural pragmatic analysis in the (advanced) learner curriculum, and the development of training tools based on the coding scheme applied to their data. No doubt, Mary, our hypothetical foreign language learner engaged in the process of what Schumann calls 'acculturation' (1976, 1978), is grateful for these developments. But their relevance to Hideki and Roberto, our hypothetical research collaborators, is much more doubtful. For a start, they aren't learning a foreign language. Nor are they attempting to come to terms with a 'target culture'. Their use of a lingua franca isn't to be measured, as the use of a foreign language might be, in terms of its deficit status in relation to native member speech act norms or politeness conventions. For Hideki and Roberto, the issue is to establish an intercultural *modus operandi*. This is precisely the area addressed by Istvan Kecskes in his paper 'Intercultural Pragmatics', which has been written specifically for this Reader and appears in print for the first time here.

Among the reasons for asking the editor of the journal *Intercultural Pragmatics* to write a 'think-piece' paper are the recent emergence of this area and the current lack of an agreed explanatory approach, issues to which Kecskes draws attention in his opening paragraph, before going on to argue that his own socio-cognitive approach provides a promising starting point.

He begins by drawing attention to the equivocal nature of intention and the need to regard it as a co-constructed phenomenon. He reminds us that interaction is characterized by misunderstanding as well as cooperation and by individual as well as societal factors. He argues that the cognitive-philosophical concepts of intention, cooperation and relevance that underlie our understanding of speech acts and implicature need to be combined with sociocultural-interactional notions such as attention, egocentrism and salience, in what he terms a socio-cognitive approach. Our *attention* is dynamic in that it focuses on what we process as salient at each point in an interaction. And since *salience* is partly determined by our earlier private or egocentric experience, the degrees of salience associated with phenomena differ from user to user. These notions are particularly relevant in accounting for intercultural communication.

Kecskes acknowledges that intracultural and intercultural communication are similar, to the extent that cultural representation is an emergent, synchronic phenomenon in both. However, they clearly differ in that cultural models provide a pre-existing resource which may be added to or modified in intracultural communication, whereas in intercultural communication cultural representation is almost entirely ad hoc. This lack of pre-existing common ground might lead us to think of interculturality as a cause of miscommunication, but this would be a mistake because of the preference intercultural interlocutors show for semantically transparent rather than formulaic language.

Kecskes argues that a second important difference between intercultural and intracultural communication lies in the level of interaction that interlocutors operate at. Intercultural communication is, Kecskes claims, discourse segment-centred, a level which enables the necessary trial-and-error process to occur. Unlike utterance-centred intracultural communication, which is amenable to the theories of utterance interpretation that constitute the backbone of pragmatic theory, intercultural communication is best analyzed by means of Centering Theory, which Kecskes applies to a short exchange involving students from Brazil, Columbia and Hong Kong.

As is clear, cross-cultural and intercultural pragmatics study very different social contexts and reflect the very different reasons users have for working in a language other than an L1. But over and above these differences, it's worth bearing in mind the important conclusion Kecskes reaches in the final sentence of his paper, that it's not enough to study only intracultural pragmatics in order to understand communication.

SHOSHANA BLUM-KULKA, JULIANE HOUSE AND GABRIELE KASPER

CROSS-CULTURAL PRAGMATICS
Requests and apologies

PRE-READING

1   Have you had any experiences – either when visiting another country or when speaking to a visitor to your own country – that have made you think about pragmatic use?
2   Spend a few minutes thinking about how you might set about investigating the differences between pragmatic use in one culture and another. It may help to think both about socio-pragmatics (the contexts in which pragmatic behaviour of particular kinds is appropriate) and pragmalinguistics (the ways in which forms accomplish pragmatic ends appropriately).
3   Make a list of typical features of (a) requests and (b) apologies.
4   Before you start to read, fill in the blanks in the following sentences with what seem to you to be the most appropriate words or phrases:
    •   The abundance of linguistic options available for requesting behaviour testifies to ...
    •   Ideally, all data should come from ...
    •   These demands for ... have ruled out the use of ethnographic methods.

IN-READING

As you read, you will come across the three sentences which you completed in your own words in Pre-reading activity (4). When you reach each of these sentences, which is marked by | , first consider whether your sentence or the authors' makes a better point and then consider whether the authors' view can be justified.

■ ■ ■

CROSS-CULTURAL PRAGMATICS: REQUESTS AND APOLOGIES
SHOSHANA BLUM-KULKA, JULIANE HOUSE AND GABRIELE KASPER

CCSARP was set up to investigate cross-cultural and intralingual variation in two speech acts: requests and apologies. These two speech acts are particularly interesting as they both constitute *face-threatening acts*, in Brown and Levinson's terms, but affect the participants' face wants in markedly different ways.

Theoretical work on requests has shown, on the one hand, the complexity of the relationship between form, meaning, and pragmatic prerequisites involved (Gordon and Lakoff 1975; Searle 1975a), and, on the other hand, the high social stakes involved for both interlocutors in choice of linguistic options. Requests are pre-event acts: they express the speaker's expectation of the hearer with regards to prospective action, verbal or nonverbal. Requests are face-threatening by definition (Brown and Levinson 1978): hearers can interpret requests as intrusive impingements on freedom of action, or even as a show in the exercise of power; speakers may hesitate to make the request for fear of exposing a need or risking the hearer's loss of face. The abundance of linguistic options available for requesting behavior testifies to the social intricacies associated with choice in mode of performance. Yet, despite the richness of the subject for both sociolinguistics and cross-cultural pragmatics, surprisingly few studies have attempted to empirically document requesting behavior in one particular society, let alone compare it across different speech communities.

[. . .]

Both speech acts chosen for the investigation, requests and apologies, are face-threatening acts and call for *redressive action*, and they both concern events that are costly to the hearer. However, the request, in requiring a future effort from the interlocutor, imposes mainly on the hearer, while the apology, as an attempt by the speaker to make up for some previous action that interfered with the hearer's interests, counteracts the speaker's face wants. By apologizing, the speaker acknowledges that a violation of a social norm has been committed and admits to the fact that he or she is at least partially involved in its cause. While requests are made to cause an event or to change one, apologies signal the fact that the event has already taken place. The fact that the request is a pre-event, whereas the apology is a post-event (Leech 1980), manifests itself in the differential modifications employed in the realization of these two acts: requests call for mitigation, compensating for their impositive effect on the hearer (e.g., Fraser and Nolen 1981; House and Kasper 1981; Rintell 1981; Walters 1981). Apologies, on the other hand, tend to be aggravated, as they themselves count as remedial work (Goffman 1971; Owen 1983) and thus are inherently hearer-supportive (Edmondson 1981; see also Fraser and Nolen 1981; Olshtain and Cohen 1983).

The general goal of the CCSARP investigation is to establish patterns of request and apology realizations under different social constraints across a number of languages and cultures, including both native and nonnative varieties.

The goals of the project are:

1. To investigate the similarities and differences in the realization patterns of given speech acts across different languages, relative to the same social constraints (cross-cultural variation).
2. To investigate the effect of social variables on the realization patterns of given speech acts within specific speech communities (sociopragmatic variation).
3. To investigate the similarities and differences in the realization patterns of given speech acts between native and nonnative speakers of a given language, relative to the same social constraints (interlanguage variation).

The study was designed to allow for reliable comparability both along the situational (sociopragmatic), cultural, and native/nonnative axes.

Method

Instrument: the discourse-completion test (DCT)

One major concern of sociolinguistic research is the manner in which data are to be collected. Ideally, all data should come from "natural" conditions: "Our goal is then to observe the way that people use language when they are not being observed"—the Observer's Paradox (Labov 1972c: 209). Unable to achieve this, we might settle for "authentic" data, recorded by participant observers during natural interactions. However, in CCSARP we were interested in getting a large sample, in seven countries, of two specific speech acts used in the same contexts. This would have been virtually impossible under field conditions. Moreover, we wished to compare speech acts not only cross-culturally, but also within the same language, as produced by native and nonnative speakers. These demands for comparability have ruled out the use of ethnographic methods, invaluable as they are in general for gaining insights into speech behavior.

Beyond the practical methodological advantages, elicited data has theoretical advantages as well. As pointed out by Hill et al. (1986: 353), "the virtue of authenticity in naturally occurring speech must be weighed against its reflection of speakers' sociolinguistic adaptations to very specific situations." Using written elicitation techniques enables us to obtain more stereotyped responses; that is "the prototype of the variants occurring in the individual's actual speech" (p. 353). It is precisely this more stereotyped aspect of speech behavior that we need for cross-cultural comparability.

Furthermore, our wish to study interlanguage (language learning) phenomena called for the use of experimentally controlled techniques. As pointed out by Kellerman (1980), hypothesis-testing of interlanguage phenomena needs identifiable, appropriate contexts that allow us to focus on specific areas of language use.

The instrument used was a discourse-completion test (DCT), originally developed for comparing the speech act realization of native and nonnative Hebrew speakers (Blum-Kulka 1982, following Levenston 1975). The test consists of scripted dialogues that represent socially differentiated situations. Each dialogue is preceded by a short description of the situation, specifying the setting, and the social distance between the participants and their status relative to each other, followed by an incomplete dialogue. Respondents were asked to complete the dialogue, thereby providing the speech act aimed at.

In the following examples of test items, (a) is constructed to elicit a request, and (b) to elicit an apology:

(a) *At the University*
Ann missed a lecture yesterday and would like to borrow Judith's notes.
Ann: _____
Judith: Sure, but let me have them back before the lecture next week.

(b) *At the College teacher's office*
A student has borrowed a book from her teacher, which she promised to return today. When meeting her teacher, however, she realizes that she forgot to bring it along.
Teacher: Miriam, I hope you brought the book I lent you.
Miriam: _____
Teacher: OK, but please remember it next week.

The questionnaire contains 16 such situations, half of which elicit requests, the other half apologies. All dialogues contain a response to the (missing) turn. This last turn in each dialogue is designed to signal illocutionary uptake. By complying with the (missing) request, and by accepting the (missing) apology, we provided the respondents with co-textual clues for the speech acts needed to complete the dialogues. In natural discourse, each of these speech acts might be negotiated across several turns. The co-textual frame provided hence further signals that this response is being understood in the given context as fully realizing a specific speech act.

In terms of content, the situations depicted by the dialogues reflect every day occurrences of the type expected to be familiar to speakers across Western cultures, specifically to the student population tested.

The situations are as follows:

S1　A student asks his roommate to clean up the kitchen the latter had left in a mess the night before.

S2　A university professor promised to return the student's term paper that day but did not finish reading it.

S3　A young woman wants to get rid of a man pestering her on the street.

S4　A student borrowed her professor's book, which she promised to return that day, but forgot to bring it.

S5　A student asks another student to lend her some lecture notes.

S6　A staff manager has kept a student waiting for half an hour for a job interview because he was called away to an unexpected meeting.

S7　A student asks people living on the same street for a ride home.

S8　The waiter in an expensive restaurant brings fried chicken instead of boeuf à la maison to a surprised customer.

S9　An applicant calls for information on a job advertised in a paper.

S10　A notoriously unpunctual student is late again for a meeting with a friend with whom she is working on a paper.

S11　A policeman asks a driver to move her car.

S12　A driver in the parking lot backs into someone else's car.

S13　A student asks a teacher for an extension on a seminar paper.

S14　The speaker offended a fellow worker during a discussion at work. After the meeting, the fellow worker comments on the incident.

S15　A university professor asks a student to give his lecture a week earlier than scheduled.

S16　The speaker has placed a shopping bag on the luggage rack of a crowded bus. When the bus brakes, the bag falls down and hits another passenger.

Situational variation. The items vary in terms of the participants' role relationship, i.e., on the dimensions of Dominance (social power) and Social Distance (familiarity) as follows:

Request situations:	*Social Distance*	*Dominance*
S1 Kitchen	$-SD$	$x = y$
S3 Street	$+SD$	$x = y$
S5 Notes	$-SD$	$x = y$
S7 Ride	$+SD$	$x < y$
S9 Information	$+SD$	$x < y$
S11 Policeman	$+SD$	$x > y$
S13 Extension	$-SD$	$x < y$
S15 Lecturer	$-SD$	$x > y$

Apology situations:

S2 Seminar paper	−SD	x > y
S4 Book	−SD	x < y
S6 Manager	+SD	x > y
S8 Waiter	+SD	x < y
S10 Meeting	−SD	x = y
S12 Driver	+SD	x = y
S14 Insult	−SD	x = y
S16 Bus	+SD	x = y

Six role constellations are represented: (a) {+SD}, {x<y/x>y}; (b) {-SD}, {x<y]/[x>y};
(c) {+SD}, {x=y}; and (d) {-SD}, {x=y}. Sex of speakers and hearers is randomly varied
across all situations, since the questionnaire is not designed to investigate this variable.

Population

The native-speaker subjects in the study were students enrolled in American, Australian, British,
Canadian, Danish, German and Israeli universities. By choosing students as our target population,
we wished to ensure as much homogeneity as possible in social class, level of income, educational
background, occupation, and age range. The samples consisted of equal numbers of males and
females in each country:

Language	Country	Subjects
Australian English	Australia	227
American English	United States	94
British English	England	100
Canadian French	Canada	131
Danish	Denmark	163
German	Germany	200
Hebrew	Israel	173

The nonnative speakers in the study were students learning the following languages:

Target language	Country	Subjects
English	Denmark	200
English	United States	34
English	Germany	200
German	Denmark	200
Hebrew	Israel	224

Procedure

Following a series of pilot tests in Hebrew and English, the project's DCT was translated into
the seven languages of the project and administered to informants on the various campuses.
Wherever necessary, the process of translation involved cultural transposition to the given
target culture's social and pragmatic system. For example, the university lecturer depicted in
several of the situations, is 'lecturer' in Hebrew, 'professor' in German, and a 'teacher' in
British English.

Data Analysis

All the data were analyzed by native speakers in the respective countries, within a shared analytical framework. The project's coding scheme is based on frames of primary features expected to be manifested in the realization of requests and apologies. The frame provides the meta-paradigm for the analysis of the data, allowing for both "zero" realizations for each feature as well as subclassifications of listed features.

The unit of analysis for both requests and apologies for the data provided by the DCT is the discourse-filler: the utterance(s) supplied by the informant in completing the test item (see Appendix for further details of the coding procedure).*

In the following, we shall list the primary features coded for requests and apologies. For a full list of the categories included in the CCSARP scheme, see Appendix.

Requests

We identify as a request sequence all the utterance(s) involved in the turn completing the dialogue in the DCT. For example:

> Judith, I missed class yesterday, do you think I could borrow your notes? I promise to return them by tomorrow.

As this example illustrates, the request sequence may include: alerters, such as address terms ('Judith'), preposed supportive moves ('I missed class yesterday'), the request proper, or Head Act ('could I borrow your notes?'), optionally elaborated with downgraders ('do you think') or upgraders and postposed supportive moves ('I promise to return them by tomorrow').

Alerters. When preceding requests, alerters serve as attention-getters, and hence are equal in function to all verbal means used for this purpose. Coding of address terms proceeds by type (nominal categories) noting variations in type of apellations (Title+ surname/Surname only, etc.) as well as semantic variations in items used ('darling, could you . . . ' as opposed to 'you fool, why don't you . . . '). (See Appendix for full list of categories.)

Supportive moves. Requests are often preceded by checks on availability ('Are you busy?') (Edmondson and House 1981) and attempts to get a precommitment ('Will you do me a favor?'). They may also be preceded, or followed, by grounders (Edmondson 1981), which provide the reason for the request ('I missed class yesterday, could I . . . ') or by promises and threats, all of which serve to persuade the hearer to do x. Some supportive moves, like grounders, can serve as requests by themselves ('I must have left my pen somewhere' responded by 'here, take mine').

Head acts. (the request proper): The Head Act is that part of the sequence which might serve to realize the act independently of other elements. Head Acts can vary on two dimensions: (a) strategy type, and (b) perspective.

(a) Strategy types. Following previous classifications of request strategy types in empirical research (Ervin-Tripp 1976; House and Kasper 1981; Blum-Kulka 1982), the CCSARP scheme classifies requests on a nine-point scale of mutually exclusive categories. The nine strategy types (on a scale of indirectness) are as follows:

1. *mood derivable:* utterances in which the grammatical mood of the verb signals illocutionary force ('Leave me alone'; 'Clean up that mess').
2. *performatives:* utterances in which the illocutionary force is explicitly named ('I am asking you to clean up the mess').

3. *hedged performatives:* utterances in which the naming of the illocutionary force is modified by hedging expressions ('I would like to ask you to give your presentation a week earlier than scheduled').

4. *obligation statements:* utterances which state the obligation of the hearer to carry out the act ('You'll have to move that car').

5. *want statements:* utterances which state the speaker's desire that the hearer carries out the act ('I really wish you'd stop bothering me').

6. *suggestory formulae:* utterances which contain a suggestion to do x ('How about cleaning up?').

7. *query preparatory:* utterances containing reference to preparatory conditions (e.g., ability, willingness) as conventionalized in any specific language ('Could you clear up the kitchen, please?'; 'Would you mind moving your car?').

8. *strong hints:* utterances containing partial reference to object or element needed for the implementation of the act ('You have left the kitchen in a right mess').

9. *mild hints:* utterances that make no reference to the request proper (or any of its elements) but are interpretable as requests by context ('I am a nun' in response to a persistent hassler).

As we move up this scale, the length of the inferential process needed for identifying the utterance as a request becomes longer; thus, while in 1., 2., and 3. illocutionary force is derivable via linguistic indicators, in 4. and 5. its understanding relies on the semantic content of the utterance (is *locution derivable*). While in 6. and 7. interpretation is aided by conventional usage, in 8. and 9. it tends to rely heavily on the context. These various means (such as grammar for 1., propositional content for 8. and 9., and conventions combining both for 7.), are all subservient to the pragmatic end of relative requestive transparency (directness). Languages may differ in the relative position granted to individual strategy types on this scale, but a distinction between three main levels of directness has been empirically shown to be valid across several languages (Blum-Kulka 1987; House 1986). These three levels are: (a) *direct strategies*, comprised of strategies 1. to 5.; (b) *conventionally indirect* strategies, comprised of strategies 6. and 7. and (c) *nonconventionally indirect* strategies, comprising strategies 8. and 9. (For further discussion of the scale see Weizman, and Blum-Kulka, this volume.)

(b) Perspective. Choice of perspective presents an important source of variation in requests. Requests can emphasize the role of the agent and be *speaker oriented* ('Can I have it?') or focus on the role of the recipient and be *hearer oriented* ('Can you do it?'). Two other possibilities are for requests to be phrased as *inclusive* ('Can we start cleaning now?') or as *impersonal* ('It needs to be cleaned').

Choice of perspective affects social meaning; since requests are inherently imposing, avoidance to name the hearer as actor can reduce the form's level of coerciveness. The four alternatives are often available to speakers within a single situation, though not necessarily for the same request strategy.

Internal modifications (downgraders and upgraders). We have defined as *internal modifers* elements within the request utterance proper (linked to the Head Act), the presence of which is not essential for the utterance to be potentially understood as a request. Thus, the omission of any or all of the bracketed parts in the following will leave the pragmatic force of the utterance as a request intact:

{Darling}, {if you are going into town tomorrow}, would you mind {awfully} cashing this cheque for me, {please}?

Such modifiers can be multifunctional in two distinct ways. First, they may act both as *indicating devices*, used to signal pragmatic force, as well as *sociopragmatic devices*, meant to affect the social impact the utterance is likely to have (Blum-Kulka 1987; House, this volume). Second, in their sociopragmatic role, they may act either as downgraders, meant to mitigate, (soften) the act or alternatively as upgraders that emphasize its degree of coerciveness (House and Kasper 1981; Faerch and Kasper, this volume). Examples of lexical and phrasal downgraders are consultative devices ('*Do you think* I could borrow your notes?') and understaters ('Could you tidy up *a bit* before they come?'), and examples of upgraders are intensifiers ('Clean up that *disgusting* mess) and expletives ('Why don't you get your *bloody ass* out of here').

Syntactic downgraders. A further factor contributing to the effect a request is going to have may be achieved by playing with syntactic elements. Being linked to the grammatical systems of the respective languages, this aspect of the analysis is realized by language specific sub-categories, such as the distinction between different types of modal verbs (can/could; will/would, etc.) in English.

Apologies

The linguistic realization of the act of apologizing can take one of two basic forms or a combination of both:

1. The most explicit realization of an apology is via an explicit *illocutionary force indicating device* (IFID) (Searle 1969: 64), which selects a routinized, formulaic expression of regret such as: (be) sorry, apologize, regret, excuse, etc. The IFID fulfills the function of signaling regret; the speaker asks forgiveness for the violation that motivated the need to apologize, thereby serving to placate the hearer. Our earlier work on apologies (Olshtain and Cohen 1983) seems to indicate that there are language specific scales of conventionality which determine preferences for IFID realizations. In English, for example, the most common form is '(be) sorry' while in Hebrew it is the word 'slixa' which means literally 'forgiveness'.
2. Another way in which one can perform an apology (with or without an IFID) is to use an utterance which contains reference to one or more elements from a closed set of specified propositions the semantic content of which relates directly to the apology preconditions. (See Olshtain, Olshtain and Vollmer, and Wolfson, Marmor, and Jones, this volume, for further discussion.) Thus, an utterance which relates to: (a) the cause for the act that the speaker did or abstained from doing, (b) the speaker's responsibility for the act that was perceived as a breach of social norms, (c) the speaker's willingness to offer repair for x, and (d) a promise of forbearance on the speaker's part (that it will never happen again) can serve as an apology (Faerch and Kasper 1984).

Olshtain and Cohen (1983) suggest the notion of an *apology speech act set* to encompass the potential range of apology strategies, any of which (i.e., an IFID and/or only an utterance of the type (b) or (c)) may count as an apology. The apology speech act set includes five potential strategies:

1. an IFID (be sorry; apologize; regret; excuse etc);
2. an explanation or account of the cause which brought about the violation;
3. an expression of the speaker's responsibility for the offence;
4. an offer of repair; and
5. a promise of forbearance.

When the speaker decides to express an apology verbally, he or she may choose one of the above-specified strategies or any combination of them.

The unit of analysis for apologies, as for requests, is the sequence of utterances used to complete the missing lines in the discourse completion test. The analysis of apologies used in the studies presented in this volume is based on a series of independent, dichotomous questions: (a) does the utterance in question contain an IFID? (b) does it contain an explanation for the cause of x? (c) does it express the speaker's responsibility for x? (d) does it convey an offer of repair from the speaker? and (e) does it contain a promise of forbearance on the speaker's part? If the answer to any of these questions is affirmative, then the utterance is assigned to that category and classified according to a list of sub-classifications. The main categories include the following (see Appendix for full list):

Ifid. Coded by language specific realizations.

Taking on responsibility. In the attempt to placate the hearer, the speaker often chooses to express responsibility for the offence which created the need to apologize. Such recognition of one's fault is face-threatening to the speaker and intended to appease the hearer. The subcategories for this strategy may be placed on a continuum from strong self-humbling on the speaker's part to a complete and blunt denial of responsibility. The acceptance of responsibility would be viewed by the hearer as an apology, while denial of responsibility would testify to the speaker's rejection of the need to apologize. Examples of the *self-humbling* end of the scale are expressions of self-deficiency ('I'm so forgetful'), and explicit self-blame ('It's my fault'), while the *rejecting responsibility* end of the scale would be represented by a complete denial of fault.

Explanation or account. A common reaction to the need to apologize is a search for self-justification by explaining the source of the offence as caused by external factors over which the speaker has no control. Depending on the situation, such an explanation can act as an apology. Explanations vary by specificity and relevance: being late can be explained by reference to the specific event that caused it ('The bus was late') or by a general statement which is implicitly brought forth as relevant to the situation ('Traffic is always so heavy in the morning').

Offer of repair. In situations where the damage or inconvenience which affected the hearer can be compensated for, the speaker can choose to offer repair in a specified or general manner, intending this as an apology; for example, 'I'll pay for the damage' in the case of an accident caused by the speaker is specific enough to count as an apology.

Promise of forbearance. In some situations the feeling of responsibility is so strong that the speaker feels the need to promise forbearance. Promise of forbearance is usually expressed by a promise that x will never happen again.

The distribution of apology strategy types across different social situations reveals which strategies are situation specific, and which can be used in any kind of situation (Olshtain and Vollmer, and Olshtain, this volume.)

Intensification. The illocutionary force of the apology can be intensified or downgraded. Intensification usually takes one or more of the following: (a) an intensifying expression within the IFID, (b) expressing explicit concern for the hearer—external to the IFID or the other strategies used, and (c) the use of multiple strategies.

Downgrading. Downgrading of an apology results from the speaker adding to the strategy which he or she uses, a minimization of the offence (when arriving late, saying 'Sorry, but we never start on time anyhow'), or a query concerning one of the preconditions of the apology ('Sorry, but you shouldn't be so sensitive' on being accused of offending a friend). The decision to perform the act of apologizing and then the decision to choose one or more strategies is affected by a number of different factors. Some of these are socio-cultural and relate to the performance of speech acts in general, such as social distance, social power, and age. Other factors are closely connected to the situational context bringing about the need to apologize. Thus, the severity of the violation x, and the perceived obligation of the speaker to apologize are, most probably, very significant factors in the choices made by the speakers. (For further discussion, see Olshtain, Vollmer and Olshtain, and Wolfson, Marmor and Jones, this volume.)

[. . .]

Note

*   The appendix referred to here and in two other places in this reading is not included in this Reader.

■ ■ ■

POST-READING

On page 3 of their work (i.e. just before the beginning of this reading), Blum-Kulka *et al.* write: 'It is only through the study of situated speech that we can hope to construe a theory interconnecting communicative functions with the contexts in which they are embedded.' Do you think that the methods of data collection and analysis that you have read about enable them to fulfil this aim? Why/why not?

HARUKO MINEGISHI COOK

WHY CAN'T LEARNERS OF JFL DISTINGUISH POLITE FROM IMPOLITE SPEECH STYLES?

PRE-READING

1   What do you understand by *impolite*? (If you have read the work of Locher and Watts, and Culpeper in Section 6, your understanding will probably be heavily influenced by these readings.)
2   Imagine three non-native English speakers, A, B and C, applying for a job requiring mother-tongue:English bilingual skills. Study each of the following statements carefully. Can you think of alternative, audience-aware ways of making each statement without changing its propositional content?

A: I am very good at English because I studied in university.
B: Since my mother is English and I lived in England for two years, I can speak, read and write English.
C: I can speak English because I lived in England when I was a child.

IN-READING

As you read, make a list of the Japanese contextualization cues discussed by Cook. As you add each item to the list, consider how a similar effect might be achieved in English.

■ ■ ■

WHY CAN'T LEARNERS OF JFL DISTINGUISH POLITE FROM IMPOLITE SPEECH STYLES?
HARUKO MINEGISHI COOK

Introduction: the indexical nature of language

Although language is a symbolic system to describe objects in the world, it is also a major tool by which we communicate who we are, what we are doing, and how we feel toward addressees and the events around us. The former is referred to as the *referential function of language*, and the latter its *indexical function*. According to Peirce (1955), there are three kinds of signs: symbols, icons, and indexes. Of these three, indexes are signs that indicate contextual information. For example, dark clouds index rain, and smoke indexes fire. Lyons (1977: 106) defines *indexicality* as "some known or assumed connexion between a sign A and its significatum C such that the occurrence of A can be held to imply the presence or existence of C." As we can see, language is full of expressions which point to the existence of particular aspects of the social context in which they are used. For example, pronouns such as *I* and *you* index the current speaker and the current addressee, respectively, in the speech context. Spatial expressions such as *here* and *there* index a place close to the speaker and a place close to the addressee, respectively, in the speech context. Indexes are interpreted only in the current speech context. This property of linguistic expressions is called *indexicality* (Silverstein 1976b; Lyons 1977; Ochs 1988; Duranti 1997). Indexes are not limited to pronouns and spatial and temporal expressions in language. Researchers working on theories of situated meaning consider most linguistic features as indexical expressions, for they are interpreted in speech contexts (e.g., Duranti and Goodwin 1992; Gumperz and Levinson 1996).

Since indexes are interpreted in context, they contextualize the referential component of an utterance. Gumperz (1982a, 1992, 1996) proposes a subclass of indexes, which are called "contextualization cues." Contextualization cues are defined as "constellations of surface features of message form . . . by which speakers signal and listeners interpret what the activity is, how semantic content is to be understood and *how* each sentence relates to what precedes or follows" (1982a: 131, emphasis in original). Although some indexes such as personal pronouns point to visually available contexts or contexts directly referred to in the preceding talk, contexts of contextualization cues are ambiguous (Gumperz 1996). Prosody, paralinguistic signs, code choice, and choice of lexical forms or formulaic expressions serve as contextualization cues.

The following examples provide some illustrations of contextualization cues in both English and Japanese:

(1) In a taped elementary school classroom session, the teacher told a student to read. The student responded, "I don't wanna read." The teacher got annoyed and said, "All right, then, sit down"

Gumperz (1982a: 147)

In this example, the student said *I don't wanna read* with a rising intonation, which serves as a contextualization cue. Gumperz states that when the tape was played, some interpreted the student's utterance as a refusal, but others, in particular black informants, interpreted it as a request for encouragement. Rising intonation in this particular context is interpreted in two contrasting ways. This example illustrates that there are different interpretive conventions held by different social groups even when the members of the different groups speak the same language.

[. . .]

A contextualization cue is a powerful tool for sense making in social interaction. While in English prosody serves as a major contextualization cue, languages such as Japanese are rich in morphological contextualization cues, which include honorifics and sentence-final particles. For example, a referential expression of gratitude used by a lower status person in a formal situation to a higher-status person can be rude if it lacks proper honorific expressions, as example (3) illustrates:

(3) Tetsudatte kurete   doomo arigatoo
     helping   giving (me) very   thank
     "Thank you very much for helping me".

Although this utterance conveys gratitude in the referential message, it is quite rude if the addressee is higher in status and/or the speech context is formal, for the utterance lacks appropriate honorific morphology. The gerundive verb *kurete* (giving [me]) should be an honorific one, *kudasatte*, to exalt the addressee, and the *doomo arigatoo* (thank you very much) should be a more polite version with the polite verb, *gozaru*, and the addressee honorific suffix, *-masu*, as in *doomo arigatoo gozaimasu*. These examples show that, in social interaction, how an utterance is said is more important than what is said. In the case of Japanese, since pragmatic information is largely encoded in the morphology, it is more salient and accountable. NSs of Japanese readily judge the utterance in (3) as rude in the above-mentioned context, contrary to what the referential message conveys.

For second and foreign language learners, learning how to interpret and use contextualization cues is extremely difficult. Gumperz (1996: 383) explains the reason why they are difficult to learn, noting that

> because of the complexity of the inferential processes involved and their inherent ambiguity, contextualization cues are not readily learned, and certainly not through direct instruction, so that . . . second-language speakers may have good functional control of the grammar and lexicon of their new language but may contextualize their talk by relying on the rhetorical strategies of their first language. Contextualization conventions are acquired through primary socialization in family or friendship circles or intensive communicative co-operation in a finite range of institutionalized environments.

By their nature, then, contextualization cues are also difficult to teach explicitly in a classroom. What makes it even more difficult to teach them is that contextualization cues often co-occur to produce certain social meaning. In Gumperz's words (1996: 383):

> As relational signs – not readily amenable to decontextualized treatment – contextualization cues signal by making salient certain lexical strings within the context of grammatical rules. Foregrounding, moreover, does not rest on any one single cue. Rather assessments build on co-occurrence judgments that simultaneously evaluate clusters of cues to generate hypothesis-like tentative – i.e., valid for the moment – assessments that draw on typified knowledge and are subject to constant change as the interaction progresses.

I will illustrate by using natural data how a collocation of contextualization cues foregrounds particular social aspects of interaction. Example (4), which comes from Okamoto's data (1998: 144), is an exchange between a salesclerk and a customer.

(4) At a women's clothes section of the department store in Osaka: A female customer
     asks a sales woman who was talking with another customer.
     C: Kore no ookii no nai?
        "Don't you have this in a larger size?"
     S: Hai shooshoo o-machi-itadakemasu ka.
        "Yes, could you please wait for a moment?"

In Japanese department stores, salesclerks are expected to serve customers in a very polite manner, and customers are entitled to receive such a service. The speakers in (4) know this norm and choose appropriate collocations of contextualization cues. The salesclerk uses *hai* (yes) and *shooshoo* (a moment), which are the more formal versions of un and *chotto*. The store clerk also uses both addressee and referent honorifics on the verb. The honorific prefix *o-* on the verb stem *machi* (wait) and auxiliary verb *itadaku* (receive) are both referent honorific form and the addressee honorific *masu* form is suffixed on the verb *itadaku* as in *itadakemasu*. A collocation of these linguistic features indexes formality, which is normally expected in the speech of a sales-clerk in a department store (except for the food section in the basement, where salesclerks prefer to be more forceful and create less distance from customers in speech). The customer in (4), on the other hand, does not use any honorifics. Her utterance ends with the plain form (nonhonorific counterpart of the *masu* form) *nai* (does not exist) and also includes *kore* (this), which is a less formal version of *kochira* (this). These co-occurring features index informality, which is normative in customers' speech to a salesclerk.

In order to speak and interpret utterances appropriately, interlocutors need to know what social role they play in a given speech event and what is the normative expectation of that role in society. They further need to know that certain linguistic features collocate in a certain speech style or register (pragmalinguistic knowledge) and that a particular co-occurrence structure is linked to certain social roles and situations (sociopragmatic knowledge). Since any inferencing processes are as complex as demonstrated here, nonnative listeners are faced with an enormous task of interpreting native speech. They must have the linguistic, sociolinguistic, pragmatic, and discoursal knowledge of the linguistic features in question, sociocultural knowledge pertinent to the speech event, and the ability to draw on these knowledge sources and match them with the input (including contextual information) in the high-speed parallel processing fashion required by the online processing of oral input. For foreign language learners, learning this inferencing process is a far greater task than for second language learners. As pointed out by Gumperz (1996), NSs acquire contextualization conventions primarily through socialization processes in the family, among friends, and in institutional environments. When language is used as a resource for dealing with social life, language is a means of communication but not an object of inspection. Typically foreign language learners are restricted to the classroom, an environment with limited input and occasion for practice. This is also an environment in which language tends to be treated as an object, and the classroom organization is teacher-fronted (Kasper 1997). Thus, we can presume that the opportunities for language socialization are very limited in the foreign language class-room. To learn to communicate in an appropriate manner in the target language, foreign language learners need to distinguish different speech styles and the social meaning associated with each style. Apparently, it is difficult to learn contextualization conventions in a foreign language classroom, in particular when learners have little positive transfer from L1 to rely on.

Are students of Japanese as a foreign language (JFL) able to distinguish polite from impolite speech styles? What factors influence their success or failure in recognizing such stylistic differences? Can learners of JFL notice co-occurring linguistic features of a particular speech style and associate the style to certain social situations, in particular, when the content of a message and the speech style are in conflict? One of the ways to test the learners' ability to understand the social meaning of an utterance is to see whether they notice the social meaning in such an instance. Does instruction in pragmatic features help learners notice them? If so, what type of instruction is most beneficial? To my knowledge, there has been no study on foreign language learners' comprehension of appropriate speech styles. This chapter examines second-year American JFL students' pragmatic judgment of a polite speech style (application for a job) after two and a half semesters of typical foreign language instruction at the university level.

The study

As a part of a regular midterm exam given to 201 level Japanese classes at the University of Hawai'i at Manoa during the fall semester of 1997, students were given a listening comprehension test. Its results are the basis of this study.

Participants

A total of 120 students in 12 sections taught by 8 instructors participated in this study. According to the instructors' subjective reports, 7 sections were average classes, 3 were below average, and 2 were above average. Thus, overall, the students who participated in this study were average students taking Japanese at the University of Hawai'i. Students who pass Japanese 102 with a grade of C or above are placed at the level of Japanese 201. Almost all the students who participated in this study were NSs of English. Only 0.9% were NSs of other languages: Chinese, Korean, Laotian, and Filipino. In addition, 0.6% of the students reported that they currently lived with or lived for a substantial length of time with a NS of Japanese, and 0.4% lived in Japan or Okinawa for more than a year. Fifty-four percent were female students, and 46% were male.

Eight instructors participated in the study, out of which seven were female and one was male. Their ages ranged from the 30s to the early 50s. Half of them were NSs of Japanese, who were raised in Japan and received their B.A. from a Japanese university, and the other half were nonnative speakers (NNSs) who were considered to be near-native speakers of Japanese and had experience living in Japan for more than a year. All eight instructors held a master's degree from the University of Hawai'i. Seven of them held the degree from the East Asian Language Department, and one from the Department of English as a Second Language. Two instructors were also doctoral students in the East Asian Language Department and were concurrently taking courses in interlanguage pragmatics and/or second language acquisition. One instructor had been teaching Japanese for 20 years, three for more than 10 years, and four for less than 10 years. All eight of the instructors were interviewed by the researcher after the results of the midterm exam were given to the students.

Material

In the question that is the focus of this study, students are given a help-wanted ad of a clothing company called Pineapple Republic that is seeking an English-Japanese bilingual clerk. The four qualifications required for this job are to speak polite Japanese, to be able to work during weekends and evenings, to be able to use Excel, and to have knowledge of Japanese fashion trends. Students then hear three short audiotaped self-introductory speeches in Japanese given by three applicants applying for this job. Each applicant's speech is played three times. They are asked to choose the most appropriate applicant and write in English the reason why they made that choice.

The appropriateness of the applicants' speech should be judged by students according to what they say (referential content of the message) and how they say it (pragmatic meaning).

In this question, as I elaborate below, one of the speakers' (Applicant A) speech was problematic in that the referential content of the message did not match the pragmatic meaning indexed by co-occurring linguistic features. On the level of the referential message, Applicant A states that she is very good at Japanese, but a collocation of features that serve as a contextualization cue indicates that her speech style is too informal for the occasion. Thus it implies that her Japanese is not good enough. Can JFL students notice the inappropriate speech style, indexed by a collocation of the linguistic features, that is in conflict with that of the referential content? If they do, can they make a pragmatic judgment similar to that of NSs? In this sense, this exam question offers a good opportunity to investigate JFL students' ability to focus on social meaning indexed by co-occurring features. The following are the texts that were read to the students three times. Three applicants' speech texts: Each applicant's speech consists of a self-introduction, a reason for application, statements of qualifications, and a closing. In the following examples, the *masu* form is marked by a single underline, the plain form by a dotted underline, and the particle *yo* and the contracted forms by a double underline.

Applicant A

INTRODUCTION

1. Watashi no namae wa Susan Suzuki <u>desu</u>. Sue to yonde kudasai.
    (My name is Susan Suzuki. Please call me Sue.)

REASON FOR APPLICATION

2. Mae ni Crazy Shirts de shigoto o shite <u>imashita</u>.
    (I used to work in Crazy Shirts.)

STATEMENTS OF QUALIFICATIONS

3. Nihongo wa watashi wa totemo yoku <u>dekimasu</u> <u>yo</u>. Daigaku de ninen benkyoo <u>shita</u> kara.
    (I am very good at Japanese *yo* because I studied in university.)
4. Sore kara senmon wa kompuuta da kara, Excel wa <u>tsukaemasu</u> <u>yo</u>.
    (And since my major is computer, I can use Excel *yo*.)
5. Shuumatsu mo yoru mo shigoto <u>daijoobu</u>.
    (It's OK to work on weekends and evenings.)
6. E, to fasshion wa KIKU terebi o yoku mit<u>eru</u> <u>n</u> <u>da</u> kara, Nihonjin ga donna fasshion ga suki ka yoku shitt<u>eru</u> <u>yo</u>.
    (Uh, as for fashion, because I often watch KIKU TV [Japanese TV], I know well what kind of fashion Japanese people like.)

CLOSING

7. Ja, doozo yoroshiku.
    (Well, please treat me well.)
8. Henji matt<u>emasu</u>.
    (I am waiting for your reply.)

Applicant B

INTRODUCTION

1. Watashi wa Jim Thomas to <u>mooshimasu</u>.
   (I am called Jim Thomas.)

REASON FOR APPLICATION

2. Hawai'i Daigaku no gakusei na node, ima shuumatsu to yoru no shigoto o sagashite <u>imasu</u>.
   (Since I am a student at the University of Hawai'i, I am looking for a job during evenings and weekends.)
3. Choodo Pineapple Republic no shigoto ga ii n ja nai ka to omotte kono teepu o tsukutte <u>imasu</u>.
   (I am making this tape thinking that the Pineapple Republic work is just right for me.)

STATEMENTS OF QUALIFICATIONS

4. Nihongo wa haha ga Nihonjin de, Nihon ni ninen hodo sunde <u>imashita</u> kara, hanasete, yomete, <u>kakemasu</u>. (Since my mother is Japanese and I lived in Japan for 2 years, I can speak, read, and write Japanese.)
5. Kompuuta wa amari suki ja nai n <u>desu</u> ga, Excel wa <u>tsukaemasu</u>.
   (I do not like computers much, but I can use Excel.)
6. Boku no shumi wa amari nai n <u>desu</u> ga, tokidoki gitaa o <u>hikimasu</u>.
   (I do not have many hobbies, but I sometimes play the guitar.)

CLOSING

7. Doozo yoroshiku onegai <u>shimasu</u>.
   (I request you to please treat me well.)

Applicant C

INTRODUCTION

1. Watashi no namae wa Keiko Grant <u>desu</u>. Kono natsu McKinley kookoo o sotsugyoo <u>shimashita</u>.
   (My name is Keiko Grant. I graduated from McKinley High School this summer.)

REASON FOR APPLICATION

2. Watashi wa fasshion ga daisuki <u>desu</u>.
   (I like fashion very much.)
3. Pineapple Republic de yoku kaimono o <u>shimasu</u>.
   (I often shop at Pineapple Republic.)
4. Mae kara, konna mise de shigoto ga shite mitai to omotte <u>imashita</u>.
   (I think that I have been wanting to work in such a store for a while.)

STATEMENTS OF QUALIFICATIONS

5. Nihongo wa kodomo no toki ni zutto Nihon ni sunde ita node <u>hanasemasu</u>.
    (I can speak Japanese because I lived in Japan when I was a child.)
6. Yomu no wa kantan na mono nara yomeru n <u>desu</u> ga, shimbun to ka wa chotto . . .
    (I can read simple things but newspaper is a little [difficult].)
7. Excel wa mada heta na n <u>desu</u> ga, nan toka <u>tsukaemasu</u>.
    (I am still not good at Excel, but I can manage it.)
8. Gambatte sugu joozu ni naritai to <u>omoimasu</u>.
    (I think that I will try to improve my skill soon.)
9. Watashi wa oboeru no ga hayai n <u>desu</u>.
    (I can learn fast.)

CLOSING

10. Doozo yoroshiku onegai <u>itashimasu</u>.
    (I request you to please treat me well.)

Table 1 shows the three applicants' self-reported qualifications (the referential content of the message). According to the referential content of the message that the three provide, Applicant A qualifies in all respects. In contrast, Applicants B and C impart information that can be interpreted negatively in applying for the job. Applicant B mentions that he does not like computers much, and Applicant C states that her Japanese and computer skills are not so good. In addition, Applicants B and C do not indicate whether or not they have the required qualifications 4 and 2, respectively. Thus, in terms of what they say (referential content of the message), it is clear that Applicant A is the best choice.

The appropriate way of presenting oneself in applying for a job in Japanese is constituted by the presence and absence of various co-occurring linguistic and nonlinguistic features. Since the speech was on audio-recorded tapes in this study, we consider only linguistic features. I call the features that are positively evaluated in this social context "positive features" and those that are negatively evaluated, "negative features." Tables 2 and 3 list the characteristics of the three applicants' speech with respect to the linguistic features that convey social meaning. The

Table 1 Self-reported qualifications of the three applicants

Qualifications	Applicant A (female)	Applicant B (male)	Applicant C (female)
1. Speak polite Japanese	speak well	able to write, speak, and read	able to speak but can't read newspaper
2. Work during weekends and evenings	yes	yes	–
3. Use computer program Excel	yes	yes (but does not like computers much)	yes (but not skillful)
4. Have knowledge of Japanese fashion trends	yes	–	interest in fashion

Table 2 Positive pragmatic features

	Applicant A (female)	Applicant B (male)	Applicant C (female)
formal form (*masu* form)	inconsistent use of *masu* (6 *masu* forms, 5 plain forms)	consistent use of *masu*	consistent use of *masu*
appropriate hedges	no	yes	yes
fixed expression	yes	yes	yes
appropriate honorific	no	yes	yes

Table 3 Negative pragmatic features*

	Applicant A (female)	Applicant B (male)	Applicant C (female)
informal form (plain form in the main clause)	5	0	0
final particle	*yo* 3	*yo* 0	*yo* 0
contracted form	*teru* 2	*teru* 0	*teru* 0
	temasu 1	*temasu* 0	*temasu* 0

positive features include the use of the formal form (*masu* form), which is marked by the morpheme -*masu* on the sentence-final verbal or *desu* as a copula, appropriate fixed expressions, hedges, and honorifics, and the negative features include the plain form on the sentence-final verbal, the final particles such as *yo*, and certain contracted forms, all of which make the speech too informal.

Both Applicants B and C consistently use the formal *masu* form, but Applicant A uses the informal form (the plain form) five out of eleven times on the verbal ending. Although the other two applicants consistently use the positive pragmatic features, Applicant A does not use two of them. Furthermore, Applicant A uses all the negative pragmatic features when the others do not use them at all. A qualitative comparison of the three applicants' speech further reveals how Applicant A's speech is inappropriate. In the sections of statements of qualifications and closing, Applicant A's speech becomes problematic. In social contexts such as a taped speech for a job application in which a consistent mannered self-presentation (acting in role on stage) is required, the *masu* form (the formal form) on the sentence-final verbal indexes the display of a good self-presentation (Cook 1999). Thus the use of the *masu* form is considered the norm in this social context, and the use of the plain form gives an impression that the speaker is too informal, for he or she does not present himself or herself properly. Applicants B and C consistently use the *masu* form in the sentence-final position whereas Applicant A uses the plain form (indicated by a dotted line in the speech text) five times.

In Japanese society, a display of humble attitude is valued, in particular in unequal power encounters. A lower-status person is expected to sound hesitant, indirect, and apologetic even when, from a Westerner's point of view, he or she has no obvious reason to do so (Mizutani and Mizutani 1978). An assertion of one's strong qualification thus needs to be modified in Japanese with a hedge or indirectness even when one applies for a job. We see a clear contrast between Applicant A and Applicants B and C in terms of assertive force. Both Applicants B and C do not assert that they are good at Japanese, but, by stating that they lived in Japan and/or have a Japanese mother, they imply that they are good in Japanese. Applicant C mentions that she is not skillful in using Excel but will try to improve, which humbles her own ability but gives a positive future perspective. Humbling one's own ability is an appropriate hedge in applying for a job in Japanese as long as one provides a positive attitude for future improvement. Another way to hedge one's assertion in Japanese is the use of the verb *to omou* (to think that). The expression *to omou* softens the speaker's position by indicating that what is said is his or her point of view (Locastro and Netsu 1997). Both Applicants B and C use this hedge, whereas Applicant A does not. Applicant B uses it when he states his reason for applying in line 3 (*Choodo Pineapple Republic no shigoto ga ii n ja nai ka to omotte* [I am making this tape thinking that the Pineapple Republic work is just right for me]). Applicant C uses this hedge when she states her reason for application and her positive outlook for skill improvement in line 4 (*Mae kara, konna mise de shigoto ga shite mitai to omotte imashita* [I think that I have been wanting to work in such a store for a while]) and in line 8 (*Gambatte sugu joozu ni naritai to omoimasu* [I think that I will try to improve my skill soon]).

However, both Applicants B and C also use expressions that give rather a negative impression as well. B states in line 5 that *Kompuuta wa amari suki ja nai n desu ga* (I do not like computers much), and C expresses in line 6 that *shimbun to ka wa chotto* (newspaper is a little [difficult]). Applicant C subtly makes this statement by omitting the word *difficult*. When the job qualifications specify knowledge of Japanese fashion trends, Applicant B does not indicate such knowledge, and Applicant C only mentions that she likes fashion in general. In contrast, Applicant A directly asserts all qualifications required for the position. She asserts her good Japanese language proficiency and her ability to use Excel, both of which she acquired at school. She also states her knowledge about Japanese fashion trends. She asserts her qualifications without an appropriate hedge but with the assertive final-particle *yo*. She states in line 3 that *Nihongo wa watashi wa totemo yoku dekimasu yo* (I am very good at Japanese *yo*), in line 4 that *Excel wa tsukaemasu yo* (I can use Excel *yo*), and in line 6 that *Nihonjin ga donna fasshion ga suki ka yoku shitteru yo* (I know well what fashion Japanese people like *yo*). Note that the other applicants do not use the particle *yo* at all. By the particle *yo*, the speaker asserts himself or herself by drawing the addressee's attention to the speaker's words (Cook 1991). The particle *yo* can be polite if it occurs with an utterance which humbles the speaker. For example, when it occurs with a refusal of a compliment, it emphasizes the speaker's humble attitude. Hence *yo* is polite in this instance. When *yo* occurs with an assertion, however, it reinforces the assertive attitude of the speaker. For this reason, its use is rude in this context. Thus, the assertions of Applicant A are judged by NSs as severely inappropriate.

In a formal context, certain contracted forms sound too informal. One of them is the form *-teru* or *-temasu*, which is formed by deleting [i] from the progressive/stative construction, *-te iru* (verbal gerund form *-te* + verb *to be* in the plain form) or *-te imasu* (verbal gerund form *-te* + verb *to be* in the *masu* form). Applicant A uses the progressive/stative construction four times in her speech. She chooses the contracted form *teru* (in line 6) twice and *temasu* (in line 8) once. In contrast, both Applicants B and C consistently use the more formal noncontracted form *-te imasu*.

In Japanese, the use of appropriate fixed expressions is very important, particularly in formal situations. It is customary to end a message that asks the addressee's favor with a fixed expression such as *doozo yoroshiku* (Please treat me well) or a more polite version, *doozo yoroshiku onegaishimasu* (I request you to please treat me well). All the applicants use one of the versions of this fixed expression; Applicant A uses the shortest version, *doozo yoroshiku*, Applicant B uses the more polite *doozo yoroshiku onegai shimasu*, and Applicant C, the most polite version with the dishonorific expression (i.e. humbling the speaker), *itashimasu* (do). Furthermore, if an applicant refers to the prospective employer's action or belongings, or mentions his or her action in relation to the prospective employer, he or she is expected to use honorifics (and dishonorifics) to exalt the prospective employer's action or belonging and humble his or her own action or belongings. When she says that *Henji mattemasu* (I'm waiting for your reply), Applicant A neither exalts the prospective employer's reply with the honorific prefix *o-* as in *o-henji* (honorable reply) nor does she humble her own action of waiting with the humble form *o-machi shite orimasu* (I am humbly waiting). In addition, she uses the informal, contracted form, *temasu*.

In sum, Applicant A's speech is far more pragmatically inappropriate than the others because of a lack of appropriate collocations of features. As indicated by the instructor's comments, Applicant A's inappropriate speech style weighs far greater than her self-reported good qualifications.

Procedure

In the listening comprehension task, students were instructed that they were to take the role of the bilingual manager of Pineapple Republic and that they would write a report in English to their supervisor as to who they thought to be the best applicant for the job and why that decision was made. They were given a help-wanted ad which lists the four qualifications for the job. After listening to the taped self-introduction of the three applicants three times, they selected who they thought to be the most qualified applicant and wrote in English their justification for their selection. [. . .]

In order to shed light on possible sources for the students' assessments, eight of the instructors whose students participated in the test were interviewed after the test results were obtained and returned to the students. The instructors were interviewed in the researcher's office. The interview was conducted in Japanese with instructors who are NSs of Japanese and in English with instructors who are NNSs of Japanese. They were asked the following six questions:

1. Were you surprised that the majority of students chose Applicant A?
2. Why do you think that the majority of students chose Applicant A or did not choose Applicant C?
3. Do you teach pragmatic functions in class?
4. If you do, how do you teach them?
5. Do your students ask about the pragmatic functions of the forms involved?
6. How do you rate this class (these classes) – is it an average or a better-than-average class?

Since the interviews were conducted more like a conversation in a friendly atmosphere, the six questions were used as a guideline. Some instructors provided more information than others. The length of the interviews varied from 15 minutes to 30 minutes. Interviews were tape-recorded. The researcher listened to the tapes and took notes. The analysis of the interviews was made based on the notes.

Results

Recognition of speech styles

As shown in Table 4, out of 120, an overwhelming 97 students (80.8%) chose Applicant A as the most desirable applicant for the job, 17 (14.2%) chose Applicant C, and 6 (5%) chose Applicant B. It became clear from the students' explanations that the main reason for choosing Applicant A was that, according to the referential content of the three applicants' speech, she satisfied all the qualifications.

Table 5 categorizes the ninety-seven students who chose Applicant A into three groups. Group 1 consists of sixty-eight students who evaluated positively Applicant A's Japanese skill. Out of them, sixty students specifically mentioned that Applicant A is very good at Japanese, which is a literal translation of her self-reported statement (*Nihongo wa watashi wa totemo yoku dekimasu yo*). The fact that these students commented that A is very good at Japanese and that they did not offer any negative comment on her speech style suggests that they focused only on the referential content and that they did not notice A's impolite manner of speech. One of the students even commented that A's manner of speaking was very polite. Another eight students positively commented on A's Japanese. Their comments, such as "A displays politeness," "A learned polite Japanese," and "A's Japanese sounds very good," again indicate that they failed to notice A's inappropriate manner of speaking. Thus, apparently, sixty-eight students in Group 1 did not notice the pragmatic meaning indexed by the linguistic features listed in Tables 2 and 3. Group 2 consists of twenty-three students who did not specifically mention Applicant A's good Japanese skill. They either stated that Applicant A can speak Japanese or that she studied Japanese for 2 years in college. It is not clear whether they noticed Applicant A's inappropriate speech style. If they did, they certainly could not judge it as a crucially negative factor for applying for a job. Group 3 consists of six students who negatively evaluated Applicant A's Japanese skill or style but still chose her as the most suitable applicant because of the other qualifications. This indicates that they do not understand that in applying for a job in Japanese, an inappropriate speech style is problematic even when the other qualifications are good.

[. . .]

Table 4 Distribution of students' choices

Applicant A	Applicant B	Applicant C	Total
97	6	17	120
80.8%	5.0%	14.2%	100%

Table 5 Reasons for choosing Applicant A

1. Positive evaluation of A's Japanese skill (A is very good at Japanese = 60) (other positive comments = 8)	68
2. No mention of A's good Japanese skill	23
3. Negative evaluation of A's Japanese skill	6
Total	97

The effects of instruction

How (and to what extent) were the co-occurring pragmatic features that constitute an appropriate formal speech style for a job application taught in the class? According to the interviews, none of the eight instructors expected this outcome at all. They were unanimously surprised. For them, it was obvious that Applicant A's speech style was definitely impolite for applying for a job. In the instructors' words, Applicant A was "out of the question." In their judgment, Applicant C was the most suitable for the position, and Applicant A was by far the worst. They thought that most students would choose either Applicant B or Applicant C. The instructors assumed that since students learned by the 201 level the pragmatic functions of the *masu* and plain forms, they would notice A's use of the plain form and could judge it impolite in this context. Six instructors mentioned that the reason why the majority of students chose Applicant A was that they focused on the referential content and that they could not pay attention to the speech style. One instructor reported that after the exam, she read the same texts twice to the students. This time she told them to pay attention to the forms. After hearing the texts twice, some students figured out why Applicant A's speech was impolite. This suggests that when students are specifically instructed to pay attention to the pragmatic function, they may recall what was taught in class. After the exam, one of the NS instructors was told by her students that Applicant A sounded enthusiastic. This comment concurs with that of two NNS instructors, who grew up in Hawai'i. They speculated that Applicant A was chosen by many students because her voice quality sounded enthusiastic and convincing. When I (as an NS of Japanese) listened to the tape, Applicant A did not sound enthusiastic at all. It seems that the voice quality of Applicant A gave an impression to some local students that she was enthusiastic. Enthusiasm may be one of the factors that contributed to the choice of Applicant A.

Among the pragmatic features listed in Tables 2 and 3, the only one that was recognized by all instructors as a factor responsible for A's impolite speech style is her use of the plain form in the main clause predicate. The distinction between the *masu* and plain forms is perhaps the most salient because all the final verbs in the main clause have to be morphologically marked by either the *masu* or the plain form. Table 6 summarizes the instructors' treatment of the *masu* and plain forms in their classrooms.

The instructors teach the functions of these forms in role-plays and conversation drills. In fact, prototypical uses of these forms are first introduced in the textbook at the 101 level and mentioned throughout the textbook whenever relevant conversations appear. For this reason, the instructors assumed that students would be able to notice any use of the plain form and judge it as inappropriate for a formal occasion such as applying for a job. Furthermore, six instructors reported that their students asked about the appropriate use of the *masu* and plain forms in class, especially when they created a skit or performed a role-play. Two reported that better students asked questions on these forms. This indicates that some students are consciously aware of this distinction when they have time to think about it but may not notice it in an online listening comprehension task. Furthermore, in reality, the situation is more complicated than a simple dichotomy of the two forms. Not all instances of the plain form mark the informal speech style. The contrast between the two forms is made only when they appear on the verbal in the main clause. Typically, in a subordinate clause the plain form occurs and it does not contrast with the *masu* form in the pragmatic function. For example, Applicant C states *Mae kara, konna mise de shigoto ga shite mitai to omotte imashita* (I think that I have been wanting to work in such a store for a while). In this utterance, the word *mitai* (want to try) is in the plain form, which is embedded in the quotation *to omotte imashita* (have been

Table 6 Instructional methods of the *masu* and plain forms

Instructor	Were masu/plain forms taught in 201 class?	What activities were used to teach them?	Did students ask about the functions of these forms?
1	no (assumed to be learned previously)	role-plays	yes (better students)
2	no	–	yes
3	yes	role-plays, conversation drills	no
4	yes (often)	role-plays	yes (better students)
5	no (assumed to be learned previously)	–	yes (a few)
6	yes	skits, dialogue	yes
7	no (assumed to be learned previously)	–	no
8	yes	role-plays	yes

thinking that). Because it is in the embedded clause, this use of the plain form does not index informality. Furthermore, whether the plain form is contrasted with the *masu* form depends on a degree of subordination. For example, two clauses that denote a cause, the *node* and *kara* clauses, differ with respect to social meaning when they occur with the plain form. In the *node* clause the plain form does not necessarily index informality, but in a *kara* clause the plain form does index informality. In this sense, it is more like an independent clause. For this reason, in formal speech, the use of the *masu* form in a *kara* clause is more appropriate. Applicant A's speech contains three *kara* clauses and each takes the plain form, which sounds too informal. In contrast, Applicant C uses a *node* clauses (*zutto Nihon ni sunde ita node*). The verb *ita* (was) is in the plain form, but because it is in the *node* clause, it does not index informality. In an online comprehension task, it must be difficult for students to differentiate a plain form in the embedded clause from that in the main clause and to assign a different pragmatic meaning to each.

Only Instructor 8 noticed pragmatic features other than the *masu* and plain forms which contributed to A's impolite speech style. She pointed out that the use of the particle *yo* was extremely impolite in this context and that a lack of hedges in A's speech further contributed to her impoliteness. She mentioned that she came to realize inappropriate pragmatic features while she was administering the midterm exam. She reported that she did not explain the function of the particle *yo* explicitly in class, except for correcting its wrong use by the students. The interviews with the instructor revealed that although students were taught at some point in their Japanese study that the particle *yo* is an assertive particle, generally no explicit instruction was given that its use is inappropriate in asserting one's qualification in a social context such as applying for a job. Furthermore, no instruction was given with respect to the function of hedges in formal social situations in Japanese society. In addition, Instructor 8 commented that during the midterm planning session, the members of the midterm exam committee did not even discuss why Applicant A's speech was pragmatically inappropriate because the inappropriateness was obvious to them. The instructors' reports on their classroom instruction suggest that other than the sentence-final *masu* and plain forms, the functions of most of the pragmatic markers listed in Tables 7.2.2 and 7.2.3 are more or less inaccessible to the instructors' awareness. This is perhaps because these pragmatic markers as contextualization cues have different indexical functions in different social contexts. They have, in Gumperz's words (1996: 383), "inherent ambiguity." NSs learned them in their socialization process as a means of real-life communication. Hence, these features are not brought to the conscious attention of the instructors or of their students. A question that suggests itself is whether Instructor 8's more explicit awareness of pragmatic features had an impact on her students' performance on the exam.

Looking at the twelve sections (i.e., classes) of Japanese instruction, we see that the results of Section 1 were markedly different from those of the rest. In this section, out of ten students only two chose Applicant A while six chose Applicant C and two chose Applicant B. Furthermore, five students who chose Applicant B or C noted that Applicant A's speech style was neither polite nor humble. In other words, half the class clearly noticed and was able to judge Applicant A's inappropriate use of the pragmatic markers. This section was taught by Instructor 8, who, when necessary, gave explicit instruction on both the functions of *masu* and plain forms and the final particles. Instructor 8 also taught another section (Section 2), in which five students out of seven (71%) chose Applicant A. According to her self-report, she taught both sections in the same method and manner. Thus, the better performance of Section 1 cannot be attributed to the instructor's teaching method. The difference between the two sections was that whereas Section 2 was an average class, Section 1 consisted of many exceptionally highly motivated students. According to Instructor 8, many students in Section 1 were interested in Japanese culture and had a strong desire to visit Japan or work with Japanese people. Interest in other cultures, societies, and their members is a part of integrative motivation (Clément et al. 1994). A comparison of the results of Section 1 and 2 suggests that students who have a high integrative motivation notice pragmatic functions that are taught.

Discussion and conclusion

In this study, contrary to the instructors' expectation, 80.8% of the students chose Applicant A, who was regarded by the instructors as by far the worst applicant because of her impolite speech style. Among the ninety-seven students who chose Applicant A, sixty-eight did not notice her impolite speech style and gave it a positive evaluation; twenty-three students either did not notice A's inappropriateness or could not judge it as such. Only six students noticed her inappropriate speech style but could not judge it as a crucially negative factor. Only 14.2% of all the students chose Applicant C, who was considered the most desirable applicant by the instructors.

Recent classroom research on interlanguage pragmatics has found that, in general, teaching pragmatics is beneficial to second and foreign language learners (Kasper 1997; Kasper and Rose 1999). So far, these findings are made largely in the areas of speech acts (Beebe and Takahashi 1989a, 1989b; Billmyer 1990a, 1990b; Olshtain and Cohen 1990; Morrow 1996), pragmatic routines and strategies (Wildner-Bassett 1994; House 1996; Tateyama et al. 1997), and conversational implicatures (Bouton 1994; Kubota 1995). If teaching pragmatics is beneficial, we would expect that the teaching of contextualization cues should not be an exception. Knowledge of inferential processes is indispensable in developing performance-based teaching and testing materials. Explicit instruction in many of the contextualization cues, however, is extremely difficult in a foreign language classroom for several reasons. First, NSs learn inferential processes through primary socialization, in which language is used as a means of communication rather than an object of inspection. Second, since these processes are typically unconscious, NSs have little awareness of how they arrived at their interpretation and what linguistic forms are involved in these processes, so even NS instructors are often not consciously aware of their pragmatic functions. Third, contextualization cues as indexes are inherently ambiguous as to which aspects of context are foregrounded. Finally, a collocation of contextualization cues often foregrounds certain social information, such as speech styles being indexed by co-occurring cues. These difficulties, however, can be overcome by the enhancement of instructors' pragmatic, sociolinguistic, and discoursal knowledge of the target language and culture. In other words, in order to teach inferential processes effectively in a foreign language classroom, the instructor needs to analyze the social context of the teaching materials and fully understand pragmatic functions of linguistic forms and what exactly constitutes a "framing" (Tannen 1993a) or expectation structure that surrounds an utterance.

Some contextualization cues are more noticeable than others. For example, the functions of the *masu* and plain forms in this study were more readily available to the consciousness of the instructors than the others as a marker of a speech style. They are also clearly explained in the textbook. This study has demonstrated that at the 201 level explicit instruction of one contextualization cue was not sufficient for the majority of the students to notice and judge an impolite speech style during a comprehension task. To teach an appropriate speech style for a given speech event, it is necessary to teach students a range of co-occurring contextualization cues that constitute that speech style. Furthermore, it is important to instruct students to pay attention to the relationship between linguistic form, its social meaning, and the social context in which that particular meaning is foregrounded, for one of the instructors' reports suggests that only when students are told to pay attention to these forms may they recognize their social meanings.

This study suggests that there may be a relationship between intrinsic motivation and an ability to understand the social meaning of contextualization cues. More studies are needed to determine the role of motivation in conversational inferencing. Furthermore, a discrepancy was found between the instructors' expectations and the students' performance in terms of the comprehension of pragmatic meanings. What the instructors considered obvious was not obvious to the students at all, which suggests that it is important for instructors to have knowledge of linguistic, pragmatic, discoursal and cultural structures of the target language as well as those of the students' native language and evaluate what needs to be explicitly taught in class.

[. . .] [T]he present study suggests that in order to understand the pragmatic meaning of a speech style, JFL students need to know a wider range of co-occurring linguistic forms and their pragmatic functions which constitute various speech registers as well as their specific cultural norms of interpretation. Is the full range of co-occurring features teachable in a JFL class? If so, what is the relative effect of different instructional approaches? Unlike a speech act, which is readily accessible to the instructor's consciousness, a range of co-occurring features such as those discussed in this study is more subtle and often beyond the consciousness of average NSs. In this sense, it is more difficult to bring it to the instructor's attention. And finally, will the results of the exam significantly improve if students are specifically instructed to pay attention to how the applicants speak? If so, making students notice at least one pragmatic feature that is explicitly taught out of the several that constitute a particular speech style helps them judge appropriateness.

Note

*   *n* is a contracted form of the nominalizer *no*. In speech, *n* occurs even when the context is rather formal. For this reason, *n* is not included in Table 3.

■ ■ ■

POST-READING

1   Which five of the following terms in the reading would you choose as keywords: *assertive particle, contextualization cue, fixed expression, foreign language learner, formal/informal form, hedge, honorific, impolite, index, pragmalinguistic knowledge, pragmatic meaning, referential content, social meaning, socialization, sociopragmatic knowledge, speech style*? Add one further term which does not occur in the reading but which represents an important theme for you.

2   How do you react to the finding that foreign language teachers typically fail to teach contextualization cues because (a) such features have 'inherent ambiguity' and (b) teachers lack awareness of their functions?

ISTVAN KECSKES

INTERCULTURAL PRAGMATICS

PRE-READING

1   This reading explores 'how the language system is put to use in social encounters between human beings who have different first languages, communicate in a common language, and, usually, represent different cultures.' With this in mind, make a list of five questions that you hope the reading will answer.
2   To what extent do you feel positive about each of the following?
     (a) an approach to pragmatics that is less idealized than usual
     (b) an approach to pragmatics that acknowledges the role of egocentrism in communication
     (c) the study of a field in which there is uncertainty about the appropriate data set
     (d) a focus on intercultures rather than culture.

Score each on a desirability scale ranging from 1–10 and total your score in order to find out what this says about you and the paper you're about to read:

30–40 – You're going to enjoy reading this paper.
20–30 – You're setting off in a positive frame of mind.
10–20 – Try not to get too angry as you read the paper.
0–10 – You need to know why some people think your approach to pragmatics is problematic, and this is your chance to find out!

IN-READING

This reading draws important distinctions between a series of complementary and contrasting concepts. When you encounter these for the first time in this text, you may not feel that you fully understand what they are used to designate. When you are sure that you do fully understand each of them, tick the appropriate box below:

☐   Interlanguage pragmatics
☐   Cross-cultural pragmatics
☐   Intercultural pragmatics

☐   The cognitive-philosophical tradition
☐   The sociocultural-interactional tradition

☐   Cooperation
☐   Egocentrism

☐   Attention / attentional state
☐   Intention / intentional structure

☐   Salience
☐   Relevance

☐   Interculturality
☐   Intraculturality

☐   Cultural model
☐   Cultural representation

■ ■ ■

INTERCULTURAL PRAGMATICS
ISTVAN KECSKES

The study of intercultural pragmatics supports a less idealized, more down-to-earth approach to communication than current pragmatic theories usually do. Whilst not denying the importance of cooperation, rapport and politeness in communicative endeavors, intercultural pragmatics also gives equal importance to egocentrism, chaos, aggression and trial-and-error in the analysis of language production. At the same time, the short history of interculturality poses a special challenge: what exactly are we to analyze, what are we to pay attention to, and what methods are we to use for our analysis? In this paper, these issues are examined against the background of recent research in pragmatics and related fields, which has shown two dominant tendencies: first, an overwhelming emphasis on the decisive role of context, socio-cultural factors and cooperation while ignoring the role of the individual's prior experience, existing knowledge and egocentrism; and second, perspectives resulting from globalization in which language is usually substituted with community practices, and intercultures are preferred to culture (e.g., Eckert 2000; Wenger 2000; Gal and Irvine 1995; Rampton 1999, 2001). I will argue that the social-cognitive approach of Kecskes (2008) and Kecskes and Zhang (2009) provides a theoretical framework within which intercultural pragmatics can be adequately described.

1 Introduction

Intercultural pragmatics is a relatively new field of inquiry. It investigates how the language system is put to use in social encounters between human beings who have different first languages, communicate in a common language, and, usually, represent different cultures (Kecskes 2004). The communicative process in these encounters is synergistic in the sense that it is a merger in which the pragmatic norms of each participant are represented to some extent. Intercultural pragmatics adopts a socio-cognitive perspective in which individual prior experience and actual situational experience are equally important in meaning construction and comprehension. Research in intercultural pragmatics may focus on any of the following: interaction between native speakers and non-native speakers, lingua franca communication when none of the interlocutors has a common L1, multilingual discourse, the language use and development of individuals who speak more than one language.

First of all, it is important to distinguish *interlanguage pragmatics, cross-cultural pragmatics* and *intercultural pragmatics*. Although these terms are often used interchangeably, they do not refer to the same fields of inquiry. *Interlanguage pragmatics* focuses on the acquisition and use of pragmatic norms in L2: how L2 learners produce and comprehend speech acts, and how their pragmatic competence develops over time (e.g., Kasper and Blum-Kulka 1993; Kasper 1998). Thus, as Boxer (2002) argues, interlanguage pragmatics focuses on the language learner's appropriation and/or acquisition of the pragmatic norms represented in the host language community. To date, many cross-sectional, longitudinal, and theoretical studies have been conducted, mainly based on L2 classroom interactions. These have enabled interlanguage pragmatics to make a significant contribution to second language acquisition research. *Cross-cultural pragmatics*, on the other hand,

> takes the view that individuals from two societies or communities carry out their interactions (whether spoken or written) according to their own rules or norms, often resulting in a clash in expectations and, ultimately, misperceptions about the other group.
>
> Boxer (2002: 151)

Cross-cultural studies focus mainly on speech act realizations in different cultures, cultural breakdowns, and pragmatic failures, such as the way some linguistic behaviors considered polite in one language may not be polite in another. A significant number of these studies use a comparative approach to the different cultural norms reflected in language use. As we shall see, the concerns of *intercultural pragmatics* are very different.

2 Tendencies in pragmatics research

The dominant theoretical view in pragmatics is the *cognitive-philosophical* line of thinking represented by neo-Gricean pragmatics, Relevance Theory, and Speech Act Theory, which maintains that communication is constituted by recipient design and intention recognition. The speaker's knowledge involves constructing a model of the hearer's knowledge relevant to the given situational context; conversely, the hearer's knowledge includes constructing a model of the speaker's knowledge relevant to the given situational context. Communication is supposed to be smooth if the speaker's intentions are recognized by the hearer through pragmatic inferences. Consequently, the main task of pragmatics is to explain how exactly the hearer makes these inferences, and to determine what is considered the speaker's meaning

In contrast, the *sociocultural-interactional* paradigm in pragmatics research considers intention to be problematic, and underlines its equivocality. According to this view, communication is not always dependent on speaker intentions in the Gricean sense (Verschueren 1999; Nuyts 2000; Mey 2001; Haugh 2008). In fact, one of the main differences between the cognitive-philosophical approach and the sociocultural-interactional approach is that the former considers intention an *a priori* mental state of speakers that underpins communication, while the latter regards intention as a *post factum* construct that is achieved jointly through the dynamic emergence of meaning in conversation. Since the two approaches represent two different perspectives, it would be difficult to reject either of them *in toto*. Kecskes and Zhang (2009) suggest that the complexity of the issue requires that we consider both the encoded and co-constructed sides of intention when analysing the communicative process.

In general, approaches to communication based on the assumption that the participants' main endeavor is to cooperate in making interaction as smooth as possible seem optimistic. This means that the strong emphasis on rapport, cooperation and politeness in pragmatics research should be supplemented by a recognition of the need for attention to the less positive aspects of communication, including break-downs, misunderstandings, struggle and linguistic aggression. This is something that has been often missed. An adequate theory of communication should, therefore, take into account both societal and individual factors, including cooperation and egocentrism.

3 The socio-cognitive approach

The socio-cognitive approach (SCA) (Kecskes 2008; Kecskes and Zhang 2009) that unites the societal and individual features of interaction appears to be an adequate theoretical framework for intercultural pragmatics. SCA treats communication as a dynamic process in which individuals are not only constrained by societal conditions but also shape them. Speakers and hearers are equal participants in the communicative process, each relying on their most accessible and salient knowledge for the production and comprehension of speech. Consequently, only a holistic interpretation of utterance and discourse from the perspective of both speaker and hearer can provide an adequate account of language communication.

The SCA to communication and pragmatics emphasizes not only the role of co-construction but also the importance of prior knowledge in the interaction. SCA points out the complex role of cultural models and private mental models, and how these are applied categorically and/or reflectively by individuals in response to socio-cultural environmental feedback mechanisms, and how this leads to and explains different meaning outcomes and knowledge transfer. In meaning construction and comprehension, individuals rely both on pre-existing encyclopedic knowledge based on their prior experience and on current knowledge created in the process of interaction.

In the socio-cognitive paradigm, communication is driven by the interplay of *cooperation* required by societal conditions and *egocentrism* rooted in the prior experience of the individual. Consequently, egocentrism and cooperation are not mutually exclusive phenomena. They are both present in all stages of communication to a different extent because they represent individual and societal traits in the dynamic process of communication. On the one hand, speakers and hearers are constrained by societal conditions, but as individuals they have their own goals, intentions, desires, etc. that are freely expressed, and recognized in the flow of interaction. This is not to deny the pragmatic theories that have grown out of the cooperation-centered Gricean approach. In recognizing the importance of egocentrism, SCA is a synthesis of the cooperation-centered view of communication and egocentrism-based approaches in cognitive psychology. Several researchers (e.g., Keysar and Bly 1995; Barr and Keysar 2005; Giora 2003) have argued that speakers and hearers are egocentric to a surprising degree, and have shown how the egocentric endeavors of interlocutors play a much more decisive role in the initial stages of production and comprehension than current pragmatic theories envision. Like House (2003), Kecskes (2007) argues that, especially in the first phase of the communicative process, instead of looking for common ground, which is absent to a great extent, lingua franca speakers articulate their own thoughts with whatever linguistic means they can easily use.

In Kecskes's SCA, communication is characterized by the interplay of two traits that are inseparable, mutually supportive and interactive:

Individual trait	Social trait
attention	intention
private experience	actual situational experience
egocentrism	cooperation
salience	relevance.

Communication is the result of the interplay of *intention* and *attention* motivated by the socio-cultural background that is privatized individually by interlocutors. The socio-cultural background is composed of the encyclopaedic knowledge of interlocutors deriving from their prior experience tied to the linguistic expressions they use and their current experience in which those expressions create and convey meaning. For instance:

(1) Professor: - Is there anything else you want to tell us about yourself?
　　Aysa: - Uh,. . . no, nothing.. ... When can I call for the result?
　　Professor: - *There is no need to contact us. We'll call you.*
　　Aysa: - Ok, but .., uhm, . . .when?
　　Professor: - Very soon.
　　　　　　　　　　　　　(Job interview for assistantship at SUNY, Albany.)

In job interviews there is usually a special load attached to some of the recurring expressions such as *There is no need to contact us. We'll call you*, which basically indicates that the interview is over. What the speaker meant differed from what the hearer inferred from the same utterance. The difference is the result of the different privatization of an utterance based on the prior experience of interlocutors. By privatization I mean the process in which an utterance is produced or interpreted based on the prior and actual situation experience of interlocutors in an actual situational context.

The socio-cognitive approach integrates the pragmatic view of cooperation and the cognitive view of egocentrism, and emphasizes that both cooperation and egocentrism are manifested to a varying extent in all phases of communication. While cooperation is an intention-directed practice measured by relevance, egocentrism is an attention-oriented trait measured by salience. Intention and attention are identified as two measurable forces that affect communication in a systematic way. The measurement of intention and attention by means of relevance and salience is distinct from earlier explanations (e.g., Sperber and Wilson 1986/1995; Wilson and Sperber 2004; Giora 2003).

4 Interculturality and intraculturality

There have been several attempts to explain the difference between interculturality and intraculturality (e.g., Samovar and Porter 2001; Ting-Toomey 1999; Gudykunst and Mody 2002). According to Samovar and Porter (2001: 95), 'intracultural communication' is 'the type of communication that takes place between members of the same dominant culture, but with slightly different values', as opposed to 'intercultural communication' which is the communication between members of two or more distinct cultures.

Several researchers make the mistake of considering interculturality as the main reason for miscommunication (e.g., Thomas 1983; Hinnenkamp 1995; Ting-Toomey 1999). In fact, some researchers (House 2003; Kecskes 2007) show the opposite to be the case. The use of semantically transparent language by non-native speakers results in fewer misunderstandings and communication breakdowns than we would expect. The insecurity experienced by lingua franca speakers makes them establish a unique set of rules for interaction which may be referred to as an 'interculture' according to Koole and ten Thije (1994: 69), or a 'culture constructed in cultural context'.

Blum-Kulka et al. (2008: 164) define interculturality as 'a contingent interactional accomplishment' from a discursive-constructivist perspective. They argue that a growing literature explores interculturality as a participant concern (e.g., Higgins 2007; Mori 2003; Markee and Kasper 2004). The socio-cognitive approach goes one step further and defines interculturality as a phenomenon that is not only interactionally and socially constructed in the course of communication, but also relies on relatively definable cultural models and norms representing the speech communities to which the interlocutors belong. Consequently, interculturality has both relatively static and emergent components. In order for us to understand the dynamic and ever-changing nature of intercultural encounters, we need to approach interculturality dialectically. Cultural constructs and models change diachronically, while cultural representation and speech production by individuals changes synchronically. **Interculturality is a situationally emergent and co-constructed phenomenon that relies both on relatively definable cultural norms and models as well as situationally evolving features.** Intercultures are created in a communicative process in which the cultural norms and models brought to the interaction from the prior experience of interlocutors blend in a synergetic way with the features created *ad hoc* in the interaction. The result is intercultural discourse in which there is mutual transformation of knowledge and communicative behavior. **Interculturality has both an *a priori* side and an emergent side that occur and act simultaneously in the communicative process.** Consequently, intercultures are not fixed phenomena, but are created in the course of a communication in which participants belonging to different L1 speech communities speak a common language while at the same time representing the different cultural norms and models that are defined by their respective L1 communities, as in this conversation involving students from Brazil, Columbia and Hong Kong:

(2) B: Have you ever heard about au pair before?
     Col: No, what is au pair?
     HK: It's a French word.
     B: . . . we come as an exchange to take care of kids.
     Col: What kids?
     B: Kids in the host family. We live with the host family.
     HK: By the way, how about the kids? How do you know what to do with them?
     B: We have to go to training.
                (Albany English Lingua Franca database collected by PhD students.)

In this conversation, the interlocutors represent three different languages and cultures (Portuguese, Cantonese, Spanish), and use English as a lingua franca. This is the prior knowledge that the participants bring to the discussion. They create an interculture, which belongs to none of them and emerges in the course of their conversation. Within this interculture, the interactants have a relatively smooth discussion about the French term *au pair*, which is used to denote a job in the USA and represents prior knowledge which some but not all of them share. There are no misunderstandings in the interaction because each participant takes care to use semantically transparent language.

Such intercultures come and go, they are neither stable nor permanent. They just occur. They are synergetic and blended. Interculturality is constituted on the spot by the speakers who participate in the interaction. Much the same might be said of intracultural communication. Indeed, the currently dominant approach is that there is no principled difference between intracultural and intercultural communication (cf. Winch 1997; Wittgenstein 2001). Although we can accept this as far as the *mechanism* of the communicative process is concerned, there is in fact a quantitative difference in the *nature and content* of intracultural and intercultural interactions. The interlocutors in an intracultural interaction rely on the prior knowledge and culture established in a relatively definable speech community, which is privatized by individuals belonging to that community. What is created on the spot enriches the given culture, contributes to it and remains within the fuzzy but recognizable confines of that language and culture. In the case of intercultural communication, however, the prior knowledge that is brought to and privatized in the interaction belongs to different cultures and languages, and what participants create on the spot will disappear rather than enrich a particular culture or language. Intercultures are *ad hoc* creations that may enhance the individual and the globalization process but can hardly be said to add to any particular culture.

Imagine an intracultural discussion of legal issues involving a lawyer and a carpenter, say, in the United States. Their discussion may not progress smoothly because the carpenter may not be very knowledgeable about legal terms. If, however, two lawyers discuss legal issues, they will certainly understand each other's technical language, although there may still be some individual differences. This is what prompts the argument that a U.S. lawyer would understand an English-speaking French lawyer better than she would understand an English-speaking carpenter. However, we must be careful about judgments like this. As I argue elsewhere (2009: 9), a person who moves from Albany, New York to New Orleans, Louisiana, makes adjustments to the new culture, and starts to say things like *I might could do this*. This cannot be compared qualitatively to the case when a person moves from Albany, New York to Lille, France. In the first case we can speak about peripheral rather than core changes in the language use of the person. Louisiana culture and Upstate New York culture can be considered sub-cultures of American culture, and Louisiana dialect and the Upstate New York dialect are dialects of American English. However, the change is different when a person moves from Albany, New York to Lille, France. Comparing Upstate New York dialect and the Picard dialect of Lille is different from comparing Upstate New York and the Louisiana dialects. In the first case we speak about dialects of different languages (English and French) while in the second case we speak about dialects of the same language (English). There is a qualitative difference between crossing language boundaries and crossing dialects. The same is true for cultures. The relationship between American and French cultures differs qualitatively from the relationship between Louisiana sub-culture and Upstate New York sub-culture and may create qualitatively different mental and behavioral changes.

There is one more major difference between intracultural and intercultural communication. Intracultural communication is dominated by preferred ways of saying things (Wray 2002) and preferred ways of organizing thoughts within a particular speech community (Kecskes 2007). This is not the case in intercultural communication because the development of 'preferred ways' requires time and conventionalization within a speech community. Human languages are very flexible. They can lexicalize whatever their speakers find it important to lexicalize. There are preferred ways of lexicalizing certain phenomena, so that Americans *shoot a film*, *dust the furniture*, *make love*, *do the dishes*, etc. One language has a word for a phenomenon that is important in that culture, and another does not. In Russian, *spargal'ki* denotes 'tools for cheating'. In Hungarian the same phenomenon is denoted by the word *puska*. But there is no word for this in English. Knowing what expressions to select and what is appropriate or inappropriate in a particular situation may be an important sign of group-inclusiveness, or, as some would say, that we are 'native'-like. In intercultural communication, this group-inclusiveness is created on the spot by speakers with different linguistic and cultural backgrounds who cannot rely on the advantageous use of the formulaic and figurative elements of a common language. In an empirical study, Kecskes (2007) demonstrated that in lingua franca communication the use of formulaic language by the participants amounted to less than 10% of the 'native' norm. Instead, lingua franca speakers relied on semantically transparent language to ensure that their interlocutors could follow what they said.

In sum, it is erroneous to think that intercultural communication differs from intracultural communication because the former is more complicated than the later and leads to more miscommunication. As we saw above, the dissimilarity is qualitative rather than quantitative, because there is a qualitative difference between crossing language boundaries and crossing dialects.

5 Linguistic pragmatics and intercultural pragmatics

Although intercultural pragmatics offers a new perspective on communicative processes and introduces a socio-cognitive angle into pragmatics research, its scope and goals should also be defined in relation to other approaches to pragmatics, such as the Neo-Gricean approach, Speech Act Theory and Relevance Theory. Issues in the pragmatics paradigm, including the semantics-pragmatics interface, literal meaning, explicature, implicature, salience, etc., are relevant to intercultural pragmatics, but in a revised way. There are three dimensions in which intercultural pragmatics shows important differences from other sub-fields in pragmatics. These are developed in sub-sections 5.1, 5.2 and 5.3.

5.1 Pragmatic theories are utterance-centered; intercultural pragmatics is discourse segment-centered

The focus of pragmatic theories is on communicative actions (speech acts, pragmatic action, utterance) while intercultural pragmatics focuses on interaction. Pragmatic theories are utterance-centered. In these theories, the most significant difference between a sentence and an utterance is that sentences are judged according to how well they make sense grammatically, while utterances are judged according to their communicative validity (Habermas 1979: 31). Following Austin, the main focus of pragmaticians is on the illocutionary meaning conveyed by an utterance in its actual situational context in intracultural communication. However, utterance analysis in intercultural pragmatics may be problematic for two reasons. On the one hand, utterances in intercultural interactions are often not regularly formed on account of language proficiency issues. On the other hand, Kecskes (2007) demonstrates that the creativity of lingua franca speakers is detectable at the discourse rather than the utterance level. A similar idea is suggested by Prodromou (2008). Consequently, in intercultural communication, it makes more sense to analyze discourse segments rather than utterances. And indeed, the criticism of intercultural interaction as characterized by miscommunication, lack of systematic coherence and a low level of creativity is seen to be invalid when we analyze the phenomenon on a discourse-segment rather than an utterance level and in the socio-cognitive paradigm in which we treat creativity and coherence as discourse in progress.

Instead of considering coherence as a formal text- and product-oriented concept, we should instead perceive it as an interactively negotiated process which is dependent on the context and the interlocutors. Coates (1995) argued that much real language data is coherent without the application of any cohesive devices. Thus coherence is closely connected to interpretability and acceptability in context, and involves both intra- and extra-textual factors. Coherence is not so much a textual phenomenon as an effect that comes about when interlocutors ascribe meaning to utterances and understand how each other's contributions cohere. As Bublitz and Lenk (1999: 157) claim, there is a 'default principle of coherence', a basic assumption that interlocutors produce coherent discourse.

One discourse level whose analytical methodology is well established in the literature is talk-in-interaction. In recent years, serious efforts have been made to introduce Conversational Analysis (CA) into second language acquisition and interlanguage pragmatics research. CA can also be used for analytic purposes in intercultural pragmatics. However, I want to explore a different methodology here, namely centering theory. Centering theory was developed by Grosz and Sidner (1986) to stress the role of purpose and processing in discourse. Their theory is compatible with SCA because it focuses on the interplay and change of intention and attention within discourse segments and underlines both *a priori* and emergent features in the discursive process. The theory attempts to relate focus of attention, choice of referring expression, and perceived coherence of utterances within a discourse segment. It provides a model of discourse structure and meaning well suited to intercultural interaction where an understanding of the ways in which focus of attention affects both the production and the understanding of various linguistic expressions in discourse is crucial.

Centering theory distinguishes three components of discourse: linguistic structure, intentional structure, and attentional state. *Linguistic structure* groups utterances into discourse segments. *Intentional structure* consists of discourse segment purposes and the relations between them. *Attentional state* is an abstraction of the focus of attention of the participants as the discourse unfolds. Attentional state, being dynamic, records the objects, properties, and relations which are salient at each point of the discourse

There are two levels of attentional state. The global level is concerned with the relations between discourse segments and the ways in which attention shifts between them; it depends on the intentional structure. The local level is concerned with changes of attention within discourse segments. *Centering* (Grosz et al. 1995), an element of the local level, pertains to the interaction between the form of linguistic expression and local discourse coherence. In particular, it relates local coherence to choice of referring expression (e.g., pronouns in contrast to definite descriptions or proper names), and argues that differences in coherence correspond in part to the different demands for inference made by different types of referring expressions, given a particular attentional state.

According to centering theory, discourses consist of constituent segments, each of which is represented as part of a discourse model. *Centers* are semantic entities that are part of the discourse model for each utterance in a discourse segment. They consist of forward-looking centers (Cf), backward-looking centers (Cb), and preferred centers (Cp).

Centering theory predicts four transition states:

CONTINUE: If the current Cb is the same as the previous one and the same as the current Cp

RETAIN: If the current Cb is the same as the previous one but different from the current Cp

SMOOTH-SHIFT: If the current Cb is different from the previous one and the same as the current Cp

ROUGH-SHIFT: If the current Cb is neither the same as the previous one nor the same as the current Cp.

This then is how Centering theory analysis would apply to the exchange considered earlier in example (2):

(3)   U1: Have you ever heard about au pair before?
               Cf: you ; au pair
       U2: No, what is au pair?
               Cf-Cb: au pair   CONTINUE
       U3: It's a French word.
               Cf-Cb: French word   CONTINUE
       U4: . . . we come as an exchange to take care of kids.
               Cf: we; kids / Cb: 0   ROUGH-SHIFT
       U5: What kids?
               Cf-Cb: kids   CONTINUE
       U6: Kids in the host family.
               Cf-Cb: kids; host family   CONTINUE
       U7: We live with the host family.
               Cf: we; / Cb: host family   RETAIN
       U8: By the way, how about the kids?
               Cf-Cb: kids   SMOOTH-SHIFT
       U9: How do you know what to do with them?
               Cf: you / Cb: them   RETAIN
       U10: We have to go to training.
               Cf-Cb: we; training   CONTINUE

Several researchers (e.g., Walker 1998; Hu and Pan 2001) have argued that the restriction of centering to operating within a discourse segment should be abandoned in order to integrate centering with a model of global discourse structure. According to Walker (1998), the within-segment restriction causes three problems. The first is that centers are often continued over discourse segment boundaries with pronominal referring expressions whose form is identical to those that occur within a discourse segment. This can be very clearly seen in the analysis in example (2). The second is that recent work has shown that listeners perceive segment boundaries at various levels of granularity so that it is unlikely that each listener will identify the same segment boundaries. The third issue is that even within a discourse segment, there are strong contrasts between utterances whose adjacent utterance is hierarchically recent and utterances whose adjacent utterance is linearly recent. Hu and Pan (2001) argued that centering theory makes wrong predictions in center computation because the theory does not distinguish a backward-looking center (Cb) from a discourse segment topic (DST). Although Cb and DST share many properties, they are conceptually different, and should thus be differentiated from each other. Cb is used to process the local coherence of discourse between utterances, while DST is used to process the more global coherence of discourse between discourse segments. In our example, the first Discourse Segment Topic is 'au pair'. The DST changes in U4 to 'kids'. However, the dialog continues implicitly to be about 'au pair'. As the utterance segments in a lingua franca are less coherent than the discourse segment as a whole, in lingua franca analysis we should focus on the DST.

We have no space here to go into a detailed explanation of how to use centering theory to analyze intercultural interaction data beyond this single example. There is no doubt, however, that this type of analysis looks very promising in intercultural pragmatics.

5.2 Intercultural communication as a trial-and-error, try-again process co-constructed by participants

Pragmatic theories look at human communication in a rather idealized way. They emphasize cooperation, rapport, politeness. While intercultural pragmatics does not deny the importance of these phenomena in human communication, it makes an attempt to give equal attention to negative features of the process, including break-downs, errors, misunderstandings and egocentrism. According to SCA, everyday communication is not conducted as a practice of recipient design and intention recognition, as current pragmatic theories tend to claim. In fact, communication is more like a trial-and-error, try-again process that is co-constructed by the participants. It appears to be a non-summative and emergent interactional achievement (Arundale 1999, 2008). This is especially true in intercultural communication, as the following exchange between a Brazilian and a Polish student demonstrates:

(4) B: And what do you do?
     P: I work at the university as a cleaner.
     B: As a janitor?
     P: No, not yet. Janitor is after the cleaner.
     B: You want to be a janitor?
     P: Of course.
                (Albany English Lingua Franca database collected by PhD students.)

The Pole could not design her production for the recipient because she did not know much about the recipient so simply relied on her lexical knowledge to get her message across. However, they worked out the problems originating from the differences in their prior experience quite smoothly

5.3 The priority of salience in production and comprehension

In pragmatic theories, relevance and cooperation are seen as the main driving forces of the communicative process. In contrast, intercultural pragmatics emphasizes the priority of *salience* both in production and comprehension. While cooperation is an intention-directed practice measured by relevance, egocentrism is an attention-oriented trait measured by salience (Kecskes 2008; Kecskes and Zhang 2009). The simplest definition of salience is that it is the most probable meaning out of all possible meanings (Kecskes 2007).

Two of the main debates in pragmatic theory focus on the controversies surrounding the conscious versus automatic processing of available contextual information and the distinction between literal and nonliteral meaning. But in fact, these issues are two sides of the same question: the literal/nonliteral distinction is closely bound up with the distinction between the automatic and conscious retrieval of information:

> Though literal meanings tend to be highly salient, their literality is not a component of salience. The criterion or threshold a meaning has to reach to be considered salient is related only to its accessibility in memory due to such factors as frequency of use or experiential familiarity.
>
> Giora (2003: 33)

Intercultural communication clearly demonstrates the priority of salience over contextual factors both in production and comprehension. Gibbs (1996: 33) argues that 'context becomes operative only at a post-access stage, guiding the selection of the contextually relevant meaning of the ambiguous words.' The critical variable in language processing is salience, and not the literalness of lexical units (Giora 2003; Kecskes 2004). The main claim of Giora's graded salience hypothesis is that salient meanings are processed automatically (though not necessarily solely), irrespective of contextual information and 'strength of bias' in the first phase of comprehension when lexical processing and contextual processing run parallel (Giora 2003: 24). Other cognitive psychologists also emphasize that the individual, egocentric endeavors of speakers and hearers play a much more decisive role in communication than current pragmatic theories envision (Keysar and Barr 2002). Language processing is anchored in the assumption that what is salient or accessible to oneself will also be accessible to one's interlocutors (Barr and Keysar 2005; Colston 2005; Kecskes 2007). This is what we call the *egocentrism* of speaker-hearer. Egocentrism is not a negative phenomenon. It is something interlocutors cannot help, cannot subdue. What is salient, based on their prior experience, is always on their mind subconsciously and automatically. This is why it is not enough to emphasize only the co-constructed, emergent aspect of the communicative process. Together with the societal factor, we must also emphasize the individual cognitive factor (prior experience). Giora's graded salience hypothesis (1997, 2003) does this, and claims that instead of postulating the priority of literal meaning, the priority of salient (i.e. conventional, familiar, frequent, predictable) meaning should be assumed.

In intercultural pragmatics, salience is an especially crucial factor. Interlocutors participating in intercultural encounters have their main prior experience rooted in different cultures and languages. They share more limited common ground than interlocutors in intracultural communication and therefore have to create most of the common ground in the course of communication. This unique situation increases the importance of the linguistic code as opposed to the situational context in meaning production and comprehension. Language as a system encodes basic meaning (usually called *literal meaning*) for each user of that code. Several studies in English lingua franca use (House 2003; Philip 2005; Kecskes 2007) have found that ELF speakers rely on semantically transparent language rather than the formulaic and/or figurative language associated with 'native'-likeness. In an empirical study, Kecskes (2007) showed that ELF users usually avoided formulaic expressions, not necessarily because they did not know them, but because they were worried that their interlocutors would not understand them properly. In other words, they were reluctant to use language that they knew, or perceived, to be figurative or less semantically transparent (see also Philip 2005). Since lingua franca speakers have different socio-cultural backgrounds and represent different cultures, the mutual knowledge they may share is knowledge of the primary meaning of words and expressions. Consequently, semantic analysability plays a decisive role in ELF speech production. This assumption was supported in Kecskes's study by the fact that the most frequently used formulaic expressions were fixed semantic units and phrasal verbs whose semantic transparency is more apparent than that of idioms, situation-bound utterances or speech formulas.

As we have seen, several studies (House 2003; Philip 2005; Kecskes 2007) demonstrate that literal meaning may play a more decisive role in intercultural communication than it does in intracultural communication. Indeed, in L1 communication, speakers frequently use the term *literally* to mark their commitment to the most salient meaning even when that meaning is figurative rather than strictly literal, as in Israel's (2002) examples:

(5)   He was literally glued to the screen
       She was literally driving him nuts in his later years.

For an L1 user, either the figurative or the literal or both meanings of an expression can be most salient depending on their private experience. However, in intercultural communication, because of the diverse prior experience of interlocutors and because of the fact that they usually learn rather than acquire the common language or lingua franca, interlocutors use the linguistic code as common ground and give priority to literal meaning as most salient. When this is not the case, miscommunication may occur, as in example (6):

(6)   Chinese: I think Peter drank a bit too much at the party yesterday.
      Turkish: Eh, tell me about it. He always drinks too much.
      Chinese: When we arrived he drank beer. Then Mary gave him some vodka.
             Later he drank some wine. Oh, too much.
      Turkish: Why are you telling me this? I was there.
      Chinese: Yes, but you told me to tell about it.
             (Albany English Lingua Franca database collected by PhD students.)

In this conversation, the use of the expression 'tell me about it' in a figurative sense leads to misunderstanding because the Chinese student processes it literally.

In both intracultural and intercultural communication, salience overrides literalness because, given the fact that lexical units encapsulate the history of their prior use, those usages will get priority in the meaning hierarchy that represents the most familiar and frequent encounters. However, while in intracultural communication the most salient meaning can be either literal or figurative or both, in intercultural communication, the most salient meaning for interlocutors is usually the literal meaning.

Although Giora (1997, 2003) argues that cognitively prominent salient meanings rather than literal meanings play the most important role in both production and comprehension, more attention in pragmatics research has been paid to comprehension than to production. Kecskes's SCA claims that salience plays as important a role in language production as in comprehension. The role of salience in language production involves a relation between prominence of entities in a ranking, and preference of a choice among alternatives. For analytic purposes, three theoretically-significant categories should be distinguished: individual salience, collective salience and situational salience. Individual salience is characterized as a natural built-in preference in the general conceptual and linguistic knowledge of the speaker, which has developed as a result of prior experience with the use of lexical items and which changes both diachronically and synchronically. Individual salience is affected by collective salience and situational salience. The former is shared with other members of the speech community and changes diachronically. This is illustrated in the following exchange from a popular sit-com:

(7)   Jill: I met someone today.
      Jane: Good for you.
      Jill: He is a police officer.
      Jane: Are you in trouble?
      Jill: Oh, no!

This conversation demonstrates how a positive or negative private experience can affect the salience an individual attaches to an expression. The collective salience tied to the expression *police officer* suggests trouble, problem, something wrong, something against the law. However, Jill may have had a positive experience with a police officer, even perhaps of a romantic nature. So when she uses the expression 'police officer', its individual salience for her differs from the collective salience. This is not, however, the case for Jane, whose utterance 'Are you in trouble?' is produced as a result of collective salience.

Situational salience may change synchronically owing to the salience of specific objects in the context of language production, and may accrue through such determinants as vividness, speaker motivation and (if you allow the coinage) recency of mention. In an actual situational context, individual salience is affected and shaped both by collective and situational salience. When the speaker is faced with the choice of a word or an expression, a ranking of the available choices is obtained on the basis of the degree of salience of entities in the generation context. The word or phrase is then selected for utterance on the basis of maximum salience.

6 Conclusion

In this paper, the basic tenets and principles of intercultural pragmatics were reviewed. Intercultural Pragmatics was defined as a field of inquiry focusing on how the language system is put to use in social encounters between interlocutors who have different first languages, communicate in a common language, and usually represent different cultures.

It was emphasized that interculturality can be described properly only in a socio-cognitive paradigm that pulls together the societal and individual features of communication and emphasizes that cooperation and egocentrism are not antagonistic in the communicative process. Interculturality was defined as a situationally emergent, co-constructed phenomenon that relies on relatively definable cultural norms and models as well as situationally evolving features. Consequently, interculturality has both an *a priori* and an emergent side, which occur and act simultaneously in the communicative process. Intercultures are created as a result of blending the cultural norms and models brought into the interaction from the prior experience of the interlocutors with the features created *ad hoc* in the interaction.

I pointed out that intercultural interactional data poses a special challenge for analysts for two reasons. Firstly, the short history of interculturality makes it difficult to decide what to analyze, what to pay attention to, and what methods to use for analysis. Second, intercultural interaction should be analyzed at the discourse-segment rather than the utterance level because coherence and creativity are clearly detectable at this level. It is not through the individual utterance that language users demonstrate that they are cooperative, but rather how they behave over the course of the conversation.

As I stated at the outset, intercultural pragmatics is a field of inquiry which supports a less idealized, more down-to-earth approach to communication than current pragmatic theories usually do. Intercultural pragmatics does not deny the importance of cooperation, rapport and politeness in communicative endeavors, but it also acknowledges the role of egocentrism, chaos, aggression and trial-and-error. For these reasons, intercultural pragmatics has an important role to play in helping us to better understand the real nature of human communication.

■ ■ ■

POST-READING

This reading has a simple two-word title, 'Intercultural Pragmatics'. Working alone or with a colleague, think of a least 6 other possible titles or title + sub-title combinations. Or if you want to give yourself a real test, try to work out possible 3- 4- 5- 6- 7- 8- 9- and 10-word titles or title + sub-title combinations.

SECTION 7 FURTHER READING

Cross-cultural studies

In order to understand how the CCSARP methodology is applied, we recommend that you should read one of the studies reported in:

Blum-Kulka, S., House, J. and G. Kasper (eds) (1989) *Cross-Cultural Pragmatics: requests and apologies*, Norwood, New Jersey: Ablex Publishing Corporation.

Particularly good are the papers by Blum-Kulka and by Blum-Kulka and House, and, for a critical perspective, the paper by Wolfson, Marmor and Jones.

Discourse-completion tests

For an objective analysis of problems associated with DCTs, read:

Rose, K. (1994) 'On the validity of DCTs in non-Western contexts', *Applied Linguistics* 15: 1–14.

Interlanguage pragmatics

Kasper, G. and Blum-Kulka, S. (eds) (1993) *Interlanguage Pragmatics*, Oxford: Oxford University Press.

Japanese sentence-final particles

If Cook's paper inspires you to find out more about the nominalizer *no* and the sentence-final particles *ne*, *yo* and *yone*, which some believe to be the unmarked norm in Japanese, read:

Cook, H.M. (1990) 'An indexical account of the Japanese sentence-final particle *no*', *Discourse Processes* 13 (4): 401–40.
Cook, H.M. (1992) 'Meanings of non-referential indexes: a case study of Japanese sentence-final particle *ne*', *Text* 12: 507–39.
Kamio, A. (1994). 'The theory of territory of information: the case of Japanese', *Journal of Pragmatics* 21 (1), 67–100.
Takubo, Y. and Kinsui, S. (1997) 'Discourse management in terms of mental spaces', *Journal of Pragmatics* 28 (6): 741–58.

For a more comprehensive book length treatment, read:

Saigo, H. (2011) *The Pragmatic Properties and Sequential Functions of the Japanese Sentence-Final Particles Ne, Yo, and* Yone, Amsterdam: John Benjamins.

Intercultural pragmatics

The first edition of the journal *Intercultural Pragmatics* (2004) includes an editorial by Kecskes and a paper by Mey which explore some of the parameters of the area, as well as an interview with Giora in which she discusses her graded salience hypothesis.

Socio-cognitive approach

The two sources Kecskes refers to are:

Kecskes, I. (2008) 'Dueling context: a dynamic model of meaning', *Journal of Pragmatics* 40 (3), 385–406.
Kecskes, I. and Zhang, F. (2009) 'Activating, seeking and creating common ground: a socio-cognitive approach', *Pragmatics & Cognition* 17 (2), 331–55.

Pragmatics and conversation – development and impairment

Introduction

HISTORICAL PRAGMATICS APART, pragmatic analyses tend to focus on spoken interaction. As such, the discipline overlaps with other linguistic approaches which also prioritize spoken interaction. Two such approaches, Conversation Analysis (henceforth CA) and Interactional Sociolinguistics, are primarily *qualitative* ethnomethodological endeavours: this means analysts focus on the minutiae of participants' turn-taking sequences but in a way that makes no (or very few) *a priori* assumptions about their social and cultural backgrounds. Where interactional sociolinguistics differs from CA is in its focus on the interactional variation exhibited by some participants and also in its interest in Gricean-based analyses of inferential processes of implicature (cf. Sections 2 and 3). By way of illustration, Gumperz (1996) posits an approach whereby analysts focus on participants' "moves", "counter-moves" and "confirmations-disconfirmations" as a means of uncovering the (prosodic, paralinguistic, lexical and/or formulaic) indexical signs that *cue* the background knowledge necessary to understand the (underlying) meaning of a given interactional sequence (cf. Section 4). Such an approach has proved to be particularly useful when investigating (breakdowns in) intercultural communication. However, as we've focussed on intercultural communication in Section 7, this section is devoted to papers that are representative of the fields of developmental pragmatics and clinical pragmatics and, at the same time, draw on insights from CA and interactional sociolinguistics (in addition to pragmatics).

We begin with an extract that reports on young children's acquisition and development of (socially) effective/appropriate interactional skills, Anat Ninio and Catherine Snow's chapter, 'Children as Conversationalists', from their (1996) monograph, *Pragmatic Development. Essays in Developmental Science*. The extract, as it is presented here, pays particular attention to children's development of turn-taking and turn-management skills - including the use of repair sequences: this helps to explain why Ninio and Snow choose to highlight influential CA-based work before beginning their analysis proper (but this section is omitted, owing to length constraints). Ninio and Snow also outline some characteristics of skilful conversation (the bulk of which we do include), before going on to document the development of turn-taking skills within children, and the problems they must overcome to become competent conversationalists themselves. We have opted to begin this first extract at the point at which Ninio and Snow reiterate their intention 'to reconcile the claim of conversational precocity . . . with evidence about conversational inadequacies of young children'. Again, due to length limitations, we omit some of their discussions in respect to 'topic selection and topic maintenance' and 'referential communication tasks', and also their extended analysis of 4-year-old Ethan's conversation with his parents (which primarily focuses on their attempts to support Ethan's 'topic development'). The edited extract nevertheless presents a coherent account of the development of young children's conversational skills and the role played by significant caregivers in that development process. In respect to the latter, for example, Ninio and Snow particularly emphasize the importance of repair sequences – by, for example, using clarification requests (including rerun requests, substitutions, partial/full repetitions, etc.). As we might expect, it is the caregivers who tend to be the primary users of such requests in the early stages – so that they might signal (the child's need to repair) 'ill-formed utterances'. This particular practice, then, serves to (implicitly) communicate to children 'an important central principle of *effective* communication': that the 'interlocutor's perspective is often different from one's own and must [therefore] be taken into account'.

The second and third papers in this section can be considered to be representative of clinical pragmatics. We include them, alongside Ninio and Snow's study, not only because of their shared interest in conversation but also because clinical pragmatics – as a field – draws upon our understanding of what constitutes a normal development of pragmatic competence (i.e. developmental studies) as a means of highlighting pragmatic deficiencies in both children and adults.

The first of our clinical pragmatics studies is Emanuel Schegloff's (1999) CA-based journal article entitled 'Discourse, pragmatics, conversation, analysis', which was originally published in *Discourse Studies*. In the extract we include here Schegloff begins by introducing the video data he analyses in this study, which relates to a commissurotomy patient referred to as Alvin, whom Eran Zaidel (a neuropsychologist) had 'been studying for quite a long time': 'commissurotomy' is the name given to a procedure whereby the corpus callosum is surgically severed, with the result that the right and left hemispheres of the brain can no longer communicate. At the time of publication, a patient who underwent such a procedure was thought to experience problems in respect to 'turn-taking, the doing of . . . commands and requests, and the range of conventional norms we ordinarily term 'etiquette' or 'politeness''. But Schegloff analyses a few seconds of one exchange between Alvin and a research assistant, Dan, as a means of demonstrating Alvin's 'capacity to parse and to grasp the talk of an interlocutor and to respond effectively in interaction' – including complying with (indirect) requests. Schegloff is at pains to point out that Alvin's 'turns' constitute gestural/physical actions as opposed to verbal ones, that is, his 'compliance, responsive attention deployment, approval solicitation, and the like' indicate Alvin's sensitivity to the orderly '*turn* organisation of the talk' rather than constituting *turns*-at–talk in and of themselves. Even so, he appears to have found evidence for communicative behaviour, which formal testing procedures missed. Schegloff believes that this is because the type(s) of laboratory 'testing' in use at the time were not really assessing behaviour such as 'commands and indirect requests per se'; rather, they were testing 'decontexted actions, actions not part of indigenously engendered courses of action'. In response, he posited the usefulness of CA in capturing participants' *actual* conversational capacities. His call has since been taken up by Sarah Lock, Ray Wilkinson and others responsible for programmes like SPPARC (*Supporting Partners of People with Aphasia in Relationships and Conversation*). SPPARC draws on CA techniques as a means of, first, identifying areas of intervention, which might aid Alzheimer's sufferers and their partners in their day-to-day communications, and, then, constructing and evaluating various means by which such individuals can change or amend particular aspects of their verbal and/or non-verbal behaviour.

Like Schegloff, Heidi Hamilton (1994) also picks up on the potential inadequacies of relying purely on lab-based language research, when seeking to understand the (lack of) pragmatic competence of Alzheimer's patients, and instead advocates an interactional sociolinguistic approach 'as a complement to traditional analyses . . . in clinical settings'. For our final extract in this section on **Pragmatics and conversation – development and impairment**, we draw from sections of the introductory chapter and Chapter 2 of Hamilton's monograph, *Conversations with an Alzheimer's Patient. An Interactional Sociolinguistic Study*. As Hamilton highlights, the primary aim of this study is to investigate how one Alzheimer's patient, referred to as Elsie, 'performs in everyday conversation as her disease progresses and how that performance both influences and is influenced by the behavior of her conversational partner'. As such, 'the conversations at the heart of this study' are 'open-end, *natural* talks' (i.e. they represent 'talking for talk's sake' as opposed to 'speech elicited as part of an experimental research protocol'), with the result that Elsie and Hamilton take turns in 'being the "expert" on topics, and both initiate, maintain and close topics at will'; which, in turn, means that, like Alvin (see above), Elsie is able to exhibit a 'fuller communicative repertoire' than lab-based studies have prototypically allowed.

We believe that the edited reading, as it is reproduced here, provides a coherent account of 'Elsie's communicative abilities and difficulties as observed in the fourteen conversations', recorded by Hamilton between November 1981 and March 1986 in her capacity as a volunteer at a healthcare centre. Hamilton has two primary focii: the extent to which Elsie demonstrates 'automaticity in language' and the extent to which she can take the 'role of the other'. In regard to automaticity, Hamilton notes that Alzheimer's patients like Elsie appear to lose the capacity to use 'more creative and higher option semantic and pragmatic systems' long before they lose the more automatic features of their language use. Elsie's more automatic language features included terms like *for goodness sake, my my* and *that's a good idea* which, through frequent long-term usage, had become stored within her 'inventory of talk'. By 'role of the other', Hamilton is referring to a "normal" interlocutor's 'ability to predetermine how another person will react to their actions by evoking in themselves the same response the other person will have'. For example, interlocutors will often help their conversational partner(s) by linguistically signalling given and new information. For Elsie, this ability became problematic as her illness progressed – to the extent that she began to present new information as though it were *given* information, and 'information . . . known to her conversational partner' as though it were new. That said, Hamilton found evidence to suggest 'Elsie's decreased ability to take the role of the other in conversation' was not 'uniformly distributed across all facets of her language use'. For example, Hamilton found evidence of 'Elsie's successful use of . . . positive politeness' (i.e. of Elsie taking the feelings of her conversational other into account) in 1982, and evidence of Elsie responding 'to questions and taking a turn-at-talk' as late as 1986 (i.e. nearing the end of the study). Hamilton then goes on to further problematize our understanding of taking 'the role of the other', by pointing out that the ("normal") interactional partners of Alzheimer patients also struggle to 'take the perspective' of their 'disabled conversational partner[s]': as a result, she suggests we should not be too ready to attribute conversational breakdowns/miscommunications to disabled interlocutors only.

ANAT NINIO AND CATHERINE E. SNOW

CHILDREN AS CONVERSATIONALISTS

PRE-READING

Before beginning the Ninio and Snow reading, write down/summarize what you know about *conversational repair*. Consider, in particular, why conversational repair might be important (a) to the 'smooth running' of conversation generally, and (b) to children's linguistic development in particular.

IN-READING

As you come to Ninio and Snow's list of seven types of clarification requests (indicated by | in the margin), stop reading and provide your own definition for each. Try to provide definitions that clearly capture the differences between 'rerun requests', 'yes-no questions that are full repetitions', 'yes-no questions that are partial repetitions', 'direct questions of the meaning of a word', 'yes-no questions that substitute new forms', 'yes-no questions that are (partial/full) repetitions but also add new material' and 'wh-questions that demand product completion concerning a missing component'.

■ ■ ■

CHILDREN AS CONVERSATIONALISTS
ANAT NINIO AND CATHERINE E. SNOW

[. . .] One goal of this chapter is to reconcile the claim of conversational precocity (which we accept) with evidence about conversational inadequacies of young children, which we will demonstrate. Their inadequacies include a tendency not to respond appropriately to many conversational-exchange starters, failures to maintain conversational topic, lack of resources for starting conversations with relative strangers, difficulties in gauging the interlocutor's state of knowledge, and other such obstacles to full participation as skilled conversationalists. Conversational skill has a number of components, some strictly linguistic and others more clearly social or interactive; young children are fairly accomplished at some yet rather poor at others.

[. . .]

Consider the following [. . .] conversational exchange between former spouses a couple of years after their divorce [taken from the play, *The Real Thing*]:

Henry: How are things with your friend? An architect, isn't he?

Charlotte: I had to give him the elbow. Well, he sort of left. I called him the architect of my misfortune.

Henry: What was the matter with him?

Charlotte: Very possessive type. I came home from a job, I'd been away only a couple of days, and he said, why did I take my diaphragm? He'd been through my bathroom cabinet, would you believe? And then, not finding it, he went through everything else. Can't have that.

Henry: What did you say?

Charlotte: I said, I didn't take my diaphragm, it just went with me. So he said, what about the tube of Duragel? I must admit he had me there.

Henry: You should have said, "Duragel!—no wonder the bristles fell out of my toothbrush."

(Stoppard 1982: 66)

Characteristics of this exchange that make it highly competent [. . .] include:

1. Rapid turn-taking. In fact, the effectiveness of the exchange as a piece of theater derives in part from the phenomenon called *latching*, or *immediate uptake*, in which each turn begins a microsecond before the previous one ends.

2. Avoidance of overlaps, interruptions, and dysfluencies. In addition to avoiding interturn pauses, competent conversations avoid periods of overlapping speech (although what is considered "overlapping" is highly culturally determined), interruptions of turns, intraturn pauses or dysfluencies that might elicit interruptions, and other violations of the joint principles "only one speaker at a time" and "at least one speaker all the time."

3. Observance of obligations to respond. Certain conversational turns absolutely require a response, whereas others simply allow one. Greetings, for example, must be returned— failure to respond to a greeting is considered a social slight. Questions, unless rhetorical, must be acknowledged even if not answered, and failure to do so is a frank violation of rules for turn exchange (one children get away with a fair amount of the time).

4. Observation of obligations as a listener. In addition to responding when required, good conversationalists are expected to display attentiveness, to indicate comprehension or lack thereof, and to give the interlocutor time and opportunity to speak. Rules for listener behavior are little emphasized in the developmental literature on conversational skill; in fact, they have been attended to primarily in cross-cultural analyses, for example, analyses suggesting that Japanese conversational rules require a more active, responsible listener than do Anglo-American rules. Clearly, though, folk politeness rules in Anglo-American culture do enjoin speakers at the least to stop and give others a turn, to attend to others' speech, and so on. And in fact, such attentiveness is prerequisite to effective timing of one's own turns and to the provision of topic-appropriate responses.

5. Topic relatedness. In good conversations, like that between Charlotte and Henry, utterances relate topically to their predecessors. This principle is sufficiently strong that its inverse is institutionalized in the Gricean maxim (Grice 1975) of relevance: No matter what answer one gets, seek an interpretation that assumes topic relevance. Children acquire this very

important principle of topic development only with great difficulty and over a very long period of time. The requirement of topic relatedness leads to many additional characteristics of conversation, for example, the availability of explicit topic-change or topic-diversion strategies (e.g., *by the way, not to change the topic but . . ., that reminds me*), as well as of formulas for topic reinstatement and topic termination. [. . .]

6. Repair strategies. Whereas scripted conversations like the one quoted here typically avoid misunderstandings and failures of uptake, normal conversations are studded with various sorts of breakdowns, and thus skilled conversationalists must control polite procedures for eliciting repairs and checking on comprehension.

[. . .]

Children's conversational skills

The paradox of children's coexistent precocity and immaturity in the realm of conversation can be explained by the need to control these various subsystems of conversational skill simultaneously. In some subsystems, for example, taking turns, children become good fairly early. In others, for example, maintaining topic relevance or observing rules of timing and obligations to respond, they are considerably less precocious. In this chapter we describe the development of children's conversational skills across these various domains.

[. . .]

Children's turn-taking

The first attempts to think about children's interactions with adults from a conversational perspective were directly influenced by the work of the conversational analysts; it was reading Sacks et al. (1974) that led Snow to analyze interactions between two British mothers and their infants using constructs like turn, first-pair part, adjacency pair, and so on (Snow 1977). In applying these constructs to parent-infant interaction, contrasts with adult-adult conversation emerged; whereas adult conversationalists take turns intentionally and [. . .] compete for the next turn, infants are liberally given credit for turns they either did not take at all (total silence) or did not intend as communicative (e.g., burps, coughs). [. . .] Infants as young as three months in Snow's study (1977), and even younger in Kaye and Charney's work (1980, 1981), were being treated as conversational partners by their mothers during face-to-face play sessions and feeding sessions; it is thus perhaps not surprising that by eight or nine months of age such children are fairly good at the turn-taking aspect of conversation, at least in dyadic situations with adult interactants. By the time they are producing their first words, children can typically sustain long bouts of well-timed turn alternations with mothers (Kaye and Charney 1980, 1981; Snow 1977). The crucial role of the sensitive adult in this accomplishment is demonstrated by the fact that, with peers, the same pattern of turn alternations only appears a couple of years later; by about age three, though, children do follow rules of turn-taking with each other (Ervin-Tripp 1979; Keenan and Klein 1975).

Once children have learned to take their turns reliably they are faced with the problem of maintaining the turn—holding the floor. This may be a more serious problem for children than for adults, since children speak relatively slowly and dysfluently; pauses and dysfluencies represent opportunities for the interlocutor to seize a turn. Adults tend to protect children's turns, but in peer-interaction situations children must learn to hold the floor long enough to finish their own turns, a challenge that becomes greater as one's playmates become more skilled in exploiting opportunities to seize the floor. By about age four, children show some control over the use of devices like sentence-initial *and* or repetitive *et puis* (and then) as floor holders, signaling that their turn is not yet complete by initiating a new syntactic unit (Jisa 1984–5; Peterson and McCabe 1987).

Much writing about conversational development has emphasized continuity—the degree to which the structure of early mother-infant interactions resembles that of adult conversational exchange. Bateson (1975), for example, referred to mother-infant interactions as *proto-conversations*, and Trevarthen (1979) has argued for infant social/communicative precocity on the basis of structural similarities between infant-adult and adult-adult interaction patterns. It is also clear, though, that such periods of adult-infant conversation-like interaction alternate with periods of interaction that do not resemble conversational turn-taking, times when both parties vocalize in unison or when long silences occur (e.g., Stern et al. 1975). The tendency of Western psychologists to emphasize the continuity identifiable in some interactions (see Collis 1985) could be taken as a reflex of precisely the same cultural tendency that leads mothers to treat infant burps or coughs as conversational turns—a cultural commitment to the principles that (1) conversation is the normal form for human interaction, and (2) babies should be accorded autonomy and interactive rights similar to those of adults.

In fact, many problems of conversational management are eased for young children (and thus the appearance of continuity is enhanced) by the availability of highly cooperative adult conversational partners. Thus, children's violations of some of the rules governing adult conversation are not considered particularly serious, and their frequent difficulties abiding by the Gricean maxims (Grice 1975) of relevance and quantity are compensated for by adult willingness to engage in extensive repair.

How do we reconcile, though, the view that young children are rather proficient in at least the turn-taking aspects of conversation with the widely accepted view that young children are egocentric (Piaget 1929) and engage in private speech—speech in which turn-taking does not occur? Herein lies one of the complexities of understanding conversational development; it is easy to characterize children as precocious or as hopelessly unskilled depending on what aspect of conversation one focuses on. In interaction with adults, children tend to stay involved in conversations and to look like good turn-takers. In interactions with peers, children are more likely to show disruption of turn-taking through engagement in private speech. One study of four-year-olds in dyadic interaction showed that almost half of the segments of talk (defined as talk focused on one topic) were monologic (Schober-Peterson and Johnson 1991); however, about half of these monologic segments were unsuccessful attempts to enter into dialogue.

Children's turn-taking failures have several possible sources. Disruptions of turn-taking in infant-adult interaction, when infants are allowed to produce contentless turns, reflect the infants' lack of skill in turn-taking itself. Later disruptions can result from the undeveloped state of other conversational skills, that is, children who know they should take a turn nonetheless fail to do so because they do not understand the interlocutor or because they cannot think of anything to say on the topic. Indeed, continuation of a conversational topic in adult-child talk is often a function more of adult responsiveness (Bloom et al. 1976) than of child-topic maintenance behaviors, although improvement in topic maintenance occurs with age [. . .]. Some violations of normal conversational responsiveness by young children may also relate to deficits in their ability to comprehend implicitly nominated topics (Bacharach and Luszcz 1979; Luszcz and Bacharach 1983) or to other cognitive limitations on control over conversational implicature.

Violations of timing

The picture presented by Sacks et al. (1974) of adult conversations with minimal overlap and minimal silence is, of course, somewhat idealized even for mature conversationalists. In addition to clear violations, such as two speakers starting simultaneously and intentional or inadvertent interruptions of one speaker by another, adult conversations include periods of simultaneous speech occasioned by back channels and by chorusing. Back channels are vocal signals from the listener indicating agreement or attentiveness, frequent in Japanese conversations. Conversations among working-class North American girls are often characterized by periods of chorusing, when one or more listeners chime in with the speaker; effective chorusing requires that the speaker introduce refrains that are sufficiently predictable that unison or at least convergent chorusing is possible (Hemphill 1989).

Although interruptions are defined as violations, it is also clear that learning to interrupt is an important aspect of acquiring conversational skill. Sometimes it is crucial to interrupt the interlocutor—when an emergency arises, for example, or when one's dinner-party conversation is being dominated by an indefatigable bore. Children do get better at interrupting ongoing adult conversations in ways that are appropriate (Sachs et al. 1990), but skillful interruption is one of those skills that even some adults do not fully control.

Cultural differences and listening behavior

Cultural differences in the occurrence of back channels show that acquiring conversational skill requires learning not just how and when to talk but how and when to listen as well. The role of the listener in conversation is culturally constructed in conformity with a larger set of rules about social interaction and is subject to social class and gender, as well as to cultural variation. The most familiar contrast is probably that between Japanese and Western listeners. [. . .]

[. . .] [M]iddle-class American conversation is constructed as an interaction in which the primary responsibility for clarity of communication rests with the speaker, who is thus required to predict or explicitly demand information about required background knowledge and consistently to monitor his or her own output for comprehensibility. Japanese interactions, on the other hand, are constructed as communicative events in which speakers have considerable latitude to be elliptical, to assume shared background knowledge, and to be unclear, because listeners are responsible to signal (non)comprehension. Japanese children are socialized rather explicitly into their role as active, interpretive, responsible listeners in interactions in which their mothers tell them, for example, that visitors to the house may not really mean what they say (Clancy 1986). Presumably, North American children are similarly socialized into an understanding of speaker responsibility through interactions in which adults demand that children clarify their intentions, provide the background information adults need to understand their narratives, make explicit unfamiliar referents, and so on (see Blum-Kulka and Snow 1992).

Topic selection and topic maintenance

A [. . .] problem for the aspirant conversationalist is the issue of topic selection. [. . .] This problem [. . .] is somewhat alleviated for adults by the availability of standard, safe, culturally prescribed topics within speech communities—the weather in England, the playoff situation in the seasonally appropriate current sport for U.S. males, feeding and sleeping problems for parents with young children, and so on.

Young children are greatly disadvantaged in the making of small talk by their ignorance of the standard, culturally determined list of topics that organizes casual conversation for adults (Kellermann et al. 1989), as well as by their lack of knowledge about those topics (they typically do not read the papers, watch TV news broadcasts, or follow professional sports). Instead, childhood conversations tend to develop around topics dictated by play—by available objects that constitute a shared focus of attention, by formal games, or by familiar fantasy themes stimulated perhaps by the availability of dress-up clothes or tea sets. Absent these, young children's conversations often decline into word play, mutual repetitions, or other relatively contentless talk (Garvey 1975).

Such vocal play is one constructive low-level solution to the inability of young children to sustain social relations through simple talk, an inability that dictates the different organization of social events for different age groups. Whereas adult parties are typically unstructured in terms of activities on the assumption that conversation will constitute the major entertainment, children's parties are tightly scheduled with games, excursions, performances, and planned activities, because parents know that a group of 5- or even 10-year-olds simply will not fill up several hours with talk. In terms of Goffman's scheme for the contexts allowing talk [. . .], young children can make use of the intersubjectivity created by joint attention and joint action to generate conversations and interaction in general, but they typically cannot establish sustained intersubjectivity through conversation alone [. . .]

[. . .]

Procedures for topic initiation

Infants as young as 11 months of age are likely to manipulate an object that has been touched by a strange adult and to replicate the adult's actions on the object while engaging in sociable activities, like maintaining eye contact with the adult, or vocalizing (Eckerman et al. 1979). Such events may be the entry into topic initiation for young children: these topic initiations are pre-linguistic, object-mediated, and nonverbal, reflecting social abilities that underlie and prepare for linguistic developments.

The kinds of object-mediated social initiatives described by Eckerman and colleagues are typically responded to, by middle-class Western mothers at least, with utterances that establish the topic linguistically, for example, naming the object (*yes, a ball!*) or signaling something about the appropriate response to it (e.g., *pretty* or *roll it to me!*). The form of the maternal utterance in response to child object-mediated topic nominations has considerable influence on how children later choose to initiate and extend topics themselves (Goldfield 1987, 1990). Mothers who reliably respond with object names have children described as *referential*, who themselves rely on naming as a conversational strategy. Mothers who respond with phatic expressions (*nice!* or *pretty!*) have children who themselves are more *expressive*.

In interaction with young children, an adult's first conversational challenge is establishing a joint topic so that conversation can ensue. There are basically two possible mechanisms for doing so: a response to the child's initiation of some topic or an utterance designed to **Direct the hearer's attention** to some object or event that can serve as a new topic [. . .]. In the Harvard sample [. . .], every parent produced at least two, and typically more, utterances designed to **Direct the child's attention** in 20 minutes of interaction at every observation (Snow et al. 1996). **Directing hearer's attention** utterances were among the most frequent adult communicative acts (Pan et al. 1996). Evidently, even middle-class American mothers, the same type who respond to their infants' burps as conversational turns, require more content for interaction with somewhat older children.

Children in the Harvard study sample also offered their parents considerable opportunity to follow up on a child-initiated topic. Child acts **Directing the hearer's attention** (DHA) were the most frequent type of interpretable communicative attempts children made at 14 months. The 52 children observed at 14 months produced a total of 374 communicative acts coded as DHA, but 317 of these were interpretable as DHA only from accompanying nonverbal behaviors, for example, pointing or showing. At 20 months, 48 children produced a total of 610 DHA acts, of which 221 relied crucially on nonverbal components. Only 15 of the 308 DHA acts produced by 38 32-month-olds relied on nonverbal components for comprehensibility. These data reflect considerable development in children's capacities to nominate conversational topics and to do so verbally rather than through gesture or action. This capacity to nominate topics verbally is prerequisite to the initiation of absent, remote, or abstract topics, which both children and their parents do more successfully as the children get older.

[. . .] Discussions of topics that are attended to jointly by parent and child are the object- or book-mediated discussions we think of as typical in interaction with young children. All of the Harvard-sample parents engaged in such talk with children of all ages, although the percentage of children participating increased, 69 percent, 94 percent, and 100 percent at 14, 20, and 32 months, respectively [. . .] Discussions of topics slightly more remote, for example, talking about one's own nonpresent toothbrush upon seeing a toothpaste ad, were coded as **Discussion related to the present;** whereas 90 percent of parents engaged in this kind of talk at all ages, only 17 percent of children did so at 14 months, although more than 50 percent did by 20 months.

Even more striking development is seen in children's ability to participate in **Discussion of the nonpresent**, for example, telling stories about past events, planning future activities, discussing theoretical issues, and so on. One child managed this at 14 months (and then only by responding to adult initiatives), but 27 percent of children observed did so by 20 months and 51 percent by 32 months. Whereas cognitive developments are clearly prerequisite to the ability to discuss nonpresent topics, new acquisitions in the domain of linguistic structures (e.g., coming to control past tense, future aspect, genericity markers, and the like) are also crucial for initiating talk about nonpresent topics. Conversely, increasing participation in the decontextualized talk coded as discussion of nonpresent topics serves as a crucial context for the continued acquisition of such linguistic structures.

Topic continuation—site of major development

Once initiated, topics need to be developed. Poor conversationalists are not necessarily unable to think of topic-initiating questions; they might think of many initiatory questions but fail to ask any follow-up questions or produce what Kaye and Charney (1981) have called *turnabouts*. When interacting with peers, children often either fail to maintain a topic (Blank and Franklin 1980) or else use relatively primitive devices to do so. Keenan and Klein (1975), for example, analyzed conversations between twins to show that exact or partial imitation was a primary device used to maintain coherence across turns. Similarly, Garvey (1975) showed that dyads used both repetition of and ritualized variations on each others' utterances to generate conver- sational exchanges up through age 5. It is striking in the exchanges Garvey described that cross- turn relevance was sometimes maintained by sound-play-based cohesion rather than true topic cohesion. Reliance on imitative devices for maintaining cross-turn cohesion declines from age 2 to age 5 (Benoit 1982). Explicit marking of cross-utterance relations with "conjuncts," like *for example, so,* and *anyway,* or with "attitudinal" expressions, like *really* or *perhaps,* is extremely rare in the speech of 6-year-olds, and 12-year-olds have not achieved adultlike frequencies of these devices (Scott 1984). This finding becomes fairly important in light of the crucial role such markers are generally assumed to play in introducing nuances of politeness, deniability, and connectedness in adult conversation (Wardhaugh 1985).

[. . .]

Individual differences in skill at topic continuation and topic maintenance

[. . .]

Because adults are inclined to take on conversational responsibilities in interactions with children, and because children in peer interactions have low-level strategies (which range from tolerating silence and parallel play to simply repeating each other's utterances) for solving the problem of conversation, seeing individual differences in children's conversational skill requires giving children harder-than-usual conversational tasks. One commonly used task is some variant of referential communication—requiring, for example, that two children communicate about objects, pictures, or maps only one of them has full access to. Although these various referential communication tasks tend to be transactional (i.e., to require transfer of information and problem solving of some sort), they can be usefully analyzed for more purely interactional features as well, for example, mechanisms for establishing joint attention, shared knowledge, and mutual understanding. [. . .]

An alternate approach puts children in a situation where conversational exchange is the only task facing them. The task, first used by Donahue et al. (1980), involves getting children to role-play the host of a talk show—a quintessential setting for purely interactive rather than transactional conversation. The child subject is told that he or she is to interview an adult, as if for a television show like Phil Donahue's or Geraldo's. Donahue and colleagues observed child pairs, but Schley and Snow (1992) used an adult interviewee who was instructed to be politely responsive but not helpful in keeping the conversation going—that is, to answer questions but not to elaborate on responses. Precisely because no transactional task is defined, the talk-show setting is one where children's skills at initiating and maintaining topics are severely tested. In fact, some children ages 7 to 12 simply could not keep going for the four minutes we had planned; adult experimenters in these circumstances, despite extensive training and instructions to respond appropriately but avoid initiations, were unable to resist the temptation to help out by starting to ask questions themselves! Schley and Snow (1992) found that children who were rated higher as conversational partners in the talk-show task (1) used open-ended questions and questions contingent upon previous utterances more often, (2) avoided silent pauses of more than a short duration, and (3) successfully elicited elaborated responses from their adult interlocutor. Conversational skill was not related, however, to dysfluencies like self-corrections, repetitions, interruptions, or vocal hesitations, even though half the children tested were not native speakers of English.

Schley and Snow's findings concerning topic extension echo those of Dorval and Eckerman (1984) [. . .] Dorval and Eckerman found large age differences in the degree to which the talk related to topics at hand, as well as in the nature of the relations among turns. Their youngest subjects, second graders, produced the highest proportion of unrelated conversational turns. Ninth graders produced a substantial proportion of factually related turns; the twelfth graders and the adults increasingly incorporated into their conversation turns that took into account the perspective of the person being discussed. [. . .] [Similarly] Bloom et al. (1976)

[. . .] found the incidence of children's utterances that were on [the] same topic immediately preceded adult utterances and that [. . .] added new information rose from 21 percent of all utterances during stage one (MLU under 1.5, ages 19 to 23 months) to 46 percent at stage five (MLU above 3.5, ages 35 to 38 months). These findings suggest that one major component of development in conversation is learning to make responses related to the previous turn [. . .]

Conversational skill can play a central role in a child's access to social interaction with peers (Corsaro 1979), in determining peer acceptance (Hemphill and Siperstein 1990), in second-language learners' access to input in their target language (Krashen 1985), and in making a positive impression on teachers and other powerful adults (Evans 1987). The impression that most children develop conversational skill relatively easily and automatically may be incorrect. Shy children, for example, show deficits as conversationalists that reveal the interface between language development and personality. Reticent children speak not only less but also less complexly than their peers, using shorter utterances, single topic turns, and fewer narratives and decontextualized descriptions of nonpresent objects (Evans 1987). Furthermore, children with language or reading disabilities (Bryan et al. 1981; Donahue 1984; Donahue et al. 1980, 1983) and mildly retarded children (Hemphill 1987; Hemphill and Siperstein 1990) show problems interacting with peers that may be traceable to lack of control over the subtleties of conversational skill. Bryan, Donahue and their colleagues found that in unstructured conversations poor conversationalists could "get along" by virtue of responding to the conversational initiatives of their more skilled peers, but when they were made responsible for the conversation by use of the talk-show task their deficiencies were revealed. Mentally retarded children showed more problems than language-matched, normally developing children with topic control, conversational assertiveness, topic initiation, and fluency, but they had few problems with topic transitions, requests for clarifications, and replies to initiations (Hemphill 1987).

[. . .]

Repair

Effective conversation requires the coordination of action, attention, and intention between two or more individuals; it is almost inevitable that the process of conversation will be characterized by occasional failures—failures of turn alternation, failures of uptake, failures of clear expression of intention. When such failures occur **and are obvious**, repair procedures must be in place to prevent breakdown of communication and a threat to the social relationship. Of course, many miscommunications are covert, unrecognized by one or another party to the conversation, or even if recognized, mutually unacknowledged (see Blum-Kulka and Weizman 1988, for examples). We focus here on breakdowns serious enough that it is impossible to continue the conversation unless they are repaired.

Normally, breakdown of message transmission is repaired by the use of clarification requests—the listener asks *Huh?* or *What did you say?* or makes some more specific request for clarification (*He gave you a what?*). Clarification is a point where the development of conversation, of communicative intent [. . .], and of extended discourse overlaps; without clarification, conversation breaks down, and topics cannot be extended. How do children acquire the ability to use clarification procedures to contribute actively to repair of conversational breakdown? How do parents use clarification questions in ways that might help children learn about pragmatic and other aspects of language?

The acquisition of clarification requests

Children hear quite a lot of adult talk they cannot understand and thus might be expected to produce clarification requests early. In fact, children do not produce such requests until about age 2 [. . .]. Children must also learn to respond appropriately to adult requests for clarification, which they hear from an early age—fairly often in response to their own uninterpretable utterances. Child-initiated requests for clarification did not emerge reliably in the Harvard study (Pan et al. 1996; Snow et al. 1996) until 20 months, when 15 of 48 children produced them, as compared with only one of 52 children at 14 months and 31 of 37 children at 32 months (see Table 8.1.1).

Furthermore, children heard relatively few parental requests for clarification, although much of what they themselves produced was uninterpretable. Only 39 of the 52 children observed at 14 months heard any clarification questions during the observation, although 100 percent of the 48 20-month-olds observed and 36 of the 37 32-month-olds observed did hear clarification requests (see Table 8.1.1). For comparison purposes we include in Table 8.1.1 information about the number of child utterances that were uninterpretable; at 14 months fewer than one-seventh of uninterpretable child utterances were responded to with requests for clarification, whereas by 20 months well over half were. Clearly, parents were responding to their children's increased language sophistication by increasingly holding children accountable for their utterances and creating contexts in which children had to learn to respond to adult clarification requests.

Child-initiated requests for clarification during the age range 14 to 32 months were both relatively rare and fairly unsophisticated in form, consisting mostly of *Huh?* or *What?* The only child-initiated clarification request at 14 months was the following:

Example [1]
Mother: look what you made. isn't that pretty? (referring to child's drawing)
Child: what(t)?
Mother: you did that. very good!

At 20 months, such examples were somewhat more frequent across the entire corpus, although a few children were particularly liberal with initiatory requests for clarification. One

Table 8.1.1 Repair utterances by children and parents

Age (in months)	Children			Parents		
	14	20	32	14	20	32
Number	52	48	37	52	48	37
Total communicative acts	3,005	5,215	5,767	17,070	15,854	9,904
Total demanding clarification acts	13	170	188	234	662	348
Number producing demands for clarification	8	35	31	39	48	36
Child-initiated demands for clarification	1	49	68	–	–	–
Number initiating demands for clarification	1	15	19	–	–	–
Uninterpretable utterances (YYY)	1,579	1,014	339	–	–	–
Number producing YYY	52	48	37	–	–	–

Source: Snow et al. (1996); Pan et al. (1996).

child at 20 months produced more initiatory clarification requests than all the other 20-months-olds together, using as well a variety of forms including *huh?* and *what?* and repeating stressed words of preceding adult utterances with a questioning intonation.

Child-initiated clarification requests were not only rare at 20 months but were also severely restricted in form. Only one example from a 20-month-old required any syntactic restructuring or analysis of the queried utterances:

> *Example [2]*
> Mother: I don't think Jane wants you to climb up on her desk, Kate.
> Child: Jane doesn't?

Every other request observed from 20-month-olds consisted of *huh, what*, or repetition of some part of the queried utterance, typically the final stressed word.

By 32 months children initiated many more clarification sequences but with formal means that were still limited mostly to *huh, what*, and repetition. Of the 188 child utterances in clarificatory sequences, 68 were child-initiated requests for clarification. Six children produced no clarificatory utterances at 32 months, whereas only one parent produced none.

Maternal clarification requests

Mothers use clarification requests in interaction with children for the standard reason—to remediate conversational breakdowns—but for additional reasons as well: as control mechanisms and as procedures for socializing children in the pragmatics of conversation. An apparent request for information can, even in adult conversation, function as a challenge to the truthfulness or acceptability of the interlocutor's utterance or as a marker of its extraordinariness on some dimension, for example:

> *The president has just resigned to join a monastery.*
> *What?*

Parents and teachers use pseudo-clarification requests in similar ways to signal to children that their statements are absurd:

> *I'm borrowing the car for the weekend.*
> *You're what?*

or that some observance of standard politeness has been omitted:

> *Gimme milk.*
> *What?*
> *Please gimme milk.*

With children under 32 months, parental requests for clarification typically focus on real communicative breakdowns but are starting to be used for derivative purposes. Anselmi et al. (1986) have reported that children ages 1;8 to 3;8 show no differences related to age or language stage in their response to clarification questions, which they respond to appropriately about 85 percent of the time. Frank, a child in the Harvard study, heard a particularly large number and rich assortment of clarification requests, to which he responded appropriately at 20 months, for example:

Example [3]

Child:	piece.
Mother:	oh you want a big piece here?
Child:	yeah.
Mother:	okay.

He could respond appropriately as well when his mother, somewhat unusually in interaction with a child so young, used a clarification request to challenge his meaning rather than to query it:

Example [4]

Child:	no!
Mother:	no?
Child:	no.
Mother:	yeah.

By 32 months, Frank was more active in clarification request sequences, reflecting the substantial opportunities for practice his mother had given him. In this excerpt from a sequence of 120 consecutive utterances all on the same topic, Frank is trying to express a complex meaning his mother never fully understands (asterisks in the example indicate deleted utterances). This conversation exemplifies how central repair sequences are to the maintenance of a topic; their mastery is thus prerequisite to the production of extended discourse:

Example [5]

1	Child:	I need a push!
2	Mother:	a what?
3	Child:	push.
4	Mother:	what kind of a push?
5	Child:	push the saw.
6	Child:	push saw.
7	Mother:	you mean, well you want me to give it [saw] to you and you push it [saw]?
8	Child:	no, put in the saw just like the man have.
9	Mother:	I don't know what you mean, just like the man has.
10	Child:	yeah it could push.
11	Mother:	make it [saw] go back and forth?
12	Child:	yeah.
13	Mother:	well you do that [make it go back and forth].

*****

17	Child:	man with saw [whining]!
18	Mother:	oh, you want me to make a man with a saw?
19	Child:	yeah push that.
20	Child:	man <has to> [?] push.
22	Child:	push.

*****

77	Child:	push saw that I have.
78	Mother:	you have?
79	Child:	yeah.
80	Child:	push saw I have.

Maternal clarification requests as feedback

The form of maternal clarification requests undergoes age-related changes, suggesting that mothers fine-tune their attempts at communication repair to children's ability to process information about reasons for the breakdown (Ninio 1986). Clarification demands made by 24 Hebrew-speaking mothers to their 10-, 18-, and 26-month-old children were examined. The dyads were videotaped at home in activities of their choice for 30 minutes. In the three groups of mothers, an average of 5.2 percent, 8.5 percent, and 12.0 percent of all maternal utterances, respectively, were clarification requests. The proportions of child utterances that were queried by at least one clarification demand were, on the average, 21.6 percent in the youngest age group, 22.2 percent in the middle group, and 17.1 percent in the oldest group. If noncommunicative babble-type vocalizations are also included in these statistics, the proportion of utterances queried increases to 39.4 percent in the youngest age group.

Clarification demands were found to belong to one of seven different types [. . .]

Rerun requests [. . .] [that] provide only a general indication that a communication was not heard or understood [. . .] The clarification request [. . .] is [thus] uninformative about the locus of the problem [. . .]

Yes-no questions that were full repetitions of the original utterance. [. . .]

Yes-no questions that were partial repetitions of the original utterance. [. . .] [S]uch clarification requests are rather ambiguous; since they stop the flow of conversation, they signal that something in the previous utterance was problematic but not why the recipient needs further confirmation of this utterance. It could be anything from needing reassurance that the previous speaker indeed had intended to say what was said, in which case there is nothing wrong with the form of the utterance, to a complete lack of understanding of what was said, because the recipient did not recognize the utterance as containing intelligible words. As a negative feedback signal this functions rather like the **Rerun request**, that is, it points to some global problem with the utterance or some part of it. Since the present speaker provides a version of what he or she had heard said, at least the previous speaker can know whether the problem was with hearing or with some other aspect of the communication. When the repetition is partial, some specific component or components of the utterance are singled out as causing the problem, but otherwise the query is as ambiguous as a full repetition.

Direct queries of the meaning of a word the child used. [. . .]

Yes-no questions that substituted new forms for all or part of the original utterance. [. . .] The substituted component or components are offered as [a] better alternative for saying what the previous speaker meant [. . .].

Yes-no questions that were repetitions, either partial or full, of the original utterance but that also added some new material to the original utterance. [. . .]

Wh-questions that demanded product completion concerning a missing component of the utterance. [. . .] These questions also provide specific information about the omission by the previous speaker of an obligatory component of the sentence. Such clarification requests give fully expllicit negative feedback signals about grammaticality.

The distribution of maternal clarification demands among these categories revealed that the type chosen by mothers was fine-tuned to the children's linguistic mastery. In the youngest age group (10-month-olds), where most child utterances were nonconventional vocalizations with or without communicative significance and only a few even approximated conventional words, most clarification requests were **Rerun requests** (66.4 percent), and almost all the rest were **Substitutions** (22.1 percent). Only 6.5 percent of all maternal clarification requests were either **Yes-no questions** or **Wh-questions** that signaled that the child's utterance lacked a necessary component. The great majority of utterances queried by a **Rerun request** were noncommunicative babble; 91 percent of all **Rerun requests** were to this type of vocalization, compared with 44 percent of **Substitutions** and none of the other types.

In the 18-month age group, where children produced mostly one-word utterances with some two-word vertical or horizontal constructions, the average proportion of **Rerun requests** declined to 22.5 percent. The proportion of **Substitutions** stayed about the same (20.6 percent). The most dramatic increase occurred in the two categories signaling a missing component, where these two together accounted for 31.4 percent of all clarification requests.

In the 26-month age group, where all children produced multiword utterances, the proportion of **Rerun requests** declined further to 13.7 percent, along with **Substitutions** (7.3 percent). The two "expansion" categories accounted for 44.8 percent of all clarification requests.

In addition, **Partial repetitions** increased from 0 percent to 1.7 percent to 8.2 percent, whereas **Full repetitions** increased from 4.9 percent to 23.9 percent to 33.2 percent, respectively, in the three age groups. **Direct queries about unintelligible words** stayed at a low 0 percent, 1.6 percent, and 1.1 percent, respectively, in the three groups.

These results indicate that children receive negative feedback about ill-formed utterances and, moreover, that this feedback is fine-tuned to what they can be expected to process and use for modifying their rule system. For very young beginning speakers, the major informative negative feedback is the **Substitution** kind; the provision of such feedback functions to teach children to substitute more conventional forms for their own nonconventional productions. It is obvious that 10-month-olds who are just beginning to produce conventional verbal forms cannot benefit from the information that they omit obligatory components from their sentences. However, these types of feedback are increasingly appropriate as children enter the multiword stage, that is, in the 18- and 26-month age groups. For older children, such teaching is provided by **Yes-no questions that expand the children's own utterance**. In the two older age groups, children's major departure from grammaticality is errors not of commission but of omission; they simply cannot yet put all the obligatory components into a sentence. It appears that mothers, in their spontaneous conversations with their children, provide explicit information about this problem, along with some direct modeling of the more conventional, full forms the children should develop toward.

Why insist on repair?

We have devoted considerable space to the consideration of conversational repair because it constitutes a lens on several issues central to an understanding of children's development of conversational skill. First, if we see turn-taking as central to conversation, it is clear that repair is necessary for turn-taking to continue smoothly. Some repair mechanisms respond directly to turn disruptions, for example, apologizing for interruptions. More common, though, are repair procedures designed to remediate breakdowns in message transmission—at the level either of the signal (*I didn't hear you*) or of the illocutionary force (*What in god's name did you mean by that?*). These repairs reveal the interlocutors' commitment to the basic presuppositions underlying conversation—that communication is possible, that information can be shared, and that different personal perspectives can be aligned. Ultimately, all of the issues we deal with under the rubric *pragmatics* have to do as well with perspective, since the simplest general formulation of all of the specific rules for speaking appropriately might be "understand and acknowledge your interlocutor's point of view."

Parents request clarification from their children for many reasons—to understand the child's message, to signal disapproval of the message, to correct the way of expressing the message. In the process, they illustrate an important central principle of effective communication: The interlocutor's perspective is often different from one's own and must be taken into account. Repair procedures lie directly on the boundary between conversation per se and extended discourse—the product of conversation in which perspective becomes a central issue.

■ ■ ■

POST-READING

1 Return to your notes from the pre-reading exercise: does your definition of conversational repair need amending in light of the understanding you've gained from reading Ninio and Snow? How might you answer (a) and (b) of the pre-reading exercise, now that you have completed your reading?

2 Ninio and Snow provide examples of several interactions between Frank and his mother, at various stages in his development. Focussing on *Example 5* only, categorize the mother's utterances, using the seven types of clarification requests listed on page 402.

3 At the end of the reading, Ninio and Snow identify 'an important central principle of effective communication: The interlocutor's perspective is often different from one's own and must be taken into account'. Do you concur with Ninio and Snow's view? Why/why not? How might Ninio and Snow's view help to explain the primacy they give to *conversational repair*?

EMANUEL A. SCHEGLOFF

DISCOURSE, PRAGMATICS, CONVERSATION, ANALYSIS

PRE-READING

As we explain above, Schegloff adopts a CA-based approach: that is, he takes as his 'officially central pre-occupation' formal interactional features such as turn-taking, sequence structure and repair (Schegloff 1999: 417) rather than, speaker *intent* and/or hearer *perception*. Is a focus on such formal interactional features problematic in your view? Why/why not? Do you find such an approach compatible with the pragmatic approaches discussed in Section 2? Why/why not?

IN-READING

1   We have marked the point at which Schegloff suggests Alvin has comprehended – and has responded appropriately to – a(n indirect) request, in the margin of the text (using |).
   *   Read through this section carefully, and identify those features which distinguish this as non-verbal compliance to a verbal request, paying particular attention to Alvin's use of gaze/eye 'signals'.
   *   According to Schegloff, Alvin may have interpreted the initial 'absence of 'approval' for his new physical position as being indicative of not moving enough, at which point he moves a little more *without being prompted to do so* (see second |). Schegloff argues that this constitutes 'a kind of sensitive micro-tuning and adjustment of conduct to interactional contingencies in a request/compliance sequence'. Re-word Schegloff's explanation, in layman's terms.

■ ■ ■

DISCOURSE, PRAGMATICS, CONVERSATION, ANALYSIS
EMANUEL A. SCHEGLOFF

[Editor's note: for this Reading, we utilise pp. 418–26, and thus omit the introduction, the sections entitled 'Is there such a thing as 'ordinary conversation'?', 'Is ordinary conversation the "basic" speech exchange system?', 'Formal accounts and the analysis of singular occurrences', 'Why a formal account of turn-taking?' and the conclusion. In the introduction, Schegloff describes a student trend of focussing upon 'diversities rather than commonalities' in the latter half of the twentieth century, which – he argues – also led to 'a focus on [communicative] *misunderstandings*' (p. 406). Schegloff then goes on to warn that 'characterizing conversation by what it is *not* – not subject to special restrictions or practices whether legal or functional, or, as some put it, talk *not* in institutional or formal contexts – makes it sound as if 'conversation' is a residual category, what is left over once we have isolated affirmatively describable *other* forms of talk-in-interaction' (p. 407, original italics). For Schegloff, however, 'ordinary conversation' is not only 'a recognizable modality of talk-in-interaction' (p. 413) in its own right, but '*the* basic medium' of the 'interactional exchange (p. 413, our italics): that is to say, 'other speech-exchange systems . . . appear to be shaped by the adaptation of the practices and organizations of ordinary conversation to their special functional needs . . . ' (p. 415). In the sections, 'Formal accounts and the analysis of singular occurrences' and 'Why a formal account of turn-taking?', Schegloff also builds a platform from which to claim 'it is ill-considered to fault [the CA] focus' on turntaking or sequence organization (as some have done) simply because it does not take 'meaning' or 'action' as 'its officially central pre-occupation; for it may be by reference to just such formal features of the talk that action, and what is vernacularly termed 'meaning', are constituted and grasped in the first instance' (pp. 417–18).]

[. . .]

The episode I examine is drawn from materials which may be of special interest to those especially concerned with matters alternatively subsumed under the rubrics 'discourse' and 'pragmatics', and with the deployment of linguistic and other resources in practical conduct, and *as* practical conduct. One of the participants comes to the occasion with challenged and suspect linguistic capacities. He is a commissurotomy patient, that is, a man whose brain hemispheres were surgically severed from one another some years earlier – an operation used to deal with otherwise intractable neurological problems. The setting is one in a series of testing sessions in which the impact of this surgery on cognitive and linguistic functioning is being examined; we look at a momentary, *non*-testing interpolation in that session.

The project from which I am drawing began with the juxtaposition of some empirical observations with one view about the localization of various aspects of linguistic functioning in the brain.

Roughly, the view held at the time these observations were made (some 8–9 years ago), and very likely still widely held (but see Perkins 1998: 307; Zaidel 1998; Zaidel et al. 1998), was that, whereas much of the neurological substrate of language – for phonology, syntax, the lexicon and semantics – is localized in the *left* hemisphere (among the naturally right handed, etc.), the so-called discourse-organizational and pragmatic functions are situated in the *right* hemisphere. Various sorts of evidence were held to support this view, drawing almost entirely on clinical and testing observations regarding various so-called 'pragmatic deficits' attendant upon cerebro-vascular insults to the right hemisphere.

What exactly should count as 'pragmatics' or 'discourse' has never been thoroughly clarified, let alone become a matter of consensus, and there is no reason to think that all the preoccupations which are treated as belonging to 'discourse' or 'pragmatics' form some sort of unified or coherent domain. Among the deficits included in the discussion of the consequences of disruption in the right hemisphere were counted an impaired capacity to enact and recognize emotional expression; problems in the use and recognition of non-literal uses of language, such as irony, metaphor, humor and, most importantly, indirection; and the compromising of other operations understood to be associated with the use of language in organized undertakings such as interaction

– including turn-taking, the doing of particular actions [. . .], such as commands and requests, and the range of conventional norms we ordinarily term 'etiquette' or 'politeness'.[1]

Through the cooperation of the neuropsychologist Eran Zaidel and the philosopher Asa Kasher, I gained access to videotapes of several testing sessions with commisurotomy patients whom Zaidel has been studying for quite a long time.[2] Although not exactly 'right-hemisphere *damaged*', persons who have had commisurotomies have undergone surgery which severed the *corpus callosum*, the pathway through which the two hemispheres of the brain 'communicate'. However intact the right hemisphere itself may be in these persons, the left hemisphere presumably has no access to its operations and products – at least according to the currently dominant version of brain function as I am given to understand it (Zaidel et al. 1998: 281, suggest four accounts of 'normally unified everyday behavior of the patients' in spite of this disconnection). In such persons we should see most clearly the effects of depriving the rest of the language faculty – what is thought of in contemporary linguistics as the very *core* of the language faculty – of the robust operation of its pragmatic and discourse components.

[. . .] [I]n order to specify in a reliable way just what the effects are, we need empirically grounded accounts of what such persons *can* do – *do* do – in circumstances embodying ordinary contingencies of interaction, and not just how they perform in testing situations which, far from neutralizing interactional contexts, themselves can constitute distinctive speech-exchange systems which confront participants with quite distinctive, and potentially complicating, interactional exigencies.[3]

The fragment, which lasts no more than a few seconds, occurs in the middle of a testing session with a man whom I call Alvin. Although Alvin does not talk in this exchange (in fact, he has been asked by the research assistant to talk as little as possible),[4] the episode displays his capacity to parse and to grasp the talk of an interlocutor and to respond effectively in interaction. For the purposes of the present discussion, the point is to see the access we get to this brief exchange with the analytic resources of so-called 'formal' treatments of turn-taking and sequence organization.

The research assistant, Dan (DG), has been administering the tests, while the Principal Investigator, Ezra (EZ), is manning the camera in an adjacent room, shooting through the doorway. As the sequence on which we focus begins (at no. 1 in the following transcript), Alvin (AA) is sitting almost motionless, watching the assistant take out and examine the next set of stimulus cards (Figure 8.2.1).

My examination of this exchange is organized around the numbers positioned above the lines of the transcript. Each number marks the locus of some observations about the sequence to that point and the import of those observations, the first of which is the gloss of the state of the interaction at the onset of this sequence just provided.

```
        1          2                              3
EZ: Alvin, can yo[u come a bit closer to the [table=
                 [((AA turning                 [((AA leans
                    to EZ))                     forward,
                                                head down))

              4            5
        =may[be even the[re?=
            [((AA eyes  [((AA grasps chair,
             up))        eyes down))
                                              6
AA: =((slides chair forward one substantial measure, then looks
     up to EZ))
```

```
                7
  EZ:  That's [good.=
              [((AA slides forward another small increment))
  AA:  =((lips part, head turns back to table, puts left hand to
                8           9
       mouth and coughs, [left hand adjusts glasses))
                         [
  DG:                    [Oh:::kay, ((puts first new stimulus card
                              on table in front of AA))
```

Let us note first, at 2, Alvin's prompt coordinated response to Ezra's use of his name as an address term; he looks to Ezra directly after Ezra has spoken his name, aligning himself as a recipient for the turn-in-progress (Goodwin 1981). That he has analyzed his name – Alvin – as doing addressing is itself, of course, an achievement. Taken as an object for 'on-line' parsing and analysis in real time, 'Alvin' can be understood in either of two ways. One is as an address term or vocative; the other is as the subject of a clause/sentence. On the former analysis, Alvin would be the addressee and, potentially,[5] the selected next speaker (the prior request that he minimize speaking to the contrary notwithstanding). On the latter analysis, the utterance would be understood as about Alvin, but addressed to the testing assistant, Dan.

Not until the word 'you' is there grammatical evidence that it is an utterance along the first of these lines which is in progress. But by the time 'you' is articulated, Alvin is already turning his head toward Ezra, so that by the time 'come a bit' is being said, Alvin is already fully oriented toward him as an aligned recipient (Figure 8.2.2).

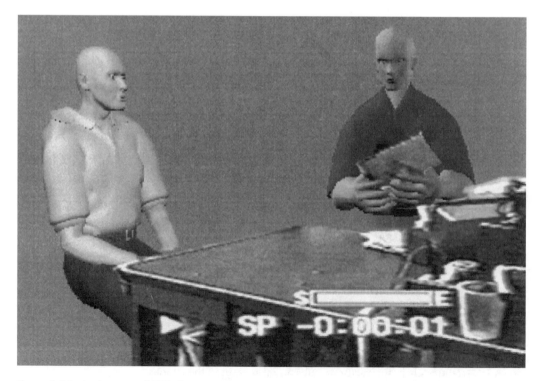

Figure 8.2.1 At the start of EZ's first turn, at 1.

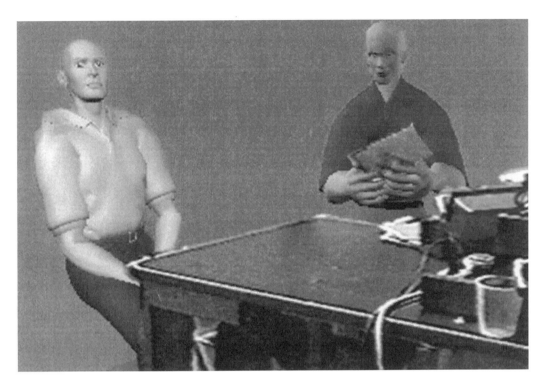

Figure 8.2.2 At the word 'you', at 2.

Since Alvin and Dan are sitting side by side, the loudness of the utterance does not differentiate them as intended recipients. Alvin has analyzed the talk for its displayed target, has recognized its first element as indicative of that, and has produced an appropriate response when he finds himself to be that target – an initial indication of discourse/pragmatic capacity, with respect both to turn-taking and sequence organizational features of the talk; for the design of this bit of talk serves to (potentially) select Alvin to occupy the next turn position and also involves constraints on what should be done there – a response to the summons, which he here realizes by gaze re-direction, in compliance with the earlier instruction to minimize talking.

By 3, Alvin has begun withdrawing his gaze and initiating a compliant response at the word 'table', which is projectable as the incipient possible completion of Ezra's turn (see Figure 8.2.3). Note that there are at least two orders of discourse/pragmatic competence involved here. The first of these is Alvin's analysis of the turn-in-progress for its imminent possible completion, displayed by his incipient gaze withdrawal – a turn-taking matter.

A second competence displayed here regards the turn's sequence-organizational status; Alvin displays an analysis of Ezra's utterance as making relevant some sort of responsive turn or action next, and 'next' means 'now'. In particular, Alvin begins to display an analysis of Ezra's turn as a *request*, and a request for an *action*, by initiating an action seeable and analyzable (by Ezra) as *compliance* with the request.

It might be noted as well that the request is in the form which many forms of conventional speech-act theory would term 'indirect'. The form '*can you* come a bit closer . . . ' in this view literally asks a question about ability or capacity. The 'request for action', has to be analyzed out of this utterance as the indirect speech act being enacted. This is just the sort of

Figure 8.2.3 At the start of the word 'table', at 3.

speech act, just the sort of non-literal usage which – in the common view – persons with a discourse/pragmatic deficit would be expected to have trouble with.[6]

Directly following 'table', with the audible continuation of talk (the 'may' of 'maybe'), at 4, Alvin apparently registers that the turn may be extended *past* its projectable point of possible completion, and his eyes begin to return to the speaker Ezra (Figure 8.2.4) – again turn-taking competence of a detailed sort.

At 5, Alvin hears in the talk that the extension of the turn past its initial possible completion is not 'generative', that is, it is not a whole new unit of talk, but involves some add-ons (or 'increments') to the prior turn-constructional unit. The previous analysis of upcoming possible completion appears then to be re-instituted; Alvin again withdraws his gaze and continues the previously initiated action, which, with the grasping of the chair, now shows itself transparently to be a compliance with the request (Figure 8.2.5); Alvin now slides his chair closer to the table by a substantial increment. Again, then, both turn-taking and sequence-organizational constraints are being grasped and met.

At 6, at the possible completion of the action designed as compliance with Ezra's request, Alvin looks to Ezra (Figure 8.2.6).

Sequence-structurally this is a third position, a position in which the initiator of a sequence (especially a sequence like a request sequence) regularly makes some assessment of, or other reaction to whatever was done as a response to the sequence initiation (i.e. in second position). Here then is a place at which orientation to sequence structure can warrant 'anticipation' of a sequence-structural, third position, uptake – a place for Alvin to look to Ezra for an assessment of the adequacy of his 'move'; has he moved 'close enough'?

Figure 8.2.4 Halfway through the word 'maybe', at 4.

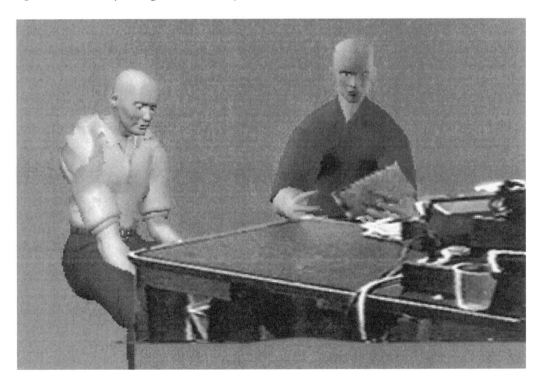

Figure 8.2.5 Halfway through the word 'there', at 5.

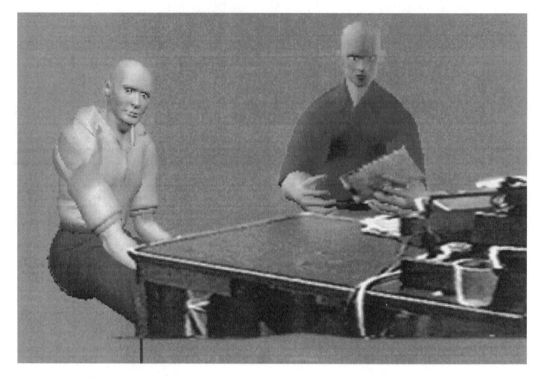

Figure 8.2.6 After forward slide of chair, at 6.

Note that here, unlike the first observation, it can *not* be by virtue of Ezra being a speaker or a source of sound that Alvin looks to him. Although Ezra does indeed deliver the type of utterance which 'belongs' in third position ('That's good'), Alvin glances toward him *before* this utterance is begun. Note again that the posture in Figure 8.2.6 is captured just before Ezra's assessment, 'That's good'. This is a gaze direction warranted by *sequence structure* (in particular, request/compliance sequence structure), a relevance structure to which Alvin, by his glance, shows himself to be oriented and attentive. Indeed, his turn to Ezra, aligning himself as recipient, may serve to prompt the assessment utterance which is then forthcoming.

Although we lack the data here, we can venture a guess that as Alvin looks to him, Ezra is neither smiling nor nodding, and that his evaluation of the adequacy of Alvin's compliance move is not clear until his utterance. In the absence of 'approval', Alvin may read the possible *in*adequacy of his response, and, *as* Ezra is saying 'That's good', at 7, Alvin is already executing a move to add another increment of compliance to what he had already done. In the video of this episode, one can see an additional small increment of sliding the chair forward during 'That's good', as if in response to the absence of validation of the previously designed compliant action. We have here not merely discourse/pragmatic competence, but a kind of sensitive micro-tuning and adjustment of conduct to interactional contingencies in a request/compliance sequence.

Upon completion of the added increment of moving closer and Ezra's assessment, it appears that Alvin has analyzed Ezra's 'That's good' as *both* the end of a turn *and* the end of a sequence. He shows this in several ways. First, he turns his head back to the table and away from Ezra; second, he adjusts his glasses (at 9; see Figure 8.2.8) – which is for him a 'work-related'

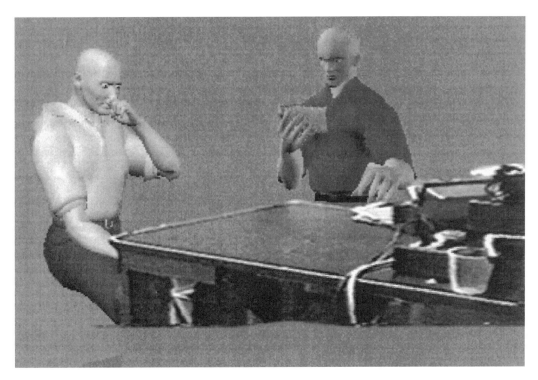

Figure 8.2.7 After turning away from camera, at 8.

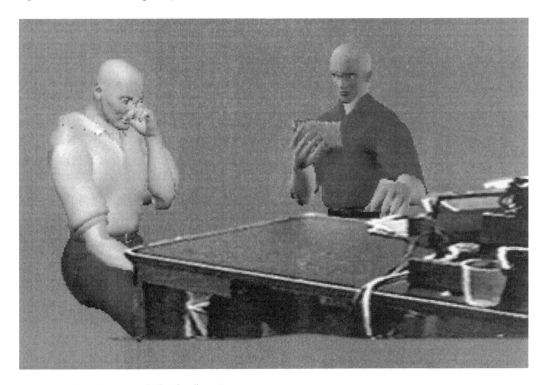

Figure 8.2.8 As Dan says "Oh:::kay", at 9.

gesture, regularly used with new or difficult stimulus tasks; third, these movements are well coordinated with the testing assistant, Dan, such that the adjustment of the glasses converges with Dan's 'Okay' and placement of the new stimulus on the table (Figure 8.2.9).

This amounts, then, to Alvin's recognition, and *collaborative constitution* with Ezra and Dan of this little sequence as a 'side sequence' (Jefferson 1972) interpolated into a larger, ongoing activity, *from* which it created a temporary departure, and *to* which there should be a return on its completion. There is then the recognition and joint construction of a *hierarchical* structuring of activities and sequences of activities.

Finally, we should register the observation that, at just the juncture between the end of the side sequence and the resumption of the 'work' activity, Alvin puts his hand to his mouth and coughs (at 8), or – to put it in terms of the etiquette with which he shows himself to be in compliance – he 'covers his mouth while coughing' (Figure 8.2.7). By placing the cough in the no-man's land between sequences (note, it comes *after* the gaze withdrawal and *before* the adjustment of glasses marking task resumption), he puts it at a relatively non-sensitive moment, when no one is an active interactional co-participant, into whose interactional space this ritually marked body adjustment is thrust. And etiquette is, of course, arguably *another* of the components of pragmatics and interactive discourse organization.

About this whole episode, with its robust and exquisitely detailed attention to compliance with an indirect request, it remains only to remark that, later on, it turned out that (according to the results of formal testing procedures) Alvin 'did not perform well on tests related to commands and indirect requests'. [. . .] Perhaps this much can be suggested here: perhaps the testing goes not so much to commands and indirect requests per se as it does to decontexted actions, actions not parts of indigenously engendered courses of action.[7]

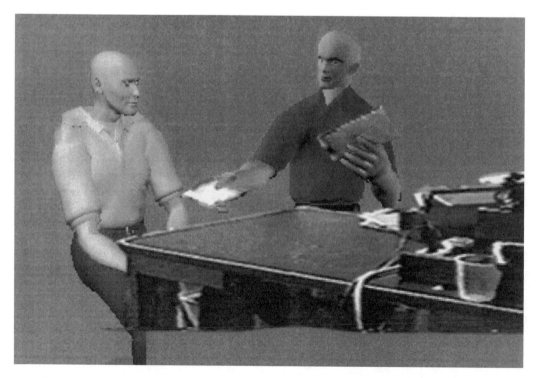

Figure 8.2.9 Dan resumes testing, after 9.

[. . .] I submit that in order to understand the physical movements which constitute the whole of Alvin's participation in this episode – indeed to come to 'see' them at all, in an analytic sense – we need to appreciate (we *have* appreciated) their status as social actions. Compliance, responsive attention deployment, approval solicitation, and the like – that is what they are. By them, Alvin displays his orientation to the relevant organizational dimensions within which this interaction is being realized and on which it is being scaffolded. The timing of his moves displays Alvin's grasp – in its *detailed course* – of the developmental structure of Ezra's talk – as composing a turn constructional unit, which is progressing toward possible completion, at which point it may be for *him* to respond, and as constituting an action which will shape the *terms* of his response within a jointly oriented-to sequence structure. These movements embody and display in this setting's situated details Alvin's and Ezra's collaborative orientation to the resources, constraints and practices of turn-taking and sequence organization as formal organizational frameworks for their concerted participation, through whose deployment the import of what is going on here is materialized, is fabricated, jointly, *by* the parties, *for* the parties.

How is all that made available to *us*, external observers? We do not encounter it in the same fashion as the participants do – micro-moment by micro-moment forward in real time, subject to the practical contingencies and exigencies of responding, and the interactional import of *non*-response. Here is where the resources of formal accounts of such structures of practice come into play. For that is what work such as the turn-taking article and accounts of adjacency pairs and their expansions are designed in part to do.

[. . .] [T]heir payoff [. . .] rests in their capacity to illuminate actual episodes of interaction, to serve as tools in the understanding of what is going on there for the parties and how it is getting done – tools like 'possible turn completion', 'transition-relevance of possible completion', 'the conditional relevance brought into play by a first pair part', etc. Formal analysis is then not an *alternative* to so-called 'substantive', or 'content-ful', or 'meaningful' or 'setting-specific' treatment of ordinary talk-in-interaction; it is an *instrument* for its *implementation*. It serves us well as professional analysts to the degree that it has accurately depicted the formal character of how ordinary participants in talk-in-interaction co-construct those episodes and undertand them in their course, and for that very reason.

[. . .] I hope that this brief analytic exercise dispels another puzzling misconception, that conversation analysis ignores the body and its deployment in interaction, as well as actions which are not verbally realized. Were that the case, we would have had nothing at all to say about one of the featured participants in this little episode. But note: even though Alvin's participation in this exchange is sensitive to the turn organization of the talk to which he is responding in a fine-grained way, and although his actions do satisfactorily answer to the relevance rules underlying the action sequence being implemented here, it would be analytically ill-conceived and ill-advised to treat his contribution to this exchange as a turn-at-talk. Even though it is a contribution to the sequence, it is not a turn-at-talk. That does not mean that it is not orderly, the product of practices of conduct in interaction. His actions have an organization to them – some of which have been mentioned informally in the preceding account – displayed launching of an action, implementation of the action, showing that the action has been brought to completion by a 'decay' of its physical movements, etc.

The description of such elements of conduct in interaction has been less developed in conversation analysis than accounts of talk, but it has not been absent (see for example [. . .] Schegloff 1984, 1998: other recent contributions are found in the work of Charles and Marjorie

Goodwin – C. Goodwin 1994, 1995; M.H. Goodwin 1997, 1998). Further development of such work is in order, as is well-considered discussion of the relationship of such action to turns at talk, but not (as is sometimes proposed) the treatment of physically implemented actions as turns-at-talk, which – in the plain meaning of the words – they are specifically not. Two sorts of work are then in prospect in this regard, if past experience is a proper guide: detailed explications of single episodes of interaction in which physically implemented actions (including gestures, postures, etc.) are elaborated (Goodwin 2000, 2003); and efforts to elucidate formal structures of practice in the deployment of the body in episodes of interaction (indeed, one such effort – Sacks and Schegloff 1975 – was delivered some 25 years ago; see also Schegloff 1998). Perhaps it will now be easier to see these two types of undertaking as mutually enabling and enriching, rather than as competitors for the allegiance of students in this area.

[. . .]

Appendix

Notational conventions employed in the transcribed episodes examined in the text include the following (a fuller glossary of conventions may be found in Ochs et al. 1996: 461–5):

:::	colons indicate stretching of the preceding sound, proportional to the number of colons
(())	double parentheses enclose descriptions of conduct rather than transcriptions of it
[	left brackets connecting two lines indicate simultaneous onset of what follows the brackets
=	equal signs at the end of one line and the start of the next indicate no break or dealy between the lines thereby connected
table	underlining indicates slight overstress on the underlined item
(1.1)	numbers in parentheses indicate silence in tenths of a second
° °	words between degree marks are markedly softer than surrounding talk in proportion to the number of degree marks.

Notes

1   For a review of much of the relevant literature, see Zaidel (1998) and Zaidel et al. (1998).

2   I would like to thank Asa Kasher and Eran Zaidel for providing access to data from their study of split-brain patients, a study supported by the USA–Israel Binational Science Foundation (grant no. 88–00116/3) and by the Israel Science Foundation (grants nos. 891/96–7 773//92–3 to Asa Kasher, Tel-Aviv University, and Eran Zaidel, UCLA), and by the USPHS NIH (grant no. NS 20187 to Eran Zaidel).

3   For a discussion of a setting which raises related issues, see Schegloff (1991: 54–7). For a more general discussion of the relationship between naturalistic and experimental research on talk-in-interaction which bears on testing as a mode of inquiry as well, see Schegloff (1996: 22–30).

4   This itself is indicative of a special speech-exchange system being in operation for the 'testing' interaction, one which is apparently sustained by the 'subject' even in this momentary intermission from it.

5   'Potentially' because addressing an utterance to someone does not, by itself, select them as next speaker. Only certain turn types, if addressed to another, select that other as next speaker. The most common such turn types are those which constitute 'first-pair parts' of adjacency pairs (Sacks et al. 1974: 716–17). The turn addressed to Alvin here, being a request, is such a first-pair part, and does select him as next.

6   I am not, of course, endorsing speech act theory here. On the contrary, the utility and relevance of its way of discriminating direct and indirect speech acts in actual talk-in-interaction is called into question here, as it is elsewhere (Schegloff 1988, 1992b: I: xxiv–xxvii). Shoshana Blum-Kulka has pointed out to me (pers. comm.) that many lines of speech act theory would now consider the form of this utterance as virtually formulaic and as not implicating the sort of analysis to which the text is addressed.

7   After reading a draft of this paper, Asa Kasher (one of the Principal Investigators in the larger study from whose material this episode was drawn) wrote (per. correspondence) that in the testing mentioned in my text 'the S did not use a command, under . . . circumstances where normal Ss do use it regularly, and that he did not react properly to non-regular indirect requests, not of the form of "could you . . ." and the like, which are usual, but rather of unusual forms ("would it be possible for you . . . ." and the like) . . . '. [. . .] My text does not question the adequacy of the tests in assessing whatever they will turn out to have assessed, only their relevance to what those who have been tested can do – demonstrably *do* do – in real life circumstances. What the tests are assessing is, of course, precisely what is at issue here – the organization of a 'language faculty'; its mapping to, and implication with, the architecture of the brain; the context-sensitivity of practices of talking-in-interaction etc.

I am reminded of a number of stories I was told by Claus Heeschen, trained as a formal linguist and aphasiologist (and my collaborator in Heeschen and Schegloff 1999), in describing his own scientific trajectory from testing as the instrument of inquiry into the speech and other conduct of aphasics to detailed examination of naturalistic records of ordinary interaction in mundane settings with friends and relatives. For example, while engaged in testing aphasic patients, he would ordinarily use rest periods during which patients had coffee to go and check his mail, etc. One day he happened to join the patients in the coffee room during the break and was astonished to hear the patients doing things while talking amongst themselves or with relatives which they had just shown themselves 'unable' to do in the preceding testing session. After that experience he undertook to try out other methods of inquiry in addition to testing, and, eventually, in preference to it.

That there may be important differences in capacity and performance between talking in the special frame of 'testing interaction' and in ordinary conversation is, then, no idiosyncratic or casual suggestion on my part; indeed, the contrast is reported by one of the Principal Investigators of this very project (as cited above from Zaidel 1998 and Zaidel et al. 1998). One payoff we may hope for from the intersection of naturalistic with other modes of inquiry is just such a specification as is at issue here of what tests (or other measurement instruments) are tapping; that is, a specification of validity.

■ ■ ■

POST-READING

1   One aspect of Schegloff's argument in this paper is that, if we are to fully understand communicative disabilities,

> [. . .] we need empirically grounded accounts of what . . . persons [with such disabilities] *can* do – *do* do – in circumstances embodying ordinary contingencies of interaction, and not just how they perform in testing situations which, far from neutralizing interactional contexts, themselves can constitute distinctive speech-exchange systems which confront participants with quite distinctive, and potentially complicating, interactional exigencies.

Put simply, we need to observe people as they engage in normal conversation, and not just rely on tests undertaken in laboratory settings. Unpack Schegloff's stance, by taking supportive and contrary views. If possible, we would encourage you to work in pairs, so that you can engage in an interactive 'real-time' debate. Where this is not possible, we would encourage you to, first, write a one page *pro*-document and, then, write a one page *anti*-document (preferably using bullet points). Once you have done this, you might want to 'take sides', by summarizing which view you find most convincing.

2   A second aspect of Schegloff's argument is that the CA approach has much to offer when it comes to understanding the intricacies of conversation, both for clinical researchers and also for students of pragmatics and discourse analysts. As before, adopt a 'supportive' and 'contrary' stance in regard to the benefits of CA (a) to clinical researchers, and (b) to students of pragmatics and discourse analysts.

HEIDI EHRENBERGER HAMILTON

CONVERSATIONS WITH AN ALZHEIMER'S PATIENT
An interactional sociolinguistic study

PRE-READING

What, if anything, do you know about Alzheimer's disease and how it progressively affects a sufferer's ability to communicate? Write down all that you know *before* beginning the reading.

IN-READING

Hamilton provides glosses/definitions for (a) 'taking the role of the other', (b) '*particular* other' versus '*generalized* other', (c) 'recipient design', (d) 'underaccommodation', (e) 'automaticity', (f) 'self-initiated' versus 'other-initiated' repair, and (g) 'metacommunicative framing language'. We have signalled the relevant sections in the reading, using a series of | in the margins so that you can provide your own definitions/glosses, *in your own words,* at the point at which you see | .

■ ■ ■

CONVERSATIONS WITH AN ALZHEIMER'S PATIENT
AN INTERACTIONAL SOCIOLINGUISTIC STUDY
HEIDI EHRENBERGER HAMILTON

Linguistic analyses of Alzheimer's disease

One manifestation of Alzheimer's disease is a progressive and apparently irreversible deterioration of the patient's ability to communicate with others. The patient may have trouble finding the appropriate word in a conversation. She may have trouble tracking and using pronouns appropriately or in understanding indirectness as it was intended. On the other hand, she may continue to be able to carry out some of the more mechanical tasks in interaction, such as taking a turn-at-talk or getting someone's attention. She may even perform better if dealing with a topic of personal importance rather than a more banal one.

[. . .]

[. . .] Most studies of Alzheimer's patients' linguistic (dis)abilities to date have involved test situations in which the patients perform various tasks (e.g. naming objects in photographs or drawings, performing transformations on sentences, and disambiguating spoken homophones). [. . .] [T]his situation has begun to change over recent years, but even today, studies which focus on discourse are carried out almost exclusively within an experimental paradigm.

[. . .]

In this study, [. . .] I hope to offer the reader an alternative, complementary approach to language pathology based on natural, interactional principles [. . .]

The observations and analyses reported in this study are based on fourteen naturally occurring conversations I had with one Alzheimer's patient, Elsie, which were tape-recorded in a 121-bed Washington, D.C.-area private health care center between November 1981 and March 1986 [when Elsie was 81 to 86 years old]. In my role of participant-observer, I was carrying out what Kitwood (1988: 176) calls a personal research approach which is meant to supplement the technical approach normally taken in studies of Alzheimer's disease. Kitwood describes the researcher's role as follows:

> The key to a personal approach is that it does not "stand outside," taking the position of a detached and unaffected observer. At its core, it works interpretively and empathetically, going far beyond the measurement of indices or the codification of behaviour. In all of this the researcher takes a personal risk . . . *It is on the ground of our own experience in relationship that we can gain some inkling of what is happening to another.* (my emphasis)

Because determinations of the extent to which one partner is interacting successfully *in a natural setting* rely on an insider's knowledge of what has been shared over time (see Blakar 1985 for discussion), I argue it is legitimate, if not imperative, for the analyst to take this role of participant-observer in an interactional study of communicative breakdown.

[. . .]

Taking the role of the other

Critical to an individual's success as a conversational partner is the ability to take the role of the other at every point in each given conversation. It is only by figuratively stepping into the mind of the addressee of our remarks that we are able to accomplish conversational coherence and maintain mutual face in interaction at the same time. Taking the role of the other is a crucial factor underlying the full range of linguistic and social decisions in interaction, such as whether to use a pronoun or a full noun phrase, when to take a turn-at-talk, and which speech acts, register, and conversational style to choose.

Mead (1934) speaks of the notion of taking the role of the other as being "basic to human social organization." He argues that only human beings possess the ability to predetermine how another person will react to their actions by evoking in themselves the same response the other person will have. Self-monitoring of one's own behavior continues, though, even in the absence of other human beings at a given time. In this case, it is not the *particular* other whose role is being taken but the *generalized* other. This generalized other is "the incorporation of the community within the individual" and is, in a sense, "the source of social conscience" (Cuzzort and King 1980: 109).

Sacks et al. (1978: 42–3) have applied the concept of taking the role of the other to participant behavior in *conversation*, whereas Mead's use of the notion of taking the role of the other applies to the full range of human behavior. Sacks and his colleagues use the term "recipient design" to describe what they call "perhaps the most general principle particularizing conversational interaction." In their analyses, they identify recipient design as operating with regard to such conversational phenomena as word selection, topic selection, ordering of sequences, and options and obligations for starting and terminating conversations. Erickson (1986) further differentiates the notion of "recipient design" into two types: (1) retrospective recipient design, in which a speaker takes what the interlocutor just did or said into account in the design of the emerging discourse, and (2) prospective recipient design, in which a speaker takes into account what she projects the interlocutor's reaction to the utterance to be in the design of that utterance.

Figurski (1987) outlines a model of person-awareness which further differentiates the notion of taking the role of the other. In this model, Figurski identifies three main dimensions of awareness: (1) target (the self or the other); (2) perspective (egocentric or allocentric); and (3) content (experience or image). The egocentric perspective towards the self results then in the awareness of one's own experience, whereas the allocentric perspective towards the self results in the awareness of how one is viewed (image) by the other. Accordingly, the egocentric perspective towards the other results in the awareness of how one views the other (image), whereas the allocentric perspective towards the other results in the awareness of the other's experience.

In taking the role of the other in conversation, interlocutors operate with various types of assumptions – including what constitutes shared background knowledge, world knowledge, social expectations, common sense, and cultural, ethnic, age, and sex stereotypes. When these assumptions prove to be wrong, and knowledge assumed to be shared is *not* shared, expectations are *not* met, or stereotypes are *not* confirmed in the interaction, interlocutors may experience interactive difficulties. [. . .] Characteristics of the conversationalists, such as age, sex, ethnic group, and disability, as well as their relationship to each other, can be expected to influence the type(s) of discourse strategies used in response to these major or minor breakdowns in communication.

[. . .]

[. . .] [The one critical factor which usually separates] an Alzheimer's disease patient and a "normal" interlocutor of the same ethnic group, [. . .] sex, age, and approximate socio-economic status is Alzheimer's disease. [. . .] If, however, age also differentiates the interlocutors, the danger exists that negative evaluations springing from interactional nonsuccess will be overextended to include healthy elderly individuals rather than just describing individuals with Alzheimer's disease. Thus, the frustration resulting from such interactional difficulties can lead "normal" individuals to construct or confirm a stereotype of the senile population or the elderly population as a whole, similar to the reinforcement of racial and ethnic stereotypes as discussed in Gumperz (1982b).

On the part of the Alzheimer's patient, the interactional frustration may result in a negative evaluation of the "normal" conversational partner or a social group he or she represents. Additionally, to the extent that the patient is aware of his or her disability, the communicative breakdown may heighten his or her own feelings of incompetence, leading to a potentially serious breakdown of mutual face in the interaction. In this case, the Alzheimer's patient may attempt to offer an excuse, however feeble, for his or her behavior which does not live up to expectations, indicating that he or she can take the perspective of the other (in Figurski's terms, an allocentric perspective on the self, resulting in awareness of how one is being viewed by the other person). Alternatively, the "normal" interlocutor may present a ready-made account for the Alzheimer's patient to accept as an explanation of his or her own apparent "temporary lapse."

In their examination of accommodation and the healthy elderly, Coupland et al. (1988) discuss the phenomenon of underaccommodation to conversational needs as a strategy sometimes found in the discourse directed to young interlocutors by elderly individuals. Characteristics of this under accommodation include greater focus on self than on the addressee and lowly attuned discourse management. [. . .] An important distinction must be made, however, between the occasional *intentional* underaccommodation in which the speaker really does wish to be unhelpful to his or her conversational partner and the *unintentional* underaccommodation which I argue characterizes much of the discourse involving Alzheimer's patients. It is not the case that the patient does not *wish* to take the role of the other, it is that he or she *cannot* take the role of the other to the extent that "normal" interlocutors can. Unfortunately, this critical difference between ill-intent and disability on the part of the speaker is not always perceived by recipients of this underaccommodation, leading to undeserved negative evaluations of the patient's behavior.

With specific reference to Elsie's communicative abilities and difficulties [. . .], probably the most obvious manifestation of Elsie's difficulty in taking the role of the other in conversation is her misuse of the information system. That is, information which is *not* known to her conversational partner is presented by Elsie as given information, or information which *is* known to her conversational partner is presented as new information. Elsie's difficulty in using pronouns falls into this category as does her occasional introduction of utterances "out of the blue" into the discourse. Problems on the lexical level include Elsie's use of neologisms, her "reassignment" of the meaning of common words, and her overuse of "empty" words. On the topical level, topic shifts perceived as inappropriate by the conversational partner may indicate Elsie's underlying difficulty in determining what her interlocutor will view as an appropriate change in topic. As Elsie's ability to take the role of the other deteriorates over time, her own needs and wishes continue to play an important role in the interactions. Elsie's discourse abilities when dealing with personally important topics appear to be more flexible and sophis-ticated than when dealing with more banal ones. Additionally, Elsie's attempts to get the attention of her conversational partner and to indicate to her conversational partner that she did not hear her utterance further indicate her abilities to see that her own needs are met. Elsie's problems in interpreting indirectness used by the "normal" interlocutor can also be framed within the discussion of taking the role of the other. If Elsie has difficulty taking the perspective of her conversational partner, she may not be able to figure out his or her possible motivation(s) for using indirectness. Brown and Levinson (1987: 268) suggest that this is a general problem of indirect uses of language: "Decoding the communicative intent relies on the mutual availability of a reasonable and particular motive for being indirect."

Elsie's decreased ability to take the role of the other in conversation does not appear to be uniformly distributed across all facets of her language use. Following Halliday (1978), we observe that Elsie's abilities to take the role of the other on a more formal procedural dimension of interaction (what Halliday calls "mode") seem to remain intact longer than do her abilities to take the role of the other regarding the management of interpersonal positions, roles, and faces (what Halliday calls "tenor"), which, in turn, seem to remain intact longer than do her abilities to take the role of the other in terms of ideational content construction (what Halliday calls "field"). Evidence of breakdowns on the ideational content construction level, such as pronoun, lexical, and topic selection, exists in our very first conversations in the fall of 1981. Evidence of Elsie's successful use of accounts and positive politeness, which indicate that she can take the feelings of her conversational other into account, can be found through our September 1982 conversation. Evidence of Elsie's awareness of procedural demands of a discourse with regard to another's perspective, such as responding to questions and taking a turn-at-talk, can be found even in the very latest conversations in 1986.

Although the above discussion of problems in taking the role of the other has been limited to Elsie, [. . .] it is important to see that this distinction between disabled and normal is not hard and fast. Following Crystal's (1984) view of language handicap as an interactive phenomenon, I wish to point out that it is not only the Alzheimer's patient who has trouble taking the perspective of her conversational other. The distortion which exists because of the physiological problem of the Alzheimer's patient makes it very difficult, if not impossible, for the "normal" partner to take the perspective of her disabled conversational partner. As McTear and King (1991) argue, the miscommunication which exists in many clinical contexts derives from the discrepancies between the mental states of the interlocutors – the healthy participant as well as the patient – rather than from some problem in the linguistic channel arising only out of the communicative disability of the patient. "Normal" individuals and Alzheimer's patients sometimes employ somewhat different discourse strategies and draw on somewhat different resources in their attempts to deal with the uncertainty which accompanies their inability to take the role of the other; this fact, however, should not be mistaken for the assignment of complete inability on the part of the disabled individual and complete ability on the part of the "normal" conversational partner. Responsibility to make sense of what is going on, to attempt to accomplish conversational coherence, to save mutual face, and to sustain the interaction belongs to both interlocutors.

Automaticity

The concept of automaticity (Whitaker 1982a, 1982b) as discussed by Tannen (1987) maintains that the more automatic a language feature or task has become over the experiences of a lifetime, the greater the chance that an individual will be able to use it appropriately. According to Bayles and Kaszniak (1987: 175), automatic processes are those which are "carried on without conscious monitoring." The phenomenon of automaticity is more easily recognized in language used by individuals with a disorder which affects various types of communication processes differentially than it is in unproblematic language produced by "normal" individuals. [. . .]

[. . .]

Besides the primarily automatic structural manipulations, such as turn-taking, which she is able to carry out in conversation, Elsie uses other types of language which seem to be more automatic than creative. These include language stored in long-term memory, such as culturally learned linguistic formulas (e.g. "Gee whiz!"), metacommunicative framing language (e.g., "I think"), and idiosyncratic ready-made language (e.g. professional jargon and terms of endearment), as well as language stored in short-term memory, such as immediate repetition of self and others, which can either be perceived as excessive (perseveration) or non-excessive.

In the rest of the chapter conversational evidence of Elsie's relative strengths and weaknesses in communication will be presented and discussed with reference to the notions of taking the role of the other and automaticity [. . .]

Conversational evidence of increasing problems in taking the role of the other

[. . .]

Conversational evidence of Elsie's increasing problems over time with other-experience awareness comes from several communicative areas: (1) the responses to word-finding difficulty in interaction and the related problem of appropriate use of reference; (2) her comprehension (or lack thereof) of indirect speaker meanings in discourse; (3) her production of self-initiated repairs; (4) her production of compliments and expressions of appreciation; and (5) her explicit use of the personal pronoun *you* in various speech acts. [. . .]

Word-finding difficulty [. . .] is one of the earliest and most obvious manifestations of the communication breakdown which accompanies Alzheimer's disease. As would be expected, then, Elsie has a great deal of difficulty, throughout the fourteen conversations, in finding words. When she cannot think of a particular word, she sometimes coins a new word (neologism), talks around the word (circumlocution), uses an already existing word to mean something else (reassignment of meaning), uses a semantically related (but different) word, or makes use of a semantically "empty" word, such as "place" or "thing." [. . .]

[. . .] Elsie's use of these different options in response to word-finding difficulty seems to be systematic. Following the conversations of fall 1982, Elsie no longer uses circumlocutions or semantically related words when she has problems finding a word. Instead, she continues to use neologisms, "empty" words, or reassigns the meaning of an unrelated word to take the "lost" word's place. In lieu of the intended word, the use of a circumlocution of a semantically related word indicates a greater other-orientation than does the use of a newly coined word, an inexplicit word, or a completely unrelated word. Clues as to the intended meaning are offered to the listener in the first two cases; in the latter three cases, the listener is offered at most an indication as to whether the speaker is referring to an inanimate object (*thing*), or a location (*place*), etc. That she stops providing a greater number of clues as to her intended meaning suggests that Elsie is no longer aware of the kinds of informational help she needs to offer her partner in order to maintain a successful conversation.

Elsie's difficulty in using reference appropriately may also be related to the word-finding difficulty just discussed. That is, if she cannot come up with the appropriate full noun phrase, she may use a pronoun instead, even though the pronoun does not provide enough information to the listener. These reference problems may, on the other hand, be traced to her problems in taking my perspective. In this interpretation, Elsie cannot realize that I do not have the referent for her pronouns in my bank of knowledge, and simply assumes that I will know what she knows. This would then be evidence of the egocentrism which has been discussed by Hutchinson and Jensen (1980) as a characteristic of Alzheimer's patients. According to this interpretation, then, Elsie's difficulties with the reference system would be part of an overall difficulty with the information system in communication. That is, Elsie presents information which is *not* known to her conversational partner as given information, or information which *is* known to her conversational partner as new information. Clearly the memory problems so prevalent in Alzheimer's disease may play a role in the patient's ability to assess what is new information for a given interlocutor. (This disruption of reference has been discussed at length in Ulatowska et al. 1990 and has been speculatively linked to the problem in taking the needs of the listener into account in Ulatowska et al. 1988, and Ripich and Terrell 1988.)

In example [1], I have just come upon Elsie reading aloud in the lounge on second floor. We exchange greetings and I ask her what she is reading about. She says she is *working on this*. Then she laughs and says *so that's was where she was (gonna go)* and immediately asks the following question:

Example [1]

ELSIE:	Where does <u>she</u> live? About the same? Where you folks do?
HEIDI:	I don't know who . . . who do you mean?
ELSIE:	Oh.
HEIDI:	I don't know who you mean.
ELSIE:	Well, let's see. What street?

(October 2, 1982)

Since there is no apparent referent for *she* in the prior discourse or in the physical environment, I do not know who Elsie is talking about. My first question requesting clarification is met with a simple *Oh*. Elsie's utterance (*well, let's see*) following my restatement that I do not know who she means seems to indicate her awareness that a problem in understanding exists on my part. However, Elsie's subsequent reformulation of her question strongly suggests that she is unable to identify what the source of my problem is, namely, that I do not know who the referent for *she* is. Her question *What street?* is simply a further specification of her initial question, indicating that she is interested in the street name rather than the city name, for example. Given that Elsie has been reading when I arrive to talk to her, it is possible that the referent for *she* is to be found in the story. Her egocentrism would prevent her from realizing that, having just arrived, I could not possibly know what she knows about the story.

Indirectness. Elsie's problems in interpreting indirect speaker meaning as used by the "normal" interlocutor may also be framed within the discussion of taking the role of the other. If Elsie has difficulty taking the perspective of her conversational partner, she may not be able to figure out his or her possible motivation(s) for using indirectness. This difficulty in interpreting indirectness has also been documented in mild Alzheimer's patients: Bayles (1985) found a significant difference between mild Alzheimer's patients and normal subjects regarding ability to judge whether an utterance in a particular context was intended literally.

Prior to example [2], I helped Elsie back to her room from the lounge where we were talking. We are now standing near her window in her room looking outside. Following a remark that she does not think it is going to rain, Elsie invites me to sit down. I need to go and visit other residents, however, and feel that I must refuse her offer to stay and talk:

Example [2]

ELSIE:	Please sit down.
HEIDI:	Oh well, that's okay. I think I should probably go and see some more people but I wanted to come and talk with you this morning.
ELSIE:	Oh <u>you mean</u>, wait a minute. <u>What what did you say?</u>
HEIDI:	I just said that I should probably go and see a couple more people before exercise class starts.
ELSIE:	Oh. for today
HEIDI:	└ Uhhuh. For today. And then I'll be back for you when the class starts if you want to join us .. for exercise.
ELSIE:	Oh <u>you mean</u> └ oh you oh I see
HEIDI:	uhhuh
ELSIE:	<u>you mean</u> then to look for us. <u>Is that what you meant?</u>
HEIDI:	└ I came to talk to you this morning └
ELSIE:	mhm
HEIDI:	because I think you're so interesting [laughs].
ELSIE:	Well, you're glad that you can stay as long as you want to stay a while. └
HEIDI:	Okay. └
ELSIE:	Yes. ┌ (. . .)
HEIDI:	└ You've
ELSIE:	┌You can sit right here.
HEIDI:	└ got such interesting things. Okay.
ELSIE:	You sit right there. (March 5, 1982)

Elsie has problems deciphering my very indirect refusal of her offer. My reluctance to say *no* directly to her prompts her to ask me several times what I mean, resulting, humorously enough, in a change in my plans. I end up staying and talking with Elsie and visit the other residents later in the day.

While example [2] illustrates the problems Elsie has in understanding the message underlying my indirect utterance, example [3] shows Elsie responding with a simple *yes* to a yes–no question which conventionally is used to trigger a more elaborate response. In his discussion of responses to yes–no questions, Yadugiri (1986) argues that a mere *yes* is inadequate in pragmatic terms to such questions which are intended to check whether a precondition holds for asking a relevant wh-question. In this example, Elsie appears to be responding to the *direct* reading, rather than the intended indirect reading, of the question. The fact that I follow up with a wh-question asking for more information indicates my expectation that the initial question would trigger a fuller response.

In example [3], I am trying to get Elsie to talk about her extensive travels and residence abroad:

Example [3]

HEIDI:	Did you ever live in someplace like India . . or uh Japan?
ELSIE:	Oh yes. In other countries ⌐of the
HEIDI:	└yeah
ELSIE:	world ⌐you mean? ⌐
HEIDI:	└mhm ⌐ └ mhm
ELSIE:	<u>Yes.</u>
HEIDI:	Which ones? Do you remember?
ELSIE:	Oh I've been to quite a few.

(March 5, 1982)

In this example, however, Elsie merely answers *yes*. Her reformulation of my question about specific countries to a more general question about *other countries of the world* indicates that she has understood the question. That she has not inferred my *intent* that the yes–no question serve indirectly as a request for a more elaborate answer is indicated by her simple answer *yes*. In response to my follow-up question, *which ones?*, Elsie says *I've been to quite a few*. This response suggests that Elsie realizes a more complete answer is expected of her, but long-term memory problems or word-finding difficulties probably do not allow a more specific response.

Against the background of memory and word-finding difficulties, an alternative interpretation of this example is possible. Perhaps Elsie *does* understand initially that more specific information is being requested of her. Knowing her limitations in providing such an answer, however, she opts to answer the direct reading of the question. Only when she is pushed by the follow-up question does she have to lay bare the fact that she cannot provide such specific information.

Self-initiated repair. In their discussion of organization of repair in conversation, Schegloff et al. (1977) differentiate between self-initiated and other-initiated repair. Whereas the use of a self-initiated repair indicates an awareness on the part of the speaker that something that she has just said or is about to say needs to be adjusted to help the listener understand her correctly, the use of an other-initiated repair indicates an awareness on the part of the listener that her communicative needs are not being met by the current speaker. In that sense, then, Elsie's use of self-repair up through our conversations in July 1985 provides evidence that on some level she is continuing to take my communicative needs into account. Example [4] shows Elsie repairing her utterance by replacing the lexical item (*bree*) with the more readily understandable item *read*:

Example [4]

> HEIDI: What do you want?
> ELSIE: I have to (bree) read.
>
> (July 4, 1985)

The phenomenon of self-repair is also reported by Illes (1989) for Alzheimer's patients in the early and middle stages of the disease. Illes suggests that this repair work shows that these patients "were aware of their own verbal difficulties as well as the presence of the interlocutor."

[. . .]

Use of compliments and expressions of appreciation. Elsie's decreasing ability to take the perspective of her partner is additionally indicated by the fact that after spring 1984 she no longer gives compliments or expresses appreciation. These communicative tasks, which had been characteristic of her conversational contributions up until that time, are examples of what Brown and Levinson (1987: 62) term "positive politeness." This refers to the orientation of one's utterance toward making the conversational partner feel wanted and liked. Examples [5] and [6] illustrate Elsie's use of positive politeness in the center. Example [5] takes place in the elevator following the exercise class. Elsie is complimenting a fellow resident of the center on her dress:

Example [5]

> ELSIE: <u>That's a very pretty dress.</u>
> HEIDI: Isn't that?
> ELSIE: <u>Isn't that pretty?</u> Ye:s.
> HEIDI: It's lovely.
> ELSIE: <u>You all have . . . yours is pretty too.</u>
> HEIDI: [laughing] Oh well, thank you.
> ELSIE: <u>and you too.</u> [laughing]
>
> (November 20, 1981)

After I support her linguistically in her compliment to the other resident, Elsie distributes compliments to all of us in the elevator, seeming to derive immense joy from making people feel good.

Even in later conversations when her utterances become more difficult to understand, Elsie's compliments are strikingly well-formed and easy to comprehend. Example [6] occurs while Elsie and I are looking at a mail-order catalogue in the lounge. At the beginning of this segment Elsie is still referring to objects represented in the catalogue:

Example [6]

> ELSIE: Now these are very (huse some of that day). Mhm. ⌉
> HEIDI: ⌐ I think ⌐ I remember
> ELSIE: ⌊ <u>Your hair</u>
>
> HEIDI: <u>is so beautiful.</u> ⌉ Well, thank you.
>
> (March 17, 1984)

During my time as a volunteer at the center, I observed time and time again that this ability to make others feel good was a crucial factor in Elsie's attracting conversational partners. Her use of positive politeness seemed in many cases to offset the uncomfortableness caused by the confusion and communicative breakdowns. By summer 1985, however, such compliments are made no longer, and expressing appreciation to the person who is responsible for a desired action is replaced by a favorable ego-centered evaluation of the situation (*oh that's good*).

Explicit use of the pronoun "you". We can also examine Elsie's use of the personal pronoun "you" in reference to her conversational partner as evidence of her increasing difficulty in taking the role of the other and the concomitant increase in the reference to herself. During our conversations together, Elsie uses the pronoun *you* to accomplish the following interactional tasks: to request information about me, to check her understanding of what I said (*you mean . . .?*), to request repetition of what I said (*What did you say?*), and to request an action on my part. Elsie's increasing difficulty in taking the role of her other is indicated by the fact that after the spring 1984 conversation, Elsie drops her requests for information about me, but continues (1) to ask questions which are critical to Elsie's own understanding of the conversation (repetitions and confirmations of understanding) and (2) to request that I carry out actions which will benefit Elsie.

[. . .]

Conversational evidence of maintained ability to use relatively automatic language

Conversational evidence of Elsie's maintained ability to use relatively automatic language comes from observations of her ability to carry out procedural tasks in the interactions as well as of her use of ready-made language both from long-term and short-term memory.

[. . .]

Procedural tasks which Elsie is able to perform even in the later conversations are of three types: (1) attention-getting devices; (2) ability to indicate that the interlocutor's utterance was not heard; and (3) structural manipulations of the conversational machinery.

[. . .]

Structural manipulations. One of the striking features of Elsie's discourse is her excellent ability to deal with the mechanical parts of conversation. [. . .]

In example [7], Elsie answers my question about going to exercise class issued in lines 1–2, but not until line 12. In between my question and her answer to it, Elsie asks three related questions, two regarding the time of the class (lines 3 and 5) and one regarding what the class is (line 7):

Example [7]

1.	HEIDI:	Hi. Would you like to go to exercise
2.		today?
3.	ELSIE:	What time? ⌈When?
4.	HEIDI:	⌊Right right now.
5.	ELSIE:	When?
6.	HEIDI:	Right now.
7.	ELSIE:	And what is that doing?
8.	HEIDI:	uh . . Well, you know that stuff we do
9.		all the time with the uh with the

10.   little cymbals that we have and we
11.   have a good time with music.
12. ELSIE: Well, I don't know yet.

(November 27, 1982)

Given her short-term memory problems, that fact that Elsie can still ask and receive answers to three related questions before giving me an answer to my question is quite amazing and is evidence, I believe, for the hypothesis that structural manipulations in conversation remain intact longer than content-level manipulations.

Ready-made language

Elsie seems able to use ready-made language in the design of her discourse. The term "ready-made language" refers to the prefabricated pieces of language discussed by Bolinger (1961: 381) which speakers do not actively create when they talk, but rather "reach for" from an ever-growing inventory of talk they have used or heard before. [. . .]

In example [8], Elsie is standing in front of the elevator following the exercise class. She seems to be somewhat confused as to whether she goes down or up on the elevator to her home floor. After I give her the answer, she uses the formula *Whatever you say* to indicate that she trusts me to tell her where she needs to go:

Example [8]

ELSIE: Don't we go down? ⌈Huh? Do we go
HEIDI: ⌊Here. You go
ELSIE: ⌈down or up?⌉
HEIDI: ⌊down.   ⌋ ⌊ You go down, Elsie.
ELSIE: Whatever you say.

(November 25, 1981)

Just prior to example [9], Elsie and I had heard the quick tongue of an auctioneer on the television set which was on in the lounge:

Example [9]

ELSIE: Oh, for goodness sake. My my.

(May 18, 1982)

Elsie apparently found his vocal techniques worthy of comment and used the formulas *for goodness sake* and *my my* to do so.

Metacommunicative framing language. Metacommunicative framing language stands outside the actual content of the discourse and comments on the speaker's relationship to the content, i.e., whether she understands it (*I don't understand, I see*), agrees with it to a certain degree (*That's right, I think, I guess, I suppose*), disagrees with it (*I doubt*), does not know (*I don't know*), does not remember it (*I don't remember, I forget, I've forgotten, I forgot*), or wants to have a moment to reflect on it (*Wait a minute, Let's see, Lemme see*).

Since there are few stances one can take *vis-à-vis* a chunk of discourse relative to the possibilities regarding *content* of the discourse chunk, and these metacommunicative comments are "reusable" in a variety of situations (and have been used over the course of a lifetime), I understand metacommunicative framing language to be a type of "ready-made" language. Elsie's successful use of metalanguage corroborates the finding of a case study by Andresen (1986) of a severely aphasic patient whose most fluent and coherent language was used to say (metacommunicatively) that he could not say anything.

Idiosyncratic language. Whereas linguistic formulas form a pool of linguistic resources which are available to any speaker in the speech community, I understand idiosyncratic ready-made language to be more individual and to a certain extent a product of the speaker's life experiences.

[. . .] In example [10], Elsie passes an elderly man in a wheelchair on her way to the elevator following exercise class:

Example [10]

ELSIE: I'm praying for you, dear honey, to help you better. Is that all right, dear honey? Honey? Yes. Lots of love to you, dear, to help you. Yeah. We've been good friends, haven't we? Haven't we, dear? And then I can go on. and uh. You can do it, honey. I'll pray for you.

(November 27, 1981)

Elsie begins and ends what she says to her fellow patient with the fact that she is praying for him to get better and will continue to do so. She expresses confidence that he can indeed get better. Although these instances all point to Elsie's earlier career in the ministry, it is her statement to herself *and then I can go on* which seems most to differentiate this chunk of discourse from one which could have been uttered by any other religious friend of the patient. It seems to shed light on an earlier time in Elsie's life when she conveyed concern, love, and confidence to whole groups of people in need of it. When Elsie thought her job was done with one person, she could move on to the next.

[. . .]

In addition to [. . .] language from Elsie's past which seems to be incorporated relatively fluently and automatically into her ongoing discourse, I understand idiosyncratic ready-made language to include other building-blocks which Elsie uses in a marked way in her discourse. These include her frequent use of amount terms, the utterance *That's a good idea* and the term of endearment *dear honey*, as well as the marked use of opposites and the conditional mood. [. . .]

The frequent use of *amount terms*, as illustrated by example [11], is very characteristic of Elsie's discourse [. . .]. In this example Elsie is responding to my question to her whether she would like to move to another chair or would rather stay near the window where she has complained about the cold:

Example [11]

ELSIE: Well, I think right now . . I just as soon do it <u>a little bit</u> cause it's gonna gonna (change) <u>some of it</u> cause the sunshine's coming in. and one was for (growin up) just <u>a little bit</u> ago (did <u>great big part</u>).

(March 5, 1982)

Her frequent use of these amount terms, especially *a little bit*, contributes to the impression of Elsie as a tentative, hedging speaker. Although it is not possible here to determine definitively whether this interpretation is justified, their frequency does seem to suggest that they are simply ready-made building-blocks being used automatically to produce a greater amount of discourse with little additional effort.

Additionally, Elsie often uses the evaluative statement *That's a good idea* in places where a positive evaluation would be appropriate as a response but where reference to *a good idea* is odd if not completely inappropriate. The fact that *that's a good idea* seems to be interchangeable in Elsie's discourse with the simpler form *that's good* suggests that it, too, is a building-block to be used automatically by Elsie in constructing her discourse. Example [12] is one of many discussions Elsie and I had about where my home was located:

Example [12]

ELSIE:	And where did you say your home was?
HEIDI:	It's uh just a couple blocks from here.
	I'm ⌐
ELSIE:	└ Oh I see. Oh that's good.
HEIDI:	I'm on Walter Road. ⌐
ELSIE:	└ You can do that.
	<u>That's a good idea.</u>

(March 5, 1982)

In this example, after positively evaluating with *Oh that's good* the fact that I only live a couple of blocks from the nursing home, Elsie produces the pragmatically odd evaluation *That's a good idea* of the fact that I live on Walter Road. The automatic usage of this phrase is indicated by an occurrence a couple of minutes earlier in the same conversation. There, following my statement that I live very close to the nursing home, Elsie's initial, automatic response was *Oh that's a good i:* which she broke off (an example of self-initiated repair) and replaced with the more appropriate *That's very good*.

[. . .]

An additional characteristic of Elsie's discourse which can be understood as part of her idiosyncratic ready-made language is her use of opposites within an utterance. Once Elsie has chosen the first half of her statement, the second half in a sense follows "automatically," as it can be produced simply by negating what went before. In example [13], Elsie is cleaning her eyeglasses and makes the following comment with the presumed meaning that sometimes she is successful cleaning her glasses and sometimes she is not:

Example [13]

ELSIE:	<u>Sometimes they'll go alright and other times they won't be.</u>

(March 5, 1982)

In this example we note that Elsie is successful at negating the adverb (*sometimes* vs. *other times*) as well as the auxiliary verb (*'ll* vs. *won't*), and continues to use the correct pronoun (*they*) and tense (future). Elsie's only problem is the mismatch between main verbs *go* and *be*, which would not even have been noticed if she had deleted the final verb following *won't*.

[. . .]

In tracking Elsie's use of ready-made language over time, it appears that the more idiosyncratic language is lost before the more culturally shared linguistic formulas. The marked use of *that's a good idea*, the professional language, the overuse of amount terms, and the use of opposites, discussed above as being characteristic of Elsie's discourse, all appear for the last time in the March 1984 conversation. The only one of Elsie's "personal" ready-made language characteristics to occur in summer 1985 is the use of terms of endearment. On the other hand, more general readymade language features, such as metacommunicative comments and linguistic formulas (*Gee whiz!, I should say so*) continue to occur in summer 1985, as does the more ephemeral repetition of the conversational partner and repetition of self in the form of perseveration. Since the idiosyncratic ready-made language phenomena are arguably what make a chunk of discourse "Elsie's talk" as opposed to someone else's, this finding fits well with the frequently observed personality changes noted by family members of Alzheimer's patients (see Bayles and Kaszniak 1987 and Campbell-Taylor 1984). It could well be that part of the reason the patient is "not the person I used to know" is that she or he is not using the *language* "I used to know."

[. . .]

■ ■ ■

POST-READING

1   Assess the usefulness of the following statement:

> "Normal" interlocutors will always engage in *intentional* underaccommodation, and interlocutors with disabilities such as Elsie's will always engage in *unintentional* underaccommodation.

What (if anything) is problematic about such a stance? Where possible, justify your answer by drawing from Hamilton and also other texts in this Reader.

2   Like Crystal (1984) and McTear and King (1991), Hamilton argues that we should not be too quick to attribute conversational breakdowns/miscommunications to disabled interlocutors only. Rather, we should accept that 'responsibility to make sense of what is going on, to attempt to accomplish conversational coherence, to save mutual face, and to sustain the interaction belongs to both interlocutors'. Drawing from Hamilton's own examples (1 through 13), identify instances where Hamilton seems to be employing 'somewhat different discourse strategies and draw[ing] on somewhat different resources' than Elsie. Are there any instances where the 'breakdown' in understanding can be attributed to Hamilton rather than to Elsie? How difficult is it to attribute communication breakdown to one (rather than both) individuals, even when one of them has a recognized communicative disability?

3   Cummings (2009: 13) has argued that many clinical pragmatics studies adopt too broad a view of pragmatics, in the sense that they focus on 'a whole range of non-linguistic behaviours' such as facial expression, gesture and eye contact, which are not 'rooted in language use' and, as such, shouldn't be considered "pragmatic". Do you think that the readings in this section provide sufficient evidence to suggest that non-linguistic behaviours such as facial expression, gesture and eye contact do, in fact, serve communicative purposes? Is there sufficient evidence to suggest a pragmatic approach *should* include, for example, gestures, especially when it can be shown that they serve a clear communicative purpose? You might find it worthwhile to return to some of the readings in Section 2, when contemplating this particular question.

SECTION 8 FURTHER READING

CA

There are a number of accessible introductions to CA – see, e.g., Sacks *et al.* (1974), Heritage (1984), Wooffitt (2005), Ten Have (2007) and Hutchby and Wooffitt 2008) – some of which also touch upon language pathology. In addition, Whitworth *et al.* (1997), Basso (2003) and Goodwin (2003) specifically focus on CA and communication discourse.

Interactional Sociolinguistics

Like Pragmatics, Interactional Sociolinguistics is a diverse field, which draws from anthropology, sociology and linguistics (including CA and Pragmatics). Researchers particularly associated with Interactional Sociolinguistics include Gumperz (1982a, 1982b, 1992, 1999), Goffman (1963, 1967, 1971, 1974) and, more recently, Schiffrin (1987, 1994, 1996).

Clinical pragmatics

Clinical researchers working within a more explicitly pragmatic paradigm include Ninio and Snow (1996), Leinonen *et al.* (2000) and Cummings (2005, 2009). For useful snapshots of pragmatic development and impairment, see, e.g., De Villiers (2010), Ryder (2010) and Rollins (2010).

Relevant journal articles

A range of developmental studies are to be found in journals such as *Child Development, Journal of Child Language, Cognitive Psychology, Developmental Psychology, Applied Linguistics, Applied Psycholinguistics, Language Sciences, Journal of Communication Disorders, Journal of Experimental Child Psychology, Journal of Pragmatics*, etc. Some of these journals also include adult-based clinical studies and/or experimental studies, as do journals such as *Cognition, Behavioural and Brain Sciences, Cognitive Science, Brain and Language, Memory and Cognition, International Journal of Language and Communication Disorders*, etc.

SECTION 9

Pragmaticians on pragmatics

Introduction

THE THREE READINGS IN THIS SECTION share the view that pragmatics
has been concerned predominantly with the recovery of propositional meaning and has
overlooked the extent to which the language we use reflects social context. The first reading,
Roman Kopytko's *Journal of Pragmatics* paper 'Against rationalistic pragmatics', rejects what
he sees as the reductionist approach adopted by Austin, Grice, and Sperber and Wilson and
asserts that we need a more empirical pragmatics. The second and third readings – Jon
Pressman's 'Pragmatics in the late twentieth century: Countering recent historiographic neglect'
and Charles Briggs's Introduction to the *Special Edition on Conflict and Violence in Pragmatic
Research* – were first published in *Pragmatics*, the journal of the *International Pragmatics
Association*. These readings reflect the perspective of the Chicago School, whose anthropological
approach places indexicality at the centre of language use.

All three authors are uncomfortable, to say the least, with the attempt to reduce the
production and recovery of meaning to a quasi-mathematical formulation. All three argue
that sociocultural considerations have been insufficiently taken account of in linguistic
pragmatics. Kopytko and Pressman, in particular, argue that privileging a means-ends view
of functional language results in illocutionary rather than pragmatic functionalism, which is
any case problematic given the unpredictability of speaker-intended perlocution. And while
Kopytko accuses the rationalists of promoting a 'decontextualized pragmatics', Pressman quotes
Silverstein's view of linguistic pragmatics as the 'idealization of how lexical expressions
propositionally or referentially function'. Going further still, Briggs sees such idealizations as
highly politicized attempts to impose an orderly framework on talk that is in reality anything
but orderly.

In the first reading, 'Against rationalistic pragmatics', Roman Kopytko rejects pragmatic
theories which account for language use solely in terms of reason. For Kopytko, linguistic
actions are motivated by a complex array of contextual phenomena, including emotional as
well as rational responses to experience. He thus goes head-to-head with the linguistic
philosophers whose proposals for interpreting utterances are based on the assumption that talk

is purely rational. He also identifies Brown and Levinson's means-ends account of politeness phenomena as a paradigm example of an explanatorily inadequate mechanism for calculating how a linguistic utterance takes into account complex sociological contexts. (As you'll recall from Section 6, Brown and Levinson reduce these contexts to just three variables, P, D and R.)

At the beginning of his paper, Kopytko challenges a number of assumptions, which he later critiques in detail. These are

(1) philosophical essentialism, or the assumption of 'pure' reason;
(2) modular pragmatics, or the isolation of reason alone as a sufficient motivation for linguistic action;
(3) reductionism, by which a complex set of sociological motivations are reduced to a simple set of schemata;
(4) the view of human beings as rational agents or model persons whose rationality is inferred from their external behaviour (which in any case doesn't always seem that rational) rather than analysed as an intrinsic psychological process;
(5) a categorical or absolutist view of reason, which is wrongly regarded as a natural, non-fuzzy category, and the failure to acknowledge that linguistic behaviour should more properly be described as exhibiting degrees of motivation; and
(6) a deductive approach which derives principles for future behaviour from previous cases, so that past instances are held to predict future instances in a nomological or rule-creating, rather than a probabilistic, way.

At the end of the reading, Kopytko concludes that explanatory theories in pragmatics are unlikely to be satisfactory when we have yet to achieve even observational adequacy. Despite his criticisms of rationalistic pragmatics, Kopytko leaves us with very little idea of what an observationally adequate empirical pragmatics would actually involve, beyond identifying 'the empirical relationship between the concepts of a pragmatic theory and the description of pragmatic phenomena.' Even so, this reading should inspire us to think more carefully about talk and the contexts in which it occurs and to be suspicious of theories supported by invented examples or by decontextualized utterances. We omit only the abstract, two incidental paragraphs and, for reasons of space and difficulty, two sub-sections from Kopytko's original paper – 2.2, which argues that pragmatic processes are fuzzy and indeterminate, and 2.3, which discusses the relationship between rationality and the achievement of intended goals.

One way of confronting the issue of observational adequacy identified by Kopytko is to use methods of data collection such as participant observation which are common in social anthropology. Pressman demonstrates that there is indeed a long tradition of ethnographically oriented pragmatics of this kind. He argues that the results obtained in this tradition have been systematically excluded from the literature with which most readers are familiar. By way of evidence, one might consider the balance of readings in this volume. Or the absence of any representation of Chicago School anthropological linguistics in Horn and Ward's benchmark volume *The Handbook of Pragmatics* (2004). Similarly, there's no reference to this tradition in either the original editors' introduction to the first edition of the *Journal of Pragmatics* (1977) or in the twenty-fifth anniversary Jubilee editorial (2002). The latter draws (not entirely approving) attention to the pre-eminence of the reductive approaches critiqued by

Kopytko and the minimalist and increasingly deductive approaches of Relevance Theory and some neo-Griceans, but it does not draw attention to the tradition that Pressman presents, which is perhaps surprising given the strong representation of the 'continental' tradition in the journal. As we think of the systematic exclusion of pragmatic theories grounded in social context, we are perhaps faced with what the editors of the Jubilee edition of the *Journal of Pragmatics* describe (with apologies to Kundera) as 'the unbearable lightness of pragmatics'.

While Pressman's overt motivation in writing this paper is countering the neglect of the Chicago School, his paper should at the same time be read as a positive argument for an ethnolinguistic approach to pragmatics. We have already encountered some of these ideas in the Verschueren reading in Section 4. Thus Pressman's insistence that 'contextual factors necessarily impinge on language form', his claim that 'the social ends accomplished by the pragmatic function of language are just as important as the propositional ends manifested by the referential function', the principle of 'calibration' and the inevitability of a metapragmatic dimension are not new in this volume. However, what Pressman adds is the historical context in which these ideas were developed.

Turning to that historical context, when you read Pressman's paper, it does help to know that Roman Jakobson (1960), to whom Pressman refers extensively, proposed six functions whose occurrence co-varies with social context. Imagine a context in which H has agreed to look after S's dog while S is on holiday. In this context, we might suppose a range of functions oriented to in S's utterance *I'm afraid D-O-G-S like going for bloody W-A-L-K-S, or rather shoe-ruining expeditions to the country*, namely:

- a *referential* function: it describes a state of affairs;
- an *expressive* function: 'bloody' indicates S's attitude to the propositional content of the utterance;
- a *conative* function: 'I'm afraid' takes account of H's presumed attitude to the propositional content of the utterance;
- a *phatic* function: the spelling aloud of 'dogs' and 'walks' acknowledges that the overhearing dog might understand and react to these two words if they were not disguised in this way;
- a *metalinguistic* function: 'or rather shoe-ruining expeditions to the country' glosses 'walks'.

And just to complete Jakobson's set, had S said 'walky-pawkies' rather than spelt 'W-A-L-K-S' aloud, S's utterance would have exhibited a *poetic* function too.

Although a lengthy description of Jakobson's functions does occur in Pressman's paper, we have edited this out to save space. Indeed, we have reduced the paper considerably, but without compromising its essential content, which includes an explanation of the background to Pressman's argument, a historical account of Chicago School functionalism, an account of Silverstein's proposals and an outline of the approaches of two other researchers in the continuing Chicago tradition.

Taking issue with the principle that general theories are to be preferred over focused local studies, Briggs criticizes the interest of pragmaticians and conversation analysts in the 'ordinary' or 'everyday' use of language, which he sees as a means of marginalizing, or even excluding, the '*extra*ordinary'. As the editor of a special edition of *Pragmatics* dedicated to the analysis of extraordinary interactions occurring in extraordinary contexts, Briggs is interested in how the particularity of a context is constructed in discourse that is unlike the discourse of more familiar interaction types. As well as reflecting Briggs's own position, this reading also refers to the work of the various contributors to the special edition it introduces. In editing the reading, we have tried to strike a balance between providing an insight into the range of extraordinary discourses featured and excising the detail which makes little sense for anyone not intending to read the special edition of the journal in its entirety.

ROMAN KOPYTKO

AGAINST RATIONALISTIC PRAGMATICS

There's no hiding the intrinsic difficulty of this reading, which is perhaps the most difficult in this volume. However, careful and repeated study of this thought-provoking paper certainly repays the effort. The more-extensive-than-usual reading activities are designed to help you with the challenge ahead.

PRE-READING

Using a 5-point scale (1 = strongly agree, 2 = agree, 3 = neutral, 4 = disagree, 5 = strongly disagree), score each of the following statements that you are about to come across in Kopytko's paper:

- Reason interacts with other faculties in a complex process of indeterminate character.
- Past experience must be viewed indeterministically, because each situation in the future will be different.
- The course and 'result' of a discourse cannot be predicted from its basic constituents, i.e. participants and social context.
- The scope of context is indefinite: minimally, it should include the participant's identity and role; assumptions about temporal, spatial, and social settings; assumptions about what participants know or take for granted; knowledge of the medium and social factors. There is no theory that could predict the relevance of such features and their impact on discourse.
- The unit of analysis of linguistic interaction must be a larger stretch of discourse than a speech act.
- The course of linguistic interaction between S and H is unpredictable and the perlocutionary effect uncertain. It is very fortunate for humans that this is so, because otherwise life would be predictively boring and linguistic interaction deterministically unbearable.
- Politeness cannot be assigned out of context to any particular structure.

IN-READING

In the second half of this reading, Kopytko refers to several pragmaticians, and particularly Brown and Levinson, about whose work on politeness you will already have formed an opinion.

At each point in the reading where you see | in the margin, review your existing opinion of the work referred to in the light of Kopytko's view.

■ ■ ■

AGAINST RATIONALISTIC PRAGMATICS
ROMAN KOPYTKO

[. . .]

1 Introduction

The main objective of this paper is to show the inadequacy of an approach to pragmatics which I will label 'rationalistic pragmatics' (henceforth: RP). In my opinion, the major claims, assumptions and postulates of RP (i.e. a type of pragmatics based on rationalistic assumptions rather than on empirical findings) may be derived from the following theoretical sources: (1) philosophical essentialism (cf. Popper 1945; Janicki 1989); (2) modular pragmatics (cf. Fodor 1983; Wilson and Sperber 1986a); (3) the principle of methodological reductionism (cf. Popper 1945); (4) the postulate of the 'rationality of human behavior' analyzed in terms of 'ideal types', 'rational agents', etc. (cf. Weber 1949; Grice 1975; Levinson 1983; Sperber and Wilson 1986; Brown and Levinson 1987): (5) categorical pragmatics (cf. Leech 1983; Rosch 1978); (6) deductive-nomological, i.e. deterministic, predictive approaches (cf. Hempel 1965).

Specifically, this critique will concentrate on the three interrelated methodological aspects of RP, i.e. *rationality, reductionism*, and *context*. The leitmotif of this triad – the question of prediction – will frequently recur. It will be claimed that neither rationality nor reduction nor context are predicative concepts in linguistic pragmatics. That is to say, they are not predictive in the deductive-nomological sense. However, the possibility of other forms of prediction, for instance of the inductive or probabilistic type, will not be denied.

It should be noticed that the construct of 'rationality' is a reduction of the human mind to one of its mental faculties. But it is doubtful whether the mind is reducible to its components. (On the cognitive-affective system, cf. Markus and Wurf (1987) and Winton (1990).)

The crucial role of context in pragmatics is indisputable. However, in the framework of RP this role is reduced.

In sum, the usefulness of the construct of 'rationality', the principle of methodological reductionism and the reduction of social to psychological facts will be questioned (cf. Durkheim 1895). Finally, context reduction in RP will be shown to lead to pragmatic paradoxes.

My arguments against RP will frequently be supported by the views of philosophers, social psychologists, sociologists and linguists.

The RP approach as represented in politeness theory (cf. Brown and Levinson 1987, henceforth: B&L) will be the primary object of my critical analysis.

2 On rationality

B&L's (1987: 58) 'Model Person'-MP is assigned a special property of *rationality*, defined as the application of a specific mode of reasoning – what Aristotle called 'practical reasoning', which guarantees inferences from ends or goals to means that will satisfy those ends. Thus, linguistic strategies will be the *means* of satisfying communicative and face-oriented *ends*, in a strictly formal system of rational 'practical reasoning'. B&L insist that their system of practical reasoning, 'Kenny logic', is "essentially parasitic on deductive reasoning". Furthermore, B&L assert that their model is predictive – "We consider that if the predictions made by our model are borne out by the data drawn from usage in a small sample of unrelated cultures and languages, strong support may be inferred for the original assumptions" (1987: 59).

2.1 The non-modular rationality

A model of social action in which individuals rationally pursue their own self-interest has a long tradition. It is associated closely with the social philosophy of Jeremy Bentham and John Stuart Mill (with precursors such as Thomas Hobbes, John Locke and David Hume), often referred to as utilitarianism. Economics, behavioral psychology and sociology (specifically, exchange theory) have been influenced by utilitarian concepts. The 'construct' in economics of *Economic Man* (methodologically analogous to that of B&L's MP) reflects the assumptions that individuals behave as if they maximize *utility*, subject to a set of constraints of which the most obvious is income. Economic Man is then 'rational', if he pursues this objective, although he may face obstacles (such as imperfect information) which prevent him from actually achieving the goal.

[. . .]

The capacity of humans to draw logical conclusions has been regarded as their most distinctive faculty. A philosophical discussion of this ability has a long tradition, going back to Plato's differentiation of will, reason and passion in Man. The tripartite nature of the soul was presented in *Phaedrus* (cf. Plato 1972), although the doctrine was already present in the *Republic*: "the career of the soul is akin to the passage of a chariot with driver, one well-mannered white steed, and one intractable and plunging black steed. The driver is reason, the white steed the spirited part (related to will) and the black steed represents the appetitive element in man – the element of desire with its lawlessness. The task of reason is to control the will and appetites and provide a unity of function among these elements of the soul" (cf. Reese 1980: 441).

In modern times, Charles S. Peirce (1931–58) seems to continue and develop the ancient Platonian distinction. Reese presents Peirce's standpoint in the following way:

> "Man has no compartmentalized faculties, as reason, will, feeling. Rather, his inner life and his nature are a compound *reason-will-feeling*. The three interpenetrate. In addition to conscious inferences, there is a semi-conscious process in which inferences continue, feelings develop, attitudes form. No reason is possible without emotion and will; no feeling or willing, which is not also inferring. We are this compound, complex process".
>
> (1980: 420)

The most important consequences of Peirce's claims (and directly relevant to the present discussion) are the following: *firstly*, the modular view of human faculties is rejected in favor of the non-modular approach (referred to in the quotation as non-compartmentalized faculties); and *secondly*, by implication a predictive, deterministic model of human behavior must be questioned because no 'pure rationality' exists. Rather, reason interacts with other faculties in a complex process of indeterminate character.

[. . .]

2.4 Rationality and essentialism

The notion of 'pure rationality' or the reduction of rational action to its essentials, where it is viewed as some kind of Weberian 'ideal type', cannot be tested and corroborated outside the social context. Furthermore, B&L's claim that MPs possess a specific property of 'rationality' is in a sense trivial, because the statement that actors are rational because their actions are rational (or the other way round: this action is rational, because its actor is rational) is tautological and unfalsifiable. Rational Behavior, e.g. in a speech encounter, depends on the interrelationship between S and H in a social context. S's and H's knowledge of social interaction (their past experience) and their mutual knowledge of one another's personality, values, goals, intentions, etc., cannot be overlooked in the assessment of the factor of rationality. (More on this in the section on context.) It should also be stressed that past experience must be viewed indeterministically, because each situation in the future will be different, and moreover, social situations are not well-defined, i.e. the number of relevant factors influencing the course and result of social interaction is unpredictable.

The achievement of goals and their analysis in terms of a cost/benefit scale is a subjective, individual matter, and cannot be divorced from an individual hierarchy of values. In practice, 'rationality' is not viewed in terms of universal values, but rather is realized according to individual values.

Furthermore, it would be a mistake to believe that the achievement of a goal is always a result of calculation (rational action). It may as well be an effect of chance, risk-taking, or the side-effect of other action (not necessarily rational), such as in the case of instinctive or habitual behavior, etc. In other words, goal achievement may be a result of unpredictable events and circumstances.

It is hardly possible to imagine what 'purely rational action' would be like, except as a decontextualized abstract notion with an actor reduced to *ad hoc* essentials, as some sort of construct. However, an actor's rationality is usually interwoven with other motives (factors), such as those proposed by Plato and which challenge the possibility of predicting the results of an action. It cannot be overlooked that in the case of social interaction not only the factors responsible for actors' behavior influence the course and result of their actions, but also the rationality of their 'strategies of action', and factors associated with the receivers and their social context. Therefore, the assumption of rationality can be viewed only in a very abstract and restricted way. A mathematical formula-like rationality or some kind of deductive reasoning can hardly be claimed to be an adequate model of human action, of social interaction, or of the phenomena of linguistic pragmatics.

2.5 Rationality and the perlocutionary effect

A theory of 'rationalistic pragmatics' adopts some form of modular pragmatics with all its weaknesses (as presented earlier), restrictiveness, and incompleteness. It has been claimed above that rationality without any criterion of 'rationality' is an unfalsifiable notion. But couldn't the rationality of an action be assessed, tested, or falsified in terms of its success or failure?

In a speech encounter, the perlocutionary effect could be such a criterion. Obviously, it cannot be seen as an absolute, or final criterion, because, for example, the positive effect of a perlocutionary act could be followed immediately by a blunder, 'faux pas', misunderstanding, etc., turning success into failure; or the long-term effects (due to unintended consequences) might be assessed differently from the short-term effects, and evaluated in a new light.

The perlocutionary effect of a speech act is unpredictable because it depends on a set of pragmatic factors which are also unpredictable. Therefore, a distinction between the intended vs. the actual perlocutionary effect has been proposed (cf. Lyons 1977: 731). The rationality of the intended perlocutionary effect should thus be assessed in terms of the actual perlocutionary effects (perhaps with the reservation that the unit of such an assessment should be a larger stretch of discourse, in order to account for a possible subsequent reevaluation of the perlocutionary effects). The actual perlocutionary effect can be assessed by S and H; by a possible O (an observer, or third party, i.e. other participants in the speech encounter); and finally by the linguist analyzing the discourse. The intended perlocutionary effect and its 'rationality' can be adequately assessed only by S; it must be conjectured or inferred (probabilistically) by the other participants in the discourse (and the linguist).

In conclusion, the perlocutionary effect does not seem to be an adequate criterion of rationality. [. . .]

2.6 Rationality and functional explanation

Finally, to conclude the question of rationality, I will make a few comments on the rationality of the functional and teleological explanations adopted both by Leech (1983) and B&L (1987). In this connection, B&L view linguistic strategies as *means* satisfying communicative and face-oriented *ends*, in a strictly formal system of rational 'practical reasoning'.

Every explanation in terms of purposes, ends, goals, plans, etc., presupposes the adoption of a functional or teleological explanation. According to Lass (1980: 69), the main difficulty with functional explanation is "that it is always irreducibly *post hoc* (in the sense of being totally non-predictive)", and that the functions invoked often seem rather fishy and devoid of principled support. Summing up the teleological problem, Lass (1980: 90) claims that there are no functional explanations because (a) we have no principled definition of 'dysfunction'; (b) we therefore cannot define what constitutes a 'function'; and because (c) there are no D-N (deductive-nomological) and probabilistic explanations in historical linguistics. (Lass presents his critique of functionalism in the context of language change.)

The problems of functionalism in sociological theory were extensively presented in Turner (1978). They mainly include (1) the question of empirical validity; (2) the question of tautology; and (3) the question of unjustified teleology. The latter problem appears when the explanation assumes the existence of aims or goals causally correlated with the process and structures that serve to realize those goals, without any possibility of proving the existence of causal sequences, the mechanisms by which the goals create or regulate structures, and the processes involved in the realization of those goals. The question of tautology may appear, when empirical hypotheses (if available at all) that should prove a non-tautological character of an explanation do not reveal the indispensable logical interrelationship (correlations) with the theory they are part of.

The problems of functional/teleological explanation have, so far, proven to be insurmountable in all fields of scientific endeavor. What is relevant for our present discussion is the non-predictability of (rational) action analyzed in terms of functional/teleological notions and, as a result, the failure of functional explanations (i.e. *ends-means* analyses). It should not be overlooked that the concept of 'want', used by B&L to analyze negative and positive face, is a teleological notion. It cannot be denied that it is possible for human beings to take action with respect to future goals. That is, some kind of 'teleology of purpose' may be claimed to underlie an intention to reach some goal. Such a kind of rational action relies on 'motivation' based on experience, knowledge of the world, personal capabilities, and (what is most important for our present argument) on *inductive expectation*, in contradistinction to B&L's claims about the rationality of practical reasoning based essentially on deductive reasoning.

Therefore, propositions like the following: *Whenever strategy X is used, goal Y is achieved*, or alternatively; *Whenever goal Y is achieved, strategy X is used* (in relation to human beings) can only be assigned an inductive certitude. By contrast, a proposition such as the following: *Whenever strategy X is used, goal Y may (probably) be achieved* is based on experience, knowledge, expectations, etc., and seems to reflect better the non-predictive character of human behavior.

3 On reductionism

The Cartesian analytical method has been a rather successful tool for explaining and defining in the natural sciences. Methodological reductionism, with its ontological claim of the reducibility of science to the claims of physics, and the methodological assumption about the priority of reduction as a method of research and explanation have been adopted almost universally by scientists in the field of natural science, although not without reservations. Popper (1974) claims that there are no examples of complete and fully successful reduction in science. As a rule, even in the case of the most successful instances of the application of the reductionist method, there always remains the unsolved, or unexplained residue. Practically, almost each attempt at full reduction meets with failure. Nonetheless, Popper does not seem to dismiss the method of reduction utterly, because according to him we can learn from our failed attempts, as well as from the successful ones.

The chances of successful reductionism in the social sciences seem to be even smaller than in the natural sciences. It was John Stuart Mill in the 19th century who advocated reductionism in sociology. Thus, social processes and phenomena are claimed to be reducible to the psychological and biological laws of individuals. Social reductionists maintained that all social laws must be derivable in principle from the psychology of 'human nature', i.e. social laws must ultimately be reducible to psychological laws. In contrast, Emile Durkheim's reaction to this extreme psychologism was to postulate an autonomous sociology, based on the notion of irreducible social fact.

3.1 *Popper on reductionism*

The defenders of an autonomous sociology (cf. Popper 1945: 90) pointed out that "no action can ever be explained by motives alone. They [i.e. the motives, R.K.] must be supplemented by a reference to the general situation, and especially to the environment. In the case of human actions, this environment is very largely of a social nature; thus our actions cannot be explained without reference to our social environment, to social institutions and to their manner of functioning. It is therefore impossible to reduce our actions to a psychological or behavioristic analysis; rather every such analysis presupposes sociology, which therefore cannot wholly depend on psychological analysis". [. . .]

3.2 *'Face' and reductionism*

For Brown and Levinson (1987) a Model Person is a willful and fluent speaker of a natural language endowed with a special property of 'face'. They assume that all competent adult members of a society have (and know each other to have) 'face' — the public self-image that every member wants to claim for her/himself. This self-image consists of two related aspects: (a) *negative face*: the basic claims to the territories, personal preserves, rights to non-distraction, i.e. to freedom of action and freedom from imposition; and (b) *positive face*: the positive self-image or 'personality' (crucially including the desire that this self-image be appreciated and approved of) claimed by interactants.

In contrast to Goffman's (1967: 5) view of face as "the positive social value a person effectively claims for himself", or "an image of self delineated in terms of approved social attributes", B&L redefine face in terms of basic *wants* in the following way: *negative face*: the want of every competent adult member that his actions be unimpeded by others; and *positive face*: the want of every member that his wants be desirable to at least some others (cf. B&L 1987: 62).

B&L go one step further than Goffman in their reductionist approach to 'face' by reducing a person's public self-image to some basic (universal) wants of human nature. They do not elaborate on the notion of 'want'; neither do they situate their concept in any psychological model or theory of basic human needs.

The value of the vague concept of 'want' in a predictive, deterministic system such as the one that B&L attempt to construct for politeness theory is doubtful. One would have to assume that the two wants (mentioned above) are encapsulated in two modules which exist in 'splendid isolation', independent of other wants, whatever these may be (e.g. the want to be challenged, opposed, or dominated) and resistant to all internal and external (social) pressures.

Generally speaking, the question of reduction of face to wants seems to be controversial and in need of justification. Face is more than just want; it is also (or perhaps primarily) a social value and norm. Someone (an actor) is afraid of losing face because of a probable loss of reputation, respect, social prestige, or any kind of social punishment. The frustration of his individual want (which may be a blow to his positive self-image), may still be less harmful than the distortion of this public self-image and its social consequences.

The reduction of politeness to face, face to self-image, self-image to want seems to be an attempt at grasping the essence (or true nature) of the defined terms. But there are serious methodological problems in the essentialist approach (cf. Popper 1945: 32), such as (1) the problem of distinguishing 'true' essential definitions from false ones; (2) the problem of avoiding an infinite regression of definitions.

Another connection of B&L's theory with essentialism is via the Weberian *Zweckrational* model of individual action (they reject the *Wertrational* model). According to Weber, *Zweckrational* (instrumental action) is action in which the actor not only compares different means to a goal but also assesses the utility of the goal itself (cf. Weber 1949). For Weber, the types of action he postulates are 'ideal types'. In addition to the two types mentioned above, he proposed *traditional* and *affective* action. He also admits that it is empirically impossible for actions not to be a mixture of two or more of the types. B&L's reductionist bias of basing their theory on one type of action, the *Zweckrational* model, will undoubtedly fail to account for the more complex cases.*

3.3 'Emergence' and discourse

An important problem for methodological reductionism is the phenomenon of 'emergence', i.e. "when two entities are combined at a higher level of integration, not all the properties of the new entity are necessarily a logical or predictable consequence of the properties of the components" (Lass 1980: 106). Emergent properties are, in principle, immune to prediction. From the linguistic point of view, emergence has two aspects: diachronic and synchronic. Diachronically, emergence is 'invention', the appearance of genuine novelty. Synchronically, it is a holistic transcendence, or the difference between the 'specific character of things' and the properties of things they are made of (cf. Lass 1980: 140). According to Popper, consciousness and language are emergent phenomena (viewed diachronically). For the present discussion, it is the synchronic emergent properties in social groups that are of primary interest. Specifically, these include the surprising and unexpected emergent properties which come to light in the course of a speech encounter due to the presence of 'specific' participants in the group; these emergences also comprise the constraining or controlling effects of a social group (e.g. all participants in a speech encounter) on the participants and all elements of their interaction (the discourse).

The emergent properties of discourse in social groups (such as the level of formality) are the 'terra incognita' of socio-pragmatics; they constitute important arguments against the use of methodological reductionism and of deterministic models in linguistics. This is so because the course and 'result' of a discourse in a group cannot be predicted from its basic constituents, i.e. participants and social context.

Last but not least, methodological reductionism may suffer from Alfred N. Whitehead's 'fallacy of misplaced concreteness' (cf. Whitehead 1967). The abstracted elements of reality (selected for heuristic purposes) may be reduced to an 'ideal type' or a conceptual model. If they are taken as a complete description of the real phenomenon and the resulting abstractions endowed with a material existence of their own, the process exemplifies 'the fallacy of misplaced concreteness', which is in effect a special case of the fallacy of reification.

There is a tendency in pragmatics towards extreme reductionism. For example, Sperber and Wilson (1986) reduce Grice's principles of conversation to one – the principle of *Relevance*. A more moderate suggestion is Horn's (1984) reduction of the four Gricean principles to two, viz. the Q-Principle – *Make your contribution sufficient; say as much as you can*; and the R-Principle – *Make your contribution necessary; say no more than you must*. Furthermore, Sperber and Wilson's theory of Relevance relies heavily on the notion of 'rationality'; thus, the participants in a speech exchange are described in purely intellectual terms of logic and reasoning, which seems to be an exception rather than a rule of conversation.

I would like to conclude these comments on methodological reductionism with an enumeration of a number of problems and contradictions that any reductionist approach in pragmatics must face. These basic problems and contradictions include the following: the contradictions between (1) a predictive model vs. inductive reasoning, and the non-predictive status of functional and teleological explanation; (2) psychological concepts (face, rationality, wants) vs. sociological methods (i.e. sociolinguistic variables such as P (power), D (social distance), R (rate of imposition)); – a fallacy related closely to Whitehead's 'fallacy of misplaced concreteness'; (3) face and rationality as objects of Popper's World 2 vs. as objects of his World 3 (exemplified by Leech's (1983) world of intersubjective social phenomena);[**] (4) the subjective orientation of individuals (voluntary intentions and motives) vs. the objective determinism of the MP; (5) social imposition of values vs. individual free will; (6) individual vs. social (group) wants; (7) mentalist pragmatics as object of World 2 vs. intersubjective pragmatics of World 3; (8) universal claims (i.e. for P, D, R) vs. descriptive goals (counter-examples); (9) the static character of a predictive model vs. the dynamic character of linguistic negotiation, transaction, etc; (10) psychological factors vs. social factors, whith psychological factors (personality, attitude, etc.) overriding the abstract social factors (e.g. the social variables P, D, R).

In conclusion, sociological explanations are not reducible to psychological and biological ones. Linguistic interaction seems to be an interplay between social and psychological factors. The predictiveness of such an interplay, although desirable, is not always attainable.

4 On context

The notion of 'context' has a significance which cannot be overlooked in pragmatics. How much information about context is required in pragmatic analysis? The scope of context is indefinite; minimally, it should include the participant's identity and role; assumptions about temporal, spatial, and social settings; assumptions about what participants know or take for granted; knowledge of the medium and social factors. There is no theory that could predict the relevance of such features and their impact on the discourse. Nonetheless, the claim that some elements of the context in a particular speech encounter may be more relevant than others does not appear to be totally unfounded. However, it should be remembered that very often such features (among other reasons, due to their ambivalent character) are not easily identified. Therefore, very tentatively and unpredictively, the relevant pragmatic context should include those elements of the (general) context that directly influence and shape the 'rationality' of the course of discourse, both in the positive and negative sense. Positively – when all participants of a speech encounter properly identify the relevant contextual features and conform to the accepted norms of linguistic interaction (i.e. maintain face, observe conversational principles, etc.); and negatively – when the course of discourse is not smooth but disturbed by unexpected contextual intrusion (e.g. *faux pas*, excitement, anger, emergent group properties, etc.).

4.1 Context and interaction

The most simplified model of linguistic interaction consists of two agents S and H involved in a dyadic speech exchange. That is, (S $\leftrightarrows$ H), interacting in some unspecified context. From the point of view of pragmatics, the scope of pragmatic context in S & H's linguistic interaction seems to be too narrow. A broader concept of context might include H as a part of S's pragmatic context and S as a part of H's context. That is so, because the abstract social parameters of P – power and D – social distance – are closely correlated with both agents, who must (to some degree) conform to the social expectations associated with these social variables.

Furthermore, the attitude of S to H and H to S may (and usually does) influence the level of politeness of a speech encounter. It should be remembered that the notion of attitude (or affect) is not a predictable concept. It is very likely that in almost every speech encounter between S and H, some kind of attitudinal 'bond' develops (negative or positive) that may influence the course (and other elements) of the discourse, for example the relative level of politeness. The level of politeness of a discourse may also be the result of transaction or negotiation between the two parties involved (or, even forced or imposed on the 'weaker' party by the 'stronger' one in a specific context).

Few would dispute the claim that the meaning (sense) of an utterance can only be understood (analyzed) in a specific pragmatic context. The relevant elements of the context associated with a particular speech encounter or genre (cf. Ventola 1987) could perhaps to some extent be enumerated in advance (with the reservation that 'the unexpected always happens'). Which are the relevant features of the context and in what way they will influence the interpretation of an utterance, can be decided only *ex post*, because interpretation is not a deterministic concept (nor is the perlocutionary effect of the utterance).

4.2 Pragmatic paradoxes

B&L's theory of politeness is not a model of linguistic interaction. Such interaction requires a minimum of two MPs, i.e. two ideal speaker-hearers endowed, according to B&L with 'face' and 'rationality', and interacting in a pragmatic context. The unit of analysis of linguistic interaction must be a larger stretch of discourse than a speech act in order to be able to account, for instance, for S's reaction to H's response in a speech exchange, or more generally, to explain S's and H's linguistic behavior in relation to the 'universe of discourse' and the specific goals of the encounter. Frequently, surprising changes of linguistic strategies, attitudes, etc. may take place in the course of a discourse, due to the intrusion of contextual factors. (For instance, the unpredictable use of forms of address in e.g. Early Modern English (*thou*/*you* in Shakespeare); such changes can only be accounted for by reference to the preceding and/or the following context (e.g. parts of discourse).)

B&L's model theory of politeness is H-biased in the sense that an S endowed with 'face' and 'rationality' (assuming that H also possesses those two properties) should react deterministically to the social parameters P, D, R, all correlated closely with the same parameters in H. That is, S is seen as a deterministic device, or an abstract concept devoid of attitudes, personality, emotions, irrationality, ignorance, values, contradictory goals, unpredictable reactions, etc. It seems, however, that all sorts of factors (psychological, social or cultural, past and present) may radically influence S's linguistic behavior. Therefore, the course of linguistic interaction between S and H is unpredictable and the perlocutionary effect uncertain. It is very fortunate for humans that this is so, because otherwise life would be predictively boring and linguistic interaction deterministically unbearable.

Methodological reductionism in pragmatics (e.g. politeness theory in terms of models (MP) and reduced social variables (P, D, R)) leads directly to a pragmatic paradox – that of a 'decontextualized pragmatics'. That is so because both the MP and the variables P, D, R must be contextually situated. Thus, for S, H is a part of his or her context defined only partially by the social variables (P, D). Furthermore, the values of P, D, R are not absolute, but rather are contextually specified. That is, the values of P, D, R (and their significance in the discourse) probably will be higher in a formal context than in an informal context (discourse). For instance, an FTA (face threatening act) of S towards H in a public setting will be more damaging to face than in a private one: independent observers of verbal interaction will assess the face damage of the interlocutors, and their assessment may differ from that of S and H. More significantly, they may impose sanctions on the culprits, which may ruin the public self-images of S and H. Furthermore, the values of P and D in an interaction between S and H and their linguistic consequences, the level of politeness, formality, etc., may be contextually controlled. For example, when two old friends appear together on the same TV show, the level of formality and politeness they show to one another may increase to conform to the conventions of the show or to meet the expectations of the viewers.

In B&L's decontextualized pragmatics, a number of questions of great significance have not been raised at all. For example, what is the relationship between the social parameters P and D in context, e.g. when D becomes superordinate in relation to P? Other problems include the context for positive vs. negative politeness; the relative relevance of the social variables P, D, R for positive vs. negative politeness; politeness in formal vs. informal discourse; politeness and audience (a third party in the discourse); the weightiness of an FTA (i.e. an estimate of risk, as expressed by B&L's formula: $W_x = D(S,H) + P(H,S) + R_x$) is also decontextualized (and over-simplified). Thus, the formula will not account for the fact that an FTA committed in public or in a formal situation (e.g. Othello's public assault of Desdemona) will be greater than in less 'face damaging' contexts. It should also be noted that such a calculation of an FTA is not only decontextualized, but also 'depersonalized' (i.e. B&L assume that an FTA is an objective notion and that all agents will react to it in the same manner). Such an approach may look 'rationally scientific', but at the same time it makes human behavior predictively unpredictive. In other words, pragmatics becomes the study of competence, not performance, and this is perhaps another example of the pragmatic paradox.

Finally, it should be remembered that no sentence is inherently polite or impolite (cf. Fraser and Nolen 1981; Zimin 1981). Politeness is a property of an act, not the act itself. Irrespective of the intention of the speaker, it is the hearer who assigns politeness to any utterance within the situation in which it was heard. Thus, politeness is a property of utterances and not of sentences, so that politeness cannot be assigned out of context to any particular structure.

5 Conclusion

In conclusion, B&L's model of politeness (or any other model of politeness) cannot be claimd to possess a predictive force resembling that of a theory in the natural sciences. A more modest approach in terms of a theory of probability would better reflect the true nature of the process of social interactions. Chomsky's (1965) ambitious requirement of explanatory adequacy in a linguistic theory can only be much admired; however, if a theory has not achieved even the level of observational adequacy, there is a danger that explanatory attempts (e.g. reduction, rationality, etc.) may prove to be only partially satisfactory, or simply fail. The problem seems to be that the methodological approach and the theoretical framework may create the illusion of coping with reality, especially in the case of tautological theory (e.g. when the rationality of an action is deduced from the assumption that the actor is rational). As to the universality of B&L's claims (i.e. the universality of face, rationality, a hierarchy of strategies), these can only be accepted with a pinch of salt. Also Popper (1983) threatens the universalists (bald on record) with the claim that probability theory attributes zero probability to universal theories.

Finally, even though the arguments presented above against 'rationalistic pragmatics' point up many of its weaknesses, they only represent a selection: a comprehensive analysis of the issue awaits to be done. The usefulness of the notion of rationality and the methodological principle of reductionism in the framework of RP (associated with a categorical, modular pragmatics and deterministic claims) has been questioned. As has been shown, context reduction in RP leads to a pragmatic paradox of 'decontextualized pragmatics' (here it should be stressed that *rationality* and *pragmatics* are both context-dependent notions). RP as an 'ideal type' seems to be a prescriptive model, i.e. it is more concerned with the question of how 'rational agents' should use their language to meet the standards of rationality and predictiveness than with describing how language is actually used by the speakers. As a matter of fact, the descriptive results of B&L's (1987) analysis are more satisfying than their theoretical assumptions (i.e. RP). A deductive relationship between the explanatory (theoretical) level and the descriptive analysis remains entirely postulatory. Furthermore, according to Popper (1963), even when an empirical hypothesis can be shown to be logically inferrable from the basic concepts of a theory, its validity depends on the truths of these concepts (premises), which is assumed, not proved.

As an alternative to RP, I suggest a unified view of empirical pragmatics, whose theoretical foundations would be based on the following features: (1) non-modular, (2) non-essentialist, (3) non-categorical, (4) non-deterministic in its view of pragmatics, (5) contextual, (6) non-reductionist in its approach to pragmatics.

The advantages (or disadvantages) of such a theory of pragmatics over RP remain to be investigated; especially its descriptive and explanatory adequacy, fruitfulness and what seems to be the most important – the empirical relationship between the concepts of a pragmatic theory and the description of pragmatic phenomena.

Note

*   See p. 287 and the note on p. 302.
** Popper's World 2 contains knowledge and his World 3 contains the linguistic realizations of such knowledge.

■ ■ ■

POST-READING

1   Return to the statements you evaluated in the pre-reading activity. Are there any that you would evaluate differently now that you have read Kopytko's paper?

2   To what extent does Kopytko's critique apply to the contributors to pragmatic theory whose work you have read earlier in this volume?

3   Is what Kopytko calls 'emergence' really our inability to adequately specify all the relevant variables so that, although he may be right to critique Brown and Levinson's work for the paucity of variables they identify, his own position is also fundamentally flawed?

4   It's often said that syntacticians seek an account of the available data that is both explanatory and predictive, i.e. that accounts for all and only the possible grammatical structures of a language in a highly deterministic way. Do you think a comparable approach to pragmatics is useful?

5   To what extent is the kind of pragmatics with which you are most familiar 'decontextualized', in that it's 'more concerned with the question of how "rational agents" should use their language to meet the standards of rationality and predictiveness than with describing how language is actually used by the speakers'?

JON F. PRESSMAN

PRAGMATICS IN THE LATE TWENTIETH CENTURY
Countering recent historiographic neglect

PRE-READING

1   Which work/s in your opinion mark(s) the beginning of linguistic pragmatics?
2   Do you agree that 'pragmatic studies within linguistics and philosophy are strongly influenced by the theoretical and methodological concerns of those disciplines, which have very little interest or expertise in the study of culture'? To what extent is this comment an appropriate judgement on the primary texts that you've read both in this Reader and elsewhere?

IN-READING

1   Section 2 of the reading: for each of the first seven paragraphs in this section, we supply a sentence starter, which you should complete when you've read the paragraph:

Paragraph 1, '*Much of what* . . .'
Sentence starter: 'Jakobson's typology, which identifies six functions in language use, . . .'

Paragraph 2, '*Although Silverstein* . . .'
Sentence starter: 'Silverstein's emic take on Jakobson's etic proposals enable him to . . .'

Paragraph 3, '*Whereas Jakobson* . . .'
Sentence starter: 'By rejecting referentiality as the predominant function, Silverstein . . .'

Paragraph 4, '*Silverstein's own work* . . .'
Sentence starter: 'In exploring the cline from purely referential to indexical-referential forms, Silverstein . . .'

Paragraph 5, '*From this data* . . .'
Sentence starter: 'Self-referentiality . . .'

Paragraph 6, '*Silverstein's interest* . . .'
Sentence starter: 'Metapragmatics, defined as the unavoidable . . ., often goes unrecognized because . . .'

Paragraph 7, '*Inherently included* . . .'
Sentence starter: 'Signs may be regarded as plurifunctional in the sense that . . .'

2   Section 4 of the reading: the functionality tree below has two wilting branches and a magnificent flower. Pause after reading each paragraph and add a label to an appropriate unlabelled branch or petal.

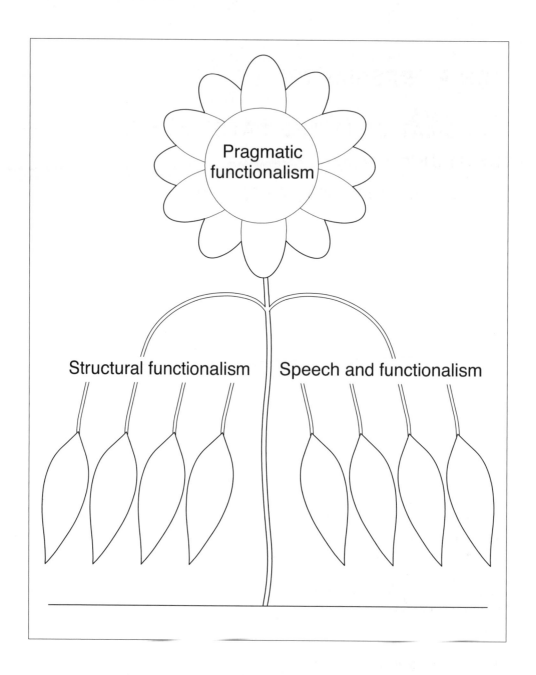

PRAGMATICS IN THE LATE TWENTIETH CENTURY COUNTERING RECENT HISTORIOGRAPHIC NEGLECT

JON F. PRESSMAN

1 Introduction

As an unavoidable consequence of the marketplace phenomenon that typifies the contemporary academy (Bourdieu 1988 [1984]), the 'factionalization' of the social and behavioral sciences into sub-disciplines, academic specializations, theoretical schools, and methodological minorities can cause grave problems for the historiography[1] of such disciplines. The study of pragmatics in the late twentieth century suffers from such a historiographic crisis. Divided into linguistic and anthropological linguistic orientations, the former is essentially unaware of the insights stemming from the latter, several exceptions notwithstanding (e.g., Verschueren 1994). In taking stock of the theoretical influences that have shaped contemporary pragmatics, clearly some relevant approaches have received little attention, or have been overlooked entirely, by the linguistic faction. One such omission is the intellectual lineage initiated by Roman Jakobson and followed up by his student, Michael Silverstein. The contributions made by these two individuals, and by students who have continued in this lineage, warrant reconsideration historiographically if for nothing more than bringing sociocultural considerations to bear on linguistic pragmatic problems. As one prominent anthropological linguist has observed, "pragmatic studies within linguistics and philosophy are strongly influenced by the theoretical and methodological concerns of those disciplines, which have very little interest or expertise in the study of culture" (Duranti 1994: 11). This paper attempts to redress this historiographic omission by enumerating on the recent contributions of Jakobson, Silverstein, and two of Silverstein's students.

Recently, Steve Caton (1993) has argued that "it is not unreasonable to date the beginning of a modern linguistic pragmatics from the publication in 1957 of Roman Jakobson's 'Shifters, verbal categories, and the Russian verb'" (1993: 335 fn.6). Pragmatics in its sociocultural application has its intellectual origins in the semiotic philosophies of Charles Peirce (1931) and Charles Morris (1938), and yet Jakobson's contributions to this now pervasive mode of inquiry in anthropological linguistics should not be overlooked. Jakobson (1976, 1977), in fact, has discussed Peirce's influence with tremendous gratitude and laments the fact that he was the first linguist who utilized the theories of this 'pathfinder' in the science of language. Borrowing certain semiotic ideas from the writings of Peirce, especially his tripartite distinction of icon, index, and symbol, as well as the Saussurean distinction between 'language' and 'parole,' the most significant point of Jakobson's 1957 article is to demarcate precisely the extent to which information about parole is encoded in grammar, referential indexes or 'shifters' cited as the linguistic signs responsible for this phenomenon.[2] Even though he never formally advanced a theory of pragmatics, it is in his 1957 paper that Jakobson (1896–1982) ushered in what would become the defining concern of anthropological linguistic pragmatics in later years. This was an insistence that the context-sensitive or pragmatic function of speech have the same scholarly attention paid to it as the referential function of speech had for some time before.

Jakobson must equally get credit for reawakening in linguistics an interest in the functional analysis of the speech event, and it is his 1960 paper, "Closing statement: linguistics and poetics," where we find his clearest conception of this approach, the so-called 'means-end' model of the Prague Linguistic Circle, as described in his 1971 [1963] paper. Whereas much of previous theory had listed general sociological functions of language use (e.g., Bühler 1990 [1934a]), the role of linguistic sign therein unclear, Jakobson proposed to begin with an analysis of the speech situation, placing the linguistic sign within it, and deriving an exhaustive typology of functions as they relate to the constituent factors of the situation. What Jakobson referred to as "the pragmatic approach to language" (1971, [1968]: 703) was this positing of a basic set of functions involved in the communicative act. That is, the referential, emotive, conative, phatic, poetic, and metalingual functions within a given speech situation vary in their relative importance and expressive salience, but are always present in the situation. In advancing such a functionalism, Jakobson showed that linguistic forms covary as the relations among components of the speech event change and are modified. Regarded as a pioneer of this functionalist approach in the analysis of the speech act, subsequently followed up by anthropological linguists Dell Hymes (1968 [1962], 1974a [1970], 1974, 1975) and Michael Silverstein (1975, 1976b, 1985a), Jakobson brought to structural linguistics a model for demonstrating that contextual factors necessarily impinge on language form itself. Jakobson's factor-function characterization of the speech event inaugurated a new perspective in the anthropology of language, supplying the basis for a pragmatic orientation that would, in later years, yield dramatic results in anthropological fieldwork and ethnolinguistic scholarship.

The aim of this paper is to outline the bedrock of a modern pragmatics inherent in Jakobson's 1960 and later works, specifically in his exegesis of the factor-function approach to the speech act. In what follows, I will trace linear movements along shared intellectual-theoretical traditions of the late twentieth century, influential trends which recreated and modified these traditions. As an exercise in intellectual history, this paper will chart Jakobson's functionalist orientation on the speech act through Silverstein's (b. 1945) retooling of such under the aegis of pragmatics, culminating with a discussion touching on the recent work of several of Silverstein's students, Charles Briggs (b. 1953) and Greg Urban (b. 1949), both of whom have made contributions to ethnolinguistics from such a pragmatic orientation. Silverstein's approach warrants attention insofar as he has integrated theoretical claims laid out separately by Jakobson in his 1957 and 1960 papers. Silverstein's formulation of pragmatics synthesizes Jakobson's 1957 notion of speech indexicality with his 1960 functional diagram of the speech event, two concepts Jakobson never himself connected. Further, Silverstein's (1985b) article presents this integration in ethnolinguistic context, and both Briggs and Urban rely on this approach in their own studies.

On a more general level, this paper seeks to address a problem in intellectual historiography. One of the unfortunate circumstances that accrues to many instances of historiography of the social and behavioral sciences is the widespread neglect of research that does not follow suit with prevailing notions of what constitutes such a exercise, or what type of content ought to be included in such a historiographical project. Aggravating the problem is the stance endorsed by some historians of intellectual property that various approaches to empirical phenomena may be discounted and judged ineffectual on grounds that the property in historiographic question differs too profoundly with their own theoretical or methodological agenda. These scholars concentrate on large portions of some historiographic achievement, yet include in their discussion only those ideas that corroborate the historiographic object from a privileged position. Well-informed proponents may be placated, chalking up such neglect to a type of historiographic ideology, however it is difficult to ignore oversights that misrepresent seminal portions of the history.

As I explained above, the situation is particularly problematic in pragmatics, a field of study consisting of both linguistic and anthropological linguistic groupings, the influence of the former superseding that of the latter only in membership count, not in the ability to account for patterned, linguistic phenomena. For example, among the four major historiographic texts on pragmatics published in the last ten to fifteen years by linguists (i.e., Gazdar 1979; Leech 1983; Levinson 1983; and Mey 1993), the overall neglect afforded anthropological linguistic insights by their counterparts, particularly the work of Silverstein, attests to the chronic lack of dissemination, and even intentional disregard, that characterizes the contemporary historiographic period. Without realizing it, one prominent historiographer epitomized the problem when he speculated "who would regard his [Silverstein's] output as in a particular way pioneering where pragmatics is concerned" (Koerner 1994: personal communication). This paper, although not initially conceived as such, offers an elaborate response to this opinion.

[. . .]

2 Jakobson's functionalism

Much of what will be discussed herein, under the general rubric of functionalism, owes its inception to Jakobson, and has been reworked by Silverstein. Silverstein studied under Jakobson in the late sixties and early seventies at Harvard University where Jakobson was Professor of Slavic Languages and Literatures and of General Linguistics, and has elaborated along semiotic-functional lines much of what Jakobson first conceptualized when he himself combined Peircean semiotics with his own Prague School structuralism. Silversteinian pragmatics, as will be made more clear, took an impetus from Jakobson's appropriation of Peirce's semiotic analysis of the sign and "although Jakobson . . . had already analyzed referential categories of grammar as 'indexical,' it was Silverstein who suggested that this sign-category might be usefully applied to the study of nonreferential uses of language" (Caton 1990: 159). Equally important to Jakobson was the fact that structuralism, of the type advocated by his Prague School colleagues, was viewed as being comprised of aggregate functions. "Structure in its proper sense . . . is a set of functions organizing atomized empirical reality" (Novák 1932 in Steiner 1978: 360). Structure, then, is predicated on a set of functions bound through internal interconnections into such a structure. Specifically, the Structuralists saw language as an instrument of communication, consisting of a number of functions which differed according to the goal for which they were utilized. However, as long as the Structuralists analyzed these functions from 'natural' language use, the multiplicity of functions served by language prevented them from arriving at any definite number of functions. Only by suspending this 'natural attitude' (i.e., by bracketing off all the social and psychological conditions of the act of communication, and taking into account only the act itself) did the Prague Structuralists arrive at the functional invariants of language (Steiner 1978: 381 fn.48). The first among the members of the Circle to take this step was Karl Bühler (1990 [1934a]) who reduced the speech event to its three basic components (speaker, listener, and topic) and ascribed to them three basic functions (expressive, appellative, and presentational). Bühler's preliminary typology of the functions of language was more fully elaborated by Jakobson (1960), and it is his typology that has achieved notable status in the anthropological literature (cf. Hymes 1968 [1962]; Silverstein 1985a).

Although Silverstein has ostensibly defined the field of pragmatics by his own original contributions, there is a definite link to be seen with the theories of his former teacher. One of the most productive tracks taken by Silverstein (and, in time, his own students) has been the application of Jakobson's multifunctional perspective of the communicative event to specific, ethnolinguistic problems. Such problems bear out the reality of some of what Jakobson put forth, combining linguistic theory with an appraisal of context-sensitive language use. To achieve this via empirically-grounded research, Silverstein had to amend to Jakobson's 'etic' framework of the speech event and its interacting components an 'emic' perspective. Emic, in this sense, demarcates a move from the strictly theoretical to the ethnological, from linguistic to ethnolinguistic. That is, "any pragmatic form is a signal that can be used both in effecting specific contextual changes and in describing them. And the description can focus on any of the components of the speech event: speaker, hearer, audience, referent, channel, signal, time, locus, or some relationship between these" (Silverstein 1981b: 15).

Whereas Jakobson was a theoretical linguist, never engaging in fieldwork in the anthropological sense, and focusing his attention primarily on Slavic languages and literatures, Silverstein and his Chicago students (Briggs and Urban) have been much more ethnographically-oriented, expanding the domain of research by focusing, in large part, on non-Western societies and languages. Such interests have much to do with Silverstein's insistence that "distinct pragmatic meanings yield distinct analyses of utterances, thereby severing our dependence on reference as the controlling functional mode of speech" (1976b: 21). The social ends accomplished by the pragmatic function of language are just as important as the propositional ends manifested by the referential function. An example of this pragmatic function is illustrated by the 'mother-in-law' language of Dyirbal which involves a special lexicon, referentially identical with the standard lexicon, that must be used in the presence of one's mother-in-law. "Use of this special language signals no change in referential content (what is being said), but only a change in situational or pragmatic context (to whom one is speaking)" (Mertz 1985: 6). Recent ethnolinguistic scholarship has, in part, dedicated itself to describing pragmatic function, and recently monographs extolling the pragmatic dimensions of language and the interaction these dimensions obtain with referentiality have been produced by a younger generation of anthropological linguists (e.g., Errington 1988; Hanks 1990), many of whom could be included in the Silversteinian intellectual lineage,[3] having had Silverstein as their intellectual mentor while working towards the doctorate in Anthropology at the University of Chicago. Their descriptions of pragmatics (referential and nonreferential indexical signification) within an ethnographic surround augment Jakobsonian 'invariant' functionalism with Silverstein's claim that "various indexical systems are superimposed one on another in any phenomenal linguistic signal and are 'in play' to different degrees, over the realtime course of using language" (Silverstein 1987a: 32).

Silverstein's own linguistic work on Worora, an Australian aboriginal language of the Northern Kimberley coast (1986), Dyirbal, an Australian aboriginal language of the Cairns Rain Forest (1976a, 1981a), and the Wasco-Wishram dialect of Chinook, an American Indian language of the Northwest coast (1972, 1974, 1976a, 1978, 1985a), attests to a concern with expanding the traditionally held belief that the referential function of speech be the basis for linguistic theory. For example, in his work on case-marking, Silverstein has demonstrated that referential indexical features, as well as purely referential ones, are to be taken into consideration when seeking to explain the patterns differentiating noun-phrases types in language (cf. Lucy 1992a: 96–99, 1992b: 68–71). In simplified terms, Silverstein's interpretation of noun-phrase types argues for a 'hierarchical' model in which those forms that depend on the immediate context of speech for their explication be marked differently than those that do not. Specifically, regular 'splits' of case marking between nominative-accusative and ergative-absolutive paradigms are shown "to be readily characterizable in terms of the resultant ordering of referential features" (Lucy 1992a: 68). In organizing these features in 'referential space,' Silverstein (1981a, 1985c, 1987b) presents a cline of extensional reference "for what the gradually more extensive groups of denotational categories differentially include by way of characterizing potential referents" (1987b: 147). What this means is that there is a gradual and uniform change in the conditions of reference as one moves in either direction along this cline. At one extreme end of the cline, denotational categories denote indexically and always refer to entities that are the very conditions for using any tokens of language at all, always presupposable in the acts of reference. These are the necessarily constituted roles of speaker and addressee. At the other end, reference heavily depends on the presupposition of syntacticosemantic category types in morphosyntactic structure, organized in linguistically-stipulated utterance formations. These types, 'segmentable natural kind things,' are "intensional categories the interrelated structure of which corresponds to the set of all possible distinct morphosyntactic patterns in a language" (Silverstein 1987b:

153) whose referential components for accomplishing extensionalization are much less dependent on indexicality for explanation. Thus, the indexical factor is most important at the one end, in the region of personal deictics, and the semanticosyntactically-based intensionalizations are most important at the other end, constituted by abstract entities of extension.

From this data, Silverstein (1987b) presents the argument that it is on the indexical end of the cline that the self-referential quality of speech, that is, the ability of forms to refer to their own relationship in the speech situation, is demonstrated. Referencing the act of speaking itself through the use of personal deictics, self-referentiality is made possible by the pragmatic function (indexicality). In such an interpretation, Silverstein not only demonstrates the relationship that the pragmatic function of language has with its referential counterpart, but points to an interesting phenomenon whereby native speakers are, for the most part, unaware of this indexical level. Silverstein offers an explanation when he explains that

> there is a marked difference in the nature of characterizability conditions on extendable objects. And it is this seemingly less obviously transparent involvement of factors of indexicality . . . that makes the experience of extending entities with [intensional syntacticosemantic] categories . . . appear to be less 'centered' in the pragmatics of the communicative event, more a matter of applying language to a decentered and 'objectively categorizable' universe 'out there,' that exists – in some sense – independent of such pragmatic events of communicating about it.
>
> (1987b: 157)

Silverstein's interest in accounting for the relationship between actual language use and native speaker awareness of such language use (1976b, 1979, 1981b) relies heavily on what he has called 'metapragmatics,' the referring to and predicating about the pragmatic function of language. Metapragmatics, in this way, is the reconstruction of an indexical signalling event, the picking out of and supplying information about a pragmatic act. Metapragmatics "is a description of an indexical signalling event" (Silverstein 1987b: 159).[4] As such, the metapragmatic function is based on referentiality and operates concurrently with the pragmatic one. "Without a metapragmatic function simultaneously in play with whatever pragmatic function(s) there may be in discursive interaction, there is no possibility of interactional coherence, since there is no framework of structure . . . in which indexical origins or centerings are relatable one to another as aggregated contributions to some segmentable, accomplishable, event(s)" (Silverstein 1993: 37). The coincidence of these two functions is described by Silverstein as "the unavoidability and transparency of metapragmatic reference" (1981a: 241). That metapragmatic reference should be unavoidable and transparent to the native speaker is, in some part, predicated on the nature of the 'marked' noun-phrase to foreground the event of speaking. The linguistic ideology of the native speaker, as will be explained, highlights awareness of the referential function of language while hindering awareness of the indexical function. Such an ideology of reference (Silverstein 1979) is caused by the inclination of native speakers to "objectify on the basis of analogies to certain pervasive surface-segmentable linguistic patterns, and act accordingly" (Silverstein 1979: 202). In other words, Silverstein makes a distinction between the linguist's trained analysis of language and the 'secondary rationalizations' of native speakers.

Inherently included in the act of speaking by virtue of the personal deictics, the transparency and unavoidable coincidence experienced by the native speaker of metapragmatic code to its pragmatic object code arises from having to functionally differentiate a 'plurifunctional' sign. Both indexical and referential sign modalities are united, even laminated, in one sign token. Specifically, the personal deictics denote by virtue of the fact that they unavoidably index their denotata, which are therefore characterizable as the pragmatic conditions presupposed by these forms. Silverstein (1987b) contends that the indexical presuppositions, hence pragmatics, of the use of each of these forms, are precisely what are extendable by them; hence, the indexical function is transparently represented in the characterizability conditions, that is, the conditions for extensional use of the denotational category. At the same time, it is clear that the very form that is the indexical signal is the signal that refers to what is indexed; hence, to isolate the indexical sign is to isolate the referential sign, and there is unavoidable coincidence of these two modalities. So we might see the denotational content of these [personal deictic] categories as a transparent and unavoidably coincident metapragmatics for their own indexical conditions of occurrence, their pragmatics. They are, in effect, INDEXICAL DENOTATIONALS, the denotational content of which is transparently metapragmatic with respect to its denotational coincident pragmatic content.

(1987b: 162)

[. . .] Clearly, Silverstein's claims establishing the unavoidable and transparent nature of metapragmatic functioning take an impetus from Jakobson's positing of a metalingual function, where language has as its object the code itself. This paper is most concerned with this avenue of Silverstein's work, and mentions his linguistic studies of case-marking only to show that empirical research underlies his semiotic-functional arguments.

Such stipulations, deriving eventually from Silverstein's own fieldwork data, are useful in ethnolinguistic scholarship insofar as they provide the neophyte researcher with at least a partial 'model' of what to expect regarding native language ideologies. Such ideologies, as "any sets of beliefs about language articulated by users as a rationalization or justification or perceived language structure and use" (Silverstein 1979: 193), are articulated by native speakers through several semiotic-functional factors, as identified by Silverstein (1981b). For example, one of the identified factors encapsulating native linguistic ideology is what Silverstein calls "unavoidable referentiality" (1981b: 5) Unavoidable referentiality is an inherent quality of plurifunctional signs by which the referential-and-predicational mode of such signs are more salient to native description than their concomitant indexical mode. Specifically, it is this factor that can be correlated to the 'unavoidability' of metapragmatic reference, as described above. However, in Silverstein's conceptualization, language function as analyzed by the trained anthropological linguist is to be kept distinct from native awareness of this function. As seen here, though, certain semiotic phenomena can be calqued from the level of language function onto the level of native speaker awareness. For example, the unavoidability and transparency of metapragmatic reference of language use finds expression in speaker awareness as unavoidable referentiality. Besnier (1993), in describing affect producing devices in Tuvaluan, contends that speakers are more aware of lexical devices (e.g., "hurry!") for marking affective meaning than of intonation and stress because the former are singular in purpose, and therefore more available to explanation. The latter, Besnier explains, "are less readily identifiable as the vehicle through which these emotional states are communicated" (1993: 194), having to be superposed on the syntactic structure of a sentence whose primary purpose is to communicate referential meaning.

[. . .]

3 Jakobson's reflexivity

[. . .]

4 Silverstein's functionalism

[. . .]

The first view on human language that falls short in terms of his pragmatic functionalist perspective is what Silverstein (1985b, 1987a) has called 'structural functionalism.' In this view, formal linguistic structure is abstracted and divorced from the actualities of speech performance. It is completely centered towards referentiality in that this theory about language, having the sentence as its ideal, posits a "formally complete object of linguistic study, in which form . . . can be systematically related to meaning" (1987a: 18), and the referential relationships that develop herein are constant, identifiable without knowledge of actual usage. It becomes increasingly apparent that what it at stake if this structural function of language is endorsed is the actual contextual knowledge of any speech event; in its place is sort of a 'synthetic,' universally-applicable, propositional knowledge of reference and predication guided by the generic matrix of grammatical constraints. It is 'structural' in this sense, positing "a particular kind of functional explanation that situates the central linguistic cognitive process in autonomous grammatical structure" (1987a: 22), independent of any facts of actual linguistic usage.

This functionalism of language is nothing more than a highly structured system which seeks to impose a symbolic template on speech. Derived from the work of Saussure and Leonard Bloomfield, in this 'formalist' approach to language, surface lexical forms, individually or in grammatical construction, have been privileged so that, taken as a set, they "specify the 'function' of the lexeme or expression in the total grammatical system of the language" (1985b: 208). Thus, the delimitation of the totality of grammatical forms to be analyzed is, implicitly, restricted to the referential-and-predicational view of language. Reference, in this sense, is taken to mean sign units in grammatical arrangements, the meaning of which is a descriptive or referring proposition. "It is this referential function of speech, and its characteristic sign mode, the semantico-referential sign, that has formed the basis for linguistic theory and linguistic analysis in the Western tradition" (Silverstein 1976b: 14). For Silverstein, reference works in conjunction with indexicality, an aspect of language forgotten in this conceptualization.

The second theory on language that falls short of a pragmatic functionalism is what Silverstein has called 'illocutionary' or 'speech-act functionalism.' In this approach, advocated by philosophers of language such as Austin, Searle, and Grice, function is seen "as the purposive, goal-oriented use of speech . . . by intentional individuals in specific situations of discourse, each usage constituting a speech act" (1987a: 23). In opposition to the asocial, unconscious predication of the first functionalism, illocutionary functionalism posits a conscious and purposive behavior. The problem, though, that arises in this conception has to do with the reception or perlocutionary effects rendered with respect to the illocutionary desire. Specifically, we cannot uniquely associate any given illocution with a particular perlocution for two reasons.

First, "illocutionary function indicating devices are not necessarily explicit clause-level material" (1987a: 29). In other words, some designations of illocutionary functions in English, for example, cannot be realized by a uniquely apparent performative at the level of code. That is, there exists a "host of such linguistic devices, usages of which have metapragmatic descriptions as conventional communication types, but . . . have no clause-level realization" (1987a: 30). Within the English language, this problem translates into an overabundance of metapragmatic illocutionary functions that do not find realization in actual performatives.

The second problem similarly deals with the absence of a one-to-one relationship between illocution and perlocutionary reception. Too few illocutions explicitly fail to designate within situational contexts perlocutionary effects that may be multiply interpreted. For example, in the illocutionary phrase, "Do you have the time?," a perlocutionary effect in the mind of the hearer might take the form of a demand or of an informational question, but there is, in the mind of the sender, a unique illocutionary intent being specified. The overall problem, then, with the illocutionary function of language stems from the fact that the degree of precision with which the illocutionary function operates in relation to perlocutionary reception is not accurate enough to rule out occasional misunderstandings within the speech event. There is no recourse towards clarification in this functionalism; a comprehensive model must be able to account for, and resolve, such a problem.

Silverstein includes among those guilty of prescribing a model of speech-act functionalism, Jakobson (1960) with his factor-function typology of the speech event, as well as the ethnography of speaking approach of Hymes (1974), and much of the pragmatics advocated by the strictly linguistic faction, as discussed in the introductory section. What bothers Silverstein about all of these approaches is the fact that they all see the activity of speaking as based on the individual's proposition-like classification model predicated on extensional reference. Such a model of language use seems to ask "when and how is it socially appropriate/correct/effective to refer-and-predicate with such-and-such forms in such-and-such context" (1987a: 24)? This account of language is essentially a diagram built from a structural analysis of a maximally appropriate referring-and-predicating event, constructed without ever questioning the ability of such an abstracted schema to adequately describe, for example, indexical systems. This account is basically "an idealization of how lexical expressions propositionally or referentially function in grammatical patterns that underlie how certain utterances can . . . function in achieving effective referring-and-predicating results" (Silverstein 1987a: 25). Silversteins insistence of the plurifunctionality of the linguistic sign, that is, the superposition of both referential and nonreferential functions in one sign, denies that reference-and-predication be the singular, functional reading. For him, the same signal serves in many functional systems simultaneously.
  [. . .]
What Silverstein calls 'pragmatic functionalism' seeks to explain linguistic structures by their occurrence in, and by their serving as indexes of, particular presupposed communicative contexts of use. The advantage that pragmatic functionalism holds over structural and illocutionary functionalism is its indexical orientation. Indexicality is the missing component in such problematic functionalisms insofar as it links the elements of speech with the existential reality that is copresent with any utterance in the first, and in the second serves to solidify a unique correspondence between intent and effect in verbal action. "The indexical or pragmatic realm of function is, in a sense, the most elementary sign function in language. It bespeaks the simple fact of the situatedness of language use as a social action in some context" (Silverstein 1985b: 225). Further, when undertaking ethnolinguistic analysis, Silverstein advocates a method directed towards discerning "the pragmatics of metapragmatic usage" (1985a: 138). This method entails not only the identification of this languages's metapragmatic construction types, but equally involves a pragmatic interpretation of such types as they are systematically distributed in discourse.

5 Ethnolinguistic studies of Warao and Shokleng

[. . .]
In another ethnographically-oriented paper, Briggs (1993) addresses the problem of multiple performances of the 'same' text. Briggs analyzes three renditions of a single Warao narrative by the same person in order to show how participants' understandings of each performance play a role in differentiating the performance events. Silverstein (1993) has discussed the 'calibration' (i.e., relationship) of metapragmatic signaling event to entextualized or reported event-structure and Briggs employs this concept, focusing on the degree to which each of three performance types treats the relationship between narrated (reported or entextualized) events and narrating (signaling) events. The first type is the monologic performance which emphasizes the integrity of the narrated event, and the 'disjoint' or separate relationship the narrating event has to the narrated one. The second type, that of dialogic performance, emphasizes the link of narrated to narrating event by way of an explicit metapragmatics which spells out exactly how the two events are to be united. The final type is the acquisition-oriented performance that, in focusing on the pedagogical instruction of social interaction,

emphasizes the process of producing a narrative, and so the calibration is reflexive, designating a relationship in which metapragmatic signaling and entextualized elements form part of the same discursive and interactional unit. In his concluding remarks, Briggs insists that his own ethnolinguistic studies of Warao have endeavored to demonstrate, most generally, that "metapragmatics does not simply enable us to disambiguate reference or to calibrate inferential processes – metapragmatics provides essential means of connecting discourse with lived experience" (1993: 207).

[. . .]

Urban received his doctorate from the University of Chicago's Department of Anthropology in 1978, and was one of Silverstein's first students to systematically apply his mentor's work on pragmatics to an anthropological context, specifically the mythology of Brazil's Shokleng Indian's.

[. . .]

For Urban, in social anthropological terms, discourse is that which functions as social glue, binding individuals to collective norms. From this understanding follows what Urban (1991) calls the 'discourse-centered approach to culture,' the primary tenant of which is that "culture is localized in concrete, publicly accessible signs, the most important of which are actually occurring instances of discourse" (1991: 1). Subsequently, Urban understands mythology not as the mental object advocated by Levi-Strauss (1955), but as concrete, unfolding discourse. This mythology-as-discourse approach has several advantages, not the least of which is the ability of the myth, insofar as it contains instances of discourse as reported speech, to embody a kind of 'theory' about the relationship between speech and action. Urban describes it in this manner:

> In a text, the speech that is reported typically has some relationship to other action that is reported, for example, the speech may be about action that has taken place or will take place, it may be a command, it may be a lie, and so on. By studying these relationships, one gains access to what might be termed the 'ethno-metapragmatic theory' the text embodies, that is, how the relationship between speech and action is conceptualized by the users of the language.
>
> (1984: 310)

As a semiotic system, language enables its users to speak about speech as well as about other types of action. In order that it be be effective for social ends, some kind of regimentation must take place whereby the culture in which it is based can appropriate this discourse for its collective needs. "Minimally, this would consist in a set of normative models which represent the consequences of using discourse in certain ways in various types of social situations. The collective social benefits or detriments could be brought, however dimly, into awareness" (Urban 1993: 242). Myths are capable of playing this normative role because, as replicative narratives, they depict the outcomes of metapragmatic activities. In myth, language is embedded in a representation of social situations and processes. Insofar as the myth enters into an indexical relationship with the world through what Urban (1993) has called 'aesthetic' representation, myth is simultaneously a metapragmatic and a pragmatic device, serving to "encode a vision of the relationship between speech and social action, but also to prescribe that relationship normatively to those who listen to it" (Urban 1984: 325). Insofar as a myth contains instances of reported speech, it necessarily also encodes a vision of language use, of how speech is embedded in social action and how it relates to nonlinguistic actions. Urban contents that:

> Such an 'ethnometapragmatic' vision is open to scrutiny by any observer. If it is open to scrutiny, however, it is also accessible for manipulation by the myth-tellers themselves,

who can shape the metapragmatic image embedded in the text to suit their own purposes. Consequently, insofar as the myth-tellers have the maintenance of the status quo among their goals, there is a natural tendency for myths to take on the design characteristics of a pragmatic device used for prescribing relationships between speech and action.

(1984: 327)

[. . .]

6 Conclusion

[. . .]

As Silverstein has demonstrated, "pragmatics as a field is the study of the way indexical features of forms as used presuppose and create the very parameters of the event of communication, which is itself intersubjectively validated as purposive interlocutor activity through a socially shared system of meanings" (1985a: 134). Pragmatics as a field of study, then, must walk the fence between linguistics and anthropology, keeping a foot in each, cautious of stumbling head-over-heels into one or the other, and attentive to a historical trajectory peopled by scholars representing both.

[. . .]

Notes

1   The term 'historiography' is broadly construed herein to indicate the activity of textual exegesis where the text under interpretation has become a commodified entity in this marketplace. The amount of time that has passed since a text became available is irrelevant, as is the complete versus incomplete status of the author's oeuvre.

2   So-called because these 'duplex signs' simultaneously shift their focus at the level of message and code.

3   Other ethnolinguists who could be included in the lineage, in addition to Briggs and Urban, include the following. Dates in parenthesis indicate the year they received their doctorate from the University of Chicago's Department of Anthropology: J. Joseph Errington (1981), Richard Parmentier (1981), William Hanks (1983), Bruce Mannheim (1983), and Steve Caton (1984).

4   This correlates with what Silverstein (1993) has called 'denotationally explicit' metapragmatic sign function. However, it also holds true for 'denotationally implicit' or 'virtual' metapragmatic functioning.

■   ■   ■

POST-READING

1   Write short definitions for *structural functionalism, illocutionary functionalism* and *pragmatic functionalism* as they are characterized by Pressman.

2   After the Kopytko reading, we asked you to react to the author's claim that 'RP as an "ideal type" seems to be a prescriptive model, i.e. it is more concerned with the question of how 'rational agents' should use their language to meet the standards of rationality and predictiveness than with describing how language is actually used by the speakers.' This observation is remarkably similar to Pressman/Silverstein's 'Such a model of language use seems to ask "when and how it is socially appropriate/correct/effective to refer-and-predicate with such-and-such forms in such-and-such context"'. Try and find three or four other close matches between Kopytko's and Pressman's texts.

3   'The linguistic ideology of the native speaker . . . highlights awareness of the referential function, which hinders awareness of the indexical function.' Do you think that pragmaticians too have failed to be sufficiently aware of the indexical function, perhaps like native speakers, for ideological reasons?

CHARLES L. BRIGGS

FROM THE IDEAL, THE ORDINARY, AND THE ORDERLY TO CONFLICT AND VIOLENCE IN PRAGMATIC RESEARCH

PRE-READING

Spend a few minutes thinking about the extent to which your own study of linguistics has favoured reaching generalizations or understanding the particular.

IN-READING

Write each of the following on separate Post-it® notes: *Noam Chomsky, generality, ordinary language, Conversation Analysis, disorder, ethnomethodology*. When you come across each in the text, decide on whether it has a positive or a negative connotation for (a) Briggs and (b) yourself. Add these judgements to the Post-it® note and stick it on the text at the place you have reached. If you come across the same term subsequently and change your view, update the Post-it® note and stick it on the text at the new place.

■ ■ ■

FROM THE IDEAL, THE ORDINARY, AND THE ORDERLY TO CONFLICT AND VIOLENCE IN PRAGMATIC RESEARCH
CHARLES L. BRIGGS

Maybe we should blame it all on Noam Chomsky. I am not referring here to his efforts to reduce the study of language to a purely cognitive domain in which only quasi-mathematical relations between formal structures are worthy of study. While its roots certainly run much deeper, pragmatics was formed in part by a reaction against Chomsky's foundational fiction: "linguistic theory is concerned primarily with an ideal speaker-hearer in a completely homogeneous speech-community" (1965: 3). If marginalizing context, dialogue, interaction, and history was the prime issue here, we could just as easily decry the power of Ferdinand de Saussure's (1959[1916]) *Course in General Linguistics* in marginalizing the study of what he called *parole* for half a century. But, conversation, indexicality, implicature, performativity, contextualization, and language ideologies have become key analytic concepts that drive research in pragmatics and adjacent fields. It is rather the chasm that separates Chomsky's political analysis, which has placed him in the international limelight as a public intellectual, and the exceedingly conservative stance he takes on the study of language. And when I say conservative here I do mean *politically* conservative—what else should we call a denial that difference, conflict, institutions, social inequality, and history shape language, an attempt to root social and political analysis out of linguistics, and the claim that scholarly endeavors exist apart from the politics of contemporary society?

For those of us who do not share Chomsky's view of language, it is easy to dismiss his often stated claim (the question comes up nearly every time he gives a public lecture) that his work in linguistics and politics have nothing to do with one another. But the buck can't stop with Chomsky, in that the potential contribution of many of the insights provide pragmatics with an alternative theoretical agenda for revealing the power of language in shaping politics and the political constitution of language lies unexploited if not, in some cases, suppressed.

[. . .]

1 Scientific idealization and the search for ordinary discourse

Scientists have long seen their task as that of discerning principles that relate to as wide a range of phenomena as possible; "universal laws" are generally accorded a privileged status, and the cachet diminishes with decreasing generality. In his *Principles of Pragmatics*, Geoffrey Leech (1983: 7) argues that "Any account of meaning in language must (a) be faithful to the facts as we observe them, and (b) must be as simple and generalizable as possible." He invokes oppositions between abstract *versus* concrete and general *versus* local in according priority to "general pragmatics," which he defines as "the study of the general conditions of the communicative use of language, and to exclude more specific 'local' conditions on language"; the latter phenomena (if one accepts the distinction he is drawing) are relegated to the domain of "socio-pragmatics" (1983: 10).

This meta-theoretical preoccupation with the abstract and general hearkens strongly back definitions of science that have prevailed since the seventeenth century. As Gruner (1977: 114) argues, the reformulation of the scientific project that emerged during this period was distinguished by a new emphasis on and the development of new methods for rendering knowledge and idealization more abstract. John Locke's *Essay Concerning Human Understanding* (1959 [1690]), which profoundly shaped modern conceptions of language (Aarsleff 1982), extended this project to the study of language (see Bauman and Briggs 1997). Even scholars who reject the particular form that this quest takes in the work of Saussure and Chomsky often accept epistemological hierarchies that privilege formulations that are framed as abstract and as applying to a wide range of cases.

This epistemological predilection leads researchers to adopt methodological strategies that concentrate on phenomena that seem to afford direct access into more abstract and general aspects of language and communication. Many researchers have privileged "everyday" or "ordinary" language use in hopes of identifying widely distributed rules, norms, strategies, structures, or processes. Leech's *Principles of Pragmatics* again provides a good case in point. Arguing that general pragmatics "will be limited . . . to a RHETORICAL model of pragmatics (1983: 11), he goes on to place his definition of rhetoric both in the tradition of and in opposition to classical senses of the term. While sharing a common concern with "the effective use of language in communication" (one might quibble here with the implication that classical rhetoric dealt with language alone), Leech (1983: 15) limits pragmatics "primarily to everyday conversation," placing the study of "more prepared and public uses of language" in secondary place.

While the clarity of Leech's definitions make his exposition an useful example, he is hardly alone. Conversation analysis (CA) in particular goes much further. As Heritage and Atkinson assert, "Within conversation analysis there is an insistence on the use of materials collected from *naturally occurring* occasions of everyday interaction by means of audio- and video-recording equipment or film" (1984: 2; emphasis in the original). Beyond placing further restrictions on the scope of the "everyday" and on how conversation must be documented, CA rests not simply on the marginalization of other types of data but on their exclusion. In spite of the commitment of conversation analysts to eschew the introduction of analytic terms and categories that do not demonstrably flow from the interaction in question, this notion of the "ordinary" or "everyday" emerges not from "the data" themselves but is rather a commonsense concept that is imposed on particular discourses. This methodological commitment involves not only searching for particular sorts of events and rejecting others but in extracting them from the particular historical, social, and cultural circumstances in which they emerge, thereby making them seem "ordinary" and facilitating their synecdochic use as exemplars of more general processes.

The contributors to this special issue depart from these epistemological and methodological premises in three crucial ways. First, they have selected data that are *extra*ordinary, involving such phenomena as physical altercations, acts of violence that result in prison sentences, contestations of national political ideologies, peace negotiations between insurgent forces and nation-states, murder trials, and political debates. Some of these events are extraordinary not simply in the sense of departing from commonsense notions of what everyday interaction is all about but by virtue of their historical significance. Asif Agha analyzes forms of "tropic aggression" that shape the course of a debate between Bill Clinton and Bob Dole that took place in the course of the 1996 presidential election in the United States.[*] This encounter clearly not only was lodged in a particular set of historical circumstances but helped to produce the political tenor of the times. Maria Eugenia Villalón and Sandra Angeleri describe a series of bold discursive moves by members of a guerrilla organization that inaugurated peace dialogues with the Colombian government. The notion that these exchanges changed the political landscape does not seem to be held by the authors alone; rather, a shared sense of being in the historical limelight seems to have enabled the parties to sustain their engagement, even if it did not prove sufficient to engender a lasting settlement.

Second, these discourses do not simply *represent* conflict and violence but themselves play a significant role in constructing violent acts and in shaping their political effects. Jan Blommaert studies political debates that center on a major policy statement on immigration in Belgium. Portrayals of the cultural and political values of Belgians *versus* immigrants that emerged in these exchanges helped to shape the very conditions of life for immigrants. Briggs examines the collaboration of Venezuelan judicial and medical authorities in construing the death of an infant as an act of infanticide. He argues that the criminal case, which was the focus of much attention in the region, modeled the discursive and political silencing of persons labeled "indigenous" and their status as objects—but never agents—of political representation and decision-making. Patricia O'Connor details the narratives that male prisoners tell about their involvement in violent confrontations that take place within the prison walls. She argues that the production of highly gendered images that take place in such storytelling positions narrators within the larger economy of violence in the prison, thereby limiting their vulnerability to lethal attack.

Third, the question of what is "ordinary" or "everyday" involves more than simply which data we select but crucially depends on how we frame and analyze them. By severing indexical links to broader social, political, and historical parameters, we can give even the most historically compelling discourses the look and feel of the mundane. These essays not only focus on discourses that are saturated with struggle and violence but show how analyzing dimensions of form and function entail close attention to conflict, discursive and other. John Haviland reports a series of arguments, most of which took place in Mexico. He argues that conventional understandings of such mechanisms as turn-taking, inference, and implicature do not adequately explain how the discourse is structured or its social consequences; grasping the peculiar patterning of these quarrels leads him to quarrel with the assumptions regarding cooperation, rationality, relevance, and politeness that underlie a number of influential formulations in pragmatics.

2 Beyond the borders of context

As linguists came to recognize the constitutive—rather than peripheral—role that indexicality placed in shaping the form, meaning, and effects of discourse (see Silverstein 1976b), mapping signal to context relations became crucial. One of the primary contributions of CA and other modes of analyses was to show that this relation is not a fixed correlation between speech and language-external settings but an ongoing process of co-construction in which discourse is both shaped by and also shapes the context; to use Heritage's (1984) phrase, utterances are "doubly contextual." There is a strong tendency within extant research, however, to extend analysis of the active social process of contextualization (Gumperz 1982b) only to the limits of what happens between the time that the tape recorder or video camera is turned on and off and only to what is audible (and, increasingly, visible); CA narrows the focus primarily to the intricate relations that link a utterance to what immediate precedes and follows it.

The contributions to this special issue point to the need to attend to a much broader set of contextual relations in order to see how discourse is embedded within and engenders conflict and violence.

[. . .]

3 Questioning purported links between discursive and social order

Another theme pertains to conceptions of order and of orderliness. It has been assumed since the seventeenth century that science is based on a quest for order. The writings of Bacon, Hobbes, Locke, and others located the search for order in the human mind and in practical activity, particularly in the development of models that reveal order in a seemingly disorderly universe, the creation of social order between disparate individuals, and the material imposition of order on the "natural world" (see Gruner 1977; Hall 1963; MacPherson 1962). For Bacon, language was inherently disorderly, an obstacle to science and society. Locke saved the day for language once again, suggesting that language was in essence rational and orderly; writing in the aftermath of the devastating English civil wars, Locke argued that speech is "the great bond that holds society together" (1959 [1690] II;148).

Those varieties of pragmatics that devote serious attention to the social nexus of language generally follow Locke in assuming not only that both signs and society are orderly but in deeming the creation of semiotic order to be a (if not the) fundamental mechanism for generating social order. As George Psathas (1995: 2) and many others have suggested, CA is centrally concerned with "the order/organization/orderliness of social action," or, in Harvey Sacks (1984) words, the proposition that "there is order at all points" in human conduct. John Lee (1987: 39) argues that CA seeks to resolve long-standing debates in sociology regarding the nature of social order by grounding its study in the analysis of natural conversation. Construing conversation as the primary site in which social order is produced on an ongoing basis provides a rationale for arguing that it constitutes a privileged locus for analyzing social action (see Sacks et al. 1974). In acknowledging Hobbes' legacy in drawing attention to the problem of social order and Talcott Parsons' (1949) contribution to its modern sociological formations, Harold Garfinkel (1991: 17) argues that discerning order in the practical activity of ordinary society is the foundational mark of ethnomethodology's oppositional identity: "Distinctive emphases on the production and accountability of order* in and as ordinary activities identity ethnomethodological studies, and set them in contrast to classic studies, as an incommensurably alternate society.[1]

The articles included in this collection form part of a growing body of work that questions order and orderliness are inherent in speech and other forms of social action as well as the functionalist arguments that seek to equate them. Several recent collections suggest that *disorderliness* may be just as ordinary in discourse and that it yields important insights into everyday as well as extraordinary moments of social life (see Briggs 1996; Grimshaw 1990; O'Connor 1995). Other studies suggest that the quest for order may be rooted more squarely in *ideologies* of language (Woolard and Schieffelin 1994 and in press), than in everyday conversation and conduct in general (Joseph and Taylor 1990), more in public culture than in culture per se (Gal and Woolard 1995).

As the papers by Agha and Villalón and Angeleri show, scholars and others often impose an image of order and cooperation on dimensions of discourse that embody disorder. Haviland's examples suggest that even such cultural and social bedrock as notions of rationality, cooperation, and politeness and the role of conversation in injecting them into social life may be contingent on lay and scholarly assumptions that privilege everyday, ordinary interactions over overly conflictual exchanges. His closing remarks on the continuities between the legal battle that took place in Zinacantan in 1982 and the violent struggle that emerged in Chiapas in 1994 are intriguing; if the legions of ethnographers who conducted research in the region had paid more attention to conflict and been less concerned with generating portraits of orderly social, cultural, and ritual systems, their work would have provided a more solid basis for foreseeing the coming conflict.

Agha's analysis should help to forestall efforts to simply replace functionalist equations of linguistic and social order with equally reductionist assertions that discursive conflict provide some sort of transparent and natural foundation for social (dis)organization and discord. A variety of metadiscursive schemes of regimentation come into play in shaping both production and reception; the relationship between formal structures, social effects, and the perception of aggression is thus less adequately characterized by notions of transparency and shared orders of structure and meaning than by attending the contingent, ongoing process of regimentation. Michael Silverstein's (1993) work on metapragmatic regimentation provides a valuable framework for sorting out these complexities.

[. . .]

This effort to link discursive and social order might lead us to recall that John Locke shaped not only notions of language and mind but also created the ideological roots and the discursive practices that helped construct and institutionalize social inequality in the modern world; he created not only a philosophy of language and mind but a political theory as well. When contemporary scholars posit direct and transparent relations between communicative and social order, whether they deem them to be inherent or achieved, they run the risk of adding further scientific legitimacy to discursive practices of social regimentation—including those that center on standardization, official monolingualism, and the measurement of "intelligence" vis-à-vis discursive skills that are selectively transmitted on the basis of race, class, and nationality. In commenting on these papers, Michael Silverstein notes the persistence of a range of different types of reductionism that are still common in work that falls under the aegis of pragmatics. He warns that what he refers to as "two textualities, the denotational and the interactional" are often conflated, thereby giving rise to analyses that attribute automatic social force to formal and functional devices—without seeing how the relationship between the two is mediated by complex webs of socio-cultural, historical, and political specificities.

In sum, these papers harness pragmatic theories and methodologies to the task of analyzing a wide range of types of violence and conflict and in revealing the discursive processes that are used in legitimating, naturalizing, and challenging them. At the same time, the authors contribute to the still nascent task of reflecting on how this shift in focus reveals the need to examine and revise key assumptions that underlie work in pragmatics and related areas in general, even research that seeks to place struggle and disorder in the margins or to displace them from research on language as a whole.

[. . .]

Notes

*   Agha treats aggression as a trope of rhetorical figure "where an utterance implements aggressive effects in use but where its aggressive qualities are masked or veiled in some way."

1   Garfinkel (1991: 18) states that the asterisk following "order" is a proxy for the "accompanying suffix: (order*) – in-and-as-of-the-working-of-ordinary-society." Note that Garfinkel (1991: 14) places CA under the aegis of ethnomethodology.

■ ■ ■

POST-READING

Re-read the final sentence of each reading in this section and decide on the extent to which each of these sentences will influence the way you think about or study pragmatics in the future.

SECTION 9 FURTHER READING

For an article that develops Kopytko's paper, read:

Kopytko, R. (2001) 'From Cartesian towards non-Cartesian pragmatics', *Journal of Pragmatics* 33: 783–804.

If you enjoy fiction and are interested in the seventeenth century background to rationalism, including the contributions to philosophy of Bacon, Descartes and Locke, you'll enjoy reading this wonderfully entertaining novel:

Pears, Iain (1997) *An Instance of the Fingerpost*, London: Jonathan Cape.

A selection of important papers relevant to the issues raised by Pressman:

Hanks, W.F. (1992) 'The indexical ground of deictic reference', in A. Duranti and C. Goodwin (eds) *Rethinking Context*, pp. 43–76, Cambridge: Cambridge University Press.
Jakobson, R. (1960) 'Closing statement: linguistics and poetics', in T.A. Sebeok (ed.) *Style in Language*, pp. 350–77, Cambridge, Massachusetts: MIT Press.
Silverstein, M. (1976b). See Section 4 Further reading.
Silverstein, M. (1985d) 'Language and the culture of gender: at the intersection of structure, usage, and ideology', in E. Mertz and R.J. Parmentier (eds) *Semiotic Mediation: sociocultural and psychological perspectives*, pp. 219–59, Orlando, Florida: Academic Press.
Silverstein, M. (2010) '"Direct" and "indirect" communicative acts in semiotic perspective', *Journal of Pragmatics* 42 (2), 337–53.

Studies in the Social and Cultural Foundations of Language, Cambridge University Press, is an excellent series that focuses on sociocultural aspects of language use. For a view of pragmatics that reflects the sociocultural approach, read volumes by Bauman and Briggs, Briggs, Duranti and Goodwin, Lucy.

SECTION 10

Theory and practice in pragmatics

Introduction

IN OUR GENERAL INTRODUCTION TO THIS READER, we met several sprinters on the starting blocks of the 100 Metre Final of the Pragmatics Olympics, all of whom had definitions of 'pragmatics' emblazoned on their vests, the most race worthy of which (or so we suggested) was 'meaning in context' . . . if only because it managed to get us off the starting blocks and racing! Once off the starting blocks, we discussed the 'centrality of context' and the meaning of 'meaning' in some detail, before introducing the various approaches to pragmatics included in this Pragmatics Reader. Having since given you the opportunity of familiarizing yourselves with the ever-growing discipline that is pragmatics at the beginning of the 21st century, and some of the philosophical, cognitive and sociocultural perspectives which make up that discipline, I now want us to consider the extent to which theory should/does feed into practice and practice should/does feed into theory within pragmatics. How you come to view this issue will probably dictate your answer to a related question – whether you feel enough is being done at the beginning of the twenty-first century to make this cross-fertilization between theory and practice happen?

The issues I raise here are designed to pick up on a point we made in the general introduction, following our broad generalizations of the foci of the continental European approach, with its perspective view, and the Anglo-American approach, with its component view: the importance of drawing a distinction between 'choosing data to illustrate a theory and being concerned to ensure that the chosen data represent a social reality on the basis of which a theory may be proposed'. Consider our acceptance that 'one could hardly study presupposition without choosing one's data very carefully, for example'. Does this effectively equate to an acceptance that presuppositional theories will not work on the type of messy data typically produced by 'muddle persons', day to day (a language/theory issue)? And, if this is the case, is this problematic for you? Or do you merely see a methodological issue here, namely, that researchers should be very selective in terms of data when discussing, e.g., presupposition from a theoretical perspective? In which case, is the careful selection of data unproblematic for presupposition-based studies? Is it, in fact, a pre-requisite for pragmatics studies regardless of the pragmatic feature under investigation and, if so, does this cause problems for some of the applied pragmatic disciplines whose datasets are far from ideal?

In the sections that follow, I offer my own tentative response to the above issues, via an exploration of some of the work of the developmental, clinical and experimental pragmaticians. My motivations for choosing these areas are numerous, but I will focus here on one. While, personally, I might want to argue that much of pragmatics is simultaneously 'theory' focussed and 'practice' focussed – not least because it seeks to explain 'meaning *in context*' – developmental pragmatics, clinical pragmatics and experimental pragmatics represent applied approaches which have as part of their remit *the study of the relationship between theory and its practical application in a clinical or experimental setting*. Hence, these disciplines are not applied in the same sense that a corpus-based approach to pragmatics is applied. By this I mean to distinguish a given researcher's use of a methodology like corpus linguistics to help explicate an existing pragmatic theory (see, e.g., Archer *et al.* 2008) from pragmatics disciplines with their own defined areas of interest – such as the study of language development in children and of language disorders in children and adults.

As my list of applied pragmatic disciplines is very specific (cf. Levinson 1983: 376; Mey 2007: 103), I should perhaps point out that I'm seeking to help to spread awareness of pragmatics sub-disciplines that, to all intents and purposes, are little known by many practitioners and students of mainstream pragmatics (Perkins 2007: 1) at the same time as providing you with an indication of the extent of two-way traffic between pragmatic theory and practice in these fields. This lack of familiarity is understandable to some extent given that books on clinical pragmatics, for example, tend to be written with practitioners in mind, and seek to demonstrate 'how various pragmatic theories and analytical frameworks may be applied in the description, treatment and assessment of communication disorders' (Perkins 2007: 1). Another related problem is that, 'because their primary interest is in application rather than theory', authors of such books 'tend to be both eclectic and uncritical with regard to the pragmatic theories they make use of' (Perkins 2007: 1). To help us to explore such issues, I begin with short descriptions of the approaches typically adopted in clinical, developmental and experimental pragmatics.

Snapshots of three applied disciplines

When you read the following descriptions of clinical, developmental and experimental pragmatics, you will get a sense of the extent to which they each draw on psychology. These multidisciplinary approaches also make use of neuroanatomy and neuroimaging techniques, in the case of clinical pragmatics, and draw on cultural psychology, anthropology and sociology, in the case of developmental pragmatics – but this multidisciplinary characteristic will not be discussed in any depth below. Rather, I focus on the origins and the initial 'language' focus of each of these disciplines, beginning with developmental pragmatics.

Developmental pragmatics – its origins and initial focus

Developmental pragmatics is the term used to capture research which has the primary goal of studying the way in which language-intact children develop their pragmatic skills and/or competence. The earliest studies were undertaken in the 1970s and 1980s, when it became obvious that clinicians needed to have a better appreciation of the pragmatic norms against which findings of impairment could be compared.

Prominent amongst the earliest researchers was Elizabeth Bates (1974, 1976), who not only pioneered the modern study of child language development, but was one of the first researchers to emphasize the pragmatic dimensions of language acquisition. As a psycholinguist, developmental psychologist and cognitive scientist, Bates was particularly interested in how the brain processes language. However, in contrast to Chomsky's 'standard' and 'extended standard theories' (1965, 1971), which promoted the idea of a language acquisition device, Bates believed that linguistic knowledge is distributed throughout the brain and hence that the acquisition of language rests on a foundation of general mental abilities. Bates and her colleagues were particularly keen to document preverbal infants' proto-imperative and proto-declarative competencies: that is, the use of a combination of intentional vocalizations and gestures by 8–10 month old infants as a means of eliciting help or obtaining desired objects (Bates *et al.* 1975). Bates believed that these vocal and gestural activities served as building blocks for toddlers' later verbal communications, even though 'the linguistic expression of communicative intents is qualitatively different from their gestural and behavioural expression' (Ninio and Snow 1996: 48). That said, it is widely believed that 'the language system, once established, soon diverges from its nonverbal origins' in the case of hearing children (Ninio and Snow 1996: 49), not least because of the grammatical component within illocutionary acts, which is lacking in preverbal communicative acts (see Dore 1975, 1978).

Ninio and Wheeler (1984) are also key figures within developmental pragmatics. Their 'Inventory of Communicative Acts' (INCA) and related systems, for example, have been used extensively to record the development of verbal communicative skills in 12–36-month-old infants (see Ninio 1984; Ninio and Goren 1993; Snow *et al.* 1996; Tsuji 2002; Zhou 2002) These systems specifically draw upon both speech act theory (Austin 1962; Searle 1976) and also ideas relating to facework (Goffman 1967, 1974) to identify and code the communicative intent of caregivers and children at two distinct levels – the level of the utterance and the level of the social interchange. The first level equates to activities such as requests/proposals, statements, refusals, etc. The second level seeks to identify the extent to which the interchange constitutes a negotiation, a marking event, an evaluation, a discussion, a performance or vocal game, an acknowledgement, metacommunication or a correction/repetition.

Clinical pragmatics – its origins and initial focus

Clinical pragmaticians share the developmental pragmaticians' interest in pragmatic development, but their foci are the factors that disrupt the developmental process in some way. They are also interested in the communicative disruptions which individuals (of any age) can experience following a cerebral injury or pathology. Pragmatic disorders commonly investigated include Altzheimer's Disease and other forms of dementia/neurodegenerative disorders, aphasia, and damage caused by stoke or traumatic brain injuries (see Section 8).

Interestingly, clinical pragmatics emerged around the same time as Austin, Searle and Grice initially proposed that language can be used 'to do things' and that 'what a sentence *says*' is not necessarily the same as 'what it may be taken to *implicate*' (Cummings 2009: 9–10, italics as in original). Like the ordinary language philosophers, clinicians were struggling with the same 'unhelpful assumptions about language', which 'had their origin in a semantic conception of language and meaning':

Under this conception, single words and sentences were regarded as the only units of meaning (the notion of discourse was completely overlooked) and meaning was based entirely on language (words and sentences had an invariant meaning that was not influenced by how speakers used these linguistic entities). The effect of these assumptions on clinical practice was that disproportionate emphasis was placed on structural language skills, often at the expense of any consideration of how clients used their language skills in a range of communicative situations. Also, despite the fact that normal language users do not produce utterances in a linguistic vacuum, assessment and treatment of language skills proceeded by and large on the basis of single word and single sentence productions. In attempting to eliminate these assumptions, or at least reduce their significance, clinicians and researchers embraced new methods of pragmatic assessment and treatment, redefined notions of treatment efficacy in pragmatic terms and even devised new nosological [i.e. disease-related] categories to reflect the clinical significance of impairments of pragmatic language skills.

(Cummings 2009: 11)

Particularly noteworthy, here, is the pioneering work of Rapin and Allen (1983, 1988) and Bishop and Rosenbloom (1987). Although they worked separately in the US and the UK respectively, both research teams identified semantic-pragmatic disorders in children who demonstrated poor language use (e.g., difficulties or delays in their ability to understand contextual meaning/inferences). Both teams also concluded (again separately) that these difficulties were not structurally-motivated but were pragmatic in nature – thereby ensuring pragmatics took on a diagnostic significance within a clinical setting.

Experimental pragmatics – its origins and initial focus

The group of mainly British/European researchers who have developed the field of experimental pragmatics share the clinical pragmaticians' interest in the semantic-pragmatic interface. However, their methods of investigation (eye tracking, timed response to stimuli, the choice of a 'best' sentence to describe X from a set of candidates, etc.) are as influenced by psycholinguists as they are by the philosophical ideas first postulated by Searle and Grice and later developed by neo-Griceans and relevance theorists. By way of illustration, some of the earliest studies undertaken by Clark and Lucy (1975) used reaction time as a means of gauging whether indirect requests take longer to comprehend than direct requests. This work was quickly extended, with a view to testing further theoretical assumptions – for example, Clark's (1979) study relating to the telephone request, 'Can you tell me what time you close?', sought to discover whether targets consider both the direct and the indirect questions inherent within the stimulus request. The most typical response, 'Yes, we close at six', was taken as evidence that targets typically address both in their answers (however, see Munro 1979 for a different analysis).

Another key figure within experimental pragmatics – the cognitive linguist, Raymond Gibbs – has also studied indirect speech acts extensively, and like Clark, in a way that feeds into theory. For example, Gibbs (1981, 1986) has 'measured' the effect of conventionality on the time/effort it takes to understand (i.e. make sense of) indirect SAs. However, it is Gibbs's work with Moise in regard to readers' comprehension of Generalized Conversational Implicatures (GCIs) which is generally taken to signal the beginning of experimental pragmatics proper (Beziodenhout 2010: 148).

Gibbs and Moise (1997) used forced-choice judgement tasks to determine whether listeners first access the semantically-encoded meaning of an utterance such as 'Robert cut a finger' (i.e. Robert cut some finger or other) and then use context to infer the GCI (Robert cut *his* finger) or whether the GCI is directly accessed (cf. Gibbs' 1994 work on the processing of idioms and metaphors). Specifically, they asked participants to read sentences containing GCI-carrying words, as well as paraphrases of these sentences, and choose which version most closely captured what was said. Interestingly, their resulting observations conflict somewhat with similar work carried out within a relevance-theoretic framework by Nicolle and Clark (1999): Gibbs and Moise found that minimal or non-enriched readings (i.e. those which were semantically encoded) were rarely chosen by the participants, and concluded that enriched meanings were directly accessed. Nicolle and Clark found that readers tended to favour the implicature paraphrases, and explained that readers had based their choice(s) on what seemed to them to closely match the original in its degree of relevance (for further detail, see Bezuidenhout 2010: 148–9). More recently, Garrett and Harnish (2007) have drawn on Bach's (1995) notion of *context*-free *impliciture* to best explain how readers in their experiments were found to favour choices involving an expansion of what is implicit in what is said (e.g., statements such as 'I've had breakfast', will generally be understood as communicating that S has had breakfast on the day of articulating the utterance).

This begs an interesting question to which we'll return later (pp. 480–1): if experimental results can be shaped, in part, by the theoretical approach that experimenters adopt, to what extent do such experiments really test the applicability of the theories themselves? Suffice it to say, Bezuidenhout (2010: 148) claims that the experimental pragmatics field was 'launched' with precisely this aim in mind – especially in regard to the 'hotly debated' issues at the semantic-pragmatic interface. This ongoing interest with the semantics-pragmatics interface also helps to explain the numerous experimental studies that have sought to explore presupposition, scalar implicatures, implicitures, metaphor and the more general theory of mind (ToM) abilities of children and impaired populations.

In the sections that follow, I briefly highlight some of the experiments and clinical studies that have been undertaken as a means of better understanding scalar implicatures and ToM abilities, and then go on to discuss the diagnostic significance of pragmatics, and the related issue of fuzzy boundaries, which – as will become clear – is seen by some as a problem, especially in regard to the application of pragmatic theory within a clinical context.

Scalar implicatures

Noveck's (2001) work on children's understanding of scalar implicatures is well known to both developmental and experimental pragmaticians. Noveck used a variety of tasks to elicit child and adult listeners' judgements about utterances containing scalar implicature triggers. These included assessing their understanding of statements such as 'There must be a parrot in the box', using truth value judgement tasks. Noveck would manipulate various scenarios, so that the puppet (which respondents were asked to evaluate) was occasionally 'underinformative': for example, the puppet would state that the parrot might be in the box, even though the informants knew the parrot was in the box. Noveck found that the younger the participants, the more likely they were to accept such underinformative statements, in spite of contrary visual evidence (between 69 and 80 per cent of 5- to 9 year-olds accepted such statements, as compared to 35 per cent of adults). Noveck also found that his child-informants accepted utterances such as 'Some elephants have trunks' as being true more than adult-informants did

(89 per cent as compared to 41 per cent). Noveck has claimed that such experiments provide proof that children are more logical than adults and that pragmatic abilities such as being able to derive – and evaluate as false – scalar implicatures like 'Not all elephants have trunks' are a late development. But subsequent work by Papafragou and Musolino (2003) and Feeney et al. (2004) has found that children as young as 6- and 7-years of age will reject under-informative statements when the context makes the pragmatically enriched response relevant, a finding which seems to lend support to the relevance-theoretic argument that semantic meanings of weak terms are readily accessible to both children and adults, while narrowed meanings are associated with extra effort. Not surprisingly, Feeney et al., Papafragou and Musolino all go on to query whether Noveck's results reflect the unnaturalness of the experimental setup and the task demands rather than the children's *actual pragmatic abilities* (see also Schegloff's and Hamilton's criticisms of laboratory-based testing conditions in Section 8).

As the above studies are comprehension oriented, it's also worth highlighting Katsos's (2007) investigation of adults' and children's (ages 5–11) comprehension and production abilities, here. Katsos used truth-value judgement tasks involving a fictional character, Mr Caveman, who needed help describing various scenarios, including the Horn scale – i.e. whether 'The elephant had pushed [some/all] of the trucks'. Katsos (2007) found that the younger children were informative speakers, that is, they were capable of giving exhaustive answers. However, they tended to be underinformative comprehenders, in the sense that they commonly accepted underinformative statements from Mr Caveman. Given that the 11-year-olds within Katsos's study showed themselves to be informative comprehenders as well as informative producers, we can hypothesize that comprehension and production are dissociated in younger children but that, as pragmatically-intact children begin to mature, they develop the heuristic mechanisms which allow them very rapid access to quantity implicatures and similar constructions.

In a follow-up experiment, Katsos found that children became even more willing to accept underinformative statements from Mr Caveman, when told that the fictional character was 'guessing'. According to Bezuidenhout (2010: 152–3), this shows that children may not always respond 'egocentrically, based on their own privileged epistemic position' but, rather, will 'take their interlocutor's epistemic situation into account' when it's deemed necessary to do so. I pick up on the egocentricity or otherwise of children below (but see also the Ninio and Snow reading in Section 8).

Centrality of intentionality

The concept of theory of mind (Premack and Woodruff 1978) – the idea that we attribute intention and other mental states (i.e. belief, knowledge, desire) to ourselves and others – is central to all three of the applied fields discussed here. This is not surprising, given the centrality of ToM abilities to communication in general. Indeed, as Doherty (2009: 152) explains, 'most of our communication involves exchanging information, mainly to change each other's mental states' and that, '[w]ithout a theory of mind, there would be little point to most conversation'. But what, if anything, can developmental pragmatics, clinical pragmatics and experimental pragmatics tell both armchair theorists and field-based researchers about ToM that they might not have surmised already through imagining or know through observation (Clark and Bangerter 2004: 25–6)?

To start with, even something as basic as pointing has been posited as a joint attention behaviour, which requires taking into account another person's mental state i.e., whether the person notices an object or finds it of interest. Some researchers, most notably, Baron-Cohen (1991) claim that proto-declarative pointing (the inclination to spontaneously reference an object in the world as of interest and to appreciate the directed attention and interests of another) is a critical precursor to the development of ToM abilities in infants. Further evidence to suggest infants quickly become 'intentional interpreters' (Meini 2010: 494) – i.e., begin to assume the other's perceptual and psychological perspective – has been posited by Baldwin (1991). In one experiment, Baldwin (1991) found that eighteen-month-old children were able to use the gaze of the adult experimenter to differentiate the verbalized intended object (i.e. an object in a bucket) from the unintended object (the object in their possession).

The centrality of intention in conjunction with the recognition that ToM abilities 'take time to become fully functional' in language-intact individuals (Matsui 2010: 469) and, in some individuals, never fully develop helps to explain the (re)occurrence in developmental (and, to some extent, clinical) studies of two inter-related questions: 'First, what type of communicative intents' can individuals express and at what age, and 'second, by what linguistic means' do they express these intents? (Ninio and Snow 1996: 15). Studies seeking to address these questions have shown, for example, that normally-developing children become capable of understanding the concept of belief around 4–5 years (Wellman et al. 2001). However, autistic children lack the ToM skills that are 'present in normally developing four-year olds' (Cummings 2009: 5). The ToM abilities of deaf and/or blind children are also frequently delayed, and in similar ways to those of autistic children according to Hobson and Bishop (2003), that is, such children demonstrate limited engagement in social interaction, infrequent comment on the world around them, etc.

As in the case of scalar implicature studies, some researchers are concerned that the task demands of ToM tests prevent some children from demonstrating their true level of ToM ability (see, e.g., Miller 2004). Nevertheless, standard false belief tasks ('location . . . ', 'content . . .' and 'appearance-reality') remain the litmus test for assessing the development of ToM (Wimmer and Perner 1983; Perner et al. 1987; Flavell et al. 1983) – although it's widely accepted that normal children who have not yet developed the capacity to pass such tests may still be able to demonstrate an understanding of pretence (Clements and Perner 1994; Leslie 1987). Around the same time as children are developing the capacity to understand false belief, they also come to understand individual differences in the interpretation of the same event (Perner and Wimmer 1985; Carpendale and Chandler 1996). In normally developing 6- to 9-year olds, this is followed by the ability to engage in white lies, irony, etc. (Winner and Leekam 1991). This growing sophistication in understanding mind continues into adulthood, before showing some signs of decline in old age in the normal adult (Happé et al. 1998), and considerable decline in Alzheimer's sufferers (see Hamilton, Section 8).

Delimiting intent

The desire to fully investigate communicative intent ensures that a clear distinction is made within developmental pragmatics between a meaningful verbal-communicative act, which requires a host of socio-cognitive capacities on the part of the speaker, and other communicative vocalisations, which do not. Put simply, to be meaningfully communicative, the speaker must have or possess:

- The will to affect the addressee by some purposeful behaviour.
- Control of communicative intentionality, that is, the formulation of intents concerned with achieving an understanding of a message by an addressee.
- Control of a range of different types of communicative intents, encompassing different types of socio-cognitive and linguistic concepts.
- The ability to express intents conventionally, effectively, and politely.

(adapted from Ninio and Snow 1996: 16)

As stated previously (page 473), if we were to unpack this a little further, we would find an influence within developmental pragmatics which is also evident in mainstream pragmatics generally: i.e. the notion of conversation as a cooperative activity (Grice 1975) involving the signalling of communicative (illocutionary) intent (Austin 1962; Searle 1969) in a way that adheres to shared socio-cultural guidelines (Goffman 1974). This is not surprising, when we consider that most developmental studies seek to determine 'how children acquire the knowledge necessary for the appropriate, effective, rule-governed employment of speech in interpersonal situations', that is, 'how children are taught to speak in pragmatically appropriate ways' (Ninio and Snow 1996: 4, 6). What this means, however, is that the study of 'background information on the social structure and familial arrangements of the society under study' is as crucial as the study of particular language features (Ninio and Snow 1996: 6).

Although the approach outlined above is not completely different from Cummings' (2009: 217–33) view of what should be included as part of pragmatics proper, Cummings is concerned about the "exclude nothing" approach within clinical pragmatics, which seems to typify pragmatic assessment protocols (e.g., Dewart and Summers' 1995 Pragmatics Profile and Bishop's 2003 Children's Communication Checklist) and also with the non-centrality of language within clinical pragmatics more generally. The two are related – at least for Cummings, who does not adhere to the view that non-linguistic factors (facial expression, gesture, eye contact, etc.) can function and/or be taken to be intent indicators in pragmatics because, in her view, language and intent cannot be separated. Indeed, she understands *language* to be '*at the centre of an account of pragmatics*' and *pragmatics* as '*always involving the intention to communicate*' (Cummings 2009: 244–9, italics as in original).

There are two observations that we might make at this point. First, there is a broad acceptance within mainstream pragmatics and other conversation-focussed fields that gestures and other non-verbal actions can be intentionally communicative, as Schegloff argues in Section 8.2. (Note, also, how a number of the more philosophical readings in this Reader draw on non-linguistic communicative examples to illustrate their theories.) The semiotic interpretation of pragmatics is especially evident in speech and language pathology, to the extent that Perkins (2007: 10) defines pragmatics as 'the use of linguistic *and non-linguistic* capacities for communicative purposes' (my italics). Second, Cummings' approach, if followed, would necessitate the exclusion of studies like Baron-Cohen et al.'s (1999) investigation of faux pas in autistic subjects, especially given that a faux pas, by definition, is unintentional. This is in spite of the fact that unintentional communication is a legitimate interest/concern within mainstream pragmatics (see, e.g., Goffman's *accidental* level of face threat and Culpeper's use of the *accidental* category in his studies of impoliteness).

These observations aside, I believe that Cummings' concerns raise broader issues regarding the difficulties associated with delimiting pragmatics and hence the diagnostic significance of pragmatic theory, and that these issues feed into the main consideration of this chapter, whether cross-fertilization between pragmatic theory and practice can and does happen. I explore each issue, in turn.

Delimiting pragmatics and the diagnostic concern

The lack of consensus amongst pragmatic theoreticians in regard to what pragmatics is and is not is well known. For the theoreticians themselves, this is not overly damaging, as they 'can treat the question of boundaries as an interesting academic point that is worthy of discussion' (Cummings 2008: 229). As Perkins (2007) and Cummings (2009) highlight, the fact that pragmatics has fuzzy boundaries is much more problematic for clinical pragmaticians. One problem discussed in some detail is that of terminology – a problem that has arisen, according to Perkins (2007: 8), 'because the terminology and conceptual apparatus of pragmatics is derived from disciplines such as linguistics, philosophy of language and sociology', that is, disciplines which tend to be 'more concerned with abstract models on the one hand and [with] the description of social behaviour on the other'. Added to this, clinicians have tended to import these terms 'wholesale and without adaptation' and, *ipso facto*, without giving adequate consideration to wider pathological issues.

A related issue raised by Perkins (2007: 8) is also worthy of brief comment: whereas pragmatic theoreticians have 'the luxury of being able to focus only on the specific features which are of interest to them', clinicians 'need to understand a condition in its entirety in order to *plan appropriate intervention*'. I have italicized the notion of planning appropriate intervention to draw attention to – and reiterate – a point made earlier: that the focus of clinical, developmental (and to a lesser extent, experimental) pragmatics will always favour application over theory. However, as Perkins (2007) points out, this does not mean that clinicians have to proceed eclectically or uncritically with regard to the pragmatic theories they make use of. Indeed, Perkins and Cummings both argue for a coming together of mainstream and clinical pragmatics, albeit from different positions. For example, the coming together has a specific *cognitive* and *linguistic* focus in Cummings' conceptualization (2009: 249–50) and requires 'all clinical investigators' to be or become 'critical of their own practice' and to better understand pragmatic concepts. However, Perkins (2007: 181) believes that a focus on the cognitive and linguistic capacities of the individual is too restrictive (both within clinical and mainstream pragmatics) – unless attention is also paid to 'interlocutor contributions' and other 'properties of the interaction'. In addition, any coming together of these two areas needs to involve two-way traffic, according to Perkins, so that the study of pragmatic impairments can also begin to impact upon pragmatic theory and/or on mainstream pragmatics more generally (2007: 8).

Perkins believes that the best means of achieving this is to treat pragmatic ability and disability within a single framework and offers us his own emergentist approach in this regard. This holistic approach allows for a number of interacting intra- and inter-personal variables during a given communication, the choice of which will be shaped in part by the underlying semiotic, cognitive and sensorimotor capacities within and between individuals. At the intra-personal level, these include signalling systems (language, gesture, facial expression), cognitive systems (ToM abilities, inference, memory), motor output systems (the vocal tract, hand movement), and sensory input systems (hearing, vision). At the interpersonal level, we might consider which meanings are explicitly encoded and which left implicit, which signalling systems are used, and which meanings are most salient/relevant. Intrapersonal and interpersonal domains, then, constitute

[. . .] dynamic systems whose integrity and equilibrium are maintained via a continuous process of compensatory adaptation. The effect of this is most plainly seen when one or more individual elements malfunction to create an imbalance within the system as a whole.

(Perkins 2007: 176)

Perkins' (2010: 234) approach is not meant to belittle the importance of language within pragmatics but rather to signal that pragmatics is as much about 'language *use*' as it is about '*language* use'. For Perkins, this means thinking beyond the level of the utterance, so that we can pay attention to both the linguistic cohesive devices (anaphora, ellipsis, information structure, pragmatic markers, etc.) that link utterances together in meaningful ways and also, importantly, utterance sequencing at a wider level (2010: 235). This brings into play not only speaker intent, but also (impairments) to ToM abilities/'role of the other' abilities, etc. (see Section 8). To summarize, Perkins is seeking to get away from a view of (linguistic) communication as 'a single, seamless process' (2007: 8) because, in his view, it backgrounds the complexities of the processes of interaction – and these complex processes are crucial to the understanding of pragmatic impairment and pragmatic abilities generally. But what would such an approach look like for mainstream pragmaticians?

Feeding theory into practice and practice into theory – a way forward?

The most significant coming together of mainstream pragmatics and an applied field in a way that explicitly tests pragmatic theory is probably most evident, currently, within experimental pragmatics. In particular, researchers have been debating the usefulness of the notions of 'what is said', 'what is implicated', and explicatures/ implicitures. This debate has inspired researchers such as Van der Henst *et al.* (2002a) to test whether, when asked the time, targets tend to favour Grice's first Quality maxim, 'Do not say what you believe to be false', as Grice seemed to assume, or the relevance-theoretic heuristic, 'Follow a path of least effort in constructing an interpretation of the utterance . . . [and s]top when your expectations are satisfied' (Wilson 2010: 396). Their experimental method involved requesting the time on three separate occasions: on the first occasion, only the request 'Do you have the time, please?' was made; on the second, the qualification 'My watch has stopped' was added to the request; and on the third, the qualification was amended to 'I have an appointment at 4.00'. Van der Henst *et al.* found that targets systematically aimed at optimal relevance rather than literal truthfulness. For example, they tended to round up their answer to the nearest five minute slot (i.e. from 11.13 to 11.15) when only the request was made, but to be much more specific when the situation seemed to dictate it (such as when the time of the 4pm appointment was growing close). Much more work needs to be done before we can begin to conclude that relevance theory has more predictive power than, for example, neo-Gricean approaches. What is noticeable, however, is the contribution of relevance theorists to experimental, developmental and impairment studies, a contribution that seems set to grow even further (see, e.g., Wilson 2010).

But is this kind of approach complimentary to the holistic approach promoted by Perkins? For example, does it take sufficient account of the non-linguistic and non-cognitive properties of the interaction, which come about because of the context (and will change from context to context)? Huang (2010b: 15) seems to believe that both the relevance-theoretic camp and the experimental pragmatics camp are beginning to complement and learn from each other, and in a way that also suggests a coming together of the Anglo-American and continental European traditions (i.e. the theoretical and the empirical). But I sense that Perkins' emergentist pragmatics will require investigations even more broad than this – i.e., ones which simultaneously seek to use the insights of discourse analysis and conversation analysis as well as relevance theory, for example. Given such an approach might feel unworkable (theoretically and methodologically) for some within mainstream pragmatics – can we find a way forward that constitutes the coming together of pragmatics in all its various guises?

One means of developing a holistic approach is to heed Clark and Bangerter's (2004: 26) advice to 'draw on'/'learn' from the three main avenues of language investigation – the *armchair*, the *laboratory* and the *field* – even when our personal focus and/or specialism might sit squarely within one or, at the most, straddle two. Experimental pragmatics has also managed to do this to some extent, as Clark and Bangerter's own work on referencing reveals. To adopt such a view is to recognize both the strengths of these avenues, and also that their weaknesses can be overcome, to some extent, via combining them. After all, 'you cannot even begin without armchair observations. You cannot easily draw causal claims outside the laboratory. And yet you cannot really know what language use is, in all its richness, without venturing into the field' (Clark and Bangerter 2004: 26). It goes without saying that such an undertaking is easier to promote than it is to execute, however, not least because of the theoretical leaps which would need to be made before cross-fertilization of any kind might take place. In fact, we might find that we have to amend or even abandon (aspects of) established theories – especially if we accepted the need (as Perkins claims) for a pragmatics that treats pragmatic ability and disability within a single framework.

Where next for pragmatics?

The goal of Section 10 has been to provide you with a snapshot of developmental, clinical and experimental pragmatics, and the extent of overlap between them and mainstream pragmatics, as a means of demonstrating the relationship between them. I have also shown how developmental, clinical and experimental pragmatics have sought to apply pragmatic theory. As there's less 'traffic' from these applied disciplines to mainstream pragmatics, to borrow Perkins' (2007) metaphor, we are presented with an important question: whether mainstream pragmatics would gain from such traffic? Ultimately, you must decide for yourselves. My own view is that we should engage with the applied pragmatics literature if only to have a more convincing argument as to why specific mainstream pragmatic approaches shouldn't/don't need to draw on these disciplines. It's more likely, however, that mainstream approaches will be strengthened by this process, and become what they sometimes claim to be now – approaches which are representative of language use in all its complexities.

I also believe that this cross-fertilization between applied and theoretic approaches (cognitive, empirical and socio-cultural) should begin to be reflected more in the classroom, as well as in future pragmatics readers and textbooks. Indeed my hope is that the second edition of this Reader will contain more readings relating to what we currently consider to be sub-disciplines of pragmatics, and that we will have a wealth of publications to report, which, like the small number that currently exist, seek to reflect pragmatics in all its variety, to bring (applied) sub-disciplines to a more mainstream audience, and to grapple with terminological ambiguity and disparity.

SECTION 10 FURTHER READING

Cummings' (2010) *Pragmatics Encyclopedia,* published by Routledge, offers a very good overview of pragmatics, including the areas discussed above. For more detailed accounts of these disciplines, see also the 'Further reading' recommended in Section 8. In particular, we recommend the following as a starting point – not least because they seek to bring these approaches to the attention of a more mainstream audience: Ninio and Snow (1996); Noveck and Sperber (2004); Perkins (2007).

Glossary

The definitions in this glossary are intentionally general. Some of the authors whose work is included in this Reader use the items listed below in more particular ways and provide their own text-specific definitions. Terms defined in this glossary which also appear in other definitions are marked with an asterisk.

Accommodation   The willingness of a hearer to accept a proposition which is conveyed or presupposed rather than formally asserted.

Activity type   A term used by Levinson (1979b) to describe a culturally recognized, goal-directed activity such as a job interview, a jural interrogation or a classroom discussion, where there are recognized constraints on participants and setting, and thus on the kinds of allowable contributions. Preferred to the term *speech event** by Levinson because activity types contain both speech and characteristic actions.

Ambiguity   The property of having two or more syntactic or semantic interpretations. Disambiguation, or determining the appropriate interpretation, may be assisted by co-text, immediate context, wider encyclopedic knowledge or a combination of these factors.

Anaphora   A means of referring to a previous item, or *antecedent*, in a discourse.

Backchannelling   The provision by an addressee during speaker discourse of non-interruptive responses such as comprehension signals.

Blending   Combining parts of separate words into a new word to convey a concept which blends the separate concepts conveyed by the feeder words (e.g., *motel* from *motorist* and *hotel*).

Calculus   A method of calculating, usually applied by mathematicians and engineers to complex and constantly varying phenomena. In the study of formal language we use a calculus to determine the truth value of complex sentences (propositional logic) and to represent intrasentential relations (predicate logic).

Cognitive model   The term used by cognitive linguistics inter-changeably with *Idealized cognitive model* or *ICM* to mean much the same thing as *frame**, *schema(ta)*, and *script*, i.e. the encyclopedic knowledge built up from previous experience in relation to which new information is assessed.

Competence   A term used by Chomsky to distinguish our innate, largely tacit knowledge of language from *performance*, the overt language which we produce in speech. Can be compared to de Saussure's *langue* and *parole*.

Conceptual and procedural encoding   A distinction made by Blakemore (1987) between the propositional meaning we convey (conceptual encoding) and the use of discourse markers (procedural encoding) to constrain the processes by which the hearer interprets the speaker's conceptually encoded material so as to facilitate the determination of the relevance of an utterance.

Conditions   Constraints which condition production or comprehension. In speech act theory, the production of utterance is constrained by the need for the speaker to be sincere, the utterance to be felicitous, etc.

Constraint   A means of limiting production or interpretation so as to ensure that only permissible forms and meanings occur.

Context   Aspects of social structure relevant in the interpretation of the context-sensitive elements of utterances. Contexts may impinge on or be created by the use of language. Presumptive contexts are said to be *distal* or *macro* and contexts created in talk are said to be *micro*.

Contextualization cue   A term first used by Gumperz (1982) to describe the way speakers index utterances to a particular social context and thus express membership by their largely unconscious choice of form, register, prosody, and even code.

Conventionalization   The process by which a pragmatic meaning may become a semantic meaning over time.

Conversation analysis (CA)   An ethnomethodological approach to talk (talk-in-interaction) which does not invoke pre-conceived categories, and whose aim is to uncover regular patterns and preferences in the allocation of turns and the structuring of talk generally.

Community of Practice   A term coined by Lave and Wenger (1991) to depict the groups to which people belong, and which usually involves *situated learning* (i.e. the process of learning through experience). The typical individual belongs to several communities of practice simultaneously – for example, groups at work, school, home, in society, etc. In some of these groups, he or she will be a core member and in others, a (more) marginal member.

Defeasibility   In philosophy, deductive inference* is termed *monotonic*, i.e. the addition of further premises does not undermine the conclusion already reached. Inductive inference is *non-monotonic*, i.e. the addition of further premises may undermine the conclusion already reached. In pragmatics, non-monotonic inferences are said to be *defeasible*, i.e. they can be cancelled by the addition of additional information. Some meanings are defeasible (e.g., that I have only one child in the utterance 'I have a child'), others, such as entailments,* are not defeasible (e.g., that I have at least one child in the utterance 'I have a child').

Deixis   The indexical property of a closed class of demonstratives such as *I*, *here* and *now*, whose reference is determined in relation to the point of origin of the utterance in which they occur. Also known as *shifters*.

Discourse marker   A form that signals a relationship between two utterances or portions of discourse without contributing to the truth-conditions of either. Although *discourse marker* is the most widely used term, other terms commonly found include *connective particle*, *discourse particle* and *pragmatic marker*.

Emic/etic   Anthropologists distinguish *emic* approaches, which reflect the perspectives members of a society have of their own culture and of those aspects of their behaviour that are significant for them, from *etic* approaches, which describe cultures from the perspective of an independent outsider. (This distinction reflects the difference between *phonemes*, which distinguish meaning, and allophones, *phonetic* realizations which do not discriminate meaning.)

Enrichment/pragmatic strengthening   An umbrella term for the process of enriching literal or propositional meaning by means of pragmatic inference.

Entailment   A meaning that is always associated with an expression so that on every occasion when the expression occurs the same meaning arises. For example, we can never say that football team A beat football team B without entailing that A scored at least one goal more than B.

Epistemic meaning   A meaning (such as that conveyed by some uses of modal auxiliaries) which encodes the degree of commitment of a speaker to what they say.

Ethnolinguistics   The study of linguistics from a cultural perspective. A term favoured in Europe over *linguistic anthropology* and *anthropological linguistics*, which are more common in USA.

Ethnography   A written description of cultural practice typically based on direct participatory experience.

Evidential   A linguistic form (such as *I remember . . .*) which conveys the evidential provenance of an utterance.

Explicature   A term used by Sperber and Wilson (1986/1995) to describe the 'full propositional form' of a sentence whose indeterminacies have been resolved by a process of inference.

Face   A term used by Goffman (1967) to describe the 'positive social value' which people claim for themselves in interaction by means of their (linguistic) actions. Brown and Levinson (1978/1987) developed Goffman's notion, distinguishing *positive face*, a person's sense of self-esteem, and *negative face*, a person's desire to determine their own course of action. They further differentiate *face-wants* (the need to have their face respected) and, following Goffman, *face-threat* (the threat to self-esteem or to freedom of action) and *facework* (language addressed to the face-wants of others).

Formalism   An approach to the study of language which views linguistic form as an autonomous entity. Formalists distinguish *sentences*, linguistic forms, from *utterances*, sentences used for a purpose, i.e. given a function.

Frame   The sociocognitive information about the expectable features of events that we hold as the result of socialization and that we draw on when judging new behaviour either as participants or as onlookers. For example, we would expect a certain level of aggressive questioning between participants within a courtroom and a televised political interview context. But we would not expect the same aggressive style at a dinner party.

Function   A description of language which focuses on its purpose or orientation rather than its form. Attempts have been made to provide taxonomies of functions by Bühler, Jakobson, and Halliday in particular.

Grammaticalization   The process by which an item comes to have a systematic relation to other items.

Ground   The background against which a *figure* is foregrounded. According to Langacker (1987, 1991), the relationship of figure and ground (*profile* and *base* in his terminology) is the most significant property of human language. The relationship between assertion and presupposition might be construed as a figure/ground relationship. According to Hanks (1992), deictics uniquely combine figure and ground in a single form.

Hedging   A means of indicating weak adherence to a conversational maxim. *Hedges* may be contrasted with *intensifiers*, which indicate strong adherence to a maxim.

Heuristic   An insight about defaults and preferences used by speakers to help them produce maximally communicative utterances or by hearers to infer optimal meaning.

Higher-level explicature   A term used by Sperber and Wilson (1986/1995) to describe the propositional attitude of the speaker, including the illocutionary force of an utterance, which the addressee must recover inferentially.

Honorifics   Forms used to encode the (high) social status of an addressee.

Iconicity   The use of linguistic form to imitate meaning, as in the use of onomatopoeia or when the order of clauses reflects the order in which the propositions they convey occurred.

Idiom   A (complex) expression whose meaning isn't predictable on the basis of its component parts. Idioms are usually language specific.

Illocutionary force indicating device (IFID)   A term invented by Searle (1969) to cover explicit performatives and items such as *please* which indicate the illocutionary force of an utterance.

Implicature   Grice's term for an inferred meaning, often with a different logical (i.e. non-truth-preserving) form from that of the original utterance. In Grice's theory, the inferential process by which a hearer derives a conversational implicature is calculable, and the implicature is defeasible (cancellable without a contradiction arising) and non-detachable (if the context holds, any item with the same meaning will have the same implicature). In Grice's proposals, implicatures may be *generalized* (inferred irrespective of context – e.g., 'some' will always implicate *not all*) or *particularized* (particular to the context of the utterance in which they arise).

Indexicality   The variability of reference of the same linguistic forms across contexts.

Indirect speech act   A functional use of language other than the one prototypically associated with the form used to convey it. For example, 'Would you mind opening the window' is a request expressed in an interrogative form.

Inference   A conclusion derived from premises. A deductive or 'logical' inference is necessarily valid; inductive inferences 'project beyond the known data' (Honderich 1995) and are probabilistic, i.e. an inductive inference may not yield the same conclusion when additional premises are adduced. The inferences that constitute pragmatic meanings are usually presumed to be inductive, although relevance theorists argue that explicatures and implicatures are deductive.

Intention   *Intentionality* is the term used by philosophers to refer to the mental ability to direct thought, and hence to perform teleological, i.e. outcome-oriented, actions. Speech acts, implicatures and instances of politeness phenomena presume intentionality.

Interlanguage   A term invented by Selinker (1972) to refer to language-learner-language, which he regarded as a fossilized intermediate system between L1 and L2. Widely used since to mean language-learner-language in general.

Language change   The phenomenon of diachronic change in natural languages that is studied by historical linguists.

Language universal   A form or function thought to exist in all languages.

Linguistic relativity   The belief that the properties of a language partly determine the way its speakers perceive the world. Advanced in the early and mid-twentieth century by Sapir and his student, Whorf – hence known as *the Sapir-Whorf hypothesis*.

Logic   The science of valid reasoning. For pragmaticians, the extent to which natural languages behave like formal languages, whether a theory of truth can serve as a sufficient theory of meaning, and theories of inference are particularly relevant logical issues.

Logical form   The representation of the propositional content of a sentence or phrase in a form that eliminates differences of word order, etc. in natural languages and makes the underlying semantics transparent.

Markedness   The extent to which a linguistic form is natural (*unmarked*) or unusual (*marked*) when compared to related forms.

Maxim   *Maxim* is the term Grice uses for the guidelines which speakers accept when contributing to conversation and which enjoin them to provide appropriately informative, well-founded, relevant contributions in a perspicuous manner. Neo-Griceans have used Grice's maxims as the basis for developing comprehensive *principles** to guide the speaker in providing interpretable utterances and the hearer in recovering intended meanings.

Meaning   The understanding that is conveyed in a communicative act. In semantics, meaning is regarded as a property of language and usually thought of as truth-conditional (see *Truth value*). So establishing what a particular expression *entails** or necessarily presupposes provides a meaning which cannot be cancelled by contextual information. In pragmatics, meaning results from the intentional use of language by a speaker in a context.

Mental representation   Thought (as distinct from the language used to represent thought).

Mental space semantics   A discourse processing model associated with Fauconnier (1985, 1997) which attempts to show how indexicality, presupposition, and implicature are constructed in a cognitive environment or *mental space*.

Metalanguage   The self-reflexive use of language to comment on or gloss instances of language use. Hence *metapragmatic* uses of language gloss the pragmatic function of (parts of) an utterance and *metasequential* uses of language gloss the conversational function of (parts of) a talk sequence.

Metapragmatics   The study of forms such as discourse markers and of the indexical properties of utterances in general which guide the hearer in the recovery of pragmatic meaning.

Metarepresentation   (The ability to construct) a mental representation of how something seems to someone else, including their beliefs and intentions.

Metonymy   The representation of an entity by one of its sub-parts, properties or attributes, as in the mention of a felicity condition as a way of accomplishing an indirect speech act.

Modality   The grammatical category traditionally associated with forms such as *likely, may* and other expressions of ability, necessity, obligation, permission, prohibition, and possibility, all of which convey propositions whose truth value is related to possible worlds. Modal forms may appear to reflect a world independent of the speaker or may reflect the speaker's perspective (*epistemic** meaning). More broadly, the notion of modality includes *hedges** and other expressions of speaker commitment as well as *evidentials.**

Modularity   The hypothesis that the mind is compartmentalized, with specific functions, such as language processing, performed by dedicated modules.

Occam's razor   The preference for a parsimonious explanation (after the fourteenth century philosopher William of Ockham).

Optimality   The highest level of match between a form and a representation such as a meaning, or between a representation and a form.

Ostension   Any means, verbal or non-verbal, of making manifest the intention to communicate.

Performative   The use of language to accomplish action. Commonly associated with speech acts (see, e.g., Austin 1962).

(Im)Politeness   The degree to which an utterance satisfies the *face-wants** of others. Brown and Levinson's proposal, in which politeness phenomena are seen as redressive and computed as a function of speaker-hearer power-distance differentials and degrees of imposition, is probably the best known example of a 'second order', i.e. theoretically focused, model. In contrast, 'first order', i.e. participant-focused approaches, argue that to be deemed to be im/polite, behaviour must go beyond what is expected by the participants, given the situation, and/or what is seen to be appropriate within a given interaction.

Polysemy The property of having related meanings which arise by a range of processes including narrowing and broadening of a principal meaning.

Pragmalinguistics A term coined by Leech (1983) to capture a user's knowledge of appropriate pragmatic forms; distinguished from *socio-pragmatics*, also coined by Leech (now usually sociopragmatics), to describe a user's knowledge of the contexts in which it's appropriate to use particular forms. Leech equates pragmalinguistics with 'general' pragmatics and sociopragmatics with culture-specific pragmatics.

Pragmatics The study of language used in contextualized communication and the usage principles associated with it.

Presupposition A meaning taken as given which does not need to be asserted. Competing theories discuss presupposition as semantic (*non-defeasible** and contributing to the truth-conditional meaning of the sentence in which it occurs), as conventional implicature (non-defeasible and non-truth-conditional) and as pragmatic (cancellable when inconsistent with speaker/hearer knowledge of the world).

Principle A term, weaker than *rule*, intended to capture the reasons for our motivation to speak or act in predictable, cooperative ways.

Projection The inheritance by a complex sentence of the property of one of the component sentences embedded within it, as, for example, in the case of *presupposition projection*.

Proposition A (typically linguistic) representation of a state of affairs about which an opinion or belief (a propositional attitude) can be expressed.

Prosody The supra-segmental phonetic features of a unit of language.

Prototype A best example, as distinct from *stereotype*, or typical example (often with negative connotations). Prototype theory holds that we recognize category members by the extent to which they are good examples rather than by the extent to which they exhibit putative criterial features.

Recursion The ability of a feature to contain a copy of itself, such as the ability of a sentence to contain another embedded sentence. Identified by Chomsky (1957, 1965) as one of the defining properties of human language and taken as the motivation for generative syntax.

Reference Most descriptions are used to *refer to* or pick out persons, objects or notions that exist in some real or imagined world. The function of picking out an object in the world by means of a linguistic description is called *referring,* and the entity picked out by this act of *reference* is called a *referent*.

Reflexivity The tendency of language to refer to its own function, speech act descriptions being particularly obvious examples of this phenomenon.

Register A linguistic repertoire associated with recognizable cultural practice.

Relational work The interpersonal work people undertake when interacting in order to maintain/enhance affinity, formality, etc. or to signal indifference, annoyance, etc.

Relevance Relevance theory holds that every utterance comes with a guarantee of its own relevance. The degree of relevance is measured by the extent to which a salient meaning is readily recovered.

Repair The term used in conversation analysis to describe the immediate correction or adjustment by the speaker or the addressee of some part of what was said.

The semantics/pragmatics interface A way of referring to the much disputed boundary between semantic and pragmatic meaning.

Sentence/speaker meaning   Terms used to capture the difference between invariant semantic meaning (sentence meaning) and occasion-specific pragmatic meaning (speaker meaning).

Sign   A form, such as a word, to which a meaning can be attached. According to Peirce, the relationship between the form and the meaning may be *iconic** (i.e. mimetic), *indexical** (interpretable in the context in which it occurs), or *symbolic* (conventional but arbitrary, thus accounting for the different terms used in different languages to refer to the same entity).

Sociopragmatics   See *Pragmalinguistics*.

Speaker attitude   The encoding of speaker perspective is also referred to as *propositional** attitude.

Speech act   The performative, or action accomplishing, aspect of language use, and particularly the (illocutionary) force associated with an utterance.

Speech event   See *Activity type*.

Structuralism   An approach in which two or more items in an internal structure are defined in relation to each other by noting the distinctive features they do not share.

Subjectification   The process by which a form that once conveyed an objective meaning comes to convey a meaning that also encodes the speaker's attitudes or beliefs. Subjectification is sometimes argued to be a motivating factor in language change.

Talk-in-interaction   A term used in *Conversation Analysis** to draw attention to the underlying principle of *turn-taking** in conversation.

Truth value   When considered as descriptions of states of affairs that exist or that might come about in some world, sentences can be judged to be true or false, and thus have a *truth-value*. Truth-conditional semantics is based on the view that if we know the conditions that must exist in the world for a sentence to be true, then we know its meaning. A central question in Gricean and post-Gricean pragmatics is how to deal with the inferences that frequently arise from the use of sentences linked by operators such as *and, if* and *or*, which are treated as truth-functional in studies of formal language.

Turn-taking   *Conversation analysis** identifies *turns* (turn-constructional units) as the principal unit in *talk-in-interaction** and studies the properties of conversational sequences (adjacency pairs, anticipation, next turn proof procedures, *repair,** etc.) and how transitions between speakers and topics occur.

Underdetermination   It's widely agreed that the semantic value of linguistic forms is underspecified, i.e. *underdetermines* the meaning the speaker seeks to convey, and so needs to be enriched or strengthened in ways particular to the contexts in which they occur.

Utterance   A sentence used by a speaker for some purpose. Thus 'I'm Maxine' is both a sentence (it has a determinate grammar) and an utterance (Maxine uses it to introduce herself).

Variation   Differences in the way language is used which can be related to aspects of social context such as age, class, gender, culture, occasion, occupation, etc. Items are said to be in *free variation* when no relation appears to exist between their use and social context. Variation may occur at phonetic, semantic, pragmatic or syntactic levels and be synchronic or, in the case of historical language change, diachronic.

References

Aarsleff, H. (1982) *From Locke to Saussure: essays on the study of language and intellectual history*, Minneapolis, Minnesota: University of Minnesota Press.

Abbott, B. (2004) 'Definiteness and indefiniteness', in L.R. Horn and G. Ward (eds) *The Handbook of Pragmatics*, pp. 122–50, Oxford: Blackwell.

Abrahams, R.D. (1962) 'Playing the dozens', *Journal of American Folklore* 75: 209–20.

Andersen, G. (1999) *Pragmatic Markers and Sociolinguistic Variation: a corpus-based study*, Ph.D. thesis, University of Bergen.

Anderson, L.B. (1986) 'Evidentials, paths of change, and mental maps: typologically regular asymmetries', in W. Chafe and J. Nichols (eds) *Evidentiality: the linguistic coding of epistemology*, pp. 273–312, Norwood, New Jersey: Ablex.

Anderson, S.R. and Keenan, E.L. (1985) 'Deixis', in T. Schopen (ed.) *Language Typology and Syntactic Description*, vol. 3 – grammatical categories and the lexicon, pp. 259–308, Cambridge: Cambridge University Press.

Anselmi, D., Tomasello, M. and Acunzo, M. (1986) 'Young children's responses to neutral and specific contingent queries', *Journal of Child Language* 13: 135–44.

Antaki, C. and Widdicombe, S. (eds) (1998) *Identities in Talk*, London: Sage.

Archer, D. (2005) *Questions and Answers in the English Courtroom (1640–1760)*, Pragmatics and Beyond New Series 135, Amsterdam and Philadelphia: John Benjamins.

——(2008) 'Verbal aggression and impoliteness: related or synonymous?', in D. Bousfield and M.A. Locher (eds) *Impoliteness in Language: studies on its interplay with power in theory and practice*, pp. 181–207, Berlin and New York: Mouton de Gruyter.

——(2010) 'The history of speech acts', in A.H. Jucker and I. Taavitsaineen (eds) *Historical Pragmatics*, pp. 379–418, Berlin and New York: Mouton de Gruyter.

Archer, D., Culpeper, J. and Davies, M. (2008) 'Pragmatic annotation', in A. Lüdeling and M. Kytö (eds) *Corpus Linguistics: an international handbook*, pp. 613–42, Berlin and New York: Mouton de Gruyter.

Ariel, M. (1994) 'Pragmatic operators', in R.E. Asher and I.M.Y. Simpson (eds) *The Encyclopedia of Language and Linguistics*, vol. 6, pp. 3250–3, Oxford: Pergamon Press.

Aristotle (384–322 BC) 'Nicomachean ethics', trans. J.A.K. Thompson (1969) *The Ethics of Aristotle: the nicomachean ethics translated*, Harmondsworth: Penguin.

Arnovick, L.K. (1995) 'Sounding and flyting the English agonistic insult: writing pragmatic history in a cross-cultural context', in M.J. Powell (ed.) *The Twenty-First LACUS Forum 1994*, pp. 600–19, Chapel Hill, North Carolina: The Linguistic Association of Canada and the United States.

——(1999) *Diachronic Pragmatics: seven case studies in English illocutionary development*, Pragmatics and Beyond New Series 68, Amsterdam and Philadelphia: John Benjamins.

Arundale, R.B. (1999) 'An alternative model and ideology of communication for an alternative to politeness theory', *Pragmatics* 9: 119–54.

——(2008) 'Against (Gricean) intentions at the heart of human interaction', *Intercultural Pragmatics* 5 (2): 231–56.

Astington, J., Harris, P. and Olson, D. (eds) (1988) *Developing Theories of Mind*, Cambridge: Cambridge University Press.

Atlas, J.D. (1989) *Philosophy Without Ambiguity: a logico–linguistic essay*, Oxford: Clarendon Press.

——(2004) 'Presupposition', in L.R. Horn and G. Ward (eds) *The Handbook of Pragmatics*, pp. 29–52, Oxford: Blackwell.

——(2005) *Logic, Meaning, and Conversation: semantical underdeterminacy, implicature, and their interface*, Oxford: Oxford University Press.

Atlas, J.D. and Levinson, S.C. (1973) *The Importance of Practical Reasoning in Language Usage: an explanation of conversational implicature*, unpublished MS, Department of Linguistics, University of Cambridge.

——(1981) 'It-clefts, informativeness and logical form', in P. Cole (ed.) *Radical Pragmatics*, pp. 1–61, New York: Academic Press.

Attardo, S. (1997) 'Locutionary and perlocutionary cooperation: the perlocutionary cooperative principle', *Journal of Pragmatics* 27: 753–79.

Auer, P. (1998) *Code-Switching in Conversation*, London: Routledge.

Austin, J.L. (1962) *How To Do Things With Words: the William James lectures delivered at Harvard University in 1955*, Oxford: Oxford University Press.

Austin, P. (1990) 'Politeness revisited: the dark side', in A. Bell and J. Holmes (eds) *New Zealand Ways of Speaking English*, pp. 277–93, Clevedon: Multilingual Matters.

Bach, K. (1982) 'Semantic nonspecificity and mixed quantifiers', *Linguistics and Philosophy* 4: 593–605.

——(1987) *Thought and Reference*, Oxford: Oxford University Press.

——(1994a) 'Conversational implicature', *Mind and Language* 9: 124–62.

——(1994b) 'Semantic slack: what is said and more', in S. Tsohatzidis (ed.) *Foundations of Speech Act Theory*, pp. 267–91, London: Routledge.

——(1995) 'Standardization vs. conventional?' *Journal of Memory and Language* 25: 181–96.

——(1997) 'The semantics–pragmatics distinction: what it is and why it matters', *Linguistische Berichte* 8: 33–50; reprinted in K. Turner (ed.) (1999) *The Semantics/Pragmatics Interface from Different Points of View*, pp. 65–84, Oxford: Elsevier.

——(1999) 'The myth of conventional implicature', *Linguistics and Philosophy* 22: 327–66.

——(2001) 'You don't say', *Synthese* 128: 15–44.

——(2004) 'Pragmatics and the philosophy of language', in L.R. Horn and G. Ward (eds) *The Handbook of Pragmatics*, pp. 463–87, Oxford: Blackwell.

——(2010) 'Impliciture vs. explicature: what's the difference?', in B. Soria and E. Romero (eds) *Explicit Communication: Robyn Carston's pragmatics*, Basingstoke: Palgrave.

Bach, K. and Harnish, R. (1979) *Linguistic Communication and Speech Acts*, Cambridge, Massachusetts: MIT Press.

Bacharach, V. and Luszcz, M. (1979) 'Communicative competence in young children: the use of implicit linguistic information', *Child Development* 50: 260–3.

Baldwin, D.A. (1991) 'Infants' contribution to the achievement of joint reference', *Child Development* 62(5): 874–90.

Ballmer, T.T. and Brennenstuhl, W. (1981) *Speech Act Classification: a study in the lexical analysis of English speech activity verbs*, Springer Series in Language and Communication, vol. 8, Berlin, Heidelberg and New York: Springer Verlag.

Bargiela-Chiappini, F. (2003) 'Face and politeness: new (insights) for old (concepts)', *Journal of Pragmatics* 35 (10–11): 1453–69.

Bar-Hillel, Y. (1971) 'Out of the pragmatic wastebasket', *Linguistic Inquiry* 2: 401–7.

Bar-Hillel, Y. and Carnap, R. (1952) 'An outline of a theory of semantic information', *MIT Technical Report* 247; reprinted in Y. Bar-Hillel (1964) *Language and Information*, pp. 221–74, Reading, Massachusetts: Addison-Wesley.

Baron-Cohen, S. (1991) 'Precursors to a theory of mind: understanding attention in others', in A. Whiten (ed.) *Natural Theories of Mind: evolution, development and simulation of everyday mindreading*, pp. 233–51, Oxford: Blackwell.

——(1995) *Mind-Blindness: an essay on autism and theory of mind*, Cambridge, Massachusetts: MIT Press.

Baron-Cohen, S., O'Riordan, M., Stone, V., Jones, R. and Plaisted, K. (1999) 'Recognition of faux pas by normally developing children and children with Asperger Syndrome or high-functioning autism', *Journal of Autism and Developmental Disorders* 29: 407–18.

Barr, D.J. and Keysar, B. (2005) 'Making sense of how we make sense: the paradox of egocentrism in language use', in H.L. Colston and A.N. Katz (eds) *Figurative Language Comprehension*, pp. 21–43, Mahwah, New Jersey: Lawrence Erlbaum.

Barron, A. (2001) *Acquisition in Interlanguage Pragmatics: learning how to do things with words in a study abroad context*, Amsterdam and Philadelphia: John Benjamins.

Barsalou, L. (1987) 'The instability of graded structure: implications for the nature of concepts', in U. Neisser (ed.) *Concepts and Conceptual Development: ecological and intellectual factors in categorization*, pp. 101–40, Cambridge: Cambridge University Press.

Bartsch, R. (1987) 'Context-dependent interpretations of lexical items', in R. Bartsch, J. van Benthem and P. van Emde-Bartsch Boas (eds) *Semantics and Contextual Expressions*, Dordrecht: Foris.

——(2002) 'Lexical semantics and pragmatics', *Linguistic Berichte* 10: 27–58.

Barwise J. and Perry, J. (1983) *Situations and Attitudes*, Cambridge, Massachusetts: MIT Press.

Basso, A. (2003) *Aphasia and Its Therapy*, New York: Oxford University Press.

Bates, E. (1974) 'The acquisition of pragmatic competence', *Journal of Child Language* 1 (2): 277–82.

——(1976) *Language and Context: studies in the acquisition of pragmatics*, New York: Academic Press.

Bates, E., Camaioni, L. and Volterra, V. (1975) 'The acquisition of performatives prior to speech', *Merrill-Palmer Quarterly* 21: 205–26.

Bateson, M.C. (1975) 'Mother–infant exchanges: the epigenesis of conversational interaction', in D. Aaronson and R.W. Rieber (eds) *Developmental Psycholinguistics and Communication Disorders*, New York: New York Academy of Sciences.

Bauman, R. and Briggs, C.L. (1997) *Authorizing Discourse: the creation of power in scholarly and popular discourse*, MS in possession of authors.

Bax, M. (1981) 'Rules for ritual challenges: a speech convention among medieval knights', *Journal of Pragmatics* 5: 423–44.

——(1991) 'Historische Pragmatik: eine Herausforderung für die Zukunft. Diachrone Untersuchungen zu pragmatischen Aspekten ritueller Herausforderungen in Texten mittelalterlicher Literatur', in D. Busse (ed.) *Diachrone Semantik und Pragmatik*, pp. 197–215, Tübingen: Niemeyer.

——(1999) 'Ritual levelling: the balance between the eristic and the contractual motive in hostile verbal encounters in Medieval romance and Early Modern drama', in A.H. Jucker, G. Fritz and F. Lebsanft (eds) *Historical Dialogue Analysis*, pp. 35–80, Amsterdam: John Benjamins.

Bayles, K.A. (1985) 'Communication in dementia', in H. Ulatowska (ed.) *The Aging Brain*, pp. 157–73, San Diego, California: College-Hill Press.

Bayles, K.A. and Kaszniak, A. (1987) *Communication and Cognition in Normal Aging and Dementia*, Boston, Massachusetts: Little, Brown and Company.

Beattie, G. (1982) 'Turn-taking and interruption in political interviews: Margaret Thatcher and Jim Callaghan compared and contrasted', *Semiotica* 39 (1/2): 93–113.

Beck, B.E.F. (1972) *Peasant Society in Konku*, Vancouver: University of British Columbia Press.

Beebe, L. and Takahashi, T. (1989a) 'Do you have a bag? Social status and patterned variation in second language acquisition', in S. Gass, C. Madden, D. Preston and L. Selinker (eds) *Variation in Second Language Acquisition*, pp. 103–25, Clevedon, Avon: Multilingual Matters.

——(1989b) 'Sociolinguistic variation in face-threatening speech acts: chastisement and disagreement', in M. Eisenstein (ed.) *The Dynamic Interlanguage: empirical studies in second language variation*, pp. 199–218, New York: Plenum Press.

Benoit, P. (1982) 'Formal coherence production in children's discourse', *First Language* 3: 161–80.

Benveniste, É. (1971) 'Subjectivity in language', in M.E. Meek (trans.) *Problems in General Linguistics*, pp. 223–30, Coral Gables, Florida: University of Miami Press.

Besnier, N. (1993) 'Reported speech and affect on Nukulaelae Atoll', in J. Hill and J. Irvine (eds) *Responsibility and Evidence in Oral Discourse*, pp. 161–81, Cambridge: Cambridge University Press.

Bezuidenhout, A.L. (2010) 'Experimental pragmatics', in L. Cummings (ed.) *The Pragmatics Encyclopedia*, pp. 148–53, London and New York: Routledge.

Bezuidenhout, A.L. and Sroda, M.S. (1998) 'Children's use of contextual cues to resolve referential ambiguity: an application of relevance theory', *Pragmatics and Cognition* 6: 265–99.

Biber, D. and Finegan, E. (1989) 'Adverbial stance types in English', *Discourse Processes* 11: 1–34.

Bierwisch, M. (1983) 'Semantische Einheiten und konzeptuelle Repräsentation lexikalischer Einheiten', in W. Motsch and R. Ruzicka (eds) *Untersuchungen zur Semantik*, pp. 61–99, Berlin: Akademie-Verlag.

Bilmes, J. (1997) 'Being interrupted', *Language in Society* 26: 507–31.

Billmyer, K. (1990a) *The Effect of Formal Instruction on the Development of Sociolinguistic Competence: the performance of compliments*, unpublished Ph.D. thesis, Philadelphia: University of Pennsylvania.

——(1990b) '"I really like your lifestyle": ESL learners learning how to compliment', *Penn Working Papers in Educational Linguistics* 6: 31–48.

Bishop, D.V.M. (2003) *The Children's Communication Checklist, Version 2 (CCC-2)*, London: Psychological Corporation.

Bishop, D.V.M. and Rosenbloom, L. (1987) 'Classification of childhood language disorders', in W. Yule and M. Rutter (eds) *Language Development and Disorders*, London: Mac Keith Press.

Blakar, R.M. (1985) 'Towards a theory of communication in terms of preconditions', in H. Giles and R.N. Clair (eds) *Recent Advances in Language Communication, and Social Psychology*, pp. 10–40, Hillsdale, New Jersey: Lawrence Erlbaum.

Blakemore, D. (1987) *Semantic Constraints on Relevance*, Oxford: Blackwell.

——(1988) '*So* as a constraint on relevance', in R. Kempson (ed.) *Mental Representations: the interface between language and reality*, pp. 183–95, Cambridge: Cambridge University Press.

——(1990) 'Performatives and parentheticals', *Proceedings of the Aristotelian Society*, New Series, Vol. 91, (1990–1), 197–213.

——(1991) 'Performatives and parentheticals', *Proceedings of the Aristotelian Society* 91: 197–214.

——(1992) *Understanding Utterances*, Oxford: Blackwell.

——(1995) 'Relevance theory', in J. Verschueren, J.-O. Östman and J. Blommaert (eds) *Handbook of Pragmatics*, pp. 442–53, Amsterdam: John Benjamins.

——(2002) *Relevance and Linguistic Meaning: the semantics and pragmatics of discourse markers*, Cambridge: Cambridge University Press.

——(2004) 'Discourse markers', in L.R. Horn and G. Ward (eds) *The Handbook of Pragmatics*, pp. 221–40, Oxford: Blackwell.

——(2007a) 'Constraints, concepts and procedural encoding', in N. Burton-Roberts (ed.) *Pragmatics*, pp. 45–66, Basingstoke: Palgrave.

——(2007b) '"Or"-parentheticals, "that is"-parentheticals and the pragmatics of reformulation', *Journal of Linguistics* 43: 311–33.

——(2008) 'Apposition and affective communication', *Language and Literature* 17 (1): 37–57.

——(2009) 'Parentheticals and point of view in free indirect style', *Language and Literature* 18 (2): 129–53.

Blank, A. (1997) *Prinzipien des lexikalischen Bedeutungswandels am Beispiel der romanischen Sprachen*, Tübingen: Niemeyer.

Blank, M. and Franklin, M. (1980) 'Dialogue with preschoolers: a cognitively-based system of assessment', *Applied Psycholinguistics* 1: 127–50.

Blass, R. (1990) *Relevance Relations in Sissala*, Cambridge: Cambridge University Press.

Blaye, A., Ackermann, E. and Light, P. (1999) 'The relevance of relevance in children's cognition', in J. Bliss, P. Light and R. Saljo (eds) *Social and Technological Resources for Learning*, pp. 120–32, Oxford: Elsevier.

Blommaert, J. (1999a) 'Investigating narrative inequality: "home narratives" of African asylum seekers in Belgium', *Working Papers on Language, power and identity* 1, available online at: http://bank.rug.ac.be/lpi/.

——(ed.) (1999b) *Language Ideological Debates*, Berlin: Mouton de Gruyter.

Blommaert, J. and Verschueren, J. (1998) *Debating Diversity: analysing the discourse of tolerance*, London: Routledge.

Bloom, L., Rocissano, L. and Hood, L. (1976) 'Adult–child discourse: developmental interaction between information processing and linguistic knowledge', *Cognitive Psychology* 8: 521–52.

Blum-Kulka, S. (1982) 'Learning how to say what you mean in a second language: a study of the speech act performance of learners of Hebrew as a second language', *Applied Linguistics* 3: 29–59.

——(1987) 'Indirectness and politeness in requests: same or different?', *Journal of Pragmatics* 11: 145–60.

——(1997) *Dinner Talk: cultural patterns of sociability and socialization in family discourse*, Mahwah, New Jersey: Lawrence Erlbaum.

Blum-Kulka, S. and Snow, C.E. (1992) 'Developing autonomy for tellers, tales, and telling in family narrative events', *Journal of Narrative and Life History* 2 (3): 187–217.

Blum-Kulka, S. and Weizman, E. (1988) 'The inevitability of misunderstandings: discourse ambiguities', *Text* 8: 219–41.

Blum-Kulka S., House, J. and Kasper, G. (eds) (1989) *Cross-cultural Pragmatics: requests and apologies*, Norwood, New Jersey: Ablex.

Blum-Kulka, S., Blondheim, M., House, J., Kasper, G. and Wagner, J. (2008) 'Intercultural pragmatics, language and society', in P. van Sterkenburg (ed.) *Unity and Diversity of Languages*, pp. 155–73, Amsterdam and Philadephia: John Benjamins.

Blutner, R. (1998) 'Lexical pragmatics', *Journal of Semantics* 15: 115–62.

——(2000) 'Some aspects of optimality in natural language interpretation', *Journal of Semantics* 17: 189–216.

——(2004) 'Pragmatics and the lexicon', in L.R. Horn and G. Ward (eds) *Handbook of Pragmatics*, Oxford: Blackwell.

——(2006) 'Embedded implicatures and optimality theoretic pragmatics', in T. Solstad, A. Grønn and D. Haug (eds) *A Festschrift for Kjell Johan Sæbø: in partial fulfilment of the requirements for the celebration of his 50th birthday*, Oslo.

——(2007a) 'Optimality theoretic pragmatics and the explicature/implicature distinction', in N. Burton-Roberts (ed.) *Pragmatics*, pp. 67–89, Basingstoke: Palgrave.

——(2007b) 'Some experimental aspects of optimality-theoretic pragmatics', Amsterdam: University of Amsterdam.

——(2009) 'Concepts and bounded rationality: an application of Niestegge's approach to conditional quantum probabilities', in L. Accardi, G. Adenier, C. Fuchs, G. Jaeger, A.Y. Khrennikov, J.-Å. Larsson and S. Stenholm (eds) *Foundations of Probability and Physics* 5, vol. 1101, pp. 302–10, New York: American Institute of Physics Conference Proceedings.

Blutner, R. and Solstad, T. (2000) 'Dimensional designation: a case study in lexical pragmatics', in R. Blutner and G. Jäger (eds) *Studies in Optimality Theory*, pp. 30–40, Potsdam: University of Potsdam.

Blutner, R. and Zeevat, H. (eds) (2004) *Optimality Theory and Pragmatics*, Houndmills, Basingstoke: Macmillan.

Blutner, R., Hendriks, P. and de Hoop, H. (2003) 'A new hypothesis on compositionality', in P.P. Slezak (ed.) *Proceedings of the Joint International Conference on Cognitive Science*, Sydney: ICCS/ASCS.

Blutner, R., de Hoop, H. and Hendriks, P. (2005) *Optimal Communication*, Stanford, California: CSLI Publications.

Blyth, C. Recktenwald, S. and Wang, J. (1990) '"I'm like, 'Say what?!'" A new quotative in American oral narrative', *American Speech* 65: 215–27.

Boase-Beier, J. (2004a) 'Knowing and not knowing: style, intention and the translation of a Holocaust poem', *Language and Literature* 13 (1): 25–35.

——(2004b) 'Saying what someone else meant: style, relevance and translation', *International Journal of Applied Linguistics* 14 (2): 276–87.

Bobrow, D.G. and Norman, D.A. (1975) 'Some principles of memory schemata', in D.G. Bobrow and A. Collins (eds) *Representation and Understanding*, pp. 131–49, New York: Academic Press.

Boër, S.E. and Lycan, W.G. (1976) *The Myth of Semantic Presupposition*, Bloomington, Indiana: Indiana Linguistics Club.

Boersma, P. and Weenik, D. (2004) *Praat: doing phonetics by computer*, available online at: www.praat.org.

Bohnemeyer, J. (1998) 'Temporal reference from a radical pragmatics perspective: why Yucatec does not need to express "after" or "before"', *Cognitive Linguistics*: 239–82.

Bolinger, D.L. (1961) 'Contrastive accent and contrastive stress', *Language* 37 (1): 83–96.

Bonnefon, J.-F., Feeney, A. and Villejoubert, G. (2009) 'When some is actually all: scalar inferences in face-threatening contexts', *Cognition* 112: 249–58.

Borg, E. (2004) *Minimal Semantics*, Oxford: Oxford University Press.

——(2007) 'Minimalism versus contextualism in semantics', in G. Preyer and G. Peter (eds) *Context-Sensitivity and Semantic Minimalism*, pp. 339–59, Oxford: Oxford University Press.

Bosch, P. (1995) 'Meanings and contextual concepts', in M. Bierwisch and P. Bosch (eds) *Semantic and Conceptual Knowledge: Arbeitspapiere des Sonderforschungsbereichs 340*, Bd. 71, pp. 79–99, Stuttgart and Tübingen: Universität Tübingen.

——(2009) 'Predicate indexicality and context dependence', in P. de Brabanter and M. Kissine (eds) *Utterance Interpretation and Cognitive Models: current research in the semantics/pragmatics interface*, vol. 20, Bingley: Emerald Group Publishing.

Bott, L. and Noveck, I.A. (2004) 'Some utterances are underInformative: the onset and time course of scalar inferences', *Journal of Memory and Language* 51 (3): 437–57.

Bourdieu, P. (1984) *Homo Academicus*, trans. P. Collier (1988), Stanford, California: Stanford University Press.

——(1990) *The Logic of Practice*, Cambridge: Polity Press.

Bousfield, D. (2007a) 'Impoliteness, preference organization and conducivity', *Multilingua* 26 (1/2): 1–33.

——(2007b) 'Beginnings, middles and ends: a biopsy of the dynamics of impolite exchanges', *Journal of Pragmatics* 39 (12): 2185–216.

Bousfield, D. and Locher, M.A. (eds) (2008) *Impoliteness in Language: studies on its interplay with power in theory and practice*, Berlin and New York: Mouton de Gruyter.

——(2008) *Impoliteness in Interaction*, Amsterdam and Philadelphia: John Benjamins.

Bouton, L. (1994) 'Can NNS skill in interpreting implicatures in American English be improved through explicit instruction? A pilot study', in L. Bouton and Y. Kachru (eds) *Pragmatics and Language Learning*, monograph series vol. 5, pp. 88–109, Urbana-Champaign: Division of English as an International Language, Urbana-Champaign, Illinois: University of Illinois.

Boxer, D. (2002) 'Discourse issues in cross-cultural pragmatics', *Annual Review of Applied Linguistics* (22): 150–67.

Breheny, R. (2006) 'Communication and folk psychology', *Mind and Language* 21 (1): 74–107.

Breheny, R., Katsos, N. and Williams, J. (2006) 'Are generalised scalar implicatures generated by default? An online investigation into the role of context in generating pragmatic inferences', *Cognition* 100: 434–63.

Briggs, C.L. (1993) 'Generic versus metapragmatic dimensions of Warao narratives: who regiments performance?', in J.A. Lucy (ed.) *Reflexive Language: reported speech and metapragmatics*, pp. 179–212, Cambridge: Cambridge University Press.

——(ed.) (1996) *Disorderly Discourse: narrative, conflict, and inequality*, New York: Oxford University Press.

——(1997) 'From the ideal, the ordinary, and the orderly to conflict and violence in pragmatic research', *Pragmatics* 7 (4): 451–9.

Brinton, L.J. (1988) *The Development of English Aspectual Systems*, Cambridge: Cambridge University Press.

——(1996) *Pragmatic Markers in English*, Berlin and New York: Mouton de Gruyter.

——(2001) 'Historical discourse analysis', in D. Schiffrin, D. Tannen and H.E. Hamilton (eds) *The Handbook of Discourse Analysis*, pp. 138–60, Oxford: Blackwell.

——(2006) 'Pathways in the development of pragmatic markers in English', in A. van Kemenade and B. Los (eds) *The Handbook of the History of English*, pp. 307–34, London: Blackwell.

Bronner, S.J. (1996) '"Your mother's like. . ." Formula in contemporary American ritual insults', in R. Aman (ed.) *Opus Maledictorum: a book of bad words*, pp. 166–77, New York: Marlowe & Company.

Bronson, B.H. (1940) 'Chaucer's art in relation to his audience', in *Five Studies in Literature*, University of California Publications in English 8, pp. 1–53, Berkeley, California: University of California.

Brown, G. (1977) *Listening to Spoken English*, London: Longman.

Brown, P. and Levinson, S.C. (1978) 'Universals in language usage: politeness phenomena', in E.N. Goody (ed.) *Questions and Politeness*, pp. 56–311, Cambridge: Cambridge University Press.

——(1987) *Politeness: some universals in language usage*, Cambridge: Cambridge University Press.

Brown, R. and Gilman, A. (1960) 'The pronouns of power and solidarity', in T.A. Sebeok (ed.) *Style in Language*, pp. 253–76, Cambridge, Massachusetts: MIT Press.

Bryan, T., Donahue, M., Pearl, R. and Sturm, C. (1981) 'Learning disabled children's conversational skills: the "TV talk show"', *Learning Disability Quarterly* 4: 250–9.

Bublitz, W. and Lenk, U. (1999) 'Disturbed coherence: "fill me in"', in W. Bublitz, U. Lenk and E. Ventola (eds) *Coherence in Spoken and Written Discourse*, pp. 153–75, Amsterdam and Philadephia: John Benjamins.

Bühler, K. (1934a) '*Sprachtheorie*', trans. D.F. Goodwin (1990) *The Theory of Language: the representational function of language*, Amsterdam: John Benjamins.

——(1934b) 'The deictic field of language and deictic words', reprinted in R.J. Jarvella and W. Klein (eds) (1982) *Speech, Place, and Action: studies in deixis and related topics*, pp. 9–30, Chichester: John Wiley & Sons.

Burns, T. (1953) 'Friends, enemies, and the polite fiction', *American Sociological Review* 18: 654–62.

Bursey, J. and Furlong, A. (2006) 'Cognitive gothic: relevance theory, iteration and style', in J. Tabbi and R. Shavers (eds) *Paper Empire: William Gaddis and the world system*, pp. 118–33, Tuscaloosa, Alabama: University of Alabama Press.

Butler, K. (1995) 'Content, context and compositionality', *Mind and Language* 10: 3–24.

Bybee, J., Perkins, R. and Pagliuca, W. (1994) *The Evolution of Grammar: tense, aspect, and modality in the languages of the world*, Chicago, Illinois: University of Chicago Press.

Calvo, C. (1992) 'Pronouns of address and social negotiation in *As You Like It*', *Language and Literature* 1: 5–27.

Campbell-Taylor, I. (1984) *Dimensions of Clinical Judgment in the Diagnosis of Alzheimer's Disease*, unpublished Ph.D. thesis, Buffalo, New York: State University of New York.

Cappelen, H. and Lepore, E. (2005a) *Insensitive Semantics*, Oxford: Blackwell.

——(2005b) 'Relevance theory and shared content', in N. Burton-Roberts (ed.) *Pragmatics*, pp. 115–35, Dasingstoke: Palgrave

Caramazza, A. and Grober, E. (1976) 'Polysemy and the structure of the subjective lexicon', in C. Rameh (ed.) *Semantics: theory and application*, pp. 181–206, Georgetown University Round Table on Language and Linguistics, Washington, District of Columbia: Georgetown University Press.

Carlson, G. (2004) 'Reference', in L.R. Horn and G. Ward (eds) *The Handbook of Pragmatics*, pp. 74–96, Oxford: Blackwell.

Carlson, L. (1984) '*Well*' in Dialogue Games: *a discourse analysis of the interjection 'well' in idealized conversation*, Amsterdam and Philadelphia: John Benjamins.

Carnap, R. (1937) *Logical Syntax of Language*, London: Routledge & Kegan Paul.

Carpendale, J.I. and Chandler, M.J. (1996) 'On the distinction between false belief understanding and subscribing to an interpretative theory of mind', *Child Development* 67: 1686–706.

Carroll, J.B. (ed.) (1956) *Language, Thought, and Reality*: *selected writings of Benjamin Lee Whorf*, Cambridge, Massachusetts: MIT Press.

Carruthers, P. and Smith, P.K. (eds) (1996) *Theories of Theories of Mind*, Cambridge: Cambridge University Press.

Carston, R. (1988a) 'Language and cognition', in F. Newmeyer (ed.) *Linguistics*, vol. 3, pp. 38–68, Cambridge: Cambridge University Press.

——(1988b) 'Implicature, explicature and truth-theoretic semantics', in R. Kempson (ed.) *Mental Representations*: *the interface between language and reality*, pp. 155–81, Cambridge: Cambridge University Press; reprinted in S. Davis (ed.) (1991) *Pragmatics*: *a reader*, pp. 33–51, Oxford: Oxford University Press; and also in A. Kasher (ed.) (1998) *Pragmatics*: *critical concepts*, vol. 4, pp. 436–64, London and New York: Routledge.

——(1993) 'Conjunction, explanation and relevance', *Lingua* 90 (2): 27–48.

——(1995) 'Quantity maxims and generalised implicature', *Lingua* 96: 213–44.

——(1996) 'Enrichment and loosening: complementary processes in deriving the proposition expressed?', *Linguistiche Berichte* 8: 103–27.

——(1998) *Pragmatics and the Explicit–Implicit Distinction*, Ph.D. thesis, University of London. (Revised version published as Carston 2002a.)

——(2002a) *Thoughts and Utterances*: *the pragmatics of explicit communication*, Oxford: Blackwell.

——(2002b) 'Metaphor, ad hoc concepts and word meaning: more questions than answers', *UCL Working Papers in Linguistics* 14: 83–105.

——(2004) 'Explicature and semantics', in S. Davis and B. Gillon (eds) *Semantics*: *a reader*, pp. 1–44, Oxford: Oxford University Press.

——(2006) 'How many pragmatic systems are there?', in M.-J. Frapolli (ed.) *Saying, Meaning, Referring*: *essays on the philosophy of Francois Recanati*, London: Palgrave.

——(2008) 'Linguistic communication and the semantics–pragmatics distinction', *Synthese* 165 (3): 321–45.

——(2009a) 'The explicit/implicit distinction in pragmatics and the limits of explicit communication', *International Review of Pragmatics* 1 (1): 35–62.

——(2009b) 'Relevance theory: contextualism or pragmaticism?', *UCL Working Papers in Linguistics* 21: 19–26.

——(2010) 'Explicit communication and "free" pragmatic enrichment', in B. Soria and E. Romero (eds) *Explicit Communication*: *Robyn Carston's pragmatics*, Basingstoke: Palgrave.

Carston, R. and Powell, G. (2006) 'Relevance theory: new directions and developments', in E. Lepore and B. Smith (eds) *Oxford Handbook of Philosophy of Language*, pp. 341–60, Oxford: Oxford University Press.

Caton, S. (1990) 'Speech styles, status, and speaker awareness', *Semiotica* 80 (1/2): 153–60.

——(1993) 'The importance of reflexive language in George H. Mead's theory of self and communication', in J.A. Lucy (ed.) *Reflexive Language*: *reported speech and metapragmatics*, pp. 315–37, Cambridge: Cambridge University Press.

Chafe, W. (1986) 'Evidentiality in English conversation and academic writing', in W. Chafe and J. Nichols (eds) *Evidentiality*: *the linguistic coding of epistemology*, pp. 261–72, Norwood, New Jersey: Ablex.

Chapman, S. (2005) *Paul Grice, Philosopher and Linguist*, Basingstoke: Macmillan.

Chapple, E.D. (1940) 'Measuring human relations: an introduction to the study of the interaction of individuals', *Genetic Psychology Monographs* 22: 3–147.

Chomsky, N. (1957) *Syntactic Structures*, Den Haag: Mouton.

——(1965) *Aspects of the Theory of Syntax*, Cambridge, Massachusetts: MIT Press.

——(1971) 'Deep structure, surface structure, and semantic interpretation', in D.D. Steinberg and L.A. Jakobovitz (eds) *Semantics*: *an interdisciplinary reader in philosophy, linguistics and psychology*, pp. 183–216, Cambridge: Cambridge University Press.

Chomsky, N. and Halle, M. (1968) *The Sound Pattern of English*, New York: Harper & Row.

Christie, C. (2007) 'Relevance theory and politeness', *Journal of Politeness Research* 3: 269–94.

Chung, S. and Timberlake, A. (1985) 'Tense, aspect, and mood', in T. Shopen (ed.) *Language Typology and Syntactic Description*, vol. III – grammatical categories and the lexicon, pp. 202–58, Cambridge: Cambridge University Press.

Clancy, P. (1986) 'The acquisition of communicative style in Japanese', in B. Schieffelin and E. Ochs (eds) *Language Socialization Across Cultures*, Cambridge: Cambridge University Press.

Clark, B. (1991) *Relevance Theory and the Semantics of Non-Declaratives*, Ph.D. thesis, University College London.

——(1993) 'Relevance and pseudo-imperatives', *Linguistics and Philosophy* 16: 79–121.

——(1996) 'Stylistic analysis and relevance theory', *Language and Literature* 5 (3): 163–78.

——(2007) '"Blazing a trail": moving from natural to linguistic meaning in accounting for the tones of English', in R.A. Nilsen, N.A. Appiah Amfo and K. Borthen (eds) *Interpreting Utterances: pragmatics and its interfaces. Essays in honour of Thorstein Fretheim*, pp. 69–81, Oslo: Novus.

——(2009) 'Salient inferences: pragmatics and *The Inheritors*', *Language and Literature* 18 (2): 173–212.

——(2011) *Relevance Theory*, Cambridge: Cambridge University Press.

Clark, B. and Lindsey, G. (1990) 'Intonation, grammar and utterance interpretation: evidence from English exclamatory-inversions', *UCL Working Papers in Linguistics* 2: 32–51.

Clark, E.V. (1978) 'From gesture to word: on the natural history of deixis in language acquisition', in J. Bruner and A. Garton (eds) *Human Growth and Development: Wolfson College lectures 1976*, pp. 85–120, Oxford: Clarendon Press.

Clark, H.H. (1979) 'Responding to indirect speech acts', *Cognitive Pscyhology* 11: 430–77.

——(1996) *Using Language*, Cambridge: Cambridge University Press.

Clark, H.H. and Bangerter, A. (2004) 'Changing ideas about reference', in I.A. Noveck and D. Sperber (eds) *Experimental Pragmatics*, pp. 25–49, Basingstoke: Macmillan.

Clark, H.H. and Gerrig, R. (1984) 'On the pretense theory of irony', *Journal of Experimental Psychology – General* 113: 121–6.

Clark, H.H. and Haviland, J. (1977) 'Comprehension and the given–new contract', in R. Freedle (ed.) *Discourse Production and Comprehension*, pp. 1–40, Hillsdale, New Jersey: Lawrence Erlbaum.

Clark, H.H. and Lucy, P. (1975) 'Inferring what was meant from what was said', *Journal of Verbal Learning and Verbal Behavior* 14: 56–72.

Clayman, S. and Heritage, J. (2002) *The News Interview: journalists and public figures on the air*, Cambridge: Cambridge University Press.

Clément, R., Dornei, Z. and Noels, K. (1994) 'Motivation, self-confidence, and group cohesion in the foreign language classroom', *Language Learning* 44: 417–48.

Clements, W.A. and Perner, J. (1994) 'Implicit Understanding of belief', *Cognitive Development* 9: 377–95.

Clover, C.J. (1980) 'The Germanic context of the Unferð episode', *Speculum* 55 (3): 444–68.

Coates, J. (1983) *The Semantics of the Modal Auxiliaries*, London: Croom Helm.

——(1987) 'Epistemic modality and spoken discourse', *Transactions of the Philological Society*, pp. 110–31, Oxford: Blackwell.

——(1995) 'The negotiation of coherence in face-to-face interaction: some examples from the extreme bounds', in M.-A. Gernsbacher and T. Givón (eds) *Coherence in Spontaneous Text*, pp. 41–58, Amsterdam: John Benjamins.

Cole, P. and Morgan, J.L. (eds) (1975) *Speech Acts*, New York: Academic Press.

Collis, G. (1985) 'On the origins of turn-taking: alternation and meaning', in M. Barrett (ed.) *Children's Single Word Speech*, New York: John Wiley & Sons.

Colston, H.L. (2005) 'On sociocultural and nonliteral: a synopsis and a prophesy', in H.L. Colston and A.N. Katz (eds) *Figurative Language Comprehension: social and cultural influences*, pp. 1–20, Hillsdale, New Jersey: Lawrence Erlbaum.

Comrie, B. (1985) *Tense*, Cambridge: Cambridge University Press.

——(1989) *Aspect*, Cambridge: Cambridge University Press.

Cook, H.M. (1990) 'An indexical account of the Japanese sentence-final particle *no*', *Discourse Processes* 13 (4): 401–40.

——(1991) 'The Japanese sentence-final particle *yo* as a non-referential indexical', *Paper presented at the Second International Cognitive Linguistics Conference*, Santa Cruz: University of California.

——(1992) 'Meanings of non-referential indexes: a case study of Japanese sentence-final particle *ne*', *Text* 12: 507–39.

——(1999) 'Situational meaning of the Japanese social deixis: the mixed use of the *masu* and plain forms', *Journal of Linguistic Anthropology* 8: 1–24.

——(2001) 'Why can't learners of JFL distinguish polite from impolite speech styles?', in K.R. Rose and G. Kasper (eds) *Pragmatics in Language Teaching*, pp. 80–102, Cambridge: Cambridge University Press.

Cooke, J. (1968) *Pronominal Reference in Thai, Burmese and Vietnamese*, Berkeley, California: University of California Press.

Corsaro, W. (1979) '"We're friends, right?" Children's use of access rituals in a nursery school', *Language in Society* 8: 315–36.

Corum, C. (1975) 'A pragmatic analysis of parenthetic adjuncts', in R.E. Grossman, L.J. San and T.J. Vance (eds) *Papers from the Eleventh Regional Meeting of the Chicago Linguistic Society*, pp. 133–41, Chicago, Illinois: University of Chicago Press.

Couper-Kuhlen, E. (1996) 'The prosody of repetition: on quoting and mimicry', in E. Couper-Kuhlen and M. Selting (eds) *Prosody in Conversation*, pp. 366–405, Cambridge: Cambridge University Press.

Coupland, N., Coupland, J., Giles, H. and Henwood, K. (1988) 'Accommodating the elderly: invoking and extending a theory', *Language in Society* 17: 1–42.

Cresswell, M. (1973) *Logics and Languages*, London: Methuen.

Crystal, D. (1984) Linguistic Encounters with Language Handicap, Oxford: Blackwell.

Crystal, D. and Davy, D. (1975) *Advanced Conversational English*, London: Longman.

Csibra, G. (2010) 'Recognising communicative intentions in infancy', *Mind and Language* 25 (2): 141–68.

Culpeper, J. (1996) 'Towards an anatomy of impoliteness', *Journal of Pragmatics* 25: 349–67.

——(1998) '(Im)politeness in drama', in J. Culpeper, M. Short and P. Verdonk (eds) *Studying Drama: from text to context*, pp. 83–95, London: Routledge.

——(2005) 'Impoliteness and entertainment in the television quiz show *The Weakest Link*', *Journal of Politeness Research* 1 (1): 35–72.

——(2009) 'Historical sociopragmatics: an introduction', *Journal of Historical Pragmatics* 10 (2): 179–86.

——(2010a) 'Historical pragmatics', in L. Cummings (ed.) *The Pragmatics Encyclopedia*, pp. 188–92, London and New York: Routledge.

——(2010b) *Impoliteness: using language to cause offence*, Cambridge: Cambridge University Press.

Culpeper, J., Bousfield, D. and Wichmann, A. (2003) 'Impoliteness revisited: with special reference to dynamic and prosodic aspects', *Journal of Pragmatics* 35 (10–11): 1545–79.

Cummings, L. (2005) *Pragmatics: a multidisciplinary perspective*, Edinburgh: Edinburgh University Press.

——(2008) *Clinical Linguistics*, Edinburgh: Edinburgh University Press.

——(2009) *Clinical Pragmatics*, Cambridge: Cambridge University Press.

——(2010a) 'Clinical pragmatics', in L. Cummings (ed.) *The Pragmatics Encylopedia*, pp. 40–3, London and New York: Routledge.

——(2010b) *The Pragmatics Encyclopedia*, London: Routledge.

Currie, G. (2006) 'Why irony is pretence', in S. Nichols (ed.) *The Architecture of the Imagination*, pp. 111–33, Oxford: Oxford University Press.

——(2008) 'Echo et feintise: quelle est la difference et qui a raison?', *Philosophiques* 35: 13–23.

Cuzzort, R. and King, E. (1980) *20th Century Social Thought*, 3rd edition, New York: Holt, Rinehart & Winston.

Cysouw, M. (2001) *The Paradigmatic Structure of Person Marking*, Ph.D. thesis, University of Nijmegen.

Dale, H.E. (1941) *The Higher Civil Service of Great Britain*, Oxford: Oxford University Press.

Dalrymple, M., Kanazawa, M., Kim, Y., Mchombo, S. and Peters, S. (1998) 'Reciprocal expressions and the concept of reciprocity', *Linguistics and Philosophy* 21: 159–210.

Davies, M. and Stone, T. (eds) (1995a) *Mental Simulation: philosophical and psychological essays*, Oxford: Blackwell.

——(eds) (1995b) *Folk Psychology*, Oxford: Blackwell.

Davis, S. (ed.) (1991) *Pragmatics: a reader*, Oxford: Oxford University Press.

Deane, P. (1988) 'Polysemy and cognition', *Lingua* 75: 325–61.

de Brabanter, P. (2010) 'Uttering sentences made up of words and gestures', in B. Soria and E. Romero (eds) *Explicit Communication: Robyn Carston's pragmatics*, Basingstoke: Palgrave.

de Klerk, V. (2005) 'Procedural meanings of *well* in a corpus of Xhosa English', *Journal of Pragmatics* 37: 1183–205.

Denison, D. (1990) 'Auxiliary + impersonal in Old English', *Folia Linguistica Historica* 9: 139–66.

de Saussure, F. (1916) *A Course in General Linguistics*, in C. Bally and A. Schehaye (eds) (1959); trans. W. Baskin, New York: McGraw-Hill.

de Swart, H. (2004) 'Marking and interpretation of negation: a bi-directional OT approach', in R. Zanuttini, H. Campos, E. Herburger and P. Portner (eds) *Negation, Tense and Clausal Architecture*: *cross-linguistic investigations*, Washington, District of Columbia: Georgetown University Press.

De Villiers, J. (2010) 'Autism spectrum disorders', in L. Cummings (ed.) *The Pragmatics Encyclopedia*, pp. 31–2, London and New York: Routledge.

Dewart, H. and Summers, S. (1995) *The Pragmatics Profile of Early Communication Skills*, Windsor: NFER Nelson.

D'hondt, S. (1999) *Conversation Analysis and History*: *practical and discursive understanding in quarrels among Dar es Salaam Adolescents*, Ph.D. thesis, University of Antwerp.

Diessel, H. (1999) *Demonstratives: form, function and grammaticalization*, Amsterdam: John Benjamins.

Dixon, R.M.W. (1980) *The Languages of Australia*, Cambridge: Cambridge University Press.

Doherty, M.J. (2009) *Theory of Mind: how children understand others' thoughts and feelings*, London: Taylor & Francis.

Donahue, M. (1984) 'Learning disabled children's conversational competence: an attempt to activate the inactive listener', *Applied Psycholinguistics* 5 (1): 21–36.

Donahue, M., Pearl, R. and Bryan, T. (1980) 'Conversational competence in learning disabled children: responses to inadequate messages', *Applied Psycholinguistics* 1: 387–403.

——(1983) 'Communicative competence in learning disabled children', in K.D. Gadow and I. Bialer (eds) *Advances in Learning and Behavior Disabilities*, vol. 2, Greenwich, Connecticut: JAI Press.

Dore, J. (1975) 'Holophrases, speech acts and language universals', *Journal of Child Language* 2: 21–40.

——(1978) 'Conditions for the acquisition of speech acts', in I. Markova (ed.) *The Social Context of Language*, Chichester: John Wiley & Sons.

Dorval, B. and Eckerman, C.O. (1984) 'Developmental trends in the quality of conversation achieved by small groups of acquainted peers', *Monographs of the Society for Research in Child Development* 49, serial no. 206.

Duranti, A. (1994) *From Grammar to Politics: linguistic anthropology in a western Samoan village*, Berkeley, California: University of California Press.

——(1997) *Linguistic Anthropology*, Cambridge: Cambridge University Press.

Duranti, A. and Goodwin, C. (eds) (1992) *Rethinking Context*, Cambridge: Cambridge University Press.

Durkheim, E. (1895) *The Rules of Sociological Method*, New York: The Free Press.

——(1915) *The Elementary Forms of the Religious Life*, London.

Eckerman, C., Whatley, J. and McGehee, L. (1979) 'Approaching and contacting the object another manipulates: a social skill of the one-year-old', *Developmental Psychology* 15: 585–93.

Eckert, P. (2000) *Linguistic Variation as Social Practice*, Oxford: Blackwell.

Eckhardt, R. (2002) 'Semantic change in grammaticalization', in G. Katz, S. Reinhard and P. Reuter (eds) *Sinn & Bedeulung: Proceedings of the 6th Annual Meeting of the Gesellschaft für Semantik*, Osnabrück: University of Osnabrück, 53–67.

Eder, D. (1990) 'Serious and playful disputes: variation in conflict talk among female adolescents', in A.D. Grimshaw (ed.) *Conflict Talk*: *sociolinguistic investigations of arguments in conversations*, pp. 67–84, Cambridge: Cambridge University Press.

Edmondson, W.J. (1981) *Spoken Discourse*: *a model for analysis*, London: Longman.

Edmondson, W.J. and House, J. (1981) *Let's Talk and Talk About It*: *a pedagogic interactional grammar of English*, Munich: Urban & Schwarzenberg.

Edwards, V. and Sienkewicz, T.J. (1990) *Oral Cultures Past and Present*: *rappin' and Homer*, Oxford: Blackwell.

Eelen, G. (1999) *Ideology in Politeness*: *a critical analysis*, Ph.D. thesis, University of Antwerp.

——(2001) *A Critique of Politeness Theories*, Manchester: St Jerome Press.

Ehlich, K. (1992) 'On the historicity of politeness', in R.J. Watts, S. Ide and K. Ehlich (eds) *Politeness in Language*: *studies in its history, theory and practice*, pp. 71–107, Berlin: Mouton de Gruyter.

——(1993) 'HIAT: a transcription system for discourse data', in J.A. Edwards and M.D. Lampert (eds) *Talking Data*: *transcription and coding in discourse research*, pp. 123–48, Hillsdale, New Jersey: Lawrence Erlbaum Associates.

Eliot, T.S. (1943) *The Four Quartets*, New York: Harcourt Brace & Company.

Enç, M. (1901) *Tense without Scope*: *an analysis of nouns as indexicals*, Ph.D. thesis, Madison: University of Wisconsin.

Enfield, N.J. (2002) '"Lip-pointing" – a discussion with special reference to data from Laos', *Gesture* 1: 185–212.

Erickson, F. (1986) 'Listening and speaking', in D. Tannen (ed.) *Languages and Linguistics*: *the interdependence of theory, data and application GURT 1985*, pp. 294–319, Washington, District of Columbia: Georgetown University Press.

Erman, B. (1987) 'Pragmatic Expressions in English: a study of "you know", "you see" and "I mean" in face-to-face conversation', *Acta Universitatis Stockholmiensis*, Stockholm: Almqvist & Wiksell.

Erman, B. and Kotsinas, U.-B. (1993) 'Pragmaticalization: the case of *ba'* and *you know*', in J. Falk, K. Jonasson, G. Meclhers and B. Nilsson (eds) *Stockholm Studies in Modern Philology*, vol. 10, Stockholm: Almqvist & Wiksell International.

Errington, J.J. (1988) *Structure and Style in Javanese*: *a semiotic view of linguistic etiquette*, Philadelphia, Pennsylvania: University of Pennsylvania Press.

Ervin-Tripp, S. (1976) 'Is Sybil there? The structure of some American English directives', *Language in Society* 5 (1): 25–66.

——(1979) 'Children's verbal turn-taking', in E. Ochs and B. Schieffelin (eds) *Developmental Pragmatics*, New York: Academic Press.

Escandell-Vidal, V. (1996) 'Towards a cognitive approach to politeness', in K. Jaszczolt and K. Turner (eds) *Contrastive Semantics and Pragmatics*, vol. II – discourse strategies, pp. 621–50, Oxford: Pergamon.

——(1998) 'Intonation and procedural encoding: the case of Spanish interrogatives', in V. Rouchota and A. Jucker (eds) *Current Issues in Relevance Theory*, pp. 169–204, Amsterdam: John Benjamins.

——(2002) 'Echo-syntax and metarepresentations', *Lingua* 112: 871–900.

Evans, G. (1981) 'Understanding demonstratives', in H. Parret and J. Bouveresse (eds) *Meaning and Understanding*, Berlin: Walter de Gruyter; reprinted in P. Ludlow (ed.) (1997) *Readings in the Philosophy of Language*, pp. 717–44, Cambridge, Massachusetts: MIT Press.

Evans, M.A. (1987) 'Discourse characteristics of reticent children', *Applied Psycholinguistics* 8: 171–84.

Faerch, C. and Kasper, G. (1984) 'Pragmatic knowledge: rules and procedures', *Applied Linguistics* 5 (3): 214–25.

Fauconnier, G. (1985) *Mental Spaces*: *aspects of meaning construction in natural language*, Cambridge, Massachusetts: MIT Press; 2nd edition (1994) Cambridge: Cambridge University Press.

——(1997) *Mappings in Thought and Language*, Cambridge: Cambridge University Press.

Fauconnier, G. and Turner, M. (2002) *The Way We Think: conceptual blending and the mind's hidden complexities*, New York: Basic Books.

——(2008) 'Rethinking metaphor', in R.W. Gibbs Jr (ed.) *The Cambridge Handbook of Metaphor and Thought*, pp. 53–66, Cambridge: Cambridge University Press.

Feeney, A., Scrafton, S., Duckworth, A. and Handley, S. (2004) 'The story of some: everyday pragmatic inference by children and adults', *Canadian Journal of Experimental Psychology* 58(2): 121–32.

Figurski, T. (1987) 'Self-awareness and other-awareness: the use of perspective in everyday life', in K. Yardley and R. Honess (eds) *Self and Identity*: *psychological perspectives*, pp. 197–210, Chichester: John Wiley & Sons.

Fillmore, C.J. (1971) *Santa Cruz Lectures on Deixis*, Bloomington, Indiana: Indiana University Linguistics Club.

——(1975) *Santa Cruz Lectures on Deixis, 1971*, Bloomington, Indiana: Indiana University Linguistics Club; reprinted as C. Fillmore (1997) *Lectures on Deixis*, Stanford, California: CSLI.

——(1982) 'Frame semantics', in Linguistic Society of Korea (ed.) *Linguistics in the Morning Calm*, pp. 111–38, Seoul: Hanshin.

——(1997) *Lectures on Deixis*, Stanford, California: CSLI.

Finell, A. (1986) However: a study of its historical developments from a functional–semantic point of view, unpublished pro gradu thesis, Åbo Akademi.

——(1989) 'Well, now and then', *Journal of Pragmatics* 13: 653–6.

——(1992) 'The repertoire of topic changers in personal, intimate letters: a diachronic study of Osborne and Woolf', in M. Rissanen, O. Ihalainen, T. Nevalainen and I. Taavitsainen (eds) *History of Englishes*: *new methods and interpretations in historical linguistics*, pp. 720–35, New York: Mouton de Gruyter.

Flavell, J.H., Flavell, E.R. and Green, F.L. (1983) 'Development of the appearance-reality distinction', *Cognitive Psychology* 15: 95–120.

Fludernik, M. (1993) *The Fiction of Language and the Languages of Fiction: the linguistic representation of speech and consciousness*, London: Routledge.

Fodor, J.A. (1975) *The Language of Thought*, New York: Crowell.

——(1983) *The Modularity of Mind: an essay on faculty psychology*, Cambridge, Massachusetts: MIT Press.

Fodor, J.A. and Lepore, E. (1996) 'The emptiness of the lexicon: critical reflections on J. Pustejovsky's *The Generative Lexicon*', RuCCS, Rutgers University, Technical Report 27.

Fodor, J. and Pylyshyn, Z.W. (1988) 'Connectionism and cognitive architecture: a critical analysis', *Cognition* 28: 3–71.

Forceville, C. (1996) *Pictorial Metaphor in Advertising*, London: Routledge.

——(1999) 'Art or ad? The influence of genre-attribution on the interpretation of images', *SPIEL* 18: 279–300.

——(2000) 'Compasses, beauty queens and other PCs: pictorial metaphors in computer advertisements', *Hermes* 24: 31–55.

——(2002) 'The identification of target and source in pictorial metaphors', *Journal of Pragmatics* 34: 1–14.

——(2005) 'Addressing an audience: time, place, and genre in Peter van Straaten's calendar cartoons', *Humor* 18 (3): 247–78.

Fortescue, M. (1984) *West Greenlandic*, London: Croom Helm.

Foster-Cohen, S.H. (2004a) 'Relevance theory and second language learning/ behaviour', *Second Language Research* 20 (3): 189–92.

——(2004b) 'Relevance theory, action theory and second language communication strategies', *Second Language Research* 20 (3): 289–302.

Franks, B. (1995) 'Sense generation: a "quasi-classical" approach to concepts and concept combination', *Cognitive Science* 19: 441–505.

Franks, B. and Braisby, N. (1990) 'Sense generation or how to make a mental lexicon flexible', *Proceedings of the 12th Annual Conference of the Cognitive Science Society*, Cambridge, Massachusetts: MIT.

Fraser, B. (1990) 'Perspectives on politeness', *Journal of Pragmatics* 6: 167–90.

Fraser, B. and Nolen, W. (1981) 'The association of deference with linguistic form', in J. Walters (ed.) 'The sociolinguistic of deference and politeness', special issue of the *International Journal of the Sociology of Language* 27: 93–111.

Frege, G. (1884) *Die Grundlagen der Arithmetik: eine logisch mathematische Untersuchung über den Begriff der Zahl*, Breslau: Köbner.

——(1892) 'Über sinn und Bedeutung' ('On Sense and Reference'), *Zeitschrift für Philosophie und Philosophische Kritik* NF 100, trans. P. Geach and M. Black (eds) (1970) *Translations from the Philosophical Writings of Gottlob Frege*, pp. 25–50, Oxford: Blackwell.

——(1918) 'Der Gedanke: eine logische Untersuchung' ('The thought: a logical inquiry'), trans. A.M. and Marcelle Quinton (1956) in *Mind* 65: 289–311; reprinted in P. Ludlow (ed.) (1997) *Readings in the Philosophy of Language*, Cambridge, Massachusetts: MIT Press.

Fretheim, T. (1998) 'Intonation and the procedural encoding of attributed thoughts: the case of Norwegian negative interrogatives', in V. Rouchota and A. Jucker (eds) *Current Issues in Relevance Theory*, pp. 205–36, Amsterdam: John Benjamins.

Fritz, G. (1995) 'Topics in the history of dialogue forms', in A.H. Jucker (ed.) *Historical Pragmatics*: *pragmatic developments in the history of English*, pp. 469–98, Amsterdam: John Benjamins.

——(1997) 'Remarks on the history of dialogue forms', in E. Pietri (ed.) *Dialoganalyse V. Referate der 5. Arbeitstagung, Paris 1994*, pp. 47–55, Beiträge zur Dialogforschung 15, Tübingen: Max Niemeyer.

Fritz, G. and Muckenhaupt, M. (1981) *Kommunikation und Grammtik Texte – Aufgaben – Analysen*, Tübingen: Gunter Narr.

Furlong, A. (1996) *Relevance Theory and Literary Interpretation*, Ph.D. Thesis, University College London.

——(2001) 'Is it a classic if no one reads it?', *Proceedings of the 24th Annual Meeting of the Atlantic Provinces Linguistics Association* (APLA), pp. 54–60, Moncton, New Brunswick: Université de Moncton.

Gal, S. and Irvine, J.T. (1995) 'The boundaries of languages and disciplines: how ideologies construct difference', *Social Research* 62: 967–1001.

Gal, S. and Woolard, K.A. (1995) 'Constructing languages and publics', special issue of *Pragmatics* 5 (2).

Garfinkel, H. (1991) 'Respecification: evidence for locally produced, naturally accountable phenomena of order, logic, reason, meaning, method, etc. in and as of the essential haecceity of immortal ordinary society (I) – an announcement of studies', in G. Button (ed.) *Ethnomethodology and the Human Sciences*, pp. 10–9, Cambridge: Cambridge University Press.

Garrett, M. and Harnish, R.M. (2007) 'Experimental pragmatics: testing for implicatures', *Pragmatics and Cognition* 15(1): 65–90.

Garvey, C. (1975) 'Requests and responses in children's speech', *Journal of Child Language* 2, 41–63.

——(1977) 'The contingent query: a dependent act in conversation', in M. Lewis and L.A. Rosenblum (eds) *Interaction, Conversation and the Development of Language*, New York: John Wiley & Sons.

Gazdar, G. (1979) *Pragmatics: implicature, presupposition and logical form*, New York: Academic Press.

Geach, P. (1950) 'Russell's theory of descriptions', *Analysis* 10: 84–8.

Geeraerts, D. (1997) *Diachronic Prototype Semantics: a contribution to historical lexicology*, Oxford: Clarendon Press.

Geis, M. and Zwicky, A. (1971) 'On invited inferences', *Linguistic Inquiry* 2: 561–6.

Gelman, S. and Markman, E. (1986) 'Categories and induction in young children', *Cognition* 23: 183–209.

Gibbs, R. (1986) 'What makes some indirect speech acts conventional?' *Journal of Memory and Language* 25: 181–96.

——(1996) 'Why many concepts are metaphorical', *Cognition* 61: 309–19.

Gibbs, R.W. Jr. (1981) 'Your wish is my command: convention and context in interpreting indirect requests', *Journal of Verbal Learning and Verbal Behavior* 20: 431–44.

——(1994) *The Poetics of Mind: figurative thought and figurative language*, Cambridge: Cambridge University Press.

Gibbs, R.W. Jr and Moise, J.F. (1997) 'Pragmatics in understanding what is said', *Cognition* 62: 51–74.

Gibbs, R.W. Jr and Tendahl, M. (2006) 'Cognitive effort and effects in metaphor comprehension: relevance theory and psycholinguistics', *Mind and Language* 21 (3): 379–403.

Gilbert, D.T. and Jones, E.E. (1986) 'Perceiver-induced constraint: interpretation of self-generated reality', *Journal of Personality and Social Psychology* 50: 269–80.

Giora, R. (1997) 'Understanding figurative and literal language: the graded salience Hypothesis', *Cognitive Linguistics* 8 (3): 183–206.

——(2003) *On our Mind: salience, context and figurative language*, Oxford: Oxford University Press.

Girotto, V., Kemmelmeier, M., Sperber, D. and van der Henst, J.-B. (2001) 'Inept reasoners or pragmatic virtuosos? Relevance and the deontic selection task', *Cognition* 81: 69–76.

Givón, T. (1979) *On Understanding Grammar*, New York: Academic Press.

——(1982) 'Evidentiality and epistemic space', *Studies in Language* 6: 23–49.

Goffman, E. (1953) *Communication Conduct in an Island Community*, unpublished Ph.D. thesis, Department of Sociology, University of Chicago.

——(1955) 'On face-work: an analysis of ritual elements of social interaction', *Psychiatry: journal for the study of interpersonal processes* 18 (3): 213–31; reprinted in E. Goffman (1967) *Interaction Ritual: essays on face-to-face behavior*, pp. 5–46, Garden City, New York: Anchor Books.

——(1963) *Stigma: notes on management of spoiled identity*, Englewood Cliffs, New Jersey: Prentice-Hall.

——(1967) *Interaction Ritual: essays on face-to-face behavior*, pp. 5–46, Garden City, New York: Anchor Books.

——(1971) *Relations in Public: microstudies of the public order*, Harmondsworth, England: Penguin.

——(1972) *Relations in Public: microstudies of the public order*, New York: Harper & Row.

——(1974) *Frame Analysis: an essay on the organization of experience*, Harmondsworth: Peregrine.

Goldfield, B. (1987) 'The contributions of child and caregiver to referential and expressive language', *Applied Psycholinguistics* 8: 267–80.

——(1990) 'Pointing, naming, and talk about objects: referential behaviour in children and mothers', *First Language* 10: 231–42.

Goodwin, C. (1981) *Conversational Organization: interaction between speakers and hearers*, New York: Academic Press.

——(1994) 'Professional Vision', *American Anthropologist* 96 (3): 606–33.

——(1995) 'Co-constructing meaning in conversations with an aphasic man', *Research on Language and Social Interaction* 28 (3): 233–60.

——(2000) 'Gesture, aphasia and interaction', in D. McNeill (ed.) *Language and Gesture*, pp. 84–98, Cambridge: Cambridge University Press.

——(2003) 'Conversational frameworks for the accomplishment of meaning in aphasia', in C. Goodwin (ed.) *Conversation and Brain Damage*, pp. 90–116, Oxford: Oxford University Press.

Goodwin, M.H. (1997) 'By-play: negotiating evaluation in story-telling', in G.R. Guy, C. Feagin, D. Schiffrin and J. Baugh (eds) *Towards a Social Science of Language: papers in honor of William Labov*, vol. 2 – social interaction and discourse structures, pp. 77–102, Amsterdam: John Benjamins.

——(1998) 'Games of stance: conflict and footing in hopscotch', in S. Hoyle and C.T. Adger (eds) *Kids' Talk: strategic language use in later childhood*, pp. 23–46, New York: Oxford University Press.

Goossens, L. (1982) 'On the development of the modals and of the epistemic function in English', in A. Ahlqvist (ed.) *Papers from the Fifth International Conference on Historical Linguistics*, pp. 74–84, Amsterdam and Philadelphia: John Benjamins.

Gordon, D. and Lakoff, G. (1975) 'Conversational postulates', in P. Cole and J. Morgan (eds) *Syntax and Semantics 3: speech acts*, pp. 83–106, New York: Academic Press.

Görlach, M. (1992) 'Text-types and language history: the cookery recipe', in M. Rissanen, O. Ihalainen, T. Nevalainen and I. Taavitsainen (eds) *History of Englishes: new methods and interpretations in historical linguistics*, pp. 736–61, Berlin: Mouton de Gruyter.

Gorrell, J.H. (1895) 'Indirect discourse in Anglo-Saxon', *Publications of the Modern Language Association of America* 10: 342–485.

Goshke, T. and Koppelberg, D. (1992) 'The concept of representation and the representation of concepts in connectionist models', in W. Ramsey, S. Stich and D. Rumelhart (eds) *Philosophy and Connectionist Theory*, Hillsdale, New Jersey: Erlbaum.

Greatbatch, D. (1986) 'Aspects of topical organization in news interviews: the use of agenda-shifting procedures by interviewees', *Media, Culture and Society* 8 (4): 441–55.

Green, G.M. (2004) 'Some interactions of pragmatics and grammar', in L.R. Horn and G. Ward (eds) *The Handbook of Pragmatics*, pp. 407–26, Oxford: Blackwell.

Grice, H.P. (1957) 'Meaning', *Philosophical Review* 66: 377–88; reprinted in H.P. Grice (ed.) (1989) *Studies in the Way of Words*, Cambridge, Massachusetts: Harvard University Press; also reprinted in D.D. Steinberg and L.A. Jakobovits (eds) *Semantics: an interdisciplinary reader*, pp. 53–9, Cambridge: Cambridge University Press.

——(1967) 'Logic and conversation: the William James lectures, Harvard University', in H.P. Grice (ed.) (1989) *Studies in the Way of Words*, Cambridge, Massachusetts: Harvard University Press.

——(1971 [1957]) 'Meaning', in D.D. Steinberg and L.A. Jakobovits (eds), *Semantics: an interdisciplinary reader*, pp. 53–9, Cambridge: Cambridge University Press.

——(1975) 'Logic and conversation', in P. Cole and J.L. Morgan (eds) *Syntax and Semantics 3: speech acts*, pp. 41–58, New York: Academic Press.

——(1978) 'Further notes on logic and conversation', in P. Cole (ed.) *Syntax and Semantics 9*, pp. 113–28, New York: Academic Press.

——(ed.) (1989) *Studies in the Way of Words*, Cambridge, Massachusetts: Harvard University Press.

Grimshaw, A.D. (1980) 'Social interactional and sociolinguistic rules', *Social Forces* 58 (3): 789–810.

——(1990) Conflict Talk: sociolinguistic investigations of arguments in conversation, Cambridge: Cambridge University Press.

Grimshaw, J. (1997) 'Projection, heads, and optimality', *Linguistic Inquiry* 28: 373–422.

Groefsema, M. (1995) '*Can, may, must* and *should*: a relevance-theoretic approach', *Journal of Linguistics* 31: 53–79.

Grosz, B.J. and Sidner, C. (1986) 'Attention, intentions, and the structure of discourse', *Computational Linguistics* 12 (3): 175–204.

Grosz, B.J., Joshi, A.K. and Weinstein, S. (1995) 'Centering: a framework for modelling the local coherence of discourse', *Computational Linguistics* 21 (2): 203–25.

Grundy, P. (2008) *Doing Pragmatics*, 3rd edition, London: Hodder Education.

Gruner, R. (1977) *Theory and Power: on the character of modern sciences*, Amsterdam: B.R. Gruner.

Gu, Y. (1990) 'Politeness in modern Chinese', *Journal of Pragmatics* 14: 237–57.

Gudykunst, W.B. and Mody, B. (2002) *Handbook of International and Intercultural Communication*, pp. 259–75, Thousand Oaks, California, and London: Sage.

Gumperz, J.J. (1982a) *Discourse Strategies*, Cambridge: Cambridge University Press.

——(ed.) (1982b) *Language and Social Identity*, Cambridge: Cambridge University press.

——(1992) 'Contextualization and understanding', in A. Duranti and C. Goodwin (eds) *Rethinking Context*, pp. 229–52, Cambridge: Cambridge University Press.

——(1996) 'The linguistic and cultural relativity of conversational inference', in J.J. Gumperz and S.C. Levinson (eds) *Rethinking Linguistic Relativity*, pp. 374–406, Cambridge: Cambridge University Press.

——(1999) 'On interactional sociolinguistic method', in S. Sarangi and C. Roberts (eds) *Talk, Work and Institutional Order*, pp. 453–72, Berlin: Mouton de Gruyter.

Gumperz, J.J. and Levinson, S.C. (eds) (1996) *Rethinking Linguistic Relativity*, Cambridge: Cambridge University Press.

Gutt, E.-A. (1998) 'Pragmatic aspects of translation: some relevance-theoretic observations', in L. Hickey (ed.) *The Pragmatics of Translation*, pp. 41–53, Clevedon: Multilingual Matters.

——(2004) 'Translation, metarepresentation and claims of interpretive resemblance', in S. Arduini and R. Hodgson (eds) *Proceedings of the International Conference on Similarity and Translation*, pp. 93–101, Rimini: Guaraldi.

Guy, G. and Vonwiller, J. (1989) 'The high rising tone in Australian English', in P. Collins and D. Blair (eds) *Australian English: the language of a new society*, pp. 21–34, St Lucia: University of Queensland Press.

Haberland, H. and Mey, J.L. (1977) 'Editorial: linguistics and pragmatics', *Journal of Pragmatics* 1 (1): 1–12.

——(2002) 'Editorial: linguistics and pragmatics: 25 years after', *Journal of Pragmatics* 34 (1): 1671–82.

Habermas, J. (1979) *Communication and the Evolution of Society*, Toronto: Beacon Press.

Haicun, L. (2005) 'Explaining phatic utterance within the theory of relevance', in A. Korzeniowska and M. Grzegorzewska (eds) *Relevance Studies in Poland*, vol. 2, pp. 81–7, The Institute of English Studies, University of Warsaw.

Haiman, J. (1985) *Natural Syntax*, Cambridge: Cambridge University Press.

Hall, A.R. (1963) *From Galileo to Newton, 1630–1720*, New York: Harper & Row.

Halliday, M.A.K. (1970) 'Language structure and social function, in J. Lyons (ed.) *New Horizons in Linguistics*, pp. 140–65, Harmondsworth: Penguin.

——(1973) *Explorations in the* Functions *of Language*, London: Edward Arnold.

——(1978) *Language as Social Semiotic*, London: Arnold.

——(1979) 'Modes of meaning and modes of expression: types of grammatical structure and their determination by different semantic functions', in D.J. Allerton, E. Carney and D. Holdcroft (eds) *Function and Context in Linguistic Analysis*: *a Festschrift for William Haas*, pp. 57–79, Cambridge: Cambridge University Press.

Hamilton, H.E. (1994) *Conversations with an Alzheimer's Patient: an interactional sociolinguistic study*, Cambridge and New York: Cambridge University Press.

Hanks, W.F. (1990) *Referential Practice*: *language and lived space among the Maya*, Chicago, Illinois: University of Chicago Press.

——(1992) 'The indexical ground of deictic reference', in A. Duranti and C. Goodwin (eds) *Rethinking Context*, pp. 43–76, Cambridge: Cambridge University Press.

——(1996) 'Language form and communicative practices', in J.J. Gumperz and S.C. Levinson (eds) *Rethinking Linguistic Relativity*, pp. 232–70, Cambridge: Cambridge University Press.

Hanson, K. (1987) 'On subjectivity and the history of epistemic expressions in English', in B. Need, E. Schiller and A. Bosch (eds) *Papers from the Twenty-Third Regional Meeting of the Chicago Linguistic Society*, pp. 133–47, Chicago, Illinois: Chicago Linguistic Society.

Happé, F. (1993) 'Communicative competence and theory of mind in autism: a test of relevance theory', *Cognition* 48: 101–19.

Happé, F., Winner, E. and Brownell, H. (1998) 'The getting of wisdom: theory of mind in old age', *Developmental Psychology* 34: 358–62.

Hardin, C. (1988) *Color for Philosophers*, Indianapolis, Indiana: Hackett Publishing.

Hardman, M.J. (1986) 'Data-source marking in the Jaqi languages', in W. Chafe and J. Nichols (eds) *Evidentiality*: *the linguistic coding of epistemology*, pp. 113–36, Norwood, New Jersey: Ablex.

Harnish, R. (1976) 'Logical form and implicature', in T. Bever, J.J. Katz and T. Langendoen (eds) *An Integrated Theory of Linguistic Ability*, pp. 313–92, New York: Crowell.

Harris, S. (1984) 'Questions as a mode of control in magistrates' courts', *International Journal of the Sociology of Language* 49: 5–27.

Haspelmath, M. (2006) 'Against markedness (and what to replace it with)', *Journal of Linguistics* 42 (1): 25–70.

Hasund, I.K. and Stenström, A.-B. (1997) 'Conflict talk: a comparison of the verbal disputes between adolescent females in two corpora', in M. Ljung (ed.) *Corpus-based Studies in English*: *papers from the seventeenth international conference on English Language Research on Computerized Corpora* (ICAME 17), pp. 119–33, Stockholm, 15–19 May 1996, Amsterdam: Rodopi.

Haugh, M. (2003) 'Anticipated versus inferred politeness', *Multilingua* 22: 397–413.

——(2008) 'Intention and diverging interpretings of implicature in the "uncovered meat" sermon', *Intercultural Pragmatics* 5 (2): 201–30.

Haviland, J. (1979) 'How to talk to your brother-in-law in Guugu Yimithirr', in T. Shopen (ed.) *Languages and Their Speakers*, pp. 161–239, Cambridge, Massachusetts: Winthrop.

Hawkins, J.A. (1991) 'Un (in)definite articles. implicatures and (un)grammaticality prediction', *Journal of Linguistics* 27: 405–42.

Heeschen, C. and Schegloff, E.A. (1999) 'Agrammatism, adaptation theory, conversation analysis: on the role of so-called telegraphic style in talk-in interaction', *Aphasiology* 13 (4/5): 365–405.

Heine, B., Claudi, U. and Hünnemeyer, F. (1991) *Grammaticalization*: *a conceptual framework*, Chicago, Illinois: University of Chicago Press.

Hempel, C. (1965) *Aspects of Scientific Explanation*, New York: The Free Press.

Hemphill, L. (1987) 'Conversational abilities in mentally retarded and normally developing children', *Paper Presented at the Biennial Meeting of the Society for Research in Child Development*, Baltimore, Maryland.

——(1989) 'Topic development, syntax, and social class', *Discourse Processes* 12: 267–86.

Hemphill, L. and Siperstein, G.N. (1990) 'Conversational competence and peer response to mildly retarded children', *Journal of Educational Psychology* 82: 1–7.

Henderson, J. (1995) 'Phonology and the grammar of Yele, Papua New Guinea', *Pacific Linguistics* Series B-112.

Hendriks, P. and de Hoop, H. (2001) 'Optimality theoretic semantics', *Linguistics and Philosophy* 24: 1–32.

Heritage, J. (1984) *Garfinkel and Ethnomethodology*, Cambridge: Polity Press.

Heritage, J. and Atkinson, J.M. (1984) 'Introduction', in J.M. Atkinson and J. Heritage (eds) *Structures of Social Action: studies in conversation analysis*, pp. 1–15, Cambridge: Cambridge University Press.

Herskovits, A. (1986) *Language and Spatial Cognition: an interdisciplinary study of the prepositions in English*, Cambridge: Cambridge University Press.

Hickmann, M. (1993) 'The boundaries of reported speech in narrative discourse: Some developmental aspects', in J.A. Lucy (ed.) *Reflexive Language: reported speech and metapragmatics*, pp. 63–90, Cambridge: Cambridge University Press.

Higgins, C. (ed.) (2007) 'A closer look at cultural differences: "interculturality" in talk-in-interaction', special issue, *Pragmatics* 17 (1): 9–22.

Hill, B., Ide, S., Ikuta, S., Kawasaki, A. and Ogino, T. (1986) 'Universals of linguistic politeness', *Journal of Pragmatics* 10: 347–71.

Hill, W.F. and Ottchen, C.J. (1995) *Shakespeare's Insults: educating your wit*, New York: Crown Trade.

Himmelmann, N. (1997) *Deiktikon, Artikel, Nominalphrase: Zur Emergenz syntaktischer Struktur*, Tübingen: Niemeyer.

Hines, C.P. (1978) 'Well. . .', in M. Paradis (ed.) *The Fourth LACUS Forum*, pp. 308–18, Columbia, South Carolina: Hornbeam Press.

Hinnenkamp, V. (1991) 'Talking a person into interethnic distinction', in L. Blommaert and J. Verschueren (eds) *The Pragmatics of Intercultural and International Communication*, pp. 91–110, Amsterdam and Philadelphia: John Benjamins.

——(1995) 'Intercultural communication', in J. Verschueren, J.-O. Östman and J. Blommaert (eds) *Handbook of Pragmatics*, Amsterdam and Philadelphia: John Benjamins.

Hobbes, T. (1651) *The Leviathan*, in C.B. MacPherson (ed.) (1968) Harmondsworth, Middlesex: Penguin.

Hobbs, J., Stickel, M., Appelt, D. and Martin, P. (1993) 'Interpretation as abduction', *Artificial Intelligence* 63: 69–142.

Hobson, R.P. and Bishop, M. (2003) 'The pathogenesis of autism: insights from congenital blindness', *Philosophical Transactions of the Royal Society of London*, Series B, 358: 335–44.

Hockett, C. (1961) 'The problem of universals in language', in J.H. Greenberg (ed.) *Universals of Language*, pp. 1–29, Cambridge, Massachusetts: MIT Press.

Hoenigswald, H. (1966) 'A proposal for the study of folk-linguistics', in W. Bright (ed.) *Sociolinguistics*, pp. 16–26, The Hague: Mouton.

Hofmann, T.R. (1993) *Realms of Meaning: an introduction to semantics*, London: Longman.

Hookway, C.J. (1995) 'Peirce, Charles Sanders', in T. Honderich (ed.) *The Oxford Companion to Philosophy*, pp. 648–51, Oxford: Oxford University Press.

Hopper, P.J. (1991) 'On some principles of grammaticalization', in E.C. Traugott and B. Heine (eds) *Approaches to Grammaticalization*, vol. 1, pp. 17–35, Amsterdam: John Benjamins.

——(2010) 'Grammaticalization', in L. Cummings (ed.) *The Pragmatics Encyclopedia*, pp. 180–2, London and New York: Routledge.

Hopper, P.J. and Traugott, E.C. (1993) *Grammaticalization*, Cambridge: Cambridge University Press.

——(2003) *Grammaticalization*, 2nd edition, Cambridge: Cambridge University Press.

Horn, L.R. (1984) 'Towards a new taxonomy of pragmatic inference: Q- and R-based implicature', in D. Schiffrin (ed.) *Meaning, Form, and Use in Context: linguistic applications*, pp. 11–42, Washington, District of Columbia: Georgetown University Press.

——(1985) 'Metalinguistic negation and pragmatic ambiguity', *Language* 61: 121–74.

——(1989) *A Natural History of Negation*, Chicago, Illinois: University of Chicago Press.

——(1992) 'The said and the unsaid', *Ohio State University Working Papers in Linguistics* (SALT II Proceedings), 40: 163–202.

——(1996) 'Presupposition and implicature', in S. Lappin (ed.) *The Handbook of Contemporary Semantic Theory*, pp. 299–320, Oxford: Blackwell.

——(1998) 'Conditionals "R" us: from IF to IFF via R-based implicature', paper presented at Stanford University, May 1998.

——(2004) 'Implicature', in L.R. Horn and G. Ward (eds) *The Handbook of Pragmatics*, pp. 3–28, Oxford: Blackwell.

——(2005) 'Current issues in neo-Gricean pragmatics', *Intercultural Pragmatics* 2 (2): 191–204.

Horn, L.R. and Bayer, S. (1984) 'Short-circuited implicature: a negative contribution', *Linguistics and Philosophy* 7: 397–414.

Horn, L.R. and Ward, G. (eds) (2004) *The Handbook of Pragmatics*, Oxford: Blackwell.

Horsfall, A.B. and Arensberg, C.A. (1949) 'Teamwork and productivity in a shoe factory', *Human Organization* 8: 13–25.

House, J. (1986) 'Cross-cultural pragmatics and foreign language teaching', in K.-R. Bausch, H. Christ and H.-J. Krumm (eds) *Probleme und Perspektiven der Sprachlehrforschung*, pp. 281–95, Frankfurt: Scriptor.

——(1990) 'Intonation structures and pragmatic interpretation', in S. Ramsaran (ed.) *Studies in the Pronunciation of English*, pp. 38–57, London: Routledge.

——(1996) 'Developing pragmatic fluency in English as a foreign language: routines and metapragmatic awareness', *Studies in Second Language Acquisition* 18: 225–52.

——(2003) 'Misunderstanding in intercultural university encounters', in J. House, G. Kasper and S. Ross (eds) *Misunderstanding in Social Life*: discourse approaches to problematic talk, pp. 22–56, London: Longman.

——(2006) 'Constructing a context with intonation', *Journal of Pragmatics* 38 (10): 1542–58.

House, J. and Kasper, G. (1981) 'Politeness markers in English and German', in F. Coulmas (ed.) *Conversational Routine*: explorations in standardized communication situations and prepatterned speech, pp. 157–85, The Hague, Netherlands: Mouton.

Hu, J. and Pan, H. (2001) 'Processing local coherence of discourse in centering theory', *Proceedings of the 15th Pacific Asia Conference on Language, Information and Computation*, Hong Kong: City University of Hong Kong.

Huang, Y. (2000) *Anaphora*: a cross-linguistic study, Oxford: Oxford University Press.

——(2004) 'Anaphora and the pragmatics–semantics interface', in L.R. Horn and G. Ward (eds) *The Handbook of Pragmatics*, pp. 288–314, Oxford: Blackwell.

——(2009) 'Neo-Gricean pragmatics and the lexicon', *International Review of Pragmatics* 1 (1): 118–53.

——(2010a) 'Implicature', in L. Cummings (ed.) *The Pragmatics Encyclopedia*, pp. 205–10, London and New York: Routledge.

——(2010b) 'Anglo-American and European continental traditions', in L. Cummings (ed.) *The Pragmatics Encyclopedia*, pp. 13–15, London and New York: Routledge.

Hutchby, I. and Wooffitt, R. (2008) *Conversation Analysis*: principles, practices and applications, 2nd edition, Cambridge: Polity Press.

Hutchinson, J.M. and Jensen, M. (1980) 'A pragmatic evolution of discourse communication in normal and senile elderly in a nursing home', in L. Obler and M. Albert (eds) *Language and Communication in the Elderly*, pp. 59–73, Lexington, Massachusetts: Lexington Books.

Hymes, D. (1962) 'The ethnography of speaking', in J.A. Fishman (ed.) (1968) *Readings in the Sociology of Language*, pp. 99–138, The Hague: Mouton.

——(1970) 'Linguistic theory and functions of speech', in J. Irvine (1974) *Foundations in Sociolinguistics*: an ethnographic approach, pp. 145–78, Philadelphia: University of Pennsylvania Press.

——(1974) 'Ways of speaking', in R. Bauman and J. Sherzer (eds) *Explorations in the Ethnography of Speaking*, pp. 433–51, Cambridge: Cambridge University Press.

——(1975) 'The pre-war Prague school and post-war American anthropological linguistics', in K. Koerner (ed.) *The Transformational-Generative Paradigm and Modern Linguistic Theory*, pp. 359–80, Amsterdam: John Benjamins.

Ifantidou, E. (1994) *Evidentials and Relevance*, Ph.D. thesis, University of London. (Published with revisions as Ifantidou, 2001.)

——(2001) *Evidentials and Relevance*, Amsterdam: John Benjamins.

——(2005a) 'Evidential particles and mind-reading', *Pragmatics and Cognition* 13 (2): 253–95.

——(2005b) 'Hearsay devices and metarepresentation', in S. Marmaridou, E. Antonopoulou and V. Nikiforidou (eds) *Reviewing Linguistic Thought*: converging trends in the 21st century, pp. 401–20, Berlin: Mouton de Gruyter.

——(2005c) 'The semantics and pragmatics of metadiscourse', *Journal of Pragmatics* 37: 1325–53.

Ifantidou-Trouki, E. (1993) 'Sentential adverbs and relevance', *Lingua* 90: 69–90.

Illes, J. (1989) 'Neurolinguistic features of spontaneous language production dissociate three forms of neurodegenerative disease: Alzheimer's, Huntington's, and Parkinson's', *Brain and Language* 37: 628–42.

Imai, K. (1998) 'Intonation and relevance', in R. Carston and S. Uchida (eds) *Relevance Theory*: applications and implications, pp. 69–86, Amsterdam: John Benjamins.

Israel, M. (2002) 'Literally speaking', *Journal of Pragmatics* 34 (4): 423–32.

Jacobs, A. and Jucker, A.H. (1995) 'The historical perspective in pragmatics', in A.H. Jucker (ed.) *Historical Pragmatics*: pragmatic developments in the history of English, pp. 3–33, Amsterdam and Philadelphia: John Benjamins.

Jacobs, G. (1999) *Preformulating the News: an analysis of the metapragmatics of press releases*, Amsterdam and Philadelphia: John Benjamins.

Jäger, G. (2004) 'Learning constraint sub-hierarchies: the bidirectional gradual learning Algorithm', in R. Blutner and H. Zeevat (eds) *Pragmatics and Optimality Theory*, pp. 251–87, Houndmills, Basingstoke: Macmillan.

Jäger, G. and Blutner, R. (2000) 'Against lexical decomposition in syntax', in A.Z. Wyner (ed.) *Proceedings of the Fifteenth Annual Conference, IATL 7*, pp. 113–37, Haifa: University of Haifa.

—— (2003) 'Competition and interpretation: the German adverb wieder ("again")', in C. Fabricius-Hansen, E. Lang and C. Maienborn (eds) *Handbook of Adjuncts*, pp. 393–416, Berlin: Mouton de Gruyter.

Jakobson, R. (1932) 'Structure of the Russian verb', in L.R. Waugh and M. Halle (eds) (1984) *Roman Jakobson: Russian and Slavic grammar studies 1931–1981*, pp. 1–14, Berlin: Mouton Publishers.

—— (1939) 'Signe zéro', in A. Sechehaye (ed.) *Mélanges de Linguistique, offerts á Charles Bally*, pp. 143–52, Geneva: Georg.

—— (1956) 'Metalanguage as a linguistic problem', in R. Jakobson (ed.) (1985) *Selected Writings VII*, pp. 113–21, Berlin: Mouton De Gruyter.

—— (1957) 'Shifters, verbal categories, and the Russian verb', in R. Jakobson (ed.) (1971) *Selected Writings II*, pp. 130–47, The Hague: Mouton.

—— (1960) 'Closing statement: linguistics and poetics', in T.A. Sebeok (ed.) *Style in Language*, pp. 350–77, Cambridge, Massachusetts: MIT Press.

—— (1963) 'Efforts toward a means–ends model of language in interwar continental linguistics', in R. Jakobson (ed.) (1971) *Selected Writings II*, pp. 522–6, The Hague: Mouton.

—— (1968) 'Language in relation to other communication systems', in R. Jakobson (ed.) (1971) *Selected Writings II*, pp. 697–708, The Hague: Mouton.

—— (1976) 'A few remarks on structuralism', *Modern Language Notes* 91: 1534–9.

—— (1977) 'A few remarks on Peirce, pathfinder in the science of language', *Modern Language Notes* 92: 1026–32

—— (1984 [1957]) 'Shifters, verbal categories, and the Russian verb', in L.R. Waugh and M. Halle (eds) *Roman Jakobson – Russian and Slavic Grammar: studies 1931–1981*, pp. 41–58, Berlin: Mouton.

—— (1985 [1956]) 'Metalanguage as a linguistic problem', in *Selected Writings VII*, pp. 113–21, Berlin: Mouton de Gruyter.

Janicki, K. (1989) *Toward Non-Essentialist Sociolinguistics*, Berlin: Mouton de Gruyter.

Jary, M. (1998) 'Relevance theory and the communication of politeness', *Journal of Pragmatics* 30: 1–19.

—— (2008) 'The relevance of complement choice: a corpus study of "believe"', *Lingua* 118: 1–18.

Jaszczolt, K. (2005) *Default Semantics: foundations of a compositional theory of acts of communication*, Oxford: Oxford University Press.

Jefferson, G. (1972) 'Side sequences', in D. Sudnow (ed) *Studies in Social Interaction*, pp. 294–338, New York: Free Press.

Jespersen, O. (1921) *Language: its nature, development and origin*, New York: Henry Holt & Company.

—— (1922) Language: its nature, development and origin, London: Allen & Unwin.

Jisa, H. (1984–5) 'French preschoolers' use of et pis ("and then")', *First Language* 5: 169–84.

Joseph, J.E. and Taylor, T.J. (eds) (1990) *Ideologies of Language*, London: Routledge.

Jucker, A.H. (1993) 'The discourse marker well: a relevance-theoretical account', *Journal of Pragmatics* 19: 435–52.

—— (1986) *News Interviews: a pragmalinguistic analysis*, Amsterdam: John Benjamins.

—— (ed.) (1995) *Historical Pragmatics: pragmatic developments in the history of English*, Amsterdam and Philadelphia: John Benjamins.

—— (2000) 'Slanders, slurs and insults on the road to Canterbury: forms of verbal aggression in Chaucer's *Canterbury Tales*', in I. Taavitsainen, T. Nevalainen, P. Pahta and M. Rissanen (eds) *Placing Middle English in Context*, pp. 369–89, Berlin: Mouton de Gruyter.

—— (2005) 'Mass media', in J.-O. Östman, J. Verschueren and E. Versluys (eds) *Handbook of Pragmatics 2003–2005*, pp. 1–18, Amsterdam: John Benjamins.

Jucker, A.H. and Taavitsainen, I. (2000) 'Diachronic speech act analysis: insults from flyting to flaming', *Journal of Historical Pragmatics* 1 (1): 67–95.

—— (eds) (2008) *Speech Acts in the History of English*, Amsterdam and Philadelphia: John Benjamins.

—— (eds) (2010) *Historical Pragmatics*, Berlin and New York: Mouton de Gruyter.

Jucker, A.H., Fritz, G. and Lebsanft, F. (eds) (1999) *Historical Dialogue Analysis*, Amsterdam and Philadelphia: John Benjamins.

Kadmon, N. (1987) *On Unique and Non-Unique Reference and Asymmetric Quantification*, Ph.D. thesis, Amherst: University of Massachusetts.

Kamio, A. (1994) 'The theory of territory of information: the case of Japanese', *Journal of Pragmatics* 21 (1): 67–100.

Kaplan, D. (1978) 'Dthat', in P. Cole (ed.) *Syntax and Semantics 9: pragmatics*, pp. 221–43, New York: Academic Press.

——(1989) 'Demonstratives', in J. Almog, J. Perry and H.K. Wettstein (eds) *Themes from Kaplan*, pp. 481–563, Oxford: Oxford University Press.

Karttunen, L. (1971) 'Some observations on factivity', *Papers in Linguistics* 4: 55–69.

——(1973) 'Presuppositions of compound sentences', *Linguistic Inquiry* IV (2): 169–93.

——(1974) 'Presupposition and linguistic context', *Theoretical Linguistics* 1 (1–2): 184–94.

Kasher, A. (ed.) (1998) *Pragmatics: critical concepts*, London and New York: Routledge.

Kasper, G. (1997) *Can Pragmatic Competence be Taught?* (Net Work #6) (HTML document), Honolulu: University of Hawai'i, Second Language Teaching and Curriculum Center; available online at: http://www.fll.hawaii.edu/nflrc/NetWorks/ NW6/ (accessed 2 May 1997).

——(1998) 'Interlanguage pragmatics', in H. Byrnes (ed.) *Learning Foreign and Second Languages: perspectives in research and scholarship*, pp. 183–208, New York: The Modern Language Association of America.

Kasper, G. and Blum-Kulka, S. (eds) (1993) *Interlanguage Pragmatics*, Oxford: Oxford University Press.

Kasper, G. and Rose, K. (1999) 'Pragmatics and second language acquisition', *Annual Review of Applied Linguistics* 19: 81–104.

Katsos, N. (2007) 'Pragmatic me, pragmatic you: the development of informativeness from a speaker's and a comprehender's perspective', paper presented at XPRAG, Berlin, December 2007.

Kaye, K. and Charney, R. (1980) 'How mothers maintain dialogue with two-year olds', in D.R. Olson (ed.) *The Social Foundations of Language and Thought*, New York: Norton.

——(1981) 'Conversational asymmetry between mothers and children', *Journal of Child Language* 8: 35–50.

Kean, M.L. (1995) *The Theory of Markedness in Generative Grammar*, unpublished Ph.D. thesis, Cambridge, Massachusetts: MIT Press.

Keating, E. (1998) 'Honor and stratification in Pohnpei, Micronesia', *American Ethnologist* 25: 399–411.

Kecskes, I. (2004) 'Lexical merging, conceptual blending, cultural crossing', *Intercultural Pragmatics* 1 (1): 1–26.

——(2007) 'Formulaic language in English lingua franca', in I. Kecskes and L.R. Horn (eds) *Explorations in Pragmatics: linguistic, cognitive and intercultural aspects*, pp. 191–219, Berlin and New York: Mouton de Gruyter.

——(2008) 'Dueling context: a dynamic model of meaning', *Journal of Pragmatics* 40 (3): 385–406.

Kecskes, I. and Zhang, F. (2009) 'Activating, seeking and creating common ground: a socio-cognitive approach', *Pragmatics and Cognition* 17 (2): 331–55.

Keenan, E.O. and Klein, E. (1975) 'Conversational competence in children', *Journal of Child Language* 1: 163–84.

Kellerman, E. (1980) *On the Need for Formal Elicitation of Data* (mimeo), Nijmegen, The Netherlands.

Kellermann, K., Broetzmann, S., Lim, T.-S. and Kitao, K. (1989) 'The conversation MOP: scenes in the stream of discourse', *Discourse Processes* 12: 27–62.

Kempson, R. (1988) 'On the grammar–cognition interface', in R. Kempson (ed.) *Mental Representations*, Cambridge: Cambridge University Press.

Kenny, A.J. (1966) 'Practical inference', *Analysis* 26: 65–75.

Keysar, B. and Barr, D.J. (2002) 'Self anchoring in conversation: why language users do not do what they "should"', in T. Gilovich, D.W. Griffin and D. Kahneman (eds), *Heuristics and biases: the psychology of intuitive judgment*, pp. 150–66, Cambridge: Cambridge University Press.

Keysar, B. and Bly, B. (1995) 'Intuitions of the transparency of idioms: can one keep a secret by spilling the beans?', *Journal of Memory and Language* 34: 89–109.

Kiefer, F. and Verschueren, J. (eds) (1988) 'Metapragmatic terms', special issue of *Acta Linguistica Hungarica* 38: 1–289.

Kienpointner, M. (1997) 'Varieties of rudeness: types and functions of impolite utterances', *Functions of Language* 4 (2): 251–87.

Kiparsky, P. and Kiparsky, C. (1970) 'Fact', in M. Bierwisch and K.E. Heidolph (eds) *Progress in Linguistics*, pp. 143–73, The Hague: Mouton; reprinted in D.D. Steinberg and L.A. Jakobovits (eds) *Semantics: an interdisciplinary reader in philosophy, linguistics and psychology*, pp. 345–69, Cambridge: Cambridge University Press.

Kirby, S. and Hurford, J. (1997) *The Evolution of Incremental Learning: language, development and critical periods*, Edinburgh: University of Edinburgh.

——(2002) 'The emergence of linguistic structure: an overview of the iterated learning model', in A. Cangelosi and D. Parisi (eds) *Simulating the Evolution of Language*, pp. 121–48, London: Springer Verlag.

Kita, S. (2003) *Pointing*: *where language, cognition, and culture meet*, Mahwah, New Jersey: Lawrence Erlbaum.

Kitwood, T. (1988) 'The technical, the personal and the framing of dementia', *Social Behaviour* 3: 161–79.

Kivimaa, K. (1968) 'Clauses in Chaucer introduced by conjunctions with appended "that"', *Commentationes Humanarum Litterarum* 43.1, Helsinki: Societas Scientarium Fennica.

Kneale, W. and Kneale, M. (1962) *The Development of Logic*, Oxford: Clarendon Press.

Knowles, G. (1987) *Patterns of Spoken English*, London: Longman.

König, E. (1991) *The Meaning of Focus Particles: a comparative perspective*, London: Routledge.

Kopytko, R. (1995) 'Against rationalistic pragmatics', *Journal of Pragmatics* 23: 475–91.

——(2001) 'From Cartesian towards non-Cartesian pragmatics', *Journal of Pragmatics* 33: 783–804.

Kortmann, B. (1997) *Adverbial Subordination: a typology and history of adverbial subordinators based on European languages*, Berlin: Mouton de Gruyter.

Krashen, S. (1985) *The Input Hypothesis*, London: Longman.

Krifka, M. (2007a) 'Approximate interpretation of number words: a case for strategic communication', in G. Bouma, I. Krämer and J. Zwarts (eds) *Cognitive Foundations of Interpretation*, pp. 111–26, Amsterdam: Koninklijke Nederlandse Akademie van Wetenschapen.

——(2007b) 'Negated antonyms: creating and filling the gap', in U. Sauerland and P. Stateva (eds) *Presupposition and Implicature in Compositional Semantics*, pp. 163–77, Houndmills, Basingstoke: Macmillan.

Kubota, M. (1995) 'Teachability of conversational implicature to Japanese EFL learners', *IRLT Bulletin* 9: 35–67.

Kumon-Nakumura, S., Glucksberg, S. and Brown, M. (1995) 'How about another piece of pie: the allusional pretense theory of discourse irony', *Journal of Experimental Psychology – General* 124 (1): 3–21.

Labov, W. (1972a) 'Rules for ritual insults', in D. Sudnow (ed.) *Studies in Social Interaction*, pp. 120–69, New York: The Free Press.

——(1972b) *Language in the Inner City: studies in the black English vernacular*, Oxford: Blackwell.

——(1972c) *Sociolinguistic Patterns*, Oxford: Basil Blackwell.

Lachenicht, L.G. (1980) 'Aggravating language: a study of abusive and insulting language', *Papers in Linguistics*: *International Journal in Human Communication* 13 (4): 607–87.

Lahav, R. (1989) 'Against compositionality: the case of adjectives', *Philosophical Studies* 55: 111–29.

——(1993) 'The combinatorial–connectionist debate and the pragmatics of adjectives', *Pragmatics and Cognition* 1: 71–88.

Lakoff, G. (1972) 'Hedges: a study in meaning criteria and the logic of fuzzy concepts', in P.M. Peranteau, J.N. Levi and G.C. Phares (eds) *Papers from the Eighth Regional Meeting of the Chicago Linguistic Society*, pp. 183–228, Chicago, Illinois: University of Chicago Press.

——(1982) 'Categories and cognitive models', *Cognitive Science Technical Report* 19, Berkeley, California: Institute for Cognitive Studies, University of California.

——(1987) *Women, Fire and Dangerous Things: what categories reveal about the mind*, Chicago, Illinois: University of Chicago Press.

——(1993) 'The Contemporary theory of metaphor', in A. Ortoney (ed.) *Metaphor and Thought*, pp. 202–51, Cambridge: Cambridge University Press.

Lakoff, G. and Johnson, M. (1980) *Metaphors We Live By*, Chicago, Illinois: University of Chicago Press.

——(1987) *Women, Fire and Dangerous Things: what categories reveal about the mind*, Chicago, Illinois: University of Chicago Press.

Lakoff, R. (1972) 'The pragmatics of modality', in P.M. Peranteau, J.N. Levi and G.C. Phares (eds) *Papers from the Eighth Regional Meeting of the Chicago Linguistic Society*, pp. 229–46, Chicago, Illinois: University of Chicago Press.

——(1973) 'The logic of politeness, or minding your p's and q's', in *Papers from the Ninth Regional Meeting of the Chicago Linguistic Society*, pp. 292–305, Chicago, Illinois: Chicago Linguistic Society.

——(1982) 'Categories: an essay in cognitive linguistics', in Linguistics Society of Korea (ed.) *Linguistics in the Morning Calm*, Seoul: Hanshin.

——(1989) 'The limits of politeness: therapeutic and courtroom discourse', *Multilingua* 8: 101–29.

Lambert, W. and Tucker, G. (1976) *Tu, Vous, Usted*, Rawley, Rowley, Massachusetts: Newbury House Publishers.

Langacker, R.W. (1978) 'The form and meaning of the English auxiliary', *Language* 54: 853–82.

——(1985) 'Observations and speculations on subjectivity', in J. Haiman (ed.) *Iconicity in Syntax*, pp. 109–50, Amsterdam: John Benjamins.

——(1987) *Foundations of Cognitive Grammar: theoretical prerequisites,* vol. 1, Stanford, California: Stanford University Press.

——(1990) 'Subjectification', *Cognitive Linguistics* 1: 5–38.

——(1991) *Foundations of Cognitive Grammar: descriptive application,* vol. 2, Stanford, California: Stanford University Press.

Langendoen, T. (1971) 'Presupposition and assertion in the semantic analysis of nouns and verbs in English', in D.D. Steinberg and L.A. Jakobovitz (eds) *Semantics: an interdisciplinary reader in philosophy, linguistics and psychology,* pp. 341–4, Cambridge: Cambridge University Press.

Lass, R. (1980) *On Explaining Linguistic Change,* Cambridge: Cambridge University Press.

Lave, J. and Wenger, E. (1991) *Situated Learning: legitimate peripheral participation,* Cambridge: University of Cambridge Press.

Lebsanft, F. (1988) *Studien zu einer Linguistik des Grußes. Sprache und Funktion der altfranzösischen Grußformeln,* Tübingen: Niemeyer.

Lee, J.R.E. (1987) 'Prologue: talking organisation', in G. Button and J.R.E. Lee (eds), *Talk and Social Organisation,* pp. 19–53, Clevedon: Multilingual Matters.

Leech, G. (1980) *Explorations in Semantics and Pragmatics,* Amsterdam: John Benjamins.

——(1983) *Principles of Pragmatics,* London: Longman.

Lehrer, A. (1990) 'Polysemy, conventionality and the structure of the lexicon', *Cognitive Linguistics* 1–2: 207–46.

Leinonen, E., Letts, C. and Rae Smith, B. (2000) *Children's Pragmatic Communication Difficulties (Disorders of Communication),* London: Whurr.

Leslie, A. (1987) 'Pretense and representation: the origins of "theory of mind"', *Psychological Review* 94: 412–26.

Leslie, A. and Happé, F. (1989) 'Autism and ostensive communication: the relevance of metarepresentation', *Development and Psychopathology* 1: 205–12.

Levenston, E. (1975) 'Aspects of testing the oral proficiency of adult immigrants to Canada', in L. Palmer and B. Spolsky (eds) *Papers on Language Testing 1967–1974,* Washington, District of Columbia: TESOL.

Levinson, S.C. (1979a) 'Pragmatics and social deixis: reclaiming the notion of conventional implicature', *Berkeley Linguistics Society* 5: 206–23.

——(1979b) 'Activity types', *Linguistics* 19: 365–79.

——(1983) *Pragmatics,* Cambridge: Cambridge University Press.

——(1987a) 'Minimization and conversational inference', in M. Bertuccelli Papi and J. Verschueren (eds) *The Pragmatic Perspective: selected papers from the 1985 International Pragmatics Conference,* pp. 61–129, Amsterdam: John Benjamins; reprinted in A. Kasher (ed.) (1998) *Pragmatics: critical concepts,* vol. 4 – presupposition, implicature and indirect speech acts, pp. 545–612, London: Routledge.

——(1987b) 'Pragmatics and the grammar of anaphora', *Journal of Linguistics* 23: 379–434.

——(1992) 'Activity types and language', in P. Drew and J. Heritage (eds) *Talk at Work,* pp. 66–100, Cambridge: Cambridge University Press.

——(1995) 'Three levels of meaning', in F.R. Palmer (ed.) *Grammar and Meaning: essays in honour of Sir John Lyons,* pp. 90–115, Cambridge: Cambridge University Press.

——(1996) 'Frames of reference and Molyneux's question: crosslinguistic evidence', in P. Bloom, M.A. Peterson, L. Nadel and M.F. Garrett (eds) *Language and Space,* pp. 109–69, Cambridge, Massachusetts: MIT Press.

——(2000a) *Presumptive Meanings: the theory of generalized conversational implicature,* Cambridge, Massachusetts: MIT Press.

——(2000b) 'Yélî Dnye and the theory of basic color terms', *Journal of Linguistic Anthropology* 10: 3–55.

——(2004) 'Deixis', in L.R. Horn and G. Ward (eds), *The Handbook of Pragmatics,* pp. 97–122, Oxford: Blackwell.

Levi-Strauss, C. (1955) 'The structural study of myth', *Journal of American Folklore* 68 (270): 428–44.

Lewis, D. (1969) *Convention: a philosophical study,* Cambridge, Massachusetts: Harvard University Press.

——(1970) 'General semantics', *Journal of Semantics* 6.3/4: 175–226.

——(1972) 'General semantics', in D. Davidson and G. Harman (eds) *Semantics of Natural Language,* pp. 169–218, Dordrecht: Reidel.

Lim, T.S. (1994) 'Facework and interpersonal relationships', in S. Ting-Toomey (ed.) *The Challenge of Facework,* pp. 209–68, Albany, New York: University of New York Press.

Lindahl, C. (1987) *Earnest Games: folkloric patterns in the Canterbury Tales,* Bloomington and Indianapolis, Indiana: Indiana University Press.

Locastro, V. and Netsu, M. (1997) '-to omoimasu and "I think": a pragmatic mismatch with academic skills consequences', unpublished manuscript.

Locher, M.A. (2004) *Power and Politeness in Action: disagreements in oral communication*, Berlin: Mouton de Gruyter.

——(2006) 'Polite behavior within relational work: the discursive approach to politeness', *Multilingua* 25 (3): 249–67.

Locher, M.A. and Bousfield, D. (2008) 'Impoliteness and power in language', in D. Bousfield and M.A. Locher (eds) *Impoliteness in Language*: *studies on its interplay with power in theory and practice*, pp. 1–13, Berlin and New York: Mouton de Gruyter.

Locher, M.A. and Watts, R.J. (2005) 'Politeness theory and relational work', *Journal of Politeness Research* 1 (1): 9–33.

——(2008) 'Relational work and impoliteness: negotiating norms of linguistic behaviour', in D. Bousfield and M.A. Locher (eds) *Impoliteness in Language*: *studies on its interplay with power in theory and practice*, pp. 77–100, Berlin and New York: Mouton de Gruyter.

Locke, J. (1959 [1690]) *Essay Concerning Human Understanding*, 2 vols, New York: Dover.

Love, N. (ed.) (2001) 'Special issue: grammaticalization', *Language Sciences* 23: 93–340.

Lucy, J.A. (1992a) *Language Diversity and Thought: a reformulation of the linguistic relativity hypothesis*, Cambridge: Cambridge University Press.

——(1992b) *Grammatical Categories and Cognition: a case study of the linguistic relativity hypothesis*, Cambridge: Cambridge University Press.

——(ed.) (1993) *Reflexive Language*: *reported speech and metapragmatics*, Cambridge: Cambridge University Press.

Ludlow, P. (ed.) (1997) *Readings in the Philosophy of Language*, Cambridge, Massachusetts: MIT Press.

Luszcz, M. and Bacharach, V. (1983) 'The emergence of communicative competence: detection of conversational topics', *Journal of Child Language* 10: 623–37.

Lyons, J. (1977) *Semantics*, Cambridge: Cambridge University Press.

McCawley, J.D. (1978) 'Conversational implicature and the lexicon', in P. Cole (ed.) *Syntax and Semantics 9*: *pragmatics*, pp. 245–59, New York: Academic Press.

MacMahon, B. (1996) 'Indirectness, rhetoric and interpretive use: communicative strategies in Browning's *My Last Duchess*', *Language and Literature* 5: 209–23.

——(2001a) 'The effects of word substitution in slips of the tongue, *Finnegans Wake* and *The Third Policeman*', *English Studies* 3: 231–46.

——(2001b) 'Relevance theory and the use of voice in poetry', *Belgian Journal of Linguistics* 15: 11–34.

——(2007) 'The effects of sound patterning in poetry: a cognitive pragmatic approach', *Journal of Literary Semantics* 36 (2): 103–20.

——(2009a) 'Metarepresentation and decoupling in *Northanger Abbey*: Part I', *English Studies* 90 (5): 518–44.

——(2009b) 'Metarepresentation and decoupling in *Northanger Abbey*: Part II', *English Studies* 90 (6): 673–94.

McNeill, D. (1992) *Hand and Mind*, Chicago, Illinois: University of Chicago Press.

McPhee, N. (1982) *The Complete Book of Insults*, London: BCA.

MacPherson, C.B. (1962) *The Political Theory of Possessive Individualism: from Hobbes to Locke*, Oxford: Oxford University Press.

McTear, M. and King, F. (1991) 'Miscommunication in clinical contexts: the speech therapy interview', in N. Coupland, H. Giles and J.M. Wiemann (eds) *'Miscommunication' and Problematic Talk*, pp. 195–214, Newbury Park, California: Sage.

Maienborn, C. (2004) 'A pragmatic explanation of the stage level/individual level contrast in combination with locatives', in B. Agbayani, V. Samiian and B. Tucker (eds) *Proceedings of the Western Conference on Linguistics (WECOL)*, vol. 15, pp. 158–70. Fresno: CSU.

——(2005) 'A discourse-based account of Spanish *ser/estar*', *Linguistics* 43 (1): 155–80.

Malone, K. (1951) *Chapters on Chaucer*, Baltimore, Maryland: Johns Hopkins Press.

Mao, L.R. (1994) 'Beyond politeness theory: "face" revisited and renewed', *Journal of Pragmatics* 21: 451–86.

Markee, N. and Kasper, G. (2004) 'Classroom talks: an introduction', *Modern Language Journal* 88 (4): 491–500.

Markus, H. and Wurt, E. (1987) 'The dynamic self-concept: a social psychological perspective', *Annual Review of Psychology*, vol. 38, pp. 299–337, New York: Annual Reviews.

Mascaro, O. and Sperber, D. (2009) 'The moral, epistemic, and mindreading components of children's vigilance towards deception', *Cognition* 112: 367–80.

Mateo Martínez, J. and Yus, F. (eds) (2006) *Revista Alicantina de Estudios Ingleses* 11 (special issue on Linguistics and the Media), Departamento de Filologia Inglesa, Universidad de Alicante.

Matlock, T. (1989) 'Matlock and the grammaticalization of evidentials', in K. Hall, M. Meacham and R. Shapiro (eds) *Proceedings of the Fifteenth Annual Meeting of the Berkeley Linguistics Society*, pp. 215–25, Berkeley, California: Berkeley Linguistics Society.

Matsui, T. (2010) 'Theory of mind', in L. Cummings (ed.) *The Pragmatics Encyclopedia*, pp. 469–71, London and New York: Routledge.

Matsumoto, Y. (1988) 'Reexamination of the universality of face: politeness phenomena in Japanese', *Journal of Pragmatics* 12 (4): 403–26.

——(1989) 'Politeness and conversational universals – observations from Japanese', *Multilingua* 8: 207–21.

Mead, G.H. (1934) *Mind, Self and Society*, Chicago, Illinois: University of Chicago Press.

Meeuwis, M. (1997) *Constructing Sociolinguistic Consensus: a linguistic ethnography of the Zairian community in Antwerp*, Ph.D. thesis, Belgium: University of Antwerp.

Mehl, D. (1974) 'The audience of Chaucer's *Troilus and Criseyde*', in B. Rowland (ed.) *Chaucer and Middle English Studies in Honour of Rossell Hope Robbins*, pp. 173–89, London: George Allen & Unwin.

Meini, C. (2010) 'Modularity of mind thesis', in L. Cummings (ed.) *The Pragmatics Encyclopedia*, pp. 275–8, London and New York: Routledge.

Mercier, H. and Sperber, D. (2009) 'Intuitive and reflective inferences', in J. Evans and K. Frankish (eds) *In Two Minds*: *dual processes and beyond*, Oxford: Oxford University Press.

Mertz, E. (1985) 'Beyond symbolic anthropology: introducing semiotic mediation', in E. Mertz and R. Parmentier (eds) *Semiotic Mediation*: *sociocultural and psychological perspectives*, pp. 1–19, Orlando, Florida: Academic Press.

Mey, J.L. (1993) *Pragmatics*, Oxford: Blackwell.

——(2001) *Pragmatics*: *an introduction*, 2nd edition, Oxford, and Malden, Massachusetts: Blackwell.

——(2005) 'What is in a (hand)book? Reflections on a recent compilation', *Intercultural Pragmatics* 2 (3): 347–53.

——(2007) 'Topics in applied pragmatics', *Journal of Pragmatics* 39 (1): 1–3.

Miller, G. and Johnson-Laird, P. (1976) *Language and Perception*, Cambridge, Massachusetts: Harvard University Press.

Mills, S. (2003) *Gender and Politeness*, Cambridge: Cambridge University Press.

——(2005) 'Gender and impoliteness', *Journal of Politeness Research* 1(2), 263–80.

Mitchell, B. (1985) *Old English Syntax*, vol. 1 – concord, the parts of speech, and the sentence, vol. 2 – subordination, independent elements, and element order, Oxford: Clarendon Press.

Mitchell, J.E. (1986) *The Formal Semantics of Point of View*, Ph.D. thesis, Amherst, Massachusetts: University of Massachusetts.

Mitchell, J. and Lapata, M. (2008) 'Vector-based models of semantic composition', *Proceedings of the ACL-08*: *HLT*, pp. 236–44, Columbus, Ohio.

Mithun, M. (1986) 'Evidential diachrony in northern Iroquoian', in W. Chafe and J. Nichols (eds) *Evidentiality*: *the linguistic coding of epistemology*, pp. 89–112, Norwood, New Jersey: Ablex.

——(1999) *The Languages of Native North America*, Cambridge: Cambridge University Press.

Mizutani, O. and Mizutani, N. (1978) *How to be Polite in Japanese*, Tokyo: Japan Times.

Montague, R. (1970) 'Universal grammar', *Theoria* 36: 373–98; reprinted in R.H. Thomason (ed.) *Formal Philosophy*: *selected papers of R. Montague*, pp. 222–46, New Haven: Yale University Press.

Montgomery, M. (1999) 'Talk as entertainment: the case of *The Mrs Merton Show*', in L. Haarman (ed.) *Talk about Shows*: *La Parola e lo Spettacolo*, pp. 101–50, Bologna: CLUEB.

Morgan, J.L. (1978) 'Two types of convention in indirect speech acts', in P. Cole (ed.) *Syntax and Semantics 9*: *pragmatics*, pp. 261–80, New York: Academic Press.

——(1993) 'Observations on the pragmatics of metaphor', in A. Ortony (ed.) *Metaphor and Thought*, pp. 124–33, Cambridge: Cambridge University Press.

Mori, J. (2003) 'The construction of interculturality: a study of initial encounters between American and Japanese students', *Research on Language and Social Interaction* 36 (2): 143–84.

Morris, C. (1938) 'Foundations of the Theory of Signs', *International Encyclopedia of Unified Science*, vol. 1, No. 2, Chicago, Illinois: University of Chicago Press.

Morrow, C. (1996) *The Pragmatic Effects of Instruction on ESL Learners' Production of Complaint and Refusal Speech Acts*, unpublished Ph.D. thesis, State University of New York at Buffalo.

Munro, A. (1979) 'Indirect speech acts are not strictly conventional', *Linguistic Inquiry* 10: 353–6.

Murray, D. (1979) 'Well', *Linguistic Inquiry* 10: 727–32.

Murray, I.R. and Arnott, J.L. (1993) 'Towards the simulation of emotion in synthetic speech: a review of the literature on human vocal emotion', *Journal of the Acoustical Society of America* 93 (2): 1097–108.

Murray, S.O. (1996) 'Ritual and personal insults in stigmatized subcultures: gay – black – Jew', in R. Aman (ed.) *Opus Maledictorum: a book of bad words*, pp. 213–35, New York: Marlowe & Company.

Navarro, M.P. (2006) 'Enrichment and loosening: an on-going process in the practice of translation: a study based on some translations of *Gulliver's Travels*', in A.M. Hornero, M.J. Luzón and S. Murillo (eds) *Corpus Linguistics: applications for the study of English*, pp. 269–86, Berlin: Peter Lang.

Ness, L. and Duncan-Rose, C. (1982) 'A syntactic correlate of style switching in *The Canterbury Tales*', in J.P. Mahler, A.R. Bomhard and E.F. Konrad Koerner (eds) *Papers from the Third International Conference on Historical Linguistics*, pp. 293–322, Amsterdam: John Benjamins.

Nevanlinna, S.-A. and Taavitsainen, I. (1993) *St Katherine of Alexandria: the Middle English prose legend in Southwell Minster MS 7*, Cambridge: D.S. Brewer.

Nicolle, S. and Clark, B. (1999) 'Experimental pragmatics and what is said: a response to Gibbs and Moise', *Cognition* 69 (3): 337–54.

Ninio, A. (1984) *Functions of speech in mother–infant interaction*, Final Science Report to the U.S.–Israel Binational Science Foundation, Jerusalem, Israel.

——(1986) 'Negative feedback on very young speakers' grammar', *Paper Presented at the Conference on Human Development*, Nashville, Tennessee, March 1986.

Ninio, A. and Goren, H. (1993) *PICA-100: parental interview on 100 communicative acts*, coding manual distributed by the Department of Psychology, Hebrew University, Jerusalem, Israel.

Ninio, A. and Snow, C.E. (1996) *Pragmatic Development: essays in developmental science*, Boulder, Colorado: Westview Press.

Ninio, A. and Wheeler, P. (1984) 'Functions of speech in mother–infant interaction: designing a coding scheme for the description and classification of verbal–social acts', in L. Feagans, G.J. Garvey and R. Golinkoff (eds) *The Origins and Growth of Communication*, Norwood, New Jersey: Ablex.

Noveck, I.A. (2001) 'When children are more logical than adults: experimental investigations of scalar implicature', *Cognition* 78 (2): 165–88.

Noveck, I.A. and Sperber, D. (eds) (2004) *Experimental Pragmatics*, Basingstoke: Macmillan.

——(2007) 'The why and how of experimental pragmatics: the case of "scalar inferences"', in N. Burton-Roberts (ed.) *Pragmatics*, Basingstoke: Palgrave.

Nunberg, G.D. (1977) *The Pragmatics of Reference*, Ph.D. thesis, New York: City University of New York. Distributed 1978, Bloomington, Indiana: Indiana University Linguistics Club.

——(1979) 'The non-uniqueness of semantic solutions: polysemy', *Linguistics and Philosophy* 3: 143–84.

——(1993) 'Indexicality and deixis', *Linguistics and Philosophy* 16: 1–44; reprinted in A. Kasher (ed.) (1998) *Pragmatics: critical concepts*, vol. V, pp. 145–84, London: Routledge.

——(1995) 'Transfers of meaning', *Journal of Semantics* 12: 109–32; reprinted in J. Pustejovsky and B. Boguraev (eds) (1996) *Lexical Semantics: the problem of polysemy*, pp. 87–109, Dordrecht: Reidel.

——(1996) 'Transfers of meaning', in Pustejovsky, J. and Boguraev, B. (eds) *Lexical Semantics: the problem of polysemy*, pp. 109–32, Oxford: Clarendon Press.

——(2004) 'The pragmatics of deferred interpretation', in L.R. Horn and G. Ward (eds) *The Handbook of Pragmatics*, pp. 344–64, Oxford: Blackwell.

Nuyts, J. (2000) 'Intentionality', in J. Verschueren, J.-O. Östman, J. Blommaert and C. Bulcaen (eds) *Handbook of Pragmatics*, Amsterdam: John Benjamins.

Obler, L. and Albert, M. (1980) 'Language and aging: a neurobehavioral analysis', in D.S. Beasley and G.A. Davis (eds) *Aging, Communication Processes and Disorders*, pp. 107–21, New York: Grune & Stratton.

Ochs, E. (1988) *Culture and Language Development*, Cambridge: Cambridge University Press.

Ochs, E., Schegloff, E.A. and Thompson, S. (eds) (1996) *Interaction and Grammar*, Cambridge: Cambridge University Press.

O'Connor, P. (ed.) (1995) 'Discourse of violence', special issue of *Discourse and Society* 61 (13): 309–18.

O'Driscoll, J. (1996) 'About face: a defence and elaboration of universal dualism', *Journal of Pragmatics* 25 (1): 1–32.

Okamoto, S. (1998) 'The use and non-use of honorifics in sales talk in Kyoto and Osaka: are they rude or friendly?', in N. Akatsuka, H. Hoji, S. Iwasaki, S. Sohn and S. Strauss (eds) *Japanese/Korean Linguistics* 7: 141–57, Stanford, California: Center for the Study of Language and Information.

Oleksy, W. (ed.) (1988) *Contrastive Pragmatics*, Amsterdam: John Benjamins.

Olshtain, E. and Cohen, A. (1983) 'Apology: a speech act set', in N. Wolfson and E. Judd (eds) *Sociolinguistics and Language Acquisition*, pp. 18–36, Rowley, Massachusetts: Newbury House.

——(1990) 'The learning of complex speech act behavior', *TESL Canada Journal* 7: 45–65.

Östman, J.-O. (1982) 'The symbolic relationship between pragmatic particles and impromptu speech', in N.E. Enkvist (ed.) *Impromptu Speech: a symposium*, Meddelanden från Stiftelsens for Åbo Akademi Forskningsinstitut 78, pp. 147–77, Åbo: Åbo Akademi.

——(1986) *Pragmatics as Implicitness*, UMI no. 8624885.

Owen, M. (1981) 'Conversational units and the use of *well . . .*', in P. Werth (ed.) *Conversation and Discourse: structure and interpretation*, pp. 99–116, London: Croom Helm.

——(1983) *Apologies and Remedial Interchanges*, The Hague, Netherlands: Mouton.

Özyürek, A. and S. Kita (2002) *Interacting with Demonstratives: encoding of joint attention as a semantic contrast in the Turkish and Japanese demonstrative systems*, unpublished MS, Nijmegen, The Netherlands: Max Planck Institute for Psycholinguistics.

Padilla Cruz, M. (2008) 'Three different pragmatic approaches to the teaching of the (im)politeness of phatic utterances in English', in C. Estébanez and L. Pérez Ruiz (eds) *Language Awareness in English and Spanish*, pp. 131–52, University of Valladolid.

——(2009) 'Understanding and overcoming pragmatic failure when interpreting phatic utterances', in R. Gómez Morón, M. Padilla Cruz, L. Fernández Amaya and M.O. Hernández López (eds) *Pragmatics Applied to Language Teaching and Learning*, pp. 87–108, Newcastle: Cambridge Scholars Publishing.

Palmer, F.R. (1986) *Mood and Modality*, Cambridge: Cambridge University Press.

Pan, B., Imbens-Bailey, A., Winner, K. and Snow, C.E. (1996) 'Communicative intents of parents interacting with their young children', *Merrill-Palmer Quarterly* 42: 72–90.

Papafragou, A. (1997) 'Modality in language development: a reconsideration of the evidence', *UCL Working Papers in Linguistics* 9: 77–105.

——(1998a) 'The acquisition of modality: implications for theories of semantic representation', *Mind and Language* 13: 370–99.

——(1998b) '*Modality and the semantics–pragmatics interface*', Ph.D. thesis, University of London. (Revised edition published as Papafragou 2000.)

——(2000) *Modality: issues in the semantics–pragmatics interface*, Amsterdam: Elsevier Science.

——(2002) 'Mind reading and verbal communication', *Mind and Language* 17 (1–2): 55–67.

——(2003) 'Aspectuality and scalar implicatures in child language', *U. Penn Working Papers in Linguistics* 9.1.

Papafragou, A. and Musolino, J. (2003) 'Scalar implicatures: experiments at the semantics–pragmatics interface', *Cognition* 86: 253–82.

Parsons, T. (1949) *The Structure of Social Action*, New York: Free Press.

Pears, I. (1997) *An Instance of the Fingerpost*, London: Jonathan Cape.

Peirce, C.S. (1931) *Collected Papers*, vol. 2, Cambridge, Massachusetts: Harvard University Press.

——(1931–58) 'Collected papers', in C. Hartshorne and P. Weiss (eds) (1977) *Collected Papers of Charles Sanders Peirce*, Cambridge, Massachusetts: Harvard University Press.

——(1955) *Philosophical Writings of Peirce*, New York: Dover.

——(1998) *The Essential Peirce*, vol. 2, Bloomington, Indiana: Indiana University Press.

Penman, R. (1990) 'Facework and politeness: multiple goals in courtroom discourse', in K. Tracy and N. Coupland (eds) *Multiple Goals in Discourse*, pp. 15–38, Clevedon and Philadelphia: Multilingual Matters.

Perkins, M.R. (1983) *Modal Expressions in English*, London: Francis Patter.

——(1998) 'Is pragmatics epiphenomenal? Evidence from communication disorders', *Journal of Pragmatics* 29: 291–311.

——(2007) *Pragmatic Impairment*, Cambridge: Cambridge University Press.

——(2010) 'Approaches to pragmatic impairment', in J.S. Damico, N. Miller and M.J. Ball (eds) *The Handbook of Language and Speech Disorders*, pp. 227–46, New York: John Wiley & Sons.

Perner, J. and Wimmer, H. (1985) '"John thinks that Mary thinks that . . ." Attributing second-order beliefs by 5- to 10-year-old children', *Journal of Experimental Psychology* 39: 437–71.

Perner, J., Leekam, S.R. and Wimmer, H. (1987) 'Three-year-olds' difficulty with false belief: the case of conceptual deficit', *British Journal of Developmental Psychology* 5: 125–37.

Perry, J. (1977) 'Frege on demonstratives', *Philosophical Review* 86: 474–97; reprinted in P. Ludlow (ed.) (1997) *Readings in the Philosophy of Language*, pp. 693–714, Cambridge, Massachusetts: MIT Press.

——(1993) *The Problem of Essential Indexicals and Other Essays*, Oxford and New York: Oxford University Press.

Peterson, C. and McCabe, A. (1987) 'The connective *and*', *First Language* 8: 19–28.

Philip, G. (2005) 'Figurative language and the advanced learner', *Research News: the newsletter of the IATEFL research SIG* 16: 16–20.

Phillipps, K.C. (1966) 'Adverb clauses in the fifteenth century', *English Studies* 47: 355–65.

Piaget, J. (1929) *The Child's Conception of the World*, New York: Harcourt Brace.

Pilkington, A. (1996) 'Introduction: relevance theory and literary style', *Language and Literature* 5 (3): 157–62.

——(2000) *Poetic Effects: a relevance theory perspective*, Amsterdam: John Benjamins.

Pinkal, M. (1995) *Logic and Lexicon: the semantics of the indefinite*, Dordrecht: Kluwer.

Plate, T.A. (2000) 'Analogy retrieval and processing with distributed vector representations', *Expert Systems: the International Journal of Knowledge Engineering and Neural Networks*, special issue on connectionist symbol processing, 17 (1): 29–40.

Plato (429–347 BC) *Phaedrus*, trans. R Hackforth (ed.) (1972) Cambridge: Cambridge University Press.

Popper, K.R. (1945) *The Open Society and Its Enemies*, London: Routledge.

——(1959) *The Logic of Scientific Discovery*, London: Hutchinson.

——(1963) *Conjectures and Refutations: the growth of scientific knowledge*, London: Routledge & Kegan Paul.

——(1974) 'Scientific reduction and the essential incompleteness of all science', in F.J. Ayala and T. Grigorievich (eds) *Studies in the Philosophy of Biology: reduction and related problems*, pp. 259–84, California: University of California Press.

——(1983) *Realism and the Aim of Science*, Totowa, New Jersey: Rowman & Littlefield.

Pouscoulous, N. and Noveck, I.A. (2009) 'Developmental aspects of the semantic/pragmatic distinction', in S. Foster-Cohen (ed.) *Advances in Language Acquisition*, Basingstoke: Palgrave.

Pouscoulous, N., Noveck, I.A., Politzer, G. and Bastide, J. (2007) 'Evidence for the production of scalar implicature in young children', *Language Acquisition*.

Premack, D. and Woodruff, D. (1978) 'Does the chimpanzee have a theory of mind?', *Behavior and Brain Sciences* 1: 515–26.

Pressman, J.F. (1994) 'Pragmatics in the late twentieth century: countering recent historiographic neglect', *Pragmatics* 4 (4): 461–89.

Preston, D. (2000) 'A renewed proposal for the study of folk linguistics', in J.K. Peyton, P. Griffen, W. Wolfram and R. Fasold (eds) *Language in Action*, pp. 113–38, Cresskill, New Jersey: Hampton Press.

Prodromou, L. (2008) *English as a Lingua Franca: a corpus-based analysis*, London: Continuum.

Psathas, G. (1995) *Conversation Analysis: the study of talk-in-interaction*, Thousand Oaks, California: Sage.

Pustejovsky, J. (1995) *The Generative Lexicon*, Cambridge, Massachusetts: MIT Press.

Pustejovsky, J. and Boguraev, B. (eds) (1996) *Lexical Semantics: the problem of polysemy*, Oxford: Clarendon Press.

Putnam, H. (1975) *Mind, Language, and Reality: philosophical papers*, vol. 2, Cambridge: Cambridge University Press.

Quine, W.V.O. (1960) *Word and Object*, Cambridge, Massachusetts: MIT Press.

——(1961) *From a Logical Point of View*, New York: Harper.

Quinn, N. (1987) 'Convergent evidence for a cultural model of American marriage', in D. Holland and N. Quinn (eds) *Cultural Models in Language and Thought*, pp. 173–92, Cambridge: Cambridge University Press.

Quirk, R., Greenbaum, S., Leech, G.N. and Svartvik, J. (1985) *A Comprehensive Grammar of the English Language*, London and New York: Longman.

Rampton, B. (1999) 'Sociolinguistics and cultural studies: new ethnicities, liminality and interaction', *Social Semiotics* 9 (3): 355–74.

Rampton, B. (2001) 'Ethnicity and the crossing of ethnic boundaries', in R. Mesthrie and R. Asher (eds) *Concise Encyclopedia of Sociolinguistics*, Oxford: Elsevier.

Rapin, I. and Allen, D.A. (1983) 'Developmental language disorders: nosological considerations', in U. Kirk (ed.) *Neuropsychology of Language, Reading and Spelling*, pp. 155–84, New York: Academic Press.

——(1988) 'The semantic–pragmatic deficit disorder: classification issues', *International Journal of Language and Communication Disorders* 33: 82–87.

Rauh, G. (1981) 'Aspects of deixis', in G. Rauh (ed.) *Essays on Deixis*, pp. 9–60, Tübingen: Gunter Narr Verlag.

Recanati, F. (1989) 'The pragmatics of what is said', *Mind and Language* 4: 295–329; reprinted in S. Davis (ed.) (1991) *Pragmatics: a reader*, pp. 97–120, Oxford: Oxford University Press.

——(1993) *Direct Reference: from language to thought*, Oxford: Blackwell.

——(1995) 'The alleged priority of literal interpretation', *Cognitive Science* 19: 207–32.

——(2001) 'What is said', *Synthese* 128: 75–91.

——(2004a) *Literal Meanings*, Cambridge: Cambridge University Press.

——(2004b) 'Pragmatics and semantics', in L.R. Horn and G. Ward (eds) *The Handbook of Pragmatics*, pp. 442–62, Oxford: Blackwell.

——(2005) 'Literalism and contextualism: some varieties', in G. Preyer and G. Peter (eds) *Contextualism in Philosophy: knowledge, meaning, and truth*, pp. 171–96, Oxford and New York: Oxford University Press.

——(2006) 'Truth-conditional pragmatics: an overview', in P. Bouquet, L. Serafini and R.H. Thomason (eds) *Perspectives on Contexts*, Stanford, California: CSLI Publications.

——(2010) 'Pragmatics and logical form', in B. Soria and E. Romero (eds) *Explicit Communication: Robyn Carston's pragmatics*, Basingstoke: Palgrave.

Redeker, G. (1991) 'Review of Schiffrin 1987', *Linguistics* 29: 1139–72.

Reed, I., Miwaoke, O., Ascan, P. and Krauss, M. (1977) *Yup'ik Eskimo Grammar*, Fairbanks, Alaska: Alaska Native Language Center.

Reese, W. (1980) *Dictionary of Modem Philosophy and Religion*, Atlantic Highlands, New Jersey: Humanities Press.

Rintell, E. (1981) 'Sociolinguistic variation and pragmatic ability: a look at learners', *International Journal of the Sociology of Language* 27: 11–34.

Ripich, D. and Terrell, B. (1988) 'Patterns of discourse cohesion and coherence in Alzheimer's disease', *Journal of Speech and Hearing Disorders* 53: 8–15.

Rissanen, M., Kytö, M. and Palander-Collin, M. (eds) (1993) *Early English in the Computer Age: explorations through the Helsinki Corpus*, Berlin: Mouton de Gruyter.

Rollins, P.R. (2010) 'Developmental pragmatics', in L. Cummings (ed.) *The Pragmatics Encyclopedia*, pp. 110–11, London: Routledge.

Romaine, S. and Lange, D. (1991) 'The use of *like* as a marker of reported speech and thought: a case of grammaticalization in progress', *American Speech* 66: 227–79.

Rosales Sequeiros, X. (2005) 'Effects of pragmatic interpretation on translation: communicative gaps and textual discrepancies', *Lincom Studies in Pragmatics* 13, Munich: Lincom.

Rosch, E. (1977) 'Human categorization', in N. Warren (ed.) *Cross-Cultural Studies in Psychology*, vol. 1, London: Academic Press.

——(1978) 'Principles of categorization', in E. Rosch and B.B. Lloyd (eds) *Cognition and Categorization*, pp. 27–48, Hillsdale, New Jersey: Erlbaum.

Rose, K. (1994) 'On the validity of DCTs in non-Western contexts', *Applied Linguistics* 15: 1–14.

Ross, J.R. (1973) 'Slifting', in M. Gross, M. Halle and M.-P. Schützenberger (eds) *The Formal Analysis of Natural Languages: proceedings of the first international conference*, pp. 133–69, The Hague and Paris: Mouton.

Ross, L. (1977) 'The intuitive psychologist and his shortcomings: distortions in the attribution process', in L. Berkowitz (ed.) *Advances in Experimental Social Psychology*, vol. 10, pp. 173–220, New York: Academic Press.

Rubba, J. (1988) *Cognitive Models and California Proposition 63: English as Official Language, MS*, San Diego, California: University of California.

——(1996) 'Alternate grounds in the interpretation of deictic expressions', in G. Fauconnier and E. Sweetser (eds) *Spaces, Worlds, and Grammar*, pp. 227–61, Chicago, Illinois: University of Chicago Press.

Rubin, E. (1915) 'Figure-ground perception', trans. from German by M. Wertheimer, in D.C. Beardslee and M. Wertheimer (eds) (1958) *Readings in Perception*, pp. 194–203, Princeton, New Jersey: Van Nostrand.

Ruhi, S. (2007) 'Higher-order intentions and self-politeness in evaluations of (im)politeness: the relevance of compliment responses', *Australian Journal of Linguistics* 27 (2): 107–45.

——(2008) 'Intentionality, communicative intentions and the implication of politeness', *Intercultural Pragmatics* 5 (3): 287–314.

Ruhi S. and Dogan, G. (2001) 'Relevance theory and compliments as phatic communication: the case of Turkish', in A. Bayraktaroglu and M. Sifianou (eds) *Linguistic Politeness Across Boundaries*, pp. 341–90, Amsterdam: John Benjamins.

Rumelhart, D.E., Smolensky, P., McClelland, J.L. and Hinton, G.E. (1986) 'Schemata and sequential thought processes in PDP models', in D.E. Rumelhart, J.L. McClelland and the PDP Research Group (eds) *Parallel Distributed Processing*, vol. 2, pp. 7–57, Cambridge, Massachusetts: MIT Press.

Ryder, N. (2010) 'Pragmatic language impairment', in L. Cummings (ed.) *The Pragmatics Encyclopedia*, pp. 338–40, London and New York: Routledge.

Sachs, J., Anselmi, D. and McCollam, K. (1990) 'Young children's awareness of presuppositions based on community membership', *Paper Presented at the Fifth International Congress for the Study of Child Language*, Budapest, Hungary.

Sacks, H. (1984) 'Notes on methodology', in J.M. Atkinson and J. Heritage (eds) *Structures of Social Action*: *studies in conversation analysis*, pp. 21–7, Cambridge: Cambridge University Press.

Sacks, H. and Schegloff, E.A. (1975) 'Home position', *Paper Delivered at the Annual Meeting of the American Anthropological Association*, San Francisco, California.

——(1979) 'Two preferences in the organization of reference to persons in conversation and their interaction', in G. Psathas (ed.) *Everyday Language: studies in ethnomethodology*, pp. 15–21, New York: Irvington.

Sacks, H., Schegloff, E.A. and Jefferson, G. (1974) 'A simplest systematics for the organization of turn taking for conversation', *Language* 50: 696–735.

Sacks, H., Schegloff, E.A. and Jefferson, G. (1978) 'A simplest systematics for the organization of turn taking for conversation', in J. Schenkein (ed.) *Studies in the Organization of Conversational Interaction*, pp. 7–55, New York: Academic Press (paper first published in *Language* 50 [1974]).

Sag, I. (1981) 'Formal semantics and extralinguistic context', in P. Cole (ed.) *Radical Pragmatics*, pp. 273–94, New York: Academic Press.

Saigo, H. (2011) *The Pragmatic Properties and Sequential Functions of the Japanese Sentence-Final Particles, Ne, Yo, and Yone*, Amsterdam: John Benjamins.

Samovar, L.A. and Porter, R. (2001) *Intercultural Communication Reader*, New York: Thomas Learning Publications.

Sbisà, M. (1995) 'Speech act theory', in J. Verschueren, J.-O. Östman and J. Blommaert (eds) *Handbook of Pragmatics*, pp. 495–506, Amsterdam: John Benjamins.

Schank, R.C. and Abelson, R.P. (1977) *Scripts, Plans, Goals and Understanding*: an inquiry into human knowledge structures, Hillsdale, New Jersey: Lawrence Erlbaum Associates.

Schegloff, E.A. (1972) 'Sequencing in conversational openings', in J.J. Gumperz and D. Hymes (eds) *Directions in Sociolinguistics*, pp. 346–80, New York: Holt, Rinehart, & Winston.

——(1979) 'Identification and recognition in telephone conversation openings', in G. Psathas (ed.) *Everyday Language*, pp. 23–78, New York: Irvington.

——(1984) 'On some gestures' relation to talk', in J.M. Atkinson and J. Heritage (eds) *Structures of Social Action*, pp. 266–96, Cambridge: Cambridge University Press.

——(1988) 'On an actual virtual servo-mechanism for guessing bad news: single case conjecture', *Social Problems* 35 (4): 442–57.

——(1991) 'Reflections on talk and social structure', in D. Boden and D.H. Zimmerman (eds) *Talk and Social Structure*, pp. 44–70, Cambridge: Polity Press.

——(1992a) 'In another context', in A. Duranti and C. Goodwin (eds) *Rethinking Context*, pp. 191–228, Cambridge: Cambridge University Press.

——(1992b) 'Introduction to volume 1', in H. Sacks, *Lectures on Conversation*, G. Jefferson (ed.) Oxford: Blackwell.

——(1996) 'Issues of relevance for discourse analysis: contingency in action, interaction and co-participant context', in E.H. Hovy and D. Scott (eds) *Computational and Conversational Discourse*: burning issues – an interdisciplinary account, pp. 3–38, Heidelberg: Springer Verlag.

——(1998) 'Body torque', *Social Research* 65 (3): 535–96.

——(1999) 'Discourse, pragmatics, conversation, analysis', *Discourse Studies* 1 (4): 405–35.

Schegloff, E.A., Jefferson, G. and Sacks, H. (1977) 'The preference for self-correction in the organization of repair in conversation', *Language* 53, 361–82.

Schelling, T. (1960) *The Strategy of Conflict*, Oxford: Oxford University Press.

Schieffelin, B., Woolard, K.A. and Kroskrity, P.V. (eds) (1998) *Language Ideologies*, Oxford and New York: Oxford University Press.

Schiffer, S.R. (1972) *Meaning*, Oxford: Clarendon Press.

Schiffrin, D. (ed.) (1984) 'Jewish argument as sociability', *Language in Society* 13 (3): 311–35.

——(1985) 'Conversational coherence: the role of *well*', *Language* 61: 640–67.

——(1987) *Discourse Markers*, Cambridge: Cambridge University Press.

——(1994) *Approaches to Discourse*, Oxford: Blackwell.

——(1996) 'Interactional sociolinguistics', in S. McKay and N.H. Hornberger (eds) *Sociolinguistics and Language Teaching*, pp. 307–28, Cambridge: Cambridge University Press.

Schley, S. and Snow, C. (1992) 'The conversational skills of school-aged children', *Social Development* 1: 18–35.

Schlieben-Lange, B. (1976) 'Für eine historische Analyse von Sprechakten', in H. Weber and H. Weydts (eds) *Sprachtheorie und Pragmatik*, pp. 113–9, Tübingen: Niemeyer.

——(1979) 'Ai las – Que planhs? Ein Versuch der historischen Gesprächsanalyse am Flamenca-Roman', *Romantistische Zeitschrift für Literaturgeschichte* 3: 1–30.

Schlieben-Lange, B. and Weydt, H. (1979) 'Streitgespräch zur Historizität von Sprechakten', *Linguistische Berichte* 60: 65–78.

——(1983) *Traditionen des Sprechens. Elemente einer pragmatischen Sprachgeschichtsschreibung*, Stuttgart: Kohlhammer.

Schober-Peterson, D. and Johnson, C. (1991) 'Non-dialogue speech during preschool interactions', *Journal of Child Language* 18: 153–70.

Scholl, B. and Leslie, A. (1999) 'Modularity, development and "theory of mind"', *Mind and Language* 14: 131–53.

Schourup, L.C. (1985) *Common Discourse Particles in English Conversations*: '*like*', '*well*', '*y'know*', New York and London: Garland.

Schrott, A. (2000) '"¿Quí los podrié contra?": interrogative acts in the *Cantar de mio Cid*. Some examples from Old Spanish on asking questions', *Journal of Historical Pragmatics* 1 (2): 263–99.

Schwenter, S.A. and Traugott, E.C. (1995) 'The semantic–pragmatic development of substitutive complex prepositions in English', in A. Jucker (ed.) *Historical Pragmatics*, pp. 243–73, Amsterdam: John Benjamins.

Scott, C. (1984) 'Adverbial connectivity in conversations of children 6 to 12', *Journal of Child Language* 11: 423–52.

Searle, J.R. (1969) *Speech Acts*, Cambridge: Cambridge University Press.

——(1975a) 'Indirect speech acts', in P. Cole and J.L. Morgan (eds) *Syntax and Semantics*: *speech acts*, vol. 3, pp. 59–82, New York: Academic Press.

——(1975b) 'A taxonomy of illocutionary acts', in K. Gunderson (ed.) *Language, Mind and Knowledge*, vol. III, pp. 344–69, Minnesota Studies in the Philosophy of Science, Minneapolis: University of Minnesota Press; reprinted in J.R. Searle (ed.) (1979) *Expression and Meaning*, pp. 1–29, Cambridge: Cambridge University Press.

——(1976) 'The classification of illocutionary acts', *Language in Society* 5: 1–25.

——(1978) 'Literal Meaning', *Erkenntniss* 13: 207–24; reprinted in J.R. Searle (1979) *Expression and Meaning*, pp. 117–36, Cambridge: Cambridge University Press.

——(1979) 'A taxonomy of illocutionary acts', in J.R. Searle (ed.) *Expression and Meaning*, pp. 1–29, Cambridge: Cambridge University Press.

——(1980) 'The background of meaning', in J.R. Searle and F. Kiefer (eds) *Speech Act Theory and Pragmatics*, pp. 221–32, Dordrecht: Reidel.

——(1983) *Intentionality*, Cambridge: Cambridge University Press.

Selinker, L. (1972) 'Interlanguage', *International Review of Applied Linguistics* (*IRAL*) X/3: 209–31.

Sell, R.D. (1992) 'Literary texts and diachronic aspects of politeness', in R.J. Watts, S. Ide and K. Ehlich (eds) *Politeness in Language*: *studies in its history, theory and practice*, pp. 109–29, Berlin: Mouton de Gruyter.

Setton, R. (1999) *Simultaneous Interpretation*: *a cognitive–pragmatic analysis*, Amsterdam: John Benjamins.

——(2005a) 'Pointing to contexts: a relevance-theoretic approach to assessing quality and difficulty in interpreting', in H.V. Dam, J. Engberg and H. Gerzymisch-Arbogast (eds) *Knowledge Systems and Translation*, pp. 275–312, Berlin and New York: Walter de Gruyter.

——(2005b) 'So what is so interesting about simultaneous interpreting?', *Skase Journal of Translation and Interpretation* 1 (1): 70–84.

——(2006) 'Context in simultaneous interpretation', *Journal of Pragmatics* 38 (3): 374–89.

Seuren, P.A.M. (1985) *Discourse Semantics*, Oxford: Blackwell.

——(1988) 'Presupposition and negation', *Journal of Semantics* 6.3/4: 175–226.

——(1995) *Western Linguistics*: *an historical introduction*, Oxford: Blackwell.

Shibatani, M. (1999) 'Honorifics', in K. Brown and J. Miller (eds) *Concise Encyclopedia of Grammatical Categories*, pp. 192–201, Amsterdam: Elsevier.

Silverstein, M. (1972) 'Chinook jargon: language contact and the problem of multilevel generative systems, Part I', *Language* 48 (2): 378–406; 'Part II' *Language* 48 (3): 596–625.

——(1974) 'Dialectal developments in Chinookan tense-aspect systems: an areal-historical analysis', *International Journal of American Linguistics* 40: S45–S99.

——(1975) 'Linguistics and anthropology', in R. Bartsch and T. Vennemann (eds) *Linguistics and Neighboring Disciplines*, pp. 157–70, Amsterdam: North Holland Publishing Company.

——(1976a) 'Hierarchy of features and ergativity', in R. Dixon (ed.) *Grammatical Categories in Australian Languages*, pp. 112–71, Canberra: Australian Institute of Aboriginal Studies.

——(1976b) 'Shifters, linguistic categories, and cultural description', in K. Basso and H. Selby (eds) *Meaning in Anthropology*, pp. 11–55, Albuquerque, New Mexico: University of New Mexico Press.

——(1978) 'Deixis and deducibility in a Wasco-Wishram passive of evidence', in C. Chiarello, H. Thompson, F. Ackerman, O. Gensler, J. Kingston, E.C. Sweetser, A.C. Woodbury, K. Whistler and J. Jaeger (eds), *Proceedings of the Fourth Annual Meeting of the Berkeley Linguistic Society*, pp. 238–53, Berkeley, California: Berkeley Linguistics Society.

——(1979) 'Language structure and linguistic ideology', in P.R. Clyne, W.F. Hanks and C.L. Hofbauer (eds) *The Elements: a parasession on linguistic units and levels*, pp. 193–247, Chicago, Illinois: Chicago Linguistic Society.

——(1981a) 'Case-marking and the nature of language', *Australian Journal of Linguistics* 1: 227–44.

——(1981b) 'The limits of awareness', *Working Papers in Sociolinguistics*, no. 84, Austin, Texas: Southwestern Educational Laboratory.

——(1985a) 'The culture of language in Chinookan narrative texts; or, on saying that . . . in Chinook', in J. Nichols and A. Woodbury (eds) *Grammar Inside and Outside the Clause: some approaches from the field*, pp. 132–71, Cambridge: Cambridge University Press.

——(1985b) 'The functional stratification of language and ontogenesis', in J. Wertsch (ed.) *Culture, Communication, and Cognition: Vygotskian perspectives*, pp. 205–35, Cambridge: Cambridge University Press.

——(1985c) 'Noun phrase categorical markedness and syntactic parametricization', in S. Choi, D. Devitt, W. Janis, T. McCoy and Z. Zhang (eds), *Proceedings of the Second Eastern States Conference on Linguistics*, pp. 337–61, Buffalo, New York: SUNY Press.

——(1985d) 'Language and the culture of gender: at the intersection of structure usage, and ideology', in E. Mertz and R. Parmentier (eds) *Semiotic Mediation: sociocultural and psychological perspectives*, pp. 119–257 Orlando, Florida: Academic Press.

——(1986) 'Classifiers, verb classifiers, and verbal categories', in V. Nikiforidou, M. VanClay, M. Niepokuj and D. Feder (eds) *Proceedings of the Twelfth Annual Meeting of the Berkeley Linguistics Society*, pp. 497–514, Berkeley, California: Berkeley Linguistics Society.

——(1987a) 'The three faces of function: preliminaries to a psychology of language', in M. Hickmann (ed.) *Social and Functional Approaches to Language and Thought*, pp. 17–38, Orlando, Florida: Academic Press.

——(1987b) 'Cognitive implications of a referential hierarchy', in M. Hickmann (ed.) *Social and Functional Approaches to Language and Thought*, pp. 125–64, Orlando, Florida: Academic Press.

——(1993) 'Metapragmatic discourse and metapragmatic function', in J.A. Lucy (ed.) *Reflexive Language: reported speech and metapragmatics*, pp. 33–58, Cambridge: Cambridge University Press.

——(2010) '"Direct" and "indirect" communicative acts in semiotic perspective', *Journal of Pragmatics* 42 (2): 337–53.

Simmel, G. (1950) *The Sociology of Georg Simmel*, trans. K.H. Wolff (ed.) Glencoe, Illinois: Free Press.

Smith, A.H. (1984) *Chinese Characteristics*, New York: Fleming H. Revell Co.

Smitherman, G. (1977) *Talkin and Testifyin: the language of black America*, Boston, Massachusetts: Houghton Mifflin.

Snow, C.E. (1977) 'The development of conversation between mothers and babies', *Journal of Child Language* 4: 1–22.

Snow, C.E., Pan, B., Imbens-Bailey, A. and Herman, J. (1996) 'Learning how to say what one means: a longitudinal study of children's speech act use', *Social Development* 5: 56–84

Southgate, V., Chevallier, C. and Csibra, G. (2009) 'Sensitivity to communicative relevance tells young children what to imitate', *Developmental Science* 12 (6): 1013–19.

Spencer-Oatey, H. (1993) 'Conceptions of social relations and pragmatic research', *Journal of Pragmatics* 20: 27–47.

——(2000) 'Rapport management: a framework for analysis', in H. Spencer-Oatey (ed.) *Culturally Speaking: managing rapport through talk across cultures*, pp. 11–46, London: Continuum.

——(2002) 'Managing rapport in talk: using rapport sensitive incidents to explore the motivational concerns underlying the management of relations', *Journal of Pragmatics* 34: 529–45.

——(2008) *Culturally Speaking: culture, communication and politeness theory*, London: Continuum.

Sperber, D. (1994) 'Understanding verbal understanding', in J. Khalfa (ed.) *What is Intelligence?*, pp. 179–98, Cambridge: Cambridge University Press.

——(2000) 'Metarepresentations in an evolutionary perspective', in D. Sperber (ed.) *Metarepresentations*, pp. 117–37, Oxford: Oxford University Press.

——(2001) 'In defense of massive modularity', in E. Dupoux (ed.) *Language, Brain and Cognitive Development: essays in honor of Jacques Mehler*, pp. 47 57, Cambridge, Massachusetts: MIT Press.

——(2005) 'Modularity and relevance: how can a massively modular mind be flexible and context-sensitive?', in P. Carruthers, S. Laurence and S. Stich (eds) *The Innate Mind: structure and content*, Oxford: Oxford University Press.

Sperber, D. and Noveck, I. (2004) 'Introduction', in I. Noveck and D. Sperber (eds) *Experimental Pragmatics*, pp. 1–24, Basingstoke: Palgrave.

Sperber, D. and Wilson, D. (1981) 'Irony and the use–mention distinction', in P. Cole (ed.) *Radical Pragmatics*, pp. 295–318, New York: Academic Press.

——(1985/6) 'Loose talk', *Proceedings of the Aristotelian Society* 86: 153–71.

——(1986) *Relevance: communication and cognition*, Oxford: Blackwell.

——(1990) 'Rhetoric and relevance', in J. Bender and D. Wellbery (eds) *The Ends of Rhetoric: history, theory, practice*, pp. 140–56, Stanford, California: Stanford University Press.

——(1995) *Relevance: communication and cognition*, 2nd edition, Oxford: Blackwell.

——(1998) 'The mapping between the mental and the public lexicon', in P. Carruthers and C. Boucher (eds) *Thought and Language*, pp. 184–200, Cambridge: Cambridge University Press.

——(2002) 'Pragmatics, modularity and mindreading', *Mind and Language* 17: 3–23.

——(2005) 'Pragmatics', in F. Jackson and M. Smith (eds) *Oxford Handbook of Contemporary Philosophy*, pp. 468–501, Oxford: Oxford University Press.

——(2008) 'A deflationary account of metaphor', in R.W. Gibbs Jr (ed.) *Handbook of Metaphor and Thought*, pp. 84–108, Cambridge: Cambridge University Press.

Sperber, D., Cara, F. and Girotto, V. (1995) 'Relevance theory explains the selection task', *Cognition* 57: 31–95.

Stalnaker, R.C. (1974) 'Pragmatic presuppositions', in M.K. Munitz and P.K. Unger (eds) *Semantics and Philosophy*, pp. 197–214, New York: New York University Press; reprinted in S. Davis (ed.) (1991) *Pragmatics: a reader*, pp. 471–82, Oxford: Oxford University Press; and also in R.C. Stalnaker (ed.) *Context and Content*, pp. 47–62, Oxford: Oxford University Press.

Stanley, J. (2000) 'Context and logical form', *Linguistics and Philosophy* 23: 391–434.

Steels, L. (1998) 'The origins of syntax in visually grounded robotic agents', *Artificial Intelligence* 103: 133–56.

Steinberg, D.D. and Jakobovitz, L.A. (eds) (1971) *Semantics: an interdisciplinary reader in philosophy, linguistics and psychology*, Cambridge: Cambridge University Press.

Steiner, P. (1978) 'The conceptual basis of Prague structuralism', in L. Matejka (ed.) *Sound, Sign and Meaning: quinquagenary of the Prague linguistic circle*, pp. 351–85, Ann Arbor, Michigan: University of Michigan Press.

Stern, D.N., Jaffe, J., Beebe, B. and Bennett, S.L. (1975) 'Vocalizing in unison and in alternation: two modes of communication within the mother–infant dyad', *Developmental Psycholinguistic and Communication Disorders* 263: 89–100.

Stoppard, T. (1982) *The Real Thing*, London: Faber.

Strawson, P. (1950) 'On referring', *Mind* 59: 320–44.

——(1952) *Introduction to Logical Theory*, London: Methuen.

Stubbs, M. (1983) *Discourse Analysis: the sociolinguistic analysis of natural language*, Oxford: Blackwell.

Swartvik, J. (1979) '*Well* in conversation', in S. Greenbaum, G. Leech and J. Swartik (eds) *Studies in English, Linguistics for Randolf Quirk*, pp. 167–77, London/New York: Longman.

Sweetser, E.E. (1990) *From Etymology to Pragmatics: metaphorical and cultural aspects of semantic structure*, Cambridge: Cambridge University Press.

Taavitsainen, I. (1995) 'Narrative patterns of affect in four genres of the *Canterbury Tales*', *Chaucer Review* 30 (2): 191–210.

——(1997) 'Genres and text types in Medieval and Renaissance English', *Poetica* 47: 49–62.

Taavitsainen, I. and Jucker, A.H. (2008) 'Speech acts now and then: towards a pragmatic history of English', in A.H. Jucker and I. Taavitsainen (eds) *Speech Acts in the History of English*, pp. 1–23, Amsterdam and Philadelphia: John Benjamins.

Takubo, Y. and Kinsui, S. (1997) 'Discourse management in terms of mental spaces', *Journal of Pragmatics* 28 (6): 741–58.

Talmy, L. (1988) 'The relation of grammar to cognition', in B. Rudzka-Ostyn (ed.) *Topics in Cognitive Linguistics*, pp. 165–205, Amsterdam: John Benjamins.

Tannen, D. (1981) 'New York Jewish conversational style', *International Journal of the Sociology of Language* 30: 133–49.

——(1987) 'Repetition in conversation: towards a poetics of talk', *Language* 63: 574–604.

——(ed.) (1993a) *Framing in Discourse*, Oxford: Oxford University Press.

——(1993b) 'What's in a frame? Surface evidence for underlying expectations', in D. Tannen (ed.) *Framing in Discourse*, pp. 14–56, Oxford: Oxford University Press.

Tanz, C. (1980) *Studies in the Acquisition of Deictic Terms*, Cambridge: Cambridge University Press.

Tateyama, Y., Kasper, G., Mui, L., Tay, H. and Thananart, O. (1997) 'Explicit and implicit teaching of pragmatic routines', in L. Bouton (ed.) *Pragmatics and Language Learning*, monograph series vol. 8, pp. 163–78, Urbana-Champaign, Illinois: Division of English as an International Language, University of Illinois at Urbana-Champaign.

Taylor, J.R. (2002) *Cognitive Grammar*, Oxford: Oxford University Press.

Taylor, K.A. (2001) 'Sex, breakfast, and descriptus-interruptus', *Synthese* 128 (1): 45–61.

Tendahl, M. and Gibbs, R.W. Jr (2008) 'Complementary perspectives on metaphor: cognitive linguistics and relevance theory', *Journal of Pragmatics* 40 (11): 1823–64.

ten Have, P. (2007) *Doing Conversation Analysis: a practical guide*, London: Sage.

Thomas, J. (1983) 'Cross-cultural pragmatic failure', *Applied Linguistics* 4 (2): 91–112.

——(1995) *Meaning in Interaction: an introduction to pragmatics*, London: Longman.

Thompson, S.A. and Mulac, A. (1991) 'A quantitative perspective on the grammaticalization of epistemic parentheticals in English', in E.C. Traugott and B. Heine (eds), *Approaches to Grammaticalization*, vol. II, pp. 313–29, Amsterdam: John Benjamins.

Ting-Toomey, S. (1999) *Communicating Across Cultures*, New York and London: The Guilford Press.

Tolson, A. (1991) 'Televised chat and the synthetic personality', in P. Scannell (ed.) *Broadcast Talk*, pp. 178–200, London: Sage.

Tomasello, M. (1999) *The Cultural Origins of Human Cognition*, Cambridge, Massachusetts: Harvard University Press.

Tracy, K. (2008) 'Reasonable hostility: situation-appropriate face attack', *Journal of Politeness Research* 4: 169–91.

Tracy, K. and Tracy, S.J. (1998) 'Rudeness at 911: reconceptualizing face and face attack', *Human Communication Research* 25 (2): 225–51.

Trask, R.L. (1999) *Key Concepts in Language and Linguistics*, London: Routledge.

Traugott, E.C. (1982) 'From propositional to textual and expressive meanings: some semantic–pragmatic aspects of grammaticalization', in W.P. Lehmann and Y. Malkiel (eds) *Perspectives on Historical Linguistics*, pp. 245–71, Amsterdam: John Benjamins.

——(1989) 'On the rise of epistemic meanings in English: an example of subjectification in semantic change', *Language* 57: 33–65.

——(1992) 'Syntax', in R.M. Hogg (ed.) *The Cambridge History of the English Language: the beginning to 1066*, vol. 1, pp. 168–289, Cambridge: Cambridge University Press.

——(1995) 'Subjectification in grammaticalization', in D. Stein and S. Wright (eds) *Subjectivity and Subjectivisation: linguistic perspectives*, pp. 31–54, Cambridge: Cambridge University Press.

——(1997) 'Semantic change: an overview', *Glot International* 2 (9/10): 3–6.

——(1999) 'The role of pragmatics in semantic change', in J. Verschueren (ed.) *Pragmatics in 1998: selected papers from the sixth International Pragmatics Conference*, vol. 2, Antwerp, Belgium, International Pragmatics Association (IPrA).

——(2002) 'From etymology to historical pragmatics', in D. Minkova and R.P. Stockwell (eds) *Studies in the History of the English Language: a millennial perspective*, pp. 19–50, Berlin: Mouton de Gruyter.

——(2004) 'Historical pragmatics', in L.R. Horn and G. Ward (eds) *The Handbook of Pragmatics*, pp. 538–61, Oxford: Blackwell.

Traugott, E.C. and Dasher, R.B. (2002) *Regularity in Semantic Change*, Cambridge: Cambridge University Press.

——(2005) *Regularity in Semantic Change*, Cambridge: Cambridge University Press.

Traugott, E.C. and König, E. (1991) 'The semantics–pragmatics of grammaticalization revisited', in E.C. Traugott and B. Heine (eds) *Approaches to Grammaticalization*, vol. 1, pp. 189–218, Amsterdam: John Benjamins.

Travis, C. (1981) *The True and the False: the domain of the pragmatic*, Amsterdam: John Benjamins.

——(1989) *The Uses of Sense: Wittgenstein's philosophy of language*, Oxford and New York: Oxford University Press.

Trevarthen, C.B. (1979) 'Instincts for human understanding and for cultural cooperation: their development in infancy', in M. von Cranach, K. Foppa, W. Lepenies and D. Ploog (eds) *Human Ethology: claims and limits of a new discipline*, Cambridge: Cambridge University Press.

Trosborg, A. (1995) *Interlanguage Pragmatics: requests, complaints and apologies*, Berlin: Mouton de Gruyter.

Tsuji, H. (2002) 'Young children expressing their communicative intents: a preliminary study of the interactions between Japanese children and their caregivers', *Educate* 2: 72–84.

Turner, J. (1978) *The Structure of Sociological Theory*, Homewood, Illinois: The Dorsey Press.

Tversky, A. and Kahneman, D. (1974) 'Judgment under uncertainty: heuristics and biases', *Science* 185: 1124–31.

Ulatowska, H., Allard, L. and Chapman, S. (1990) 'Narrative and procedural discourse and aphasia', in Y. Joannette and H. Brownell (eds) *Discourse Ability and Brain Damage*, pp. 180–98, New York: Springer Verlag.

Ulatowska, H., Allard, L., Donnell, A., Bristow, J., Hayes, S., Flower, A. and North, A. (1988) 'Discourse performance in subjects with dementia of the Alzheimer type', in H. Whitaker (ed.) *Neuropsychological Studies of Nonfocal Brain Damage*, pp. 108–31, New York: Springer Verlag.

Underhill, R. (1988) '*Like* is, like, focus', *American Speech* 63: 234–46.

Urban, G. (1984) 'Speech about speech in speech about action', *Journal of American Folklore* 97 (385): 310–28.

——(1991) *A Discourse-Centered Approach to Culture*: native south American myths and rituals, Austin, Texas: University of Texas.

——(1993) 'The represented functions of speech in Shokleng myth', in J.A. Lucy (ed.) *Reflexive Language*: reported speech and metapragmatics, pp. 241–60, Cambridge: Cambridge University Press.

Urmson, J.O. (1952) 'Parenthetical verbs', *Mind* 61: 480–96.

Vandepitte, S. (1989) 'A pragmatic function of intonation', *Lingua* 79: 265–97.

Van der Auwera, J. (1997) 'Conditional perfection', in A. Athenasiadou and R. Dirven (eds) *On Conditionals Again*, pp. 169–90, Amsterdam: John Benjamins.

Van der Henst, J-B. and Sperber, D. (2004) 'Testing the cognitive and the communicative principles of relevance', in I. Noveck and D. Sperber (eds) *Experimental Pragmatics*, pp. 141–69, Basingstoke: Palgrave.

Van der Henst, J-B., Carles, L. and Sperber, D. (2002a) 'Truthfulness and relevance in telling the time', *Mind and Language* 17 (5): 457–66.

Van der Henst, J.-B., Politzer, G. and Sperber, D. (2002b) 'When is a conclusion worth deriving? A relevance-based analysis of indeterminate relational problems', *Thinking and Reasoning* 8 (1): 1–2.

Vanderveken, D. and Kubo, S. (2002) *Essays in Speech Act Theory*, Amsterdam: John Benjamins.

van Geenhoven, V. and Warner, N. (eds) (1999) *Annual Report 1998, MPI for Psycholinguistics*, Nijmegen, The Netherlands.

van Kemenade, A. and Los, B. (2006) *The Handbook of the Historicity of English*, Oxford: Blackwell.

Van Rooy, R. (2004) 'Signalling games select Horn strategies', *Linguistics and Philosophy* 27: 493–527.

Vega Moreno, R. (2007) *Creativity and Convention*: the pragmatics of everyday figurative speech, Amsterdam: John Benjamins.

Venezky, R.L. and Healey, A. (eds) (1980) *A Microfiche Concordance to Old English*, Newark, Delaware, and Toronto: University of Delaware Press.

Ventola, E. (1987) *The Structure of Social Interaction*: a systematic approach to the semiotics of service encounters, London: Frances Pinter.

Verschueren, J. (1985a) *What People Say They Do with Words*: prolegomena to an empirical–conceptual approach to linguistic action, Norwood, New Jersey: Ablex.

——(1985b) *International News Reporting*: metapragmatic metaphors and the U-2, Amsterdam and Philadelphia: John Benjamins.

——(ed.) (1987) *Linguistic Action*: some empirical–conceptual studies, Norwood, New Jersey: Ablex.

——(1989a) 'English as object and medium of (mis)understanding', in O. García and R. Otheguy (eds) *English Across Cultures – Cultures Across English*: a reader in cross-cultural communication, pp. 31–53, Berlin: Mouton de Gruyter.

——(1989b) 'Language on language: toward metapragmatic universals', *Papers in Pragmatics* 3 (2): 1–144.

——(1994) 'The pragmatic perspective', in J.-O. Östman, J. Verschueren and E. Versluys (eds) *Handbook of Pragmatics*: manual, pp. 1–22, Amsterdam: John Benjamins.

——(1995a) 'The conceptual basis of performativity', in M. Shibatani and S. Thompson (eds) *Essays in Semantics and Pragmatics*, pp. 299–321, Amsterdam and Philadelphia: John Benjamins.

——(1995b) 'The pragmatic return to meaning: notes on the dynamics of communication, degrees of salience, and communicative transparency', *Journal of Linguistic Anthropology* 5: 127–56.

——(1996) 'Contrastive ideology research: aspects of a pragmatic methodology', *Language Sciences* 18 (3/4): 589–603.

——(1999) *Understanding Pragmatics*, London: Arnold.

——(2000) 'Notes on the role of metapragmatic awareness in language use', *Pragmatics* 10 (4): 439–56.

Verschueren, J., Östman, J.-O. and Blommaert, J. (eds) (1995) *Handbook of Pragmatics*, Amsterdam: John Benjamins.

Vološinov, V.N. (1930) *Marksizm i Filosofiya Yazika* (Marxism and the philosophy of language), Leningrad.

Vygotsky, L.S. (1978) *Mind in Society: the development of higher psychological processes*, Cambridge, Massachusetts: Harvard University Press.

Walker, M.A. (1998) 'Centering, anaphora resolution, and discourse structure', in M.A. Walker, A.K. Joshi and E.F. Prince (eds) *Centering in Discourse*, Oxford: Oxford University Press.

Walters, J. (1981) 'Variation in the requesting behavior of bilingual children', *International Journal of the Sociology of Language* 27: 77–92.

Wardhaugh, R. (1985) *How Conversation Works*, Oxford: Blackwell.

Warner, A. (1990) 'Reworking the history of English auxiliaries', in S.M. Adamson, V. Law, N. Vincent and S. Wright (eds) *Papers from the Fifth International Conference on English Historical Linguistics*, pp. 537–58, Amsterdam and Philadelphia: John Benjamins.

Wartburg, W. von (1966) *Französisches Etymologisches Wörterbuch*, Basel: Zbinden.

Wartenberg, T.E. (1990) *The Forms of Power: from domination to transformation*, Philadelphia: Temple University Press.

Watts, R.J. (1984) 'An analysis of epistemic possibility and probability', *English Studies* 65: 129–40.

——(1986) 'Relevance in conversational moves: a reappraisal of *well*', *Studia Anglica Posnaniensia* 19: 37–59.

——(1991) *Power in Family Discourse*, Berlin: Mouton de Gruyter.

——(2003) *Politeness*, Cambridge: Cambridge University Press.

——(2006) 'Impoliteness as an aspect of relational work', *Paper Presented at Linguistic Impoliteness and Rudeness Conference (LIAR): confrontation and conflict in discourse*, University of Huddersfield, UK.

Watts, R.J. and Trudgill, P. (2002) *Alternative Histories of English*, London: Routledge.

Watzlawick, P., Beavin, J.H. and Jackson, D.D. (1967) *Pragmatics of Human Communication: a study of interactional patterns, pathologies and paradoxes*, New York: Norton.

Weber, M. (1949) *The Methodology of the Social Sciences*, trans. E. Shils and H. Finch (eds) Glencoe, Illinois: Free Press.

Weigand, E. (1988) 'Historische Sprachpragmatik am Beispiel: Gesprächsstrukturen im Nibelungenlied', *Zeitschrift für Deutsches Altertum und Deutsche Literatur* 117: 159–73.

Weissenborn, J. and Klein, W. (1982) *Here and There: cross-linguistic studies on deixis and demonstration*, Amsterdam: John Benjamins.

Wellman, H.M., Cross, D. and Watson, J. (2001) 'Meta-analysis of theory-of-mind development: the truth about false belief', *Child Development* 72(3): 655–84.

Welte, W. (1993) *Englische Semantik*, Frankfurt am Main: Peter Lang.

Wenger, E. (2000) 'Communities of practice and learning systems', *Organization* 7 (2): 225–46.

Wettstein, H.K. (1984) 'How to bridge the gap between meaning and reference', *Synthese* 58: 63–84; reprinted in S. Davis (ed.) (1991) *Pragmatics: a reader*, pp. 160–74, Oxford: Oxford University Press.

Wharton, T. (2009) *Pragmatics and Non-Verbal Communication*, Cambridge: Cambridge University Press.

——(2010a) 'H.P. Grice', in L. Cummings (ed.) *The Pragmatics Encyclopedia*, pp. 182–3, London and New York: Routledge.

——(2010b) 'Speech act theory', in L. Cummings (ed.) *The Pragmatics Encyclopedia*, pp. 452–6, London and New York: Routledge.

——(2010c) 'Maxims of conversation', in L. Cummings (ed.) *The Pragmatics Encyclopedia*, pp. 256–9, London and New York: Routledge.

Whitaker, H. (1982a) *Automatization of Language*, lecture given at Georgetown University, March.

——(1982b) *Automaticity*, paper presented at the conference on formulaicity, Linguistic Institute, University of Maryland.

Whitehead, A.N. (1967) *Science and the Modern World*, New York: The Free Press.

Whitworth, A., Perkins, L. and Lesser, R. (1997) *Conversation Analysis Profile for People with Aphasia*, London: Whurr Publishers.

Wichmann, A. (2000) *Intonation in Text and Discourse: beginnings, middles and ends*, London: Longman.

Wierzbicka, A. (1987) *English Speech Act Verbs: a semantic dictionary*, Sydney: Academic Press.

——(1991) *Cross-Cultural Pragmatics: the semantics of human interaction*, Berlin: Mouton de Gruyter.

Wildner-Bassett, M. (1994) 'Intercultural pragmatics and proficiency: "polite" noises for cultural appropriateness', *International Review of Applied Linguistics (IRAL)* XXX/1: 3–17.

Wilkins, D. and Hill, D. (1995) 'When "go" means "come": questioning the basicness of basic motion verbs', *Cognitive Linguistics* 6: 209–59.

Wilkins, D., Hill, D. and Levinson, S.C. (1995) 'Bedeutet KOMMEN and GEHEN in verschiedenen Sprachen immer dasselbe?', *Max-Planck-Gesellschaft Jahrbuch*: 307–12, Munich: Max-Planck-Gesellschaft.

Willett, T. (1988) 'A cross-linguistic survey of the grammaticalization of evidentiality', *Studies in Language* 12: 51–97.

Wilson, D. (1975) *Presuppositions and Non-Truth-Conditional Semantics*, London, New York and San Francisco: Academic Press.

——(1991) 'Types of non-truth-conditional meaning', unpublished MS, University College London.

——(2000) 'Metarepresentation in linguistic communication', in D. Sperber (ed.) *Metarepresentation: a multidisciplinary perspective*, pp. 411–48, Oxford: Oxford University Press.

——(2003) 'Relevance and lexical pragmatics', *Italian Journal of Linguistics/Rivista di Linguistica* 15 (2): 273–91.

——(2005) 'New directions for research on pragmatics and modularity', *Lingua* 115: 1129–46; reprinted in S. Marmaridou, K. Nikiforidou and E. Antonopoulou (eds) *Reviewing Linguistic Thought: converging trends for the 21st century*, pp. 375–400, Berlin: Mouton de Gruyter.

——(2009a) 'Parallels and differences in the treatment of metaphor in relevance theory and cognitive linguistics', *Studies in Pragmatics* (Journal of the Pragmatics Society of Japan) 11: 42–60.

——(2009b) 'Irony and metarepresentation', *UCL Working Papers in Linguistics* 21: 183–226.

——(2010) 'Relevance theory', in L. Cummings (ed.) *The Pragmatics Encyclopedia*, pp. 393–8, London and New York: Routledge.

Wilson, D. and Carston, R. (2006) 'Metaphor, relevance and the emergent property issue', *Mind and Language* 21 (3): 404–33.

——(2007) 'A unitary approach to lexical pragmatics: relevance, inference and ad hoc concepts', in N. Burton-Roberts (ed.) *Pragmatics*, pp. 230–59, Basingstoke: Palgrave.

——(2008) 'Metaphor and the "emergent property" problem: a relevance-theoretic approach', *The Baltic International Yearbook of Cognition, Logic and Communication*, vol. 3 (2007), pp. 1–40.

Wilson, D. and Sperber, D. (1981) 'On Grice's theory of conversational implicature', in P. Werth (ed.) *Conversation and Discourse*, pp. 155–78, London: Croom Helm; reprinted in A. Kasher (ed.) (1998) *Pragmatics: critical concepts*, vol. II, pp. 347–67, London: Routledge.

——(1986a) 'Pragmatics and modularity', in A.M. Farley, P.T. Farley and K.-E. McCullough (eds) *Chicago Linguistics Society 22: papers from the parasession on pragmatics and grammatical theory*, pp. 67–84.

——(1986b) 'Inference and implicature', in C. Travis (ed.) *Meaning and Interpretation*, pp. 45–76, Oxford and New York: Blackwell.

——(1988) 'Mood and the analysis of non-declarative sentences', in J. Dancy, J. Moravcsik and C. Taylor (eds) *Human Agency: language, duty and value*, pp. 77–101, Stanford, California: Stanford University Press.

——(1990) 'Linguistic form and relevance', *UCL Working Papers in Linguistics* 2, 95–111.

——(1992a) 'On verbal irony', *Lingua* 87: 53–76.

——(1992b) 'Reference and relevance', *University College Working Papers in Linguistics* 4: 167–92.

——(1993) 'Linguistic form and relevance', *Lingua* 90 (2): 1–25.

——(1998) 'Pragmatics and time', in R. Carston and S. Uchida (eds) *Relevance Theory: applications and implications*, pp. 1–22, Amsterdam: John Benjamins.

——(2002) 'Truthfulness and relevance', *Mind and Language* 111: 583–632.

——(2004) 'Relevance theory', in L.R. Horn and G. Ward (eds) *The Handbook of Pragmatics*, pp. 607–32, Oxford: Blackwell.

Wilson, D. and Wharton, T. (2006) 'Relevance and prosody', *Journal of Pragmatics* 38 (10): 1559–79.

Winch, P. (1997) 'Can we understand ourselves?', *Philosophical Investigations* 20 (3): 193–204.

Wimmer, H. and Perner, J. (1983) 'Beliefs about beliefs: representation and constraining function of wrong beliefs in young children's understanding of deception', *Cognition* 13: 103–28.

Winner, E. and Leekam, S. (1991) 'Distinguishing irony from deception: understanding the speaker's second-order intention', *British Journal of Developmental Psychology* 9: 257–70.

Winter, Y. (2001) 'Plural predication and the strongest meaning hypothesis', *Journal of Semantics* (18): 333–65.

Winton, W. (1990) 'Language and emotion', in H. Giles and P.W. Robinson (eds) *Handbook of Language and Social Psychology*, pp. 33–49, Chichester: John Wiley & Sons.

Wittgenstein, L. (1953) *Philosophical Investigations*, trans. G.E.M. Anscombe (2001) 3rd edition, Oxford/Malden: Blackwell.

Wooffitt, R. (2005) *Conversation Analysis and Discourse Analysis: a comparative and critical introduction*, London: Sage.

Woolard, K.A. and Schieffelin, B.B. (1994) 'Language ideology', *Annual Review of Anthropology* 23: 55–82.

Wray, A. (2002) *Formulaic Language and the Lexicon*, Cambridge: Cambridge University Press.

Yadugiri, M.A. (1986) 'Some pragmatic implications of the use of *yes* and *no* in response to *yes-no* questions', *Journal of Pragmatics* 10: 199–210.

Yongping, R. (2002) 'A relevance-theoretical account of politeness', *Modern Foreign Language* 25 (4): 26–39.

Yule, G. (1996) *Pragmatics*, Oxford: Oxford University Press.

Yus, F. (1998) 'Relevance theory and media discourse: a verbal-visual model of communication', *Poetics* 25: 293–309.

——(2006) 'Relevance theory', in K. Brown (ed.) *Encyclopedia of Language and Linguistics*, 2nd edition, vol. 10, pp. 512–19, Amsterdam: Elsevier.

——(2010) 'Relevance theory', in B. Heine and H. Narrog (eds) *Oxford Handbook of Linguistic Analysis*, pp. 679–701, Oxford: Oxford University Press.

Zaidel, E. (1998) 'Language in the right hemisphere following callosal disconnection', in B. Stemmer and H.A. Whitaker (eds) *Handbook of Neurolinguistics*, pp. 369–83, San Diego, California: Academic Press.

Zaidel, E., Zaidel, D. and Bogen, J.E. (1998) 'Disconnection syndrome', in J.G. Beaumont, E.M. Kenealy and M.J.C. Rogers (eds) *The Blackwell Dictionary of Neuropsychology*, pp. 279–85, Oxford: Blackwell.

Zajac, M. (2004) 'Polish quantified sentences. From logical form to explicature: an analysis of selected examples from a corpus of young Poles' everyday conversation', in E. Mioduszewska (ed.) *Relevance Studies in Poland*, pp. 143–53, The Institute of English Studies, University of Warsaw.

Zegarac, V. and Clark, B. (1999) 'Phatic interpretations and phatic communication', *Journal of Linguistics* 35: 321–46.

Zhou, J. (2002) *Pragmatic Development of Mandarin-Speaking Children from 14 Months to 32 Months*, Nanjing, China: Nanjing Normal University Press.

Zimin, S. (1981) 'Sex and politeness: factors in first and second language use', in J. Walters (ed.) 'The sociolinguistic of deference and politeness', special issue of the *International Journal of the Sociology of Language* 27: 35–58.

Zipf, G.K. (1949) *Human Behavior and the Principle of Least Effort: an introduction to human ecology*, New York: Hafner.

Zwarts, J. (2003) 'Lexical competition: "round" in English and Dutch', in P. Dekker and R. van Rooy (eds) *Proceedings of the Fourteenth Amsterdam Colloquium*, pp. 229–34, Amsterdam: ILLC.

——(2006) 'Om en rond: een semantische vergelijking', *Nederlandse Taalkunde* 11 (2): 101–23.

Zwarts, J., Hogeweg, L., Lestrade, S. and Malchukov, A. (2009) 'Semantic markedness in gender oppositions, blocking and fossilization', *Language Typology and Universals* 62 (4): 325–43.

Index

Page numbers in **bold** type indicate an authoritative treatment
Page numbers following 'G' indicate Glossary entries